The Art of Critical Reading

BRUSHING UP ON YOUR READING, THINKING, AND STUDY SKILLS

SECOND EDITION

Cabana
567-4054

Peter Mather ◆ **Rita McCarthy**

retired from
Glendale Community College
Glendale, Arizona

Glendale Community College
Glendale, Arizona

McGraw-Hill
Higher Education

Boston   Burr Ridge, IL   Dubuque, IA   New York   San Francisco   St. Louis
Bangkok   Bogotá   Caracas   Kuala Lumpur   Lisbon   London   Madrid   Mexico City
Milan   Montreal   New Delhi   Santiago   Seoul   Singapore   Sydney   Taipei   Toronto

The McGraw-Hill Companies

McGraw-Hill
Higher Education

THE ART OF CRITICAL READING: BRUSHING UP ON YOUR READING, THINKING, AND STUDY SKILLS, Second Edition

Published by McGraw-Hill, a business unit of The McGraw-Hill Companies, Inc., 1221 Avenue of the Americas, New York, NY, 10020. Copyright © 2009 by The McGraw-Hill Companies, Inc. All rights reserved. No part of this publication may be reproduced or distributed in any form or by any means, or stored in a database or retrieval system, without the prior written consent of The McGraw-Hill Companies, Inc., including, but not limited to, in any network or other electronic storage or transmission, or broadcast for distance learning. Some ancillaries, including electronic and print components, may not be available to customers outside the United States.

This book is printed on acid-free paper.

Printed in China

3 4 5 6 7 8 9 0 CTP/CTP 0 9

ISBN   978-0-07-338569-3 (Student Edition) MHID 0-07-338569-7
ISBN   978-0-07-332650-4 (Instructor's Edition) MHID 0-07-332650-X

Vice-president/Editor-in-chief: *Michael Ryan*
Sponsoring editor: *John Kindler*
Development editor: *Gillian Cook*
Editorial coordinator: *Jesse Hassenger*
Marketing manager: *Tamara Wederbrand*
Senior production editor: *Mel Valentín*
Manuscript editor: *Thomas Briggs*
Lead production supervisor: *Randy Hurst*
Senior design manager: *Preston Thomas*
Interior designer: *Glenda King*
Cover designer: *Margarite Reynolds*
Media project manager: *Thomas Brierly*
Senior photo research coordinator: *Natalia C. Peschiera*
Photo researcher: *Inge King*
Art editor: *Emma Ghiselli*
Cover image: © John Foxx/Getty Images, © *Cross-Cut*, 1998 (acrylic on canvas), Colin Booth, Private Collection/The Bridgeman Art Library, © Yasuhide Fumoto/Getty Images
Typeface: *10/13 Palatino*
Compositor: *Aptara, Inc.*
Printer: *CTPS*

Library of Congress Cataloging-in-Publication Data

Mather, Peter.
    The art of critical reading / Peter Mather, Rita McCarthy.—2nd ed.
        p. cm.
    Includes index.
    ISBN-13: 978-0-07-338569-3 (alk. paper)
    ISBN-10: 0-07-338569-7 (alk. paper)
    1. Reading (Higher education) 2. Critical thinking. 3. Study skills. I. McCarthy, Rita. II. Title.
LB2395.3.M27 2009
428.4071'1—dc22

2008017006

www.mhhe.com

Peter dedicates this book to his late parents,
Carl and Dorothy; and his brother and sister-in-law,
John and Peggy.

Rita dedicates this book to her mother, Bertha;
her sons, Ryan and Steve; her daughter-in-law, Bonnie;
her grandchildren, Zachary and Kate;
and especially her husband, Greg.

About the Authors

Dr. Peter Mather—Dr. Mather earned his B.A. in government from the University of Redlands, his first M.A. in African studies from the University of California, Los Angeles, his second M.A. in reading from California State University, Los Angeles, and his Ed.D. in curriculum and instruction from the University of Southern California. Before recently retiring, he taught reading at the secondary, adult education, and community college levels for close to 30 years. While at Glendale Community College, he taught both developmental and critical and evaluative reading. He also taught American government and was the college director of the America Reads/Counts program. In addition to being the coauthor of *Reading and All That Jazz*, now in its third edition, and *Racing Ahead with Reading*, he has published articles in the *Journal of Reading*.

Ms. Rita Romero McCarthy—Ms. McCarthy earned her B.A. in sociology and history from the University of California, Berkeley, and her M.A. in education from Arizona State University. She has taught at the elementary, secondary, and college levels. For the past 20 years, she has taught English as a second language, developmental reading, and critical and evaluative reading at Glendale Community College. She is the coauthor of *Reading and All That Jazz* and *Racing Ahead with Reading*. Ms. McCarthy has also published articles in professional journals and other media; most of these have been concerned with the use of bibliotherapy. She has also published reading lists for beginning and remedial readers.

Brief Contents

Contents

Preface to the Instructor

In 2005, we published the first edition of *The Art of Critical Reading*, a textbook that uses the theme of art to highlight an exciting and engaged approach to reading and learning. This year we are proud to present the second edition in full color.

The Art of Critical Reading was designed as a higher-level sequel to our popular *Reading and All That Jazz*, now in its third edition. Like *Jazz*, *The Art of Critical Reading* is designed to draw readers in with its engaging exercises and its reading selections, which are taken from a variety of sources: college textbooks, newspapers, magazines, and classic and contemporary literature. As with *Jazz*, the purpose of this book is to assist college students in developing the skills they need for reading, understanding, and critically evaluating textbooks and other college-level reading. While *Art* may be appropriate for a more advanced audience than is *Jazz*, it is still a book that will motivate and engage readers through its theme, its exciting reading selections, and its stimulating visuals and exercises.

Theme and Title

We chose art as the theme of this book because, like written texts, art is a form of communication. Like works of literature, works of art range from the easily understood to the enigmatic and thought provoking. In art, the viewer may dislike the unfamiliar, at least at first, but when he or she understands the "language" of art and its structure, the visual experience becomes richer. So, too, with written works. In the case both of written texts and art, the better a person understands the purpose and structure of the material, the more likely it is that that person will be able to interpret it accurately and enjoy it.

Art, like literature, sharpens our perceptions of life and requires us to re-examine our thoughts. Both artists and writers compose their works with a purpose in mind. And both artists and writers draw from their own personal experiences and backgrounds to convey their emotional or intellectual messages. Both viewers of art and readers of literature must bring their own perspectives to bear when engaged in evaluation and interpretation.

We emphasize the theme by introducing each chapter with a major work of art so that students may reach a deeper understanding of it. To enhance students' experience of the works of art, we include journal prompts to encourage students to form their own opinions and share them with their instructors and classmates. Throughout the text, we have included provocative selections on a range of art-related topics, such as graffiti, public art, Egyptian artifacts, prehistoric cave art, art theft, the *Mona Lisa*, and the Vietnam War Memorial. We conclude with a section on body art and performance art from a popular cultural anthropology textbook. Our hope is that students will find much material in this book, both visual and written, to stimulate and enrich.

Reading Selections and the Questions That Follow

The reading selections in this book were chosen, first, for their excellence. Many of the authors are famous or award winning. We also chose readings with contemporary relevance and interest. We tried to find selections that would broaden students' general knowledge about current events and be otherwise informative and useful. Finally, we sought readings that would appeal to a diverse audience. The selections address a wide variety of disciplines, from art to psychology to ethics to science. They also come from a wide variety of sources: while *The Art of Critical Reading* emphasizes textbook selections, it also presents other kinds of material students are likely to encounter in their college classes—works of literature as well as selections from magazines and newspapers.

While most of the selections are nonfiction, we also include poetry, fables, and cartoons. And although we emphasize contemporary material, we also include some classics. The one trait all the selections share is that they will enable students to clarify their own values as they experience events through someone else's eyes. Although most of the selections have not previously appeared in a reading textbook, instructors can use them with confidence, as they have been tested in our classes and in those of our colleagues.

The questions following the reading selections require students to engage in recalling, understanding, interpreting, and evaluating. They come in various formats—multiple-choice, true-or-false, fill-in-the-blank, matching, discussion, and written-response. The objective questions are written in the style of questions asked on standardized tests such as the CLAST and the TASP. The open-ended questions for discussion and writing are included to give students practice in analyzing, synthesizing, and evaluating. Such questions give students the opportunity to bring their personal experiences to bear, and they are organized in such a way as to lead students to a greater understanding of the selections. Such questions rarely have a right or wrong answer; instead, they are meant to provoke discussion and encourage debate.

Organization of the Text

This book is organized along two dimensions. First, each successive part of the book focuses on different skills that an effective critical reader must master. Second, the book begins with a narrow perspective, focusing on students' personal experience, and then moves to increasingly broader perspectives, focusing in turn on interpersonal, social, national, and international issues. The book becomes increasingly challenging as it progresses, both in the selections presented and the critical reading skills taught:

- **Part 1 explores the skills likely to lead to a successful college experience.** Material presented in this section includes an overview of creative and critical thinking skills, an introduction to study skills, and discussions about stress, locus of control, and strategies for combating procrastination. The Introduction in Part 1 is meant to be completed in the first week of class. The objective questions and short written assignments that follow the selections will allow instructors to assess the skills of individual students and the class as a whole.

- **Part 2 reviews the basic skills needed for effective critical reading.** Focusing on the processes and structures of reading, Part 2 reviews skills that include identifying the topic, identifying the main idea and supporting details, and determining the author's purpose. Students practice recognizing and using transition words and patterns of organization, as well as identifying homonyms and other confusing words. The selections, which include fables, poems, and anecdotes, touch on themes of perception, motivation, risk taking, and ethics.

- **Part 3 emphasizes reading as an interpretive and analytical process.** The goal of Part 3 is to enable students to become proficient at reading between the lines.

Topics introduced in Part 3 include inference, figurative language, and author's tone. Themes include animals and nature. Selections include material from such noted authors as Annie Dillard, Sandra Cisneros, Diane Ackerman, Farley Mowat, and Laura Hillenbrand (author of *Seabiscuit*).

- **Part 4 concentrates on developing critical reading and thinking skills.** Topics discussed include fact and opinion, the author's point of view, bias, propaganda techniques, and the structure of an argument. Selections cover such varied topics as health supplements, the Vietnam War Memorial, cultural literacy, and the Declaration of Independence and Bill of Rights. In Part 4, students are given an opportunity to evaluate evidence with material that covers the theme of death and dying, from varied perspectives.

- **Part 5 is devoted to improving study skills.** Throughout the book, we introduce students to study skills such as SQ3R, outlining, mapping, and annotating. Part 5 asks students to apply these skills to part of a chapter about body and performance art taken from a popular college anthropology textbook.

- **The Appendices** address the skills needed to use a thesaurus and to interpret visual aids effectively. The section on visual aids—tables, charts, graphs, maps—is designed to be used as an independent unit or in conjunction with specific reading selections.

Organization of the Chapters

Each chapter begins with an overview of the chapter topic and a discussion of the key terms needed for understanding the topic, followed by short exercises designed to help students understand and master the topic, and then by longer reading selections that further develop the topic. Introducing each of the longer reading selections is a section titled "Getting the Picture," which engages students with the subject of the upcoming selection. It is followed by a "Bio-sketch" of the author, which in turn is followed by a section entitled "Brushing Up on Vocabulary." Following the selections are a variety of exercises. Directions for longer written assignments, some of which will call for research by students, follow each selection. Review tests are interspersed throughout the text to reinforce skills and remind students that while individual skills may be practiced in isolation, the reading process is cumulative.

The exercises in each chapter are sequential, progressing from relatively easy to quite difficult. These exercises use many different formats in order to maintain student interest. The instructor should feel free to pick and choose among the exercises in accord with the needs of particular students or classes. The exercises are designed so that the instructor can have the students work individually or in groups.

Special Features of *The Art of Critical Reading*

In addition to the wide range of readings and challenging questions that test and reinforce student learning, we've included several special features that will reinforce skills crucial to succeeding in college:

- **Quotations in the margins that prompt student journal writing and discussion.** These quotations respond in provocative ways to reading selections and encourage students to reflect on the implications of what they have read.

- **Internet activities.** The Internet activities included in the text are directly related to the issues raised in the reading selections; some encourage students to delve more deeply into the lives and work of featured authors.

- **Study techniques.** We've included coverage of a variety of study techniques—from annotating and summarizing to outlining and mapping—to reinforce the basic skills students need to succeed in college.

- **Test-taking tips.** We conclude each chapter with tips for taking objective and essay exams. We also include a section on coping with test-taking anxiety.

- **Developing a college-level vocabulary.** There are 10 vocabulary units, each of which introduces students to a set of Latin or Greek word parts or homonyms. Students learn college-level words associated with these word parts and then practice the key words by means of verbal analogies and crossword puzzles.

New to this Edition

One thing you'll notice immediately is the beautiful, full-color design, which adds a new dimension of interest to the artworks, cartoons, and other visuals throughout the text.

You'll also notice that the reading selections are now designed to look as they would have when they appeared in their original contexts. In other words, reading selections taken from newspapers are set to look like news articles; those from magazines, like magazine articles; and those from popular books and textbooks, like excerpts from books.

In response to suggestions from our reviewers, we have placed more emphasis on the overall theme of art. There is now at least one art-related selection in each chapter. We have also included more textbook reading selections in this second edition.

Because this textbook is meant to encourage critical and evaluative reading, we have added selections on creativity and critical thinking. To encourage analysis by students, we have added more questions to the "In Your Own Words" section of the text and more assignments to the "Art of Writing" section.

Renewed emphasis has been placed on vocabulary development. The vocabulary units are now integrated into the chapters, and each reading selection now has a section on vocabulary in context. Unlike in many reading textbooks, the vocabulary exercises are varied and include creative activities as well as matching and fill-in-the blank exercises and crossword puzzles.

We have also provided more opportunities for students to practice synthesis by comparing and contrasting reading selections and artworks. And more opportunities are provided to deal with issues that are of real concern to today's students, such as cheating, food and health, relationships, and school and community.

Teaching and Learning Aids Accompanying the Book

Supplements for Instructors

- **Annotated Instructor's Edition (ISBN: 0-07-332650-X).** The Annotated Instructor's Edition contains the full text of the Student Edition plus answers to the objective exercises and some suggested answers to open-ended questions.

- **Partners in Teaching Listserv.** From current theory to time-tested classroom tips, this listserv and newsletter offer insight and support to teachers of developmental English from some of the most experienced voices in the field. To join, send an e-mail message with your name and e-mail address to english@mcgraw-hill.com.

- **Online Learning Center (www.mhhe.com/mather).** This password-protected site houses many resources for instructors, including:

  - **Instructor's Manual and Test Bank.** Available online for easy downloading, the Instructor's Manual and Test Bank, written by the authors of the textbook, are a robust resource providing innovative teaching tips, vocabulary quizzes, unit tests, supplementary activities, and useful connections to other resources, such as poems, movies, and political and cultural events.

- *PowerPoint Slides.* Also available on the instructor's site are PowerPoint slides on which the instructional content of each chapter is summarized for overhead projection.

Supplements for Students

- Online Learning Center (www.mhhe.com/mather). Our companion website offers journal prompts for each chapter, links to direct students to reliable Web sources, search exercises to give students practice at finding reliable sites on their own, and much, much more.

- Study Smart (www.mhhe.com/studysmart). This innovative study-skills tutorial for students is an excellent resource for the learning lab or for students working on their own at home. Teaching students strategies for note taking, test taking, and time management, Study Smart operates with a sophisticated answer analysis that students will find motivating. Available on CD-ROM or online, Study Smart is free when packaged with a McGraw-Hill text.

- Word Works. These Merriam-Webster and Random House reference works are available at low cost when ordered with *The Art of Critical Reading:*

  - *Merriam-Webster's Notebook Dictionary.* A compact word resource conveniently designed for 3-ring binders, *Merriam-Webster's Notebook Dictionary* includes 40,000 entries for widely used words with concise, easy-to-understand definitions and pronunciations.

  - *The Merriam-Webster Dictionary.* This handy paperback dictionary contains over 70,000 definitions yet is small enough to carry around in a backpack, so it's always there when it's needed.

  - *Random House Webster's College Dictionary.* This authoritative dictionary includes over 160,000 entries and 175,000 definitions—more than any other college dictionary—and the most commonly used definitions are always listed first, so students can find what they need quickly.

  - *Merriam-Webster's Collegiate Dictionary & Thesaurus CD-ROM.* This up-to-the-minute electronic dictionary and thesaurus offers 225,000 definitions, 340,000 synonyms and related words, and 1,300 illustrations.

  - *Merriam-Webster's Notebook Thesaurus.* Conveniently designed for 3-ring binders, *Merriam-Webster's Notebook Thesaurus* provides concise, clear guidance for over 157,000 word choices.

  - *Merriam-Webster Thesaurus.* This compact thesaurus offers over 157,000 word choices and includes concise definitions and examples to help students choose the correct word for the context.

  - *Merriam-Webster's Vocabulary Builder.* *Merriam-Webster's Vocabulary Builder* focuses on more than 1,000 words, introduces nearly 2,000 more, and includes quizzes to test the student's progress.

- Novel Ideas. These Random House and HarperCollins paperbacks are available at a low cost when packaged with the text:

  The Monkey Wrench Gang (Abbey); Things Fall Apart (Achebe); The Lone Ranger and Tonto (Alexie); Integrity (Carter); The House on Mango Street (Cisneros); Heart of Darkness (Conrad); Pilgrim at Tinker Creek (Dillard);

*Love Medicine (**Erdrich**); Their Eyes Were Watching God (**Hurston**); Boys of Summer (**Kahn**); Woman Warrior (**Kingston**); One Hundred Years of Solitude (**Marquez**); Clear Springs (**Mason**); All the Pretty Horses (**McCarthy**); House Made of Dawn (**Momaday**); Joy Luck Club (**Tan**); Essays of E. B. White* (White).

For more information or to request copies of any of the above supplementary materials for instructor review, please contact your local McGraw-Hill representative at 1-800-338–3987 or send an e-mail message to english@mcgraw-hill.com.

Acknowledgments

No textbook can be created without the assistance of many people. First, we relied on the thoughtful reactions and suggestions of our colleagues across the country who reviewed this project at various stages:

Jesus Adame, *El Paso Community College*

Edy Alderson, *Joliet Junior College*

Heidi Beck, *Seattle University*

Julia Bickel, *Indiana Wesleyan University*

Helen Carr, *San Antonio College*

Gertrude Coleman, *Middlesex College*

Marion Duckworth, *Valdosta State College*

Amy Girone, *Arizona Western College*

Suzanne Gripenstraw, *Butte College*

John Grether, *St. Cloud State University*

Joan Hellman, *Community College of Baltimore*

Suzanne Hughes, *Florida Community College*

Lorna Keebaugh, *Taft College*

Sandi Komarrow, *Montgomery College*

Leon Lanzbom, *San Diego Mesa College*

Mary D. Mears, *Macon State College*

Ronald Mossler, *Los Angeles Valley Community College*

Elizabeth Nelson, *Tidewater Community College*

Mary Nielsen, *Dalton State College*

Cindy Ortega, *Phoenix College*

Carol Saunders, *Chipola College*

Margaret Sims, *Midlands Technical College*

Peggy Strickland, *Gainesville Junior College*

Margaret Triplet, *Central Oregon Community College*

Richard S. Wilson, *Community College of Baltimore County*

Lynda Wolverton, *Polk Community College*

Cynthia Ybanez, *College of Southern Maryland*

In addition to our reviewers, our friends and colleagues at Glendale Community College offered their thoughts and supported our efforts: Dave Gallet, Darlene Goto, R.J. Merrill, Mary Jane Onnen, Brendan Regan, David Rodriguez, Linda Smith, Scott Kozak, and Russ Sears. A special thanks to Pam Hall, who loaned us so many art books and provided invaluable advice. Others who helped us were Marilyn Brophy, Roberta Delaney, Nancy Edwards, Cindy Gilbert, Tom Mather, Cindy Ortega, Lynda Svendsen, and Gwen Worthington.

We'd also like to thank the people at McGraw-Hill who worked to produce this text. First, there were our editors at McGraw-Hill. Sarah Touborg, our original editor, provided the inspiration to write the book, while Alexis Walker and Jane Carter guided the first edition. John Kindler, our sponsoring editor, has kept the process of creating a second edition running smoothly and has always been willing to discuss our ideas. With her unfailing common sense and good humor, our developmental editor, Gillian Cook, has made the creation of the second edition a true pleasure. Thanks also to Thomas Briggs, manuscript editor, Natalia Peschiera and Inge King, photo editors, Emma Ghiselli, art editor, Mel Valentín, production editor, and Randy Hurst, production supervisor. A special thanks to our local McGraw-Hill sales rep, Sherree D'Amico, for providing us with so many of the textbooks we have cited in the text.

To all the people who participated with us in creating this book, we offer our sincerest thanks.

Peter Mather
Rita McCarthy

Preface to the Student

"Everyone who knows how to read has it in their power to magnify themselves, to multiply the ways in which they exist, to make their lives full, significant, and interesting."
—ALDOUS HUXLEY

Some of you are just beginning college. Some of you have already taken college classes. Regardless of how much college experience you have, this book is designed to help you become better at reading, understanding, and evaluating college-level material. In this book, you will be given an opportunity to practice your reading skills on the sorts of materials that you will encounter in other college courses, including excerpts from college textbooks, literature, newspapers, and popular fiction and nonfiction. Along the way, you will learn how to be a critical reader. The word *critical* derives from the Greek word *kriticos*, which means "one who is able to judge." A critical reader is someone who is able to make judgments about a piece of writing. Critical reading goes beyond mere comprehension. It includes the ability to interpret, analyze, and evaluate what you read. Your college classes are designed to expose you to new information and ideas on many subjects. They are also meant to stimulate you to think critically about what you are reading and learning. This book will make you a better critical reader.

Art and reading both involve critical thinking. Artists such as painters, sculptors, and photographers engage in critical thinking as they go about creating a work of art. They think critically about the concept or idea or feeling they wish to convey and also about how best to express this perspective in the work of art. And viewers of a work of art must employ critical thinking in seeking to understand its meaning. Similarly, authors think critically when working to communicate their thoughts in their writings, and readers think critically in seeking to understand an author's message and their own reaction to it. Art and reading share something else too—they both involve specific skills that can be improved by effort and practice. Thus, the title of this book: *The Art of Critical Reading*.

The first part of this book discusses personal skills, such as handling stress and avoiding procrastination. The next part of the book broadens the focus to look at such topics as personal health and environmental concerns. The book then expands its focus as it discusses political issues, such as those relating to the Declaration of Independence and the Bill of Rights, and social issues such as cheating.

The following pages illustrate how this book works. Spending a few minutes getting to know the features and organization of the text will help you to get the most out of *The Art of Critical Reading*.

WALKTHROUGH

Chapter openers include a work of art and questions that will stimulate you to think critically about this work of art. These chapter openers will not only expose you to great works of art; they will also provide you with important opportunities to practice "reading" visuals critically.

The Author's Purpose and the Rhetorical Modes

CHAPTER 3

The Oath of the Horatii (1784) BY JACQUES-LOUIS DAVID
Photo: G. Blot/C. Jean. Louvre, Paris. Réunion des Musées Nationaux/Art Resource, NY.

View and Reflect
In the painting, three brothers are swearing an oath to their father to defeat their enemies or die for Rome.
1. What are the brothers receiving from their father?
2. Compare the postures and attitudes of the men to those of the women. How do the hands of the men and women express their respective attitudes?
3. What does the woman in black in the background of the painting appear to be doing?
4. Notice the three arches in the background of the painting. Where else does the artist repeat this theme of a group of three?
5. What do you think the artist's purpose was in creating this painting?
6. How does the painting illustrate risk-taking behavior?
7. What is the dominant color in the male grouping? What might that color represent?

119

Each chapter begins with an expanded explanation of the topic and a discussion of key terms needed to understand it. Short examples and exercises are included in these sections to help you master the topic and prepare you for the related readings that follow.

DETERMINING THE AUTHOR'S PURPOSE

Highlight or underline the definitions of the key terms. Then write a paraphrase of each definition in the margin.

Inform

Entertain

Persuade

Audience

Specific purpose

Most writers create a story, essay, article, or poem with at least one **general purpose** in mind. Because most writers do not directly state their general purpose, the reader must use indirect clues to determine it. We can identify the general purpose by asking the question "Why did the author write this?" Usually, this purpose will fall into one of three broad categories: to inform, to entertain, or to persuade.

An author whose purpose is **to inform** will provide readers with knowledge or information. Ordinarily, the material will be presented in an objective, neutral fashion. Authors who write textbooks presenting factual material often have this purpose in mind. Articles in newspapers are also usually meant to inform.

An author whose purpose is **to entertain** will tell a story or describe someone or something in an interesting way. A piece of writing meant to entertain will often make an appeal to the reader's imagination, sense of humor, or emotions. Such writing may be either fiction or nonfiction. Witty, unusual, dramatic, or exciting stories usually have entertainment as their purpose.

Finally, the author's purpose may be **to persuade.** Persuasion goes beyond merely entertaining or providing information. This kind of writing tries to change the reader's opinions by appealing to emotions or intellect. If making an emotional argument, the author may use vividly descriptive passages designed to manipulate the reader's feelings. If making an appeal to intelligence, the author will employ logic and reasoning. Political literature is a common form of writing meant to persuade. Newspaper editorials ordinarily have persuasion as their purpose also.

Authors take into account their **audience** (those they are writing for) when they choose their **general purpose.** Writers of fiction usually want to entertain readers by creating interesting characters and stories. If an author writes an article for a wellness magazine, the general purpose will probably be to provide information promoting good health. If an author writes a letter to solicit campaign contributions for a political candidate, the general purpose will be to persuade people to give money.

In addition to a general purpose, authors also usually have a **specific purpose,** which reveals more detailed information about the article than the general purpose. Take the wellness example above. The general purpose is to inform. The specific purpose might be "to inform people about foods that protect against cancer."

Sometimes an author may have more than one purpose in mind. For instance, an author might want both to entertain and to persuade. Or the author might write an entertaining article that also provides information about something important. In these instances, usually one of the author's purposes will be primary. To determine the general and primary purpose, first identify the main idea and the key details that support that idea. Then note the author's choice of words. Is the vocabulary neutral and unbiased? Is it meant to influence our judgment in some way? Finally, note the source of the article or passage. Often the publication that the article or passage comes from will help you identify the author's primary purpose.

Read the paragraph below, and identify the writer's topic, main idea, and general and specific purposes.

The viewpoint, now gaining momentum, that would allow individuals to "make up their own minds" about smoking, air bags, safety helmets, and the like ignores some elementary social realities. The ill-informed nature of this viewpoint is camouflaged by the appeal to values that are dear to most Americans. The essence of the argument is that what individuals do with their lives and limbs, foolhardy though it might

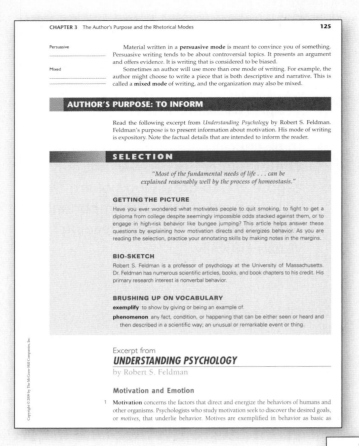

The reading selections are preceded by a "Getting the Picture" section, which includes information that will help you understand what you are about to encounter. A "Bio-sketch" of the author follows; this section will provide you with information about the writer's life or writing experience. "Brushing Up on Vocabulary" sections will provide you with an overview of unfamiliar words in the selection.

The Comprehension Checkup following the reading selections consists of objective questions to test your understanding of what you have just read; the "Vocabulary in Context" exercises are provided to help you to build your word knowledge; "In Your Own Words" and "The Art of Writing" exercises ask you to reflect on and write about the selection you've just encountered, enriching your experience and giving you another opportunity to polish your skills; and the "Internet Activity" following the reading selection provides a jumping-off point for learning more about the topic or the author of the selection.

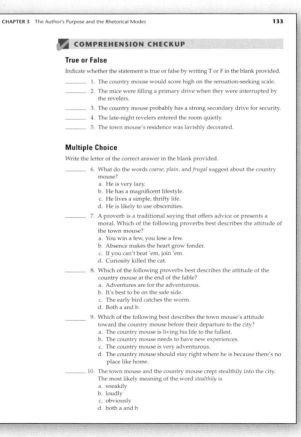

12. A. A good painting should shock or jolt the senses.
    B. A good painting should give me a feeling of peace and security.
13. A. People who ride motorcycles must have some kind of unconscious need to hurt themselves.
    B. I would like to drive or ride a motorcycle.

Scoring   Give yourself one point for each of the following responses: 1A, 2A, 3A, 4B, 5A, 6B, 7A, 8A, 9B, 10B, 11A, 12A, 13B. Find your total score by adding up the number of points and then use the following scoring key:

    0–3 very low sensation seeking
    4–5 low
    6–9 average
    10–11 high
    12–13 very high

15   Keep in mind, of course, that this short questionnaire, for which the scoring is based on the results of college students who have taken it, provides only a rough estimate of your sensation-seeking tendencies. Moreover, as people get older, their sensation-seeking scores tend to decrease. Still, the questionnaire will at least give you an indication of how your sensation-seeking tendencies compare with those of others.

Source: "Motivation and Emotion," from Robert S. Feldman, *Understanding Psychology,* 5th ed., pp. 326–327, 329. Copyright © 1999. Reprinted by permission of The McGraw-Hill Companies, Inc.

COMPREHENSION CHECKUP

Topic and Main Idea

1. What is the topic of this article? _____

2. What is the article's main idea? _____

STUDY TECHNIQUE 4

Outlining

An outline is an orderly arrangement of ideas going from the general to the specific. An outline shows the relationship and importance of ideas by using a system of Roman numerals for main headings (I, II, III, etc.), capital letters for subheadings (A, B, C, etc.), and numbers for sub-subheadings (1, 2, 3, etc.). Whether you are using outlining to organize class notes or a reading selection, only the most important points should be included.

A partial outline of the previous selection follows. Complete the outline by filling in the missing information in your own words.

I. *Motivation* is defined as _____

"Study Technique" boxes offer tips for mastering your college-level work; these can be applied not only to the material you are encountering in this text but in all your college courses.

TEST-TAKING TIP

After the Test Is Returned

After taking a test, think about what happened. Was it what you expected and prepared for? In what ways did it surprise you? Did it cover both lecture and textbook material? Or focus on one or the other? Think about how to change your approach to the course and the next test to take into account what you learned from the format of this test.

At some point, you will get your test back. Or you could ask to see it. This is another opportunity for you. Go over the test to see where your weaknesses are. What sorts of questions did you have the most trouble with? Many students have trouble with questions phrased in the negative, such as, Which of the following is not a valid conclusion that can be drawn from the evidence below? Did you have trouble with questions of this sort? If so, try to remedy this deficiency in your test prepa-

ration before the next test. You also need to go back and learn the material better that gave you trouble, because you may see questions about this material again on future tests, such as a midterm or final exam.

If you did poorly on the test, you may want to make an appointment with your instructor to talk about it. Maybe you need to be working with the instructor or a tutor out of class. Or maybe you should become part of a study group. You might even be taking the course before you're ready for it; maybe you should take some other courses first.

The key point is to treat past tests as learning experiences for what they tell you about your test preparation, how you're doing in the course, and what changes you can make to do better. Above all, maintain a positive attitude.

"Test-Taking Tips" at the end of each chapter provide helpful hints for mastering the process of taking an exam.

VOCABULARY   Homonyms and Other Confusing Words (Unit 2)

loose   An adverb or adjective meaning "free or released from fastening or attachment." *The dog was running* loose *in the neighborhood instead of being on a leash.*

lose   A verb meaning "to come to be without." *If G.E. and Honeywell merge, Carol will probably* lose *her job.*

passed   A verb, the past tense of the verb *pass. The quarterback* passed *the ball to the tight end, who ran for a touchdown. The E.S.L. student* passed *the TOEFL exam. My grandfather* passed *away last year.* Each of these sentences uses the word *passed* as a verb expressing action.

past   A noun meaning "former time." *In the* past, *students used typewriters instead of computers.*
Also, an adjective meaning "former." *One of our* past *presidents was Harry Truman.*
Also, an adverb meaning "going beyond something." *Motel 6 is just* past *the Fashion Square shopping center.*

Study Skills

PART 5

CHAPTER IN PART 5

CHAPTER 13 Organizing Textbook Information 572

Jean Puy. Study, or The Schoolgirl, c. 1933–34

Musée National d'Art Moderne, Centre Pompidou, Paris, France. Bridgeman Art Library. ©2009 Artists Rights Society (ARS), New York/ADAGP, Paris.

571

The Study Skills covered in Part 5 will reinforce the skills you've been learning throughout the book and will help you master the material you encounter in all your college courses.

The Vocabulary Units in various chapters help you to build your vocabulary by showing you how to interpret words based on the common word parts of which they're made.

VOCABULARY   Prefixes (Unit 3)

The following prefixes all indicate numbers:

uni—one	qua(d)—four	sept—seven
mono—one	tetra—four	hept—seven
bi—two	quint—five	oct—eight
di—two	pent—five	
du(o)—two		nov—nine
	hex—six	
tri—three	sex—six	dec, dek—ten

unify   to make or become a single unit

unicameral   -cam- means "chamber." *Unicameral* refers to a legislative body made up of only one house or chamber.

bicameral   having two groups in the lawmaking body. The *bicameral* U.S. Congress is made up of the Senate and the House of Representatives.

univalve   having a shell composed of a single piece, such as a snail

bivalve   having a shell composed of two parts hinged together, such as a clam or oyster.

monochromatic of or pertaining to only one color, as in *monochromatic* pottery. It was obvious that Regis, who wore a gray tie, gray shirt, and gray slacks, preferred a *monochromatic* style of dress.

monogram   initials of a person's name in a design, such as are used on articles of clothing or stationery.

monolith   -lith means "stone," so a monolith is a single block or piece of stone of considerable size, sometimes carved into a column or large statue. The sphinx of Egypt is a *monolith*.

monotonous   sounded or uttered in one unvarying tone; lacking in variety. At the graduation ceremony, many were displeased with the keynote speaker because of his *monotonous* speaking style.

monocle   an eyeglass for one eye

monorail   a single rail serving as a track for cars. Taking the *monorail* at Disneyland adds to the excitement.

monosyllabic   having only one syllable, like *what* or *how*

biracial   consisting of or representing members of two separate races. Tiger Woods, whose mother is Asian and father is black, is *biracial*.

bipartisan   made up of or supported by two political parties. Support for education is *bipartisan*.

bifocals   eyeglasses in which each lens has two parts, one for reading and seeing nearby objects and the other for seeing things further away. Benjamin Franklin invented *bifocals* in 1784.

bisect   -sect means "to cut," so *bisect* means to cut or divide into two equal parts

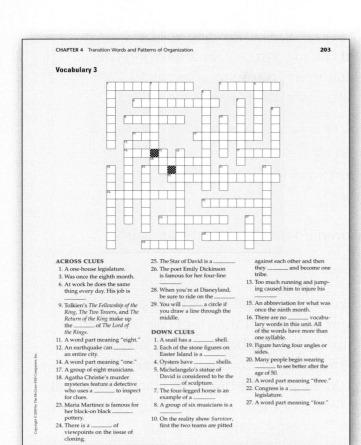

Vocabulary 3

ACROSS CLUES

1. A one-house legislature.
3. Was once the eighth month.
6. At work he does the same thing every day. His job is _____.
9. Tolkien's *The Fellowship of the Ring, The Two Towers,* and *The Return of the King* make up the _____ of *The Lord of the Rings.*
11. A word part meaning "eight."
12. An earthquake can _____ an entire city.
14. A word part meaning "one."
17. A group of eight musicians.
18. Agatha Christie's murder mysteries feature a detective who uses a _____ to inspect for clues.
23. Maria Martinez is famous for her black-on black _____ pottery.
24. There is a _____ of viewpoints on the issue of cloning.

25. The Star of David is a _____.
26. The poet Emily Dickinson is famous for her four-line _____.
28. When you're at Disneyland, be sure to ride on the _____.
29. You will _____ a circle if you draw a line through the middle.

DOWN CLUES

1. A snail has a _____ shell.
2. Each of the stone figures on Easter Island is a _____.
4. Oysters have _____ shells.
5. Michelangelo's statue of David is considered to be the _____ of sculpture.
7. The four-legged horse is an example of a _____.
8. A group of six musicians is a _____.
10. On the reality show *Survivor,* first the two teams are pitted

against each other and then they _____ and become one tribe.
13. Too much running and jumping caused him to injure his _____.
15. An abbreviation for what was once the ninth month.
16. There are no _____ vocabulary words in this unit. All of the words have more than one syllable.
19. Figure having four angles or sides.
20. Many people begin wearing _____ to see better after the age of 50.
21. A word part meaning "three."
22. Congress is a _____ legislature.
27. A word part meaning "four."

The Crossword Puzzles are fun exercises that will help you improve both your vocabulary and your reading comprehension.

The Appendices will help you learn to interpret visual aids (like graphs, charts, and maps), use a thesaurus, master vocabulary word parts, and write summaries that avoid plagiarism.

These features will serve as familiar guideposts and handy references as you make your way through the book. The structure will help you in understanding the book's content, even as the activities and exercises assist you in learning and remembering the material.

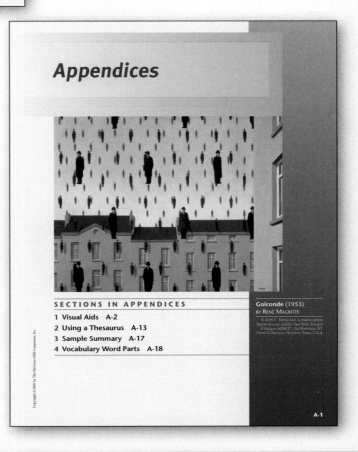

Appendices

SECTIONS IN APPENDICES

Golconde (1953)
BY RENÉ MAGRITTE

© 2009 C. Herscovici, London/Artists Rights Society (ARS), New York, Banque d'Images, ADAGP/ Art Resource, NY. Menil Collection, Houston, Texas, U.S.A.

A-1

We hope that your experience using *The Art of Critical Reading* will be entirely successful. If you have comments or suggestions for improving the way this textbook works, we'd like to hear from you. Send an email to **english@mcgraw-hill.com**, and our editors will gladly pass it along.

> *"Every child is an artist. The problem is how to remain an artist once he grows up."*
> —PABLO PICASSO

View and Reflect

In your journal, consider why most children do not grow up to be artists.

Crossword Puzzle

On the next page, you will find a crossword puzzle that will introduce you to the material covered in this book. The answers to some of the clues can be found in the Preface to the Student, which describes what the book is about and why it was written. Clues can also be found in the Table of Contents and the Index. The Table of Contents shows you the major divisions of the book. The Index, found at the back of the book, is an alphabetical listing of many important topics and the page numbers on which the information is located. Happy hunting!

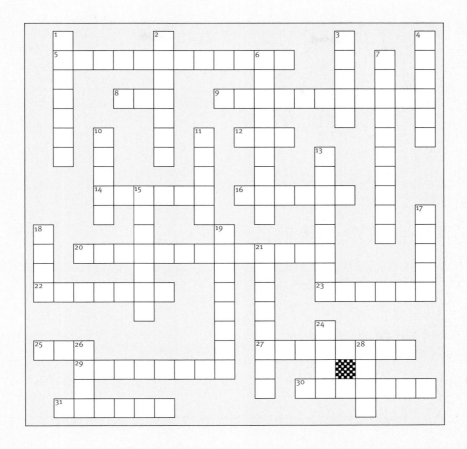

ACROSS CLUES

5. Chapter 4 discusses patterns of _____.

8. The first word in the title of the selection in Chapter 13 is _____ and the Aesthetic.

9. Charles Finney's selection discusses the western diamondback _____.

12. A discussion of similes, metaphors, and personification is found in Chapter _____.

14. The last name of the coauthor of this book who attended the University of Redlands.

16. An author whose purpose is to _____ will provide readers with knowledge or information.

20. Marian Wright Edelman was born in the state of _____.

22. Chapter 2 discusses topics, main ideas, and _____.

23. One type of pattern of organization is called cause and _____.

25. According to Vocabulary Unit 3, the prefix for nine is _____.

27. The last name of the coauthor of this book who has taught ESL classes.

29. One type of pattern of organization is called _____ and illustration.

30. Study Technique 6 is titled _____.

31. Figurative language compares two or more _____ things.

DOWN CLUES

1. In Chapter 4, there is a compare and contrast of two artworks: Manet's _____ and Cassatt's The Boating Party.

2. Most reading selections begin with a section titled "Getting the _____."

3. One type of logical fallacy is called _____ analogy.

4. Frida Kahlo was married to Diego _____.

6. Study Technique 4 is titled _____.

7. Laura Hillenbrand wrote a book about the racehorse _____.

10. Dave Barry wrote for the _____ Herald.

11. Study Technique 3 will teach you how to write summaries of _____ articles.

13. An author's purpose may be to _____ a reader or to try to change the reader's opinion.

15. If you learn by doing, your learning style would be called _____.

17. Chapter _____ discusses the difference between fact and opinion.

18. _____ stacking is one type of propaganda technique.

19. According to the Preface to the Student, the word "critical" came from the Greek word _____.

21. Michael J. Fox wrote the book _____.

24. _____ Ying Lin designed the Vietnam Veterans Memorial.

26. Study Technique 9 will teach you how to make a _____ Diagram.

28. All chapters end with test-taking _____.

Learning How to Be a Successful Student

The School of Athens (1510)
BY RAPHAEL

Scala/Art Resource, NY

Introduction

Three Musicians (1921) BY PABLO PICASSO

View and Reflect

1. This painting by Picasso is quite large. In fact, the three musicians, who include a Harlequin and a monk, are approximately life-size. What instruments are recognizable in the painting?
2. What animal is depicted on the left? Although the animal's body parts are disconnected, what parts can you clearly recognize?
3. What is the overall mood of the painting? Is it a solemn or happy occasion?
4. The painting is done in the cubist style, which tries to portray three-dimensional objects in two-dimensional space. The result is a flat, jigsaw puzzle effect. Which parts of the painting give the feeling of something being cut out and pasted on paper?

Oﾠ ne of the desired outcomes of a college education is the ability to think critically. But it's important to be able to think creatively as well. A creative thinker can generate many solutions to a problem, and a critical thinker can determine which solution is the best.

The selections that follow will explain the processes of creative and critical thinking.

SELECTION

Bull's Head
(1943) BY PABLO
PICASSO

"Intelligence and creativity are not the same thing."

GETTING THE PICTURE

The influential artist Pablo Picasso once said, "Every child is an artist. The problem is how to remain an artist once he grows up." Picasso, noted for his creativity, meant that children are unafraid to try new things even at the risk of feeling foolish or experiencing failure. As we age, many of us place more emphasis on saving face, being practical, and thinking inside the box.

Picasso, as the story goes, took a walk around his yard one day and saw an old, rusted bicycle. He took the seat and the handlebars back to his studio and welded them together to create his famous sculpture of the head of a bull. The selection below explains the creative process and the characteristics of creative thinkers like Picasso who don't just think of a bicycle seat as something to sit on. Perhaps, after reading the selection, you'll be able to unleash some of your own creative energy.

BIO-SKETCH

John Santrock is a professor of psychology and human development at the University of Texas. He is the author of many popular, well-regarded textbooks.

BRUSHING UP ON VOCABULARY

divergent differing; deviating; having no finite limits

convergent coming together; merging

Excerpt from
PSYCHOLOGY
by John Santrock

Creativity

1   What does it mean to be creative? **Creativity** is the ability to think about something in novel and unusual ways and to come up with unconventional solutions to problems. Intelligence and creativity are not the same things. Many highly intelligent people produce large numbers of products, but the products are not necessarily novel. Highly creative people defy the crowd, whereas people who are highly intelligent but not creative often try simply to please the crowd.

2   Creative people tend to be divergent thinkers. **Divergent thinking** produces many answers to the same question. In contrast, the kind of thinking required on conventional intelligence tests is **convergent thinking.** For example, a typical item on an intelligence test is "How many quarters will you get in return for 60 dimes?" There is only one correct

answer to this question. However, the following question has many possible answers: what image comes to mind when you hear the phrase "sitting alone in a dark room"?

3   Thinking further about intelligence and creativity, most creative people are quite intelligent, but the reverse is not necessarily true. Many highly intelligent people are not very creative.

Steps in the Creative Process

4   The creative process has often been described as a five-step sequence:

1. *Preparation.* You become immersed in a problem or an issue that interests you and arouses your curiosity.

2. *Incubation.* You churn ideas around in your head. This is the point at which you are likely to make some unusual connections in your thinking.

3. *Insight.* At this point, you experience the "Aha!" moment when all the pieces of the puzzle seem to fit together.

4. *Evaluation.* Now you must decide whether the idea is valuable and worth pursuing. Is the idea really novel, or is it obvious?

5. *Elaboration.* This final step often covers the longest span of time and the hardest work. This is what the famous twentieth-century American inventor Thomas Edison was talking about when he said that creativity is 1 percent inspiration and 99 percent perspiration. Elaboration may require a great deal of perspiration.

Characteristics of Creative Thinkers

5   Creative thinkers tend to have the following characteristics:

6   • *Flexibility and playful thinking.* Creative thinkers are flexible and play with problems, which gives rise to a paradox. Although creativity takes hard work, the work goes more smoothly if it is taken lightly. In a way humor greases the wheels of creativity. When you are joking around, you are more likely to consider any possibility. Having fun helps to disarm the inner censor that can condemn your ideas as off base.

7   • *Inner motivation.* Creative people often are motivated by the joy of creating. They tend to be less inspired by grades, money, or favorable feedback from others. Thus creative people are motivated more internally than externally.

"Creativity requires the courage to let go of certainties."

—Erich Fromm

8   • *Willingness to risk.* Creative people make more mistakes than their less imaginative counterparts. It's not that they are less proficient but that they come up with more ideas, more possibilities. They win some, they lose some. For example, the twentieth-century Spanish artist Pablo Picasso created more than 20,000 paintings. Not all of them were masterpieces. Creative thinkers learn to cope with unsuccessful projects and see failure as an opportunity to learn.

9   • *Objective evaluation of work.* Despite the stereotype that creative people are eccentric and highly subjective, most creative thinkers strive to evaluate their work objectively. They may use an established set of criteria to make judgments or rely on the judgments of respected, trusted others.

Living a More Creative Life

"The world is but a canvas to the imagination."

—Henry David Thoreau

10   Here are recommendations for achieving a more creative life:

11   • *Try to be surprised by something every day.* Maybe it is something you see, hear, or read about. Become absorbed in a lecture or a book. Be open to what the

world is telling you. Life is a stream of experiences. Swim widely and deeply in it, and your life will be richer.

12 • *Try to surprise at least one person every day.* In a lot of things you do, you have to be predictable and patterned. Do something different. Ask a question you normally would not ask. Invite someone to go to a show or a museum you have never visited.

13 • *Write down every day what surprised you and how you surprised others.* Most creative people keep a diary, notes, or lab records to ensure that experiences are not fleeting or forgotten.

14 • *When something sparks your interest, follow it.* The world is our business. We can't know which parts are more interesting until we make a serious effort to learn as much about as many aspects of it as possible.

15 • *Take charge of your schedule.* Figure out which time of the day is your most creative time. Carve out time for yourself when your creative energy is at its best.

16 • *Spend time in settings that stimulate your creativity.* Many report their highest levels of creativity occur when they are walking, jogging, driving, or swimming. These activities are semiautomatic in that they take only a certain amount of attention while leaving some free to make connection among ideas. Highly creative people also report coming up with novel ideas in the deeply relaxed state we are in when we are half-asleep, half-awake.

> "The best way to have a good idea is to have lots of ideas."
> —Linus Pauling

17 To evaluate the extent to which you engage in creative thinking complete the following chart.

How Creative Is Your Thinking

Rate each of the following items as they apply to you on a scale from 1 = not like me at all, 2 = somewhat unlike me, 3 = somewhat like me, 4 = very much like me.

1. I am good at coming up with lots of new and unique ideas. _4_
2. I like to brainstorm with others to creatively find solutions to problems. _4_
3. I'm a flexible person and like to play with my thinking. _3_
4. I like to be around creative people, and I learn from how they think. _4_
5. I like to be surprised by something every day. _4_
6. I wake up in the morning with a mission. _4_
7. I search for alternative solutions to problems rather than giving a pat answer. _4_
8. I know which settings stimulate me to be creative, and I try to spend time in those settings. _3_
9. I tend to be internally motivated. _4_

Total your scores for all 9 items. Your creativity score is __34__. If you scored 32–36 points, you likely are a creative thinker. If you scored 27–31 points, you are inclined to be creative, but could benefit from thinking about some ways to get more creativity in your life. If you scored 26 or below, seriously think about ways to become more creative.

Source: pp. 408–411 from PSYCHOLOGY WITH IN-PSYCH CD-ROM AND POWERWEB, 7/e by John Santrock. Copyright © 2003. Reprinted by permission of McGraw-Hill Companies, Inc.

COMPREHENSION CHECKUP

True or False

Indicate whether the statement is true or false by writing T or F in the blank provided.

_F_ 1. Intelligence and creativity are precisely the same thing.

_T_ 2. Many highly intelligent people are not very creative.

_F_ 3. In the creative process, evaluation takes the most time and requires the hardest work.

_T_ 4. Humor is an asset in the creative process.

_F_ 5. External motivation plays a large part in the creative process.

_T_ 6. Creative people have a positive attitude toward failure.

_F_ 7. Most creative thinkers are highly eccentric.

_T_ 8. To live a creative life, the author recommends being open to new experiences.

_F_ 9. Predictability is an essential characteristic of the creative life.

_T_ 10. People sometimes come up with creative ideas when they are doing a physical activity that requires little mental energy.

Vocabulary Practice

Answer the following in the blank provided.

1. You put your car in *reverse*. Are you are going forward or backward?
   backward

2. Your cousin is *proficient* at typing. Is she skilled or unskilled?
   skilled

3. If you come up with a *novel* way to travel, are you coming up with something that is new or something that has been done before? _new_

4. If you are *striving* for an A in class, are you making a strong effort or a weak one? _strong_

5. If you got a *fleeting* glimpse of a friend at a basketball game, did you see a great deal of her or very little? _very little_

6. If you *defied* your commander, are you being obedient or disobedient?
   disobedient

7. If your thinking is *flexible*, can you change your mind about something, or must you "stick to your guns"? _change mind_

8. If you take a test with all multiple-choice questions, are you taking an *objective* test or a *subjective* one? _objective_

9. If you *disarm* an alarm system, are you turning it on or off?
   off

10. If the label on the medicine bottle says, "For *external* use only," should you swallow the medicine? _No_

11. Give an example of something that is completely *predictable*.
_____

12. What is wrong with using *stereotypes*? _____
_____

In Your Own Words

In Your Own Words

1. Give your own definition of *creativity*.

2. What does the author mean when he says, "Humor greases the wheels of creativity"?

3. It has been suggested by various creativity experts that the testing process could be improved to allow for more creative responses. For instance, professors might give more points for the most unusual correct answers to a question. Or professors might ask questions that have more than one correct answer and then give credit based on the number of correct answers a student gives. What do you think about these suggestions? Should test-makers be encouraged to allow for more creative responses?

4. Study the following problems to determine how creative you are.
   a. What objects can you think of that begin with the letters "br"?
   b. How could discarded aluminum cans be put to use?
   c. How many uses can you think of for a newspaper?
   d. What would happen if everyone suddenly lost the sense of balance and could no longer stay upright?

5. How is Garfield illustrating creative problem solving in the cartoon below?

GARFIELD ®

GARFIELD © 1995, PAWS INC. Reprinted with permission of UNIVERSAL PRESS SYNDICATE. All rights reserved.

6. Which of the following is more likely an example of creative thinking? Explain the reasons for your choice.
   a. A 16-year-old trying to come up with as many reasons as she can to explain her poor grades to avoid being grounded.
   b. A 16-year-old taking a multiple-choice test.

7. When a group tries to come up with as many solutions to a problem as possible, it's called *brainstorming*. Why is this technique considered a creative thinking strategy?

The Art of Writing

A **paradox** is a statement that seems contradictory to common sense but nevertheless may be true. A coach who says to his formerly undefeated team that "this was a good loss" is stating a paradox because most of us don't think of a loss as something positive. In this case, the coach probably meant that the team had grown complacent and needed a wake-up call.

It is a paradox that doing nothing is often more tiring than working hard or that standing appears to be more tiring than walking.

One of the most famous literary paradoxes comes from the poem *The Rime of the Ancient Mariner* by Samuel Taylor Coleridge. A paraphrase of it is, "Water, water, everywhere, and not a drop to drink." The poet is referring to being adrift in the sea, parched with thirst, and yet surrounded by salty water.

Can you think of some paradoxes of your own? Try to come up with several, and include an explanation for each.

Internet Activity

At the end of many reading selections, you will find one or more suggested Internet activities. Although we have checked each site, websites do come and go, and URLs change frequently. If the Internet site mentioned in the activity is no longer available, then use a search engine like Google <www.google.com> or Yahoo! <www.yahoo.com> to find a similar site.

Check out the following website to try out some creative thinking activities. Can activities like these help you become a more creative individual?

http://www.mycoted.com/Category:Creativity_Techniques

Study the following tests of divergent thinking. How would you complete each drawing?

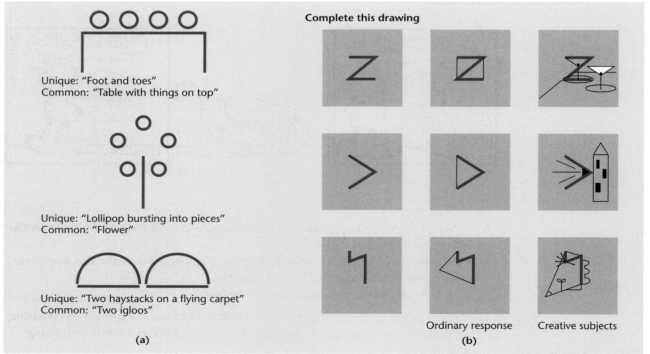

From Dennis Coon, *Approach to Mind and Behavior,* 10th ed., pp. 361. Copyright © Thomson Learning. Reprinted with permission of Wadsworth, a division of Thomson Learning: www.thomsonrights.com. Fax 800-730-2215.

SELECTION

"Nampeyo's success became a pattern that other Indian artists would follow."

GETTING THE PICTURE

The craft of ceramics involves making objects from clay, a naturally occurring earth substance. Nearly every known culture has practiced the craft of ceramics, and civilizations in the Middle East understood the basic techniques as early as 5000 B.C.E. One method for creating ceramic pots is known as *coiling*. The ceramist rolls out ropelike strands of clay, then coils them upon one another and joins them together. The coils can then be smoothed to produce a uniform, flat wall. The early Native American peoples of the southwestern United States made extraordinarily fine pots by this method. In the twentieth century, their craft was revived by a few supremely talented and creative individuals, including the famous Nampeyo, whose work is described in the selection below.

Source: Information from Mark Getlein, *Gilbert's Living with Art,* New York: McGraw-Hill, 2005, p. 278.

Nampeyo, Hopi potterymaker, seated, with examples of her work.

The National Archives

BIO-SKETCH

Now retired, Duane Preble was a professor of art at the University of Hawaii from 1961 to 1991. Preble currently serves on the Board of Trustees of Hawaii's major art museum, the Honolulu Academy of Arts.

BRUSHING UP ON VOCABULARY

abstract emphasizing line and color in a nonrepresentational design.

curator the person in charge of a museum or art collection.

shards fragments of broken earthenware.

Excerpt from
ARTFORMS

by Duane Preble

Shaping Her People's Heritage: Nampeyo (1857?–1942)

1   Traditional Native American ceramic arts had fallen into decline when Nampeyo first learned the trade from her grandmother. Most Indians in the Hopi region of Arizona, and even the Pueblo peoples of New Mexico, made very little pottery. The encroachment of mass produced goods, coupled with the severe poverty of both regions, led most Native families in the late nineteenth century to buy low-priced dishes and cooking utensils from white traders rather than pursue the ancient and time-consuming art of ceramics. Nampeyo's fusion of artistic talent and interest in the past sparked a pottery revival that spread throughout the Southwest and continues to this day.

2   The date of her birth is uncertain, since no one kept close records of such things in the village of Hano on land that the Hopis called First Mesa. She was born into the

Snake Clan, and was given the name Nampeyo, which means "Snake That Does Not Bite." There were no paved roads leading to the village, and the nearest city—Winslow, Arizona—was three days' journey away. In that isolated environment, Nampeyo grew up. Her family responded to her early artistic interests by sending her to a neighboring village to learn pottery-making from her grandmother, one of the few who still made pots. Her grandmother's large water jars were rather simply decorated, with only one or two designs on the face of each one.

3   Sometime in the middle 1890s, Nampeyo began picking up broken shards of pottery from the near-by site of an ancient Hopi village called Sikyatki. This village had been abandoned well before the Spanish Conquest. The ancient pottery fragments were more ornate and abstract than the basic symbols that Nampeyo had been painting; she was fascinated by the ancient designs and began to incorporate them into her own pots.

4   In 1895, the anthropologist Jesse Walter Fewkes arrived to dig and study the ruins of Sikyatki, and his presence transformed Nampeyo's work. Her husband was one of several assistants to Fewkes; he helped with the digging and told the anthropologist what he knew about the ancestral customs of the Hopi peoples. Fewkes and his assistants and students unearthed hundreds of burials, finding many more examples of ancient Hopi pottery in excellent condition. It was traditional to bury the dead with a seed jar, a low container with a narrow opening at the top, as a symbol of spiritual rebirth. These jars had abstract designs in brown or black over a rich yellow body. Her husband brought pieces home for Nampeyo, and soon she met Fewkes and accompanied him on digs.

5   Nampeyo invigorated her pottery by her sustained exposure to the work of her ancestors. She copied, studied, and practiced the ancient symbols. She mastered the shape of the traditional seed jar. Because the clay in the ancient pots was of finer quality than she was used to making, she sought new places to dig better clay from the earth. Fewkes, keenly interested in this revival of ancient techniques, took Nampeyo to Chicago so that she could demonstrate her knowledge to the curators of the Field Museum of Natural History. She also demonstrated her skills to tourists and archaeologists at the Grand Canyon.

"All acts performed in the world begin with imagination."

—Barbara Grizzuti Harrison

6   Once she learned the vocabulary of symbols, she found that she could freely adapt and combine them, rather than merely copy ancient models. She told an anthropologist, "When I first began to paint, I used to go to the ancient village and pick up pieces of pottery and copy the designs. That is how I learned to paint. But now I just close my eyes and see designs and I paint them." Fewkes referred to her as a "thorough artist."

7   Probably Nampeyo's biggest surprise was that non-native Americans were interested in buying her pots. She discovered that there was a ready market for pottery with the ancient designs. In this effort she was a pioneer. The relatively rare ancient pottery had always found buyers among a few select collectors; however, when Nampeyo began making pots in that style, to her delight she found that she could easily sell her entire production. She used the new income to support her entire extended family, and alleviate some of the poverty on First Mesa.

8   Nampeyo's success became a pattern that other Indian artists would follow. In the Pueblo of San Ildefonso, Maria Martinez and her husband, in collaboration with anthropologist Edgar Hewitt, soon reintroduced ancient black pottery from that Pueblo. Lucy Lewis of Acoma was similarly inspired by ancient designs. The revival of Pueblo

and Hopi pottery contributed to the creation, in 1932, of the Native American Arts and Crafts Board, the first government attempt to encourage Native creators to practice their traditional art forms.

9   Nampeyo continued to produce work herself until she began to lose her eyesight in the 1920s. Her husband painted some of her designs until his death in 1932. Today her great-granddaughters continue the tradition.

Source: Duane Preble, et al., *Artforms: An Introduction to the Visual Arts, 7th Edition*, pp. 215–216. Copyright © 2002. Reprinted by permission of Pearson Education Inc., Upper Saddle River, NJ.

 COMPREHENSION CHECKUP

True or False

Indicate whether the statement is true or false by writing T or F in the blank provided.

___F___ 1. Nampeyo learned the art of pottery making from her aunt and cousins.

___T___ 2. Nampeyo had obtained samples of pottery from the ruins of Sityaki before the arrival of Fewkes.

___T___ 3. Nampeyo's art began with basic symbols and gradually evolved into more complex designs.

___F___ 4. Nampeyo's skill in making pots lives on in her sons.

___F___ 5. Nampeyo began to lose her sight in the 1930s.

___T___ 6. Nampeyo's work was largely derivative in the beginning of her career but became more original as time passed.

___T___ 7. The clay used in the ancient pots was of a superior quality to that in Nampeyo's early work.

___T___ 8. When Nampeyo began making money from her pots, she shared the proceeds with her family.

___T___ 9. Before Nampeyo, no one was interested in collecting ancient pottery.

___T___ 10. Nampeyo's pot designs were more ornate than her grandmother's.

Multiple Choice

Write the letter of the correct choice in the blank provided.

_____ 1. Which of the following best states the main idea of the selection?
a. Probably Nampeyo's biggest surprise was that non-native Americans were interested in buying her pots.
b. Fewkes referred to her as a "thorough artist."
c. Nampeyo invigorated her pottery by her sustained exposure to the work of her ancestors.
d. Nampeyo's fusion of artistic talent and interest in the past sparked a pottery revival that spread throughout the Southwest and continues to this day.

_____ 2. The author wrote this selection to
   a. persuade the reader to support the art of indigenous peoples
   b. describe in detail the beautiful pots created by Nampeyo
   c. explain how a gifted artist revived a Native American art form
   d. tell the story of the ancient Hopi

_____ 3. In paragraph 8, the examples of Maria Martinez and Lucy Lewis illustrated
   a. that other Native American artists followed in the footsteps of Nampeyo
   b. the rivalry between fellow artists
   c. the importance of excavating ancient sites
   d. the usefulness of seed jars

_____ 4. The tradition of pottery making had fallen into decline because of
   a. the amount of time required to make a pot
   b. the availability of cheap dishes
   c. the lack of appropriate clay
   d. both a and b

_____ 5. The seed jars of the early Hopi had all of the following characteristics *except*
   a. they were decorated with abstract designs.
   b. they were a symbol of spiritual rebirth.
   c. they were always completely white.
   d. they were low with a narrow opening.

_____ 6. Nampeyo visited all of the following places *except*
   a. the Field Museum of Natural History in Chicago
   b. the Grand Canyon
   c. the Pueblo of San Ildefonso
   d. the ruins of Sikyatki

_____ 7. All of the following were mentioned as being instrumental in Nampeyo's success *except*
   a. her grandmother, who introduced her to the art of pottery making
   b. the late Senator Barry Goldwater, who was an avid collector of her pots
   c. her husband, who brought ancient pottery shards home to her
   d. the anthropologist Jesse Walter Fewkes, who allowed her to accompany him on digs

_____ 8. The village of Hano
   a. is located on the First Mesa
   b. is largely isolated
   c. is on Hopi land
   d. all of the above

_____ 9. If something is relatively rare, it means that it
   a. can be found readily
   b. is somewhat hard to find
   c. has been cooked too much
   d. is commonplace

_____ 10. Nampeyo is considered to be a pioneer. This means that she
   a. helped settle the West
   b. initiated something
   c. guided the way for others to follow
   d. both b and c

Vocabulary Practice

Fill in the blanks with a word from the list below. Not all of the words will be used.

alleviate	extended	isolated	sparked
collaboration	fusion	ornate	sustained
coupled	incorporate	pioneer	
encroachment	invigorated	revival	

1. The _Ornate_ Palace of Versailles, home to the kings of France, welcomes thousands of visitors each year.

2. Many people take medication to _alleviate_ the painful symptoms of arthritis.

3. Amelia Earhart, the first woman to pilot an airplane across the Atlantic Ocean, was a _pioneer_ in the field of aviation.

4. There has been a _____ of interest in the music of the sixties.

5. Realizing that everyone had forgotten to invite Brittany to the office party, Caroline hurriedly _____ an invitation.

6. After a workout at the gym and a long swim in the heated pool, Greg felt _____.

7. After the blizzard, the people in the small village were left completely _____ from emergency services and supplies.

8. In many places along the coast, the _encroachment_ of the sea on the land is causing concern.

9. In the three-car crash, many observers were surprised that no one _____ any injuries.

10. Their close _____ on the project resulted in many gains for the company.

In Your Own Words

1. What characteristics do you think innovators possess? What makes someone decide to attempt something that hasn't been done before?

2. In what ways did Nampeyo's family encourage her artistic talent? How can we encourage more people to participate in the arts?

3. Many of the great painters spent years copying the masters before developing their own distinct styles. Is it necessary to copy others before you can develop your own vision?

4. Do you think anthropologists would be able to investigate digs today the way Fewkes did in 1895? What is likely to happen today if an anthropologist proposes to dig in ancient burial grounds?

Written Assignment

Give a detailed description of a piece of pottery. Try to make your description so vivid that someone could draw a picture of it based on your words.

Internet Activity

Visit one of the following websites to learn more about Nampeyo. Write a few short paragraphs giving additional biographical information about her that was not included in the reading selection.

www.statemuseum.arizona.edu/nampeyo

www.meyna.com/nampeyo.html

SELECTION

"Critical thinkers analyze the evidence supporting their beliefs and probe for weaknesses in their reasoning."

GETTING THE PICTURE

To succeed as a college student, you will need to be able to read, write, and think critically. The following selection from a popular introductory psychology textbook defines the process of critical thinking.

BIO-SKETCH

After earning a doctorate in psychology from the University of Arizona, Dennis Coon taught for 22 years at Santa Barbara City College in California. He recently returned to Tucson, Arizona, to teach, write, edit, and consult. Although he has written two college textbooks that have been used by 2 million students, his real passion is teaching introductory psychology classes.

BRUSHING UP ON VOCABULARY

empirical testing gathering verifiable information from experience or experiments.

guru a leader or person with some authority and respect. Originally, a *guru* was a Hindu spiritual leader or guide.

anecdotal evidence information gathered about a person through a series of observations rather than through systematic research. Teachers often collect *anecdotal* information about their students through firsthand observation.

Excerpt from
APPROACH TO MIND AND BEHAVIOR
by Dennis Coon

Critical Thinking—Uncommon Sense

1   Most of us would be skeptical when buying a used car. But all too often, we may be tempted to "buy" outrageous claims about topics such as "channeling," dowsing, the occult, the Bermuda Triangle, hypnosis, UFOs, numerology, and so forth. Likewise, most of us easily accept our ignorance of subatomic physics. But because we deal with human behavior every day, we tend to think that we already know what is true and what is false.

"Thought is the strongest thing we have. Work done by true and profound thought— that is a real force."
—Albert Schweitzer

2   For these, and many more reasons, learning to think critically is one of the lasting benefits of getting an education. Facts and theories may change. Thinking and problem-solving skills last a lifetime.

3   Critical thinkers are willing to ask hard questions and challenge conventional wisdom. For example, many people believe that punishment (such as a spanking) is a good way to reinforce learning in children. Actually, nothing could be farther from the truth. That's why a critical thinker would immediately ask: "Does punishment work? If so, when? Under what conditions does it not work? What are its drawbacks? Are there better ways to guide learning?"

4   The core of critical thinking is a willingness to actively evaluate ideas. It is, in a sense, the ability to stand outside yourself and reflect on the quality of your own thoughts. Critical thinkers analyze the evidence supporting their beliefs and probe for weaknesses in their reasoning. They question assumptions and look for alternate conclusions. True knowledge, they recognize, comes from constantly revising and enlarging our understanding of the world.

5   Critical thinking is built upon four basic principles:

6   1. *Few "truths" transcend the need for empirical testing.* It is true that religious beliefs and personal values may be held without supporting evidence. But most other ideas can be evaluated by applying the rules of logic and evidence.

7   2. *Evidence varies in quality.* Judging the quality of evidence is crucial. Imagine that you are a juror in a courtroom, judging claims made by two battling lawyers. To judge correctly, you can't just weigh the evidence. You must also critically evaluate the *quality* of the evidence. Then you can give greater weight to the most credible facts.

8   3. *Authority or claimed expertise does not automatically make an idea true.* Just because a teacher, guru, celebrity, or authority is convinced or sincere doesn't mean you should automatically believe them. It is unscientific and self-demeaning to just take the word of an "expert" without asking, "What evidence convinced him or her? How good is it? Is there a better explanation?" This is especially true of information on the Internet, which is often inaccurate.

9   4. *Critical thinking requires an open mind.* Be prepared to consider daring departures and go wherever the evidence leads. However, it is possible to be so "open-minded" that you simply become gullible. Critical thinkers try to strike a balance between open-mindedness and healthy skepticism. Being open-minded means that you consider all possibilities before drawing a conclusion; it is the ability to change your views under the impact of new and more convincing evidence.

A Case Study of Critical Thinking

10   An anxious mother watches her son eat a candy bar and says, "Watch, it's like lighting a fuse on a firecracker. He'll be bouncing off the walls in a few minutes." Is she right? Will a "sugar buzz" make her son "hyper"? Does eating excessive amounts of sugar adversely affect children's behavior? What are the implications of this claim? If it is true, children who eat sugar should display measurable changes in behavior.

11   *Anecdotal Evidence.* What evidence is there to support the claim? It should be easy to find parents who will attest that their children become high-strung, inattentive, or unruly after eating sugar. However, parents are not likely to be

objective observers. Beliefs about "sugar highs" are common and could easily color parents' views.

12   *Casual Observations.*   Perhaps it would help to observe children directly. Let's say you decide to watch children at a birthday party, where you know large amounts of sugary foods will be consumed. As predicted by the claim, children at the party become loud and boisterous after eating cake, ice cream, and candy. How persuasive is this evidence? Actually, it is seriously flawed. Birthday parties expose children to bright lights, loud noises, and unfamiliar situations. Any of these conditions, and others as well, could easily explain the children's "hyper" activity.

13   *Authority.*   For nearly 50 years, many doctors, teachers, nutritionists, and other "experts" have emphatically stated that sugar causes childhood misbehavior. Should you believe them? Unfortunately, most of these "expert" opinions are based on anecdotes and casual observations that are little better than those we have already reviewed.

14   *Formal Evidence.*   The truth is, parents, casual observers, and many authorities have been wrong. Dr. Mark Wolraich and his colleagues recently reviewed 23 scientific studies on sugar and children. In each study, children consumed known amounts of sugar and were then observed or tested. The clear-cut conclusion in all of the studies was that sugar does not affect aggression, mood, motor skills, or cognitive skills.

15   Studies like those we just reviewed tend to be convincing because they are based on systematic, controlled observation. But don't just accept the investigators' conclusions. It is important to review the evidence yourself and decide if it is convincing.

Source: From *Approach to Mind and Behavior,* 10th ed., pp. 44–45. Copyright © Thomson Learning. Reprinted with permission of Wadsworth, a division of Thomson Learning: www.thomsonrights.com. Fax 800-730-2215.

 ## COMPREHENSION CHECKUP

Fill in the Blanks

Fill in the blanks with details from the selection.

1. Critical thinking refers to an ability to evaluate, compare, analyze, _critique_, and synthesize information.

2. The core of critical thinking is a willingness to actively _evaluate_ ideas.

3. _Empirical_ testing is needed to evaluate most ideas.

4. The quality of the _evidence_ must be critically evaluated.

5. Even the evidence of an _authority_ must be evaluated.

6. Critical thinkers must keep an open _mind_.

7. The problem with anecdotal evidence is that people are not _objective_ observers.

8. Casual _observations_ is not always reliable.

9. An authority might want to offer an expert _opinion_.

10. You should _review_ the evidence yourself to determine if it is convincing.

Vocabulary Practice

Using a dictionary, define the following words. Then use ten of the words in a sentence. You may change or add endings. The paragraph number in parentheses tells you where the word is located in the selection.

1. skeptical (1) _____ having doubt _____
2. conventional (3) _____
3. reinforce (3) _____ Strengthen _____
4. drawbacks (3) _____ disadvantages _____
5. probe (4) _____ search or examine thoroughly _____
6. transcend (6) _____ rise above or go beyond the ordinary limits of _____
7. crucial (7) _____ of vital or critical importance _____
8. credible (7) _____ Capable of being believed _____
9. demeaning (8) _____ lowering in dignity or standards _____
10. gullible (9) _____ Easily decieved or cheated _____
11. open-minded (9) _____
    _____
12. adversely (10) _____
13. attest (11) _____ Conforming to accepted standards _____
14. unruly (11) _____
15. color (11) _____
16. boisterous (12) _____ rough and noisy _____
17. flawed (12) _____ imperfect _____
18. anecdotes (13) _____ Short accounts of incidents or events _____

In Your Own Words

1. Many advertisers claim that you can increase your ability to think critically by doing mental exercises. Do you think these exercises are likely to work?
2. What is the difference between critical thinking and negative thinking?

The Art of Writing

1. In a few paragraphs, explain the following: To think critically, you must be willing to think creatively.
2. Pick one of the following real-life situations, and explain how you arrived at your solution.
    a. You are no longer getting along with your live-in girlfriend/boyfriend. You want her/him to move out, but you'd still like to remain friends.
    b. Your neighbor's new puppy barks for large parts of the night, and as a result, you're not getting enough sleep. You're close friends with the neighbor, who has done you a lot of favors in the past. How do you solve the problem?
    c. Your girlfriend/boyfriend has resumed smoking after quitting for two years. You can't stand to be around second-hand smoke. What do you do?

3. Which basic principle of critical thinking is illustrated by the following cartoon? Explain your choice.

New Yorker Cartoon BY SAM GROSS

S.GROSS

"For God's sake, think! Why is he being so nice to you?"

Internet Activity

Consult the following website:

http://www.virtualsalt.com/crebook1.htm

Evaluate the author's suggestions. Which ones do you think might work for you?

CRITICAL THINKING AND PROBLEM SOLVING

Several problems are given below. They are meant to test your critical thinking and problem-solving abilities. To solve them, you need to look at each problem in a different way. Be cautious about making assumptions.

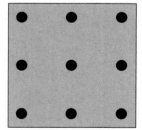

The nine-dot problem. The answer is found on page 30.

a. Nine dots are arranged in a square. Can you connect them by drawing four continuous straight lines without lifting your pencil from the paper?

b. Unscramble each set of letters to make a word that uses all the letters:

MEST   _____

LFAE   _____

DUB   _____

STKAL   _____

OTOR   _____

LTEPA   _____

Now try a new list:

FINEK   _____

OPONS   _____

KROF   _____

PUC   _____

SDIH   _____

LTEPA   _____

c. See how many of the following questions you can answer correctly.

1. Argentinians do not have a fourth of July. T or F?

2. How many birthdays does the average person have?

3. A farmer had 19 sheep. All but 9 died. How many sheep did the farmer have left?

4. Some months have 30 days, some have 31. How many months have 28 days?

5. I have two coins that together total 30 cents. One of the coins is not a nickel. What are the two coins?

6. If there are twelve one-cent candies in a dozen, how many two-cent candies are there in a dozen?

d. How many uses can you think of for a newspaper? The answer is found on page 30.

SELECTION

*"And do not ever stop learning and improving your mind,
because if you do, you are going to be left behind."*

GETTING THE PICTURE

The following selection is from a college commencement speech delivered by Marian Wright Edelman at Washington University in St. Louis, Missouri, on May 15, 1992. The eight lessons she mentions in the speech were meant to serve as "road maps" for graduating seniors. Because Edelman does not feel that she "has all the answers," students were urged to "ignore, revise, or use all or any of the lessons as they see fit." Edelman, who considers her life a testament to the American Dream, hopes that her words of advice might aid some in "developing a positive passion in life."

BIO-SKETCH

Marian Wright Edelman, the youngest of five children, was born in 1939 in Bennettsville, South Carolina. In the days when African-Americans were not allowed in city parks, Edelman's father built a park for them behind his church. Edelman graduated from Spelman College, a historically African-American college in Atlanta, went on to graduate from Yale Law School, and became the first African-American admitted to the Mississippi Bar. She has written many articles and books, including her autobiographical bestseller, *The Measure of Our Success: A Letter to My Children and Yours.* She is the founder and president of the Children's Defense Fund, has served on many boards, and has received numerous honorary awards. She is married to Peter Edelman, a professor at Georgetown Law School. They have three sons and two granddaughters.

BRUSHING UP ON VOCABULARY

free lunch something acquired without due effort or cost. The term originated in the 1800s from the custom of taverns offering free food to their patrons to encourage them to buy drinks. Today *free lunch* is often used in a pejorative way.

cut corners do something in the easiest or least expensive way; act illegally. The term was first used in the late 1800s. It originally meant to go around a corner as closely as possible so as to reduce the distance traveled, thereby saving time.

SELECTION *continued*

expediency regard for what is advantageous rather than for what is right or just. The word *expediency* is derived from the Latin *expedire,* meaning "to free one caught by the foot."

illiterate *illiterate* is derived from the Latin word *litera,* meaning "letter." So an *illiterate* is someone who does not know letters—that is, someone who lacks the ability to read.

integrity adherence to moral and ethical principles; honesty. The word *integrity* is derived from the Latin *integer,* meaning "a whole number." The word later came to mean "in one piece."

Commencement Address

by Marian Wright Edelman

Washington University
St. Louis, Missouri
May 15, 1992

1   I WANT TO SHARE A FEW LESSONS of life taken from a letter that I wrote to my own three wonderful sons. I recognize that you can take or leave these lessons, but you won't be able to say that you were never told them. Let me give you a few of them.

"The lust for comfort, that 2   The first lesson is, there is no free lunch. Do not feel entitled to anything
stealthy thing that enters   you do not sweat or struggle for. Your degree will get you in the door, but it
the house a guest and then   will not get you to the top of the career ladder or keep you there. You have got
becomes a host,   to work your way up hard and continuously.
and then a master." 3   Remember not to be lazy. Do your homework. Pay attention to detail. Take
—Kahlil Gibran   care and pride in your work. Take the initiative in creating your own opportunity and do not wait around for other people to discover you or do you a favor. Do not assume a door is closed; push on it. Do not assume if it was closed yesterday that it is closed today. And do not ever stop learning and improving your mind, because if you do, you are going to be left behind.

4   Lesson two is, assign yourself. Daddy used to ask us whether the teacher gave us any homework and if we said no, he said, well, assign yourself some. Do not wait around for somebody else to direct you to do what you are able to figure out and do for yourself. Do not do just as little as you can to get by.

5   Do not be a political bystander or grumbler. Vote. Democracy is not a spectator sport. Run for political office. But when you do run and when you do win, don't begin to think that you or your reelection are the only point. If you see a need, do not ask, "Why doesn't somebody do something?" Ask, "Why

don't I do something?" Hard work and persistence and initiative are still the non-magic carpets to success for most of us.

6   Lesson three: Never work just for money. Money will not save your soul or build a decent family or help you sleep at night. We are the richest nation on earth with the highest incarceration rate and also with some of the highest drug addiction and child poverty rates in the world.

7   Do not confuse wealth or fame with character. Do not tolerate or condone moral corruption or violence, whether it is found in high or low places, whatever its color or class. It is not okay to push drugs or to use them even if every person in America is doing it. It is not okay to cheat or to lie even if every public- and private-sector official you know does. Be honest and demand that those who represent you be honest. Do not confuse morality with legality. Dr. King once noted that everything Hitler did in Nazi Germany was legal. Do not give anyone the proxy for your conscience.

8   Lesson four: Do not be afraid of taking risks or being criticized. If you do not want to be criticized, do not do anything, do not say anything, and do not be anything. Do not be afraid of failing. It is the way you learn to do things right. It doesn't matter how many times you fall down. All that matters is how many times you get up. Do not wait for everybody to come along to get something done. It is always a few people who get things done and keep things going.

"To bring up a child in a way he should go, travel that way yourself once in a while."

—Josh Billings

9   This country desperately needs more wise and courageous shepherds and fewer sheep who do not borrow from integrity to fund expediency.

10   Lesson five: Take parenting and family life seriously, and insist that those you work for and who represent you also do so. Our nation mouths family values that we do not practice or honor in our policies.

11   I hope that your generation will raise your sons to be fair to other people's daughters and share parenting responsibilities. I am the mother of three sons, so I have told them to "share," and not just help with, family life.

12   I hope that you will stress family rituals and be moral examples for your children, because if you cut corners, they will too. If you lie, they will too. If you spend all of your money on yourself and tithe no portion of it for your university or civic causes or religious life, they will not either.

13   Lesson six is please remember and help America remember that the fellowship of human beings is more important than the fellowship of race and class and gender in a democratic society. Be decent and fair and insist that others do so in your presence. Do not tell, do not laugh at or acquiesce in racial, ethnic, religious, or gender jokes or any practice intended to demean rather than enhance another human being. Walk away from such jokes. Make them unacceptable in your presence.

14   And let us not spend a lot of time uselessly pinning and denying blame rather than healing our divisions. Rabbi Abraham Heschel put it aptly when he said, "We are not all equally guilty, but we are all equally responsible for building a decent and just America."

15   Lesson seven: Listen for the "sound of the genuine" within yourself. Einstein said, "Small is the number of them that see with their own eyes and feel with their own heart." Try to be one of them.

16   Howard Thurman, the great black theologian, said to my Spelman colleagues in Atlanta, Georgia, "There is in every one of us something that waits and listens for the sound of the genuine in ourselves, and it is the only true guide you'll ever have. And if you cannot hear it, you will all of your life spend your days on the ends of strings that somebody else pulls."

"Knock the 't' off of the 'can't'."
—George Reeves

17   You will find as you go out from this place so many noises and competing demands in your lives that many of you may never find out who you are. I hope that you will learn to be quiet enough to hear the sound of the genuine within yourself so that you can then hear it in other people.

18   Lesson eight: Never think life is not worth living or that you cannot make a difference. Never give up. I do not care how hard it gets; and it will get very hard sometimes. An old proverb reminds us that when you get to your wit's end, remember that is where God lives.

19   Harriet Beecher Stowe said that when you get into a tight place and everything goes against you, till it seems as though you cannot hang on for another minute, never give up then, for that is just the place and the time the tide will turn.

20   I do not care how bad the job market is. I do not care how hard the challenges seem to be. Hang in with life. And do not think you have to win or win immediately or even at all to make a difference. Sometimes it is important to lose for things that matter. And do not think you have to make a big difference to make America different.

21   My role model was an illiterate slave woman, Sojourner Truth, who could not read or write, but she could not stand second-class treatment of women and she hated slavery. My favorite Sojourner story came one day when she was making a speech against slavery, and she got heckled by a man who stood up in the audience and said, "Old slave woman, I don't care any more about your antislavery talk than for an old fleabite." And she snapped back and said, "That's all right. The Lord willing, I'm going to keep you scratching."

22   So often we think we have got to make a big difference and be a big dog. Let us just try to be little fleas biting. Enough fleas biting strategically can make very big dogs very uncomfortable. I am convinced that together fleas for justice, and fleas in schools and religious congregations, and fleas in homes as parents committed to a decent American society are going to transform our nation and make it un-American for any child to be poor or without health care in our rich land.

23   Finally, let me just hope that you will understand that you cannot save your own children without trying to help save other people's children. They have got to walk the same streets. We have got to pass on to them a country that was better than the one that we inherited.

24   What do you think would happen if every American, if every one of you, reached out and grabbed the hand of a child and committed yourself to seeing that no child is left behind? I hope that you will think about doing that, because everything that we hold dear as a people with faith depends on each of us committing to leaving no American child behind.

COMPREHENSION CHECKUP

Multiple Choice

Write the letter of the correct answer in the blank provided.

_____ 1. Which of the following does Edelman consider key to career success?
- a. If you are special, someone will "discover" you.
- b. A good degree is all you need.
- c. Look at the big picture and ignore the details.
- d. Keep working hard.

_____ 2. Edelman would agree with which of the following?
- a. If someone asks you to do a task, and another task needs to be done as well, do both tasks without waiting to be asked.
- b. If you see a need, try to fill it.
- c. Don't do any more homework than you have to.
- d. Both a and b

_____ 3. With respect to parents and their children, Edelman would agree with which of the following statements?
- a. Parents should serve as moral role models for their children.
- b. Our nation takes family values seriously.
- c. Good parenting is not as important today as it was 50 years ago.
- d. Children are not likely to emulate their parents' attitudes and beliefs.

_____ 4. Edelman is passionate about
- a. trying hard and taking initiative
- b. the importance of leading a moral life
- c. protecting and helping children
- d. all of the above

_____ 5. Edelman mentioned in the excerpt that failure
- a. is to be avoided at all costs
- b. is the way that you learn to do things right
- c. is something you should be ashamed of
- d. is rarely experienced by successful people

_____ 6. Edelman would agree with which of the following?
- a. We should care only about our own children.
- b. How children are raised doesn't matter much for society.
- c. Our society should make a commitment to protecting and nurturing all of its children.
- d. How parents' behave doesn't have much effect on how their children behave.

_____ 7. Edelman is likely to admire those who
- a. spend all of their money on themselves
- b. donate money to charitable causes
- c. marry into money
- d. work hard to become powerful and famous

_____ 8. Edelman is likely to agree with which of the following?
- a. It's every person for her- or himself.
- b. The end justifies the means.
- c. If corporate CEOs are lying, it's okay for you to lie as well.
- d. Lying and cheating to succeed are not acceptable.

True or False

Indicate whether the statement is true or false by writing T or F in the blank provided.

_____T_____ 9. Edelman's role model was Sojourner Truth.

_____F_____ 10. Edelman likely feels that one vote is relatively insignificant in the scheme of things.

_____F_____ 11. Edelman agrees that people should try to avoid being criticized.

_____T_____ 12. Edelman believes that something can be legal and still not be moral.

_____T_____ 13. Edelman believes that it is important to listen to yourself.

_____F_____ 14. Edelman believes that the easy path is the best one.

_____T_____ 15. Edelman believes that the little contributions people make over time can make a big difference.

Vocabulary in Context

Look through the paragraph indicated in parentheses to find a word that matches the definition given below.

1. having a right or claim to something (paragraph 2) _____

2. confinement; imprisonment (6) _____

3. disregard; overlook; excuse (7) _____

4. power or agency to act for another (7) _____

5. just right; fittingly; appropriately (14) _____

6. a person who specializes in the study of divine things or religious truth (16)

_____

7. associates; fellow members of a profession (16) _____

8. harassed with impertinent questions; shouted insults (21) _____

Choose one of the following words to complete the sentences below. Use each word only once. Be sure to pay close attention to the context clues provided.

continuously	corruption	initiative	persistence	pinned
rituals	snickered	strategic	tide	tithe

1. Despite many obstacles to her academic success, Estella refused to

   give in, and finally her _____ paid off with a $10,000 scholarship to the college of her choice.

2. Ruben took the _____ in collecting 10,000 signatures to get the proposal for a light-rail system on the ballot.

3. When Carrie got an F in English, she _____ the blame on everyone but herself.

4. Because she was _____ in pain from her leukemia, her doctor decided to try radiation as a palliative treatment.

5. Even though Marcus was on a fixed income, he was able to _____ a portion of his salary to his new church.

6. The audience _____ when the microphone went dead, but the politician continued with his speech completely unaware.

7. One of my daily _____ is a 45-minute walk with my friend Marilyn.

8. In many reality television shows, the players form _____ alliances in order to win.

9. The _____ turned against him, and he lost the election.

10. The new mayor's biggest job is to weed out _____ in governmental agencies.

Vocabulary in Context

Without using a dictionary, define the following phrases.

1. political bystander (paragraph 5) _____

2. spectator sport (5) _____

3. mouths family values (10) _____

4. wit's end (18) _____

5. tight place (19) _____

6. hang in (20) _____

7. second-class treatment (21) _____

In Your Own Words

1. What is your personal reaction to each of Edelman's lessons? What do Edelman's lessons say about her as a person? What are Edelman's priorities in life?

2. The following is an excerpt from a speech given by President Theodore Roosevelt.

> It is not the critic who counts;
> Not the man who points out
> Where the strong man stumbled,
> Or where the doer of great deeds
> Could have done them better.
> The credit belongs to the man
> Who is actually in the arena;
> Whose face is marred
> By dust and sweat and blood;
> Who strives valiantly;
> Who errs and comes up short
> Again and again;
> And who, while daring greatly;
> Spends himself in a worthy cause;
> So that his place may not be
> Among those cold and timid souls
> Who know neither victory nor defeat.

Which of Edelman's lessons does Roosevelt's speech support? In what ways is their advice the same?

The Art of Writing

1. Create a top-five list of suggestions of your own by drawing on knowledge that you learned the hard way. Include a short explanation for each of your choices. Try to give a personal anecdote illustrating each suggestion.

2. Colin Powell, secretary of state under George W. Bush, put together the following list of rules based on lessons he learned the hard way:

Colin Powell's Rules

1. It ain't as bad as you think. It will look better in the morning.
2. Get mad; then get over it.
3. Avoid having your ego so close to your position that when your position falls, your ego goes with it.
4. It can be done!
5. Be careful what you choose. You may get it.
6. Don't let adverse facts stand in the way of a good decision.
7. You can't make someone else's choices. You shouldn't let someone else make yours.
8. Check small things.
9. Share credit.
10. Remain calm. Be kind.
11. Have a vision. Be demanding.
12. Don't take counsel of your fears or naysayers.
13. Perpetual optimism is a force multiplier.

Source: From Colin Powell with Joseph E. Persico, MY AMERICAN JOURNEY, p. 603. Copyright © 1995 by Colin L. Powell. Used by permission of Random House Inc.

Write a paragraph explaining your reaction to each of Powell's rules. Write a description of Powell based on what these rules say about him.

Internet Activities

1. The website below gives you additional information about Marian Wright Edelman's background:

   www.womenshistory.about.com

   Visit this site, and then write a short paragraph about what you find interesting about Edelman's life.

2. Use a search engine like <www.google.com> or <www.yahoo.com> to locate information about one of the following individuals mentioned in Edelman's commencement speech: Sojourner Truth, Howard Thurman, Harriet Beecher Stowe, Dr. Martin Luther King, Jr., Albert Einstein, or Rabbi Abraham Heschel. What contributions did the individual you selected make to American society?

My Uncle Terwilliger on the Art of Eating Popovers
BY DR. SEUSS

"Life is the sum of all your choices."

—Albert Camus

The late Theodore Seuss Geisel (1904–1991) was known to millions of readers (adult as well as children) as Dr. Seuss. In his lifetime, he wrote and illustrated over 40 books, many of which are children's classics. Among the best known are *Horton Hears a Who, Hop on Pop, How the Grinch Stole Christmas,* and, of course, *The Cat in the Hat.* Critics praised his books, saying that he dispensed "nonsense with sense." After reading the poem below, explain the meaning in your own words. How does the poem relate to the previous selection?

My uncle ordered popovers
from the restaurant's bill of fare.
And, when they were served,
   he regarded them
with a penetrating stare . . .
Then he spoke great Words of Wisdom
as he sat there on that chair:
"To eat these things," said my uncle,
"you must exercise great care.
You may swallow down what's solid . . .
BUT . . . you must spit out the air!"
And . . . as you partake of the world's
   bill of fare,
that's darned good advice to follow.
Do a lot of spitting out the hot air.
And be careful what you swallow.

Source: "My Uncle Terwilliger on the Art of Eating Popovers" from *Seuss-isms* by Dr. Seuss. Copyright © 1997 by Dr. Seuss Enterprises, L.P. Used by permission of Random House Children's Books, a division of Random House, Inc.

_____

_____

_____

_____

_____

VOCABULARY   Introduction

"The investigation of the meaning of words is the beginning of education."

—Antisthenes

To be a successful college student, you need a college-level vocabulary. Improving your vocabulary will make you a better reader, speaker, and writer. Is there a painless way to improve your vocabulary? The answer is "No." Developing a college-level vocabulary requires effort. But there are some effective techniques that can help. These techniques are described below.

Context

When you come across an unfamiliar word in your reading, the first step you should take toward discovering its meaning is to look for context clues. The context of a word is what surrounds it and includes the sentence it appears in, other nearby sentences, and even the whole article. Try placing your finger over the unfamiliar word, and see if you can supply another word or phrase that gives the sentence meaning.

For example, see if you can figure out the meaning of the italicized word from the context of the sentence:

> Ellen's multiple sclerosis became increasingly *debilitating* to the point that she could no longer walk unaided and had to consider using a wheelchair.

You could go to the dictionary to look up the definition of *debilitating*, but you can probably guess from context clues that *debilitating*, at least as it appears in this sentence, means "to make feeble or weak."

Remember that if you are reading a light novel for enjoyment, the exact meaning of a word may not be as important as when you are reading a textbook.

Structure

The Greeks and Romans devised a system for creating words by putting together smaller word parts. To the main part of the word, which is called the root, they attached prefixes, which come before the root, and suffixes, which come after it.

This way of building words allows you to discover the meaning of a word by breaking it down into its parts. Knowing the meaning of the word's parts should help you decipher the word's meaning. Let's try an example:

> As a confirmed *misogamist,* it was unlikely Barry would be making a trip to the altar anytime soon.

The word *misogamist* has in it the word parts *mis* and *gam*. *Mis* means "hate" and *gam* means "marriage." So a *misogamist* is someone who hates marriage, or matrimony. In this book, we have included eight vocabulary units that familiarize you with more than a hundred word parts.

Dictionary

Often when people come across a word they don't know, their first impulse is to look it up in the dictionary. But this should be your last recourse for determining the meaning of a word. It's best first to try to determine a general meaning of the word by paying attention to context clues and word structure. If these techniques don't give you a sure enough sense of what the word means, then go to the dictionary to confirm or clarify the meaning. In the dictionary, you may find several different definitions for a particular word. You need to pick the one that fits the word in its sentence. Context clues will help you pick the right definition. For example, suppose in your reading you come across the following sentence, and you don't know what the word *steep* means:

> To make good sun tea, you need to *steep* several tea bags in a large jar of water out in the sun for several hours.

You look *steep* up in your dictionary and find several definitions. The first definition may be "having an almost vertical slope." The second definition may be "unduly high; exorbitant." But it is the third definition, "to soak in a liquid," that seems to fit. So now you know that to make sun tea, you must let the tea bags soak in water.

Combination

In trying to determine the meaning of an unfamiliar word, you may need to employ all of these techniques in combination. Take the following example:

> Because of his *premonition* that he would not live to see his eighty-third birthday, he made the effort to say good-bye to all of his loved ones.

Look at the context, which suggests that the word has something to do with thoughts or feelings about the future. Now look at the word parts. *Pre* means "before" and *mon* means "warn." Now you are getting closer to the meaning in this sentence. The word *premonition* as used here has a meaning similar to "forewarning." Now go to the dictionary. You will find the definitions "impression that something evil is about to happen" and "strong feeling or prediction." Now you have a better grasp of what the word means. The man had a strong feeling warning him that he would be dead before his eighty-third birthday.

Homonyms

As part of our vocabulary study, we will also learn about homonyms. Although homonyms are not a technique for discovering the meaning of an unfamiliar word, we discuss them because misuse of homonyms is common. *Homo* means "same" and *nym* means "name." So homonyms are words or phrases with the same "name" or pronunciation but different spellings or meanings.

Look at the following sentence:

> Because Tomoko *already* knows all of her colors and shapes and most of the letters of the alphabet, I'd say she's *all ready* for kindergarten.

In this example, *already* means "previously," and *all ready* means "completely prepared." People often confuse these two homonyms, as they do other homonyms. In the two sections on homonyms, you will learn how to use many homonyms correctly.

Verbal Analogies

A verbal analogy is an equation that uses words instead of numbers. Many standardized tests have sections that feature verbal analogies. Verbal analogies test not only your knowledge of vocabulary words but also your ability to see relationships between words and the concepts the words represent. The verbal analogies in this text are presented in the following format:

A : B :: C : D

This is read as "A is to B as C is to D." Here is a sample verbal analogy:

day : night :: light : dark

This is read as "day is to night as light is to dark." The analogy indicates that the relationship between *day* and *night* and the relationship between *light* and *dark* are the same. The relationship is one of opposition. *Day* is the opposite of *night*, and *light* is the opposite of *dark*.

In this book, questions for verbal analogies will look like this:

day : night :: light : _____

Your job is to find the word that fits into the blank. Here the answer is *dark*.

Word analogies can involve many kinds of relationships. Some common relationships that appear in word analogies are synonym, antonym, and cause-and-effect. Each vocabulary unit will introduce a new kind of word analogy. As we progress through the vocabulary units, the word analogies will become more difficult.

Thesaurus

A thesaurus, a special kind of word book organized by categories, enables you to refine your writing by helping you select precisely the right word for any given situation. Many of us use the same word over and over because we cannot think of an appropriate synonym. A thesaurus gives synonyms for the most common nouns, verbs, adjectives, and adverbs in the English language. In the following sentence, you can choose from any of the italicized synonyms to convey your meaning more precisely:

As the famous fashion model made her way down the runway, the audience noted that she was extremely *slender, slim, svelte, lithe, skinny, lean, thin.*

"The difference between the right word and the almost right word is the difference between lightning and the lightning bug."

—Mark Twain

You will learn about using a thesaurus in the Appendix.

Answers

(a) The nine-dot problem can be solved by extending the lines beyond the square formed by the dots.

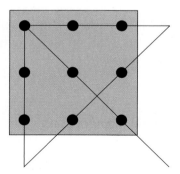

(d) Here are some starters. You can: read it, write on it, line your garbage can with it, wrap packages with it, wipe your feet on it, lay it down on the floor before you paint, train your dog with it, make a kite out of it, wipe windows with it, use it to keep your head dry if it is raining, use it as a dust pan and so on!

Life in College and Beyond

The Scream (1893) BY EDVARD MUNCH

View and Reflect

1. What is your initial response to the painting? What overall impression does it convey?
2. What do you think the landscape is meant to represent? The receding figures on the bridge? The two ships in the background? What does the combination of elements in the painting suggest?
3. What do you think the figure in the foreground is meant to represent? What does the face resemble as it screams? Use one word to describe the overall feeling of the painting.

STUDY TECHNIQUE 1

Underlining, Highlighting, Annotating

As you work through this book (and as you proceed through college), you will be introduced to a wide variety of reading selections. **Underlining** or **highlighting** important words or phrases in these selections will help you remember the authors' key points. When underlining or highlighting, be careful not to overdo it. The goal is to mark just the important points to save you from having to reread. **Annotating,** another technique for helping you remember what you're reading, is particularly useful when reading textbook material. When you annotate, you write notes to yourself, often in the margins of the book. You might write down abbreviations or symbols to identify key ideas or terms. A list of things you might want to identify, with suggested abbreviations, appears below.

MI (main idea)

T (thesis)

S (summary)

Ex (example)

Def (definition)

? (questions, needs clarification)

* (important point)

KV (key vocabulary)

SELECTION

"Respond ineffectively to stress, and eventually it will take a toll on your sense of wellness."

GETTING THE PICTURE

In this selection from a popular health textbook, you will learn about stress and how you can lower it. After reading the bio-sketch and vocabulary sections, you will practice marking and annotating a section of a textbook. Look at the sample margin notes and underlining in the first section of the reading selection below, and follow this example in marking and annotating the remainder of the textbook material on stress.

BIO-SKETCH

Both writers of this textbook teach at the Stanford University Medical School. Paul M. Insel is an adjunct clinical associate professor in the Department of Psychiatry and Behavioral Sciences, and Walton T. Roth is a professor of psychiatry and behavioral medicine. Roth is also the chief of psychiatric consultation services at the Veterans Administration Medical Center in Palo Alto.

BRUSHING UP ON VOCABULARY

hippocampus a lower portion of the brain that consolidates short-term memories into long-term memories.

biological predispositions tendencies or inclinations based on biology rather than background or experiences.

Excerpt from
CORE CONCEPTS IN HEALTH
by Paul M. Insel and Walton T. Roth

Stress: The Constant Challenge

Ex
Ex
Ex
Ex

As a college student, you may be in one of the most stressful periods of your life. You may be on your own for the first time, or you may be juggling the demands of college with the responsibilities of a job, a family, or both. Financial pressures may be intense. Housing and transportation may be sources of additional hassles. You're also meeting new people, engaging in new activities, learning new information and skills, and setting a new course for your life. Good and bad, all these changes and challenges are likely to have a powerful effect on you both physically and psychologically. Respond ineffectively to stress, and

MI

eventually it will take a toll on your sense of wellness. Learn effective responses, however, and you will enhance your health and gain a feeling of control over your life.

Test Your Knowledge

____All____ 1. Which of the following events can cause stress?
   a. taking out a loan
   b. failing a test
   c. graduating from college
   d. watching a hockey game

____F____ 2. True or false: About twice as many male college students as female college students report feeling frequently overwhelmed.

____T____ 3. True or false: High levels of stress can impair memory and cause physical changes in the brain.

____All____ 4. Which of the following may be caused or aggravated by stress?
   a. headaches
   b. irritable bowel syndrome
   c. insomnia
   d. high blood pressure

Answers

1. *All four.* Stress-producing factors can be pleasant or unpleasant and can indicate physical challenges and the achievement of personal goals as well as what would commonly be perceived as negative events.

2. *False.* In recent surveys, about 20 percent of male and 40 percent of female college students report feeling frequently overwhelmed. Female college students are more likely to report financial worries, and they spend more time in potentially stress-producing activities such as volunteer work, housework, and child care.

3. *True.* Low levels of stress may improve memory, but high stress levels impair learning and memory and, over the long term, may shrink an area of the brain called the hippocampus.

4. *All four.* Stress—interacting with heredity, personality, social environment, and behavior—increases one's vulnerability to many health problems.

Everybody talks about stress. People say they're "overstressed" or "stressed out." They may blame stress for headaches or ulcers, and they may try to combat stress with aerobic classes—or drugs. But what is stress? And why is it important to manage it wisely?

MI—Stress usually associated with negative events

Most people associate stress with negative events: the death of a close relative or friend, financial problems, or other unpleasant life changes that create nervous tension. But stress isn't merely nervous tension. And it isn't something to be avoided at all costs. In fact, only death brings complete freedom from stress. Consider this list of common stressful situations or events.

- Interviewing for a job
- Running in a race
- Being accepted to college
- Going out on a date
- Watching a baseball game
- Getting a promotion

MI—Can be related to physical challenges, pers. goals

Can modify your behavior

Obviously stress doesn't arise just from unpleasant situations. Stress can also be associated with physical challenges and the achievement of personal goals. Physical and psychological stress-producing factors can be pleasant or unpleasant. The actions you take in response to stress are influenced by your biological predispositions, past experiences, and current circumstances. While you cannot change who you are or what you've been through in the past, you *can* modify your current behavior and seek out people, places, and experiences that will improve your ability to deal with stress. In other words, what is crucial is how you respond, whether in positive, life-enhancing ways or in negative, counterproductive ways.

What Is Stress?

Just what is stress, if such vastly different situations can cause it? In common usage, "stress" refers to two different things: situations that trigger physical and emotional reactions *and* the reactions themselves. We'll be using the more precise term **stressor** for situations that trigger physical and emotional reactions and the term **stress response** for those reactions. A date and a final exam, then, are stressors; sweaty palms and a pounding heart are symptoms of the stress response. We'll use the term **stress** to describe the general physical and emotional state that accompanies the stress response. A person on a date or taking a final exam experiences stress.

Each individual's experience of stress depends on many factors, including the nature of the stressor and how the stressor is perceived. Responses to stressors include physical changes and emotional and behavioral responses.

How High Is Your Stress Level?

Many symptoms of excess stress are easy to self-diagnose. To help determine how much stress you experience on a daily basis, answer the following questions:

1. Are you easily startled or irritated?
2. Are you increasingly forgetful?

3. Do you have trouble falling or staying asleep?

4. Do you continually worry about events in your future?

5. Do you feel as if you are constantly under pressure to produce?

6. Do you frequently use tobacco, alcohol, or other drugs to help you relax?

7. Do you often feel as if you have less energy than you need to finish the day?

8. Do you have recurrent stomachaches or headaches?

9. Is it difficult for you to find satisfaction in simple life pleasures?

10. Are you often disappointed in yourself and others?

11. Are you overly concerned with being liked or accepted by others?

12. Are you concerned that you do not have enough money?

Experiencing some of the stress-related symptoms or answering "yes" to a few questions is normal. However, if you experience a large number of stress symptoms or you answered "yes" to a majority of the questions, you are likely experiencing a high level of stress. Take time out to develop effective stress-management techniques. Your school's counseling center can provide valuable support.

Symptoms of Excess Stress

PHYSICAL SYMPTOMS	EMOTIONAL SYMPTOMS	BEHAVIORAL SYMPTOMS
Dry mouth	Anxiety or edginess	Crying
Excessive perspiration	Depression	Disrupted eating habits
Frequent illnesses	Fatigue	Disrupted sleeping habits
Gastrointestinal problems	Hypervigilance	Harsh treatment of others
Grinding of teeth	Impulsiveness	Increased use of tobacco, alcohol, or other drugs
Headaches	Inability to concentrate	
High blood pressure	Irritability	Problems communicating
Pounding heart	Trouble remembering things	Social isolation

Top 20 Stressful Life Events

Death of a spouse
Divorce
Marital separation
Jail term
Death of a close family member
Personal injury or illness
Marriage
Fired at work
Marital reconciliation
Retirement
Change in health of family member
Pregnancy
Sex difficulties
New family member
Business readjustment
Change in financial status
Death of a close friend
Change to a different line of work
Change in number of arguments with spouse
Mortgage or loan for major purchase (home, etc.)

Thomas H. Holmes and Richard H. Rahe, "The Social Readjustment Rating Scale," *Journal of Psychosomatic Research,* Vol. 11, No. 2, August 1967. Copyright © 1967 with permission of Elsevier Ltd.

Mind/Body/Spirit: Healthy Connections

Meaningful connections with others can play a key role in stress management and overall wellness. A sense of isolation can lead to chronic stress, which in turn can increase one's susceptibility to temporary illnesses like colds and to chronic illnesses like heart disease. Although the mechanism isn't clear, social isolation can be as significant to mortality rates as factors like smoking, high blood pressure, and obesity.

There is no single best pattern of social support that works for everyone. However, research suggests that having a variety of types of relationships may be important for wellness. To help determine whether your social network measures up, circle whether each of the following statements is true or false for you.

Ⓣ F   1. If I needed an emergency loan of $100, there is someone I could get it from.

Ⓣ F   2. There is someone who takes pride in my accomplishments.

(T) F   3. I often meet or talk with family or friends.

(T) F   4. Most people I know think highly of me.

T **(F)**   5. If I needed an early morning ride to the airport, there's no one I would feel comfortable asking to take me.

T **(F)**   6. I feel there is no one with whom I can share my most private worries and fears.

T **(F)**   7. Most of my friends are more successful making changes in their lives than I am.

T **(F)**   8. I would have a hard time finding someone to go with me on a day trip to the beach or country.

To calculate your score, add the number of true answers to questions 1–4 and the number of false answers to questions 5–8. If your score is 4 or more, you should have enough support to protect your health. If your score is 3 or less, you may need to reach out. There are a variety of things you can do to strengthen your social ties:

"Without friends, no one would choose to live, though he had all the goods."

—Aristotle

- Foster friendships. Keep in regular contact with your friends.

- Keep your family ties strong. Participate in family activities and celebrations.

- Get involved with a group. Choose activities that are meaningful to you and that include direct involvement with other people.

- Build your communication skills. The more you share your feelings with others, the closer the bonds between you will become.

Source: From Paul Insel, CORE CONCEPTS IN HEALTH, 9/e, pp. 29–31, 43. Copyright © 2002 McGraw-Hill Companies, Inc. Used with permission.

COMPREHENSION CHECKUP

Multiple Choice

Write the letter of the correct answer in the blank provided.

_____ 1. An event that triggers stress is called a
   a. response
   b. stressor
   c. headache
   d. none of the above

_____ 2. Stress is best described as
   a. something completely under your control
   b. something rarely experienced by college students
   c. a physical and emotional response to a stressor
   d. a realistic and positive outlook on life

_____ 3. Which of the following could be a potential stressor?
   a. having to visit a relative you dislike
   b. failing a final exam
   c. the unexpected death of a relative
   d. all of the above

_____ 4. High levels of stress can
   a. aggravate high blood pressure
   b. contribute to insomnia
   (c.) both a and b
   d. improve memory

_____ 5. All of the following are correlated with high mortality rates except
   a. smoking
   b. social isolation
   (c.) marriage
   d. high blood pressure

True or False

Indicate whether the statement is true or false by writing T or F in the blank provided.

____F___ 6. Stress arises only from unpleasant situations.

____T___ 7. Excessive sweating may be a physical symptom of stress.

____T___ 8. Chronic stress can lead to heart disease.

____T___ 9. Healthy connections with others may play a role in the management of stress.

____F___ 10. Having good relationships with others is unlikely to contribute to wellness.

Vocabulary Practice

Choose the word from the following list that best completes each sentence.

chronic	isolation	overly	temporary
counter-productive	juggling	overwhelmed	triggered
	mortality	recurrent	
crucial	obesity	susceptible	
impair			

1. People who have too many problems that they can't solve may feel overwhelmed.

2. A smoker is likely to have a higher mortality rate than a nonsmoker.

3. Because many young children have unhealthy diets and fail to get enough exercise, obesity has become a problem of national concern.

4. The refusal of the airline to discuss improving employee benefits trigged a walkout by baggage handlers and flight attendants.

5. The prisoner was deemed a threat to others and so was placed in isolation.

6. In winter, people are more susceptible to colds and flu.

7. Working parents today are so busy because they are _juggling_ many roles.

8. It is of _____ importance that you come to each class session prepared.

9. The substitute teacher was _____ until the regular teacher returned from maternity leave.

10. Exposure to loud noises at an early age may _____ the ability to hear later in life.

11. He had the same _____ dream about flying every night. Unfortunately, he woke up only after he had fallen out of bed.

12. If a parent is _____ protective, a young child might not develop a sense of self-sufficiency.

13. If you have _____ throat infections, your doctor might recommend having your tonsils removed.

14. It might be _____ to work long hours at a job if your grades in school suffer as a result.

In Your Own Words

1. What is the difference between a stressor and stress? What are some of your stressors?

2. In what ways does the college experience contribute to the stress level of students?

3. Can stress be positive? Give an example of positive stress in your life.

4. What physical reactions does stress cause in the body?

5. Describe some healthy ways to deal with stress.

The Art of Writing

In a brief essay, respond to one of the items below.

1. Keep track of your own stress for several days. Try to determine what events are likely to trigger a stress response in you. Is your home life, work life, or school life the most stressful? Is your life more or less stressful than you expected?

2. Interview a friend or family member who seems to handle stress well. What strategies does this person use to successfully cope with stress?

Internet Activity

1. Stress has been linked to many illnesses. To find a list of the negative effects of stress on people's health, go to:

   www.stressless.com/AboutSL/StressFacts.cfm

   Write a paragraph describing what you learned about stress and disease.

2. Take the Quick Stress Assessment at:

   www.stressless.com/AboutSL/StressTest.cfm

Use what you learn to evaluate how well you are handling your personal stressors.

3. To find information on stress management, click "Psychology at Work" on the American Psychological Associations's Help Center:

    http://helping.apa.org

Stress at Work

MOST STRESSFUL JOBS	LEAST STRESSFUL JOBS
Air traffic controller	Bookkeeper
Customer-service or complaint worker	Civil engineer
Inner-city high school teacher	Forester
Journalist	Millwright
Medical intern	Natural scientist
Miner	Repairman
Police officer	Sales representative
Secretary	Telephone-line worker
Stockbroker	Therapist
Waiter	Toolmaker

Source: The American Institute of Stress.

LOCUS OF CONTROL

Locus of control is the perception of the amount of personal control you believe you have over events that affect your life. In general, people with an **external locus of control** believe they have little control over the events in their life, whereas people with an **internal locus of control** believe they have a good deal of control over these events. Study the cartoon below. Do you think the cartoon illustrates someone who has an internal or external locus of control? Do you think it is more stressful to have an internal or external locus of control?

Frank and Ernest

FRANK & ERNEST: © Thaves/Dist. By Newspaper Enterprise Association, Inc.

To determine your locus of control, take the following test.

For each numbered item below, circle the answer that best describes your beliefs.

1. a. Grades are a function of the amount of work students do.
   b. Grades depend on the kindness of the instructor.

2. a. Promotions are earned by hard work.
   b. Promotions are a result of being in the right place at the right time.

3. a. Meeting someone to love is a matter of luck.
   b. Meeting someone to love depends on going out often and meeting many people.

4. a. Living a long life is a function of heredity.
   b. Living a long life is a function of following healthy habits.

5. a. Being overweight is determined by the number of fat cells you were born with or developed early in life.
   b. Being overweight depends on what you eat and how much.

6. a. People who exercise regularly make time for exercise in their schedules.
   b. Some people just don't have the time for regular exercise.

7. a. Winning at poker depends on betting correctly.
   b. Winning at poker is a matter of being lucky.

8. a. Staying married depends on working at the marriage.
   b. Marital breakup is a matter of being unlucky in having chosen the wrong marriage partner.

9. a. Citizens can have some influence on their governments.
   b. There is nothing an individual can do to affect governmental functions.

10. a. Being skilled at sports depends on being born well coordinated.
    b. Those skilled at sports work hard at learning their skills.

11. a. People with close friends are lucky in meeting people.
    b. Developing close friendships takes hard work.

12. a. Your future depends on whom you meet and on chance.
    b. Your future is up to you.

13. a. Most people are so sure of their opinions that their minds cannot be changed.
    b. A logical argument can convince most people.

14. a. People decide the direction of their lives.
    b. For the most part, we have little control of our futures.

15. a. People who don't like you just don't understand you.
    b. You can be liked by anyone you choose to like you.

16. a. You can make your life a happy one.
    b. Happiness is a matter of fate.

17. a. You evaluate how people respond to you and make decisions based upon these evaluations.
    b. You tend to be easily influenced by others.

18. a. If voters studied nominees' records, they could elect honest politicians.
   b. Politics and politicians are corrupt by nature.

19. a. Parents, teachers, and bosses have a great deal to say about one's happiness and self-satisfaction.
   b. Whether you are happy depends on you.

20. a. Air pollution can be controlled if citizens would get angry about it.
   b. Air pollution is an inevitable result of technological progress.

You have just completed a scale measuring locus of control. To determine your locus of control, give yourself one point for each of the following responses:

Item	Response	Item	Response
1	a	11	b
2	a	12	b
3	b	13	b
4	b	14	a
5	b	15	b
6	a	16	a
7	a	17	a
8	a	18	a
9	a	19	b
10	b	20	a

Scores above 10 indicate internality and scores below 11 indicate externality. Of course, there are degrees of each, and most people find themselves scoring near 10. "Internals" tend to take credit for their successes and accept blame for their failures. "Externals" credit the environment for their successes as well as blame it for their failures. What kind of person are you? Does your score reflect the way you typically think about yourself?

"Locus of Control," p. 124 from Jerrold Greenberg, *Comprehensive Stress Management*, 6/e. Copyright © McGraw-Hill Companies, Inc. Used with permission.

Internet Activity

The Discovery Channel has a website that includes several self-assessment tests in the areas of health, nutrition, personality, and locus of control. Go to the website and take a test that interests you. Then write a paragraph discussing your findings.

http://health.discovery.com/tools/assessments.html

SELECTION

"Charles Schwab was very strong in math, science, and sports (especially golf), which helped him get into Stanford. But anything involving English 'was a disconnect.'"

GETTING THE PICTURE

The article excerpted below describes individuals who used creative problem-solving techniques to overcome their personal limitations.

BIO-SKETCH

Betsy Morris, senior writer for *Fortune,* has firsthand experience with dyslexia. Her son Johnny was diagnosed with dyslexia at age 7. Over the years, Morris learned a lot from watching Johnny deal with dyslexia. In particular, she came to admire his "patience, perseverance, and his ability not to give up when things don't come easily." Today, Johnny, now 12 years old, is doing well and has become a good reader. "I still hate math, though," he says.

BRUSHING UP ON VOCABULARY

dead-end a situation with no escape or solution. The term originated in the late 1800s and referred specifically to a passageway that has no exit, and so halts all progress.

perilously involving great risk; dangerous. The word *perilous* originated from the Latin *periculum,* which referred to the danger of going on a trip. Historically, travel was dangerous and uncomfortable, and as a result was "full of peril."

trivia matters or things that are unimportant or inconsequential. In Latin, *tri* means "three" and *via* means "way." In ancient Rome, at the point where three roads crossed, the women would meet to talk and gossip on the way back from the market.

late-bloomer someone who matures after the usual or expected time. The term originally referred to roses that failed to bloom when they were expected to do so.

humility the quality or state of being humble or modest. The word comes from the Latin *humus,* or earth, and originally referred to people who prostrated themselves on the ground because they didn't think much of themselves.

OVERCOMING DYSLEXIA   by BETSY MORRIS

1   Consider the following four dead-end kids.

2   One was spanked by his teachers for bad grades and a poor attitude. He dropped out of school at 16. Another failed remedial English and came perilously close to flunking out of college. The third feared he'd never make it through school—and might not have without a tutor. The last finally learned to read in third grade, devouring Marvel comics, whose pictures provided clues to help him untangle the words.

"You must have long-range goals to keep you from being frustrated by short-range failures."

—*Charles C. Noble*

Dyslexic Achievers
Scott Adams, "Dilbert" creator
Dr. Baruj Benaceraff, Nobel Prize winner
James Carville, political consultant
Cher, singer, actress
Charles "Pete" Conrad Jr., astronaut
Erin Brockovich Ellis, activist
Dr. Fred Epstein, brain surgeon
Fanny Flagg, writer, actress
Brian Grazer, producer
Whoopi Goldberg, actress
Reyn Guyer, Nerf ball developer
Dr. Edward Hallowell, psychiatrist
Florence Haseltine, M.D., Ph.D.
Bill Hewlett, cofounder, Hewlett-Packard
John R. Horner, paleontologist
Bruce Jenner, Olympic gold medalist
Thomas Kean, former governor
Sylvia Law, professor
Jay Leno, host of *The Tonight Show*
Paul B. MacCready, inventor
David Murdock, CEO, Dole Food
Nicholas Negroponte, director, MIT Media Lab
Robert Rauschenberg, artist
Nelson Rockefeller, governor, vice-president
Nolan Ryan, Baseball Hall of Famer
Raymond Smith, former CEO, Bell Atlantic
Wendy Wasserstein, playwright
Thomas J. Watson Jr., former CEO, IBM
Henry Winkler, actor, director

3   These four losers are, respectively, Richard Branson, Charles Schwab, John Chambers, and David Boies. Billionaire Branson developed one of Britain's top brands with Virgin Records and Virgin Atlantic Airways. Schwab virtually created the discount brokerage business. Chambers is CEO of Cisco systems. Boies is a celebrated trial attorney, best known as the guy who beat Microsoft.

4   In one of the stranger bits of business trivia, they have something in common: They are all dyslexic. So is billionaire Craig McCaw, who pioneered the cellular phone industry; John Reed, who led Citibank to the top of banking; Donald Winkler, who until recently headed Ford Financial; Gaston Caperton, former governor of West Virginia and now head of the College Board; Paul Orfalea, founder of Kinko's; and Diane Swonk, chief economist of Bank One. The list goes on. Many of these adults seemed pretty hopeless as kids. All have been wildly successful in business. Most have now begun to talk about their dyslexia as a way to help children and parents cope with a condition that is still widely misunderstood.

5   What exactly is dyslexia? The everyman definition calls it a reading disorder in which people jumble letters, confusing *dog* with *god*, say, or *box* with *pox*. The exact cause is unclear; scientists believe it has to do with the way a developing brain is wired. Difficulty reading, spelling, and writing are typical symptoms. But dyslexia often comes with one or more other learning problems, as well, including trouble with math, auditory processing, organizational skills, and memory. No two dyslexics are alike—each has his own set of weaknesses and strengths. About 5 percent to 6 percent of American public school children have been diagnosed with a learning disability. 80 percent of the diagnoses are dyslexia-related. But some studies indicate that up to 20 percent of the population may have some degree of dyslexia.

6   A generation ago this was a problem with no name. Boies, Schwab, and Bill Samuels Jr., the president of Maker's Mark, did not realize they were dyslexic until some of their own children were diagnosed with the disorder, which is often inherited. Samuels says he was sitting in a school office, listening to a description of his son's problems, when it dawned on him: "Oh, shit. that's me." Most of the adults had diagnosed themselves. Says Branson: "At some point, I think I decided that being dyslexic was better than being stupid."

7   Stupid. Dumb. Retard. Dyslexic kids have heard it all. According to a March 2000 Roper poll, almost two-thirds of Americans still associate learning disabilities with mental retardation. That's probably because dyslexics find it so difficult to learn through conventional methods. "It is a disability in learning," says Boies. "It is not an intelligence disability. It doesn't mean you can't think."

8   He's right. Dyslexia has nothing to do with IQ; many smart, accomplished people have it, or are thought to have had it, including Winston Churchill and Albert Einstein. Sally Shaywitz, a leading dyslexia neuroscientist at Yale, believes the disorder can carry surprising talents along with its well-known disadvantages. "Dyslexics are over represented in the top ranks of people who are unusually insightful, who bring a new perspective, who think out of the box," says Shaywitz, codirector of the Center for Learning and Attention at Yale.

Did they or didn't they have dyslexia?

Probably they did.
Winston Churchill
Leonardo da Vinci
Thomas Edison
Albert Einstein
Michelangelo
General George S. Patton
Woodrow Wilson
W. B. Yeats

9   Dyslexics don't outgrow their problems—reading and writing usually remain hard work for life—but with patient teaching and deft tutoring, they do learn to manage. Absent that, dyslexia can snuff out dreams at an early age, as children lose their way in school, then lose their self-esteem and drive. "The prisons are filled with kids who can't read," says Caperton. "I suspect a lot of them have learning disabilities."

10   Dyslexia is a crucible, particularly in a high-pressure society that allows so little room for late-bloomers. "People are either defeated by it or they become much more tenacious," says McCaw. Don Winkler, a top financial services executive at Bank One and then at Ford Motor, remembers coming home from school bloodied by fights he'd had with kids who called him dumb. Kinko's founder, Paul Orfalea, failed second grade and spent part of third in a class of mentally retarded children. He could not learn to read, despite the best efforts of parents who took him to testers, tutors, therapists, special reading groups, and eye doctors. As young class-mates read aloud, Orfalea says it was as if "angels whispered words in their ears."

11   In his unpublished autobiography, Orfalea says that to a dyslexic, a sentence is worse than Egyptian hieroglyphics. "It's more like a road map with mouse holes or coffee stains in critical places. You're always turning into blind alleys and ending up on the wrong side of town." He finally graduated but not before be-ing "invited to leave . . . practically every high school in Los Angeles." One prin-cipal counseled his mother to enroll him in trade school, suggesting that Orfalea could become a carpet layer. His mother went home and tearfully told her hus-band, "I just know he can do more than lay carpet."

12   Charles Schwab was very strong in math, science, and sports (especially golf), which helped him get into Stanford. But anything involving English "was a disconnect." He couldn't write quickly enough to capture his thoughts. He couldn't listen to a lecture and take legible notes. He couldn't memorize four words in a row. He doesn't think he ever read a novel all the way through in high school. He was within one unit of flunking out of Stanford his freshman year. "God, I must be really dumb in this stuff," he used to tell himself. "It was hor-rible, a real drag on me." So horrible that Schwab and his wife, Helen, created a foundation to help parents of children with learning disorders.

13   It was as if Schwab and the others were wearing a scarlet letter: "D" for dumb. Until about five years ago Chambers kept his dyslexia a secret. As CEO, he says, "you don't want people to see your weaknesses." One day a little girl at Cisco's Bring Your Children to Work Day forced him out of the closet. Chambers had called on her, and she was trying to ask a question before a crowd of 500 kids and parents. But she couldn't get the words out. "I have a learning disability," she said tearfully.

14   Chambers cannot tell this story without choking up himself. "You could im-mediately identify with what that was like," he says. "You know that pain. She started to leave, and you knew how hurt she was in front of the group and her parents." Chambers threw her a lifeline. "I have a learning disability too," he said. In front of the crowd, he began talking to her as if they were the only two people in the room. "You've just got to learn your way through it," Chambers told her. "Because there are some things you can do that others cannot, and

there are some things others can do you're just not going to be able to do, ever. Now my experience has been that what works is to go a little bit slower. . . ."

15   It was the kind of coaching that proved crucial to nearly everybody we talked to: mentors who took a genuine interest, parents who refused to give up, tutors who didn't even know what dyslexia was. Winkler recalls that his parents refused to let their fear of electrocution stand in the way of his fixing every iron and toaster in the neighborhood. "I wired every teacher's house," he says. "I got shocked all the time." His parents owned a mom-and-pop shop in Phillipsburg, N.J. His mother cleaned houses to pay for his tutoring. Chambers, who read right to left and up and down the page, says his parents, both doctors, claim they never once doubted his abilities, even though he says, "I absolutely did." His parents' faith was important to him. So was his tutor, Mrs. Anderson. Even today Chambers remembers tutoring as excruciating. "It might have been once or twice a week," he says, "but it felt like every day." Nonetheless, he adds, "Mrs. Anderson had an influence on my life far bigger than she might have ever realized."

16   If you could survive childhood, dyslexia was a pretty good business boot camp. It fostered risk taking, problem solving, resilience. School was a chess game that required tactical brilliance. Schwab sat mostly in the back of the room. But he was conscientious and charming, and gutsy enough to ask for extra help. Boies took a minimum of math and avoided foreign languages and anything involving spatial skills. Orfalea worked out a symbiotic relationship with classmates on a group project at USC's Marshall Business School; they did the writing, he did the photocopying (and got the germ of the idea that led to Kinko's).

"Faith is the substance of things hoped for, the evidence of things not seen."
—Hebrews 11:1

17   At Vanderbilt Law School, Samuels spent a lot of time in study-group discussions. "That's how I learned the cases," he says. His friends helped with the reading; he paid for the beer. Better than most people, dyslexics learn humility and how to get along with others. It's probably no accident that Kinko's, Cisco, and Schwab have all been on *Fortune's* list of the best places to work. "I never put people down, because I know what that feels like," says Branson, who seldom asks for a résumé either "because I haven't got one myself."

"Failure is delay, not defeat. It is a temporary detour, not a dead-end street."
—William Arthur Ward

18   By the time these guys got into business, they had picked themselves up so many times that risk taking was second nature. "We're always expecting a curve ball," says Samuels. Schwab remembers how hard it was to watch his friends receive awards and become General Motors Scholars, Merit Scholars, Baker Scholars. "I was so jealous," he says. Later on, he thought, some of the prize-winners had trouble dealing with adversity.

19   If as kids, the dyslexic executives had learned the downside of their disorder inside out, as adults they began to see its upside: a distinctly different way of processing information that gave them an edge in a volatile, fast-moving world. "Many times in business, different is better than better," says Samuels. "And we dyslexics do different without blinking an eye."

Source: Betsy Morris, "Overcoming Dyslexia," *Fortune,* May 13, 2002, pp. 55–70. Copyright © 2002 Time Inc. All rights reserved.

COMPREHENSION CHECKUP

Matching

Match the quotation with the speaker. Write the letter of the speaker in the appropriate blank. (Some speakers will be used more than once.)

a. Richard Branson   f. Paul Orfalea

b. David Boies   g. Charles Schwab

c. Sally Shaywitz   h. John Chambers

d. Craig McCaw   i. Donald Winkler

e. Gaston Caperton   j. Bill Samuels Jr.

_____J.___ 1. "Many times in business, different is better than better, and we dyslexics do different without blinking an eye."

_____B.___ 2. "It is a disability in learning. It is not an intelligence disability. It doesn't mean you can't think."

_____C.___ 3. "Dyslexics are overrepresented in the top ranks of people who are unusually insightful, who bring a new perspective, who think out of the box."

_____E.___ 4. "The prisons are filled with kids who can't read. I suspect a lot of them have learning disabilities."

_____D.___ 5. "People are either defeated by it or they become much more tenacious."

_____F.___ 6. "It's more like a road map with mouse holes or coffee stains in critical places."

_____G.___ 7. "God, I must be really dumb in this stuff."

_____H.___ 8. "You've just got to learn your way through it."

_____I.___ 9. "I wired every teacher's house. I got shocked all the time."

_____A.___ 10. "I never put people down, because I know what that feels like."

_____J.___ 11. "We're always expecting a curve ball."

_____A.___ 12. "At some point, I think I decided that being dyslexic was better than being stupid."

Multiple Choice

Write the letter of the correct answer in the blank provided.

_____ 1. Morris suggests all of the following about dyslexia *except*
   a. dyslexia has nothing to do with IQ
   b. typical symptoms of dyslexia are difficulty reading, writing, and spelling
   c. dyslexia is the same in all individuals
   d. dyslexia is not likely to be outgrown

_____ 2. What is the meaning of the word *devouring* as used in paragraph 2?
   a. scrutinizing
   b. collecting
   c. tearing apart
   d. taking in greedily with the senses or intellect.

_____ 3. In paragraph 3, when the author refers to Charles Schwab, Richard Branson, John Chambers, and David Boies as losers, she is being
   a. serious
   b. facetious
   c. cheerful
   d. optimistic

_____ 4. As described in paragraph 4, a *pioneer* is a person who
   a. first settled a region, opening it up for the occupation by others
   b. a soldier detailed to make roads in advance of the main body
   c. a person who is among the earliest in any field of inquiry, enterprise, or progress
   d. an organism that successfully establishes itself in a barren area

_____ 5. When the author refers to an *everyman definition* in paragraph 5, she means
   a. a definition commonly used by the typical or average person
   b. a definition used by people who are not in the medical or scientific field
   c. both a and b
   d. none of the above

_____ 6. In paragraph 6, the expression *dawned on* means
   a. became clear; registered
   b. sank in; came as a realization
   c. began to be perceived or understood.
   d. all of the above

_____ 7. What is the meaning of the word *snuff* as used in paragraph 9?
   a. extinguish
   b. suppress
   c. crush
   d. all of the above

_____ 8. *Crucible* in paragraph 10 refers to
   a. a short-term effect
   b. a temporary setback
   c. a severe test or trial having a lasting influence
   d. a momentous undertaking

_____ 9. As described in paragraph 10, a *tenacious* person is likely to be
   a. persistent
   b. capricious
   c. infallible
   d. disenchanted

True or False

Indicate whether the statement is true or false by writing T or F in the blank provided.

___T___ 1. Chambers kept his dyslexia a secret because as CEO he felt that it was inadvisable to reveal his weaknesses.

___T___ 2. One reason Chambers revealed his secret was because he felt a great deal of empathy for the little girl with the learning disability.

___F___ 3. A *resilient* person is someone who is inflexible.

_____I_____ 4. A relationship that is mutually beneficial to two parties could be called *symbiotic*.

_____I_____ 5. As children, dyslexics can see the benefits of having dyslexia, but adults can see only the liabilities.

_____F_____ 6. Fully 60 percent of the male population is prone to dyslexia to varying degrees.

_____F_____ 7. Dyslexia does not have a genetic component.

_____I_____ 8. Dyslexics may have difficulty learning things in a conventional manner.

_____F_____ 9. Dyslexia is usually outgrown by the time of puberty.

_____I_____ 10. If something is *excruciating*, it causes great physical or mental suffering.

In Your Own Words

1. Dr. Mel Levine (professor of pediatrics at the University of North Carolina Medical School and an expert on learning differences) says, "Schools reward well-roundedness, but so many of the most successful people have brains that are rather specialized." The dyslexic business leaders profiled in the *Fortune* magazine article by Betsy Morris all say that children should be allowed to specialize. For instance, Charles Schwab suggests that foreign language requirements should be abandoned, and Paul Orfalea says the same about trigonometry. What do you think? How much of the basic school curriculum should be modified to suit individual learners' needs?

2. Paul Orfalea recalls that as he was growing up his mother used to console him by saying that in the long run "the A students work for the B students, the C students run the businesses, and the D students dedicate the buildings." What is your opinion?

3. Our current educational system places a great deal of emphasis on good grades and high test scores to the disadvantage of the dyslexic. Do you think the emphasis should be changed?

The Art of Writing

In a brief essay, respond to the item below.

> David Boies, in addition to being dyslexic himself, has two dyslexic sons. One graduated from Yale Law School despite childhood testing that indicated he would not be able to accomplish very much. Boies thinks our current educational climate does not allow for late-bloomers. "In this environment," he says, "you get children who think they are masters of the universe, and children who think they are failures, when they're 10 years old. They're both wrong. And neither is well served by that misconception."

Vocabulary Puzzle

Directions: Use the vocabulary words to complete the puzzle.

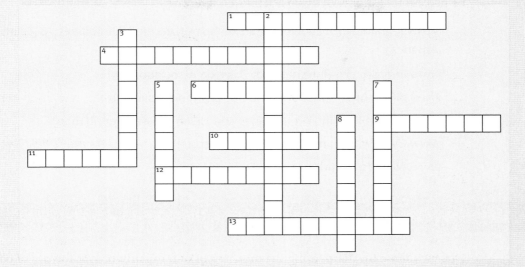

adversity	dawned	jumble	symbiotic
conscientious	excruciating	mentors	tenacious
conventional	fostered	resilience	volatile
crucial			

ACROSS CLUES

1. Causing intense suffering
4. Conforming to established practice
6. Persistent
9. Wise and trusted counselors or teachers
10. Began to be perceived
11. To confuse mentally

12. Misfortune; unfavorable circumstance
13. Ability to recover readily from adversity

DOWN CLUES

2. Meticulous; careful
3. Characterized by sudden changes
5. Of vital importance

7. Mutually beneficial relationship between two persons
8. Promoted the growth and development of

Internet Activity

Consult two of the following websites, and discuss information that you think would be helpful for parents of dyslexic children to know:

www.ldanatl.org/factsheets/dyslexia.html (Learning Disabilities Association of America)

www.Interdys.org (International Dyslexia Association)

www.NCLD.org (National Center for Learning Disabilities)

www.Schwablearning.org (Charles and Helen Schwab Foundation)

www.Cyberwink.com (Don Winkler's website)

www.Allkindsofminds.org (Mel Levine's Institute)

VOCABULARY | Words in Context

One technique for discovering the meaning of unfamiliar words is the use of context clues. By paying attention to what an author is saying, we can often discover the meanings of words without having to look them up in the dictionary. As you will see, often our own background or experiences also will help us determine the meanings of unfamiliar words. Here are some common techniques for using context to determine the meaning of new words.

Definition

Sometimes a writer provides us with a definition of a word somewhere within the sentence or nearby sentences, especially if the word is one that we are likely to be unfamiliar with.

Every year many people buy self-help audio tapes containing *subliminal* messages to help them relieve stress. These tapes contain messages that are supposedly below the level of human consciousness.

Subliminal here is simply defined as "below the level of consciousness."

Synonym

A synonym, which is another word with a similar meaning, may be used elsewhere in the sentence.

Massages are thought to provide *therapeutic* benefits by relieving stress; however, their curative powers do not extend to all patients.

You can infer from this sentence that *therapeutic* and *curative* have similar meanings.

Antonym

Sometimes you can determine the meaning of a word by finding an antonym, a word with an opposite meaning, somewhere in the sentence.

Juana's house was very well-maintained, but her sister's house was *dilapidated*.

You can see that the writer is making a contrast, and that *well-maintained* is the opposite of *dilapidated*.

Examples

Sometimes examples illustrate the meaning of a word.

> Terry has such *boundless* energy that even after working a full shift and taking care of her two small children, she still wants to go out dancing with her husband at night.

This example suggests to you that *boundless* means "infinite or vast."

Explanation

Sometimes a writer simply gives the reader an explanation of what a word means.

> The Russian gymnastic team was *disconsolate* after its loss to the Romanians. No amount of kind words from coaches and fans could raise the spirits of the young athletes.

The writer is telling you that the word *disconsolate* means "persistently sad or unhappy."

Experience

This way of discovering the meaning of a word draws on your personal experience.

> Have you ever been seated next to someone in a restaurant whose *loquaciousness* on a cell phone made you ask to be moved to another table?

Perhaps you have experienced this or a similar situation, and you can infer that *loquaciousness* means "talkativeness."

Knowledge of Subject

Here you have just enough familiarity with the subject the writer is discussing to enable you to figure out the meaning of the unfamiliar word.

> Mark labored under the *delusion* that he could pass calculus without attending class and studying.

You can guess that Mark was fooling or *deluding* himself and that *delusion* is a "false or mistaken belief."

Combination

You can use a number of these strategies at the same time to decipher the meaning of a word.

> The man at the party was a real *introvert*. He sat quietly in a corner of the room by himself working a crossword puzzle.

Here you probably used explanation, experience, and familiarity with the subject to determine that *introverts* are persons who are much more focused on their own inner thoughts and feelings than on the social environment.

Exercise 1: Context Clues

Now define the following words, without consulting your dictionary. First, give your own definition for the italicized word, and then, indicate the method(s) you used to arrive at the definition. The first example is done for you.

1. Because Americans are eating better and have access to better medical care, their *longevity* is increasing.

   Definition: <u>length of life</u>

   Method(s) used: <u>example, knowledge of subject, explanation, maybe experience</u>

2. Nudists claim it is a *liberating* experience to be without the restrictions of clothes.

   Definition: _____

   Method(s) used: _____

3. Pictures of *emaciated* and starving children filled the news as the famine in the war-torn country continued.

   Definition: _____

   Method(s) used: _____

4. *Badgered* by her children's constant pleas for a big-screen TV, the young mother finally gave in.

   Definition: _____

   Method(s) used: _____

5. Walter's *obeisance* to his brother was a source of irritation to Nancy, who couldn't figure out why Walter always deferred to him.

   Definition: _____

   Method(s) used: _____

6. After her divorce, Reyna tried to *obliterate* all evidence of her former husband by throwing out his clothes, pictures, and CDs.

   Definition: _____

   Method(s) used: _____

7. Jonathan Swift, author of *Gulliver's Travels*, did not like people in the *aggregate*, but he could tolerate them as individuals.

   Definition: _____

   Method(s) used: _____

Exercise 2: Context Clues

Use context clues to determine the meaning of the italicized words. Circle the clue word(s).

1. Tomoko tried to *pacify* her young son by giving him a lollipop, but her efforts to satisfy him failed.

2. John Lennon of the Beatles had an *innate* talent for music, but despite his natural ability, he still had to work hard to achieve success.

3. We have taken to calling our *inquisitive* neighbor "Mrs. Nosy Parker."

4. At his death, his property was distributed to his children in a just and *equitable* manner.

5. The doctor determined that constant ear infections had robbed the elderly woman of her *equilibrium*, so he prescribed a walker to help her maintain her balance.

6. Just as muscles can *atrophy* from lack of exercise, so too the mind can waste away from lack of use.

7. The *flippant* remark to his teacher earned Joel a detention. The teacher did not like Joel's joking attitude.

8. Many remarked about his *ostentatious* life style, but he refused to modify his showy ways.

9. Vincent was in a *pensive* mood, and he remained quietly thoughtful even while sitting in a noisy cafeteria.

10. Scientists have offered many explanations for why dinosaurs became *extinct*, but none of these explanations can fully explain their disappearance.

11. Venus Williams is an *agile* tennis player. Her coordination has saved many a shot.

Exercise 3: Context Clues with Nonsense Words

Try to determine the meaning of each made-up word by noting context clues.

1. Your dog or cat *donahs* by means of barks and meows. Do you think barking and meowing is a real language?

   donahs: _____

2. In most of the rock videos produced in the United States, females are generally irrelevant, presented simply as *feruna*, or ornaments, for the male performers.

   feruna: _____

3. Many American parents use television as an electronic *rennoo*, sitting their children down in front of it while they go off to do other things.

   rennoo: _____

4. Many youngsters at an increasingly early age are being exposed to a great deal of *zantun* on television, such as people being stabbed, poisoned, run over, or strangled.

   zantun: _____

5. As introverts age, they tend to become more introspective. On the other hand, people who were *metix* when they were young tend to remain just as outgoing and interested in other people as they age.

   metix: _____

6. Each of us has an area around us called our personal bubble. We may open that bubble to those we perceive as friendly, but we are careful to keep people we perceive as *sistos* away.

   sistos: _____

7. Throughout history, some form of patriarchy, a system in which men dominate women, has been the norm. There are no records of a true *kikitus*, a social system in which women dominate men.

    kikitus: _____

8. Arlie Hochschild pointed out that in the typical American home with both spouses working, the wife after putting in eight hours comes home and does a second shift of cooking, cleaning, and child care. Many men get out of performing tasks at home by demonstrating *ibil*. When it's their turn to cook, they burn the food. When they go to the grocery store, they forget the shopping list. They don't pick up an object unless they fall over it. Some even forget where they left the kids.

    ibil: _____

Exercise 4: Context Clues

Use the context to determine the missing words. Briefly describe the clue or clues that you found.

1. Some students have a strong fear of success. They often "play dumb" with their friends or back away from winning in sports or school. Because success is perceived as stressful, they are more comfortable with _____.

    Clue: _____

2. Both men and women are prone to fear of success. But women have an additional burden. If women define success as masculine, they are more likely to avoid it in order to be perceived as _____ by their peers.

    Clue: _____

3. Avoiding success is not always undesirable. An overemphasis on achievement can be just as bad. In the United States, there are many successful but unhappy workaholics. A truly successful life strikes a _____ between achievement and other needs. A happy medium is sometimes best.

    Clue: _____

4. What does it take to achieve great success? Many great Olympic athletes began with quite ordinary skills. It was their drive and determination that made them truly _____.

    Clue: _____

5. Parents can raise high achievers by nurturing dedication and hard work. The parents of Olympic athletes supported their child's interest and emphasized doing one's _____ at all times.

    Clue: _____

6. Most of us cannot achieve elite performance, but all of us can improve our everyday motivation. If you fail, regard it as a sign that you need to work _____, not that you lack ability.

    Clue: _____

SQ3R Study Method

SQ3R is a technique for reading and studying textbook material that was developed by Dr. Francis P. Robinson over 50 years ago. SQ3R stands for survey, question, read, recite, and review. Research shows that using the SQ3R method can help you improve both your reading comprehension and your grades.

A. **Survey** (Orient yourself to the assignment)
   1. Read introductory and summary paragraphs.
   2. Read headings and subheadings.
   3. Look at illustrations and tables.

At this stage, look at key parts of the article to achieve a general idea of how the article is structured and what it is all about.

B. **Question** (Find the main points)
   1. Ask who, what, where, when, why, and how.
   2. Contrast the material in front of you to previous material and to your background knowledge.
   3. Turn headings and subheadings into questions.

At this stage, you will formulate questions about the material you would like to have answered.

C. **Read** (Read actively instead of passively)
   1. Look for answers to your questions.
   2. Underline or highlight key words or phrases.
   3. Make notes in margins.
   4. Summarize key points in your own words.

The goal of this stage is to read the material in an active, questioning, purposeful way. While you are reading, keep in mind the questions you have already formulated. Don't hesitate to read the material a second or third time. How often you should read something depends on how difficult it is. Reading something a second or third time is like seeing a movie over again—new details and meanings begin to appear.

D. **Recite** (Demonstrate your understanding of the material)
   1. Put the information you have learned into your own words.
   2. Recite the main points from memory.
   3. Organize the material through outlining, mapping, diagraming, or similar techniques.

Say the answers to your original questions either to yourself or out loud. Be sure you can recite the answers to the who, what, where, when, why, and how questions you orignally posed.

E. **Review** (Memory is improved by repetition)
   1. Review material frequently.
   2. Practice giving answers.

Just as you shouldn't hesitate to read material more than once, you shouldn't hesitate to test yourself on it more than once. Continual review is the key to learning material and remembering it.

Find Your Procrastination Quotient

FRANK & ERNEST® by Bob Thaves

FRANK & ERNEST: © Thaves/Dist. By Newspaper Enterprise Association, Inc.

Do you procrastinate? Do you wait until the last minute to accomplish a task, such as a homework assignment? Do you recognize yourself in the Frank and Ernest cartoon above? To assess your tendency for procrastination, take the test that follows. Look at the statements and circle the number that best applies.

1. I invent reasons and look for excuses for not acting on a problem.

   STRONGLY AGREE 4 3 2 1 **STRONGLY DISAGREE**

2. It takes pressure to get me to work on difficult assignments.

   STRONGLY AGREE 4 3 2 1 **STRONGLY DISAGREE**

3. I take half measures that will avoid or delay unpleasant or difficult tasks.

   STRONGLY AGREE 4 3 2 1 **STRONGLY DISAGREE**

4. I face too many interruptions and crises that interfere with accomplishing my major goals.

   STRONGLY AGREE 4 3 2 1 **STRONGLY DISAGREE**

5. I sometimes neglect to carry out important tasks.

   STRONGLY AGREE 4 3 2 1 **STRONGLY DISAGREE**

6. I schedule big assignments too late to get them done as well as I know I could.

   STRONGLY AGREE 4 3 2 1 **STRONGLY DISAGREE**

7. I'm sometimes too tired to do the work I need to do.

   STRONGLY AGREE 4 3 2 1 **STRONGLY DISAGREE**

8. I start new tasks before I finish old ones.

   STRONGLY AGREE 4 3 2 1 **STRONGLY DISAGREE**

9. When I work in groups, I try to get other people to finish what I don't.

   STRONGLY AGREE 4 3 2 1 **STRONGLY DISAGREE**

10. I put off tasks that I really don't want to do but I know that I must do.

    STRONGLY AGREE 4 3 2 1 **STRONGLY DISAGREE**

Scoring: Total the numbers you have circled. If the score is below 20, you are not a chronic procrastinator and you probably have only an occasional problem. If your score is 21–30, you have a minor problem with procrastination. If your score is above 30, you procrastinate quite often and should work on breaking the habit.

If you do procrastinate often, why do you think you do it? Are there particular subjects or classes or kinds of assignments on which you are more likely to procrastinate?

Find your procrastination quotient" from Robert S. Feldman, *Power Learning*, 2/e, p. 44. Copyright © 2003 McGraw-Hill Companies, Inc. Used with permission.

AND ONE MORE THING!

Many of us, despite our best intentions, are chronic procrastinators. We are forever putting off into the far distant future things that need to be accomplished today. Obviously, to be successful in school, as well as life, this bad habit needs to be changed.

SELECTION

"Think about the successful people you know.
Are any of them procrastinators?"

GETTING THE PICTURE

Practice your SQ3R techniques with this reading selection. Read the first paragraph, the first sentence of subsequent paragraphs, the subheadings, and the information in bold type. Then read the questions at the end. What do you already know about this topic? Did you know that procrastination can lead to health problems? College students who put off doing their assignments have more headaches, colds, and stomach pains than students who complete their assignments on time. Before you start reading, come up with some questions of your own. Then read the selection completely at least once; articulate what you have learned; and, finally, review the material and answer your own questions.

BIO-SKETCH

In 1997, Stedman Graham, former professional athlete, founder of Athletes Against Drugs, and corporate and community leader, published *You Can Make It Happen: A Nine-Step Plan for Success.* The following is an excerpt from Chapter 9, "Win by a Decision."

BRUSHING UP ON VOCABULARY

procrastinate to put off doing something unpleasant or burdensome until a future time.

gridlock a blockage; a paralysis. The word refers to a traffic jam, as at a busy intersection, in which no vehicle is able to move in any direction.

Excerpt from

You Can Make It Happen

by Stedman Graham

WIN BY A DECISION

1 If you want to pursue a better life, you need a process and a method for making better decisions, a process that uses all of your creative and analytical powers, all the resources at your command. Big decisions require big thinking.

Often, the only difference between you and someone you admire is that they have made the decision to make their lives better. There is a traditional African proverb that says, "If it is to be, it's up to me...."

2   Napoleon Hill, author of the classic *Think and Grow Rich*, has noted that successful people make decisions quickly and firmly once they have reviewed all the information available. Unsuccessful people, he said, make decisions slowly and change them often. He claimed also that ninety-eight out of a hundred people never make up their minds about their major purpose in life because *they simply can't make a decision and stick with it.* I hope to help you change that percentage by becoming one of those people who can make good life decisions.

3   One of the biggest obstacles to the decision-making process is something I am very familiar with: procrastination. I come from a long line of procrastinators. It might have been longer, but they kept putting off having more of us. Some say that not making a decision is a decision in itself, one with many implications. I've worked at overcoming my tendency to procrastinate, which is the tendency to put things off. One in five Americans is a chronic procrastinator, according to DePaul University professor Joseph R. Ferrari, coauthor of *Procrastination and Task Avoidance: Theory, Research and Treatment*. Ferrari has identified two types of procrastinators: the *arousal* type and the *avoidance* type. The first kind of procrastinator puts things off because they get a thrill out of doing things at the buzzer and in a last-minute rush. The second type puts things off to avoid them for a wide number of reasons ranging from fear of failure to simply wanting to avoid doing something they consider to be unpleasant. Those who procrastinate because they have a fear of failure believe that they are better off not trying than trying and failing. Mark Twain was the literary hero of procrastinators. His motto was *"Never put off till tomorrow what you can do the day after tomorrow."*

4   Here are a few other common phrases you'll hear from serious procrastinators:

This just isn't the right time to make that decision.

I have a few other important matters to deal with first.

My schedule just won't give me the time for that matter.

I've been meaning to get to that.

I'll tackle that when I've got more experience.

You wouldn't believe all the stuff I have to do before I can get to that.

Tomorrow, I promise you.

I just have to get away from all the distractions to focus on that.

I'm waiting to make a bigger move.

There is probably a safer (better, faster, easier) way of doing this. I'll wait for it.

5   Do any of these sound familiar to you? Procrastinators are creative in making excuses, even if they can't do anything else. The question they always get from people around them is "What are you waiting for...?"

6 Decision-making gridlock is a serious problem if you are interested in pursuing your vision for a better life. Often, it is based in fear, whether your particular brand is fear of success or fear of failure or just fear of pulling your head out of the ground (or from wherever you might have stuck it). Think about the successful people you know. Are any of them procrastinators? Do they spend days looking before they leap? Or do they go after what they want? I was going to come up with a list to help you overcome this problem but . . . just kidding.

7 The self-defeating habit of procrastination is a fairly common trait. There are three theories as to why you put things off that are vitally important:

1. You are just lazy.

2. You are self-destructive.

3. You like being stuck because it brings you sympathy.

8 As you can tell, these theories do not paint a pretty picture of the procrastinator's personality. None of them really explains the problem or deals with it in a very logical manner. No one is born lazy. Only truly demented people enjoy causing pain and mental torment to themselves. Sympathy may be one form of attention, but it is hardly uplifting or inspiring.

9 Recent studies of procrastination have found that people who put things off as a matter of habit are often troubled with feelings of hopelessness, low self-esteem, guilt, or fear. Procrastination is also the province of perfectionists, who put things off because they are waiting for the perfect time to produce the perfect results.

10 Here are a few tips to help my fellow procrastinators out there get beyond their "but's" and past their "one day I'm gonna's."

EIGHT SMALL STEPS FOR GETTING PAST PROCRASTINATION

11 1. *Take small bites.* Have you ever been to one of those Mexican restaurants that advertise Burritos As Big As Your Head? They aren't exaggerating, much. But you don't order one and then say, "I think I'll wait for a better time to eat this." No, you get to work on it. You don't try to do it in one huge bite, however; you eat that giant burrito one small bite at a time. This is not only good for digestion, it is good for decision making.

12 2. *Begin now!* Without even giving yourself time to think of excuses, sit down now and start the process and force yourself to keep at it for at least an hour. Set a time to pick up where you left off.

13 3. *Slam the door on critics.* If you feel that you can't make a decision because someone is holding you back, break free of that sense of helplessness and victimization. Sometimes you have to go against the sentiments of those around you in order to make decisions that open opportunities for yourself. You can't expect others to always share your vision. Don't let anything or anyone stand

"Whatever piece of business you have in hand, before stopping, do all the labor pertaining to it which can then be done."

—Abraham Lincoln

between you and your freedom to make decisions that improve your life. It is simply impossible to always reach a consensus.

14   4. *Lighten up.* Procrastinators tend to take themselves far too seriously. You are significant only within a very limited scope. The world is not focused on your every move. The sun will still come up tomorrow. The stars will still shine tonight. No matter what you do, the future of the galaxy is not resting on your shoulders. If the thought of making a decision is weighing so heavily that you can't make it, you need to step away and regain perspective so that you don't take yourself so seriously. Do something to take your mind off the decision and to lighten your mood. Take a walk, visit a friend who cheers you up, read a comic novel, or take in a comedy at the movie theater or on television. Get out of that dark mood.

15   5. *Think of the carrot, not the stick.* Those who put things off sometimes do it because they focus on the difficulties and demands of taking an action rather than on the rewards that await them. Focus on the solution, not the problem. Keep your mind on the rewards and results of your decision rather than on the process itself. After all, how many times have you fretted and worried about doing something, only to discover that it was not nearly as painful as you had imagined? Don't dream of all the work involved; dream of the rewards you will reap when you have taken action and gone after what you want from life.

16   6. *Bring in a coach.* These days people have personal fitness trainers, personal bankers, personal speech coaches, personal accountants, personal nutrition advisers. Why not bring in a friend or family member to be your antiprocrastination coach? Give them a list of the things you need to do and order them to dog you until you do them. Provide the whip if you feel it is necessary. Drastic procrastination calls for drastic action.

17   7. *Live in the moment.* I knew of a fellow who came to the end of his life and realized that he had accomplished nothing that he had wanted to do. He lamented this fact to a friend of his, *I don't know how I wasted my whole life.* The friend observed that he hadn't started out to waste his whole life. First, he had wasted a minute of it, then an hour, then a day, then a week, a month, a year, a decade, and *then* his whole life. Take a clue, and do the opposite. Use up every minute, every hour, every day, until you have made the most of your entire life.

18   8. *Don't demand perfection.* Tell yourself there is not going to be a *perfect* time to get started, and that you don't have to be *perfect* in your performance. Compromise and start immediately and rough out the task, and then build upon it. No one is standing over your shoulder demanding that you make no mistakes. . . . You are far more likely to succeed if you work to please yourself, without feeling pressured to meet the standards of others.

Source: Pp. 224–230 reprinted with the permission of Simon & Schuster Adult Publishing Group from YOU CAN MAKE IT HAPPEN: A Nine-Step Plan for Success by Stedman Graham. Copyright © 1997 by Graham-Williams Group. All rights reserved.

COMPREHENSION CHECKUP

Fill in the Blanks

Drawing on what you learned from the selection, fill in the blanks with an appropriate word or phrase.

1. What is the selection about? _____

2. Of the eight tips presented by Stedman Graham, list the four that you find most helpful.

   a. _____

   b. _____

   c. _____

   d. _____

3. Name the two types of procrastinators.

   a. _____

   b. _____

4. There are three theories that attempt to explain why people procrastinate. List them below and give an example or illustration for each one.

   a. _____

   _____

   b. _____

   _____

   c. _____

   _____

Multiple Choice

Write the lettesr of the correct answer in the blank provided.

_____ 1. Graham would agree with which of the following?
   a. Successful people decide things impulsively.
   b. It's not possible to improve one's basic outlook on life.
   c. Procrastinators are capable of changing their decision-making habits.
   d. Before you decide on any important actions, carefully gather opinions from friends and family.

_____ 2. All of the following are typical of procrastinators *except*
   a. taking a project one step at a time
   b. expecting perfection
   c. worrying about possible failure
   d. taking themselves far too seriously

_____ 3. Graham suggests that procrastination can lead to
   a. feelings of hopelessness
   b. poor self-esteem
   c. guilt-ridden feelings
   d. all of the above

_____ 4. What is the meaning of the word *demented* as used in paragraph 8?
   a. very fine
   b. easily hurt
   c. mentally ill
   d. spoiled

_____ 5. According to Graham, procrastinators like which of the following excuses?
   a. I'll do it tomorrow!
   b. I'll wait for an easier way.
   c. I'm too distracted right now.
   d. All of the above

True or False

Indicate whether the statement is true or false by writing T or F in the blank provided.

___T___ 6. According to Graham, many procrastinators have perfectionistic tendencies.

___F___ 7. Graham has probably never had a tendency to procrastinate.

___T___ 8. Graham suggests that many procrastinators should take themselves far less seriously.

___T___ 9. Some people procrastinate because they like the attention and sympathy such behavior brings.

___F___ 10. The word *lamented* in paragraph 17 means "celebrated."

Vocabulary in Context

Choose one of the following words to complete each of the sentences below. Use each word only once. Be sure to pay close attention to the context clues provided.

chronic	consensus	drastic	lamented	logical	scope
compromise	demented	fretted	literary	perspective	vitally

1. The ___scope___ of a paperback dictionary that has 50,000 entries is far less than that of a hardback dictionary with 180,000 entries.

2. Her ___chronic___ neck pain was probably caused by a pinched nerve.

3. Marcy ___fretted___ about her son's withdrawn behavior and his sudden tendency to stay in his room all day.

4. Not that many people realize that Steve Martin, the zany comedian, also has ___literary___ talent and has published two well-received novels.

5. Because the squabbling couple refused to ___compromise___ with each other, the marriage counselor recommended the dissolution of the marriage.

6. After the medical lab results came in, the doctor said that no
drastic measures were necessary and instead advised a cautious
wait-and-see approach.

7. In contrast to when I was a teenager, the _perspective_ I now have on life
is entirely different.

8. Many environmentalists say that it is _vitally_ important that the
United States reduce its dependence on fossil fuels.

9. At the funeral, many of those present _lamented_ the loss of the young
fireman who had given his life to rescue a little girl trapped inside a burning
apartment.

10. The public defender argued that his client should not receive the death
penalty because his client had a long history of mental problems and was
demented .

11. Although Brian attends the biology class, he fails to attend the required lab sessions; therefore, it is _logical_ to assume that he might not pass the class.

12. It was the _consensus_ of all members of my family that my decision to
drop out of school was a mistake.

In Your Own Words

What is the main idea of this poem? How does the poem relate to the previous
selection?

> Walk around feeling like a leaf
> Know you could tumble any second.
> *Then* decide what to do with your time.
>
> —*Naomi Shihab Nye*

Source: Naomi Shihab Nye, last stanza from "The Art of Disappearing" in *Words Under the Words*.

The Art of Writing

In a brief essay, respond to the item below.

Find something in your life that you feel needs improvement. Think about how
you could go about making this improvement. Identify three specific things you
could do that would move you toward your goal. For example, your goal might be to
lose 15 pounds. Your three specific actions might be (1) to go running three times a
week, (2) to allow yourself no fast food on weekends, and (3) to substitute diet sodas
for regular sodas. Decide how long you're going to stick to your three specific actions.
Be sure to answer the following questions: What are you going to try to improve in
your life? What specific actions are you going to take to reach your goal? How long
are you going to persevere?

Internet Activity

Stedman Graham gives readers general pointers for dealing with procrastination.
The University of Buffalo has put together a website to help students overcome
procrastination:

http://ub-counseling.buffalo.edu/stressprocrast.shtml#intr

Consult the site and list a few of the tips you find there.

SELECTION

"For once, Leonardo's genius let him down."

GETTING THE PICTURE

Leonardo da Vinci (1452–1519) was born the illegitimate son of a local lawyer in the small town of Vinci. He was a painter and an inventor. His most famous portrait is the *Mona Lisa*. The following selection discusses the restoration of another of his famous

Before the Restoration.

After the Restoration.   Scala/Art Resource, NY. S. Maria delle Grazie, Milan, Italy

SELECTION *continued*

works of art, *The Last Supper*. Leonardo painted *The Last Supper* on a monastery wall in Milan. It depicts the Passover meal that Jesus shared with his disciples before he was brought to trial and crucified. In the painting, Leonardo illustrates the moment when Jesus said to his disciples, "One of you shall betray me." Judas, the betrayer, who is seated fourth from the left of Jesus, clutches in his hand a bag containing the 30 pieces of silver he was paid for identifying Jesus.

BIO-SKETCH

Mark Getlein is a painter and an author of textbooks on art-related subjects.

BRUSHING UP ON VOCABULARY

plague a contagious disease that causes many deaths. It can also mean something that causes trouble or annoyance.

innovation a new device or new way of doing something.

bypassed ignored a popular practice.

precarious uncertain; insecure

impregnated spread throughout

Excerpt from
RESTORATION
by Mark Getlein

1   Unwise restorations have been the plague of many a great work of art, and there can be no better example than Leonardo da Vinci's *Last Supper*. Leonardo worked on this masterpiece during the years 1495 to 1497. Always a great one for innovation, he bypassed the established wall painting technique and devised an experimental method for this project. For once Leonardo's genius let him down. What may have been his greatest work soon became a ruin. Within ten years, the painting was said to be flaking badly; within about fifty years, the biographer Giorgio Vasari wrote that "Nothing is visible but a dazzling mass of blots."

2   The first major restoration was undertaken in 1726, and five others followed. Each of these restorations did more harm than good. One used a harsh solvent that dissolved Leonardo's colors. Another applied a strong glue that attracted dirt. Yet another restorer managed to give one of the Apostle's six fingers on one hand.

3   To make matters worse, the physical environment of the *Last Supper* could scarcely have been more precarious. Sharp variations in heat and humidity forced the paint off the wall, bringing deep cracks to the surface. Sometime in the 18th century, well-meaning friars in the monastery installed a curtain across the mural—which had the effect of trapping moisture on the wall and scraping off yet more paint each time the curtain was drawn back. French soldiers of Napoleon who occupied the monastery in 1796 took turns throwing rocks at the mural and climbing ladders to scratch out the Apostles' eyes. A bomb fell on the monastery during

World War II, missing the wall by a yard. It's a miracle that anything is left at all, and little is left.

4 Finally, nearly five hundred years after Leonardo put down his brushes, sensible measures were taken to save the mural. A Milanese restorer, Dr. Pinan Brambilla, began a major restoration in 1977; the project would last more than twenty years. Dr. Brambilla had assets earlier restorers lacked—modern microscopes, chemicals, and measuring devices. Through sensitive probing, she could determine what was Leonardo's work and what was somebody else's—and remove the latter. In areas where nothing is left of Leonardo's paint, she did not attempt to reconstruct the imagery, but simply painted in a neutral color.

5 It has not been easy. Dr. Brambilla's eyesight was permanently altered, and she suffers chronic pain in her shoulders and back. She says, "I often have to clean the same piece a second time, or even a third or fourth. The top section of the painting is impregnated with glue. The middle is filled with wax. There are six different kinds of plaster and several varnishes, lacquers, and gums. What worked on the top section doesn't work in the middle. And what worked in the middle won't work on the bottom. It's enough to make a person want to shoot herself."

6 Inevitably, Dr. Brambilla will have to cope with people who want to shoot *her*. Every art historian in the world will have an opinion about her restoration, and many of those opinions will be negative, even outraged. Still, she remains philosophical about her project. "I am at peace with what I have done here," she says.

Source: From Mark Getlein, *Gilbert's Living with Art,* 8th ed. New York: McGraw-Hill, p. 111. Copyright © 2008 McGraw-Hill. Reprinted by permission of the McGraw-Hill Companies, Inc.

"A successful person is one who can lay a firm foundation with the bricks that others throw at him or her."
—David Brinkley

"Criticism is prejudice made plausible."
—H. L. Mencken

 COMPREHENSION CHECKUP

Multiple Choice

Write the letter of the correct answer in the blank provided.

_____ 1. The selection is about
   a. the restoration of *The Last Supper*
   b. Dr. Brambilla
   c. art
   d. Leonardo da Vinci

_____ 2. How many restorations of *The Last Supper* were there before Dr. Brambilla's?
   a. 5
   b. 6
   c. 7
   d. 8

_____ 3. Which of the following materials have been applied to *The Last Supper* during restorations?
   a. a harsh solvent
   b. strong glue
   c. chemicals
   d. all of the above

_____ 4. One can conclude from the reading that
- a. all artwork should be restored
- b. all art historians agree that Dr. Brambilla has done a good job
- c. art restoration can be difficult
- d. techniques of art restoration have not improved for hundreds of years

_____ 5. Which of the following has led to the current condition of the mural?
- a. installing a curtain to cover it
- b. soldiers throwing rocks at it
- c. variations in heat and humidity
- d. all of the above

True or False

Indicate whether each statement is true or false by writing T or F in the blank provided.

__F__ 6. All of the restorations of *The Last Supper* have used the same techniques.

__T__ 7. Dr. Brambilla worked on the restoration project for more than 20 years.

__F__ 8. Dr. Brambilla was not able to determine what was originally painted by Leonardo and what was painted by someone else.

__F__ 9. Leonardo originally painted six fingers on one hand of one of the Apostles.

__T__ 10. The selection implies that Leonardo's experimental wall-painting technique was not a success.

Vocabulary in Context

Write the letter of the correct answer in the blank provided.

_____ 1. All of the following could be considered assets *except*
- a. money in the bank
- b. stocks and bonds
- c. a bankrupt company
- d. a college education

_____ 2. If your mother tells you that dropping out of school is *unwise*, she means that
- a. it is a good idea
- b. it is not a good idea
- c. it is not wise
- d. both b and c

_____ 3. When you *undertake* something, you
- a. decide not to do it
- b. agree to do it
- c. refuse to do it
- d. get angry but do it anyway

_____ 4. In paragraph 2, the words *harm* and *good* are
- a. synonyms
- b. homonyms
- c. antonyms
- d. digraphs

_____ 5. If you have a *chronic* disease, it is likely to
  a. go away after a short while
  b. continue for a long time
  c. come back again and again
  d. both b and c

_____ 6. When something is *visible,* it is
  a. capable of being seen
  b. not perceptible to the eye
  c. concealed
  d. none of the above

_____ 7. Which of the following is more likely a *neutral* color?
  a. red
  b. purple
  c. beige
  d. green

_____ 8. An antonym for *sensible* is
  a. foolish
  b. practical
  c. reasonable
  d. imaginative

_____ 9. If you are feeling *philosophical* about losing your wallet, you are feeling
  a. frustrated
  b. stressed
  c. accepting
  d. depressed

_____ 10. A *harsh* chemical is one that is
  a. soft
  b. gentle
  c. strong
  d. pleasant

In Your Own Words

1. How does Mark Getlein feel about Dr. Brambilla's restoration of *The Last Supper*? What clues enable you to reach this conclusion?

2. What does the reading suggest about the character of Dr. Brambilla? How did she handle the stress of the renovation? Do you think art restoration is a stressful job? Why or why not?

The Art of Writing

Study the original *Last Supper* and Dr. Brambilla's restoration. Do you think that effort should be made to restore great works of art? Or would it be better just to leave them as they now are? Write a paragraph discussing the issue.

Vocabulary Puzzle

Directions: Use the vocabulary words to complete the puzzle.

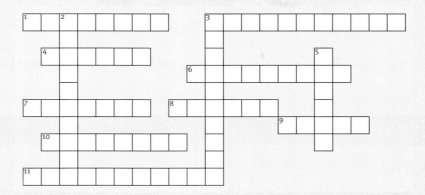

bypassed	genius	monastery	precarious
chronic	impregnated	mural	restoration
friars	innovation	plague	solvents

ACROSS CLUES

1. Elias, taking his complaint directly to the school board, _____ the teacher, the principal, and the superintendent of his school.

3. When he got home from the all-night party, he discovered that his clothes were _____ with smoke.

4. Many people consider Albert Einstein to be a _____ .

6. A _____ is a residence where monks live in religious seclusion.

7. Lifetime smokers often develop a _____ cough.

8. Traffic congestion is a _____ of modern life.

9. *Mixtec Culture* is a famous _____ by Mexican artist Diego Rivera.

10. Many common cleaning _____ have been found to be harmful to the environment.

11. Has any historical building in your community gone through a _____ process?

DOWN CLUES

2. Standing on the top step of a ladder puts a person in a _____ position.

3. The computer is a wonderful _____.

5. _____, like monks, lead austere religious lives.

Internet Activities

1. Type "Leonardo da Vinci inventions" into an Internet search engine. Click on a website that discusses Leonardo's inventions, and write a few sentences about one that you find interesting.

2. Dan Brown in *The Da Vinci Code* claims that one of the disciples seated close to Jesus in Leonardo's *Last Supper* is not John, but instead Mary Magdalene. Type in "da Vinci's *Last Supper*" and see what you find.

TEST-TAKING TIP

Be Prepared

Sometime in the next few weeks you will take a test in one of your classes. Although this advice may seem obvious, you need to prepare for the test. Don't wait until late the night before to begin studying the material. That's too late. Following are some suggestions for preparing for the test.

1. Read the course material before it is discussed in class. Every evening review the day's class notes.

2. Practice the SQ3R method of studying. Annotate and highlight your textbook and class notes.

3. Begin reviewing for a test days in advance. If you learn best by listening, read the material out loud. If you learn best by seeing, make an outline of the material. If you learn best by being physically involved, copy your notes.

4. Find out what the test is going to cover. Your instructor may give you a study guide or sample questions. If not, put together your own study guide and sample questions. What points has the instructor emphasized? What do you think are the most important points?

5. Find out what kind of test it's going to be—multiple choice, true-false, short answer, short essay, or a combination. Knowing what to expect will guide your preparation and ease your anxiety.

The most important test-taking tip is—be prepared!

Discovering Meaning Through Structure

Steam-boat, (1923)
BY FERNAND LEGER

Musée National Fernand Leger, Biot, France.
Photo: Erich Lessing/Art Resource,
NY © ARS, NY

CHAPTERS IN PART 2

Topics, Main Ideas, and Details

Carte Blanche (1965) BY RENÉ MAGRITTE

© 2009 C. Herscovici, Brussels/Artists Rights Society (ARS),
New York. Banque d'Images, ADAGP/Art Resource, NY.
National Gallery of Art, Washington, DC, U.S.A.

View and Reflect

1. *Carte Blanche* was created by the highly imaginative painter René Magritte. What does the painting illustrate about perception, which is the theme of this chapter? Is the scene you are viewing physically possible?

2. Do the trees hide or reveal the woman and the horse? Can you see the woman and the horse in the open spaces in the painting?

3. What is the topic of the painting? The main idea?

4. What is the definition of *carte blanche*? In what way does the definition apply to the painting?

TOPICS AND MAIN IDEAS

Most paragraphs are about a particular **topic** or **subject.** The topic is usually a single word or phrase and is often the noun that is mentioned most frequently in a paragraph. We can identify the topic by asking ourselves, "What is this all about?" or "Who is this all about?"

Paragraphs are supposed to be organized around a main idea with all sentences supporting this **main idea,** or key point, of the paragraph. The main idea can be identified by asking, "What key point does the author want me to know about the topic?"

The main idea may be directly stated in a paragraph—usually, but not always, in the first or last sentence—or it can be implied. When trying to find a main idea that is directly stated, it helps to remember that you are looking for a general statement, not a specific one. When main ideas are implied, you, the reader, are responsible for coming up with a general statement that unites the author's key details. This general statement should be no more than one sentence long.

Details are supporting sentences that reinforce the main idea. While the main idea is a general statement, supporting details provide specific information, such as facts, examples, or reasons, that explain or elaborate on the main idea.

As an illustration of the difference between main ideas and details, study the invitation below. The main idea of the invitation is the fact that a reception is going to be held. The details tell us who the reception is for and when and where it will occur.

 **Jon Yukio Higuchi
"All Fired Up"**

November 12 - December 5, 2002

Glendale Community College
Student Union Gallery

*You are invited to an open Reception
on:*
**Tuesday, November 12, 2002
6:00 p.m. - 8:00 p.m.**

Glendale Community College
6000 West Olive/Dunlap Ave.
Glendale, AZ 85302

 HIGUCHI CERAMIC DESIGNS
by
Jon Yukio Higuchi

Wedding Vessel
14"w x 9 3/4"h

Sponsored by the Evening Students Association

Jon Yukio Higuchi, "All Fired Up" invitation. Copyright © 2002. Used by permission of Jon Yukio Higuchi. Photo: Cheryl Miller.

Those supporting sentences that directly reinforce the main idea are called **major** supporting details, and those sentences that serve only to reinforce the major supporting details are called **minor** supporting details.

Read the following paragraph from *Gilbert's Living with Art* by Mark Getlein. The topic of the paragraph is perception.

1. In visual perception, our eyes take in information in the form of light patterns; the brain processes these patterns to give them meaning. The mechanics of perception work much the same way for everyone, yet in a given situation we do not all perceive the same things. The human eye cannot take in all available visual information. Our world is too complex, and we are constantly bombarded with an incredible range of visual images. To avoid overloading our mental circuits, the brain responds only to that visual information required to meet our needs at one moment.

The next paragraph contains a main idea sentence and a series of examples that support it. The topic of this paragraph, and the others that follow, is also perception.

2. It is easier to cope with our complex visual world if we simplify our perceptions and see according to our immediate needs. Suppose you are motoring along a busy street. Your eyes "see" everything, but what does your brain register? If you are the car's driver, you will see the traffic signs and lights, because awareness of such details is necessary. If you are hungry, your attention may be attracted by fast-food signs. If you are looking for a specific address, you will focus on building numbers and block out nearly everything else.

Identify the main idea sentence in paragraph 3 below.

3. Studies indicate that the brain is often more important than the eyes in determining what each of us sees as we move through the world. The brain's ability to control perception is obvious when we study ambiguous figures, such as the classic one reproduced here. When you first look at this drawing, you may see a white vase. Or you may see two dark profiles. Even after you have been made aware of the two images, you must consciously work at going back and forth between them. You can feel your brain shifting as it organizes the visual information into first one image and then the other.

Vase-profile illusion

Paragraph 3 expresses the main idea in the first sentence and then gives us an example that illustrates it.

To gain understanding of how main ideas and major and minor supporting details work together in a paragraph, read the following paragraph and study the outline that follows.

4. While perception can cause us to miss seeing what is actually present in the visual field, it can also do the reverse: cause us to "see" what is not present. The brain supplies information to create a kind of order it requires, even though that information may not be recorded by the eyes. In the illustration of wavy forms you may see a

perfect white circle, but there is no circle. There is only the illusion of a white circle created by breaks in the wavy forms. This is just another trick our brains play on us as part of the phenomenon of perception.

"Restoration" from Mark Getlein, *Gilbert's Living with Art*, 6th ed., New York: McGraw-Hill, 2002, p. 11. Copyright © 2002 McGraw-Hill. Reprinted by permission of The McGraw-Hill Companies, Inc.
From Mark Getlein, *Gilbert's Living with Art*, 6th ed., New York: McGraw-Hill, 2002, p. 274. Copyright © 2002 McGraw-Hill. Reprinted by permission of The McGraw-Hill Companies, Inc.

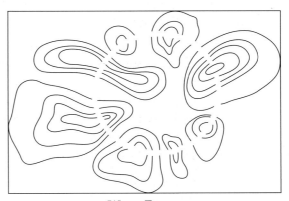

Wavy Forms
"Wavy Forms," from Mark Getlein, *Gilbert's Living with Art*, 6th ed.,
New York: McGraw-Hill, 2002, p. 274. Copyright © 2002 McGraw-Hill.
Reprinted by permission of The McGraw-Hill Companies, Inc.

Key: MI (main idea), MSD (major supporting detail), msd (minor supporting detail)

I. Perception can cause us to miss seeing what is there and can cause us to "see" what is not there. (MI)
   A. The brain supplies information to create order in what our eyes see. (MSD)
      1. You see a perfect white circle in the wavy forms. (msd)
      2. In this way, our brains trick us. (msd)

It is wise to remember that while all paragraphs have a topic, not all paragraphs have main ideas. Some background or descriptive paragraphs, which are meant to set the tone or mood of a piece of writing, may not have any main idea at all.

Exercise 1: Locating Topics in Textbook Material

Locate the topic of each paragraph. Remember to ask the question "Who or what is the paragraph about?"

1. Tickets for athletic events and musical concerts sometimes get resold for much greater amounts than the original price—a market transaction known as "scalping." For example, an original buyer may resell a $75 ticket to a concert for $200, $250 or more. Reporters sometimes denounce scalpers for "ripping off" buyers by charging "exorbitant" prices. But is ticket scalping really undesirable? Not on economic grounds! We must first recognize that such ticket resales are voluntary transactions. If both buyer and seller did not expect to gain from the exchange, it would not occur! There are no losers or victims here. Both buyer and seller benefit from the transaction. The scalping market simply redistributes assets (game or concert tickets) from those who would rather have the money to those who would rather have the tickets.

Paragraph From Campbell R. McConnell, *Economics*, 17th ed., 2008, p. 55.

Topic: _____

During a one-month period in 2001, 30.7 percent of high school students had ridden in a vehicle driven by a person who had been drinking alcohol.

2. Alcohol consumption exacts an alarming toll on college students. Students who drink more frequently die in traffic accidents, receive citations for driving under the influence/driving while intoxicated (DUI/DWI), damage personal or public property, argue or fight, attempt suicide, experience or commit sexual abuse, miss classes, receive failing grades, suffer academic probation, or drop out of college more often than do those who are not drinkers. Most campus rapes occur when the victim, the assailant, or both have been drinking.

Paragraph from Clinton Benjamin, et al., *Human Biology,* New York: McGraw-Hill, 1997.

Topic: _____

3. Anyone who has roomed with a noisy person, worked in a noisy office, or tried to study with a party going on in the next room can attest to the effect of noise on one's level of stress. Noise can raise blood pressure, increase heart rate, and lead to muscle tension. Noise has been found to be related to job dissatisfaction and to result in irritation and anxiety. Most disturbing is noise that constantly changes in pitch, intensity, or frequency. We may become used to more common and stable noise and almost ignore it. People who live near airports, for example, seem to not even hear the planes after a while. However, just because you become accustomed to the noise or are able to tune it out doesn't mean you are not being affected by it.

Paragraph from Jerrold Greenberg, *Comprehensive Stress Management,* 9th ed., New York: McGraw-Hill, 2006, p. 77. Copyright © 2006 McGraw-Hill Companies, Inc. Used with permission.

Topic: _____

4. In the traditional cultures of Asia, arranged marriages were the rule. Marriages were designed to further the well-being of families, not of the individuals involved. Marriage was traditionally seen as a matter of ancestors, descendants, and property. Supporters of these traditions point out that love is a fleeting emotion and not a sensible basis for such an important decision. Today, arranged marriages are still very common in India, in many Muslim nations, and in sub-Saharan Africa. However, it appears that this tradition is rapidly deteriorating, often in proportion to the degree of Western influence.

Paragraph from Curtis Byer, et al., *Dimensions of Human Sexuality,* 5th ed., New York: McGraw-Hill, 1999, p. 39.

Topic: _____

"When people are bored, it is primarily with their own selves."

—Eric Hoffer

5. If you are like most people, you have indulged in fake listening many times. You go to history class, sit in the third row, and look squarely at the instructor as she speaks. But your mind is far away, floating in the clouds of a pleasant daydream. Occasionally you come back to earth: the instructor writes an important term on the chalkboard, and you dutifully copy it in your notebook. Every once in a while the instructor makes a witty remark, causing others in the class to laugh. You smile politely, pretending that you have heard the remark and found it mildly humorous. You have a vague sense of guilt that you are not paying close attention, but you tell yourself that any material you miss can be picked up from a friend's notes. Besides, the instructor is talking about road construction in ancient Rome and nothing could be more boring. So, back you go into your private little world. Unfortunately, fake listening has two

drawbacks: (1) You miss a lot of information, and (2) you can botch a personal or business relationship.

Paragraph from Hamilton Gregory, *Public Speaking for College and Career,* 4th ed., New York: McGraw-Hill, 1996, p. 27.

Topic: _____

6. The number of Americans living alone more than doubled between 1970 and 2000, a much greater increase than the 16 percent growth in married couples. By 2000, 26.7 million Americans were living alone; one of every four occupied dwelling units had only one person in it. The high incidence of divorce, the ability of the elderly to maintain their own homes alone, and the deferral of marriage among young adults have contributed to the high rate of increase in the number of single-person households.

Paragraph from Michael Hughes, *Sociology the Core,* 7th ed., 2005, p. 345. Copyright © 2005 McGraw-Hill Companies, Inc. Used with permission.

Topic: _____

Exercise 2: Locating Main Ideas in Textbook Material

Locate the main idea sentence of each paragraph. The main idea can be identified by asking the question "What key point does the author want me to know about the topic?"

Paragraphs in items 1–5 from David G. Myers, *Social Psychology,* 8th ed., New York: McGraw-Hill, 2005, pp. 157–160. Copyright © 2007 McGraw-Hill Companies, Inc. Used with permission.

"Anxiety is fear of one's self."

—Wilhem Stekel

1. We infer our emotions by observing our bodies and our behaviors. For example, a stimulus such as a growling bear confronts a woman in the forest. She tenses, her heartbeat increases, adrenaline flows, and she runs away. Observing all this, she then experiences fear. At a college where I am to lecture, I awake before dawn and am unable to get back to sleep. Noting my wakefulness, I conclude that I must be anxious.

Main idea: _____1st_____

2. James Laird instructed college students to pull their brows together and frown while experimenters attached electrodes to their faces. The act of maintaining a frown caused students to report feeling angry. Those students induced to make a smiling face reported feeling happier and found cartoons more humorous. We have all experienced this phenomenon. We're feeling crabby, but then the phone rings or someone comes to the door and elicits from us warm, polite behavior. "How's everything?" "Just fine, thanks. How are things with you?" "Oh, not bad. . . ." If our feelings are not too intense, this warm behavior may change our whole attitude. It's tough to smile and feel grouchy. When Miss Universe parades her smile, she may, after all, be helping herself feel happy. Going through the motions can trigger the emotions.

Main idea: _____Last_____

3. Your gait can affect how you feel. When you get up from reading this chapter, walk for a minute taking short, shuffling steps with eyes downcast. It's a great way to feel depressed. Want to feel better? Walk for a minute taking long

strides with your arms swinging and your eyes straight ahead. Can you feel the difference?

Main idea: _____1st_____

4. It appears that unnecessary rewards sometimes have a hidden cost. Rewarding people for doing what they already enjoy may lead them to attribute their doing it to the reward. This undermines their self-perception that they do it because they like it. If you pay people for playing with puzzles, they will later play with the puzzles less than those who play without being paid. If you promise children a reward for doing what they intrinsically enjoy (for example playing with magic markers) then you will turn their play into work.

Main idea: _____1st_____

"Take away the cause and the effect ceases."

—Miguel de Cervantes

5. An old man lived alone on a street where boys played noisily every afternoon. The din annoyed him, so one day he called the boys to his door. He told them he loved the cheerful sound of children's voices and promised them each 50 cents if they would return the next day. Next afternoon the youngsters raced back and played more lustily than ever. The old man paid them and promised another reward the next day. Again they returned, whooping it up, and the man again paid them; this time 25 cents. The following day they got only 15 cents, and the man explained that his meager resources were being exhausted. "Please, though, would you come to play for 10 cents tomorrow?" The disappointed boys told the man they would not be back. It wasn't worth the effort, they said, to play all afternoon at his house for only 10 cents. This folk tale illustrates the result of bribing people to do what they already like doing; they may then see their action as externally controlled rather than intrinsically appealing.

Main idea: _____last_____

Exercise 3: Locating Supporting Details in Textbook Material

In previous exercises, we have seen that the main idea in a paragraph is frequently located at either the beginning or end of the paragraph. However, the main idea may also appear in other locations within a paragraph, such as in the middle or at both the beginning and the end. Wherever the main idea is located, it must be supported by details. Most authors provide examples, illustrations, major points, reasons, or facts and statistics to develop their main idea. While a main idea can be either directly stated somewhere in the paragraph or implied, supporting details are always directly stated. The ability to recognize supporting details is of crucial importance in the reading process. Locating supporting details will tell you whether you have correctly identified the main idea.

For those of you who are visual learners, diagrams showing the development of a paragraph and the position of the main idea and supporting details might be helpful. The topic of each of the following paragraphs is perceptual organization.

After reading the explanation for each type of paragraph, write several key supporting details on the line provided.

Paragraphs in items 1–4, 6–8 from Richard Schaefer, *Sociology*, 3rd ed., New York: McGraw-Hill, 2000, pp. 54, 56, 158. Copyright © 2000 McGraw-Hill. Reprinted by permission of The McGraw-Hill Companies, Inc. Paragraph in item 5 from Wayne Weiten, *Psychology Applied to Modern Life*, 6th ed., Belmont, CA: Wadsworth, 2000, p. 161.

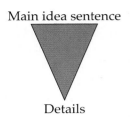

Main idea sentence

Details

1. *Much of perception is based on prior experience.* For instance, Colin Turnbull tells of the time he took a Pygmy from the dense rain forests of Africa to the vast African plains. The Pygmy had never before seen objects at a great distance. Hence, the first time he saw a herd of buffalo in the distance, he thought it was a swarm of insects. Imagine his confusion when he was driven toward the animals. He concluded that he was being fooled by witchcraft because the "insects" seemed to grow into buffalo before his eyes.

In paragraph 1, the main idea is stated in the first sentence. The author states the main idea and then provides an example to illustrate it. A diagram of this type of paragraph would be a triangle with the point aiming downward. The main idea is represented by the horizontal line at the top.

Supporting details: _____

_____

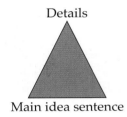

Details

Main idea sentence

2. A college professor was attacked by an actor in a staged assault. Immediately after the event, 141 witnesses were questioned in detail. Their descriptions were then compared to a videotape of the staged "crime." The total accuracy score for the group (on features such as appearance, age, weight, and height of the assailant) was only *25 percent* of the maximum possible. This incident dramatically demonstrates why witnesses to crimes so often disagree. *As you can see, impressions formed when a person is surprised, threatened, or under stress are especially prone to distortion.*

In paragraph 2, the author gives an example at the beginning and uses the main point to draw a conclusion. A diagram for this type of paragraph places the main idea at the bottom of the triangle.

Supporting details: _____

_____

Details

Main idea sentence

Details

3. Harness yourself to a hang glider, step off a cliff, and soar. No matter how exhilarating, your flight still wouldn't provide a true "bird's eye" view. *Many birds see the world in ways that would seem strange to a human.* For example, pigeons, ducks, and humming-birds can see ultraviolet light, which adds an extra color to their visual palette. Homing pigeons and many migrating birds perceive polarized light, which aids them in navigation. The American woodcock can survey a 360-degree panorama without moving its eyes or head.

In paragraph 3, the author begins with an example, states the main idea, and then concludes with additional examples. Because the main idea is in the middle, the diagram resembles a diamond.

Supporting details: _____

_____

_____

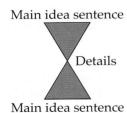

Main idea sentence

Details

Main idea sentence

4. *Psychologists are gradually convincing lawyers, judges, and police officers of the fallibility of eyewitness testimony.* In one typical court case, a police officer testified that he saw the defendant shoot the victim as both stood in a doorway 120 feet away. Measurements made by a psychologist showed that at that distance light from the dimly lit doorway was extremely weak—less than a fifth of that from a candle. To further show that identification was improbable, a juror stood in the

doorway under identical lighting conditions. None of the other jurors could identify him. The defendant was acquitted. Even in broad daylight, eyewitness testimony is untrustworthy. After a horrible DC-10 airliner crash in Chicago in 1979, 84 pilots who saw the accident were interviewed. Forty-two said the DC-10's landing gear was up, and 42 said it was down! As one investigator commented, the best witness may be a "kid under 12 years old who doesn't have his parents around." *These and other incidents are being used by psychologists to demonstrate to legal professionals the unpredictability of eyewitness testimony.*

In paragraph 4, the author begins with the main idea, provides detailed illustrations of it, and concludes with a restatement of the main idea. A diagram of this type of paragraph would have an hourglass shape.

Supporting details: _____

_____

_____

Main idea not directly stated

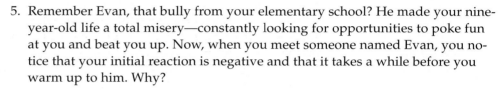

5. Remember Evan, that bully from your elementary school? He made your nine-year-old life a total misery—constantly looking for opportunities to poke fun at you and beat you up. Now, when you meet someone named Evan, you notice that your initial reaction is negative and that it takes a while before you warm up to him. Why?

In paragraph 5, the main idea is not stated in any specific sentence. Instead, all of the sentences are working together to create a word picture in your mind. Because no one sentence is clearly the main idea, a diagram of this paragraph might resemble a square or a rectangle.

Now practice what you have learned. Identify the main idea in the paragraphs below. Then draw a diagram of the paragraph and list some supporting details.

6. In a literal sense, language may color how we see the world. Researchers Berlin and Kay have noted that humans possess the physical ability to make millions of color distinctions, yet languages differ in the number of colors that are recognized. The English language distinguishes between yellow and orange, but some other languages do not. In the Dugum Dani language of New Guinea's West Highlands, there are only two basic color terms—*modla* for "white" and *mili* for "black." By contrast, there are 11 basic terms in English. Russian and Hungarian, though, have 12 color terms. Russians have terms for light blue and dark blue, while Hungarians have terms for two different shades of red.

Diagram: _____

Main idea: _____

Supporting details: _____

_____

_____

_____

7. We convey a great deal about how we feel in our facial expressions, but this can be a real problem when people of different cultures interpret facial expressions differently. Curious about cultural differences, researchers Tang and Shioiri decided to experiment by showing medical students in Japan and the United

States photos of seven basic emotions: anger, contempt, disgust, fear, happiness, sadness, and surprise. They discovered that the two groups agreed on only one facial expression: surprise. About 96 percent on both sides came to that conclusion.

Diagram: ▼ _____

Main idea: _____

Supporting details: _____

_____

_____

8. Journalist Naomi Wolf has used the term *the beauty myth* to refer to an exaggerated ideal of beauty, beyond the reach of all but a few females. When females carry adherence to "the beauty myth" to an extreme, they may develop eating disorders such as anorexia or undertake costly but unnecessary cosmetic surgery procedures. In a *People* magazine "health" feature, a young actress stated that she knows it is time to eat when she passes out on the set. Unrealistic standards of appearance and body image can have a destructive effect on young girls and adult women.

Diagram: ▲ _____

Main idea: _____

Supporting details: _____

_____

_____

Exercise 4: Identifying Main and Supporting Ideas and Diagramming Paragraphs in Textbook Material

The main idea sentence appears at different locations in the following paragraphs. Write the number of the main idea sentence on the line. Then draw a diagram of the paragraph and list numbers of the supporting detail sentences.

Information is from Ronald B. Adler and Neil Towne, *Looking Out/Looking In*, 10th ed. Fort Worth: Harcourt Brace, 2002, pp. 96, 111, 115–117.

A. (1) A person with high self-esteem is more likely to think well of others. (2) Someone with low self-esteem is more likely to have a poor opinion of others. (3) Your own experience may bear this out: Persons with low self-esteem are often cynical and quick to ascribe the worst possible motives to others, whereas those who feel good about themselves are disposed to think favorably about the people they encounter. (4) As one writer put it, "What we find 'out there' is what we put there with our unconscious projections. (5) When we think we are looking out a window, it may be, more often than we realize, that we are really gazing into a looking glass." (6) Our self concepts influence how we think about ourselves and interact with others.

Main idea sentence: _____ Diagram: _____ ▲ _____

Supporting details: _____

B. (1) We often judge ourselves more charitably than we do others. (2) When others suffer, we often blame the problem on their personal qualities. (3) On the other hand, when we're the victims, we find explanations outside ourselves. (4) Consider a few examples. (5) When *they* botch a job, we might think they weren't listening well or trying hard enough; when *we* make the mistake, the problem was unclear directions or not enough time. (6) When *he* lashes out angrily, we say he's being moody or too sensitive; when *we* blow off steam, it's because of the pressure we've been under. (7) When *she* gets caught speeding, we say she should have been more careful; when *we* get the ticket, we deny we were driving too fast or say, "Everybody does it."

Main idea sentence: _____ Diagram: ▼ _____

Supporting details: _____

C. (1) At one time or another you've probably seen photos of sights invisible to the unaided eye: perhaps an infrared photo of a familiar area or the vastly enlarged image of a minute object taken by an electron microscope. (2) You've also noticed how certain animals are able to hear sounds and smell odors that are not apparent to humans. (3) Experiences like these remind us that there is much more going on in the world than we are able to experience with our limited senses; in fact, we're only aware of a small part of what is going on around us. (4) For instance, most people who live in large cities find that the noises of traffic, people, and construction soon fade out of their awareness. (5) Others can take a walk through the forest without distinguishing one bird's call from another or noticing the differences among various types of vegetation. (6) On a personal level, we've all had the experience of failing to notice something unusual about a friend—perhaps a new hairstyle or a sad expression—until it's called to our attention.

Main idea sentence: _____ Diagram: ◆ _____

Supporting details: _____

D. (1) The kind of work we do often influences our view of the world. (2) Imagine five people taking a walk through the park. (3) One, a botanist, is fascinated by the variety of trees and plants. (4) The zoologist is looking for interesting animals. (5) The third, a meteorologist, keeps an eye on the sky, noticing changes in the weather. (6) The fourth companion, a psychologist, is totally unaware of nature, instead concentrating on the interaction among the people in the park. (7) The fifth person, being a pickpocket, quickly takes advantage of the others' absorption to make some money. (8) Our occupational roles shape our perceptions.

Main idea sentence: _____ Diagram: ⯊ _____

Supporting details: _____

E. (1) Even within the same occupational setting, the different roles that participants have can affect their perceptions. (2) Consider a typical college classroom, for example. (3) The experiences of the instructor and students often are quite dissimilar. (4) Having dedicated a large part of their lives to their work, most professors see their subject matter—whether French literature, physics, or speech communication—as vitally important. (5) Students who are taking the course to satisfy a general education requirement may view the subject quite differently: maybe as one of many obstacles that stand between them and a degree, maybe as a chance to meet new people.

Main idea sentence: _____ Diagram: ▼ _____

Supporting details: _____

F. (1) Because we're exposed to more input than we can possibly manage, the first step in perception is the selection of which data we will attend to and which we will ignore. (2) Something that is louder, larger, or brighter stands out. (3) This explains why—other things being equal—we're more likely to remember extremely tall or short people and why someone who laughs or talks loudly at a party attracts more attention (not always favorable) than do quiet guests. (4) *Repetitious stimuli, repetitious stimuli, repetitious stimuli*—also attract attention. (5) **ATTENTION IS ALSO FREQUENTLY RELATED** to contrast *or* change in **STIMULATION.** (6) Put differently, unchanging people or things become less noticeable. (7) Selection isn't just a matter of attending to some stimuli; it also involves ignoring other cues.

Main idea sentence: _____ Diagram: ⧗ _____

Supporting details: _____

SELECTION

"Over the years, I learned to smother the rage I felt at so often being taken for a criminal."

GETTING THE PICTURE

The first paragraph of the essay "Black Men and Public Space" by Brent Staples illustrates how perception affects behavior. By providing the reader with a riveting description, it serves as an introduction to the author's key ideas. In the paragraphs that follow, Staples discusses the effects of being a victim of stereotyping. At the end of the essay, he describes his creative solution to signaling his safe intentions to others.

BIO-SKETCH

Brent Staples, born in 1951, grew up in a family with an alcoholic father. He had little hope of attending college, but a special program gave him extra academic help. After graduating from Widener College (now Widener University) with a B.A. in 1973, he went on to earn his Ph.D. in psychology from the University of Chicago in 1982. Staples is currently a journalist who writes about political and cultural issues for *The New York Times.* His book *Parallel Time: Growing Up in Black and White* won the Anisfield Wolff Book Award.

BRUSHING UP ON VOCABULARY

warren a mazelike place containing many passageways; a building or area containing many inhabitants in crowded quarters. The word originally referred to a game park.

wee very early; small or tiny

BLACK MEN AND PUBLIC SPACE   by BRENT STAPLES

1   My first victim was a woman—white, well-dressed, probably in her early twenties. I came upon her late one evening on a deserted street in Hyde Park, a relatively affluent neighborhood in an otherwise mean, impoverished section of Chicago. As I swung onto the avenue behind her, there seemed to be a discreet, uninflammatory distance between us. Not so. She cast back a worried glance. To her, the youngish black man—a broad six feet two inches with a beard and billowing hair, both hands shoved into the pockets of a bulky military jacket—seemed menacingly close. After a few more quick glimpses, she picked up her pace and was soon running in earnest. Within seconds she disappeared into a cross street.

2   That first encounter, and those that followed, signified that a vast, unnerving gulf lay between nighttime pedestrians—particularly women—and me.

3   After dark, on the warrenlike streets of Brooklyn where I live, I often see women who fear the worst from me. They seem to have set their faces on neutral, and with their purse straps strung across their chests bandolier-style, they forge ahead as though bracing themselves against being tackled. I understand, of course, that the danger they perceive is not a hallucination. Women are particularly vulnerable to street violence, and young black males are drastically overrepresented among the perpetrators of that violence. Yet these truths are no solace against the kind of alienation that comes of being ever the suspect, a fearsome entity with whom pedestrians avoid making eye contact.

4   Over the years, I learned to smother the rage I felt at so often being taken for a criminal. Not to do so would surely have led to madness. I now take precautions to make myself less threatening. I move about with care, particularly late in the evening. I give a wide berth to nervous people on subway platforms during the wee hours, particularly when I have exchanged business clothes for jeans. If I happen to be entering a building behind some people who appear skittish, I may walk by, letting them clear the lobby before I return, so as not to seem to be following them. I have been calm and extremely congenial on those rare occasions when I've been pulled over by the police.

5   And on late-evening constitutionals I employ what has proved to be an excellent tension-reducing measure. I whistle melodies from Beethoven and Vivaldi and the more popular classical composers. Even steely New Yorkers hunching toward nighttime destinations seem to relax, and occasionally they even join in the tune. Virtually everybody seems to sense that a mugger wouldn't be warbling bright, sunny selections from Vivaldi's *Four Seasons.* It is my equivalent of the cowbell that hikers wear when they know they are in bear country.

COMPREHENSION CHECKUP

True or False

Indicate whether the statement is true of false by writing T or F in the blank provided.

_____T_____ 1. In the essay, Brent Staples describes the intimidating effect he has on nighttime pedestrians.

_____T_____ 2. The first woman described in the essay perceived Staples as a threat to her safety.

_____F_____ 3. It does not bother Staples to be alienated from those he encounters on the streets.

_____T_____ 4. Staples has learned to stifle the anger he feels at being taken for a criminal because of his race.

_____T_____ 5. Staples monitors his movements to make himself appear less threatening to others.

_____F_____ 6. Staples behaves in the same manner whether dressed in casual clothes or business wear.

_____T_____ 7. Staples does not want to appear as though he is following someone when he enters a building.

_____F_____ 8. When pulled over by a policeman, Staples is quick to express his anger and indignation.

_____T_____ 9. Staples whistles classical music selections to indicate to others that he is unlikely to be a mugger.

_____T_____ 10. Whistling classical music provides a measure of safety for Staples.

Vocabulary in Context

Each item below includes a sentence from the selection. Using the context clues from this sentence, determine the best meaning of the italicized words.

1. I came upon her late one evening on a deserted street in Hyde Park, a relatively *affluent* neighborhood in an otherwise mean, *impoverished* section of Chicago.

   affluent: _____wealthy_____

   impoverished: _____poor_____

2. As I swung onto the avenue behind her, there seemed to be a *discreet*, uninflammatory distance between us.

   discreet: _____good_____

3. To her, the youngish black man—a broad six feet two inches with a beard and billowing hair, both hands shoved into the pockets of a bulky military jacket— seemed *menacingly* close.

   menacingly: _____threat_____

4. After a few more quick *glimpses*, she picked up her pace and was soon running in *earnest*.

   glimpses: _____brief look_____

   earnest: _____serious state of mind_____

5. That first *encounter*, and those that followed, signified that a *vast*, unnerving gulf lay between nighttime pedestrians—particularly women—and me.

   encounter: ___To meet___

   vast: ___amount___

6. They seem to have set their faces on *neutral*, and with their purse straps strung across their chests *bandolier-style*, they *forge* ahead as though bracing themselves against being tackled.

   neutral: ___not favoring either side___

   bandolier-style: ___carrying ammunition___

   _____

   forge: ___to move___

Vocabulary Practice

Using the context clues from each sentence below, choose the best definition for the italicized word, and write the appropriate answer letter in the blank.

_____ 1. The danger they perceive is not a *hallucination*. (paragraph 3)
  a. an illusion
  b. an aggravation
  c. an outrage

_____ 2. Women are particularly *vulnerable* to street violence. (3)
  a. hardened
  b. susceptible
  c. oblivious

_____ 3. Yet these truths are no *solace*. (3)
  a. comfort
  b. criticism
  c. contempt

_____ 4. The kind of *alienation* that comes of being ever the suspect (3)
  a. detraction
  b. correction
  c. separation

_____ 5. A fearsome *entity* (3)
  a. demonstrator
  b. being
  c. worker

_____ 6. Learned to *smother* the rage (4)
  a. instigate
  b. stifle
  c. create

_____ 7. Give a wide *berth* to nervous people (4)
  a. follow
  b. reality
  c. space

_____ 8. Calm and extremely _congenial_ (4)
   a. angry
   b. sarcastic
   c. friendly

_____ 9. On late-evening _constitutionals_ (5)
   a. demonstrations
   b. initiations
   c. walks

In Your Own Words

1. What kinds of things do you look for when you are trying to decide whether a stranger is threatening?

2. What steps do you take to make yourself less threatening to others when you are out late at night?

Internet Activity

Racial profiling occurs when people are treated differently because of characteristics that are associated with race, most prominently skin color. In the last few years, many discussions of racial profiling have appeared in the media, especially about racial profiling by law-enforcement agencies. Using an Internet search engine like Google <www.google.com> or Yahoo! <www.yahoo.com>, explore the Internet to find discussions or articles about racial profiling. Write a paragraph describing what you learned about racial profiling. Based on what you learned, do you have an opinion about whether law-enforcement agencies should be allowed to engage in racial profiling?

Excerpt from
LOOKING OUT/LOOKING IN
by Loretta Malandro and Larry Barker

Did you know that some people are more likely to get mugged than others because of their body language? To assess your "muggability rating," read the article below.

The Look of a Victim

1   Little Red Riding Hood set herself up to be mugged. Her first mistake was skipping through the forest to grandma's house. Her second mistake was stopping to pick flowers. At this point, as you might remember in the story, the mean, heavy wolf comes along and begins to check her out. He observes, quite perceptively, that she is happy, outgoing, and basically unaware of any dangers in her surrounding environment. The big bad wolf catches these nonverbal cues and splits to grandma's house. He knows that Red is an easy mark. From this point we all know what happens.

2   Body movements and gestures reveal a lot of information about a person. Like Little Red Riding Hood, pedestrians may signal to criminals that they are easy targets for mugging by the way they walk. When was the last time you assessed your "muggability rating"? In a recent study two psychologists set out to identify those

body movements that characterized easy victims. They assembled "muggability rat-ings" of sixty New York pedestrians from the people who may have been the most qualified to judge—prison inmates who had been convicted of assault.

3   The researchers unobtrusively videotaped pedestrians on weekdays between 10:00 A.M. and 12 P.M. Each pedestrian was taped for six to eight seconds, the approximate time it takes a mugger to size up an approaching person. The judges (prison inmates) rated the "assault potential" of the sixty pedestrians on a ten-point scale. A rating of one indicated someone was "a very easy rip-off," of two, "an easy dude to corner." Toward the other end of the scale, nine meant a person "would be heavy; would give you a hard time," and ten indicated that the mugger "would avoid it, too big a situation, too heavy."

4   The results revealed several body movements that characterized easy victims: "Their strides were either very long or very short; they moved awkwardly, raising their left legs with their left arms (instead of alternating them); on each step they tended to lift their whole foot up and then place it down (less muggable sorts took steps in which their feet rocked from heel to toe). Overall the people rated most mug-gable walked as if they were in conflict with themselves; they seemed to make each move in the most difficult way possible."

Source: "The Look of a Victim," from Dr. Loretta Malandro and Dr. Larry Barker in *Nonverbal com-munication*. Copyright © 1988 McGraw-Hill. Reprinted by permission of Dr. Loretta Malandro.

◢ COMPREHENSION CHECKUP

Multiple Choice
Write the letter of the correct answer in the blank provided.

_____ 1. The main idea of paragraph 1 is expressed in the
   a. first sentence of the paragraph
   b. second sentence of the paragraph
   c. third sentence of the paragraph

_____ 2. The wolf is aware that Little Red will be easy to mug because
   a. she is an observant person
   b. she is oblivious to her surroundings
   c. she is a nature lover

_____ 3. The main idea of paragraph 2 is expressed in the
   a. first sentence of the paragraph
   b. third sentence of the paragraph
   c. fourth sentence of the paragraph

_____ 4. Persons convicted of assault were chosen to participate in the study because
   a. they were readily available
   b. they were not in a position to say no
   c. they knew what characteristics they had looked for in a potential victim

_____ 5. The body movements of the subjects most likely to be mugged indicate that
   a. they were well-coordinated
   b. they walked with a heel-to-toe motion
   c. they walked awkwardly

———— 6. If someone is *unobtrusively* videotaping, they are
      a. paying little attention to their subjects
      b. observing without calling attention to themselves
      c. interacting with those they are observing

REVIEW TEST: *Main Ideas and Details in Textbook Material*

Each of the following groups contains a series of related statements: One of the statements gives a main topic, another statement gives a main idea, and two or more statements give supporting details. Identify the role of each statement in the space provided using the following abbreviations:

T for topic

MI for main idea

SD for supporting detail

———— 1. a. Around 500 B.C., in what is today China, the ancient Scythians burned *Cannabis* and inhaled the hallucinogenic smoke.

———— b. The legendary Emperor Shen Nung recommended marijuana for the treatment of gout, absent-mindedness, female disorders, and constipation.

———— c. The use of *Cannabis* can be traced back to ancient China where the hemp plant was valued for its fiber and medicinal properties.

———— d. Early history of *Cannabis* in China

———— 2. a. Hookahs, or water pipes, for smoking hashish were frequently found in bazaars and marketplaces.

———— b. Arabic literature is replete with references to *Cannabis,* as can be seen in the famous *Thousand and One Nights.*

———— c. Use of *Cannabis* in the Muslim world

———— d. The use of *Cannabis* was commonplace throughout the Muslim world, including the Middle East and Africa.

———— 3. a. Spread of *Cannabis* to France

———— b. By the middle of the nineteenth century, Paris hashish clubs were frequent meeting places for intellectuals, writers, poets, and artists.

———— c. Napoleon's troops, returning from a campaign in North Africa, first popularized hashish smoking.

———— d. Then French intellectuals, who believed that the psychoactive properties of hashish enhanced their creative abilities, promoted the use of *Cannabis.*

———— e. The use of *Cannabis* spread in France in the mid-1800s.

———— 4. a. During the 1930s, American society began to turn against the use of *Cannabis* by passing laws and launching educational campaigns.

———— b. The U.S. Congress enacted the Federal Marijuana Tax Act of 1937, which regulated the sale of *Cannabis* and resulted in its virtual elimination from the nation's pharmacopoeia.

_____ c. The Federal Bureau of Narcotics undertook an "educational campaign" to make the public aware of the dangers of marijuana use.

_____ d. The crackdown

_____ 5. a. *Cannabis* can damage lung tissue, much like nicotine.

_____ b. The effects of marijuana on the male reproductive system show decreased sperm production and decreased testosterone levels.

_____ c. Even moderate use of marijuana impairs learning, short-term memory, and reaction time.

_____ d. Adverse effects of marijuana use

_____ e. Studies have discovered harmful side effects of *Cannabis* use.

_____ 6. a. Medical uses in chemotherapy and glaucoma

_____ b. While over the centuries marijuana has been employed to treat numerous ailments, today it is used in contemporary medicine for the treatment of glaucoma and as an aid to chemotherapy.

_____ c. Marijuana can significantly reduce ocular pressure in patients with glaucoma.

_____ d. The side effects of chemotherapy, which include nausea, vomiting, and loss of appetite, are reduced by the use of marijuana cigarettes.

_____ 7. a. Perception of time and space may be distorted, and minutes may seem like hours.

_____ b. *Cannabis* has significant mind-altering effects.

_____ c. Marijuana and psychoactive effects

_____ d. For instance, marijuana is associated with a sense of euphoria and calmness.

Review Test Information from Estelle Levetin, *Plants and Society,* 4th ed., New York: McGraw-Hill, 2006, pp. 355–57. Copyright © 2006 McGraw-Hill Companies, Inc. Used with permission.

PARAPHRASING

When you **paraphrase** something, you express the author's meaning in your own words. Often, you will substitute synonyms for some words (but you may have to leave the key words the same), and you will need to change the phrasing of the original passage. Usually, a paraphrase is shorter than the original passage, but it can also be the same length as the original or even longer.

The ability to paraphrase is important when you review ideas and also when you formulate an implied main idea. Here's an example with two possible paraphrases:

Original: "The man who most vividly realizes a difficulty is the man most likely to overcome it." (Joseph Farrell)

Paraphrase 1: The man who clearly recognizes a problem is the one likely to solve it.

Paraphrase 2: You are more likely to solve a problem if you first recognize clearly that a problem exists.

The first paraphrase replaces key words with synonyms so it is very like the original, and some teachers might consider this plagiarism. The second paraphrase is original because it not only replaces key words with synonyms but also conveys the ideas without using the phrasing of the original.

Now try to paraphrase the passages below. Be sure you use your own words, and do not rely on the phrasing of the original. When you finish, check to make sure that you have captured the meaning of the original.

Exercise 5: Paraphrasing Quotations

Working in a group, paraphrase the following quotations. When you finish, check to make sure the meaning of both statements is the same.

1. Even if you're on the right track, you'll get run over if you just sit there. (Will Rogers)

   _____

   _____

2. One man's justice is another's injustice; one man's beauty another's ugliness; one man's wisdom another's folly. (Ralph Waldo Emerson)

   _____

   _____

3. A toe of the stargazer is often stubbed. (Russian proverb)

   _____

   _____

4. If we could read the secret history of our enemies, we should find in each man's life sorrow and suffering enough to disarm all hostility. (Henry Wadsworth Longfellow)

   _____

   _____

5. You are only what you are when no one is looking. (Robert C. Edwards)

   _____

   _____

6. I have always thought the actions of men the best interpreters of their thoughts. (John Locke)

   _____

   _____

7. Do not use a hatchet to remove a fly from a friend's forehead. (Chinese proverb)

   _____

   _____

8. The things which hurt, instruct. (Benjamin Franklin)

_____

_____

9. If a man deceives me once, shame on him; if he deceives me twice, shame on me. (Anonymous)

_____

_____

Exercise 6: Paraphrasing a Poem

Read the poem below carefully, noting the key words and main ideas. Then explain the meaning of the poem in your own words.

Six Men of Indostan
BY JOHN G. SAXE

It was six men of Indostan
    To learning much inclined,
Who went to see the elephant
    Though all of them were blind
That each by observation
    Might satisfy his mind.

The first approached the elephant
    And, happening to fall
Against the broad and sturdy side,
    At once began to bawl:
"Why, bless me! But the elephant
    Is very much like a wall!"

The second, feeling of the tusk,
    Cried: "Ho! What have we here
So very round and smooth and sharp?
    To me, 'tis very clear,
This wonder of an elephant
    Is very like a spear!"

The third approached the animal.
    And, happening to take
The squirming trunk within his hands
    Thus boldly up he spake:
"I see," quoth he, "the elephant
    Is very like a snake!"

The fourth reached out his eager hand
    And felt about the knee:

"What most this wondrous beast is like
    Is very plain," quoth he:
"Tis clear enough the elephant
    Is very like a tree!"

The fifth who chanced to touch the ear
    Said: "e'en the blindest man
Can tell what this resembles most—
    Deny the fact who can:
This marvel of an elephant
    Is very like a fan!"

The sixth no sooner had begun
    About the beast to grope
Then, seizing on the swinging tail
    That fell within his scope,
"I see," quoth he, "the elephant
    Is very like a rope!"

And so these men of Indostan
    Disputed loud and long,
Each in his own opinion
    Exceeding stiff and strong:
Though each was partly in the right,
    And all were in the wrong.

"Six Men of Indostan," by John G. Saxe.

_____

_____

_____

_____

_____

_____

_____

Exercise 7: Paraphrasing a Fable

Explain the meaning of the fable below in your own words.

The Cracked Pot

1   A water bearer in India had two large pots, each hung on each end of a pole which he carried across his neck. One of the pots had a crack in it, and while the other pot was perfect and always delivered a full portion of water at the end of a long walk from the stream to the master's house, the cracked pot arrived only half full.

2   For a full two years this went on daily, with the bearer delivering only one and a half pots full of water to his master's house. Of course, the perfect pot was proud of its accomplishments, perfect to the end for which it was made. But the poor cracked pot was ashamed of its own imperfections, and miserable that it was able to accomplish only half of what it had been made to do. After two years of what it perceived to be a bitter failure, it spoke to the water bearer one day by the stream.

3   "I am ashamed of myself, and want to apologize to you."

4   "Why?" asked the bearer. "What are you ashamed of?"

5   "I have been able, for these past two years, to deliver only half my load because this crack in my side causes water to leak out all the way back to your master's house. Because of my flaws, you have had to do all of this work, and you don't get full value for your efforts," said the pot.

6   The water bearer felt sorry for the old cracked pot, and in his compassion he said, "As we return to the master's house, I want you to notice the beautiful flowers along the path."

7   Indeed, as they went up the hill, the old cracked pot took notice of the sun warming the beautiful wild flowers on the side of the path, and this cheered it some. But at the end of the trail, it still felt bad because it had leaked out half of its load, and so again the pot apologized to the bearer for its failure.

"Accept the place divine 8   The bearer said to the pot, "Did you notice that there were flowers only on
providence has found for your side of the path, but not on the other side? That's because I have always
you." known about your flaw and I took advantage of it. I planted flower seeds on
—Ralph Waldo Emerson your side of the path and every day while we walk back from the stream, you've watered them. For two years I have been able to pick these beautiful flowers to decorate my master's table. Without you being just the way you are, he would not have this beauty to grace his house."

Moral: Know that in our weakness we find our strength.

_____

_____

_____

_____

_____

_____

_____

Islamic Folk Stories

BY NASREDDIN HODJA

Nasreddin Hodja was born in Turkey in the early thirteenth century. He served as a religious leader (*imam*) and judge in his village. His folk stories are famous throughout the Middle East, Turkey, Hungary, Russia, and parts of Africa. All of his stories use humor to teach a fundamental lesson about human relationships and are designed to sharpen our perceptions of human failings.

After reading each fable, write the lesson or moral. Then reduce the key information in the fable to one sentence.

Source: "Islamic Folk Stories," from Charles Downing, *Tales of Hadja.* Copyright © 1964. Charles Downing, New York: Henry Z. Walck, Inc., 1965, pp. 21, 90-91, 44.

1 1. One day the Hodja and his son went on a short journey, the boy seated on a donkey. On the way they met some people coming in the opposite direction.

2 "That's modern youth for you," they said. "The son rides on a donkey and lets his poor old father walk!"

3 When they had gone, the boy insisted that his father take his place on the donkey. The Hodja mounted the donkey, and his son walked at his side. They met some more people.

4 "Just look at that!" they said. "There is a full-grown man riding on the donkey, while his poor little son has to walk!"

5 So, Hodja pulled his son on the donkey, too. After awhile, they saw a few more people coming down the road.

6 "Poor animal!" they said. "Both of them are riding on it and it is about to pass out."

7 "The best thing to do," said Nasreddin, when they had disappeared from sight, "is for both of us to walk. Then there can be no such arguments."

8 So they continued their way walking beside the donkey. It was not long before they met another group.

"Don't judge any man until you have walked two moons in his moccasins."
—Native American saying

9 "Just look at those fools," they said pointing to the Hodja and his son. "They plod along in the heat of the sun, and their donkey takes it easy!"

10 "You will have learned, my boy," said the Hodja, when they had gone, "just how difficult it is to escape the criticism of wagging tongues!"

Moral: _____

_____

Main idea sentence: _____

_____

1 2. The Hodja was invited to an important banquet, and he went in his everyday clothes. No one paid any attention to him whatsoever, and he remained hungry and thirsty, and very bored. Eventually he slipped out of the house unobserved and made his way home. Here he changed into his best clothes, putting on a magnificent turban, a fine silk robe, and a large fur coat over all. Then he made his way back to the banquet.

2 This time he was welcomed with open arms. The host bade him sit beside him, and offered him a plate covered with the choicest delicacies.

3 The Hodja took off his fur coat and held it to the plate.

4 "Eat, my beauty!" he said.

5 "Sir, what are you doing?" exclaimed his astonished host.

6 "It was the fur coat, not the man inside, which conjured up these delicacies," replied the Hodja. "Let it then eat them!"

Moral: _____

_____

Main idea sentence: _____

_____

1 3. A poor man was passing through Ak-Shehir with only a piece of dry bread between himself and starvation. As he passed by an eating house, he saw some very appetizing meatballs frying in a pan over the charcoal fire, and carried away by the delicious smell, he held his piece of dry bread over the pan in the hope of capturing some of it. Then he ate his bread, which seemed to taste better. The restaurant owner, however, had seen what was going on, and seizing the man by the scruff of his neck, dragged him off before the magistrate, who at this time happened to be Nasreddin Hodja, and demanded that he be compelled to pay the price of the pan of meatballs.

2 The Hodja listened attentively, then drew two coins from his pocket.

3 "Come here a minute," he said to the restaurant owner.

4 The latter obeyed, and the Hodja enclosed the coins in his fist and rattled them in the man's ear.

5 "What is the meaning of this?" said the restaurant owner.

6 "I have just paid you your damages," said the Hodja. "The sound of money is fair payment for the smell of food."

Moral: _____

_____

Main idea sentence: _____

_____

_____

"Islamic Folk Stories," from Charles Downing, *Tales of Hadja.* Copyright © 1964. Charles Downing, New York: Henry Z. Walck, Inc., 1965, pp. 21, 90–91, 44.

FORMULATING IMPLIED MAIN IDEAS IN TEXTBOOK MATERIAL

Not all main ideas are directly stated. Sometimes we have to look closely at the details the author has provided in order to determine the main idea. In the paragraphs below, the main idea is implied rather than stated. Read the paragraphs and try to identify the main idea. Then check to see whether you have identified it correctly.

Source: Paragraphs in items 1–8 from David Myers, *Social Psychology,* 8th ed., New York: McGraw-Hill, 2005, pp. 422, 434–436, 438–439, 441. Copyright McGraw-Hill. Reprinted by permission of The McGraw-Hill Companies, Inc.

1. What do you look for in a potential date? Sincerity? Good looks? Character? Conversational ability? Sophisticated, intelligent people are unconcerned with such superficial qualities as good looks; they know "beauty is only skin deep" and

"you can't judge a book by its cover." At least they know that's how they *ought* to feel. As Cicero counseled, "Resist appearance." However, there is now a cabinet full of research studies showing that appearance *does* matter. The consistency and pervasiveness of this effect is disconcerting. Good looks are a great asset.

"He had but one eye, and the pocket of prejudice runs in favor of two."

—Charles Dickens

The topic of this paragraph is appearance or looks. The implied main idea is: Looks matter, and people who believe that they do not are probably deceiving themselves.

In the next example, the topic is attractiveness and dating. To formulate the main idea, we must pay attention to the attitudes of both young men and young women as described in the paragraph.

2. Like it or not, a young woman's physical attractiveness is a moderately good predictor of how frequently she dates. A young man's attractiveness is slightly less a predictor of how frequently he dates. Does this imply, as many have surmised, that women are better at following Cicero's advice? Or does it merely reflect the fact that men more often do the inviting? If women were to indicate their preferences among various men, would looks be as important to them as they are to men? Philosopher Bertrand Russell thought not: "On the whole women tend to love men for their character while men tend to love women for their appearance." To see whether indeed men are more influenced by looks, researchers conducted a series of experiments. The result: The more attractive a woman was, the more the man liked her and wanted to date her again. And the more attractive the man was, the more she liked him and wanted to date him again.

From the details presented, we can conclude that both men and women put value on opposite-sex physical attractiveness. Our implied main idea should be stated something like this:

Main idea: When it comes to dating, looks appear to matter as much to young women as to young men.

You can see that determining an implied main idea requires you to reduce all of the key information contained in the paragraph to one sentence.

In order to formulate the main idea, it is sometimes helpful, first, to identify the topic and then to ask *who, what, where, when, why,* and *how* about the topic. Read the following paragraph, and try to determine the main idea for yourself before checking the main idea provided.

3. Not everyone can end up paired with someone stunningly attractive. So how do people pair off? Judging from research by Bernard Murstein and others, they pair off with people who are about as attractive as they are. Several studies have found a strong correspondence between the attractiveness of husbands and wives, of dating partners, and even of those within particular fraternities. Experiments confirm this matching phenomenon. When choosing whom to approach in social settings, knowing the other is free to say yes or no, people usually approach someone whose attractiveness roughly matches their own.

Who: men and women

What: pair off

Where: in social settings

When: during interactions with each other

Why: attempting to seek a good physical match

How: by picking people as attractive as they are

The topic of this paragraph is the matching phenomenon. If we look at all the key details, our main idea will look something like this:

Main idea: People tend to pair themselves with others who are similarly attractive.

The next paragraph provides an explanation for couples who are not similarly attractive.

4. Perhaps this research prompts you to think of happy couples who are not equally attractive. In such cases, the less attractive person often has compensating qualities. Each partner brings assets to the social marketplace. The value of the respective assets creates an equitable match. Personal advertisements exhibit this exchange of assets. Men typically offer wealth or status and seek youth and attractiveness; women more often do the reverse: "Attractive, bright woman, 26, slender, seeks warm, professional male." Moreover, men who advertise their income and education, and women who advertise their youth and looks, receive more responses to their ads. The asset-matching process helps explain why beautiful young women often marry older men of higher social status.

   Who: men/women

   What: offer compensating qualities

   Where: in the social marketplace

   When: in relationships

   Why: to achieve an equitable match

   How: by bartering youth and beauty for wealth and status

When you put together these key details, you should arrive at a main idea that looks something like this:

Main idea: Everyone brings assets to the social marketplace, and people choose partners who have similarly valuable assets.

Now look closely at these paragraphs discussing the social significance of physical attractiveness.

5. In an experiment, Missouri fifth-grade teachers were given identical information about a boy or girl but with the photograph of an attractive or unattractive child attached. The teachers perceived the attractive child as more intelligent and successful in school. Think of yourself as a playground supervisor having to discipline an unruly child. Might you show less warmth and tact to an unattractive child? The sad truth is that most of us assume what we might call a "Bart Simpson effect"—that homely children are less able and socially competent than their beautiful peers.

The main idea of this paragraph is directly stated in the last sentence because the "Bart Simpson effect" is illustrated by the remaining sentences.

In the next paragraph, the main idea is implied because no one sentence is broad enough to cover all of the key details. Try formulating the main idea by expanding the first sentence.

6. What is more, we assume that beautiful people possess certain desirable traits. Other things being equal, we guess beautiful people are happier, sexually warmer, and more outgoing, intelligent, and successful, though not more honest or concerned with others. Added together, the findings define a physical-attractiveness stereotype: *What is beautiful is good*. Children learn the stereotype

quite easily. Snow White and Cinderella are beautiful—and kind. The witch and the stepsisters are ugly—and wicked. As one kindergarten girl put it when asked what it means to be pretty, "It's like to be a princess. Everybody loves you."

Main idea: We assume that beautiful people possess certain desirable traits, and we also assume that what is beautiful is good.

In the next few paragraphs, the topic and part of the main idea are provided for you. Use the *who, what, where, when, why,* and *how* strategy to complete the main idea.

7. Undoubtedly, there are numerous advantages to being beautiful. However, attraction researchers report there is also an ugly truth about beauty. Exceptionally attractive people may suffer resentment from those of their own sex. They may be unsure whether others are responding to their inner qualities or just to their looks, which in time will fade. Moreover, if they can coast on their looks, they may be less motivated to develop themselves in other ways.

Topic: The negatives of attractiveness

Main idea: While there are many advantages to being beautiful, there are also

_____.

8. To say that attractiveness is important, other things being equal, is not to say that physical appearance always outranks other qualities. Attractiveness probably most affects first impressions. But first impressions are important—and are becoming more so as societies become increasingly mobile and urbanized and as contacts with people become more fleeting. Though interviewers may deny it, attractiveness and grooming affect first impressions in job interviews. This helps explain why attractive people have more prestigious jobs and make more money.

"Clothes and manners do not make the man; but when he is made, they greatly improve his appearance."

—Henry Ward Beecher

Topic: First impressions

Main idea: Physical appearance doesn't always outrank other qualities, but it does affect

_____.

Exercise 8: Formulating Implied Main Ideas in Textbook Material

Who Is Attractive?

Each of the following paragraphs are concerned with attractiveness. Formulate the implied main idea for each paragraph.

1. Attraction has been described as if it were an objective quality like height, which some people have more of, some less. Strictly speaking, attractiveness is whatever the people of any given place and time find attractive. This, of course, varies. Even in a given place and time, people (fortunately) disagree about who's attractive.

Implied main idea: _____

_____

_____

2. What makes an attractive face depends somewhat on the person's sex. Consistent with men historically having greater social power, people judge

women more attractive if they have "baby-faced" features, such as large eyes, that suggest nondominance. Men seem more attractive when their faces—and their behaviors—suggest maturity and dominance. People across the world show remarkable agreement about the features of an ideal male face and female face when judging any ethnic group. For example, "attractive" facial and bodily features do not deviate too drastically from average. People perceive noses, legs, or statures that are not unusually large or small as relatively attractive. Perfectly symmetrical faces are another characteristic of strikingly attractive people. So in many respects, perfectly average is quite attractive.

Implied main idea: _____

_____

3. Women favor male traits that signify an ability to provide and protect resources. Males prefer female characteristics that signify reproductive capacity. Judging from yesterday's Stone Age figurines to today's centerfolds and beauty pageant winners, men everywhere have felt most attracted to women whose waists are 30 percent narrower than their hips—a shape associated with peak sexual fertility. When judging males as potential marriage partners, women, too, prefer a waist-to-hip ratio suggesting health and vigor. This makes evolutionary sense because a muscular hunk was more likely than a scrawny fellow to gather food, build houses, and defeat rivals. But today's women prefer even more those with high incomes.

Implied main idea: _____

_____

4. Let's conclude this discussion of attractiveness on an upbeat note. First, a 17-year-old girl's facial attractiveness is a surprisingly weak predictor of her attractiveness at ages 30 and 50. Sometimes an average-looking adolescent becomes a quite attractive middle-aged adult. Second, not only do we perceive attractive people as likable, we also perceive likable people as attractive. Perhaps you can recall individuals who, as you grew to like them, became more attractive. Their physical imperfections were no longer so noticeable. When people are warm, helpful, and considerate, they *look* more attractive. Discovering someone's similarities to us also makes the person seem more attractive.

Implied main idea: _____

_____

5. Moreover, love sees loveliness. The more in love a woman is with a man, the more physically attractive she finds him. And the more in love people are, the *less* attractive they find all others of the opposite sex. "The grass may be greener on the other side, but happy gardeners are less likely to notice." To paraphrase Benjamin Franklin, when Jill is in love, she finds Jack more handsome than his friends.

Implied main idea: _____

_____

SELECTION

"My definition of a good sculpture is 'a sculpture that looks at least vaguely like something.'"

GETTING THE PICTURE

In this selection, Dave Barry is poking fun at modern art. Like much of the viewing public, he is not sure that nonrepresentational art is actually art at all.

BIO-SKETCH

Dave Barry is best known for writing his syndicated column for *The Miami Herald*. He is also a best-selling author. *The New York Times* called Mr. Barry the funniest man in America.

BRUSHING UP ON VOCABULARY

velveteen a cotton fabric with soft velvet pile.

Pomodoro Arnaldo Pomodoro was born in Italy in 1926. He has had many exhibitions in Italy, other European countries, and the United States. He is best known for his artistic stage designs and his modern sculptures located near public buildings.

Excerpt from

Dave Barry Is Not Taking This Sitting Down

by Dave Barry

1   LIKE MANY MEMBERS OF THE UNCULTURED, Cheez-It–consuming public, I am not good at grasping modern art. I'm the type of person who will stand in front of a certified modern masterpiece painting that looks, to the layperson, like a big black square, and quietly think: "Maybe the actual painting is on the other side."

"Perpetual modernness is the measure of merit in every work of art."
—Ralph Waldo Emerson

2   I especially have a problem with modernistic sculptures, the kind where you, the layperson, cannot be sure whether you're looking at a work of art or a crashed alien spacecraft. My definition of a good sculpture is "a sculpture that looks at least vaguely like something." I'm talking about a sculpture like Michelangelo's *David.* You look at that, and there is no doubt about what the artist's message is. It is: "Here's a naked man the size of an oil derrick."

3   I bring this topic up because of an interesting incident that occurred recently in Miami. . . . Miami tends to have these interesting incidents, and one of them occurred a little while ago when Dade County purchased an office

building from the city of Miami. The problem was that, squatting in an area that the county wanted to convert into office space, there was a large ugly wad of metal, set into the concrete. So the county sent construction workers with heavy equipment to rip out the wad, which was then going to be destroyed.

4   But guess what? Correct! It turns out that this was NOT an ugly wad. It was art! Specifically, it was Public Art, defined as "art that was purchased by experts who are not spending their own personal money." The money of course comes from the taxpayers, who are not allowed to spend this money themselves because (1) they probably wouldn't buy art, and (2) if they did, there is no way they would buy the crashed-spaceship style of art that the experts usually select for them.

5   The Miami wad is in fact a sculpture by the famous Italian sculptor Pomodoro (like most famous artists, he is not referred to by his first name, although I like to think it's "Bud"). This sculpture cost the taxpayers $80,000, which makes it an important work of art. In dollar terms, it is 3,200 times as important as a painting of dogs playing poker, and more than 5,000 times as important as a velveteen Elvis.

"Art is the expression
of an enormous preference."
—Wyndham Lewis

6   Fortunately, before the sculpture was destroyed, the error was discovered, and the Pomodoro was moved to another city office building, where it sits next to the parking garage, providing great pleasure to the many taxpayers who come to admire it.

7   I am kidding, of course. On the day I went to see it, the sculpture was, like so many pieces of modern taxpayer-purchased public art, being totally ignored by the actual taxpaying public, possibly because it looks—and I say this with all due artistic respect for Bud—like an abandoned air compressor.

8   So here's what I think: I think there should be a law requiring that all public art be marked with a large sign stating something like: "NOTICE! THIS IS A PIECE OF ART! THE PUBLIC SHOULD ENJOY IT TO THE TUNE OF 80,000 CLAMS!"

9   Also, if there happens to be an abandoned air compressor nearby, it should have a sign that says: "NOTICE! THIS IS NOT ART!" so the public does not waste time enjoying the wrong thing. The public should enjoy what the experts have decided the public should enjoy. That's the system we use in this country, and we're going to stick with it. . . .

Source: From *Dave Barry is Not Taking This Sitting Down,* by Dave Barry. Copyright © 2000 by Dave Barry. Used by permission of Crown Publishers, a division of Random House, Inc.

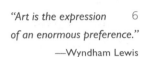

COMPREHENSION CHECKUP

The Main Idea

What is the main idea of this selection? _____

_____

_____

True or False

Indicate whether the statement is true or false by writing T or F in the blank provided.

_F_ 1. By calling Pomodoro "Bud," Barry is expressing respect for Pomodoro.

_T_ 2. Barry has an appreciation for realistic sculpture such as Michelangelo's *David*.

_T_ 3. When Barry refers to himself as a member of the "Cheez-It–consuming public," he means that his tastes are simple and unrefined.

_T_ 4. The Pomodoro sculpture was almost destroyed by construction workers.

Agree or Disagree

Indicate whether Dave Barry is likely to agree or disagree by writing A or D in the blank provided.

_D_ 5. Modern art is worthy of our respect.

_A_ 6. Taxpayers rather than "experts" are better judges of art.

_D_ 7. The more expensive a piece of art is, the more merit it has.

_A_ 8. It is often difficult to tell the difference between modern art and junk.

_A_ 9. The public, given a choice, would probably not select the modern art that is often on display outside public buildings.

Vocabulary in Context

Match the vocabulary word from the selection (on the left) with the most appropriate definition (on the right), and write the letter in the space provided. Refer to the paragraph in the selection for context clues.

_F_ grasping (paragraph 1)   a. dollars

_H_ certified (1)   b. extraterrestrial

_C_ layperson (1)   c. nonexpert

_B_ alien (2)   d. sitting

_D_ squatting (3)   e. large quantity

_E_ wad (3)   f. comprehending; understanding

_G_ convert (3)   g. change

_A_ clams (8)   h. guaranteed; confirmed

In Your Own Words

Why does Barry mention that Dade County placed the sculpture next to a parking garage? Do you think that Barry considers a parking garage an appropriate location for the sculpture? Why or why not?

The Art of Writing

In a brief essay, respond to the questions below.

Is there any public art in your area that became controversial? Why did it become controversial? Was it because of the cost? Was it because of the appearance of the artwork? Was it a combination of factors? How was the controversy resolved?

Internet Activities

1. Go to the *Miami Herald* website:

    www.miami.com.mld/miamiherald/

Type in Dave Barry's name, select a column by Barry, and print it. After reading the column, state Barry's main idea in your own words. List the details that Barry gives to support his main idea.

2. Study the cartoon "Eye of the Beholder." How does this cartoon illustrate Dave Barry's main idea?

_____

_____

_____

Eye of the Beholder

Cartoon: Eye of the Beholder, Jeff MacNelly. Copyright © 1997 Tribune Media Services, Inc.
Reprinted with permission.

SELECTION

*"In this particular circumstance, the people for whom
the art was intended chose to reject the art."*

GETTING THE PICTURE

The proverb "Beauty is in the eye of the beholder" implies that beauty is highly relative and that people will have varied opinions about what is actually beautiful. What is

SELECTION *continued*

pleasing to the eye of one of us is an eyesore to another. So too with art. People will have varied opinions about what constitutes art. In the selection below, taken from a popular art history textbook, the author Rita Gilbert describes a controversy over a work of modern art.

BIO-SKETCH

Rita Gilbert wrote her first edition of *Living with Art* in 1985. Her fourth edition of the book won a first-place award for outstanding design and production at the 1995 New York Book Show. Mark Getlein has taken over as author of this textbook. Getlein has written a variety of textbooks including *A History of Art in Africa* and *The Longman Anthology of World Literature*. As a painter, he is able to help students understand both the intellectual and practical processes of creating art.

BRUSHING UP ON VOCABULARY

dismantle   to take apart. *Dismantle* in Old French literally meant "to divest of a mantle or cloak." *Dismantle* derives from the French word part *des,* meaning "off," and *mantler,* meaning "to cloak." In Middle French, *demanteler* meant to tear down the walls of a fortress.

integrity   the state of being whole or entire; honesty. *Integrity* derives from the Latin word *integer,* which refers to a whole number in mathematics.

Excerpt from
GILBERT'S LIVING WITH ART
by Mark Getlein

Public Art

1   Rarely has the question "What is art?" caused such a public uproar as in a controversy that erupted in New York City in the early 1980s. At the center of the drama was a monumental sculpture by Richard Serra, entitled *Tilted Arc,* a 12-foot-high, 120-foot-long steel wall installed in a plaza fronting a government building in lower Manhattan.

2   Commissioned by the Art-in-Architecture division of the General Services Administration, *Tilted Arc* was part of a program that allocates 0.5 percent of the cost of federal buildings to the purchase and installation of public art. Soon after the sculpture's installation, however, the public for whom it was intended spoke out, and their message was a resounding *"That's* not art!" More than 7,000 workers in surrounding buildings signed petitions demanding the sculpture's removal. Opponents of the work had numerous complaints. *Tilted Arc,* they maintained, was ugly, rusty, and a target for graffiti. It blocked the view. It disrupted pedestrian traffic, since one had to walk all the way around it rather than straight across the plaza. It ruined the plaza for concerts and outdoor ceremonies. At a public hearing, one man summed

up the opposition view: "I am here today to recommend its relocation to a better site—a metal salvage yard."

3   Artists, dealers, and critics rushed to the sculpture's defense. The sculptor himself argued vehemently against any attempt to move *Tilted Arc*, maintaining that it had been commissioned specifically for that site and any new location would destroy its artistic integrity.

4   The battle raged for many months, and while there were dissenting voices from all sides, it shaped up principally as a struggle between the art establishment (pro) and the general public (con). At last, in an unusual editorial, *The New York Times*—a newspaper that heavily supports the arts—took a stand. "One cannot choose to see or ignore *Tilted Arc*, as if it were in a museum or a less conspicuous public place. To the complaining workers in Federal Plaza, it is, quite simply, unavoidable. . . . The public has to live with *Tilted Arc*; therefore the public has a right to say no, not here."

5   This time the public won, and the question "What is art?" was answered by a kind of popular referendum, a majority decision. *Tilted Arc* was dismantled and removed in March of 1989.

6   Does this outcome mean that *Tilted Arc* is not art, or that it isn't good art? No, it does not mean either of those things. It means simply that, in this particular circumstance, the people for whom the art was intended chose to reject the art. And similar circumstances have, very likely, occurred since the earliest artists of prehistory began painting on the walls of their caves.

Source: From Mark Getlein, *Gilbert's Living with Art,* 8th ed., New York: McGraw-Hill, 2008, p. 283. Copyright © McGraw-Hill. Reprinted by permission of The McGraw-Hill Companies, Inc.

 COMPREHENSION CHECKUP

Multiple Choice

Write the letter of the correct answer in the blank provided.

_____ 1. By choosing to use the words *uproar, controversy,* and *erupted* in the first paragraph, the author implies that
     a. the public was moderately interested
     b. the sculpture provoked a swift and strong reaction
     c. unhappiness with the sculpture developed slowly

_____ 2. From the context of paragraph 2, it can be determined that the word *resounding* most nearly means
     a. cheerfully expressed
     b. quietly voiced
     c. loudly uttered

_____ 3. The public expressed all of the following misgivings about *Tilted Arc* except
     a. it disrupted vehicular traffic
     b. it was ugly and a target for graffiti
     c. outdoor ceremonies and concerts were no longer feasible

_____ 4. A synonym for the word *vehemently* as used in paragraph 3 is
      a. ardently
      b. compassionately
      c. silently

_____ 5. *The New York Times* took the following basic position in its editorial:
      a. Because the public and the federal workers could not avoid the sculpture, their opinion about whether it should stay counted for a lot.
      b. Because the sculpture could be disassembled and relocated elsewhere, it should be moved to a more welcoming location.
      c. Because it was commissioned specifically for the site and the sculptor opposed its removal, it should stay.

True or False

Indicate whether the statement is true or false by writing T or F in the blank sprovided.

"The monument sticks like a fishbone in the city's throat."

—Robert Cowell

___T___ 6. The author suggests that similar rejections of public art have occurred in the past.

___T___ 7. A *dissenting* opinion expresses an opposing viewpoint.

___F___ 8. A *conspicuous* place is one that is hard to find or see.

Tilted Arc (1981), Richard Serra

_____ T _____ 9. We can assume that *The New York Times* cast the deciding vote in the tiebreaker between the art establishment and the general public.

_____ F _____ 10. The sculptor felt that it was in the public's best interest to relocate the sculpture to a place where it would be enjoyed and appreciated.

In Your Own Words

1. Many artists argue that photographs can depict something lifelike far better than any painting can. They conclude that paintings should not be aimed at replicating reality. Do you believe that paintings should present lifelike portrayals of their subjects?

2. What makes a work of art good or successful? How important is it that a work of art display technical skill? Or does it count for more that it be imaginative or provocative?

3. Does a piece of art need to communicate a single clear message to be good?

4. What is your opinion of *Tilted Arc*? Should it have been dismantled?

The Art of Writing

In a brief essay, respond to one of the items below.

1. Do you agree with the conclusion drawn by *The New York Times* that the sculpture should be removed? Explain why.

2. Do you think that the public should always have the final say on whether a work of public art should be displayed or should remain on display? Why or why not?

3. Richard Serra is featured in the Arts section of *Time* (June 4, 2007, pp. 65–67). (Go to http://www.time.com/serra.) Read the profile of the artist and write a brief summary. What is your impression of the two sculptures presented in the profile?

Internet Activity

Read an online biography of Richard Serra, and view some of his other sculptures. You might consult one of the following:

http://www.pbs.org/art21/artists/serra/index.html

http://www.artcyclopedia.com/artists/serra_richard.html

Does the information provided give you a different perspective on Serra from that of the reading selection? What is your opinion of his work?

Vocabulary Puzzle

Directions: Use the vocabulary words to complete the puzzle.

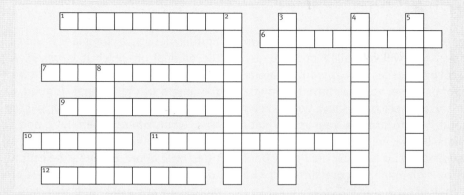

allocates	dismantled	referendum	salvage
commissioned	dissenting	relocation	uproar
conspicuous	integrity	resounding	vehemently

ACROSS CLUES

1. Taken apart
6. Angrily; ardently
7. Easily seen or noticed
9. Movement to a different place
10. A state of noisy disturbance or excitement
11. Gave an official order for
12. The state of being whole, entire, complete

DOWN CLUES

2. Disagreeing
3. Loudly uttered
4. Submission of a proposed public measure to a direct popular vote
5. Sets apart for a particular use
8. Something saved from destruction or waste

STUDY TECHNIQUE 3

Summarizing Short Articles

Summarizing, or restating main ideas in your own words, is a skill you will be called upon to use both in your college classes and at work. In literature classes, for example, you may have to provide a brief summary of a story to show you've read and understood it or to provide your reader with the main points before you offer an analysis. In biology classes, you may have to provide a brief summary of an experiment before detailing the process and equipment you used. Later in life, you may also need to provide summaries. For instance, if you become a nurse, you may need to summarize a patient's condition; if you become a sportswriter, you may need to summarize the action in a basketball game; if you become a police officer, you may need to summarize the events leading up to an accident.

When you write a summary, you need to present only the main idea and key supporting details in order of importance. Because it omits minor supporting details, a summary is much shorter than the original on which it is based. A good rule of thumb is that a summary should be one-fourth of the length of the original. A good way to identify key supporting details is to answer as many of the *who, what, where, when, why,* and *how* questions about the selection as apply. (Not all these questions will apply to every selection.) Remember, too, that the goal of a summary is brevity; in other words, always make sure that your summary contains only the main idea and key supporting details and does not include information more than once. Omit all trivia and repetition!

Also keep in mind that you are reporting the author's viewpoints and not your own. When writing a summary, never write something like "I feel" or "I think" or "It seems to me." What matters in a summary is what the author thinks. When reading over your summary, make sure you delete all expressions of your own thoughts and opinions.

Exercise 9: Writing a Summary

Directions: You just read an excerpt from Mark Getlein's "Public Art." Try to write a summary of this excerpt. Begin by identifying the main idea.

Main Idea: _____

_____

_____

Now locate the main supporting details by answering as many of the question words as possible:

Who: _____

What: _____

Where: _____

When: _____

Why: _____

How: _____

Next, list five to six of the main supporting details in your own words.

1. _____

_____

2. _____

_____

3. _____

_____

4. _____

_____

5. _____

_____

6. _____

_____

You are now ready to draft your summary.

_____

_____

_____

_____

_____

_____

_____

_____

_____

_____

_____

After writing your summary, read it over. Delete any information that is not crucial to supporting the main idea. Delete any trivia or repetition and any expressions of your own opinion. Is your presentation of information logical? If not, reorganize the information in a more logical way. Now revise your summary.

Internet Activity

The National Endowment for the Arts, created by Congress in 1965, is an independent governmental agency that funds "projects of artistic excellence." One of its services is to publish articles on various topics related to the arts. One such article, written by Marc Pally, titled "The Enterprise of Process: Notes on Planning Public Art" (1998), provides guidance for making decisions about proposed public-art projects. You will find this article at

http://www.nea.gov/resources/lessons/PALLY.html

Write a paragraph describing Pally's recommendations. Or write a paragraph explaining how Pally's recommendations might have led to better decision making about *Tilted Arc*.

TEST-TAKING TIP

Day of the Test

The day of the test has arrived. Make sure you have the proper equipment with you—pens, pencils, dictionary, blue books, and so on. Stay calm. By now you should have a good idea what's going to be on the test, and you should be prepared for it.

Now look at the test. Read through the whole test. Look on both sides of all the pages. How many questions are there? Think about how much time you want to devote to each question.

Always save time to check over your answers. Don't lose points because you accidentally skipped a question. And remember to write legibly and put your name on the test paper!

Don't be concerned if some people in the class finish the test much more quickly than you do. You don't know whether those students did well on the test or poorly.

VOCABULARY   Homonyms and Other Confusing Words (Unit 1)

As you learned in the introduction, homonyms are words or phrases that sound the same but that have different spellings or meanings. In addition to homonyms, we have included in this section other troublesome words that you might need to practice. Mastering these words will help you make a good impression in written assignments.

The short poem below illustrates the importance of using words correctly. Can you spot the mistakes?

> English spelling can seam like a maize,
> And put won strait into a hays,
> Butt now never fear,
> The spell-checker is hear,
> And its sew well-deserving of prays.
>
> —*Anonymous*

allusion	A noun meaning "a casual or passing reference to something." *The author made an* allusion *to Aphrodite, the Greek goddess of love and beauty.*
illusion	A noun meaning "something that deceives by producing a false or misleading impression of reality." *The hikers, exhausted and suffering from dehydration, saw a lake up ahead of them. But as they got closer, they realized it was just a cruel* illusion.
alot	A mistake for *a lot. There is no such word as* alot.
a lot	"Many, much." *Peggy felt* a lot *better after getting a good night's sleep.*
allot	A verb meaning "to assign a portion." *Each heir to the family fortune was* allotted *an equal share of the estate.*

already	An adverb meaning "previously." *With just a few minutes left in the game, the Cardinals thought they had* already *won.*
all ready	"Completely prepared." *After gathering her supplies and buying her textbooks, Antoinette felt* all ready *to start school.*

Think about this sentence: She is *all ready* to go to the game because she is *already* dressed.

altogether	An adverb meaning "wholly, entirely." *"There is* altogether *too much violence in public schools," complained the president of the Parent Teacher Association.*
all together	"All at the same place or time." *The family reunion brought the family* all together.
censure	A verb meaning "to strongly disapprove of or officially reprimand." *The senator was* censured *because he had accepted campaign contributions from foreign countries.*
censor	A verb meaning "to examine for the purpose of suppressing or deleting." *The Harry Potter books by J. K. Rawling are being* censored *by school libraries across the country.*
cite	A verb meaning "to quote or mention in support." *You may need to* cite *your sources in your English term paper.*
site	A noun meaning "position or location." *The* site *of the Vietnam War Memorial is in Washington D.C.*
desert	A noun meaning "a dry sandy region with little or no plant life." *The Sahara Desert is the largest* desert *in the world.*
desert	A verb meaning "to leave without intending to return." *Marcia wanted to know how Jan could* desert *her husband after fourteen years of marriage.* (The pronunciation is the same as dessert.) Also, a noun meaning "deserved reward or punishment." *The attorney who had cheated many of his elderly clients out of their retirement funds received his just* deserts *when he was disbarred.* (The pronunciation is the same as desserts.)
dessert	A noun meaning "something sweet served at the end of a meal." *Is your favorite* dessert *cake, ice cream, or something else?*

Think about this sentence: Cactus candy is a delectable *dessert* that comes from *desert* cacti.

die	A verb meaning "to cease to live." *Most of our past presidents have already* died.
dye	A noun meaning "a coloring substance." *Did you use* dye *to change the color of your hair?* Also, a verb meaning "to color with a dye." *She* dyed *her hair shocking pink to go with her dress.*
emigrate	A verb meaning "to leave one country or region and settle in another." *Many people in the United States have ancestors who* emigrated *from Ireland.*
immigrate	A verb meaning "to come to a new country to settle." *Millions of people have* immigrated *to the United States in search of a better life for themselves and their families.*

Think about this sentence: Oksana's parents *emigrated* from Russia in 1944, *immigrating* first to France and then later to the United States.

fewer	An adjective meaning "not many," refers to number. *Fewer* is used before a plural noun. *There are* fewer *words in a paperback dictionary than in a hardbound one.*
less	An adverb meaning "not as much or as many." *Less* is used to refer to things that cannot be counted. *Many people feel that they should be spending* less *time at work and more time at home with their families.*
formally	An adverb meaning "marked by form or ceremony." *The young couple* formally *announced their engagement at a special dinner party.*
formerly	An adverb meaning "at an earlier time; in the past." *The candidate running for president was* formerly *a U.S. senator.*
its	A possessive pronoun meaning "the one or ones that belong to it." *The dog always knew where to find* its *bowl when it was time to eat.*
it's	A contraction for "it is or it has." *The dark clouds indicate that* it's *about to rain.*
later	An adverb or adjective meaning "coming after the usual or proper time." *Later* is the comparative form of *late. The students wanted to postpone the test until a* later *date.*
latter	An adjective meaning "being the second of two mentioned things." *Matt's parents said he could play only one sport in high school; when they gave him a choice between playing football or being on the track team, he chose the* latter. Also, an adjective meaning "near to the end." *The use of the Internet became very popular during the* latter *part of the 1990s.*

Think about this sentence: Of the first two versions of his story, I prefer the *latter*, but the version he came up with *later* is the best of all.

lie	A noun meaning "something said that is not true." *Mary did not want to go to Cara's birthday party, so she told a little white* lie *and said she had to babysit that night.*
lie	A verb meaning "to say what is not true." *Perjury is* lying *under oath.* Also, a verb meaning "to rest or recline; to exist in a horizontal position." *Lie* is an intransitive verb; that is, it cannot take a direct object. *The dog often* lies *on the couch even though she knows she is supposed to stay off the furniture.* The past tense of the verb *lie* is *lay: Despite having scolded her, she* lay *down there again yesterday.* The present participle of *lie* is *lying: I knew when she had been* lying *on the furniture, because it was covered with hair.* The past participle of *lie* is *lain: She had* lain *on the couch every day without reproach while my mother was visiting.*
lay	A verb meaning "to put down so as to rest on, in, or against something." Lay is a transitive verb; that is, it requires a direct object. *If I* lay *any more books there, the table will break.* The past tense of *lay* is *laid: I* laid *a book down on the table last week, and now I can't find it.* The present participle of *lay* is *laying: I have been* laying *my books on the table all week.* The past participle of *lay* is *laid: In fact, I had* laid *my books down in the same spot for weeks.*

■ Homonym Quiz

Drawing on what you've learned here, fill in the blanks with an appropriate homonym.

1. Margo was _____ late for work when she stopped to answer the phone.
   already/all ready

2. "Class," said Mrs Walker, "let's sing the last part one more time _____."
   altogether/all together

3. The _____ of the disaster has been closed indefinitely.
   cite/site

4. He _____ from Brazil in 1948 and has not returned until recently.
   emigrated/immigrated

5. There were three _____ students in class today than on Tuesday.
   fewer/less

6. No one knew that the law student was _____ a convicted murderer.
   formally/formerly

7. _____ not a good day to visit Soon Yi. She's in bed with the flu.
   Its/It's

8. As he grew disenchanted with his work, he started arriving at the office _____.
   later/latter

9. Only fresh fruits or low-calorie _____ are on my diet.
   deserts/desserts

10. I just _____ that file down on the counter five minutes ago.
    lay/laid

Write a sentence of your own using *lain* correctly.

_____

_____

Vocabulary Puzzle

Directions: Use words from Homonyms Unit 1 to complete the puzzle.

ACROSS CLUES

3. The student was _____ his backpack on the wrong desk.
5. Tim went to bed much _____ than he should have.
6. Mr. Tang _____ in the hospital after a lengthy illness.
7. The senator was _____ because he made false statements to members of Congress while under oath.
8. _____ John Grisham has written eight successful novels.
10. Was the husband _____ to his wife about where he had been last night? Or, was he telling the truth?
11. Tina added a large mirror to her dining room to give the _____ of more space.
15. Sue and Anna are softball players. The former plays catcher and the _____ plays shortstop.
17. Too many children _____ by drowning in unsupervised swimming pools.
18. We usually eat a low-cal _____ after a fattening meal.
19. The _____ is an area with an arid climate.
21. The workers were going to _____ the foundation for the house next week.
22. The cow gave birth to _____ first calf.
23. The movie was _____ before it was shown on TV.
26. Patty was _____ her hair to match her school colors.
27. Thailand was _____ called Siam.

DOWN CLUES

1. They were dressed _____ in tux and tails to go to the Winter Ball.
2. Some students would do better in college by taking _____ classes.
4. The author made an _____ to a character in *Romeo and Juliet*.
5. The woman was _____ on the ground when the paramedics arrived.
9. Juan _____ (d) from Mexico three years ago.
11. Many people now residing in other countries would like to _____ to the United States.
12. The officer told the suspect to _____ the gun down and put his hands in the air.
13. Every four years the Olympics are held at a different _____. In 2000, they were held in Australia.
14. The members of the class of 1980 will not be _____ again until the next reunion.
16. I should have eaten a lot _____ at our Thanksgiving dinner.
19. Should euthanasia be available for the _____?
20. Steve did not need to take college algebra because he had _____ taken it in high school.
23. Always make sure you _____ your references properly.
24. When he missed work, he _____ to his boss about being sick.
25. On St. Patrick's Day, some people _____ their beer green.

117

The Author's Purpose and the Rhetorical Modes

The Oath of the Horatii (1784) BY JACQUES-LOUIS DAVID

Photo: G. Blot/C. Jean. Louvre, Paris. Réunion des Musées Nationaux/Art Resource, NY.

View and Reflect

In the painting, three brothers are swearing an oath to their father to defeat their enemies or die for Rome.

1. What are the brothers receiving from their father?
2. Compare the postures and attitudes of the men to those of the women. How do the hands of the men and women express their respective attitudes?
3. What does the woman in black in the background of the painting appear to be doing?
4. Notice the three arches in the background of the painting. Where else does the artist repeat this theme of a group of three?
5. What do you think the artist's purpose was in creating this painting?
6. How does the painting illustrate risk-taking behavior?
7. What is the dominant color in the male grouping? What might that color represent?

DETERMINING THE AUTHOR'S PURPOSE

Copyright © 2009 by The McGraw-Hill Companies, Inc.

Highlight or underline the definitions of the key terms. Then write a paraphrase of each definition in the margin.

Inform
_____
_____

Entertain
_____
_____

Persuade
_____
_____

Audience
_____
_____

Specific purpose
_____
_____
_____

Most writers create a story, essay, article, or poem with at least one **general purpose** in mind. Because most writers do not directly state their general purpose, the reader must use indirect clues to determine it. We can identify the general purpose by asking the question "Why did the author write this?" Usually, this purpose will fall into one of three broad categories: to inform, to entertain, or to persuade.

An author whose purpose is **to inform** will provide readers with knowledge or information. Ordinarily, the material will be presented in an objective, neutral fashion. Authors who write textbooks presenting factual material often have this purpose in mind. Articles in newspapers are also usually meant to inform.

An author whose purpose is **to entertain** will tell a story or describe someone or something in an interesting way. A piece of writing meant to entertain will often make an appeal to the reader's imagination, sense of humor, or emotions. Such writing may be either fiction or nonfiction. Witty, unusual, dramatic, or exciting stories usually have entertainment as their purpose.

Finally, the author's purpose may be **to persuade.** Persuasion goes beyond merely entertaining or providing information. This kind of writing tries to change the reader's opinions by appealing to emotions or intellect. If making an emotional argument, the author may use vividly descriptive passages designed to manipulate the reader's feelings. If making an appeal to intelligence, the author will employ logic and reasoning. Political literature is a common form of writing meant to persuade. Newspaper editorials ordinarily have persuasion as their purpose also.

Authors take into account their **audience** (those they are writing for) when they choose their **general purpose.** Writers of fiction usually want to entertain readers by creating interesting characters and stories. If an author writes an article for a wellness magazine, the general purpose will probably be to provide information promoting good health. If an author writes a letter to solicit campaign contributions for a political candidate, the general purpose will be to persuade people to give money.

In addition to a general purpose, authors also usually have a **specific purpose,** which reveals more detailed information about the article than the general purpose. Take the wellness example above. The general purpose is to inform. The specific purpose might be "to inform people about foods that protect against cancer."

Sometimes an author may have more than one purpose in mind. For instance, an author might want both to entertain and to persuade. Or the author might write an entertaining article that also provides information about something important. In these instances, usually one of the author's purposes will be primary. To determine the general and primary purpose, first identify the main idea and the key details that support that idea. Then note the author's choice of words. Is the vocabulary neutral and unbiased? Is it meant to influence our judgment in some way? Finally, note the source of the article or passage. Often the publication that the article or passage comes from will help you identify the author's primary purpose.

Read the paragraph below, and identify the writer's topic, main idea, and general and specific purposes.

The viewpoint, now gaining momentum, that would allow individuals to "make up their own minds" about smoking, air bags, safety helmets, and the like ignores some elementary social realities. The ill-informed nature of this viewpoint is camouflaged by the appeal to values that are dear to most Americans. The essence of the argument is that what individuals do with their lives and limbs, foolhardy though it might be, is their own business, and that any interference would abridge their rights. However, no civil society can survive if it permits each person to maximize his or her freedoms without concern for the consequences of one's act on others. If I choose to drive without a seat belt or air bag, I am greatly increasing my chances, in case of an accident, of being impaled on the steering wheel or exiting via the windshield. It is not just my body that is jeopardized; my careening auto which I cannot get back under control, will be more likely to injure people in other autos, pedestrians, or riders in my car. The individual who chooses to act irresponsibly is playing a game of heads I win, tails the public loses. All too often, the unbelted drivers, the smokers, the unvaccinated, the users of quack remedies, draw on public funds to pay for the consequences of their unrestrained freedom of choice. Their rugged individualism rapidly becomes dependency when cancer strikes, or when the car overturns, sending the occupants to hospitals for treatment paid for at least in part by the public, through subsidies for hospitals and medical training. But the public till is not bottomless, and paying for these irresponsible acts leaves other public needs without funds.

Source: Paragraph from Amitai Etzioni, "When Rights Collide," in *Psychology Today,* October, 1977. Copyright © 1977 Amitai Etzioni. Used by permission of the author.

Topic:	Individual liberty vs. social responsibility
Main idea:	No civil society can survive if it permits each person to maximize his or her freedom without concern for the consequence of one's act on others.
General purpose:	To persuade
Specific purpose:	To persuade us that there needs to be a balance between individual liberty and social responsibility

The following exercises will give you some practice in determining an author's general purpose.

Exercise 1: Determining the Author's Purpose

Label each sentence according to its general purpose: to inform (I), to entertain (E), or to persuade (P).

___E___ 1. Did you ever wonder how all the best athletes make sports seem so easy? The behind the back passes, the triple lutzes, the holes in one; on TV it looks so easy. We sit in our armchairs and say, "I could do that. How hard could it be?" The truth is, if we could do that, we'd be out there doing it. I think that if I had the talent, right now I'd be doing some triple lutzes. What is a lutz anyway? Are three of them a good thing? Do you have to do it in tights? Because if you have to do it in tights, I may have a problem with it.

From Tom Mather, *Voyages in the Toilet Dimension,* self-published, 1999, p. 35.

___I___ 2. Stealing goods from retail merchants is a very common crime; it constitutes about 15 percent of all larcenies. A recent survey in Spokane, Washington, revealed that every twelfth shopper is a shoplifter, and that men and women are equally likely to be offenders. Perhaps shoplifting is so frequent because it is a low-risk offense, with a detection rate of less than

1 percent. Shoppers are extremely reluctant to report shoplifters to the store management. According to one study, of those apprehended for shoplifting, approximately 45.5 percent are actually prosecuted. It is also estimated that men are slightly more likely than women to be shoplifters, and that 41 percent of offenders are white, 29 percent are black, and 16 percent are Hispanic. More than half of shoplifting events occur between the hours of 12:00 P.M. and 6:00 P.M. A study conducted in New South Wales with juvenile offenders in detention revealed that their reasons for shoplifting ranged from excitement, peer pressure, thrills, or fun; to obtaining clothes, food, or money for drugs or alcohol; to relieving boredom or stress.

From Frieda Adler et al., *Criminology and the Criminal Justice System,* 6th ed., New York: McGraw-Hill, 2007, p. 292.

_____E_____ 3. The Sound of Music: Enough Already

There was a time when music knew its place. No longer. Possibly this is not music's fault. It may be that music fell in with a bad crowd and lost its sense of common decency. I am willing to consider this. I am willing even to try and help. I would like to do my bit to set music straight in order that it might shape up and leave the main stream of society. The first thing that music must understand is that there are two kinds of music—good music and bad music. Good music is music that *I* want to hear. Bad music is music that *I* don't want to hear. I do not under any circumstances enjoy hold buttons. But I am a woman of reason. I can accept reality. I can face the facts. What I cannot face is the music. Just as there are two kinds of music—good and bad—so there are two kinds of hold buttons—good and bad. Good hold buttons are hold buttons that hold one silently. Bad hold buttons are hold buttons that hold one musically. When I hold I want to hold silently. That is the way it was meant to be.

From Fran Leibowitz, *The Leibowitz Reader,* New York: Vintage Books, 1994, pp. 137–138.

_____P_____ 4. Cheating jeopardizes the basic fairness of the grading process. Widespread cheating causes honest students to become cynical and resentful, especially when grades are curved and the cheating directly affects other students. Cheating may also have long-term effects. Taking the easy way in college may become a habit that can spill over into graduate school, jobs, and relationships. And consider this: would you want a doctor, lawyer, or accountant who had cheated on exams handling your affairs? Cheating sabotages your own academic and personal growth. Don't cheat!

From John Gardener, *Your College Experience,* Belmont, CA: Wadsworth, p. 221.

Exercise 2: Identifying the Clues That Indicate the Author's Purpose and Main Idea

Read each of the following paragraphs to determine whether the author's primary purpose is (1) to entertain, (2) to persuade, or (3) to inform. Indicate the clues that enabled you to make your decision. Then, in the space provided, write the stated or implied main idea.

1. Put an alien creature from outer space in front of a television, and it would have very little idea of what family life is like in the United States. It would conclude

that most adults are men, most adults are not married, almost no one is over age 50, very few adults have children, most mothers don't work for pay, and child care is simply not an issue. The fact is that *Friends, Third Rock from the Sun, Frasier, Ally McBeal*, and similar programs present fantasy lives that most households find fascinating, but not exactly true to their lives. Eight out of 10 adults in the United States think that almost no TV family is like their own; nearly half find *no* TV family like theirs. Katharine Heintz-Knowles, a communications professor at the University of Washington, carried out content analyses of 150 episodes of 92 different programs on commercial networks over a two-week period. She found that of the 820 TV characters studied, only 38 percent were women, only 15 percent could be identified as parents of minor children, and only 14 percent were over age 50. Only 3 percent of the TV characters faced recognizable conflicts between work and family, and no TV family made use of a child care center.

Richard Schaefer, *Sociology, 3/e*, p. 288. Copyright © 2000. Reprinted by permission of McGraw-Hill Companies, Inc. Copyright © 2000 McGraw-Hill Companies, Inc. Used with permission.

Purpose: _____   Clues: _____

Main idea: _____

2. Good manners are back, and for a good reason. As the world becomes increasingly competitive, the gold goes to the team that shows off an extra bit of polish. The person who makes a good impression will be the one who gets the job, wins the promotion, or clinches the deal. Manners and professionalism must become second nature to anyone who wants to achieve and maintain a competitive edge. The lesson is this: You can have good credentials, but a good presentation is everything. You can't neglect etiquette, or somewhere in your career you will be at a competitive disadvantage because of your inability to use good manners or to maintain your composure in tense situations.

From William G. Nickels et al., *Understanding Business*, 8th ed., New York: McGraw-Hill, 2008, p. 6. Copyright © 2008 McGraw-Hill. Used by permission of The McGraw-Hill Companies, Inc.

Purpose: _____   Clues: _____

_____

Main idea: _____

_____

3. If there's one thing this nation needs, it's bigger cars. That's why I'm excited that Ford is coming out with a new mound o' metal that will offer consumers even more total road-squatting mass than the current leader in the humongous-car category, the popular Chevrolet Suburban Subdivision—the first passenger automobile designed to be, right off the assembly line, visible from the Moon. I don't know what the new Ford will be called. Probably something like the "Ford Untamed Wilderness Adventure." In the TV commercials, it will be shown splashing through rivers, charging up rocky mountainsides, swinging on vines, diving off cliffs, racing through the surf, and fighting giant sharks hundreds of feet beneath the ocean surface—all the daredevil things that cars do in Sport Utility Vehicle Commercial World, where nobody ever drives on an actual road. Anyway, now we have the new Ford, which will be *even larger* than the Subdivision, which I imagine means it will have separate decks for the

various classes of passengers. And it will not stop there. This is America, darn it, and Chevrolet is not about to just sit by and watch Ford walk away with the coveted title of Least Sane Motor Vehicle. No, cars will keep getting bigger. I see a time, not too far from now, when people will haul their overdue movies back to the video-rental store in full-size, 18-wheel tractor-trailers with names like The Vagabond. It will be a proud time for all Americans, a time for us to cheer for our country.

From *Dave Barry is Not Taking This Sitting Down,* by Dave Barry. Copyright © 2000 by Dave Barry. Used by permission of Crown Publishers, a division of Random House, Inc.

Purpose: _____   Clues: _____

_____

Main idea: _____

4. In the traditional cultures of Asia, arranged marriages were the rule. Marriages were designed to further the well-being of families, not of the individuals involved. Marriage was traditionally seen as a matter of ancestors, descendants, and property. Supporters of these traditions point out that love is a fleeting emotion and not a sensible basis for such an important decision. However, most of these traditional cultures have a literature as well as a history full of love-smitten couples who chose death rather than marriage to the person selected by their respective families.

From Curtis Byer et al., *Dimensions of Human Sexuality,* 5th ed. New York: McGraw-Hill, 1999, p. 39.

Purpose: _____   Clues: _____

Main idea: _____

AN INTRODUCTION TO THE RHETORICAL MODES

Highlight or underline the definitions of the key terms. Then write a paraphrase of each definition in the margin.

Narrative

_____

Descriptive

_____

_____

Expository

_____

_____

In longer reading selections, the main idea is often called the **thesis.** The thesis of an essay, just like the main idea of a paragraph, expresses the most important point the writer is trying to make. The thesis is sometimes called the *controlling idea,* because its primary purpose is to hold the essay or story together.

In the process of creating written work, most writers select a **rhetorical mode of writing** that helps them achieve their purpose. There are four primary rhetorical modes: narration, description, exposition, and persuasion.

Material written in a **narrative mode** tells a story, either true or fictional. In narrative writing, the events of a story are usually ordered chronologically (by time).

With material written in a **descriptive mode,** the emphasis is on providing details that describe a person, place, or object. The writing may use figurative language and include material that appeals to one or more of the five senses. Descriptive writing most commonly deals with visual perceptions.

An author who is trying to explain something will likely use an **expository mode.** Expository writing explains ideas and how things work. It is more likely to be logical and factual. Much of the material that you read in your textbooks follows an expository mode.

Persuasive
_____

Mixed
_____
_____

Material written in a **persuasive mode** is meant to convince you of something. Persuasive writing tends to be about controversial topics. It presents an argument and offers evidence. It is writing that is considered to be biased.

Sometimes an author will use more than one mode of writing. For example, the author might choose to write a piece that is both descriptive and narrative. This is called a **mixed mode** of writing, and the organization may also be mixed.

AUTHOR'S PURPOSE: TO INFORM

Read the following excerpt from *Understanding Psychology* by Robert S. Feldman. Feldman's purpose is to present information about motivation. His mode of writing is expository. Note the factual details that are intended to inform the reader.

SELECTION

"Most of the fundamental needs of life . . . can be explained reasonably well by the process of homeostasis."

GETTING THE PICTURE

Have you ever wondered what motivates people to quit smoking, to fight to get a diploma from college despite seemingly impossible odds stacked against them, or to engage in high-risk behavior like bungee jumping? This article helps answer these questions by explaining how motivation directs and energizes behavior. As you are reading the selection, practice your annotating skills by making notes in the margins.

BIO-SKETCH

Robert S. Feldman is a professor of psychology at the University of Massachusetts. Dr. Feldman has numerous scientific articles, books, and book chapters to his credit. His primary research interest is nonverbal behavior.

BRUSHING UP ON VOCABULARY

exemplify to show by giving or being an example of.

phenomenon any fact, condition, or happening that can be either seen or heard and then described in a scientific way; an unusual or remarkable event or thing.

Excerpt from
UNDERSTANDING PSYCHOLOGY
by Robert S. Feldman

Motivation and Emotion

1 **Motivation** concerns the factors that direct and energize the behaviors of humans and other organisms. Psychologists who study motivation seek to discover the desired goals, or *motives*, that underlie behavior. Motives are exemplified in behavior as basic as

drinking to satisfy thirst or as inconsequential as taking a stroll to get exercise. To the psychologist specializing in the study of motivation, underlying motives are assumed to steer one's choice of activities. The study of motivation, then, consists of identifying why people seek to do the things they do.

2   In just an instant, John Thompson's life changed. That's all it took for an auger, an oversized, drill-like piece of farm equipment powered by a tractor, to rip off both of his arms when he slipped, falling against the rotating machinery.

3   Yet it was in the moments following the accident that Thompson demonstrated incredible bravery. Despite his pain and shock, he ran 400 feet to his house. Using the bone hanging from his left shoulder to open the door, he ran inside and dialed for help with a pen gripped in his teeth. When emergency crews arrived 30 minutes later, he told them where to find ice and plastic bags so that his severed arms could be packed for possible surgical reattachment. Thompson's rescuers came none too soon: By the time surgery could start, he had lost half his blood.

4   What explains John Thompson's enormous motivation to stay alive? Like many questions involving motivation, this one has no single answer. Clearly, biological aspects of motivation were at work: He obviously experienced a powerful *drive* to keep himself alive before he lost so much blood that his life would drain away.

"Always in a moment of extreme danger things can be done which had previously been thought impossible." 5
—General Erwin Rommel

5   A **drive** is a motivational tension, or arousal, that energizes behavior in order to fulfill some need. Many basic kinds of drives, such as hunger, thirst, pain avoidance, and need for air and sleep, are related to biological needs of the body. These are called *primary drives*. Primary drives contrast with *secondary drives,* in which no obvious biological need is being fulfilled. In secondary drives, needs are brought about by prior experiences and learning. Many secondary drives are related to learned motives for power, affiliation, approval, status, security, and achievement. Some people have strong needs to achieve academically and in their careers. We can say that their achievement need is reflected in a secondary drive that motivates their behavior.

6   We usually try to satisfy a primary drive by reducing the need underlying it. For example, we become hungry after not eating for a few hours and may raid the refrigerator, especially if our next scheduled meal is not imminent. If the weather turns cold, we put on extra clothing or raise the setting on the thermostat in order to keep warm. If our body needs liquids in order to function properly, we experience thirst and seek out water.

7   The reason for such behavior is homeostasis, a basic motivational phenomenon underlying primary drives. **Homeostasis** or "steady state" is the process by which an organism strives to maintain some optimal level of internal biological functioning by compensating for deviations from its usual, balanced internal state. Most of the fundamental needs of life, including the need for food, water, stable body temperature, and sleep, can be explained reasonably well by the process of homeostasis.

8   Unfortunately, the process of homeostasis does not explain behaviors in which the goal is not to reduce a drive, but rather to maintain or even to increase a particular level of excitement or arousal. For instance, some behaviors seem to be motivated by nothing more than curiosity. Anyone who has rushed to pick up newly delivered mail, who avidly follows gossip columns in the newspaper, or who yearns to travel to exotic places, knows the importance of curiosity in directing behavior.

9   Similarly, many of us go out of our way to seek thrills through such activities as riding a roller coaster and steering a raft down the rapids of a river. In both of these cases,

"What makes life dreary is want of motive."

—George Eliot

rather than seeking to reduce an underlying drive, people appear to be motivated to *increase* their overall level of stimulation and activity. In order to explain this phenomenon, psychologists have devised an alternative: arousal approaches to motivation.

10   According to **arousal approaches to motivation,** each of us tries to maintain a certain level of stimulation and activity. If our stimulation and activity levels become too high, we try to reduce them. But, if the levels of stimulation and activity are too low, we will try to *increase* them by seeking sensation.

11   People vary widely in the optimal level of arousal that they seek out, with some people needing especially high levels of arousal. For example, psychologists have hypothesized that individuals such as comic John Belushi, DNA researcher Sir Francis Crick, daredevil Evel Knievel, and bank robbers Bonnie and Clyde exhibited a particularly high need for arousal. Such people may attempt to avoid boredom by seeking out challenging situations.

12   It is not just the celebrated who pursue arousal; many of us characteristically seek out relatively high levels of stimulation. You can get a sense of your own characteristic level of stimulation by completing the questionnaire.

Do You Seek Out Sensation?

13   How much stimulation do you crave in your everyday life? You will have an idea after you complete the following questionnaire, which lists some items from a scale designed to assess your sensation-seeking tendencies. Circle either *A* or *B* in each pair of statements.

14   1. A. I would like a job that requires a lot of traveling.
         B. I would prefer a job in one location.

    2. A. I am invigorated by a brisk, cold day.
        B. I can't wait to get indoors on a cold day.

    3. A. I get bored seeing the same old faces.
        B. I like the comfortable familiarity of old friends.

    4. A. I would prefer living in an ideal society in which everyone was safe, secure, and happy.
        B. I would have preferred living in the unsettled days of our history.

    5. A. I sometimes like to do things that are a little frightening.
        B. A sensible person avoids activities that are dangerous.

    6. A. I would not like to be hypnotized.
        B. I would like to have the experience of being hypnotized.

    7. A. The most important goal of life is to live it to the fullest and to experience as much as possible.
        B. The most important goal of life is to find peace and happiness.

    8. A. I would like to try parachute jumping.
        B. I would never want to try jumping out of a plane, with or without a parachute.

    9. A. I enter cold water gradually, giving myself time to get used to it.
        B. I like to dive or jump right into the ocean or a cold pool.

    10. A. When I go on a vacation, I prefer the comfort of a good room and bed.
        B. When I go on a vacation, I prefer the change of camping out.

    11. A. I prefer people who are emotionally expressive, even if they are a bit unstable.
        B. I prefer people who are calm and even-tempered.

12. A. A good painting should shock or jolt the senses.
     B. A good painting should give me a feeling of peace and security.

13. A. People who ride motorcycles must have some kind of unconscious need to hurt themselves.
     B. I would like to drive or ride a motorcycle.

Scoring   Give yourself one point for each of the following responses: 1A, 2A, 3A, 4B, 5A, 6B, 7A, 8A, 9B, 10B, 11A, 12A, 13B. Find your total score by adding up the number of points and then use the following scoring key:

   0–3 very low sensation seeking
   4–5 low
   6–9 average
   10–11 high
   12–13 very high

15   Keep in mind, of course, that this short questionnaire, for which the scoring is based on the results of college students who have taken it, provides only a rough estimate of your sensation-seeking tendencies. Moreover, as people get older, their sensation-seeking scores tend to decrease. Still, the questionnaire will at least give you an indication of how your sensation-seeking tendencies compare with those of others.

Source: "Motivation and Emotion," from Robert S. Feldman, *Understanding Psychology,* 5th ed., pp. 326–327, 329. Copyright © 1999. Reprinted by permission of The McGraw-Hill Companies, Inc.

COMPREHENSION CHECKUP

Topic and Main Idea

1. What is the topic of this article? _____

    _____

2. What is the article's main idea? _____

    _____

STUDY TECHNIQUE 4

Outlining

An outline is an orderly arrangement of ideas going from the general to the specific. An outline shows the relationship and importance of ideas by using a system of Roman numerals for main headings (I, II, III, etc.), capital letters for subheadings (A, B, C, etc.), and numbers for sub-subheadings (1, 2, 3, etc.). Whether you are using outlining to organize class notes or a reading selection, only the most important points should be included.

A partial outline of the previous selection follows. Complete the outline by filling in the missing information in your own words.

I. *Motivation* is defined as _____

   _____

STUDY TECHNIQUE 4 *continued*

II. *Drive* is defined as _____

_____

A. *Primary drive* is defined as _____

_____

   1. An example of a primary drive is _____

_____

   2. Another example of a primary drive is

_____

B. Secondary drive is defined as _____

_____

   1. An example of a secondary drive is

_____

   2. Another example of a secondary drive is

_____

III. Reasons for Motivation

A. *Homeostasis* is defined as _____

_____

   1. An example of homeostasis is _____

_____

   2. Other examples of homeostasis are

_____

_____

B. *Arousal* is defined as _____

_____

   1. An example of arousal is _____

_____

   2. Another example of arousal is _____

_____

True or False

Indicate whether the statement is true or false by writing T or F in the blank provided.

____T____ 1. Primary drives are based on biological needs that must be met for survival.

____T____ 2. Regulation of body temperature is a primary drive.

____T____ 3. Trying to win a skateboarding contest is a secondary drive.

____F____ 4. Affiliation is the need to maintain distance from others.

____T____ 5. The word *homeostasis* means "steady state."

____F____ 6. All individuals need precisely the same amount of stimulation.

Primary or Secondary Need

Indicate whether each of the following is a primary (P) or a secondary (S) need.

7. ____P____ sleep

8. ____P____ thirst

9. ____S____ achievement

10. ____P____ food

Vocabulary Practice

For each item look through the paragraph indicated in parentheses to find a word that matches the definitions below.

1. Illustrated by example (paragraph 1)   e _ _ m _ _ _ f _ _ _

2. Trivial; irrelevant (1)   _ _ c _ _ _ _ q _ _ _ _ _ _ _

3. guide (1)   _ _ e _ _

4. fundamental; basic (1)   _ _ _ _ r _ _ i _ _

5. impending (6)   _ _ m _ _ _ n _

6. occurrence (7)   _ _ e _ _ _ e _ _ _

7. making up for (7)   _ o _ _ _ n _ _ _ _ _ _

8. departures from the norm (7)   _ _ _ _ _ t _ _ n _

9. longs for (8)   _ _ _ r _ s

10. most favorable (11)   _ _ t _ _ a _

11. recklessly daring person (11)   d _ _ _ _ _ _ _ i _

12. energized (14)   i _ _ _ _ _ _ _ _ e _

13. to shock or startle (14)   _ o _ _

In Your Own Words

1. What do you think accounts for the amazing determination and will to live that some people demonstrate in times of personal challenge?

2. Why do you think people pursue activities such as paragliding or bungee jumping?

3. Mentally list some primary and some secondary drives you have satisfied today. How did each influence your behavior?

4. Do you think heredity influences motivation?

5. What are your goals? Why do you pursue them? How vigorously do you try to reach them? When are you satisfied? When do you give up?

The Art of Writing

In a brief essay, respond to the questions below.

> Think about yourself and try to identify your secondary drives. How would you describe them? How do they affect your behavior? Make sure you give some specific examples. For instance, you have a strong secondary drive to achieve. This has motivated you to increase your class load and graduate from college in just three years.

Internet Activity

The *type T personality* has been described by various psychologists as a thrill-seeking or risk-taking personality. Do some research on the type T personality. You might want to first consult Frank Farley in *Psychology Today*, May 1986.

AUTHOR'S PURPOSE: TO ENTERTAIN

The following fable by Aesop has entertainment as its primary purpose. It is an example of the **narrative** mode of writing. Notice that the significant events of the story are told in chronological order.

SELECTION

*"Gradually, when things seemed quiet, the country
mouse crept out from his hiding place and whispered
good-bye to his elegant friend."*

GETTING THE PICTURE

Do you think that people who live in cities have a different perspective on life than people who live in rural areas? If you think this, what are some of the differences you see?

BIO-SKETCH

Aesop, a Greek slave, lived from about 620 to 560 B.C.E. According to legend, Aesop was eventually freed because the fables he told exhibited such great wisdom. As a free man, he traveled to Athens, Greece, where he quickly made an enemy of the ruler and was condemned to death.

Many of Aesop's best fables draw parallels between animals and humans in order to illustrate key moral principles and universal lessons. Aesop is responsible for many familiar expressions that have survived to this day, such as "sour grapes," "don't cry over spilt milk," "actions speak louder than words," and "look before you leap."

BRUSHING UP ON VOCABULARY

morsel a little bite. *Morsel* is derived from the Latin word *morsum*, meaning "bitten."

condescend This word is derived from the Latin prefix *de*, meaning "down," "down from," and "away." The meaning of "stoop to the level of inferiors" was first recorded in 1435. The fable states that "the town mouse *condescended* to nibble a little here and there." This means that the town mouse was "politely willing to do something that he thought was beneath his dignity."

rustic The English language is almost always uncomplimentary to the "country cousin." *Rustic* is derived from the Latin word *rus*, meaning "open land, country." In 1585, it acquired the meaning "rough, awkward," and then in 1594, that of "simple and plain."

The Country Mouse and the
Town Mouse

BY AESOP

1   ONCE UPON A TIME A COUNTRY MOUSE, who had a friend in town, invited him to pay a visit in the country for old acquaintance's sake. After the invitation was accepted, the country mouse, though plain, coarse,

and somewhat frugal, opened his heart and pantry to honor his old friend and to show him the proper hospitality. There was not a morsel which he had carefully stored that he did not bring forth out of its larder—peas and barley, cheese parings and nuts—with the hope that the quantity would make up for what he feared was wanting in quality to suit the taste of his elegant guest. In turn, the town mouse condescended to nibble a little here and there in a dainty manner while the host sat munching a blade of barley straw.

2 In their after-dinner chat the town mouse said to the country mouse, "How is it, my good friend, that you can endure this boring and crude life? You live like a toad in a hole. You can't really prefer these solitary rocks and woods to streets teeming with carriages and people. Upon my word of honor, you're wasting your time in such a miserable existence. You must make the most of your life while it lasts. As you know, a mouse does not live forever. So, come with me this very night, and I'll show you all around the town and what life's about."

3 Overcome by his friend's fine words and polished manner, the country mouse agreed, and they set out together on their journey to the town. It was late in the evening when they crept stealthily into the city and midnight before they reached the large house, which was the town mouse's residence. There were couches of crimson velvet, ivory carvings, and everything one could imagine that indicated wealth and luxury. On the table were the remains of a splendid banquet from all the choicest shops ransacked the day before to make sure that the guests, already departed, would be satisfied.

4 It was now the town mouse's turn to play host, and he placed his country friend on a purple cushion, ran back and forth to supply all his needs, and pressed dish upon dish on him and delicacy upon delicacy. Of course, the town mouse tasted each and every course before he ventured to place it before his rustic cousin, as though he were waiting on a king. In turn, the country mouse made himself quite at home and blessed the good fortune that had brought about such a change in his way of life.

5 In the middle of his enjoyment, however, just as he was thinking contemptuously of the poor meals that he had been accustomed to eating, the door suddenly flew open, and a group of revelers, who were returning from a late party, burst into the room. The frightened friends jumped from the table and hid themselves in the very first corner they could reach. No sooner did they dare creep out again than the barking of dogs drove them back with even greater terror than before. Gradually, when things seemed quiet, the country mouse crept out from his hiding place and whispered good-bye to his elegant friend.

6 "This fine mode of living may be all right for those who like it," he said. "But I'd rather have a crust in peace and safety than all your fine things in the midst of such alarm and terror."

Source: The Country Mouse and the Town Mouse, Aesop.

✔ COMPREHENSION CHECKUP

True or False

Indicate whether the statement is true or false by writing T or F in the blank provided.

___F___ 1. The country mouse would score high on the sensation-seeking scale.

___T___ 2. The mice were filling a primary drive when they were interrupted by the revelers.

___T___ 3. The country mouse probably has a strong secondary drive for security.

___F___ 4. The late-night revelers entered the room quietly.

___T___ 5. The town mouse's residence was lavishly decorated.

Multiple Choice

Write the letter of the correct answer in the blank provided.

_____ 6. What do the words *coarse, plain,* and *frugal* suggest about the country mouse?
   a. He is very lazy.
   b. He has a magnificent lifestyle.
   c. He lives a simple, thrifty life.
   d. He is likely to use obscenities.

_____ 7. A proverb is a traditional saying that offers advice or presents a moral. Which of the following proverbs best describes the attitude of the town mouse?
   a. You win a few, you lose a few.
   b. Absence makes the heart grow fonder.
   c. If you can't beat 'em, join 'em.
   d. Curiosity killed the cat.

_____ 8. Which of the following proverbs best describes the attitude of the country mouse at the end of the fable?
   a. Adventures are for the adventurous.
   b. It's best to be on the safe side.
   c. The early bird catches the worm.
   d. Both a and b.

_____ 9. Which of the following best describes the town mouse's attitude toward the country mouse before their departure to the city?
   a. The country mouse is living his life to the fullest.
   b. The country mouse needs to have new experiences.
   c. The country mouse is very adventurous.
   d. The country mouse should stay right where he is because there's no place like home.

_____ 10. The town mouse and the country mouse crept stealthily into the city. The most likely meaning of the word *stealthily* is
   a. sneakily
   b. loudly
   c. obviously
   d. both a and b

Vocabulary in Context

Look through the paragraph indicated in parentheses to find a word that matches the definition below.

1. thrifty (paragraph 1) _____

2. place where food is kept or stored; pantry (1) _____

3. very full; swarming; abounding (2) _____

4. searched thoroughly; plundered (3) _____

5. urged upon (4) _____

6. scornfully (5) _____

7. merrymakers (5) _____

8. method; way of acting or behaving (6) _____

In Your Own Words

1. What is the main idea of the fable?

2. Working with a partner, paraphrase one of the paragraphs of the fable. Be sure to keep the characters and setting the same.

3. What is the significance of the ending of the fable? What is meant by the last sentence? Explain.

4. Determine which of the following proverbs is more likely to express the attitude of the country mouse. Explain your choice.

    "A life lived in fear is a life half-lived."

    "Better safe than sorry."

    "Nothing ventured, nothing gained."

    "Variety is the spice of life."

    "Acorns were good till bread was found."

The Art of Writing

In a brief essay, respond to one of the items below.

1. Are you more like the country mouse or the town mouse? Why?

2. Explain how the intrusion of the revelers and the barking dogs was a threat to the homeostasis of the mice. What do you see as the secondary drives of each mouse? Make reference to the previous article if necessary.

Internet Activity

The following website has a collection of more than 665 of Aesop's fables:

   www.Aesopfables.com.

Select three fables you find interesting, and print them. Think about the meaning of the fables and how the moral might apply to your own life. Describe your conclusions in a short paragraph.

AUTHOR'S PURPOSE: TO PERSUADE

The following is a poem by Judith Ortiz Cofer. The poem's purpose is to persuade, and it is written in a persuasive mode.

SELECTION

"Finally, you must choose between standing still in the one solid spot you have found, or you keep moving and take the risk."

GETTING THE PICTURE

What idea is Ortiz Cofer trying to convince us to accept? What course of action is she recommending?

BIO-SKETCH

Judith Ortiz Cofer was born in Puerto Rico in 1952 and is currently a professor of English and creative writing at the University of Georgia. A recipient of the O. Henry Award for a short story, she has also published two volumes of poetry: *Peregrina* in 1986 and *Triple Crown* in 1987. *The Meaning of Consuelo* was published in 2003.

Crossings

BY JUDITH ORTIZ COFER

Step on a crack. ★
In a city of concrete it is impossible
to avoid disaster indefinitely.
You spend your life peering
downward, looking for flaws,
but each day more and more fissures
crisscross your path, and like the lines
on your palms, they mean something
you cannot decipher.
Finally, you must choose between
standing still in the one solid spot you
have found, or you keep moving
and take the risk:
Break your mother's back.

★"Step on a crack, break your mother's back"—a rhyme children say while they avoid stepping on the cracks in a sidewalk. Stepping on a crack is supposed to bring bad luck.

Source: Judith Ortiz Cofer, "Crossings," from *Reaching for the Mainland and Selected New Poems.* Copyright © 1987 Bilingual Press/Editorial Bilingue, Arizona State University, Tempe, AZ. Reprinted with permission.

COMPREHENSION CHECKUP

In Your Own Words

Try to explain the meaning of the poem in your own words.

_____

_____

_____

_____

_____

_____

The next article discusses extreme sports. Read the article and think about its purpose and the rhetorical mode the author uses. Then answer the questions that follow.

SELECTION

"America has always been defined by risk; it may be our
predominant national characteristic."

GETTING THE PICTURE

In recent years, the young and the fit have been besieged with invitations to participate in man-made "life tests." They are asked, "Do you have what it takes?" And told, "Just do it." Increasingly, reality movies and TV programs like *Survivor* occupy our national attention. As you are reading the article below, try to determine what's behind this preoccupation with testing the limits.

BIO-SKETCH

Karl Taro Greenfeld is a Japanese-American writer—author of *Speed Tribes: Days and Nights with Japan's Next Generation* (1994)—and editor for *Time* magazine's Asian edition.

BRUSHING UP ON VOCABULARY

acronym a word formed by combining the initial letters or syllables of a series of words. It comes from the Greek *akros,* meaning "tip," and *onym,* meaning "name." Large numbers of *acronyms* first began to appear during World War I when WAAC (Women's Army Auxiliary Corps) and similar words were formed. The trend accelerated during World War II with terms such as RADAR (radio detecting and ranging). Some common acronyms are AIDS (acquired immunodeficiency syndrome), NAFTA (North American Free Trade Agreement), and MADD (Mothers Against Drunk Driving).

orgy the word came to us from the Greek word *orgia,* meaning "secret ceremonies." The Greeks held nighttime religious rituals in honor of Dionysius, the Greek god of wine. These *orgia* involved drinking, singing, dancing, and acts of sex. The current meaning is much the same except that the religious element has been eliminated.

SELECTION *continued*

bespeak a British term meaning "to speak for or order in advance."

pandemic an epidemic that spreads over a large area, possibly even worldwide. The term comes from the Greek word *pandemos,* meaning "disease of all the people."

perilous involving grave risk; hazardous; dangerous. A long time ago, travel was a highly dangerous undertaking. The word *perilous* comes from the Latin *periculum,* which means, "the danger of going forth to travel."

manifestation clearly evident; an outward indication. From the Latin *manus,* which means "hand," and *festus,* which means "struck." Something that is *manifest* to the senses is something that can be touched or struck by the hand.

pansy a dainty flower with velvety petals and a "thoughtful face." The word is derived from the French *penser,* meaning "to think." The word is also a slang term for an effeminate man.

contemplate to consider thoughtfully. The ancient Roman priests carefully considered various signs or omens that were revealed to them inside the temples of their gods. *Contemplate* is derived from *con,* meaning "with," and *templum,* meaning "temple."

© Oliver Furrer/Brand X/JupiterImages

LIFE ON THE EDGE   by KARL TARO GREENFELD

1   FIVE . . . FOUR . . . THREE . . . TWO . . . ONE . . . SEE YA!" And Chance McGuire, 25, is airborne off a 650-foot concrete dam in Northern California. In one second he falls 16 feet, in two seconds 63 feet, and after three seconds and 137 feet he is flying at 65 m.p.h. He prays that his parachute will open facing away from the dam, that his canopy won't collapse, that his toggles will be handy, and that no ill wind will slam him back into the cold concrete. The chute snaps open, the sound ricocheting through the gorge like a gunshot, and McGuire is soaring, carving S turns into the air, swooping over a winding creek. When he lands, he is a speck on a path along the creek. He hurriedly packs his chute and then, clearly audible above the rushing water, lets out a war whoop that rises past those mortals still perched on the dam, past the commuters puttering by on the roadway, past even the hawks who circle the ravine. It is a cry of defiance, thanks, and victory; he has survived another BASE jump.

2   McGuire is a practitioner of what he calls the king of all extreme sports. BASE is an acronym for building, antenna, span (bridge), and earth (cliffs). BASE jumping has one of the sporting world's highest fatality rates: in its 18-year history, 46 participants have been killed. Yet the sport has never been more popular, with more than a thousand jumpers in the U.S. and more seeking to get into it every day.

3   It is an activity without margin for error. If your chute malfunctions, don't bother reaching for a reserve—there isn't time. There are no second chances.

4   Still, the sport's stark metaphor—a human leaving safety behind to leap into the void—may be perfect with our times. As extreme a risk-taker as McGuire seems, we may all have more in common with him than we know or care to admit. America has embarked on a national orgy of thrill seeking and risk taking. Extreme sports like BASE jumping, snowboarding, ice climbing, skateboarding and paragliding are merely the most vivid manifestation of this new national behavior.

5   The rising popularity of extreme sports bespeaks an eagerness on the part of millions of Americans to participate in activities closer to the metaphorical edge, where danger, skill, and fear combine to give weekend warriors and professional athletes alike a sense of pushing out personal boundaries. According to American Sports Data, a consulting firm, participation in so-called extreme sports is way up. Snowboarding has grown 113 percent in five years and now boasts nearly 5.5 million participants. Mountain biking, skateboarding, scuba diving, you name the adventure sport—the growth curves reveal a nation that loves to play with danger. Contrast that with activities like baseball, touch football, and aerobics, all of which have been in steady decline throughout the '90s.

"Life has no romance without risk."

—Sarah Doherty, first one-legged person to scale Mount McKinley

6   The pursuits that are becoming more popular have one thing in common: the perception that they are somehow more challenging than a game of touch football. "Every human being with two legs, two arms, is going to wonder how

fast, how strong, how enduring he or she is," says Eric Perlman, a mountaineer and filmmaker specializing in extreme sports. "We are designed to experiment or die."

7   And to get hurt. More Americans than ever are injuring themselves while pushing their personal limits. In 1997, the U.S. Consumer Safety Commission reported that 48,000 Americans were admitted to hospital emergency rooms with skateboarding-related injuries. That's 33 percent more than the previous year. Snowboarding E.R. visits were up 31 percent; mountain climbing up 20 percent. By every statistical measure available, Americans are participating in, and injuring themselves through, adventure sports at an unprecedented rate.

8   Consider Mike Carr, an environmental engineer and paraglider pilot from Denver who last year survived a bad landing that smashed 10 ribs and collapsed his lung. Paraglider pilots use feathery nylon wings to take off from mountaintops and float on thermal wind currents—a completely unpredictable ride. Carr also mountain bikes and climbs rock faces. He walked away from a 1,500-foot fall in Peru in 1988. After his recovery, he returned to paragliding. "This has taken over many of our lives," he explains. "You float like a bird out there. You can go as high as 18,000 feet and go for 200 miles. That's magic."

9   America has always been defined by risk; it may be our predominant national characteristic. It's a country founded by risk-takers fed up with the English Crown and expanded by pioneers—a word that seems utterly American. Our heritage throws up heroes—Lewis and Clark, Thomas Edison, Frederick Douglass, Teddy Roosevelt, Henry Ford, Amelia Earhart—who bucked the odds, taking perilous chances.

10   Previous generations didn't need to seek out risk; it showed up uninvited and regularly: global wars, childbirth complications, diseases and pandemics from the flu to polio, dangerous products, and even the omnipresent cold-war threat of mutually assured destruction. "I just don't think extreme sports would have been popular in a ground-war era," says Dan Cady, professor of popular culture at California State University at Fullerton. "Coming back from a war and getting onto a skateboard would not seem so extreme."

11   But for recent generations, many of these traditional risks have been reduced by science, government, or legions of personal-injury lawyers, leaving Boomers and Generations X and Y to face less real risk. Life expectancy has increased. Violent crime is down. You are 57 percent less likely to die of heart disease than your parents; smallpox, measles, and polio have virtually been eradicated.

"The greater the difficulty, the more glory in surmounting it."

—Epicurus

12   Combat survivors speak of the terror and the excitement of playing in a death match. Are we somehow incomplete as people if we do not taste that terror and excitement on the brink? People are [taking risks] because everyday risk is minimized and people want to be challenged," says Joy Marr, 43, an adventure racer who was the only woman member of a five-person team that finished the 1998 Raid Gauloises, the grandaddy of all adventure races. This is a

sport that requires several days of nonstop slogging, climbing, rappelling, rafting, and surviving through some of the roughest terrain in the world. Says fellow adventure racer and former Army Ranger Jonathan Senk, 35: "Our society is so surgically sterile. It's almost like our socialization just desensitizes us. Every time I'm out doing this I'm searching my soul. It's the Lewis and Clark gene, to venture out, to find what your limitations are."

13   Psychologist Frank Farley of Temple University believes that taking conscious risk involves overcoming our instincts. He points out that no other animal intentionally puts itself in peril. "The human race is particularly risk-taking compared with other species," he says. He describes risk-takers as the Type T personality, and-the U.S. as a Type T nation. He breaks it down further, into Type T physical (extreme athletes) and Type T intellectual (Albert Einstein, Galileo). He warns there is also Type T negative, that is, those who are drawn to delinquency, crime, experimentation with drugs, unprotected sex, and a whole litany of destructive behaviors.

14   All these Type Ts are related, and perhaps even different aspects of the same character trait. There is, says Farley, a direct link between Einstein and BASE jumper Chance McGuire. They are different manifestations of the thrill-seeking component of our characters: Einstein was thrilled by his mental life, and McGuire—well, Chance jumps off buildings.

15   McGuire, at the moment, is driving from Hollister to another California town, Auburn, where he is planning another BASE jump from a bridge. Riding with him is Adam Fillipino, president of Consolidated Rigging, a company that manufactures parachutes and gear for BASE jumpers. McGuire talks about the leap ahead, about his feelings when he is at the exit point, and how at that moment, looking down at the ground, what goes through his mind is that this is not something a human being should be doing. But that's exactly what makes him take the leap: that sense of overcoming his inhibitions and winning what he calls the gravity game. "Football is for pansies," says McGuire. "What do you need all those pads for? This sport [BASE jumping] is pushing all the limits. I have a friend who calls it suicide with a kick."

16   When a BASE jumper dies, other BASE jumpers say he has "gone in," as gone into the ground or gone into a wall. "I'm sick of people going in," says Fillipino. "In the past year, a friend went in on a skydive, another drowned as a result of a BASE jump, another friend went in on a jump, another died in a skydiving plane crash. You can't escape death, but you don't want to flirt with it either." It may be the need to flirt with death, or at least take extreme chances, that has his business growing at the rate of 50 percent a year.

"Who does nothing   17   Without some expression of risk, we may never know our limits and
need hope for nothing."   therefore who we are as individuals. "If you don't assume a certain amount
—J. C. F. von Schiller   of risk," says paraglider pilot Wade Ellet, 51, "you're missing a certain amount of life." And it is by taking risks that we may flirt with greatness. "We create technologies, we make new discoveries, but in order to do that, we have to

18 That's certainly what's driving McGuire and Fillipino as they position themselves on the Auburn bridge. It's dawn again, barely light, and they appear as shadows moving on the catwalk beneath the roadway. As they survey the drop zone, they compute a series of risk assessments. "It's a matter of weighing the variables," Fillipino says, pointing out that the wind, about 15 m.p.h. out of the northwest, has picked up a little more than he would like. Still, it's a clear morning, and they've climbed all the way up here. McGuire is eager to jump. But Fillipino continues to scan the valley below them, the Sacramento River rushing through the gorge.

19 Then a white parks-department SUV pulls up on an access road that winds alongside the river. Park Rangers are a notorious scourge of BASE jumpers, confiscating equipment and prosecuting for trespassing. Fillipino contemplates what would happen if the president of a BASE rig company were busted for an illegal jump. He foresees trouble with his bankers, he imagines the bad publicity his business would garner, and he says he's not going. There are some risks he is simply not willing to take.

Source: From Karl Taro Greenfield, "Life on the Edge," *Time*, 9/6/99, pp. 29–36. © 1999 Time Inc. Reprinted by permission.

COMPREHENSION CHECKUP

True or False

Indicate whether the statement is true or false by writing T or F in the blank provided.

____F____ 1. BASE jumping has an extremely low fatality rate.

____F____ 2. Park Rangers are generally supportive of BASE jumping.

____T____ 3. The BASE jumpers described in the article weigh many variables before deciding to perform a BASE jump.

____T____ 4. Fillipino was reluctant to endanger his business interests with a jump off the Auburn bridge.

____T____ 5. People who are Type T negative are attracted to unlawful activities.

Multiple Choice

Write the letter of the correct answer in the blank provided.

_____ 6. Thes author's primary purpose in writing this article was to
   a. entertain the reader with a good story about Chance McGuire and friends
   b. persuade people to try extreme sports
   c. provide information about BASE jumping and other extreme sports.
   d. convince the reader that extreme sports should be outlawed

_____ 7. It is suggested in the article that
   a. extreme sports will eventually be replaced by regular sports
   b. extreme sports are responsible for many physical injuries
   c. our national heritage is replete with stories of heroic individuals who took risks
   d. both b and c

_____ 8. It is suggested in the article that
   a. our ancestors faced real adversity in the form of disease and war
   b. persons with Type T personalities especially enjoy challenges
   c. some persons who do not face real adversity in their lives turn to extreme sports to fill this void
   d. all of the above

_____ 9. What is the most likely meaning of *weekend warrior* as used in paragraph 5?
   a. a person who likes to take chances in the summer months
   b. a person who encounters physical challenge and adversity on a daily basis
   c. a person who works hard during the week and relaxes on the weekend
   d. a person who engages in rigorous physical activity primarily on the weekend

_____ 10. Chance McGuire disparages those who
   a. have "gone in"
   b. participate in conventional sports
   c. believe paragliding is superior to BASE jumping
   d. take unwarranted risks

Vocabulary in Context

Using the context clues provided, define the following words. Then consult your dictionary to see how accurate your definition is.

1. clearly *audible* above the rushing water, lets out a war whoop (paragraph 1)

   Definition: _____

2. If your chute *malfunctions*, don't bother reaching for a reserve (3)

   Definition: _____

3. a human leaving safety behind to leap into the *void* (4)

   Definition: _____

4. smallpox, measles, and polio have virtually been *eradicated* (11)

   Definition: _____

5. experimentation with drugs, unprotected sex, and a whole *litany* of destructive behaviors (13)

   Definition: _____

Missing Letters

Fill in the missing letter for each word below. Then place that letter on the line of the quote following to complete General Patton's statement.

prac ——— itioner

confisc ——— ting

star ———

p ——— ril

s ——— ourge

vari ——— bles

steri ——— e

per ——— hed

——— nprecedented

contemp ——— ate

predomin ——— nt

ricoche ——— ing

manif ——— station

boun ——— aries

omnip ——— esent

inh ——— bitions

pan ——— y

bespea ———

——— peck

"_____. That is quite different from being rash."

—*General George S. Patton*

In Your Own Words

1. Have you ever tried an extreme sport? Do you think the benefits of participating in an extreme sport outweigh the risks? Based on the article, can you identify some common characteristics of those who participate in extreme sports?

2. Should the law place restrictions on extreme sports? What sorts of restrictions should apply?

3. Do you think that life is more risky today than it was 50 years ago? In what ways might contemporary life be more risky? In what ways might it be less risky?

The Art of Writing

In a brief essay, respond to the item below.

"Extreme athletes put not only themselves in danger by their activity; rescue workers who rescue extreme skiers from avalanches and medical workers called on to helicopter-lift athletes in trouble out of the rugged terrain are also put at risk." Is this fair?

Internet Activity

To learn more about extreme sports, consult one of the following websites:

http://expn.go.com

www.adventuresports.com

www.extreme.com

http://espn.go.com/extreme/index.html

Summarize your findings.

Dean Dunbar, an extreme-sports enthusiast, has been an active participant in a variety of extreme sports despite a degenerative eye condition.

To read about Dunbar, go to www.awezome.com and click on Extreme Dreams. Summarize your findings.

SELECTION

GETTING THE PICTURE

Do you think that graffiti can be art? Or is graffiti always just vandalism? What problems has your town or city had with graffiti? Has your city allowed any graffiti to be painted as "art"?

BIO-SKETCH

Charisse Jones is an award-winning journalist who is currently a New York correspondent for *USA Today*. She is a former staff writer for the *Los Angeles Times* and *The New York Times*. While at the *LA Times*, she cowrote one of the ten stories that won the Pulitzer Prize for coverage of the Rodney King riots in Los Angeles.

BRUSHING UP ON VOCABULARY

graffiti markings as initials, slogans, or drawings, written or sketched on a sidewalk, wall, and so on. Also called *aerosol art*. Graffiti began in the late 1960s in the South Bronx. It includes "wild style" colorful murals and "scratchiti," a type of etching commonly found on the windows of subway trains.

tag a graffiti signature.

tagging writing a tag or a nickname of the writer as often and as artistically as possible.

TATS Cru a 1980s group of graffiti writers who became commercial artists. They now paint graffiti-style murals on walls for clients like Chivas Regal and Coca-Cola.

Mecca a place that attracts many people with interests in common. Mecca is a city in west Saudi Arabia. It is the birthplace of Muhammad, and thus the spiritual center of Islam. Muslims face in the direction of Mecca when they pray, and they are expected to go on a pilgrimage to Mecca at least once in their lives.

Leaving Their Mark Behind

by CHARISSE JONES

1   DAVIDE PERRÉ CAME here to paint, not the portraits and landscapes that might be displayed in a SoHo gallery, but the blank walls and scarred storefronts of New York City.

2   "I'd been to a lot of places, but I had to see New York," said Perré, 25, a graffiti artist from Dusseldorf, Germany, who has left his mark in spray paint from Australia to Argentina.

3   But while he gets permission from property owners before spray-painting a mural, Perré has seen many of his friends get arrested for doing the same. And he admits that nowadays, among the energetic, rebellious ranks of graffiti writers, there might be just a little fear.

4   "If somebody really likes to 'bomb,' they don't care," he says, using street lingo for writing your name on a wall. But "they may be afraid of the vandals squad."

5   When it comes to graffiti, New York City is Mecca, twice. It is the beacon for graffiti writers around the world who feel they haven't arrived until they have scrawled their name along a subway car or made a pilgrimage to 106th Street and Park Avenue, the graffiti writers' "hall of fame."

6   But it is also a model for government officials from Tokyo to Copenhagen, who having seen New York launch an anti-graffiti offensive that has led to the arrest of hundreds of vandals and the virtual eradication of graffiti from public property. Those officials look to New York for advice on how to fight the scourge in their own cities.

7   There were 1,657 arrests for graffiti offenses for the year ending June 30, a 34% increase over the previous year. The city's subway trains and sanitation trucks, once rolling canvasses for graffiti writers, are not allowed to leave their yards with a mark on them—and any train that gets marked along its route is taken out of service and washed clean.

8   A citywide database links vandals to their graffiti monikers, or "tags." And city officials are increasingly using the vandals' own snapshots of their spray-can handiwork to prosecute.

9   "They'll come over and film themselves tagging the train, and then we'll arrest them and use the videotape against them," says Agostino Cangemi, assistant counsel and chairman of the mayor's anti-graffiti task force. "They usually intend to stay a day, but they end up staying a lot longer because they get caught up in our judicial process."

10   Perhaps no other city is as linked in the public imagination with the scrawl of graffiti as New York, an image cemented in the 1970s and '80s with the rising popularity of rap music and genre film classics such as *Wild Style* and *Beat Street*.

11   "There are a lot of people who, when they come, say, 'Where's the trains with the graffiti on them?'" says Hector Nazario, aka "Nicer," who went from a graffiti "crew" member as a teenager to the co-founder of an advertising agency that uses graffiti as its medium. "In a lot of people's minds, that's what New York looks like."

12   When Mayor Giuliani took office in 1994, he made graffiti a major target of his campaign to improve New Yorkers' quality of life. Currently, the city spends roughly $25 million a year on its anti-graffiti efforts, Cangemi says, and everyone from a Japanese chapter of the Guardian Angels to government officials

in Montreal have asked local officials for advice on controlling graffiti.

13 A citywide anti-graffiti task force, created in 1995, includes representatives from about 20 city agencies, Cangemi says. An anti-graffiti coordinator collects information from police precincts, each of which has a designated liaison to deal with graffiti problems. And no fewer than three vandal squads target the issue.

14 "I believe when that phrase 'quality-of-life crimes' began to be used, that was one of the turning points for viewing graffiti as something more than just scrawling on a wall by a young person," says Mariela Stanton, chief of the anti-bias and youth-gang bureau for the Queens County district attorney's office.

15 While graffiti offenses can be felonies, they are usually misdemeanors committed by anyone from gang members marking territory to first-time offenders experimenting with a spray can to "crews" that exist solely to create graffiti, Stanton says.

16 And though officials say such identifications are more akin to handwriting analysis than fingerprints when it comes to accuracy, some prosecutors are beginning to rely more on police experts who can link a vandal to his "tag," even when there is no eyewitness to the crime.

17 "It's only been in the last few months that we looked at this new way of putting a case together," Stanton says, adding that courts are slowly becoming more receptive to such expert testimony. "I think the courts are more ready to take graffiti seriously. . . . So we're in a new mindset to start looking at new ways of prosecution."

18 Expert testimony, usually thought of as a way to help convict those who commit more serious crimes, is just one of the legal devices being used against graffiti vandals. Police officers go undercover and use surveillance to catch vandals in the act.

19 On Staten Island, where first-time offenders can be sentenced to 100 hours of community service and be ordered to reimburse property owners, police officers have a database with more than 450 names and tags.

20 "Arrests are up, and incidents of graffiti are down," says Capt. Frank Belcastro, head of the police department's Staten Island task force. "And the reason we really target graffiti is because when you have graffiti in an area, it creates an atmosphere where people believe they can engage in criminal conduct without fear of retribution."

21 But one man's vandalism is another man's art. And while graffiti artists say the crackdown has quelled some illegal activity, the subculture, celebrated in movies, underground magazines, books and even a current exhibition on hip-hop at the Brooklyn Museum of Art, continues to thrive.

22 "They caught one or two, but they can't stop the other hundred who are coming behind these kids," Nazario says. "For some kids, it's their way of sticking their hand out of a crowd and saying, 'I exist.'"

23 Though Nazario, 33, does not condone vandalism, he says he remembers the rush he felt as a teenager when the subway was his canvas.

24 "Being from the Bronx, I could paint a train here and it would be my rolling gallery," he says, "because it would ride through Manhattan and end up in Brooklyn or Queens. Then it would ride back, and everyone in New York would see it."

25 His ad agency in the Bronx, TATS cru, is a gathering place for graffiti artists from around the world. And Davide Perré is one of them. Perré, along with his twin brother, Raoul, graduated from

"Art is not an end in itself, but a means of addressing humanity."

—Modest Mussorgsky

breaking the law in Germany—scribbling on trains and even the Berlin Wall—to etching characters and murals for business owners in the USA.

26   For many graffiti writers visiting from overseas, "they paint, take a picture and go home," says Davide Perré, who

now lives in New York. "They don't have to go to the Empire State Building."

27   The pictures, while they could become evidence, are apparently worth the risk.

28   "That's enough for them," Nazario says, "because in this art form you learn nothing lasts forever."

Source: Charisse Jones, "Leaving their mark behind," *USA Today*, 11/22/2000, p. 19A. Copyright © 2000. Reprinted with permission.

COMPREHENSION CHECKUP

True or False

Indicate whether the statement is true or false by writing T or F in the blank provided.

_____ T 1. According to the selection, graffiti artists have become more fearful that tagging will lead to their arrest.

_____ F 2. Since the start of the campaign to eradicate graffiti in New York City, activity by graffiti vandals has escalated.

_____ T 3. Government officials across the country look to New York to provide advice on how to solve the graffiti problem in their own communities.

_____ F 4. Graffiti arrests have plummeted since New York began its anti-graffiti campaign.

_____ T 5. "Nicer" has successfully made the transition from former graffiti crew member to businessman.

_____ T 6. Former mayor Rudy Giuliani saw graffiti as a quality-of-life issue for New Yorkers.

_____ F 7. Most graffiti offenses are considered to be felonies.

_____ F 8. Identifying a graffiti artist by his "tag" is similar to doing a sophisticated fingerprint analysis.

_____ T 9. Expert testimony is increasingly being used against graffiti vandals.

_____ T 10. Law enforcement officials target graffiti because they say graffiti fosters other criminal conduct.

Multiple Choice

Write the letter of the correct answer in the blank provided.

_____ 1. The best statement of the main idea is which?
   a. The mayor's anti-graffiti task force has dealt a death blow to graffiti writers.
   b. Despite New York City's crackdown on graffiti, many taggers still practice their form of artistic expression.
   c. In the near future, graffiti is likely to be revered as a form of folk art.
   d. Graffiti artists want to be known in their neighborhoods.

_____ 2. The purpose of the selection is to
   a. persuade the reader to report graffiti activity to the authorities
   b. defend the artistic merits of graffiti
   c. discuss the lifestyle of the typical graffiti artist
   d. inform the reader about graffiti as art and graffiti as vandalism

_____ 3. Unlike many artists, graffiti artists know that their work is
   a. likely to be of a permanent nature
   b. likely to be of a transitory nature
   c. valued by the public at large
   d. likely to be exhibited in fine establishments

_____ 4. For some graffiti artists, pictures of their work are
   a. worth the risk
   b. used by the police as evidence against them
   c. a way for the police to overcome the lack of an eyewitness to a crime
   d. all of the above

_____ 5. New York City has responded to the proliferation of graffiti by
   a. hiring more police
   b. using guards to patrol the premises of key city structures
   c. launching a campaign to narrowly define the term art
   d. hiring an anti-graffiti coordinator

_____ 6. In New York City, graffiti is regarded as
   a. a common activity by young people who wish to assert themselves
   b. a cry of help
   c. a problem that needs to be dealt with by the proper authorities
   d. solely a gang activity

_____ 7. Paragraphs 5 and 6 discuss
   a. the popularity of New York to graffiti writers
   b. the history of Mecca
   c. the success of New York's anti-graffiti efforts
   d. both a and c

_____ 8. New York City makes its case against graffiti artists in all of the following ways *except*
   a. by means of surveillance
   b. by using undercover police officers
   c. by refusing to sell spray cans to minors
   d. by linking a vandal to his tag

Vocabulary in Context

First, use context clues to give your own definition for the italicized word. Next, give the dictionary definition. Finally, write your own sentence using the italicized word in the same way that it is used in the selection.

   Example:

   rebellious ranks of graffiti writers (paragraph 3) __defiant_____

   Dictionary Definition: fighting or struggling against authority or any type of control

   Sentence: The ____rebellious_____ two-year-old refused to eat a balanced diet.

1. *beacon* for graffiti writers (5) _____

   Dictionary definition: _____

   Sentence: _____

2. virtual *eradication* of graffiti (6) _____

   Dictionary definition: _____

   Sentence: _____

3. how to fight the *scourge* (6) _____

   Dictionary definition: _____

   Sentence: _____

4. an image *cemented* in the 1970s (10) _____

   Dictionary definition: _____

   Sentence: _____

5. designated *liaison* to deal with graffiti (13) _____

   Dictionary definition: _____

   Sentence: _____

6. ordered to *reimburse* property owners (19) _____

   Dictionary definition: _____

   Sentence: _____

7. it creates an *atmosphere* (20) _____

   Dictionary definition: _____

   Sentence: _____

8. without fear of *retribution* (20) _____

   Dictionary definition: _____

   Sentence: _____

9. *quelled* some illegal activities (21) _____

   Dictionary definition: _____

   Sentence: _____

10. does not *condone* vandalism (23) _____

    Dictionary definition: _____

    Sentence: _____

In Your Own Words

In Phoenix, Arizona, a law was passed banning the sale of spray paint to minors. In addition, the Phoenix Police Department created a hotline for reporting graffiti activity, and community groups painted over graffiti in their neighborhoods weekly. The measures appear to have worked. Of the original 100 "crews" of graffiti artists, it is estimated that only a few remain. What problems has your town or city had with graffiti? What has your community done to eradicate graffiti? Why do you think the public in general is so opposed to graffiti?

The Art of Writing

In a brief essay, respond to either item below.

1. Graffiti is considered by some experts to be an expression of pride, self-worth, and personal affirmation. Others consider it to be a form of language. What is your opinion? Taking into account your understanding of graffiti, how severe do you think the penalties should be for youthful offenders who tag?

2. Over the years, the legendary artists Christo and Jean-Claude have created numerous colossal "projects." For instance, at various times, they have "wrapped" a whole section of the Australian coastline, a historic bridge in France, and the German Parliament building in plastic sheeting. They became overnight celebrities when they set up white nylon sheeting for 24 miles over the hills of northern California. Although Christo's and Jean-Claude's structures are physically present for only a short time, they live on afterward in sketches, photographs, and videos. When Christo was criticized for the transitory nature of his work, he replied, "I think it takes much greater courage to create things to be gone than to create things that will remain" (*Living with Art*, p. 287).

   Write a paragraph comparing and contrasting the structures produced by Christo and the work of graffiti artists. In what ways do Christo and graffiti artists have similar philosophies of art? In what ways are their philosophies of art different? (See page 572.)

Internet Activities

1. Want to check out graffiti "art"? Consult the following site, which features a collection of more than 3,000 examples of graffiti gathered from around the world. Be careful, though; some graffiti may contain offensive language or images.

   www.graffiti.org

2. The Perré twins, Davide and Raoul, are among the hundreds every year who flock to New York City to try their hand at graffiti. When the Perrés first decided to make the trip from their native Germany, they consulted a website called "Art Crimes: The Writing on the Wall," which appears at www.graffiti.org and is known in their circle as the "international graffiti yellow pages." Visit the site and briefly summarize your findings.

REVIEW TEST: *Context Clue Practice Using Textbook Material*

Use the context to determine the meaning of the italicized word(s).

1. What are the odds that you'll be involved in some kind of violent act within the next seven days? 1 out of 10? 1 out of 100? 1 out of 1,000? 1 out of 10,000? According to George Gerbner, the answer you give may have more to do with how much TV you watch than with the actual risk you face in the week to come. Gerbner, former dean of the Annenberg School of Communication at the University of Pennsylvania, claims that heavy television users develop an exaggerated belief in "a mean and scary world." The violence they see on

the screen *cultivates* a social *paranoia* that resists notions of trustworthy people or safe environments. (p. 385)

cultivates: _____

paranoia: _____

2. On any given week, two-thirds of the major characters in prime-time programs are caught up in some kind of violence. Heroes are just as involved as villains, yet there is great inequality as to age, race, and gender of those on the receiving end of physical force. Old people and children are harmed at a much greater rate than young or middle-aged adults. In the pecking order of "victimage," blacks and Hispanics are killed or beaten more than their Caucasian counterparts. Gerbner notes that it's risky to be "other than clearly white." It's also dangerous to be female. The opening lady-in-distress scene is a favorite dramatic device to *galvanize* the hero into action. And finally, blue-collar workers "get it in the neck" more often than white-collar executives. (p. 387)

galvanize: _____

3. Not surprisingly, more women than men are afraid of dark streets. But for both sexes the fear of victimization *correlates* with time spent in front of the tube. People with heavy viewing habits tend to overestimate criminal activity, believing it to be ten times worse than it really is. In actuality, muggers on the street *pose* less bodily threat than injury from cars. (p. 389)

correlates: _____

pose: _____

4. Those with heavy viewing habits are suspicious of other people's motives. They subscribe to statements that warn people to expect the worst:

"Most people are just looking out for themselves."

"In dealing with others, you can't be too careful."

"Do unto others before they do unto you."

Gerbner calls this *cynical* mind-set the "mean world syndrome."

The Annenberg evidence suggests that the minds of heavy TV viewers become *fertile* ground for *sowing* thoughts of danger. (p. 389)

cynical: _____

fertile: _____

sowing: _____

5. Gerbner also explains the constant viewer's greater *apprehension* by the process of *resonance*. Many viewers have had at least one firsthand experience with physical violence—armed robbery, rape, bar fight, mugging, auto crash, military combat, or a lover's quarrel that became vicious. The actual *trauma* was bad enough. But he thinks that a repeated symbolic portrayal on the TV screen can cause the viewer to replay the real-life experience over and over

in his or her mind. Constant viewers who have experienced physical violence get a double dose. (p. 391)

apprehension: _____

resonance: _____

trauma: _____

6. Because advertising rates are tied directly to a program's share of the market, television professionals are experts at gaining and holding attention. Social critics *decry* the *gratuitous* violence on television, but Stanford psychologist Albert Bandura denies that aggression is unrelated to the story line. The scenes of physical violence are especially compelling because they suggest that violence is a preferred solution to human problems. Violence is presented as a strategy for life. (p. 369)

decry: _____

gratuitous: _____

7. On every type of program, television draws in viewers by placing attractive people in front of the camera. There are very few overweight bodies or pimply faces on TV. When the *winsome* star roughs up a few hoods to help the lovely young woman, aggression is given a positive cast.

winsome: _____

8. Using violence in the race for ratings not only draws an attentive audience, it transmits responses that we, as viewers, might never have considered before. The media expand our repertoire of behavioral options far beyond what we would discover by trial and error and in ways more varied than we would observe in people we know. Bandura says it's fortunate that people learn from *vicarious* observation, since mistakes could prove costly or fatal. Without putting himself at risk, Tyler Richie, a 10-year-old boy, is able to discover that a knife fighter holds a switchblade at an inclined angle of forty-five degrees and that he jabs up rather than lunging down. We hope that Ty will never have an occasion to put his knowledge into practice. (p. 370)

vicarious: _____

9. We observe many forms of behavior in others that we never perform ourselves. Without sufficient motivation, Ty may never imitate the violence he sees on TV. Bandura says that the effects of TV violence will be greatly *diminished* if a youngster's parents punish or disapprove of aggression. Yet Ty also shares responsibility for his own actions. (p. 371)

diminished:_____

Paragraphs in items 1–9 from Em Griffin, *A First Look at Communication Theory*, 6th ed., New York: McGraw-Hill, 2006.

● TEST-TAKING TIP

After the Test Is Returned

After taking a test, think about what happened. Was it what you expected and prepared for? In what ways did it surprise you? Did it cover both lecture and textbook material? Or focus on one or the other? Think about how to change your approach to the course and the next test to take into account what you learned from the format of this test.

At some point, you will get your test back. Or you could ask to see it. This is another opportunity for you. Go over the test to see where your weaknesses are. What sorts of questions did you have the most trouble with? Many students have trouble with questions phrased in the negative, such as, Which of the following is not a valid conclusion that can be drawn from the evidence below? Did you have trouble with questions of this sort? If so, try to remedy this deficiency in your test prepa-

ration before the next test. You also need to go back and learn the material better that gave you trouble, because you may see questions about this material again on future tests, such as a midterm or final exam.

If you did poorly on the test, you may want to make an appointment with your instructor to talk about it. Maybe you need to be working with the instructor or a tutor out of class. Or maybe you should become part of a study group. You might even be taking the course before you're ready for it; maybe you should take some other courses first.

The key point is to treat past tests as learning experiences for what they tell you about your test preparation, how you're doing in the course, and what changes you can make to do better. Above all, maintain a positive attitude.

VOCABULARY   Homonyms and Other Confusing Words (Unit 2)

loose	An adverb or adjective meaning "free or released from fastening or attachment." *The dog was running* loose *in the neighborhood instead of being on a leash.*
lose	A verb meaning "to come to be without." *If G.E. and Honeywell merge, Carol will probably* lose *her job.*
passed	A verb, the past tense of the verb *pass. The quarterback* passed *the ball to the tight end, who ran for a touchdown. The E.S.L. student* passed *the TOEFL exam. My grandfather* passed *away last year.* Each of these sentences uses the word *passed* as a verb expressing action.
past	A noun meaning "former time." *In the* past, *students used typewriters instead of computers.* Also, an adjective meaning "former." *One of our* past *presidents was Harry Truman.* Also, an adverb meaning "going beyond something." *Motel 6 is just* past *the Fashion Square shopping center.*

Think about this sentence: This *past* week has *passed* by quickly.

peace	A noun meaning "freedom from dissension or hostilities." *The United States would like Israelis and Palestinians to agree on terms for* peace.
piece	A noun meaning "a limited portion or quantity of something." *Do you want a big* piece *of pumpkin pie or a small one?*
personal	An adjective meaning "concerning a particular person." *Our* personal *lives are often quite different from our public lives.*
personnel	A noun meaning "the body of persons employed in an organization." *The airline employed a wide variety of* personnel, *including pilots, baggage handlers, and ticketing agents.*

Think about this sentence: Sometimes it is not a good idea to share too much *personal* information with other *personnel* in your office.

rain	A noun meaning "water that falls to earth in drops formed from moisture in the air." *It often seems like we have either too much or too little* rain.
rein	A noun meaning "a leather strap fastened to each end of a bit for guiding or controlling an animal." *The stagecoach driver held on tightly to the horses'* reins.
reign	A noun meaning "period of rule or government by a monarch." *The thousand-year* reign *of kings in France came to an end with the execution of King Louis the XVI.*
right	An adjective meaning "in accordance with what is good, proper, just." *The student circled the* right *answer on the quiz. After two years working as a waitress, Emily made the* right *decision to return to college.*
	Also, an adjective meaning "opposite of left." *At 18 months, Zachary uses his* right *hand to throw a ball.*
	Also, a noun meaning "something that is due to anyone by just claim." *The court gave Carl the* right *to see his daughter on weekends and holidays.*
rite	A noun meaning "a formal ceremony." *Fraternities have increasingly fallen into trouble with school authorities for having initiation* rites *that include hazing.*
write	A verb meaning "to form words or letters; to send a message in writing." *When did you first learn how to* write *your name?*
wright	A combining form meaning "a person who makes or builds something." *William Shakespeare is one of the most famous play*wrights.

Think about this sentence: It is *right* that we should attend the last *rites* of the well-known play*wright*.

stationary	An adjective meaning "not moving." *The cyclist bought a* stationary *bike so that he could practice riding indoors during the winter.*
stationery	A noun meaning "writing paper." *The new bride bought special* stationery *to use for her thank-you notes.*
their	An adjective meaning "possession." *Their apartment was located near the college.*

there	An adverb meaning "direction." *Notice how the word* here *appears in the word* there. *The student union is over* there.
	Also, a pronoun used to begin a sentence or phrase. There *is an e-mail message waiting for you.*
they're	A contraction for "they are." They're *all packed and ready to go on their trip.*

Think about this sentence: *They're* supposed to be in class, so why do I see them over *there* talking with *their* friends.

tortuous	An adjective meaning "full of twists and turns." *Although it can be a grand adventure, rafting the* tortuous *Colorado River can also be dangerous.*
torturous	An adjective meaning "involving great pain or agony." *Prior to the use of local anesthetics, extracting a tooth was a* torturous *business.*
vain	An adjective meaning "having an excessively high opinion of oneself." *Carly Simon wrote a well-known song titled "You're So* Vain." *Supposedly it's about Mick Jagger of* The Rolling Stones.
	Also, an adjective meaning "futile." *The joint rescue effort was a* vain *attempt to free the sailors trapped in the submarine.*
vein	A noun meaning "any blood vessel that carries blood back to the heart from some part of the body." *Surface* veins *are often visible just under the skin.*
vane	A noun, a short form of weather *vane.* *The weather* vane *indicated the direction the wind was blowing.*
weather	A noun meaning "the state of the atmosphere with respect to wind, temperature, cloudiness, etc." *The dry* weather *during the summer led to many forest fires.*
whether	A conjunction used to introduce two or more alternatives. *It makes no difference to me* whether *or not he comes to the party.*
who	A subjective pronoun meaning "what person or persons or which person or persons." *I don't believe you did that paper all by yourself.* Who *helped you?* (Here *who* is the subject of the sentence.)
whom	A pronoun used as the object of a verb or preposition. *To* whom *do you want to give the money?* (Here *whom* is an object of the preposition *to*.) *Whom will you meet after the game.* (Here *you* is the subject of the sentence and *whom* is the direct object of the verb *meet*.)
who's	A contraction of "who is." Who's *going with me to the movie tonight?*
whose	A possessive adjective meaning "done by whom or which or having to do with whom or which." Whose *car is this? Your lights are on! The Ford F-150 is a truck* whose *popularity is never in doubt.*
your	A possessive adjective meaning "belonging to you or done by you." Your *classes have been scheduled for mornings only, so that you can work in the afternoons.*
you're	A contraction for "you are." You're *on the list to receive tickets to the rock concert.*

■ Homonym Quiz

Fill in the blanks with an appropriate homonym.

1. The _____ department can't release _____ information.
   personal/personnel   personal/personnel

2. I don't like to teach in that classroom because the desks are all _____.
   stationary/stationery

3. You just got here. _____ not already thinking about leaving, are you?
   Your/You're

4. _____ going to do the grocery shopping this week?
   Who's/Whose

5. I found _____ car keys under the sofa cushion.
   your/you're

6. I don't know _____ the gym is open on Labor Day or not.
   weather/whether

7. Tina pleaded in _____ to get Sara taken away from her abusive mother.
   vain/vein/vane

8. The road into the mountains was becoming increasingly _____.
   tortuous/torturous

9. Farmers are worried about their crops because of too little _____.
   rain/rein/reign

10. How could you _____ your lunch money? You just had it in your hand.
    loose/lose

Write a sentence of your own using *passed* correctly.

_____

Now that you have studied the vocabulary in Unit 2, practice your new knowledge by completing the crossword puzzle on the following page.

Vocabulary 2

ACROSS CLUES

1. _____ car are we going to take?

2. Juan and Luz Garza purchased _____ new home in December.

3. Boot Camp is considered a _____ of passage for soldiers.

8. Objects are _____ unless moved.

9. The bus passengers were scared when the bus began its descent down the _____ mountain road.

11. The _____ treaty ending World War II was signed aboard the U.S.S. *Missouri.*

13. The _____ manager at Hewlett-Packard hired several new computer technicians.

16. Some people don't believe it matters _____ we have a Republican or a Democrat in the White House.

17. Is _____ going to be a test on homonyms tomorrow?

21. The cowboy saw a snake and pulled on his horse's _____.

23. _____ going to win the World Series this year?

24. What are you going to do if you _____ your cleaning deposit on the apartment?

25. Some people think that "might makes _____."

DOWN CLUES

1. Arthur Miller, who wrote *Death of a Salesman*, is a famous play _____.

4. Before the invention of the Aqua-Lung, diving was _____.

5. Jacob's uncle _____ away at the age of 90.

6. You might want to go to a _____ store to buy school supplies.

7. Katie hoped her _____ tooth would fall out quickly because she wanted money from the tooth fairy.

10. Queen Elizabeth II has had a long _____.

12. The _____ outside was unbearably hot and humid.

14. The candidate admitted that he had made mistakes in the _____.

15. You need to supply a list of _____ references when you apply for a job.

18. *Did Rosa's mother _____ from Peru or Colombia?

19. _____s carry blood back to the heart.

20. The weather _____ indicated a strong wind from the north.

22. _____ chances of doing well in college are better if you attend class regularly.

23. _____ was our most intelligent president?

*Answer found in Homonyms (Vocabulary Unit 1).

Transition Words and Patterns of Organization

The Cardsharps (1594) BY MICHELANGELO MERISI DA CARAVAGGIO

Kimbell Art Museum, Fort Worth, TX. Photo: Erich Lessing/Art Resource, NY.

View and Reflect

1. What is the man in the background doing with his right hand?
2. What is the man to the right side of the picture doing behind his back?
3. What is the person to the left of the picture doing? Is he aware of what the other two people are doing?
4. What are your feelings about what's happening in the painting?

TRANSITION WORDS

When you are reading, it is important to pay close attention to **transition words.** These special words show the relationships between ideas within sentences and within paragraphs. Just as good drivers learn to watch the road ahead closely, using signposts or markers to make their trips easier and safer, good readers learn to pay attention to the author's transition words, making the writing clearer and more comprehensible.

Look at the sentences below. The addition of a transition word signaling a contrast makes a big difference in our ability to understand Juan's situation.

1. Juan was very eager to buy a new home. The thought of leaving the familiar surroundings of his apartment filled him with dread.

2. Juan was very eager to buy a new home. *However,* the thought of leaving the familiar surroundings of his apartment filled him with dread.

The first example doesn't really make a lot of sense. If Juan is so eager to buy a home, why is he filled with dread? The addition of the transition word in the second sentence makes the situation clear. Although Juan wants to buy a home, he is understandably reluctant to give up his safe and comfortable surroundings.

Now look at these two sentences:

1. Trent did poorly in his math classes. He decided to switch his major to economics.

2. *Because* Trent did poorly in his math classes, he decided to switch his major to economics.

The first example makes us guess at the relationship between the two sentences. The addition of the transition word clarifies this relationship.

Below is a list of transition words, divided into groups by the information they convey. Review this list and then complete the exercises that follow.

TRANSITION WORDS

Words that can be used to show **classification or division (categories):**

break down	combine, combination	lump
category, categorize	divide, division	split
class and subclass	group, grouping	type
classify, classification	kind	

Words that can be used to show **cause-and-effect** relationships:

as a consequence	due to	result, resulting
as a result	for	since
because	for this reason	so
begin	hence	then
bring(s) about	lead(s) to	therefore
consequently	reaction	thus

continued

TRANSITION WORDS (continued)

Words that can be used to show **comparison:**

all	both	like
and	in comparison	likewise
as	just as	similar, similarly

Words that can be used to show **contrast:**

although, though	(in) (by) contrast	on the other hand
but	in opposition	rather than
despite	instead	opposite
even so	nevertheless	unlike
however	on the contrary	yet

Words that can be used to show **steps in a process:**

after	finally	preceding
afterward(s)	first, second, third	process
at last	later	step
at this point	next	subsequently
at this stage	now	then

Words that can be used to show **examples:**

(for) example	specific	(to) demonstrate
(for) instance	specifically	(to) illustrate, illustration
(in) particular	such as	
particularly		

Words that can be used to **define:**

call, called	describe(s), described	refer(s) to
concept	label	term, terminology
define(s), defined	mean(s), meaning	
definition	name	

Words that can be used to show **chronological order:**

after	during	in the year(s)
always	earlier	later
any month (May, etc.)	era, period	next
any season (winter, etc.)	finally	preceding, previous
any time (12:00, etc.)	first, second, etc.	presently
any year (2003, etc.)	following	soon
at last	frequently	then
before	immediate, immediately	until
currently	in the meantime	when

Exercise 1: Using Transition Words

Directions: Insert the appropriate transition word into the following sentences. Be sure your completed sentences make sense.

1. The tendency to explain most events in terms of oneself or one's environment is (definition) _____ *locus of control.*

2. Developed by psychologist Julian Rotter, the idea is that people fall into either of two (classification or division) _____ : those with internal locus of control perceive that they are mostly responsible for what happens to them (both the good and the bad), while those with external locus of control consider their environment to be responsible.

3. Some evidence suggests that most of us are neither true internals nor true externals (contrast) _____ are a mixture of the two. Thus, we tend to see ourselves as responsible for our *successes* (contrast) _____ attribute our *failures* to our environment.

4. (example) _____, football players explain a win as being due to their athletic skills but blame the condition of the field for a loss.

5. (comparison) _____, in games that combine skill and chance, winners easily attribute their successes to their skill while losers attribute their losses to chance.

6. When I win at Scrabble, it's (cause and effect) _____ of my verbal dexterity; when I lose, it's (cause and effect) _____ "Who could get anywhere with a Q without a U?"

7. Politicians attribute their success to (steps in a process) _____ their hard work, _____ their reputation, and _____ their strategy. They attribute their losses to factors beyond their control.

SOME COMMON PATTERNS OF ORGANIZATION

Writers organize their supporting sentences and ideas using **patterns of organization.** Some common patterns of organization are:

1. Classification and division
2. Cause and effect
3. Examples and illustrations
4. Comparison and contrast
5. Listing
6. Steps in a process
7. Definition
8. Chronological order

A writer's chosen pattern of organization will affect the transition words that are used. In the sections that follow, we will discuss patterns of organization and the relationships between patterns of organization and transition words.

The reading selections in this chapter, dealing with ethical and unethical behavior, will give you an opportunity to study some of these patterns of organization and their associated transition words.

CLASSIFICATION OR DIVISION

Classification is the process of organizing information into categories. A category is created by noticing and defining group characteristics. The categories we create make it easier to analyze, discuss, and draw conclusions.

Often paragraphs are organized using classification. In the paragraphs below, the author organizes lying into three specific categories. This makes it easier for us to understand and remember the information being presented. Read the paragraphs and then study the outline that follows.

Lies, Lies, Lies

"No one means all he says and yet very few say all they mean."

—Henry Adams

St. Augustine identified eight **kinds** of lies, not all of them equally serious but all sins nonetheless. The number Mark Twain came up with, not too seriously, was 869. In practice, there are probably as many lies as there are liars, but lying can be roughly **classified** according to motive and context. No hard boundaries exist between these **categories,** since some lies are told for more than one purpose. Most lies fall within a spectrum of three broad **categories.**

1. *Lies to protect others, or "I love your dress."* Most "little white lies" belong here, well-intentioned deceptions designed to grease the gears of society. In this context, people want to be fooled. No one expects, and few would welcome, searing honesty at a dinner party. And the couple who leaves early, saying the babysitter has a curfew, would not be thanked by the hostess if the truth were told: "Frankly we're both bored to tears."

On rare occasions, lying to protect others can literally be a matter of life and death. Anne Frank survived as long as she did because those sheltering her and her family lied to the Nazis. The French Resistance during World War II could not have operated without deception. Military and intelligence officials will, as a matter of routine, lie to protect secret plans or agents at risk.

2. *Lies in the interest of the liar, or "The dog ate my homework."* Here rest the domains, familiar to everyone, of being on the spot, of feeling guilty, of fearing reprimand, failure, or disgrace, and on the other side of the ledger, of wishing to seem more impressive to others than the bald facts will allow. In this **category,** the liar wants to get away with something. If a lie turneth away wrath, or wins a job, or a date on Saturday night, why not tell it? Or so the theory goes.

3. *Lies to cause harm, or "Trust me on this one."* These are the lies people fear and resent the most, statements that will not only deceive them but also trick them into foolish or ruinous courses of behavior. Curiously, though, lying to hurt people just for the heck or fun of it is probably quite rare. Some perceived advantage prompts most lies. If there is no benefit in telling a lie, most people won't bother to make one up.

Source: From Paul Gray, "Lies, Lies, Lies," *Time,* 10/5/92, pp. 32–35. © 1992 Time Inc. Reprinted by permission.

I. People differ on how many kinds of lies there are (MI)
   A. St. Augustine—8 (MSD)
   B. Mark Twain—869 (MSD)
II. There are three basic categories of lies (MI)
   A. Lies to protect others (MSD)
      1. Little white lies (msd)
      2. Lying to save lives (msd)
         a. Anne Frank (msd)
         b. Military and intelligence officials (msd)
   B. Lies in the interest of the liar (MSD)
      1. Lies to avoid failure and disgrace (msd)
      2. Lies to seem more impressive (msd)
   C. Lies to cause harm (MSD)
      1. Lies to deceive (msd)
      2. Lies to trick (msd)

Exercise 2: Classification and Division

Directions: Fill in the blank with an appropriate transition word from the list below. Some of the transitions words will fit in more than one of the sentences, but use each one only once. Make sure the sentence makes sense with the transition word you choose.

category   classes   classify   combine   divide   grouping   split

1. According to criminologist Albert Cohen, we can _____ young urban males into three general categories.

2. The first _____ is called *corner boy,* because it describes a person who hangs out in the neighborhood with his peers, spending the day in some group activity such as gambling or athletics.

3. We can further _____ young urban males by identifying those individuals who are striving to live up to middle-class standards.

4. This _____ is referred to as *college boy.*

5. The final category, *delinquent boy,* can be _____ into two groups: those who eventually become law-abiding citizens and those who do not.

6. The *college boy* category is the smallest of the _____, while the *corner boy* is the largest.

7. According to Cohen, we can _____ all three groups to form a subculture that has its own norms, beliefs, and values that are distinct from those of the dominant culture.

Information from Freda Adler, et al., *Criminology,* 6th ed., New York: McGraw-Hill, 2008, p. 145.

CAUSE AND EFFECT

In a cause-and-effect relationship, one thing causes another thing to happen. The second event is the effect or result of the first event. Try reading the following anecdote to locate cause-and-effect relationships.

It's Saturday morning. Bob is just about to set off on a round of golf when he real-izes that he forgot to tell his wife that the guy who fixes the washing machine is coming around at noon. **So** Bob heads back to the clubhouse and phones home.

"Hello," says a little girl's voice.

"Hi, honey, it's Daddy," says Bob. "Is Mommy near the phone?"

"No, Daddy. She's upstairs in the bedroom with Uncle Frank."

After a brief pause, Bob says, "But you haven't got an Uncle Frank, honey!"

"Yes, I do, and he's upstairs in the bedroom with Mommy!"

"Okay, **then.** Here's what I want you to do. Put down the phone, run upstairs and knock on the bedroom door and shout to Mommy and Uncle Frank that my car has just pulled up outside the house."

"Okay, Daddy!"

A few minutes later, the little girl comes back to the phone.

"Well, I did what you said, Daddy."

"And what was the **result?**"

"Well, Mommy jumped out of bed with no clothes on and ran around screaming; **then** she tripped over the rug and fell down the front steps and she's just lying there. I think she's dead."

"Oh my God! And what was the **reaction** of Uncle Frank?"

"He jumped out of bed with no clothes on, and **then** he was all scared and **so** he jumped out the back window into the swimming pool. He must have for-gotten that last week you took out all the water to clean it, **so** he hit the bottom of the swimming pool and is just lying there, not moving. He may be dead, too."

There is a long pause, **then** Bob says, "Swimming pool? Is this 854-7039?"

Now complete the followings sentences, inserting the effect of the given cause.

1. Because Bob forgot to tell his wife about the repairman, he _____.

2. Because the little girl informed Mommy and Uncle Frank that Daddy was home, they _____

3. Because Bob called the wrong number, he _____.

Exercise 3: Cause and Effect

Directions: Fill in the blank with an appropriate transition word or phrase from the list below. Some of the transition words will fit in more than one of the sentences, but use each one only once. Make sure the sentence makes sense with the transition word you choose.

as a consequence   as a result   because   cause   therefore

1. _____ of skepticism about the validity of lie detector tests, many employers have turned instead to written "integrity tests."

2. Repeatedly, lie detectors have been proved to be unreliable indicators of lying. _____, the American Psychological Association has ad-opted a resolution stating that the evidence for the effectiveness of polygraphs "is still unsatisfactory."

3. The many sources of possible error in the use of lie detectors _____ operators to make mistakes when trying to judge another person's honesty.

4. _____ U.S. federal law bars employers from using polygraphs as screening devices for most jobs.

5. For now, _____, you can be assured that any secrets you may harbor will remain hidden.

Information from Robert S. Feldman, *Understanding Psychology,* 5th ed., New York: McGraw-Hill, 1999, p. 353.

EXAMPLES AND ILLUSTRATION

A paragraph of examples usually gives a general statement of the main idea and then presents one or more concrete examples or illustrations to provide support for this idea. The terms *example* and *illustration* are often used interchangeably, but an illustration can be thought of as an example that is longer and more involved. A main idea might be supported by only one "illustration." Many writers place the most important or convincing example or illustration either first, as an attention-getter, or last, as a dramatic climax.

The following paragraphs provide an illustration of the main idea that most people are basically trustworthy.

"I think that we may safely trust a good deal more than we do."

—Henry David Thoreau

How about some good news for a change? Something to consider when you are in a people-are-no-darn-good mood?

Here's a phrase we hear a lot: "You can't trust anybody anymore." Doctors and politicians and merchants and salesman. They're all out to rip you off, right?

It ain't necessarily so.

To **demonstrate,** a man named Steven Brill tested the theory, in New York City, with taxicab drivers. Brill posed as a well-to-do foreigner with little knowledge of English. He got into several dozen taxis around New York City to see how many drivers would cheat him. His friends predicted in advance that most would take advantage of him in some way.

One driver out of thirty-seven cheated him. The rest took him directly to his destination and charged him correctly. Several refused to take him when his destination was only a block or two away, even getting out of their cabs to show him how close he already was. The greatest irony of all was that several drivers warned him that New York City was full of crooks and to be careful.

You will continue to read stories of crookedness and corruption—of policemen who lie and steal, doctors who reap where they do not sew, politicians on the take. Don't be misled. They are news because they are the exceptions. The evidence suggests that you can trust a lot more people than you think. The evidence suggests that a lot of people believe that. A recent survey by Gallup indicates that 70 percent of the people believe that most people can be trusted most of the time.

Who says people are no darn good? What kind of talk is that?

Source: From Robert L. Fulghum, *All I Really Need to Know I Learned in Kindergarten,* pp. 59–60. Copyright © 1986, 1988 by Robert L. Fulghum. Used by permission of Random House, Inc.

Exercise 4: Example

Directions: Fill in the blank with an appropriate transition word or phrase from the list below. Some of the transitions will fit in more than one of the sentences, but use each one only once. Make sure the sentence makes sense with the transition you choose.

example   for instance   particular   specifically   such as

1. A variety of strategies are used to steal vehicles for financial gain. _____, the "strip and run" strategy occurs when a thief steals a car, strips it for its parts, and then abandons the vehicle.

2. Another _____ is the "scissors job," which occurs when scissors are jammed into certain ignition locks in mostly American-made cars, allowing the thief to start the car easily.

3. Some strategies involve deceit, _____ the "valet theft," which takes place when a thief dresses and poses as a valet attendant, opens the car door for the driver, takes the keys, and quickly drives away.

4. The "insurance fraud scheme," which occurs when a car owner reports his or her car stolen and hides the car for approximately 30 days, or until after the claim is paid, is another _____ strategy that involves deceit.

5. A combination of motor vehicle theft and robbery is _____ known as "carjacking."

Information from Freda Adler, et al., *Criminology and the Criminal Justice System,* 6th ed., New York: McGraw-Hill, 2008, p. 295.

COMPARISON-CONTRAST

A comparison shows similarities, while a contrast shows differences. Sometimes a writer both compares and contrasts at the same time. In the paragraphs that follow, the author compares and contrasts amateur and professional burglars and burglaries.

"The study of crime begins with the knowledge of oneself."

—Henry Miller

George Rengert and John Wasilchick conducted extensive interviews with sub-urban burglars in an effort to understand their techniques. They found significant **differences** with respect to several factors.

1. *The amount of planning that precedes a burglary.* **Unlike** amateurs, professional burglars plan more.

2. *The extent to which a burglar engages in systematic selection of a home.* Most burglars examine the obvious clues, such as presence of a burglar alarm, a watchdog, mail piled up in the mailbox, and newspapers on a doorstep. **On the other hand,** more experienced burglars look for subtle clues such as closed windows coupled with air conditioners that are turned off.

In addition, Rengert and Wasilchick examined the use of time and place in burglary, and they discovered that time is a critical factor to all burglars, for three reasons.

Both amateur and professional burglars must minimize the time spent in targeted places so as not to reveal an intent to burglarize.

Also, opportunities for burglary occur only when a dwelling is unguarded or unoccupied, usually during daytime. (Many burglars would call in sick so often that they would be fired from their legitimate jobs, **while** others simply quit their jobs because they interfered with their burglaries.)

Further, burglars have "working hours." Many have time available only during a limited number of hours, particularly if they have a legitimate job. One experienced burglar stated that "the best time to do crime is between 8:00 and 9:00 A.M. when mothers are taking the kids to school." **In contrast,** another stated that the best time is in the middle of the afternoon when people are at work.

Source: Information from Freda Adler, et al., *Criminology,* 5th ed., New York: McGraw-Hill, 2004, pp. 219–220.

Exercise 5: Comparison-Contrast

Directions: Fill in the blank with an appropriate transition word from the list below. Some of the transitions will fit in more than one sentence, but use each one only once. Make sure the sentence makes sense with the transition word you choose.

    although   but   despite   even   nevertheless   while   yet

1. Our society seems to endorse one set of beliefs _____ glorifying just the opposite.

2. Examples of this glorification include Al Capone and Jesse James, who are in some ways cultural heroes _____ they were known criminals.

3. We have also glorified business executives, _____ we know that business executives are sometimes exploitative, as in the movie *Wall Street.*

4. We are dismayed by the amount of violence and crime in our society; _____ the television programs that play on these themes are the most popular.

5. _____ the fact that we condemn lying, politicians who tell the truth are rejected by voters.

6. We profess to be a country that cherishes our constitution and due process rights; _____, we clap and cheer in movie theaters when "Dirty Harry" types kill the "bad guys."

Information from Jocelyn M. Pollock, *Ethics in Crime and Justice,* 3rd ed., Belmont, California: Wadsworth, 1998, p. 18.

Exercise 6: Comparison-Contrast

Directions: Compare and contrast Cassatt's *The Boating Party* with Manet's *Boating.* Mary Cassatt painted *The Boating Party* twenty years after Manet's *Boating* and was probably inspired by the earlier work.

The Boating Party (1893–1894).   BY MARY CASSATT

Chester Dale Collection. Image courtesy of the Board of Trustees, National Gallery of Art, Washington, D.C.

Boating (1874).   BY EDOUARD MANET

The Metropolitan Museum of Art, H. O. Havemeyer Collection, Bequest of Mrs. H. O. Havemeyer, 1929 (29.100.15). Image © The Metropolitan Museum of Art.

1. How does each artist frame or draw the viewer's attention to the central characters? Where is the focus in each painting?

2. How would you characterize the women and the men in each of these paintings, their personalities, and their relationship to one another?

3. What does each painting seem to be saying about gender-role stereotypes?

4. If you didn't know which of these works was painted by a man and which was painted by a woman, what would you surmise about the artists' gender? Why?

(From Duane Preble, *Artforms*, 8th ed. Englewood Cliffs, NJ: Prentice-Hall, 2002, p. 455).

STUDY TECHNIQUE 5

Creating a Comparison–Contrast Chart

A comparison-contrast chart, like the one here, shows similarities, differences, or similarities and differences between two or more things. When studying closely related topics or reading texts that use the comparison-contrast pattern of development, consider creating a comparison-contrast chart to help you sort out and remember similarities and differences.

The comparison-contrast chart at right lists the differences and similarities discussed in the excerpt on suburban burglars on page 167. Completing this chart will help you learn the main supporting details discussed in the excerpt.

SUBURBAN BURGLARS
Differences

AMATEURS	PROFESSIONALS
1. Plan less	1. Plan more
2. Examine obvious clues	2. _____

Similarities

1. Both must minimize time spent in targeted places.

2. Opportunities are usually best in the daytime.

3. _____

REVIEW TEST: *Main Ideas, Details, Purpose, Patterns of Organization, Transitions*

Read the following humorous poem and then answer the questions that follow.

BRUSHING UP ON VOCABULARY

Jesse and Frank James outlaws in the nineteenth century who robbed trains and banks in spectacular style. It is believed that Jesse was killed by a member of his own gang.

vaudeville a form of theatrical entertainment popular in the late nineteenth and early twentieth centuries that often included comedians, singers, dancers, and trained animals. Even though skits were short, audiences often pelted the performers with food when they didn't like the act.

Elizabeth Barrett Browning and Robert Browning English poets of the nineteenth century. Elizabeth is best known as the author of the words "How do I love thee? Let me count the ways," Robert is best known for his narrative poems, such as "My Last Duchess."

Crime at Its Best
BY STODDARD KING

Disgusted with crimes that are piffling and messy,
We think of the James brothers, Frankie and Jesse,
Who never degraded the clan of James
By writing "confessions" and signing their names.

When poverty hovered o'er Jesse and Frank,
They saddled their horses and held up a bank,
(A calling in which it is wrong to engage)
But they never appeared on the vaudeville stage.

Though Jesse was tough and his brother was tougher,
They never made readers of newspapers suffer
By reading the sob sisters' sorrowful sobbing
Of how they read Browning before going robbing.
The gang that they worked with was surely a bad one,
But as for smart lawyers, I doubt that they had one;
Insanity dodges they never were pleading,
And that's why their life makes such excellent reading.

A movie rights offer they'd both have resented,
(Provided that movies had then been invented).
So in spite of our virtue, it's hard to suppress
A sneaking affection for Frank and for Jess.

Source: Stoddard King, "Crime at Its Best," from *Norton Book of Light Verse,* edited by Russell Baker, p. 202. Copyright © 1986 Russell Baker. Used by permission of W. W. Norton & Company, Inc.

1. What is the main idea of the poem? _____

_____

2. What specific qualities does the author admire in the James Brothers?

_____

_____

3. What does the author have to say about lawyers? _____

_____

4. What does the title mean? _____

_____

5. What commentary is the author making about our society? _____

_____

6. What is the author's primary purpose—to entertain, to inform, or to persuade?

_____

7. What pattern of development does the poem use? Point out transition words
    that the author used. _____

_____

8. Write a paraphrase of one of the stanzas (in prose), making sure to retain the
    meaning of the poem.

_____

_____

LISTING

When an author simply lists information without regard to order, the pattern of organization is referred to as listing or enumeration. Sometimes, authors use numbers (1, 2, 3), letters (a, b, c), or bullets (•) to point out the individual items in the list. Other times, they say *first, second, third*, etc. or *in addition, next*, or *finally*. Often, a colon will be used as punctuation at the start of a list. A variation of the word *follow* may indicate that a list is about to begin. In the excerpt below, the late columnist Ann Landers lists a series of "lies."

And the Third Biggest Lie Is . . .
BY ANN LANDERS

Dear Readers:
A while back, I was asked to print the three biggest lies in the world. I was able to come up with only two: "I'm from the government and I'm here to help you," and "The check is in the mail."

I asked my readers if they could supply the third biggest lie. Thousands rose to the occasion. The mail was simply wonderful. Here's a sampling:

From Lebanon, Pa.: It's a good thing you came in today. We have only two more in stock.

Sparta, Wis.: I promise to pay you back out of my next paycheck.

Woodbridge, N.J.: Five pounds is nothing on a person with your height.

Harrisburg, Pa.: But officer, I only had two beers.

Hammond, Ind.: You made it yourself? I never would have guessed.

Eau Claire, Wis.: It's delicious, but I can't eat another bite.

Charlotte, N.C.: Your hair looks just fine.

Philadelphia: It's nothing to worry about—just a cold sore.

Mechanicsburg, Pa.: It's a terrific high and I swear you won't get hooked.

Dallas: The river never gets high enough to flood this property.

Manassas, Va.: The delivery is on the truck.

Tacoma, Wash.: Go ahead and tell me. I promise I won't get mad.

Billings, Mont.: You have nothing to worry about, honey. I've had a vasectomy.

Philadelphia: The three biggest lies: I did it. I didn't do it. I can't remember.

Chicago: This car is like brand new. It was owned by two retired schoolteachers who never went anywhere.

Boston: The doctor will call you right back.

Montreal: So glad you dropped by. I wasn't doing a thing.

U.S. Stars and Stripes: You don't look a day over 40.

Washington, D.C.: Dad, I need to move out of the dorm into an apartment of my own so I can have some peace and quiet when I study.

Windsor, Ont.: It's a very small spot. Nobody will notice.

Cleveland: The baby is just beautiful!

New York: The new ownership won't affect you. The company will remain the same.

Holiday, Fla.: I gave at the office.

Lansing, Mich.: You can tell me. I won't breathe a word to a soul.

Huntsville, Ala.: The puppy won't be any trouble, Mom. I promise I'll take care of it myself.

Minneapolis: I'm a social drinker, and I can quit anytime I want to.

Barrington, Ill.: Put the map away. I know exactly how to get there.

Troy, Mich.: You don't need it in writing. You have my personal guarantee.

Greenwich, Conn.: Sorry, the work isn't ready. The computer broke down.

Phoenix: I'll do it in a minute.

Elkhart, Ind.: The reason I'm so late is we ran out of gas.

Scarsdale, N.Y.: Our children never caused us a minute's trouble.

Detroit: This is a very safe building. No way will you ever be burglarized.

Glendale, Calif.: Having a great time. Wish you were here.

Source: "And The Third Biggest Lie is . . ." by permission of Esther P. Lederer and Creators Syndicate, Inc. Used with permission.

STEPS IN A PROCESS

In the steps-in-a-process pattern, something is explained or described in a step-by-step manner. A transition word often introduces each step. Scientific writing commonly follows this pattern. In addition, anyone demonstrating how to make or do something will probably use this pattern.

In the paragraphs that follow, the author gives a step-by-step account of psychologist Lawrence Kohlberg's theory of moral development. The first two paragraphs are outlined for you as an example. Complete the outline of the third paragraph.

According to Lawrence Kohlberg, moral reasoning develops in **three stages.** In the **first stage,** the preconventional level, children's moral rules and moral values consist of do's and don'ts to avoid punishment. A desire to avoid punishment and a belief in the superior power of authorities are the two central reasons for doing what is right. According to the theory, until the ages of 9 to 11, children usually reason at this level. They think, in effect, "If I steal, what are my chances of getting caught and being punished?" According to Kohlberg, most delinquents and criminals reason at the preconventional level.

Most adolescents reason at **stage two,** the conventional **stage. At this stage,** individuals believe in and have adopted the values and rules of society. Moreover, they seek to uphold these rules. They think, in effect, "It is illegal to steal and therefore I should not steal, under any circumstances."

"Those who are too lazy and comfortable to think for themselves and be their own judges obey the laws. Others sense their own laws from within."

—Hermann Hesse

At the postconventional **level, the final stage,** individuals examine customs and social rules according to their own sense of moral principles and duties. They think, in effect, "One must live within the law, but certain ethical principles, such as respect for human rights, supersede the written law when the two conflict." This **level** of moral reasoning is generally seen in adults after the age of 20.

Source: Information from Freda Adler et al., *Criminology,* 6th ed., p. 86. Copyright © 2007 McGraw-Hill Companies, Inc. Used with permission.

I. There are three stages of moral reasoning.
   A. Stage one: the preconventional level
      1. Moral code of do's and don'ts
      2. Two reasons for doing what is right
         a. Avoid punishment
         b. Superior power of authority
      3. Ages 9–11
      4. Delinquents and criminals reason at this level.
   B. Stage two: the conventional stage
      1. Individuals have adopted society's moral code.
      2. Adolescents
   C. _____
      1. Individuals examine customs according to their own sense of moral values.
      2. Personal and ethical principles supersede _____.
      3. Adults after _____.

Exercise 7: Steps in a Process

Directions: Fill in the blank with an appropriate transition word from the list below. Some of the transitions will fit in more than one of the sentences, but use each one only once. Make sure the sentence makes sense with the transition you choose.

final   next   process   second   step   subsequently

Study Links Proficiency in Lying to Teen Popularity

Whether Pinocchio or a president, a liar can remain a beloved figure. In fact, a new research study suggests that the best teenage liars are often the most popular kids.

1. As a first _____, the study, conducted by Robert Feldman, a University of Massachusetts psychologist, looked at the nonverbal behavior of 32 young people ages 11 to 16.

2. At the _____ stage, the young persons' social skills were evaluated, yielding an assessment of their popularity.

3. _____, they were individually videotaped both lying and telling the truth about whether they liked a drink they had been given.

4. As a final step in the _____, 58 college students were asked to watch the videotapes and judge how much each teenager really liked the drink.

5. _____, researchers concluded that girls were better at lying than boys.

6. The _____ analysis showed a strong link between the most socially adept teenagers and the best deceivers.

Study Links Proficiency . . . Information from *The Arizona Republic,* 10/28/00.

DEFINITION

A paragraph that uses definition will clarify or explain a key term. Definitions can be developed by providing dictionary meanings or personal meanings. They can also be developed through examples or by comparing and contrasting the key term with other terms.

In the paragraphs below, the authors of *Criminology* attempt to clarify the meaning of *burglary* by providing concrete illustrations, describing distinguishing characteristics, and comparing and contrasting this word to other, similar words. Read the paragraphs and then study the map that follows.

Burglary

A "burg," in Anglo-Saxon terminology, was a secure place for the protection of one-self, one's family, and one's property. If the burg protects a person from larceny and assault, what protects the burg? The burghers, perhaps. But there had to be a law behind the burghers. And that was the law of burglary, which made it a crime to break and enter the dwelling of another person at night with the intention of committing a crime therein. (Of course it had to be at night, because during the day the inhabitants could defend themselves, or so it was thought.) The common law defined "burglary" as:

> The breaking and entering of the dwelling house of another person at night with the intention to commit a felony or larceny inside

By "breaking," the law **meant** any trespass (unauthorized entry), but usually one accompanied by a forceful act, such as cracking the lock, breaking a windowpane, or scaling the roof and entering through the chimney. The "entering" was complete as soon as the perpetrator extended any part of his or her body into the house in pursuit of the objective of committing a crime in the house. The house had to be a "dwelling," but that **concept** was extended to cover the "curtilage," the attached servants' quarters, carriage houses, and barns. The dwelling also had to be that of "another." And as we mentioned, the event had to occur at "night," which was **defined** as between sundown and sunup.

The most troublesome **term** has always been the "intention to commit a felony or larceny" (even a petty or misdemeanor larceny) inside the premises. How can we know what a burglar intends to do? The best evidence of intent is what the burglar actually does inside the premises. Any crime the burglar commits inside is considered evidence of criminal intention at the moment the burglar broke and entered the dwelling.

Source: Burglary Information from Freda Adler et al., *Criminology,* 6th ed., pp. 309–310. Copyright © 2008 McGraw-Hill Companies, Inc. Used with permission.

"The home of everyone is to him his castle and fortress, as well as his defence against injury and violence, as for his repose."

—Edward Coke

Exercise 8: Definition

Directions: Fill in the blank with an appropriate transition word or phrase from the list below. Some of the transitions will fit in more than one of the sentences, but use each one only once. Make sure the sentence makes sense with the transition you choose.

describe   is called   means   refers to   term

1. The label "amateur thieves" _____ occasional offenders who take advantage of a chance to steal when little risk is involved.

2. This _____ that most "amateur thieves" commit few crimes; some commit only one crime.

3. A person _____ a "professional thief" when he or she makes a career of stealing.

4. The term "professional thief" also is used to _____ persons who take pride in their profession, are imaginative and creative in their work, and accept its risks.

5. The _____ "larceny" refers to theft or stealing and is the most prevalent crime in our society.

STUDY TECHNIQUE 6

Mapping

Mapping is a technique you can use to organize material you are studying. Similar to outlining, it shows how the main points relate to each other. Unlike outlining, however, it is more visual and less formal. Visual learners may find this a more helpful technique than outlining.

The map below shows the major points and how they relate to one another for the excerpt on burglary (page 175).

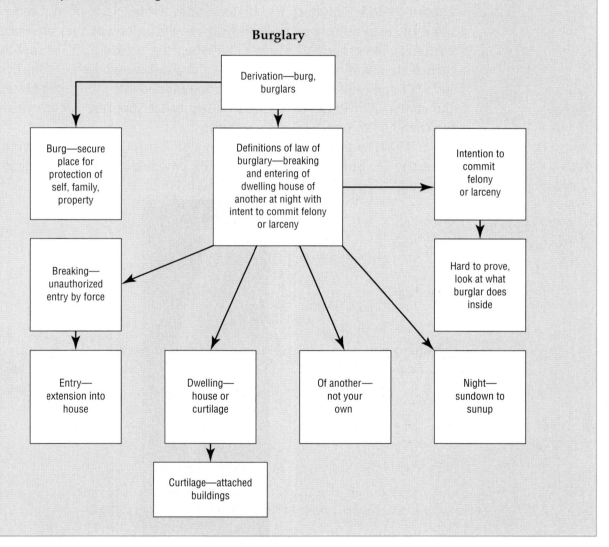

Burglary

Derivation—burg, burglars

Burg—secure place for protection of self, family, property

Definitions of law of burglary—breaking and entering of dwelling house of another at night with intent to commit felony or larceny

Intention to commit felony or larceny

Hard to prove, look at what burglar does inside

Breaking— unauthorized entry by force

Entry— extension into house

Dwelling— house or curtilage

Of another— not your own

Night— sundown to sunup

Curtilage—attached buildings

CHRONOLOGICAL ORDER

The word *chronological* comes from the Greek root *chron*, which means "time." The chronological pattern of organization involves arranging events in the order in which they actually happened. For this reason, historical essays and other articles that are date-oriented are usually organized by this method. Paragraphs written with this pattern are usually very easy to recognize.

The following paragraphs are in the chronological pattern.

Brancusi's Bird: Manufactured Metal or Work of Art

"A work of art is an exaggeration."

—Andre Gide

A trial held in New York City in **1928** demonstrated just how hard it can be to agree on what constitutes "art." Edward Steichen, a prominent American photographer, purchased a bronze sculpture entitled *Bird in Space* from the Romanian artist Constantin Brancusi, who was living in France. In **1926,** Steichen imported the sculpture to the United States, whose laws do not require payment of customs duty on original works of art as long as they are declared to customs on entering the country. But when the customs official saw the *Bird,* he balked. It was not art he said: it was "manufactured metal." Steichen's protests fell on deaf ears. The sculpture was admitted into the United States under the category of "Kitchen Utensils and Hospital Supplies," which meant that Steichen had to pay $600 in import duty.

In **1927,** with the financial backing of Gertrude Vanderbilt Whitney, an American sculptor and patron of the arts, Steichen appealed the ruling of the

Bird in Space (1923),
CONSTANTIN BRANCUSI

The Metropolitan Museum of Art, Bequest of Florene M. Schoenborn, 1995. Image © The Metropolitan Museum of Art.

customs official. The ensuing trial received a great deal of publicity. Witnesses discussed whether the *Bird* was a bird at all, whether the artist could make it a bird by calling it one, whether it could be said to have characteristics of "bird-ness," and so on. The conservative witnesses refused to accept the work as a bird because it lacked certain biological attributes, such as wings and tail feathers. The more progressive witnesses pointed out that it had birdlike qualities: upward movement and a sense of spatial freedom. The court decided in favor of the plaintiff. The *Bird* was declared a work of art, and Steichen finally got his money back.

In **today's** market a Brancusi *Bird* would sell for millions of dollars.

Information from Laurie S. Adams, *Art Across Time,* 3rd ed., New York: McGraw-Hill, 2007, p. 5.

STUDY TECHNIQUE 7

Time Lines

A time line is a specialized way of organizing information. Time lines are useful when material needs to be organized chronologically by dates, such as in a history class, although they could also be useful in almost any other class.

All that a time line does is list dates in chronological order along a line and then assign information to the dates. You can make a time line vertically (up and down) or horizontally (across). How specific you want to make a time line (that is, the number of dates and the amount of information you assign to each date) depends on the reading material and your needs.

Complete the time line with information from "Brancusi's Bird." Additional historical dates have been added to put the information in perspective.

1876   Birth date of Constantin Brancusi

1904   Brancusi moves to Paris

1926   _____

1927   _____

1928   _____

1957   Brancusi dies

1973   Steichen dies

Exercise 9: Chronological Order

Directions: Fill in the blank with an appropriate transition word from the list below. Some of the transitions will fit in more than one of the sentences, but use each one only once. Make sure the sentence makes sense with the transition you choose.

currently   finally   first   next   previously   then

1. _____, at Disney World, home of Donald Duck, Mickey and Minnie Mouse, Goofy, and their friends, illegal behavior is successfully controlled in an environment that does not have the sterile, fortresslike appearance so often associated with security.

2. The _____ security measure occurs in the parking lot with advice to lock your car and remember that you have parked at a particular lot—for example, "Donald Duck 1."

3. _____, with friendly greetings of "Have a good time," watchful eyes surround visitors on the rubber-wheeled train into Never-Never Land.

4. The _____ line of defense is crowd control, which is omnipresent, yet unobtrusive, with signposts guiding you through the maze of monorails, rides, and attractions.

5. Physical barriers have _____ been strategically placed to prevent injury and regulate the movement of adults and children alike.

6. _____, Mickey Mouse and Goofy actors monitor movements, making Disney World one of the safest locations in the United States.

REVIEW TEST: *Identifying Patterns of Organization in Textbook Material*

Identify the pattern of organization by noting the transitional words.

1. Over the years, television has changed many sports. For example, the World Series is now played in chilly October temperatures at night on the East Coast and in late afternoon on the West Coast, thereby ensuring that the games will be shown on television during prime time in the eastern and central time zones. In another instance, professional basketball playoffs now include 16 of the 27 NBA teams, and the season stretches into June, providing TV with more high-rated games. And the National Hockey League has expanded the pauses in play following certain penalties to more than 30 seconds to allow time for commercials.

   Pattern: _____

   Clues: _____

2. For years, the National Association of Broadcasting (NAB) enforced restrictions on liquor advertising. First, NAB decreed that no hard liquor could be advertised on radio or television. Next, broadcasters were prohibited from showing anyone drinking beer or wine in a commercial; glasses could be hoisted, but no sipping was allowed. Finally, it was decided that currently active sports figures could not appear in beer or wine commercials.

   Pattern: _____

   Clues: _____

3. The tendency to blame the media for society's woes seems to be escalating. The general public seems convinced that media influences are creating and fostering antisocial behavior and are the reason for all that is wrong with society. These arguments are supported by members of Congress who have tried to curtail the violence on television, blaming it for the increase in violence in our cities. The end result was the introduction of the V-chip in television sets to allow parents to control the types of programs their children watch.

   Items 1–3, 7 from James R. Wilson, *Mass Media Mass Culture*, 5th ed., New York: McGraw-Hill, 2001, pp. 31, 361, 6, 357, 217, 218. Copyright © 2001 McGraw-Hill. Reprinted by permission of The McGraw-Hill Companies, Inc.

   Pattern: _____

   Clues: _____

4. We can divide readers into three types. The most enthusiastic readers are known as bibliophiles—book lovers who consume 50 or more books a year. Bibliophiles started the phenomenon of neighborhood book groups, in which friends and acquaintances gather to discuss a book that they've all read. The second category is the casual reader—those who enjoy reading but find the time to read only a few books a year. The last category, required readers, might read extensively, but they read only what they have to for their job or studies. Many students at both the high school and college levels are required readers. Textbook sales would be nonexistent without students, and the sales of classic literature are highly dependent on college students.

   Paragraph from George Rodman, *Mass Media in a Changing World*, 2/e, p. 90. Copyright © 2008 McGraw-Hill Companies, Inc. Used with permission.

   Pattern: _____

   Clues: _____

5. The largest circulating newspaper in the United States happens to be the *National Enquirer*. This popular publication's success can be traced back to 1952, when Generoso (Gene) Pope purchased the *New York Enquirer*. He immediately began filling the newspaper with stories about crime, sex, and violence. In 1958, Pope expanded the *Enquirer* into a national publication and began selling it in supermarkets. He toned down the sex and violence to appeal to a broader audience and began focusing on stories about celebrity gossip, government waste, psychic predictions, life-threatening accidents, and medical advice. At the conclusion of the O. J. Simpson murder trial in 1995, many news reporters conceded that the *Enquirer* had probably covered the story better than anyone else. Much of that credibility was lost in the final years of the 1990s as the *Enquirer* continued to print weekly stories accusing numerous people of being responsible for the death of JonBenet Ramsey of Colorado. Today, *National Enquirer* reporters are among the highest paid in the nation, and the paper covers major news events with teams of journalists and photographers.

   Paragraph from James R. Wilson, *Mass Media, Mass Culture*, 5/e, pp. 175–176. Copyright © 2001 McGraw-Hill Companies, Inc. Used with permission.

   Pattern: _____

   Clues: _____

6. People are defined as illiterate if they can't read because they never learned how. Some experts suggest that as many as one in five Americans are functionally illiterate. This term refers to those who may have some basic skills but cannot read even a simple children's story with comprehension. Alliterates are defined as those who can read but don't. They include people who dislike the act of reading and people who just never picked up the habit. Some experts estimate that as many as 15 percent of Americans are alliterates. According to Gallup polls, fewer books are read in the United States, per capita, than in any other English-speaking country.

   Paragraph from George Rodman, *Mass Media in a Changing World*, 2/e, p. 90.

   Pattern: _____

   Clues: _____

7. Getting a person to buy or rebuy a product involves far more than simply running an ad in a newspaper or a commercial on television. There are three main steps in the selling process: awareness, trial, and reinforcement. *Awareness* is the easiest step. Through repetition and other advertising techniques, consumers are made aware that a product exists. *Trial*, the second step, involves getting people to try the product by sending free samples through the mail, handing them out in stores, giving away discount coupons, and offering price reductions. *Reinforcement* is the necessary third step to persuade users to buy the product again.

   Pattern: _____

   Clues: _____

8. Buffalo herds played a crucial role in most Plains Indians' culture—providing almost all the basic necessities. Indians ate the buffalo meat, made clothing and teepees out of the hides, used the fats for cosmetics, fashioned the bones into tools, made thread from the sinews, and even burned dried buffalo droppings as fuel. To settlers, however, the buffalo were barriers to western expansion. The herds interfered with construction, knocked over telegraph poles and fences, and could derail trains during stampedes.

   Other cultural differences caused misunderstandings between settlers and Native Americans. Among Anglo-Americans, capitalism fostered competition and frontier living promoted individualism. On the other hand, Plains Indians lived in tribes based on kinship ties. As members of an extended family that included distant cousins, Indians were taught to place the welfare of the group over the interest of the individual. The emphasis within a tribe was on cooperation rather than competition. Some tribes might be richer than other tribes, but there was seldom a large gap between the rich and the poor within a tribe.

   Another major cultural difference between the newly arriving settlers and the Plains Indians was their attitudes toward the land. Most Native Americans had no concept of private property. Chief Joseph of the Nez Perce eloquently expressed the view: "The earth was created by the assistance of the sun, and it should be left as it was. . . . The country was made without lines of demarcation, and it is no man's business to divide it."

   Native Americans refused to draw property lines and borders because of how they viewed the place of people in the world. Unlike Whites who tended to see land, plants, and animals as resources to be exploited, Native Americans, stressed the unity of all life—and its holiness.

   Paragraph from James Kirby Martin, *America and Its People,* 5/e, p. 443.

   Pattern: _____

   Clues: _____

ADDITIONAL TRANSITION WORDS

Summary and Conclusion	Spatial Order
finally	above
hence	below
in brief	beyond
in conclusion	front
in short	left
in summary	near
over all	next to
so	on top
therefore	right
thus	underneath
to conclude	center
to sum up	

Emphasis	Concession
as indicated	although
as noted	despite
certainly	even though
here again	in spite of
It's important to remember	
once again	
to emphasize	
to repeat	
truly	
unquestionably	
without a doubt	

Reversal	Addition
granted that	again
instead	also
nevertheless	and
still	another
unlike	as well as
yet	besides
	further
	furthermore
	in addition
	moreover
	too

While lists of transition words are helpful, the groupings of the words given in this section are not perfect, and many of these words may be used in more than one category. The only reliable way to determine the function of a transition word is by studying the context of the sentence and the paragraph.

CHEATING

When asked why they cheated, college students generally absolved themselves of responsibility, blaming their actions on the instructor or fellow students. Their responses also reflect concern about grades and time pressures.

COLLEGE STUDENTS' TOP 10 REASONS FOR CHEATING

Rank	Reason for Cheating
1	The instructor assigns too much material.
2	The instructor left the room during the test.
2*	A friend asked me to cheat, and I couldn't say no.
4	The instructor doesn't seem to care if I learn the material.
5	The course information seems useless.
6	The course material is too hard.
6*	Everyone else seems to be cheating.
8	I'm in danger of losing a scholarship because of low grades.
9	I don't have time to study because I'm working to pay for school.
10	The people sitting around me made no effort to protect their work.

*Tied

SOURCE: Listing based on Valerie J. Haynes, George M. Diekhoff, Emily E. LaBeff, and Robert E. Clark, "College Cheating: Immaturity, Lack of Commitment and the Neutralizing Attitude," *Research in Higher Education,* 1986, Vol. 25, No. 4, pp. 347–354.

CALVIN AND HOBBES © 1993 Watterson. Reprinted by permission of Universal Press Syndicate. All rights reserved.

Internet Activity

Consult either of the following websites to get updated information on the ethical beliefs and practices of high school and college students.

www.academicintegrity.org (Center for Academic Integrity)

www.josephsoninstitute.org (Josephson Institute of Ethics)

If available, print a recent ethics survey or report card.

SELECTION

*"Now Petroski can spend hours making points
about pencils."*

GETTING THE PICTURE

To conclude the section on transition words and patterns of organization, read this selection about the pencil, an object so commonplace that we take it for granted.

According to Mark Getlein, author of *Gilbert's Living with Art*, the pencil has been responsible for more drawings than any other medium. This is because pencils are cheap, readily available, and easy to work with, *and* mistakes can be erased. Despite the pencil's lowly status, Getlein says that some of the most beautiful drawings we know of have been created with graphite pencil.

BIO-SKETCH

Lewis J. Lord is a former writer for *U.S. News & World Report*. Lewis Lord has made a career out of writing about objects that seem trivial but that have had a tremendous impact on our lives, such as the paper clip, the zipper, and the aluminum beverage can. His previous books include *Paperboy: Confessions of a Future Engineer, Invention by Design,* and *The Evolution of Useful Things.*

BRUSHING UP ON VOCABULARY

Mikado a comic opera by Gilbert and Sullivan about a Japanese tailor who becomes an executioner.

Ernest Hemingway a twentieth-century American author whose memorable books include *The Old Man and the Sea, The Sun Also Rises,* and *For Whom the Bell Tolls.*

John Steinbeck a twentieth-century American author best known for *Of Mice and Men, The Grapes of Wrath,* and *East of Eden.*

Manhattan Project the code name for the U.S. project to develop an atomic bomb during World War II.

Dixie a term referring to the southern states in the United States. The term derives from the song "Dixie," which was written by a northerner but was played to generate enthusiasm for the southern cause during the Civil War.

THE LITTLE ARTIFACT THAT COULD by LEWIS J. LORD

1   There once was a time when Professor Henry Petroski regarded the pencil as . . . well . . . just a pencil. He used it a lot, but what he knew about it would not blunt the soft tip of a Dixon Ticonderoga No. 1. Despite two decades as an engineer, he was not even aware of how the pencil got its lead, of how graphite was sandwiched between two pieces of wood. "It's something I never thought about," he confesses. "People don't think much about pencils."

2   Now Petroski can spend hours making points about pencils. For instance, he can tell you how to judge a pencil by its ferule, the metal that connects the wood and the eraser ("the best are brass, with painted stripes") . . . how New York's Eagle Pencil Company, one day after Pearl Harbor, renamed its best-selling Mikado the Mirado . . . how Ernest Hemingway got in the mood for writing by sharpening dozens of No. 2s . . . how Abraham Lincoln, whose tariff policy protected the infant U.S. pencil industry, reportedly wrote the Gettysburg Address with a pencil made in Germany. And for etymology's sake, he can report that *pencil* derives from *peniculus,* a Latin word for brush.

"We only think when we are confronted with a problem."

—John Dewey

3   Petroski first contemplated the pencil when he read a *Journal of Applied Mechanics* article on BOPP's, or broken-off pencil points. Its author, in reporting how BOPP's occur, raised one question that went unanswered. Why do pencil points break at a slant rather than straight across the lead? As a civil-engineering professor at Duke University specializing in why things fail, Petroski considered the problem a personal challenge, which he eventually solved in an equation-packed article of his own. But he didn't stop there. The more he examined the lowly pencil, the more he perceived it as a wonder, as complex and as grand as a space shuttle or the Golden Gate Bridge. He emerged with a theme that he wanted to share with his students and the world: "To scrutinize the trivial can be to discover the monumental."

4   No academic journal has room for all that Petroski can say about one of civilization's most common artifacts, but his book, *The Pencil,* makes a start. In 434 pages, Petroski establishes the pencil as a paradigm of design and invention in the history of engineering. His pet claim is that the pencil, which creates and reshapes ideas, is mightier than the pen, which makes them permanent.

5   Petroski's pencil pokes through the crannies of American life. In the early 1900s, for instance, some educators opposed the addition of erasers to pencils. "The easier errors may be corrected," they argued, "the more errors will be made." The barons of the pencil industry were equally rigid in their labor policies. Jersey City's Joseph Dixon Crucible Company, when it made one third of America's pencils in the 1870s, carefully counted each day's output. If one pencil was missing from a factory room, every employee in that room was to be fired.

6   Yet, for engineers, the main story is the pursuit of a better pencil, a contest that has been international almost from the start. England ruled as the world's

first pencil power, in the 17th and 18th centuries, simply because it possessed the best-known source of graphite, commonly called lead. When France and England went to war in 1793, the French ran out of pencils. So Paris hired a young engineer, Nicolas-Jacques Conté, to make a new kind of lead—an effort that Petroski likens to the Manhattan Project of World War II. Conté's invention—a baked mixture of graphite, dust, clay and water—is still the world's basic pencil lead. Yet it was Germany that cashed in on Conté's technology and dominated the market until recently.

7   America emerged as a pencil power 100 years ago partly because the world's best pencil wood—hard to warp or splinter—came from red cedars of the South. The advantage faded as those trees vanished, and pencil-makers resorted to sending "cedar cruisers" across Dixie to buy cedar stumps, fence posts, and old planks from barns. Eventually, other woods were dyed and perfumed to look and smell like cedar from Georgia and Florida. As usual, America had the best ads. Eagle's Mirado went "30 miles for a nickel," and Eberhard Faber's Van Dyke was "good to the last half-inch."

8   John Steinbeck, who blunted 60 pencils in 6 hours of writing a day, looked for years for "the perfect pencil." Some days, his soft Blackwings "floated over the paper just wonderfully." Other days, they fractured and he went to a harder point, the Mongol No. $2\frac{3}{8}$. The pencil that Steinbeck sought will never exist, Petroski says, "because no artifact is perfect." But the professor describes many pencils as very good. Four brands with striped ferules—Mongol, Mirado, Velvet, and Ticonderoga—are deemed America's best yellow models, rivals of the costlier Blackwing.

9   The impending death of the pencil has been forecast for decades, first with the arrival of the ballpoint pen, then with the word processor. But the world pencil market—14 billion pencils a year, including 2 billion made in the U.S.— keeps growing. America's challenge, Petroski says, is staying ahead of high-quality imports from Europe, Japan, and the third world, including "places that were making baskets a half-century ago."

10   What about the pencil of the future? Some say it is already here, made of plastic. But Petroski likens the plastic pencil to New Coke. "It doesn't have the right feel. Who wants a pencil that bends?" His bet is on wood.

From Lewis J. Lord, "The Little Artifact That Could," *U.S. News & World Report,* January 22, 1990. Copyright © 1990 U.S. News & World Report, L.P. Reprinted with permission.

COMPREHENSION CHECKUP

Multiple Choice

Write the letter of the correct answer in the blank provided.

_____ 1. The author's primary purpose in writing this selection was to
   a. entertain the reader
   b. persuade people to buy pencils
   c. provide information about Petroski and the history of the pencil
   d. discuss the impending "death" of the pencil

_____ 2. The organizational pattern of paragraph 2 is primarily
   a. definition
   b. compare and contrast
   c. chronological order
   d. examples

_____ 3. The words *derives from* in paragraph 2 indicate
   a. cause and effect
   b. definition
   c. conclusion
   d. concession

_____ 4. In paragraph 3, the words *lowly* and *grand* and also the words *trivial* and *monumental* are
   a. homonyms
   b. antonyms
   c. synonyms
   d. rhymes

_____ 5. In paragraph 5, the transition words *for instance* indicate
   a. addition
   b. reversal
   c. spatial order
   d. example

_____ 6. In paragraph 6, the transition word *yet* indicates
   a. addition
   b. concession
   c. emphasis
   d. reversal

_____ 7. In paragraph 6, what kind of relationship does the following statement indicate: "[The] French ran out of pencils. So Paris hired a young engineer . . . to make a new kind of lead"?
   a. compare/contrast
   b. cause/effect
   c. example
   d. classification/division

_____ 8. The word *ferrules* in paragraph 8 means
   a. the wooden part of the pencil
   b. the eraser
   c. the graphite
   d. the metal strip around the eraser

_____ 9. You could conclude from this selection that
   a. the pencil will be replaced by the computer
   b. wood pencils will probably be around for a long time to come
   c. mechanical pencils are superior to wooden pencils
   d. pens are superior to pencils because ink is more permanent

_____ 10. The meaning of *artifact* as used in the selection is
   a. a handmade object belonging to an earlier time or cultural stage
   b. an object made by human hands; a simple tool
   c. an object found at an archaeological excavation
   d. a non-natural structure accidentally introduced into something being studied

True or False

Indicate whether the statement is true or false by writing T or F in the blank provided.

_____T_____ 11. More pencils are made abroad than in the United States.

_____F_____ 12. Petroski is identified as a student at Duke University.

_____F_____ 13. The Mikado pencil was made in Japan.

_____T_____ 14. Steinbeck sometimes made use of 60 pencils in a single day.

_____T_____ 15. Some educators did not welcome the addition of erasers to the pencil.

Vocabulary Matching

Match the vocabulary words in Column A with their definitions in Column B. Place the correct letter in the space provided.

Column A

_____G_____ 1. artifact

_____A_____ 2. confronted

_____H_____ 3. contemplated

_____F_____ 4. crannies

_____B_____ 5. expounded

_____I_____ 6. impending

_____D_____ 7. infant

_____C_____ 8. jargon

_____E_____ 9. paradigm

_____J_____ 10. scrutinize

Column B

a. faced

b. explained; interpreted

c. specialized language

d. something in a very early stage

e. a model; a pattern

f. chinks and cracks

g. a thing made by human hands

h. seriously thought about

i. about to happen

j. examine closely

In Your Own Words

The author makes several pencil "puns" or plays on words. For instance, in paragraph 1, he says, "What he knew about it [the pencil] would not blunt the soft tip of a Dixon Ticonderoga No. 1" Find the puns and explain the meaning of each (including the one above). Hint: Check paragraphs 2 and 5.

Optional: Try creating a pencil pun of your own.

The Art of Writing

In a short essay, explain what Professor Petroski means when he says, "To scrutinize the trivial can be to discover the monumental."

Internet Activities

1. Explore the Internet to find answers to these questions. Consult the following site: www.pencils.com. Or type "history of pencils" into a search engine.

   a. Why are the majority of pencils in the United States yellow?

   b. Do most European pencils have erasers?

   c. What do the various grades of pencil leads mean? Which grade is required for use on most standardized tests?

2. Do research on artists well known for their pencil drawings. One such example is Ingres' *Nicolo Paganini*, a portrait of the violinist. In addition, many of Picasso's preliminary sketches for *Guernica* were done in pencil, as were many of Leonardo da Vinci's drawings of horses and other animals. Do you think the pencil drawings convey as much emotion as works done in other media, such as ink or water color?

TEST-TAKING TIP

Dealing with Test-Taking Anxiety

While the key to success in test taking is generally adequate preparation, you also need to maintain a positive attitude and stay relaxed. Take the following test to help you determine whether anxiety over test taking may be interfering with your ability to get a good grade.

TEST ANXIETY SCALE

To assess your test-anxiety level, rate yourself from 1 to 5 on each of the following statements.

1—never   2—rarely   3—sometimes
4—often   5—always

1. I have trouble sleeping the night before a test.

    1   2   3   4   5

2. I have visible signs of nervousness right before a test (sweaty palms, shaky hands).

    1   2   3   4   5

3. I have butterflies in my stomach or feel nauseated before a test.

    1   2   3   4   5

4. I am irritable and hard to be around before a test.

    1   2   3   4   5

5. I worry about how others are doing on the test.

    1   2   3   4   5

6. My mind goes blank during the test, or I am unable to recall information.

    1   2   3   4   5

7. I have difficulty choosing answers.

    1   2   3   4   5

8. I make mistakes on easy questions or put answers in the wrong places.

    1   2   3   4   5

9. I am always afraid that I will run out of time.

    1   2   3   4   5

10. I remember the information that I forgot after I have turned in the test.

    1   2   3   4   5

If you gave yourself five or more 4s or 5s, you may be highly anxious about tests. In that case, you should try the following relaxation techniques:

1. Take several long, deep breaths to calm yourself. After a few minutes, close your eyes and imagine a favorite place. Make this mental scene as detailed as you can.

2. Try to relax your whole body, starting with your feet. Work your way up through your body—your legs, torso, chest, arms, neck, head, and face.

3. If permissible, suck on a piece of hard candy.

4. View the test as an opportunity for self-discovery and not as a win/lose proposition.

If you feel that your anxiety is overwhelming, get help from your college counseling center.

VOCABULARY   Prefixes (Unit 3)

The following prefixes all indicate numbers:

uni—one	qua(d)—four	sept—seven
mono—one	tetra—four	hept—seven
bi—two	quint—five	oct—eight
di—two	pent—five	
du(o)—two		nov—nine
	hex—six	
tri—three	sex—six	dec, dek—ten

unify	to make or become a single unit
unicameral	*-cam-* means "chamber." *Unicameral* refers to a legislative body made up of only one house or chamber.
bicameral	having two groups in the lawmaking body. The *bicameral* U.S. Congress is made up of the Senate and the House of Representatives.
univalve	having a shell composed of a single piece, such as a snail
bivalve	having a shell composed of two parts hinged together, such as a clam or oyster.
monochromatic	of or pertaining to only one color, as in *monochromatic* pottery. It was obvious that Regis, who wore a gray tie, gray shirt, and gray slacks, preferred a *monochromatic* style of dress.
monogram	initials of a person's name in a design, such as are used on articles of clothing or stationery.
monolith	*-lith* means "stone," so a monolith is a single block or piece of stone of considerable size, sometimes carved into a column or large statue. The sphinx of Egypt is a *monolith*.
monotonous	sounded or uttered in one unvarying tone; lacking in variety. At the graduation ceremony, many were displeased with the keynote speaker because of his *monotonous* speaking style.
monocle	an eyeglass for one eye
monorail	a single rail serving as a track for cars. Taking the *monorail* at Disneyland adds to the excitement.
monosyllabic	having only one syllable, like *what* or *how*
biracial	consisting of or representing members of two separate races. Tiger Woods, whose mother is Asian and father is black, is *biracial*.
bipartisan	made up of or supported by two political parties. Support for education is *bipartisan*.
bifocals	eyeglasses in which each lens has two parts, one for reading and seeing nearby objects and the other for seeing things further away. Benjamin Franklin invented *bifocals* in 1784.
bisect	*-sect* means "to cut," so *bisect* means to cut or divide into two equal parts

bigamy	the act of marrying one person while already legally married to another
dichotomy	division into two parts or kinds. *-tomy* is derived from the Latin word *temnien,* meaning "to cut." In the United States, there is a *dichotomy* of viewpoints on the issue of the death penalty.
duplex	a house having separate apartments side by side
duplicate	to make an exact copy of; to double
triplicate	to make three copies of; to triple
triple	made up of three. He ordered a *triple* cone with vanilla, strawberry, and chocolate. A hit in baseball that lets the batter get to third base.
triannual	done, occurring, or issued three times a year, as in a *triannual* magazine.
trilogy	a set of three plays, novels, or other creative works, which form a group, although each is a complete work on its own. *Star Wars, The Empire Strikes Back,* and *The Return of the Jedi* make up a *trilogy.*
quadrangle	an open area surrounded by buildings on all four sides, such as is often seen on college campuses; a plane having four sides.
quatrain	a stanza or poem of four lines, such as in this example by Emily Dickinson:

"Hope" is the thing with feathers
That perches in the soul
And sings the tune without the words
And never stops—at all.

"Hope is the thing with feathers" reprinted by permission of the publishers and the Trustees of Amherst college from THE POEMS OF EMILY DICKINSON, Thomas H. Johnson, ed., Cambridge, Mass.: The Belknap Press of Harvard University Press. Copyright © 1951, 1955, 1979, 1983 by the President and Fellows of Harvard College.

quadriceps	a large, four-part muscle at the front of the thigh
quadricentennial	*cen-* means "100" and *-enn-* means "year," so a *quadricentennial* is a 400th anniversary. The United States will celebrate its *quadricentennial* in 2176.
tetrapod	*-pod* means "foot," so a *tetrapod* is a vertebrate having four legs or one that is descended from a four-legged ancestor.
quintessence	the fifth element; a perfect type or example of something. Works by Picasso are the *quintessence* of modern art.
pentathlon	an athletic contest with five different track and field events
hexagram	a six-pointed starlike figure. The Star of David is a *hexagram.*
sextet	a group of six singers or players
heptagon	a seven-sided figure
octet	a group or stanza of eight lines; a company of eight singers or musicians.

decimate	to destroy or kill a large part of. Florida was *decimated* by the hurricane. In the sixteenth century, the word *decimate* meant to kill every tenth man arbitrarily as punishment for mutiny.
September	originally the seventh month. Our calendar evolved from the original Roman calendar, which began in March instead of January. You can see that making March the first month makes *September* the seventh month.
October	originally the eighth month
November	originally the ninth month
December	originally the tenth month

Completing Verbal Analogies

The easiest type of analogy question involves synonyms, or words that have the same meaning. Analogy questions involving synonyms can be expressed as "*A* means the same as *B*; *C* means the same as *D*." An example is shown below.

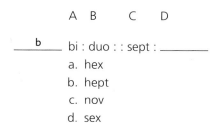

```
         A   B      C     D

___b___  bi : duo : : sept : _____
         a. hex
         b. hept
         c. nov
         d. sex
```

You must first look at the relationship between A and B. The relationship between A and B is one of sameness. *Bi* and *duo* both mean "two." They are synonyms; they mean the same thing. This means that the relationship between C and D must also be one of sameness. *Sept* means "7." We learned previously that *hept* also means "7." Therefore, *hept*, or choice (b), is the correct answer.

The complete analogy reads as follows:

bi : duo :: sept : hept
"bi" is to "duo," as "sept" is to "hept."

Complete the following analogies.

```
_____ 1.  sex : hex : : quad : _____
             a. uni
             b. quint
             c. pent
             d. tetra

_____ 2.  uni : mono : : bi : _____
             a. di
             b. nov
             c. tri
             d. dec
```

_____ 3. quint : pent : : sex : _____
    a. hept
    b. hex
    c. dec
    d. dek

_____ 4. dek : dec : : di : _____
    a. duo
    b. ped
    c. pod
    d. mono

Now that you have studied the vocabulary in Unit 3, practice your new knowledge by completing the crossword puzzle on the following page.

Vocabulary 3

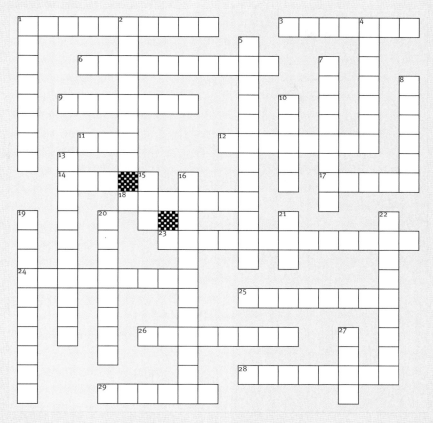

ACROSS CLUES

1. A one-house legislature.
3. Was once the eighth month.
6. At work he does the same thing every day. His job is _____.
9. Tolkien's *The Fellowship of the Ring*, *The Two Towers*, and *The Return of the King* make up the _____ of *The Lord of the Rings*.
11. A word part meaning "eight."
12. An earthquake can _____ an entire city.
14. A word part meaning "one."
17. A group of eight musicians.
18. Agatha Christie's murder mysteries feature a detective who uses a _____ to inspect for clues.
23. Maria Martinez is famous for her black-on black _____ pottery.
24. There is a _____ of viewpoints on the issue of cloning.

25. The Star of David is a _____.
26. The poet Emily Dickinson is famous for her four-line _____.
28. When you're at Disneyland, be sure to ride on the _____.
29. You will _____ a circle if you draw a line through the middle.

DOWN CLUES

1. A snail has a _____ shell.
2. Each of the stone figures on Easter Island is a _____.
4. Oysters have _____ shells.
5. Michelangelo's statue of David is considered to be the _____ of sculpture.
7. The four-legged horse is an example of a _____.
8. A group of six musicians is a _____.
10. On the reality show *Survivor*, first the two teams are pitted against each other and then they _____ and become one tribe.
13. Too much running and jumping caused him to injure his _____.
15. An abbreviation for what was once the ninth month.
16. There are no _____ vocabulary words in this unit. All of the words have more than one syllable.
19. Figure having four angles or sides.
20. Many people begin wearing _____ to see better after the age of 50.
21. A word part meaning "three."
22. Congress is a _____ legislature.
27. A word part meaning "four."

Interpreting What We Read

Person Throwing a Stone at a Bird (1926)
BY JOAN MIRO

Digital Image © The Museum of Modern Art, NY, U.S.A. Licensed by Scala/Art Resource, NY © ARS, NY

Inference

Reverence (1989) BY JIM SARDONIS

© Jim Sardonis/www.sardonis.com

View and Reflect

1. What feeling about whales has the sculptor portrayed?
2. What do you think it feels like to stand before this sculpture? Would the sculpture be as imposing if it were done on a smaller scale
3. How does the sculptor convey the strength of the whale? Would it have been as effective to have depicted the entire whale?
4. The sculpture rises out of the ground as if it were a living entity. Does it seem like a natural part of the landscape in winter? How would it appear in summer?

INTRODUCTION TO INFERENCE SKILLS

A good reader makes educated guesses based upon observable details. We use our intuition and experiences to create a likely interpretation of what is happening in a story, while being careful that our interpretation is logical and realistic. The detective stories by Sir Arthur Conan Doyle featuring the fictional detective Sherlock Holmes clearly show the reasoning process in drawing inferences. Holmes's extraordinary powers of observation and deduction enable him to solve mysteries that baffle lesser detectives. His companion is Dr. Watson, who records his many successes. The following excerpt from *A Study in Scarlet* is narrated by Watson.

1 "I wonder what that fellow is looking for?" I asked, pointing to a stalwart, plainly dressed individual who was walking slowly down the other side of the street, looking anxiously at the numbers. He had a large blue envelope in his hand, and was evidently the bearer of a message.

2 "You mean the retired sergeant of Marines," said Sherlock Holmes.

3 "Brag and bounce!" thought I to myself. "He knows that I cannot verify his guess."

4 The thought had hardly passed through my mind when the man whom we were watching caught sight of the number on our door, and ran rapidly across the roadway. We heard a loud knock, a deep voice below, and heavy steps ascending the stair.

5 "For Mr. Sherlock Holmes," he said, stepping into the room and handing my friend the letter.

6 Here was an opportunity of taking the conceit out of him. He little thought of this when he made that random shot. "May I ask, my lad," I said, in the blandest voice, "what your trade may be?"

7 "Commissionaire, sir," he said, gruffly. "Uniform away for repairs."

8 "And you were?" I asked, with a slightly malicious glance at my companion.

9 "A sergeant, sir, Royal Marine Light Infantry, sir. No answer? Right, sir."

10 He clicked his heels together, raised his hand in salute and was gone. . . .

11 "How in the world did you deduce that?" I asked.

12 "Deduce what?" said he, petulantly.

13 "Why, that he was a retired sergeant of Marines. . . ."

14 "It was easier to know it than to explain why I know it. If you were asked to prove that two and two made four, you might find some difficulty, and yet you are quite sure of the fact. Even across the street I could see a great blue anchor tattooed on the back of the fellow's hand. That smacked of the sea. He had a military carriage, however, and regulation side whiskers. There we have the marine. He was a man with some amount of self-importance and a certain air of command. You must have observed the way in which he held his head and swung his cane. A steady, respectable, middle-aged man, too, on the face of him—all facts that led me to believe he had been a sergeant."

Source: From Sir Arthur Conan Doyle, *A Study in Scarlet.*

"All of us are watchers—of television, of time clocks, of traffic on the freeway, but few are observers. Everyone is looking; not many are seeing."

—Peter M. Leschak

Now study the Gary Larson cartoon. In the cartoon, just as Sherlock Holmes used clearly observable details to make his deduction about the retired sergeant, the hunter/sleuth is using the same type of detail to determine that a deer has "bedded down for the night." Is the hunter using all the available clues? Which ones has he ignored?

You can see how you have to be good at drawing inferences to understand cartoons.

The Far Side® by Gary Larson

"See how the vegetation has been trampled flat here, Jimmy? That tells me where a deer bedded down for the night. After a while, you'll develop an eye for these things yourself."

SELECTION

"Poor Barney is dead an soon I shell be the same."

GETTING THE PICTURE

Most critical readers make inferences as they go along and then, as they are provided more clues by the author, either reject these inferences or subject them to further analysis. At the conclusion of the story, they assemble all of these valid inferences, just as you must do in the following science fiction tale.

Barney

BY WILL STANTON

1   AUGUST 30TH. We are alone on the island now, Barney and I. It was something of a jolt to have to sack Tayloe after all these years, but I had no alternative. The petty vandalisms I could have forgiven, but when he tried to poison Barney out of simple malice, he was standing in the way of scientific progress. That I cannot condone.

2   I can only believe the attempt was made while under the influence of alcohol, it was so clumsy. The poison container was overturned and a trail of powder led to Barney's dish. Tayloe's defense was of the flimsiest. He denied it. Who else then?

3   *September 2nd.* I am taking a calmer view of the Tayloe affair. The lonely life here must have become too much for him. That, and the abandonment of his precious guinea pigs. He insisted to the last that they were better suited than Barney to my experiments. They were more his speed, I'm afraid. He was an earnest and willing worker, but something of a clod, poor fellow.

4   At last I have complete freedom to carry on my work without the mute reproaches of Tayloe. I can only ascribe his violent antagonism toward Barney to jealousy. And now that he has gone, how much happier Barney appears to be! I have given him complete run of the place, and what sport it is to observe how his newly awakened intellectual curiosity carries him about. After only two weeks of glutamic acid treatments, he has become interested in my library, dragging the books from the shelves, and going over them page by page. I am certain he knows there is some knowledge to be gained from them had he but the key.

1. What kind of animal do you think Barney is? _Guinea pig_.
2. What does the narrator infer about Tayloe's relationship to Barney? _____ _Tayloe is jealous of Barney._
3. What has Barney gained since Tayloe's dismissal? _____ _Barney is happier._
4. What can we infer is the likely intent of the scientific experiments? _____ _An experiment to test the intelligence of the guinea pig._

5   *September 8th.* For the past two days I have had to keep Barney confined and how he hates it. I am afraid that when my experiments are completed I shall have to do away with Barney. Ridiculous as it may sound there is still the possibility that he might be able to communicate his intelligence to others of his kind. However small the chance may be, the risk is too great to ignore. Fortunately there is, in the basement, a vault built with the idea of keeping pests out, and it will serve equally well to keep Barney in.

6   *September 9th*. Apparently I have spoken too soon. This morning I let him out to frisk around a bit before commencing a new series of tests. After a quick survey of the room he returned to his cage, sprang up on the door handle, removed the key with his teeth, and before I could stop him, he was out the window. By the time I reached the yard I spied him on the rim of the well, and I arrived on the spot only in time to hear the key splash into the water below.

7   I own I am somewhat embarrassed. It is the only key. The door is locked. Some valuable papers are in separate compartments inside the vault. Fortunately, although the well is over forty feet deep, there are only a few feet of water in the bottom, so the retrieving of the key does not present an impossible problem. But I must admit Barney has won the first round.

1. Why does Barney dispose of the key in this manner? _____
_____

2. What has Barney accomplished by getting rid of the key? _____
_____

3. Do you think Barney is aware of the writer's intentions toward him? _____

8   *September 10th*. I have had a rather shaking experience, and once more in a minor clash with Barney I have come off second best. In this instance I will admit he played the hero's role and may even have saved my life.

9   In order to facilitate my descent into the well I knotted a length of three-quarter-inch rope at one-foot intervals to make a rude ladder. I reached the bottom easily enough, but after only a few minutes of groping for the key, my flashlight gave out and I returned to the surface. A few feet from the top I heard excited squeaks from Barney, and upon obtaining ground level I observed that the rope was almost completely severed. Apparently it had chafed against the edge of the masonry and the little fellow perceiving my danger had been doing his utmost to warn me.

10   I have now replaced that section of rope and arranged some old sacking beneath it to prevent a recurrence of the accident. I have replenished the batteries in my flashlight and am now prepared for the final descent. These few moments I have taken off to give myself a breathing spell and to bring my journal up to date. Perhaps I should fix myself a sandwich as I may be down there longer than seems likely at the moment.

1. What conclusion does the scientist make about the probable cause of the accident? _____
_____

2. Why does he assume Barney is a hero? _____
_____

11   *September 11th*. Poor Barney is dead an soon I shell be the same. He was a wonderful ratt and life without him is knot worth livving. If anybody reeds this

please do not disturb anything on the island but leeve it like it is as a shryn to Barney, espechilly the old well. Do not look for my body as I will caste myself into the see. You mite bring a couple of young ratts and leeve them as a living memorial to Barney. Females—no males. I sprayned my wrist is why this is written so bad. This is my laste will. Do what I say an don't come back or disturb anything after you bring the young ratts like I said. Just females.

Goodby

Source: From Will Stanton, "Barney," from *Fifty Short Science Fiction Tales*. Copyright © 1951 Will Stanton.

1. Who is the likely writer of this last journal entry? _____

2. What specific requests does this writer make? _____

   _____

3. Why does the writer want everyone to stay away? _____

   _____

4. Would a sprained wrist account for the sudden grammatical and spelling errors?

   _____

5. How did Tayloe's dismissal benefit the final author? Why was it essential for him to remove Tayloe from the scene? _____

   _____

6. What parts of this story are the opposite of what you expected them to be? _____

   _____

7. Which group is the author poking fun of in this story? _____

8. In what ways do you think Stanton would like to see this group be more responsible? _____

   _____

Vocabulary in Context

Using the context clues below and in the reading selection, choose the best definition for the italicized word, and write the appropriate answer letter in the blank. You may use your dictionary if necessary.

_b___ 1. *petty* vandalisms (paragraph 1)
   a. subordinate
   b. small, minor
   c. peevish

_a___ 2. simple *malice* (1)
   a. spite
   b. charity
   c. sickliness

_c___ 3. cannot *condone* (1)
   a. amplify
   b. make dense
   c. excuse

_____ 4. something of a *clod* (3)
    a. lump of clay
    b. large heavy shoe
    c. oaf

_____ 5. *mute* reproaches (4)
    a. muffle the sound
    b. silent
    c. shared

_____ 6. only *ascribe* (4)
    a. attribute
    b. restrain
    c. occupy

_____ 7. violent *antagonism* (4)
    a. unknown
    b. anxiety
    c. hostility

_____ 8. *frisk* around (6)
    a. search for concealed weapon
    b. romp
    c. dive

_____ 9. *commencing* a new series of tests (6)
    a. starting
    b. assuming
    c. preserving

_____ 10. *facilitate* my descent (9)
    a. make superficial
    b. make easier
    c. make worthy

_____ 11. a *rude* ladder (9)
    a. elemental
    b. ignorant
    c. crude

_____ 12. *chafed* against (9)
    a. irritated
    b. fretted
    c. rubbed

_____ 13. prevent a *recurrence* (10)
    a. repercussion
    b. repetition
    c. restoration

_____ 14. *replenished* the batteries (10)
    a. stocked
    b. perfected
    c. replaced

_____ 15. final *descent* (10)
    a. birth, lineage
    b. step downward
    c. devalue

A Remote-Controlled Rat: Using Robotics, Researchers Give Upgrade to Lowly Rats; Study Sees Job for Rodents at Disaster Sites

by KENNETH CHANG

GETTING THE PICTURE

The previous selection described a very intelligent rat who in the end was able to best a scientist. The selection below describes an ongoing experiment with rats, to harness their native abilities.

1   PROVIDING A BIOLOGICAL TWIST TO ROBOTICS, scientists have fitted live rats with remote controls to guide them through mazes, past obstacles, and even up trees by typing commands on a laptop computer up to half a mile away.

2   The approach, which takes advantage of an animal's innate ability to do things like climb over rocks, could ultimately be applied to inspecting a disaster area, said the scientists, who report their findings in May's issue of the journal *Nature*.

3   "An animal, especially a rat, has much greater facility for getting around a difficult terrain" than would a robot engineered from scratch, said the senior author of the paper, Dr. John K. Chapin, a professor at the State University of New York's Downstate Medical Center in Brooklyn.

4   The researchers do not commandeer the rat's brains and directly command the animals, zombielike, where to go. Rather, they take advantage of well-worn techniques of training animals by providing rewards.

5   The difference is that in the rats, both the stimuli and the reward are piped directly into the brain, and both can be sent by radio signals from some distance away.

6   Three wires were implanted into the brain of each rat. A pulse of current along one wire stimulated a region of the brain that made the rat feel as if its left whiskers had been touched.

7   A second wire led to the sensing region of the right whiskers. The third was connected to the part of the brain's pleasure center, the medial forebrain bundle.

8   The researchers trained the rats to turn left or right when they felt a stimulus in the corresponding whiskers, rewarding them with a pulse of euphoria in the pleasure center.

9   Strapped on the rat is a tiny backpack containing the antenna for receiving radio signals and a small microprocessor that dispenses the electrical pulses to the rat's brain. The researchers also attached tiny video cameras to get a rat's eye view.

10   Pressing the keys on the researchers' laptop computer sent the radio commands to the rat: the J key to steer the rat left, L to turn it to the right, and K to provide the reward.

11   The researchers also used a joystick like that used in video games to guide the rats up ladders, down stairs, and across narrow ledges.

12   Unlike robots, animals can quickly adapt to a new terrain. The researchers were able to take the rats, which had never been outdoors, and make them climb trees, scurry along branches, turn around and come back down.

13   "Our robot friend was astounded," Dr. Chapin said. "He knew what it would

take to have a machine climb a tree having never seen a tree, having never come close to solving that physical problem."

14   That versatility could find use in search-and-rescue operations, Dr. Chapin said.

15   While robots can survive high temperatures, toxic chemicals, and even tumbles of several stories in height, remote-controlled animals might be able to penetrate through tiny spaces that robots cannot.

16   Dr. Robin R. Murphy, director of the Center for Robot-Assisted Search and Rescue who helped coordinate the use of robots at the World Trade Center wreckage, described the research as "very interesting," but added, "I don't think it's appropriate for search and rescue."

17   The rats would be easily distracted by blood or remains, Dr. Murphy said, adding, "Unfortunately, a lot of this is what rats usually treat as food." Human rescuers and victims would be disconcerted by the sight of rats scurrying around.

18   "The rats could scare weakened victims to death," Dr. Murphy said.

19   But she added that remote-controlled animals might be of use in less chaotic environments, like searches for land mines.

20   Dr. Chapin said he thought many of the problems could be solved.

21   A wireless computer network could ferry data between a pack of rats so that if one rat were out of direct radio contact with the operator, its signal could still be transmitted through the network, Dr. Chapin said.

22   And over time, perhaps people could learn to like rats.

23   "Maybe if it becomes widely known there are these rescue rats," Dr. Chapin said, "people wouldn't be scared."

Source: From Kenneth Chang, "A Remote-Controlled Rat," *New York Times,* May 2, 2002, p. A20. Copyright © 2002 by The New York Times Co. Reprinted with permission.

COMPREHENSION CHECKUP

True or False

Indicate whether each statement is true or false by writing T or F in the space provided.

___F___ 1. Dr. Chapin believes that a robot can be better than a rat at climbing over rocks.

___T___ 2. The experiment with rats operated under the principle of rewarding good behavior.

___T___ 3. Rats can quickly adapt to a new terrain even if they have had no previous experience with it.

___T___ 4. Three wires deliver electrical cues to the rat.

___F___ 5. If the rat turns in the desired direction, it receives a sensation of pain.

Completion

List three advantages of using a rat at a disaster site.

1. _____

2. _____

3. _____

List three disadvantages of using a rat at a disaster site.

1. _____

2. _____

3. _____

Vocabulary Practice

Write the letter of the word that is not related in meaning to the other words in the set.

1. __b__ a. innate   b. extrinsic   c. inherent   d. inborn
2. __c__ a. facility   b. capability   c. difficulty   d. ease
3. __c__ a. euphoria   b. elation   c. gloom   d. well-being
4. __d__ a. dispensed   b. apportioned   c. provided   d. hoarded
5. __b__ a. scurry   b. creep   c. hasten   d. scoot
6. __d__ a. versatility   b. adaptability c. flexibility   d. rigidity
7. __c__ a. disconcerted b. perplexed   c. composed   d. confused
8. __c__ a. chaotic   b. disordered   c. harmonious   d. disorganized

In Your Own Words

1. What can you infer about Dr. Chapin's feelings about the experiment? Does he think it likely that it will be practical to use rats in search-and-rescue missions?

2. What does Dr. Murphy believe about the feasibility of using rats in rescue operations? Cite specific details from the selection to support your conclusions.

3. How do you feel about controlling animals by means of remote-control devices?

4. Do you think that rats should be employed by the U.S. military to sniff out explosives? By law enforcement to sniff out illegal drugs or other contraband?

5. Some people are comfortable using animals such as rats in experiments of this sort, but not animals such as dogs, cats, or monkeys. How do you feel about this issue? Do you have concerns about turning animals into robots serving humans? Explain your reasoning.

Internet Activity

Use a search engine such as Google <www.google.com> or Yahoo! <www.yahoo.com> to locate information about recent developments in animal experimentation. Summarize your findings.

The Art of Writing

In a brief essay, respond to the item below.

Other scientists weighed in with their opinions when this study was first published. One scientist concluded that "rat-patrols" were certainly feasible and that it was "better them than us." Howard Eichenbaum, professor of psychology at Boston University, said that while it was certainly cheaper to turn a rat into a robot than attempt to build a robot to function like a rat, he worried about the ethics of the situation. "We're talking about making animals behave like machines," he said. Finally, some scientists worried that this new "rat technology" could fall into enemy hands. If so, these so-called robo-rats could be guided into government buildings where they could act as suicide bombers. Respond to each of these opinions by the experts, and give your own opinion.

DRAWING INFERENCES FROM TEXTBOOK MATERIAL

After reading the following excerpts from college textbooks, choose the statement that can be directly inferred from the material, and write the appropriate letter in the blank.

ETHICAL ISSUES

As a graduate student in sociology at Washington State University, Rik Scarce studied radical environmental and animal-rights activists who sometimes break the law to dramatize their cause. When a group calling itself the Animal Liberation Front claimed responsibility for a raid on a university laboratory, in which 23 mink, mice, and coyotes were released and hydrochloric acid was poured on computers (causing an estimated $150,000 in damage), Scarce was subpoenaed to appear before a grand jury. Scarce acknowledged that he knew a prime suspect in the case quite well, but refused to answer any further questions. He argued that testifying about his sources not only would cause environmental activists to refuse to speak with him, curtailing his own research, but also would affect the sociological research effort as a whole. Sources would be less likely to trust other social scientists, and social scientists might shy away from controversial research that required confidentiality. Scarce went to jail rather than violate his commitment to confidentiality.

Source: "Ethical Issues" from Craig Calhoun, *Sociology,* 7th ed., New York: McGraw-Hill, 1997, p. 42.

"You are remembered for the rules you break."

—Douglas MacArthur

_____ 1.   We can infer that
    a. the judge in this case was not persuaded by Scarce's argument
    b. the courts agree that information collected during sociological research is confidential
    c. Scarce actually knew nothing about who had raided the laboratory
    d. just as journalists are allowed to protect their sources, so are sociologists

A FRIEND NAMED BO

1   Any of us would be lucky to have a friend such as Bo. Bo is a wonderful companion, loyal and giving unselfishly of time and affection. He is ever-ready to help, and in return, he asks for little.

2   But Bo was trained to be this way.

3   Bo is a 5-year-old golden retriever and labrador mix, a dog trained to be a helpmate to his owner, Brad Gabrielson. Gabrielson has cerebral palsy, and he has little control over his muscles. Yet with the help of Bo, Gabrielson can lead a life of independence.

4   Bo's abilities are many. If the doorbell rings, he answers the door. If Gabrielson drops something, Bo will pick it up. If Gabrielson is thirsty, Bo brings him a drink. One time, when Gabrielson fell, Bo left the apartment, went across the hall to a neighbor's door, where he scratched and barked. When the neighbor proved not to be home. Bo went upstairs to another neighbor's apartment.

5   When that neighbor—who had never encountered Bo before—came to the door, Bo led him downstairs, carefully tugging his hand. As the neighbor helped Gabrielson, Bo stood careful watch at his side. Said Gabrielson later, "On my own, I would have had to lie there . . . until my fiancée got home six hours later." But, he continued, "Bo came over and licked my face, to make sure I was all right, that I responded. Then he went to look for help." And Gabrielson stopped worrying.

Source: "A Friend Named Bo" from Robert S. Feldman, *Understanding Psychology,* 5th ed., p. 184. Copyright © 1999 McGraw-Hill Companies, Inc. Used with permission.

_____ 2.   We can infer that
     a. Gabrielson fell as a result of his own carelessness
     b. Gabrielson stopped worrying because he knew that his fiancée would turn up shortly and take care of him
     c. Gabrielson stopped worrying because he trusted that Bo would find help
     d. Gabrielson stopped worrying because his cell phone was nearby

FIDDLER ON THE MUD

1   What lives in mud, feeds on mud, and finds mates by calling and waving across the mud? But, of course—fiddler crabs, creatures remarkable in many ways but best known as the ultimate experts in mud.

2   The many species of fiddler crabs (Uca) are inhabitants of mud and sand flats in estuaries and other sheltered coasts. Fiddlers are deposit feeders. They feed at low tide, using their pincers to scoop mud up into the mouth. The detritus in the mud is extracted with the help of brushlike mouth parts. Water is pumped from the gill chambers into the mouth to make the lighter detritus float and thus help separate it from the mud. The detritus is swallowed, and the clean mud is spat out on the substrate in neat little balls.

3   Fiddlers are active at low tide and retreat into their burrows at high tide. Each burrow has an entrance (revealed by the neat little balls of mud around it) that the occupant can plug when the tide comes in. At the next low tide, crabs emerge from home to feed and do whatever healthy, active fiddlers like to do.

4   Fiddlers have an interesting sex life. Males feature one tremendously enlarged claw, either right or left. It is brightly colored or highlighted with markings in many species. Females have a much smaller pair, which are used in feeding, as in the case of the males' small pincer. Males use their claw to advertise their sex—to tell females they mean business and to threaten any other males that may be in their way. They wave the claw at low tide on territories established around their burrows. Males entice any interested females into their burrows, and a female may visit a few pads before deciding on a particular one. Males

often fight for prospective mates. They fight very carefully: A lost claw means disaster. It takes many molts to regenerate one that is big enough to get the crab back in action, and crabs whose claws are too small or that don't have the right moves can get pretty lonely!

5   In those areas coinhabited by several species of fiddlers, waving is used to prevent a male from attracting females of the wrong species. Some species wave up and down, others sideways. The angle and frequency of waving also vary, and bowing, fancy steps, and other body movements may form part of the ritual. Some beat the claw on the ground, and males of many species even produce sound by vibrating a joint of the large claw. It pays to advertise!

Source: "Fiddler on the Mud" from Peter Castro in *Marine Biology,* 6th ed., New York: McGraw-Hill, 2007, p. 268. Copyright © McGraw-Hill. Reprinted by permission of The McGraw-Hill Companies, Inc.

_____ 3.   We can infer that
    a. the small pincer is useful to female fiddler crabs, but not to males
    b. both sexes of fiddler crabs use the small pincer for feeding
    c. male fiddler crabs use the small pincer to attract female fiddler crabs
    d. a male fiddler crab can quickly regenerate a large claw

_____ 4.   We can infer that
    a. the male crab makes use of his large claw to attract female crabs of the right species
    b. male fiddler crabs threaten other male fiddler crabs with their large claw
    c. you can tell the species of a male fiddler crab by how it waves its large claw
    d. all of the above

_____ 5.   We can infer that
    a. the fiddler crab's diet consists of mud
    b. the fiddler crab's diet consists of the detritus that is extracted from mud
    c. larger, stronger fiddler crabs eat smaller, weaker ones
    d. fiddler crabs extract nutrition from sea water

DEVOTION TO ANIMALS

1   Hinduism is distinctive among world religions for its kindness to animals. A devout Hindu does not kill or eat animals. Cows often wander along Indian streets, and cars and taxis take care to drive around them. Furthermore, visitors to some Hindu temples may find monkeys and even mice well fed and running free. Several extremely popular gods, such as Ganesha and Hanuman, have animal features; and gods such as Shiva and Vishnu are regularly portrayed in the company of their animal companions. A Shiva temple would often be thought incomplete without a statue of Nandi, the bull who is Shiva's vehicle.

2   This devotion to animals in Hinduism has several possible origins: an ancient deification of certain animals, such as the elephant and tiger; the desire to neutralize dangerous or mischievous animals, such as the snake, rat, and monkey;

and even a sense that human beings and animals have the same origin (a belief also common in oral religions). Belief in reincarnation has undoubtedly also played a role. When they see animals and insects, many Hindus see prehuman beings who in their spiritual evolution will eventually become human themselves. This brings a feeling of closeness to nonhuman forms of animal life.

3

Among the animals, cows receive special veneration. In rural India, to have a cow is to have milk and butter, fuel (dried dung), and the warmth and comfort associated with household pets. With a cow, one is never utterly destitute. Affection for the cow may represent a vestige of earlier matriarchal society—hinted at by the commonly used term *gau mata*, "mother cow." (The fact that Muslims butcher cows is a source of terrible friction between the Hindus and Muslims in India.)

Source: "Devotion to Animals" from Michael Molloy in *Experiencing the World's Religions: Tradition, Challenge and Change,* 4th ed., New York: McGraw-Hill, pp. 102–103. Copyright © 2008.

> *"I consider myself a Hindu, Christian, Moslem, Jew, Buddhist, and Confucian."*
> —Gandhi

_____ 6.   We can infer that
   a. Hindus generally view animals as evil
   b. Hindus are ordinarily protective of animals
   c. a Muslim is unlikely to eat cow meat
   d. ownership of a cow in Hindu society is a terrible burden

NO CATTLE, NO DIGNITY

Along with the rest of their country, the Dinka of Sudan have been involved in a war that has torn apart the nation since 1955. Before the war caused institutions to collapse in southern Sudan, the Dinka were the south's richest and proudest tribe. They were high court judges, civil administrators, and doctors, as well as farmers and cowherds. But the loss of cattle changed all that. Cattle stood at the heart of virtually every important tradition and ceremony in Dinka life. Cattle have always been the Dinka's highest form of wealth, but the war caused the loss of many herds. The loss has caused the Dinka to change their myths and adopt new sources of food. The loss of cattle has also changed marriage. An offering of cattle to the bride's family was traditionally the central transaction at a dowry celebration. Nowadays the negotiations are still held, but they are about handshakes and pledges. There is no livestock available to change hands. Despite the loss of life and land caused by war, the loss of cattle may represent the biggest impact of the war on the Dinka. A change in this single part of culture has caused changes throughout the culture.

> *"There is nothing permanent except change."*
> —Heraclitus

Source: "No Cattle, No Dignity" from Michael Hughes in *Sociology: The Core,* 7th ed., p. 53. Copyright © 2005 McGraw-Hill. Reprinted by permission of The McGraw-Hill Companies, Inc.

_____ 7.   We can infer that
   a. sheep serve an important ceremonial function in Dinka society
   b. the destruction of war has not touched the Dinka's cattle herds
   c. the loss of cattle has had a devastating impact on Dinka society
   d. dowry exchanges in Dinka culture still feature an exchange of cattle

VENOMOUS SNAKES ARE FEW

1   Modern snakes and lizards make up 95 percent of living reptiles. Snakes evolved from lizards during the Cretaceous period and became adapted to burrowing. They lack limbs, so their prey must be subdued and swallowed without the benefit of appendages for manipulating food. Most snakes, like the boas and pythons, are powerful constrictors, suffocating their struggling prey with strong coils. Smaller snakes, such as the familiar garter snakes and water snakes, frequently swallow their food while it is still alive. Still others use toxic saliva to subdue their prey, usually lizards. It is likely that snake venom evolved as a way to obtain food and is used only secondarily in defense.

2   There are two major groups of venomous snakes. Elapids are represented in the United States by the coral snakes, which inhabit the southern states and display bright bands of red, yellow (or white), and black that completely encircle the body. In these snakes, the fangs, which are modified teeth, are short and permanently erect. The venom is a powerful neurotoxin that usually paralyzes the nervous system. Actually, coral snakes are responsible for very few bites—probably because of their secretive nature, small size, and relatively mild manner.

3   Vipers, represented in the United States by pit vipers such as the copperhead and cottonmouth and about 15 species of rattlesnakes, make up the remaining venomous snakes of the United States. They have a sophisticated venom delivery system terminating in two large, hollow, needlelike fangs that can be folded against the roof of the mouth when not in use. The venom destroys the victim's red blood cells and causes extensive local tissue damage. These snakes are readily identified by the combination of heat-sensing facial pits, elliptical pupils in the eyes, and a single row of scales on the underside of the tail. None of our harmless snakes has any combination of these characteristics.

4   First aid for snakebite is not advised if medical attention is less than a few hours away; application of a tourniquet, incising the wound to promote bleeding, and other radical treatments often cause more harm than good. The best method of treating snakebite is through the use of prescribed antivenin, a serum containing antibodies to the venom. A hospital stay is required because some people are allergic to the serum.

5   Most people are not aware that snakes are perhaps the greatest controllers of disease-carrying, crop-destroying rodents because they are well adapted to following such prey into their hiding places. Also, snakes are important food items in the diets of many other carnivores, particularly birds of prey such as hawks and owls. Their presence in an ecosystem demonstrates the overall health of the environment.

Source: "Venomous Snakes Are Few" from Sylvia Mader in *Biology,* 8th ed., New York: McGraw-Hill, 2004, p. 569. Copyright © 2004 McGraw-Hill. Reprinted by permission of The McGraw-Hill Companies, Inc.

_____ 8.   We can infer that
         a. it is difficult to distinguish elapids from vipers
         b. coral snakes are responsible for the majority of poisonous snake
            bites in the United States
         c. snakes perform an important function in their ecosystems
         d. a tourniquet should always be applied to a snakebite to keep
            venom from reaching the heart and causing cardiac arrest

DRAWING INFERENCES FROM LITERATURE

SELECTION

*"When autumn came the men decided to look for the
rattler's den and execute mass slaughter."*

GETTING THE PICTURE

The essay that follows is a classic. Charles Finney describes the life-and-death cycle of the western diamondback rattlesnake. Pay particular attention to how well suited the diamondback was to the environment before the arrival of man.

BIO-SKETCH

Charles Finney (1905–1984) was born in Sedalia, Missouri. He attended the University of Missouri and worked for the *Arizona Daily Star* in Tucson, Arizona, in various writing capacities from 1930 to 1970. His most famous book, *The Circus of Dr. Lao,* earned the 1935 National Booksellers Award for the most original novel. In addition to his other novels, he contributed short stories to various magazines such as *The New Yorker* and *Harper's.* This short story, "The Gladiator," has been selected for publication in nine literature anthology textbooks.

BRUSHING UP ON VOCABULARY

nemesis an unconquerable opponent or rival. The word is derived from the ancient Greek goddess of divine retribution. The goddess Nemesis punished the pretentious with her mighty sword.

chaparral cock-roadrunner a large (two-foot-long) terrestrial cuckoo residing in the arid regions of the western United States, Mexico, and Central America.

to homestead to acquire or settle on unclaimed land. A law was passed in the 1860s that offered up to 160 acres of land to any man who paid a registration fee, lived on the land for five years, and cultivated or built on it.

flank the side of an animal or person, between the ribs and the hip.

rendezvous an agreement to meet at a certain time or place. The word is borrowed from Middle French and literally means "to present yourself."

The Life and Death of a Western Gladiator

BY CHARLES FINNEY

1   HE WAS BORN ON A SUMMER MORNING IN the shady mouth of a cave. Three others were born with him, another male and two females. Each was about five inches long and slimmer than a lead pencil.

2   Their mother left them a few hours after they were born. A day after that his brothers and sisters left him also. He was all alone. Nobody cared whether he lived or died. His tiny brain was very dull. He had no arms or legs. His skin was delicate. Nearly everything that walked on the ground or burrowed in it, that flew in the air or swam in the water or climbed trees was his enemy. But he didn't know that. He knew nothing at all. He was aware of his own existence, and that was the sum of his knowledge.

3   The direct rays of the sun could, in a short time, kill him. If the temperature dropped too low he would freeze. Without food he would starve. Without moisture he would die of dehydration. If a man or a horse stepped on him he would be crushed. If anything chased him he could run neither very far nor very fast.

4   Thus it was at the hour of his birth. Thus it would be, with modifications, all his life.

5   But against these drawbacks he had certain qualifications that fitted him to be a competitive creature of this world and equipped him for its warfare. He could exist a long time without food or water. His very smallness at birth protected him when he most needed protection. Instinct provided him with what he lacked in experience. In order to eat he first had to kill; and he was eminently adapted for killing. In sacs in his jaws he secreted a virulent poison. To inject that poison he had two fangs, hollow and pointed. Without that poison and those fangs he would have been among the most helpless creatures on earth. With them he was among the deadliest.

6   He was, of course, a baby rattlesnake, a desert diamondback, named Crotalus atrox by the herpetologists Baird and Girard and so listed in the *Catalogue of North American Reptiles* in its issue of 1853. He was grayish brown in color with a series of large dark diamond-shaped blotches on his back. His tail was white with five black crossbands. It had a button on the end of it.

7   Little Crotalus lay in the dust in the mouth of his cave. Some of his kinfolk lay there too. It was their home. That particular tribe of rattlers had lived there for scores of years.

8   The cave had never been seen by a white man.

9   Sometimes as many as two hundred rattlers occupied the den. Sometimes the numbers shrunk to as few as forty or fifty.

10   The tribe members did nothing at all for each other except breed. They hunted singly; they never shared their food. They derived some automatic degree of safety from their numbers, but their actions were never concerted

toward using their numbers to any end. If an enemy attacked one of them, the others did nothing about it.

11   Young Crotalus's brother was the first of the litter to go out into the world and the first to die. He achieved a distance of fifty feet from the den when a Sonoran racer, four feet long and hungry, came upon him. The little rattler, despite his poison fangs, was a tidbit. The racer, long skilled in such arts, snatched him up by the head and swallowed him down. Powerful digestive juices in the racer's stomach did the rest. Then the racer, appetite whetted, prowled around until it found one of Crotalus's little sisters. She went the way of the brother.

12   Nemesis of the second sister was a chaparral cock. This cuckoo, or roadrunner as it is called, found the baby amid some rocks, uttered a cry of delight, scissored it by the neck, shook it until it was almost lifeless, banged and pounded it upon a rock until life had indeed left it, and then gulped it down.

13   Crotalus, somnolent in a cranny of the cave's mouth, neither knew nor cared. Even if he had, there was nothing he could have done about it.

14   On fourth day of his life he decided to go out into the world himself. He rippled forth uncertainly, the transverse plates on his belly serving him as legs.

15   He could see things well enough within his limited range, but a five-inch-long snake can command no great field of vision. He had an excellent sense of smell. But having no ears, he was stone deaf. On the other hand, he had a pit, a deep pockmark between eye and nostril. Unique, this organ was sensitive to animal heat. In pitch blackness, Crotalus, by means of the heat messages recorded in his pit, could tell whether another animal was near and could also judge its size. That was better than an ear.

16   The single button on his tail could not, of course, yet rattle. Crotalus wouldn't be able to rattle until that button had grown into three segments. Then he would be able to buzz.

17   He had a wonderful tongue. It looked like an exposed nerve and probably was exactly that. It was forked, and Crotalus thrust it in and out as he traveled. It told him things that neither his eyes nor his nose nor his pit told him.

18   Snake fashion, Crotalus went forth, not knowing where he was going, for he had never been anywhere before. Hunger was probably his prime mover. In order to satisfy that hunger, he had to find something smaller than himself and kill it.

19   He came upon a baby lizard sitting in the sand. Eyes, nose, pit, and tongue told Crotalus it was there. Instinct told him what it was and what to do. Crotalus gave a tiny one-inch strike and bit the lizard. His poison killed it. He took it by the head and swallowed it. Thus was his first meal.

20   During his first two years Crotalus grew rapidly. He attained a length of two feet; his tail had five rattles on it and its button. He rarely bothered with lizards anymore, preferring baby rabbits, chipmunks, and round-tailed ground squirrels. Because of his slow locomotion he could not run down these agile little things. He had to contrive instead to be where they were when they would pass. Then he struck swiftly, injected his poison, and ate them after they died.

21   At two he was formidable. He had grown past the stage where a racer or a roadrunner could safely tackle him. He had grown to the size where other

desert dwellers—coyotes, foxes, coatis, wildcats—knew it was better to leave him alone.

22   He found "her" on a rainy morning. Of that physical union six new rattle-snakes were born. Thus Crotalus, at two, had carried out his major primary function: he had reproduced his kind. In two years he had experienced every-thing that was reasonably possible for desert diamondback rattlesnakes to experience except death.

23   He had not experienced death for the simple reason that there had never been an opportunity for anything bigger and stronger than himself to kill him. Now, at two, because he was so formidable, that opportunity became more and more unlikely.

24   He grew more slowly in the years following his initial spurt. At the age of twelve he was five feet long. Few of the other rattlers in his den were older or larger than he.

25   He had a castanet of fourteen segments. It had been broken off occasionally in the past, but with each new molting a new segment appeared.

26   His first skin-shedding back in his babyhood had been a bewildering experience. He did not know what was happening. His eyes clouded over until he could not see. His skin thickened and dried until it cracked in places. His pit and his nostrils ceased to function. There was only one thing to do and that was to get out of that skin.

27   Crotalus managed it by nosing against the bark of a shrub until he forced the old skin down over his head, bunching it like the rolled top of a stocking around his neck. Then he pushed around among rocks and sticks and branches, literally crawling out of his skin by slow degrees. Wriggling free at last, he looked like a brand new snake. His skin was bright and satiny, his eyes and nostrils were clear, his pit sang with sensation.

28   For the rest of his life he was to molt three or four times a year. Each time he did it he felt as if he had been born again.

29   At twelve he was a magnificent reptile. Not a single scar defaced his rippling symmetry. He was diabolically beautiful and deadly poison.

30   His venom was his only weapon, for he had no power of constriction. Yellowish in color, his poison was odorless and tasteless. It was a highly complex mixture of proteids, each in itself direly toxic. His venom worked on the blood. The more poison he injected with a bite, the more dangerous the wound. The pain rendered by his bite was instantaneous, and the shock accompanying it was profound. Swelling began immediately, to be followed by a ghastly oozing. Injected directly into a large vein, his poison brought death quickly, for the victim died when it reached his heart.

31   At the age of twenty Crotalus was the oldest and largest rattler in his den. He was in the golden age of his viperhood.

32   He was six feet long and weighed thirteen pounds. His whole world was only about a mile in radius. He had fixed places where he avoided the sun when it was hot and he was away from his cave. He knew his hunting grounds thoroughly, every game trail, every animal burrow.

33   He was a fine old machine, perfectly adapted to his surroundings, accustomed to a life of leisure and comfort. He dominated his little world.

34   But men were approaching. Spilling out of their cities, men were settling in that part of the desert where Crotalus lived. They built roads and houses, set up fences, dug for water, planted crops.

35   They homesteaded the land. They brought new animals with them—cows, horses, dogs, cats, barnyard fowl.

"The greatest joy in nature is the absence of man."
—Bliss Carman

36   The roads they built were death traps for the desert dwellers. Every morning new dead bodies lay on the roads, the bodies of the things the men had run over and crushed in their vehicles.

37   That summer Crotalus met his first dog. It was a German shepherd which had been reared on a farm in the Midwest and there had gained the reputation of being a snake-killer. Black snakes, garter snakes, pilots, water snakes; it delighted in killing them all. It would seize them by the middle, heedless of their tiny teeth, and shake them violently until they died.

38   This dog met Crotalus face to face in the desert at dusk. Crotalus had seen coyotes aplenty and feared them not. Neither did the dog fear Crotalus, although Crotalus then was six feet long, as thick in the middle as a motorcycle tire, and had a head the size of a man's clenched fist. Also this snake buzzed and buzzed and buzzed.

39   The dog was brave and a snake was a snake. The German shepherd snarled and attacked. Crotalus struck him in the underjaw; his fangs sank in almost half an inch and squirted big blobs of poison into the tissues of the dog's flesh.

40   The shepherd bellowed with pain, backed off, groveled with his jaws in the desert sand, and attacked again. He seized Crotalus somewhere by the middle of his body and tried to flip him in the air and shake him as, in the past, he had shaken slender black snakes to their death. In return, he received another poison-blurting stab in his flank and a third in the belly and a fourth in the eye as the terrible, writhing snake bit wherever it could sink his fangs.

41   The German shepherd had enough. He dropped the big snake and in sick, agonizing bewilderment crawled somehow back to his master's homestead and died.

42   The homesteader looked at his dead dog and became alarmed. If there was a snake around big enough to kill a dog that size, it could also kill a child and probably a man. It was something that had to be eliminated.

43   The homesteader told his fellow farmers, and they agreed to initiate a war of extermination against the snakes.

44   The campaign during the summer was sporadic. The snakes were scattered over the desert, and it was only by chance that the men came upon them. Even so, at summer's end, twenty-six of the vipers had been killed.

"Nature thrives on patience; man on impatience."
—Paul Boese

45   When autumn came the men decided to look for the rattler's den and execute mass slaughter. The homesteaders had become desert-wise and knew what to look for.

46   They found Crotalus's lair, without too much trouble—a rock outcropping on a slope that faced south. Cast-off skins were in evidence in the bushes. Bees

flew idly in and out of the den's mouth. Convenient benches and shelves of rock were at hand where the snakes might lie for a final sunning in the autumn air.

47   They killed the three rattlers they found at the den when they first discovered it. They made plans to return in a few more days when more of the snakes had congregated. They decided to bring along dynamite with them and blow up the mouth of the den so that the snakes within would be sealed there forever and the snakes without would have no place to find refuge.

48   On the day the men chose to return nearly fifty desert diamondbacks were gathered at the portals of the cave. The men shot them, clubbed them, smashed them with rocks. Some of the rattlers escaped the attack and crawled into the den.

49   Crotalus had not yet arrived for the autumn rendezvous. He came that night. The den's mouth was a shattered mass of rock, for the men had done their dynamiting well. Dead members of his tribe lay everywhere. Crotalus nosed among them, tongue flicking as he slid slowly along.

50   There was no access to the cave anymore. He spent the night outside among the dead. The morning sun warmed him and awakened him. He lay there at full length. He had no place to go.

51   The sun grew hotter upon him and instinctively he began to slide toward some dark shade. Then his senses warned him of some animal presence near by; he stopped, half coiled, raised his head and began to rattle. He saw two upright figures. He did not know what they were because he had never seen men before.

52   "That's the granddaddy of them all," said one of the homesteaders. "It's a good thing we came back." He raised his shotgun.

Source: From "The Life and Death of a Western Gladiator," by Charles Finney.

 COMPREHENSION CHECKUP

Main Ideas, Supporting Details, and Purpose

Drawing on what you learned from the selection, answer the questions or fill in the blanks appropriately.

1. What is the author's main idea? _____

   _____

2. What was the author's purpose in writing the essay? _____

   _____

   _____

3. How does the author want the reader to feel about rattlesnakes at the end of the

   essay ? _____

   _____

4. The rattlesnake "senses" the presence of other animals by using its _____.

5. The group of rattlesnakes described in the story lived in a _____.

True or False

Indicate whether each statement is true or false by writing T or F in the blank provided.

_T_ 1. The rattlesnake's weapon is its virulent poison.

_F_ 2. Rattlesnakes work in concert to kill their prey.

_F_ 3. The baby rattlesnake is taught by older snakes how to fend for itself.

_T_ 4. The homesteaders waged a war of extermination against the rattlesnakes.

_____ 5. Without the power of constriction, the rattlesnake would be among the most helpless creatures on earth.

_T_ 6. Crotalus was killed by the homesteaders. *implied yes*

look for this

Vocabulary in Context

Look through the paragraph indicated in parentheses to find a word that matches the definition below.

1. actively poisonous (paragraph 5)

2. sleepy (13)

3. to plan with ingenuity; devise (20)

4. confusing or completely puzzling (26)

5. fiendishly; wickedly (29)

6. occurring at irregular intervals (44)

7. assembled (47)

8. shelter or protection from danger (47)

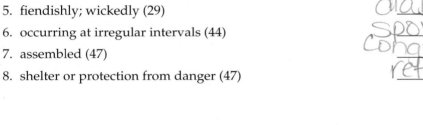

virulent
somnolent
contrive
bewildering
diabolically
sporadic
congregated
refuge

Vocabulary Puzzle

Directions: Use the vocabulary words below to complete the crossword puzzle.

agile	dehydration	fang	symmetry
cave	delicate	litter	tidbit
ceased	den	sac	whet
concerted	eminently	slim	writhe
defaced			

ACROSS CLUES

2. a cave used as a place of shelter
3. fragile; easily damaged
4. stimulate
6. quick; nimble
7. abnormal loss of water from the body (or tissue)
10. planned or devised together
11. the means by which poison is injected
13. excellence of proportion
14. a hollow in the earth

DOWN CLUES

1. number of young brought forth at one birth
2. marred
5. a small morsel of food
8. highly; very
9. baglike structure containing fluid
10. stopped; discontinued
12. twist
13. slender

In Your Own Words

1. Some people are very fearful of snakes, even harmless ones. What do you think causes this irrational fear?

2. What are some things people can do to avoid being bitten by a rattlesnake while hiking or camping in the wilderness?

3. How did the snake come to be so vilified in Western culture? Do you think movies like *Anaconda* or *Snakes on a Plane* help or harm the snake's reputation?

4. Have you ever been bitten by a snake? Do you know anyone who has been bitten? Did you know that the strength of a snake's venom varies depending on how old the snake is, when it last ate, and what time of day the strike occurs? How much it affects a person also depends on how deeply the fangs penetrate and how much venom is injected. How should a person be treated after a snake bite?

The Art of Writing

Explore your own feelings about snakes. Are you fearful of them or respectful? Does your particular culture view snakes in a specific way? Write a short essay giving your opinion of humans' treatment of snakes.

Internet Activities

1. Consult the following website to research the history of snakes and the mythology associated with them. Write a few paragraphs discussing what you learn.

   http://www.umass.edu/nrec/snake_pit/pages/begin.html

2. There are many different kinds of rattlesnakes. To learn more about rattlesnakes, including one that is an albino, visit the website sponsored by the American International Rattlesnake Museum in Albuquerque, New Mexico:

   www.rattlesnakes.com

   First, read about two different kinds of rattlesnakes, and then make a list of their similarities and differences. What can you infer about the rattlesnake's ability to survive? Is it well equipped to survive in the modern world or is it in danger of extinction?

DRAWING INFERENCES FROM CARTOONS

Study the cartoon by Gary Larson below and then write an appropriate caption or main idea sentence for it.

The Far Side® by Gary Larson

"Freeze, Earl! Freeze! ... Something rattled!"

THE WOLF IN FABLES   by AESOP

GETTING THE PICTURE

While many people see the wolf as a symbol of untamed wilderness, others view the wolf as a vicious animal. Fables and fairy tales such as "Little Red Riding Hood" and "The Three Little Pigs" have emphasized the cunning and deceitfulness of the "Big Bad Wolf."

What inferences can you draw from these fables by Aesop about the characteristics of a wolf? List them after reading the selection.

THE WOLF AND THE CRANE

A wolf devoured his prey so ravenously that a bone got stuck in his throat, and in extreme agony, he ran and howled throughout the forest, beseeching every animal he met to pull out the bone. He even offered a generous reward to anyone who succeeded in pulling it out. Moved by his pleas as well as the prospect of the money, a crane ventured her long neck down the wolf's throat and drew out the bone. She then modestly asked for the promised reward, but the wolf just grinned and bared his teeth.

"Ungrateful creature!" he replied with seeming indignation. "How dare you ask for any other reward than your life? After all, you're among the very few who can say that you've put your head into the jaws of a wolf and were permitted to draw it out safely."

Moral: *Expect no reward when you serve the wicked, and be thankful if you escape injury for your pains.*

Source: The Wolf and the Crane from *Aesop's Fables,* edited by Jack Zipes, pp. 17. Copyright by Jack Zipes. Used by permission of Dutton Signet, a division of Penguin Putnam group (USA) Inc.

THE SHEPHERD BOY AND THE WOLF

A shepherd boy, who tended his flock not far from a village, used to amuse himself at times by crying out "Wolf! Wolf!" His trick succeeded two or three times, and the whole village came running to his rescue. However, the villagers were simply rewarded with laughter for their pains.

One day the wolf really did come, and the boy cried out in earnest. But his neighbors thought that he was up to his old tricks and paid no attention to his cries. Consequently, the sheep were left at the mercy of the wolf.

Moral: *Even when liars tell the truth, they are never believed.*

Source: The Shepherd Boy and the Wolf from *Aesop's Fables,* edited by Jack Zipes, pp. 22. Copyright by Jack Zipes. Used by permission of Dutton Signet, a division of Penguin Putnam group (USA) Inc.

Drawing on what you learned from these two fables, list four characteristics of the wolf.

_____

1. _____
2. _____
3. _____
4. _____

Based on what you already know and what you learned from these fables, explain the following sayings in your own words.

1. It's important to keep the wolf from one's door.

_____

2. Beware a wolf in sheep's clothing.

_____

3. He is as hungry as a wolf.

_____

4. It's bad manners to wolf your food down.

_____

5. He has many girlfriends and is such a wolf.

_____

6. What inferences can you draw about the wolf from these sayings?

_____

SELECTION

"Once I had become aware of the strong feeling of property rights which existed amongst the wolves, I decided to use this knowledge to make them at least recognize my existence."

GETTING THE PICTURE

The following selection was written in the early 1960s by Farley Mowat, a noted conservationist. Mowat was hired by the Canadian government to investigate the claim that hordes of wolves were slaughtering arctic caribou. He was sent to live alone in the arctic tundra where he was supposed to establish contact with the wolves so he could better understand their behavior. This brief excerpt describes his initial contact with the wolf he came to call "George."

BIO-SKETCH

Farley Mowat, born and raised in Canada, considers himself to be a "Northern Man." He says that he likes to think he is a "reincarnation of the Norse saga men and, like them, [his] chief concern is with the tales of men, and other animals, living under conditions of natural adversity." The recipient of numerous awards, Mowat's two best-known works, *A Whale for the Killing* (1984) and *Never Cry Wolf* (1963), were made into popular movies.

BRUSHING UP ON VOCABULARY

cognizance perception or knowledge. To take *cognizance* of something is to notice or recognize it. *Cognizance* comes from the Latin *cogni*, which means "to come to know."

baleful harmful or threatening harm; ominous, deadly.

inviolate kept sacred or unbroken, intact.

diurnal done or happening in the daytime. The first part of the word does not come from *di*, meaning "two," but from *dies* meaning "day."

nocturnal the opposite of *diurnal*—means "done or happening at night."

cache a place in which stores of food are hidden.

austerely very plainly or simply, with no ornamentation or luxury.

epitome a good example that shows all the typical qualities.

Excerpt from

Wolf Songs

BY FARLEY MOWAT

GEORGE

1   Quite by accident I had pitched my tent within ten yards of one of the major paths used by the wolves when they were going to, or coming from their hunting grounds to the westward; and only a few hours after I had taken up residence one

of the wolves came back from a trip and discovered me and my tent. He was at the end of a hard night's work and was clearly tired and anxious to go home to bed. He came over a small rise fifty yards from me with his head down, his eyes half-closed and a preoccupied air about him. Far from being the preternaturally alert and suspicious beast of fiction, this wolf was so self-engrossed that he came straight on to within fifty yards of me, and might have gone right past the tent without seeing it at all, had I not banged my elbow against the teakettle, making a resounding clang. The wolf's head came up and his eyes opened wide, but he did not stop or falter in his pace. One brief, sidelong glance was all he vouchsafed to me as he continued on his way.

2   It was true that I wanted to be inconspicuous, but I felt uncomfortable at being so totally ignored. Nevertheless, during the two weeks which followed, one or more wolves used the track past my tent almost every night—and never, except on one memorable occasion, did they evince the slightest interest in me.

3   By the time this happened I had learned a good deal about my wolfish neighbors, and one of the facts which had emerged was that they were not nomadic roamers, as is almost universally believed, but were settled beasts and the possessors of a large permanent estate with very definite boundaries.

4   The territory owned by my wolf family comprised more than a hundred square miles, bounded on one side by a river but otherwise not delimited by geographical features. Nevertheless there *were* boundaries, clearly indicated in wolfish fashion.

5   Anyone who has observed a dog doing his neighborhood rounds and leaving his personal mark on each convenient post will have already guessed how the wolves marked out *their* property. Once a week, more or less, the clan made the rounds of the family lands and freshened up the boundary markers—a sort of lupine beating of the bounds. This careful attention to property rights was perhaps made necessary by the presence of two other wolf families whose lands abutted on ours, although I never discovered any evidence of bickering or disagreements between the owners of the various adjoining estates. I suspect, therefore, that it was more of a ritual activity.

6   In any event, once I had become aware of the strong feeling of property rights which existed amongst the wolves, I decided to use this knowledge to make them at least recognize my existence. One evening, after they had gone off for their regular nightly hunt, I staked out a property claim of my own, embracing perhaps three acres, with the tent at the middle, and *including a hundred-yard-long section of the wolves' path*.

7   Staking the land turned out to be rather more difficult than I had anticipated. In order to ensure that my claim would not be overlooked, I felt obliged to make a property mark on stones, clumps of moss, and patches of vegetation at intervals of not more than fifteen feet around the circumference of my claim. This took most of the night and required frequent returns to the tent to consume copious quantities of tea; but before dawn brought the hunters home the task was done, and I retired, somewhat exhausted, to observe results.

8   I had not long to wait. At 0814 hours, according to my wolf log, the leading male of the clan appeared over the ridge behind me, padding homeward with his usual air of preoccupation. As usual he did not deign to glance at the tent; but when he reached the point where my property line intersected the trail, he stopped as abruptly as if he had run into an invisible wall. He was only fifty yards from me and with my binoculars I could see his expression very clearly.

9   His attitude of fatigue vanished and was replaced by a look of bewilderment. Cautiously he extended his nose and sniffed at one of my marked bushes. He did not seem to know what to make of it or what to do about it. After a minute of complete indecision he backed away a few yards and sat down. And then, finally, he looked directly at the tent and at me. It was a long, thoughtful, considering sort of look.

10   Having achieved my object—that of forcing at least one of the wolves to take cognizance of my existence—I now began to wonder if, in my ignorance, I had transgressed some unknown wolf law of major importance and would have to pay for my temerity. I found myself regretting the absence of a weapon as the look I was getting became longer, yet more thoughtful, and still more intent.

11   I began to grow decidedly fidgety, for I dislike staring matches, and in this particular case I was up against a master, whose yellow glare seemed to become more baleful as I attempted to stare him down.

12   The situation was becoming intolerable. In an effort to break the impasse I loudly cleared my throat and turned my back on the wolf (for a tenth of a second) to indicate as clearly as possible that I found his continued scrutiny impolite, if not actually offensive.

13   He appeared to take the hint. Getting to his feet he had another sniff at my marker, and then he seemed to make up his mind. Briskly, and with an air of decision, he turned his attention away from me and began a systematic tour of the area I had staked out as my own. As he came to each boundary marker he sniffed it once or twice, then carefully placed *his* mark on the outside of each clump of grass or stone. As I watched I saw where I, in my ignorance, had erred. He made his mark with such economy that he was able to complete the entire circuit without having to reload once, or to change the simile slightly, he did it all on one tank of fuel.

14   The task completed—and it had taken him no longer than fifteen minutes—he rejoined the path at the point where it left my property and trotted off towards his home—leaving me with a good deal to occupy my thoughts.

15   Once it had been formally established, and its existence ratified by the wolves themselves, my little enclave in that territory remained inviolate. Never again did a wolf trespass on my domain. Occasionally, one in passing would stop to freshen up some of the boundary marks on his side of the line, and, not to be outdone in ceremony, I followed suit to the best of my ability. Any lingering doubts I might have had as to my personal safety dissolved, and I was free to devote all my attention to a study of the beasts themselves.

16   Very early in my observations I discovered that they led a well-regulated life, although they were not slavish adherents to fixed schedules. Early in the evenings the males went off to work. They might depart at four o'clock or they might delay until six or seven, but sooner or later off they went on the nightly hunt. During this hunt they ranged far afield, although always—as far as I could tell—staying within the limits of the family territory. I estimated that during a normal hunt they covered thirty or forty miles before dawn. When times were hard they probably covered even greater distances, since on some occasions they did not get home until the afternoon. During the balance of the daylight hours they slept—but in their own peculiarly wolfish way, which consisted of curling up for short wolf-naps of from five to ten minutes' duration; after each of which they would take a quick look about, and then turn round once or twice before dozing off again.

17   The females and the pups led a more diurnal life. Once the males had departed in the evening, the female usually went into the den and stayed there, emerging only occasionally for a breath of air, a drink, or sometimes for a visit to the meat cache for a snack.

18   This cache deserves special mention. No food was ever stored or left close to the den; and only enough was brought in at one time for immediate consumption. Any surplus from a hunt was carried to the cache, which was located in a jumble of boulders half-a-mile from the den, and stuffed into crevices, primarily for the use of the nursing female who, of course, could not join the male wolves on extended hunting trips.

19   The cache was also used surreptitiously by a pair of foxes who had their own den close by. The wolves must have known of the location of the foxes' home, and probably knew perfectly well that there was a certain amount of pilfering from their cache; but they did nothing about it even though it would have been a simple matter for them to dig out and destroy the litter of fox pups. The foxes, on their side, seemed to have no fear of the wolves, and several times I saw one flit like a shadow across the esker within a few yards of a wolf without eliciting any response.

20   Later I concluded that almost all the dens used by the Barren Land wolves were abandoned fox burrows which had been taken over and enlarged by the wolves. It is possible that the usefulness of the foxes as preliminary excavators may have guaranteed them immunity; but it seems more likely that the wolves' tolerance simply reflected their general amiability.

21   During the day, while the male wolves took it easy, the female would be reasonably active about her household chores. Emerging boisterously from the close confines of the den, the pups also became active—to the point of total exhaustion. Thus throughout the entire twenty-four-hour period there was usually something going on, or at least the expectation of something, to keep me glued to the telescope.

22   After the first two days and nights of nearly continuous observing I had about reached the limits of my endurance. It was a most frustrating situation. I did not dare to go to sleep for fear of missing something vital. On the other

hand, I became so sleepy that I was seeing double, if not triple, on occasion; although this effect may have been associated with the quantities of wolf-juice which I consumed in an effort to stay awake.

23   I saw that something drastic would have to be done or my whole study program would founder. I could think of nothing adequate until, watching one of the males dozing comfortably on a hillock near the den, I recognized the solution to my problem. It was simple. I had only to learn to nap like a wolf.

24   It took some time to get the knack of it. I experimented by closing my eyes and trying to wake up again five minutes later, but it didn't work. After the first two or three naps I failed to wake up at all until several hours had passed.

25   The fault was mine, for I had failed to imitate *all* the actions of a dozing wolf, and, as I eventually discovered, the business of curling up to start with, and spinning about after each nap, was vital to success. I don't know why this is so. Perhaps changing the position of the body helps to keep the circulation stimulated. I *do* know, however, that a series of properly conducted wolf-naps is infinitely more refreshing than the unconscious coma of seven or eight hours' duration which represents the human answer to the need for rest.

26   Unfortunately, the wolf-nap does not readily lend itself to adaptation into our society, as I discovered after my return to civilization when a young lady of whom I was enamored at the time parted company with me. She had rather, she told me vehemently, spend her life with a grasshopper who had rickets, than spend one more night in bed with me.

27   As I grew more completely attuned to their daily round of family life I found it increasingly difficult to maintain an impersonal attitude toward the wolves. No matter how hard I tried to regard them with scientific objectivity, I could not resist the impact of their individual personalities. Because he reminded me irresistibly of a Royal Gentleman for whom I worked as a simple soldier during the war, I found myself calling the father of the family George, even though in my notebooks, he was austerely identified only as Wolf "A."

28   George was a massive and eminently regal beast whose coat was silver-white. He was about a third larger than his mate, but he hardly needed this extra bulk to emphasize his air of masterful certainty. George had presence. His dignity was unassailable, yet he was by no means aloof. Conscientious to a fault, thoughtful of others, and affectionate within reasonable bounds, he was the kind of father whose idealized image appears in many wistful books of human family reminiscences, but whose real prototype has seldom paced the earth upon two legs. George was, in brief, the kind of father every son longs to acknowledge as his own.

29   His wife was equally memorable. A slim, almost pure-white wolf with a thick ruff around her face, and wide-spaced, slightly slanted eyes, she seemed the picture of a minx. Beautiful, ebullient, passionate to a degree, and devilish when the mood was on her, she hardly looked like the epitome of motherhood; yet there could have been no better mother anywhere. I found myself calling her Angeline, although I have never been able to trace the origin of her name in the murky depths of my own subconscious. I respected and liked George very

much, but I became deeply fond of Angeline, and still live in hopes that I can somewhere find a human female who embodies all her virtues.

30   Angeline and George seemed as devoted a mated pair as one could hope to find. As far as I could tell they never quarreled, and the delight with which they greeted each other after even a short absence was obviously unfeigned. They were extremely affectionate with one another, but, alas, the many pages in my notebook which had been hopefully reserved for detailed comments on the sexual behavior and activities of wolves remained obstinately blank as far as George and Angeline were concerned.

31   Distressing as it was to my expectations, I discovered that physical lovemaking enters into the lives of a pair of mated wolves only during a period of two or three weeks early in the Spring, usually in March. Virgin females (and they are all virginal until their second year) then mate; but unlike dogs, who have adopted many of the habits of their human owners, wolf bitches mate with only a single male, and mate for life.

32   Whereas the phrase "till death us do part" is one of the more amusing mockeries in the nuptial arrangements of a large proportion of the human race, with wolves it is a simple fact. Wolves are also strict monogamists, and although I do not necessarily consider this an admirable trait, it does make the reputation for unbridled promiscuity which we have bestowed on the wolf somewhat hypocritical.

Source: "George," from "Good Old Uncle Albert," by Farley Mowat, from *Wolf Songs*, edited by Robert Busch, San Francisco. Reprinted by permission of Sierra Club books.

 ## COMPREHENSION CHECKUP

Multiple Choice

Write the letter of the correct answer in the blank provided.

_____ 1. If the author were reading this selection out loud, he would most likely sound
　　　　a. solemn
　　　　b. admiring
　　　　c. angry
　　　　d. perplexed

_____ 2. From this article, you could conclude that the author
　　　　a. has a genuine affection for animals
　　　　b. considers hunting a favorite pastime
　　　　c. is a rancher who is afraid that wolves will kill his cattle
　　　　d. dislikes outdoor life

_____ 3. The word *offensive* in the last line of paragraph 12 means
　　　　a. illegal
　　　　b. insulting
　　　　c. damaging
　　　　d. aggressive

_____ 4. From paragraph 22, you could infer that the "wolf-juice" the author consumed is most likely
   a. coffee
   b. beer
   c. tea
   d. milk

_____ 5. All of the following are examples of how male and female wolves behave *except*
   a. male and female wolves are promiscuous
   b. the males hunt for food while the females stay close to the den
   c. the males rest during the day while the females do household chores
   d. male and female wolves are likely to mate for life

_____ 6. The writer's main purpose in writing this selection is to
   a. relate humorous anecdotes about the wolf
   b. describe the wolf's behavior and habitat
   c. explain why wolves are disappearing from the wild
   d. persuade hunters to treat the wolf with more respect

_____ 7. The information presented in paragraphs 25–26 supports which of the following statements?
   a. Mowat discovered that a wolf-nap is far less refreshing than seven hours of sound sleep.
   b. Mowat discovered that all of the actions of a dozing wolf must be enacted to have a successful wolf-nap.
   c. Mowat discovered that by taking wolf-naps, he was not endearing himself to a particular lady friend.
   d. both b and c

_____ 8. Paragraphs 28–29 provide details that primarily
   a. describe the physical and personality characteristics of George and Angeline
   b. demonstrate the superiority of wolf characteristics in contrast to humans
   c. describe the paternal and maternal characteristics of the wolf
   d. all of the above

_____ 9. Which of the following occurred first?
   a. The lead wolf backed away and sat down.
   b. The author marked "his" property.
   c. The author turned his back on the wolf.
   d. The lead wolf made his mark and then trotted off toward home.

_____ 10. Which of the following observations best support the author's contention that the wolves led a well-regulated life?
   a. While the males were gone, the females and pups retreated to the den.
   b. During the balance of daylight hours, they slept.
   c. Early in the evenings the wolves went off to hunt.
   d. All of the above

Vocabulary in Context

Each item below includes a sentence from the selection. Using the context clues provided, write a preliminary definition for the italicized word. Then look up the word in a dictionary and write the appropriate definition.

1. "Far from being the *preternaturally* alert and suspicious beast of fiction, this wolf was so self-engrossed that he came straight on to within fifty yards of me." (paragraph 1)

   Your definition: _____

   Dictionary definition: _____

2. "The wolf's head came up and his eyes opened wide, but he did not stop or *falter* in his pace." (1)

   Your definition: _____

   Dictionary definition: _____

3. "One brief, sidelong glance was all he *vouchsafed* to me as he continued on his way." (1)

   Your definition: _____

   Dictionary definition: _____

4. "It was true that I wanted to be *inconspicuous*, but I felt uncomfortable at being so totally ignored." (2)

   Your definition: _____

   Dictionary definition: _____

5. "Nevertheless, during the two weeks which followed, one or more wolves used the track past my tent almost every night—and never, except on one memorable occasion, did they *evince* the slightest interest in me." (2)

   Your definition: _____

   Dictionary definition: _____

6. "Once a week, more or less, the clan made the rounds of the family lands and freshened up the boundary markers—a sort of *lupine* beating of the bounds." (5)

   Your definition: _____

   Dictionary definition: _____

7. "In order to ensure that my claim would not be overlooked, I felt obliged to make a property mark on stones, clumps of moss, and patches of vegetation at intervals of not more than fifteen feet around the *circumference* of my claim." (7)

   Your definition: _____

   Dictionary definition: _____

8. This took most of the night and required frequent returns to the tent to consume *copious* quantities of tea." (7)

   Your definition: _____

   Dictionary definition: _____

9. As usual he did not *deign* to glance at the tent; but when he reached the point where my property line *intersected* the trail, he stopped as abruptly as if he had run into an invisible wall." (8)

   Your definition: _____

   Dictionary definition: _____

   Your definition: _____

   Dictionary definition: _____

Vocabulary Practice

Complete the sentences with one of the following vocabulary words.

abutted	embodies	monogamist	temerity
adherent	enamored	murky	transgressed
aloof	enclave	nomadic	unassailable
bestowed	hypocritical	pilfering	unbridled
ebullient	immunity	surreptitiously	vehemently

1. Having lived in ten homes in the last two years, he led a _____ existence.

2. Her property directly _____ mine.

3. By the time he was 18, he had _____ most laws.

4. For his vacation, he wanted to find a quiet _____ far off the beaten path.

5. Don't bother offering her dessert because she is a strong _____ of the Atkins diet.

6. After missing his 12:30 curfew, Danny _____ crept through the house while hoping his parents wouldn't awaken.

7. Susan was caught _____ small items from the store.

8. He was granted _____ in exchange for his testimony.

9. Joe is so _____ with Rosa that I think a wedding will occur shortly.

10. Despite unrelenting pressure from the prosecutor, the defendant _____ proclaimed his innocence.

11. He is a man of such integrity that his word is considered _____.

12. At the funeral, Mark stood _____ from the rest of the family.

13. Her _____ personality helps to explain why so many people choose to be around her.

14. Sara searched through the _____ water trying in vain to find her diamond ring.

15. She _____ all the traits of an excellent student.

16. Several players had the _____ to criticize the coach for conducting extended practices.

17. He was a committed _____ who had been married for over forty years to the same wife.

18. Regis _____ the $1,000,000 prize on the winning contestant.

19. It's _____ for Karen to lecture about healthy life choices when she continues to smoke.

20. Nothing can beat a young child's _____ enthusiasm for summer vacation.

In Your Own Words

1. Mowat discovered that in many instances the myths of wolf behavior are not the same as the reality. List as many discrepancies between the two as you can find.

2. Mowat asserted his property rights by "marking" the boundaries of his territory. How is the lead wolf's response contrary to what we might typically expect?

3. Mowat comes to admire the wolves in many respects and in some instances feels that their lifestyle is superior to ours. What specific aspects of wolf behavior does Mowat admire?

4. An artist could probably paint a picture using Mowat's descriptions of George and Angeline. Give a brief synopsis of each one, including character traits. What key details does Mowat use in order to portray the wolves in human terms?

5. Explain the symbiotic relationship between the wolves and foxes.

The Art of Writing

In a brief essay, respond to one of the items below.

1. You have now read three selections on wolves. Write a brief profile of the wolf.

2. In the United States, one of the most controversial conservation issues is the reintroduction of wolves into areas where they have long been extinct. One group feels that parks such as Yellowstone need wolves to preserve an ecological balance. These groups note that an overabundance of deer is currently overgrazing vast areas of the park. Because wolves are a natural predator of deer, they would help control the deer population. On the other hand, many feel that the wolf is detrimental to human beings, and the loudest opposition to reintroduction comes from the ranching community, which is fearful of massive livestock loss.

   Come up with several suggestions for resolving the dispute between the two groups. If necessary, go to the library or the Internet and do additional research.

Internet Activity

One of the best websites about wolves is sponsored by *Nova* of the Public Broadcasting System. Check out its website at

www.pbs.org/wgbh/nova/wolves

Then take a short quiz to see how much you know about the relationship between the domestic dog and the wolf. Finally, print an article of interest to you, and list some inferences that can be drawn from it.

SELECTION

"As race day approached, the names War Admiral and Seabiscuit were on everyone's lips. Even President Roosevelt was swept up in the fervor."

GETTING THE PICTURE

In 1938, the racehorse Seabiscuit was a cultural icon. Then-president Franklin Delano Roosevelt was so caught up in the competition between Seabiscuit and War

AP Images

Admiral that he made several important advisors wait to see him while he listened to the race on the radio. When Laura Hillenbrand began her research for her book *Seabiscuit*, she was struck by how the assembled cast of characters—automobile magnate Charles Howard; Tom Smith, the original Horse Whisperer; and jockeys Red Pollard and George Woolf—all represented the pioneering spirit of the Old West. All were tough gamblers who were not afraid to take a chance. Hillenbrand was fascinated by the irony of Howard making his fortune by replacing horses with cars, yet achieving fulfillment by racing the horse many consider the greatest of all thoroughbreds.

BIO-SKETCH

Laura Hillenbrand has been writing about horse racing since 1988. She is a winner of the Eclipse Award, the highest journalistic award in thoroughbred racing. A long-time sufferer of chronic fatigue syndrome, Hillenbrand's poor health made writing *Seabiscuit* truly a labor of love. Mostly housebound, she conducted phone interviews of more than 100 people for the book, which took over four years to write. Hillenbrand, who currently lives in Washington, D.C., served as a consultant for the Universal Pictures movie of the same name that featured Tobey Maguire in a lead role. *Seabiscuit* was named a *New York Times* Notable Book of the Year for 2001.

BRUSHING UP ON VOCABULARY

bush-league an old baseball expression for minor and semiprofessional baseball leagues. Their games were usually played in uncomfortable and primitive conditions. Since many players in the "bush league" are either beginners or past their prime, the term refers to someone or something amateurish or incompetent.

Cinderella a fairy tale recorded by Charles Perrault. In the story, a young girl is forced by her stepmother and stepsisters to wear rags and do manual labor. When a nearby prince holds a ball, Cinderella's fairy godmother transforms her into an elegant lady and sends her off to the royal palace. There she meets the prince, who falls in love with her. But at the stroke of midnight, she assumes her previous ragged state and flees, leaving her glass slipper behind. The prince discovers her despite her ragged appearance when the glass slipper fits on her foot. They are married and "live happily ever after." The name *Cinderella* is sometimes applied to a person, group, or animal who undergoes a sudden transformation and becomes a winner.

underdog something or someone expected to lose in a contest or conflict.

shell-shocked an early term for combat or battle fatigue.

Excerpt from

Seabiscuit

BY LAURA HILLENBRAND

THE RACE OF THE CENTURY

1   In 1938, near the end of a decade of monumental turmoil, the year's number-one newsmaker was not Franklin Delano Roosevelt, Adolf Hitler, Lou Gehrig, or Clark Gable. It was an undersized, mud-colored, crooked-legged racehorse named Seabiscuit.

2   He came from nowhere. He spent nearly two seasons floundering in the lowest ranks of racing, misunderstood and mishandled. Then he attracted the attention of racehorse trainer Tom Smith, a mysterious, virtually mute refugee from the vanishing frontier who bore with him generations of lost wisdom about the secrets of horses. Smith recognized something in Seabiscuit.

3   His boss, California automobile magnate Charles Howard, agreed that the little horse had grit, and bought him cheap. "We had to rebuild him, both mentally and physically," Howard recalled later. "But you don't have to rebuild the heart when it's already there, big as all outdoors."

4   The third member of Seabiscuit's team of handlers, Red Pollard, was in his twelfth year of a failing career as a jockey and part-time prizefighter when Tom Smith hired him. His experience with horses at countless bush-league racetracks had given him insight into the minds of hard-used, nervous animals, and he quickly won Seabiscuit's trust.

5   One of the first things he did was tell Smith that the whip, used so liberally by the horse's former rider, had to be put away. "Treat him like a gentleman," said Pollard. "He'll run his heart out for you."

6   And run he did. Seabiscuit began winning races. His reputation spread, aided by radio, which enabled a vast number of citizens to experience his triumphs. Millions upon millions of people, torn loose by the Depression from their jobs, their savings, their homes, were desperate to lose themselves in anything that offered affirmation. Spectator sports were enjoying explosive growth, and none more than thoroughbred racing. When Seabiscuit, the Cinderella horse, burst onto the scene, something clicked.

7   Seabiscuit's growing legion of fans were eager for him to race against the era's other equine superstar, Triple Crown–winner War Admiral, son of the legendary Man o' War.

8   War Admiral had the same imperious, lordly way of his father. He was a hellion who spun and fought at the gate, tossed the starters aside, and lunged through false starts. Once under way, he had awesome, frightening speed. No horse in his age group could stay with him. The sleek blue blood awaited a horse who would take the true measure of his greatness. It would never have

occurred to anyone in the East that this horse might be the stocky California contender, Seabiscuit.

9   In the fall of 1938 a contest between the two horses was finally arranged. Seabiscuit and War Admiral were set to race against each other at Maryland's Pimlico racetrack on November 1, in what was universally hailed as the race of the century.

10   Unfortunately, Red Pollard would not be riding Seabiscuit. Some five months earlier, on June 23, Red had been warming up a horse for a friend when the animal spooked and bolted; running at 30 m.p.h, the horse smashed Red's leg against the corner of a barn; nearly severing it below the knee.

11   His best friend, a jockey named George "Iceman" Woolf, took over as Seabiscuit's rider for the race. Woolf called Pollard, who was still in the hospital, to talk strategy.

"Fortune favors the bold."

—Terence

12   Like virtually everyone else, the Iceman believed that War Admiral simply had more God-given ability than Seabiscuit. How, he asked Pollard, should he run this race?

13   Pollard surprised him. He proceeded from the assumption, shared by almost no one else outside the Seabiscuit camp, that his horse had the speed to take the lead. He advised his friend to do something completely unexpected and perhaps unprecedented: When jockey Charley Kurtsinger launched War Admiral in his final drive for the wire, Woolf should let him catch up.

14   Pollard was sure that if Woolf let War Admiral challenge him, Seabiscuit would run faster and try harder than if Woolf attempted to hold the lead alone. "Maybe you would call it a kind of horse psychology," he explained. "Once a horse gives Seabiscuit the old look-in-the-eye, he begins to run to parts unknown. He might loaf sometimes when he's in front and think he's got a race in the bag. But he gets gamer and gamer the tougher it gets."

"But risks must be taken because the greatest hazard in life is to risk nothing."

—Dear Abby

15   It was an enormous risk. If Pollard was wrong about Seabiscuit, then his strategy would hand the victory to War Admiral. But Woolf recognized that his friend understood the horse better than he did. He came to view the race as Pollard did, as a test of toughness, and he had never seen a horse as tenacious as Seabiscuit. "Seabiscuit's like a hunk of steel—Solid. Strong.," he once said. "Admiral has speed, good speed . . . speed when unopposed. But he's not game." Of Seabiscuit he said, "You could kill him before he'd quit."

16   Woolf agreed to do exactly what Pollard told him to do. He and Smith brought Seabiscuit to Pimlico and went to work.

17   As race day approached, the names War Admiral and Seabiscuit were on everyone's lips. Even President Roosevelt was swept up in the fervor. A rumor that he was going to "denounce one of the horses" during a Fireside Chat made the rounds, but he kept his allegiance secret. "The whole country is divided into two camps," wrote Dave Boone in the *San Francisco Chronicle*. "People who never saw a horse race in their lives are taking sides. If the issue were deferred another week, there would be a civil war between the War Admiral Americans and the Seabiscuit Americans."

18   In the track offices, horsemen gathered for the post-position draw. Both horses' handlers wanted the rail, which, if the horse could hold it, would ensure the shortest trip around the track. If Seabiscuit got the rail, the experts believed he might have a glimmer of a chance. If War Admiral got it, they believed the race would be over before it began.

19   War Admiral drew the rail.

20   On the day of the race, a Tuesday, a vast, agitated throng banged against Pimlico's fences six hours before the start. All morning long, automobiles and special trains disgorged thousands of passengers from every corner of the nation and the world.

21   By race time the grandstand and clubhouse were full to bursting, and the infield was packed with the overflow crowd. Fans stood upon every rooftop, fence, tree limb, and telephone pole as far as a mile from the start, hoping to catch a glimpse of the race.

22   Reporters massed by the railings in the press box. War Admiral was the toast of the newsmen; every single *Daily Racing Form* handicapper had picked him to win, as had some 95 percent of the other sportswriters. Only a small and militant sect of California writers was siding with Seabiscuit. War Admiral was also the heavy favorite in the betting, but reporters mingling in the crowd found that most racegoers were rooting for the underdog.

23   At 4 P.M. the two horses and their riders stepped onto the track before a crowd, wrote sportswriter Grantland Rice, "keyed to the highest tension I have ever seen in sport, the type of tension that locks the human throat."

"No animal admires another animal."

—Blaise Pascal

24   It took two tries to get the race started. First Woolf pulled Seabiscuit out of the walk-up because something felt wrong to him. Then War Admiral unraveled at the starting line, whirling in circles.

25   They lined up for the third time. Seabiscuit and War Admiral walked up to the starting line together. The flagman's hand hovered high in the air, and then the flag flashed down as the strangely hushed track clanged with the sound of the bell. War Admiral and Seabiscuit burst off the line at precisely the same instant.

26   For thirty yards, the two horses hurtled down the track side by side, their strides settling into long, open lunges, their speed building and building.

27   A pulse of astonishment swept over the crowd. War Admiral, straining with all he had, was losing ground. First Seabiscuit's nose forged past him—then his throat, then his neck. War Admiral was kicking so hard that his hind legs appeared to be thumping into his girth, but he couldn't keep up.

28   An incredible realization sank into Charley Kurtsinger's mind: *Seabiscuit is faster.* Up in the press box, the California contingent roared.

29   After a sixteenth of a mile, Seabiscuit was half a length ahead and screaming along. He kept pouring it on, flicking his ears forward. The spectators were in a frenzy.

30   Kurtsinger was shell-shocked. His lips were pulled back and his teeth clenched. In a few seconds, Woolf and Seabiscuit had stolen the track from him,

nullifying his post-position edge and his legendary early speed. Kurtsinger didn't panic. War Admiral, though outfooted, was running well, and he had a Triple Crown winner's staying power. Seabiscuit was going much, much too fast for so grueling a race. He couldn't possibly last.

31   As the two horses banked into the first turn, Woolf remembered Pollard's advice to reel Seabiscuit in. He eased back ever so slightly on the reins and felt the horse's stride shorten. With nothing but the long backstretch ahead of him, Woolf carried out Pollard's instructions. Edging Seabiscuit a few feet out from the rail, he tipped his head back and called back to Kurtsinger: "Hey, get on up here with me! We're supposed to have a horse race here! What are you doing lagging back there?"

32   Bounding forward in a gigantic rush, War Admiral slashed into Seabiscuit's lead. A shout rang out in the crowd, "Here he comes! Here he comes!" Woolf heard the wave of voices and knew what was happening. In a few strides, War Admiral swooped up alongside him. A few more, and he was even. Kurtsinger thought: *I'm going to win it.* The grandstand was shaking.

33   The horses stretched out over the track. Their strides, each twenty-one feet in length, fell in perfect sync. The speed was impossible; at the mile mark, a fifteen-year-old track record fell under them, broken by nearly a full second. The track rail hummed up under them and unwound behind.

34   The stands were boiling over. Spectators were fainting by the dozens. As 40,000 voices shouted them on, War Admiral found something more. He thrust his head in front.

35   Woolf glanced at War Admiral's beautiful head, sweeping through the air like a sickle. He could see the depth of the colt's effort in his large amber eye, rimmed in crimson and white. "His eye was rolling in its socket as if the horse was in agony," Woolf later recalled.

36   Woolf dropped low over the saddle and called into Seabiscuit's ear, asking him for everything he had. Seabiscuit gave it to him. War Admiral tried to answer, clinging to Seabiscuit for a few strides, but it was no use. He slid from Seabiscuit's side as if gravity were pulling him backward. Seabiscuit's ears flipped up. Woolf made a small motion with his hand.

37   "So long, Charley." He had coined a phrase that jockeys would use for decades.

38   When he could no longer hear War Admiral's hooves beating the track, Woolf looked back. He saw the black form some thirty-five feet behind, still struggling to catch him. Woolf felt a stab of empathy. "I saw something in the Admiral's eyes that was pitiful," he would say later. "He looked all broken up. I don't think he will be good for another race. Horses, mister, can have crushed hearts just like humans."

39   The Iceman straightened out and rode for the wire, his face down. Seabiscuit sailed into history four lengths in front, running easy.

40   Up in the hospital, Red Pollard greeted reporters with a rhyme:

> *"The weather was clear, the track fast*
> *War Admiral broke first and finished last."*

41   "Well, what did you think of it?" one asked him.

42   "Seabiscuit did just what I'd thought he'd do," Pollard said. "He made a rear admiral out of War Admiral."

43   An envelope from Woolf arrived. Inside was $1,500, half the jockey's purse.

Source: "The Race of the Century," from Laura Hillenbrand, *Seabiscuit: An American Legend,* New York: Ballantine Books, 2001, pp. xvii–xix, 257,259–260, 267–277. Copyright © 2001 by Laura Hillenbrand.

COMPREHENSION CHECKUP

Multiple Choice

Write the letter of the correct answer in the blank provided.

_____ 1. The author suggests all of the following about drawing the rail position *except*
    a. if the horse can hold it, the rail position ensures the shortest trip around the track
    b. if War Admiral drew the rail, track experts believed the race could not be won by Seabiscuit
    c. Seabiscuit did not like to run along the inside rail
    d. the handlers of Seabiscuit and the handlers of War Admiral wanted the rail position

_____ 2. The author suggests all of the following *except*
    a. War Admiral was favored to win by those betting
    b. California writers remained loyal to Seabiscuit
    c. most racegoers were rooting for War Admiral to win
    d. *Daily Racing Form* handicappers picked War Admiral to win

_____ 3. Jockey Charley Kurtsinger didn't panic when he realized that Seabiscuit was faster because he felt that
    a. War Admiral was running well
    b. Seabiscuit could not possibly maintain that pace throughout the race
    c. he could let Seabiscuit exhaust himself and then run him down
    d. all of the above

_____ 4. As described in paragraph 15, a *tenacious* horse is likely to be
    a. persistent
    b. stubborn
    c. obstinate
    d. all of the above

_____ 5. A *glimmer* of a chance in paragraph 18 refers to
    a. a slight chance
    b. a faint chance
    c. both a and b
    d. none of the above

∨ True or False

Indicate whether the statement is true or false by writing T or F in the blank provided.

___T___ 6. The race was so exciting that many fans watching the action unfold beneath them fainted.

___T___ 7. At one point in the race, Charley Kurtsinger thought he was going to win.

___F___ 8. A person who gives in easily is displaying a lot of *grit*.

___F___ 9. A synonym for *sleek* is "rough."

___F___ 10. Red Pollard and Charley Kurtsinger were best friends.

Sequence

Number the sentences in the order in which they occur in the reading selection.

_____ a. An envelope from Woolf arrives with $1,500 inside.

_____ b. Woolf talks strategy with Pollard, who is still in the hospital recuperating.

_____ c. It took two tries to get the race started.

_____ d. War Admiral drew the rail.

_____ e. Seabiscuit sailed into history four lengths in front, running easy.

_____ f. Red Pollard injures his leg.

_____ g. After a sixteenth of a mile, Seabiscuit was half a length ahead and screaming along.

_____ h. War Admiral thrust his head in front.

_____ i. Charles Howard, automobile magnate, bought Seabiscuit cheap.

_____ j. War Admiral and Seabiscuit burst off the line at precisely the same instant.

_____ k. A crowd gathers six hours before the official start of the race.

Matching

Match the quotation with the speaker. Write the letter of the speaker in the appropriate blank. (Some speakers will be used more than once.)

a.	Charles Howard	c.	George Woolf
b.	Red Pollard	d.	Dave Boone

_____ 1. "If the issue were deferred another week, there would be a civil war between the War Admiral Americans and the Seabiscuit Americans."

_____ 2. "So long, Charley."

_____ 3. "Once a horse gives Seabiscuit the old look-in-the-eye, he begins to run to parts unknown."

_____ 4. "He made a rear admiral out of War Admiral."

———— 5. "But you don't have to rebuild the heart when it's already there, big as all outdoors."

———— 6. "His eye was rolling in its socket as if the horse was in agony."

———— 7. "He'll run his heart out for you."

———— 8. "You could kill him before he'd quit."

———— 9. "The weather was clear, the track was fast, War Admiral broke first and finished last."

———— 10. "Horses, mister, can have crushed hearts just like humans."

Vocabulary in Context

Look through the paragraph indicated in parentheses to find a word that matches the definition below.

1. a state of great confusion; agitation (paragraph 1)   *Turmoil*

2. struggling helplessly (2)   *floundering*

3. silent, refraining from speech (2)   *mute*

4. a person of great importance in a particular field (3)   *magnate*

5. of or pertaining to a horse (7)   *equine*

6. domineering in a haughty manner (8)   *imperious*

7. to idle away time (14)   *loaf*

8. passion; zeal (17)   *fervor*

Vocabulary Puzzle

Directions: Use the vocabulary words below to complete the crossword puzzle.

contingent   frenzy   mingling   tenacious
disgorged   glimmer   sect   unraveled
empathy   grit   spooked
forged   grueling   sync

ACROSS CLUES

2. sympathy
5. representative group
6. indomitable spirit; pluck
8. faint glimpse; inkling
10. ejected; yielded
12. extreme mental agitation; frantic
14. exhausting

DOWN CLUES

1. frightened
3. a group deviating from generally accepted thought
4. fell apart
7. blending
9. stubborn
11. harmony
13. moved ahead with increased speed

In Your Own Words

1. How did this story make you feel? Why do you think so many people got so caught up in the life of one horse?

2. What character traits did Seabiscuit have? What lessons can humans learn from his attitude?

The Art of Writing

Like Seabiscuit, Barbaro, the 2006 Kentucky Derby winner, was another "tough" horse. When he was euthanized on January 29, 2007, millions who had never even been to a horse race mourned his loss. His death, instead of being relegated to the sports section, was front-page news. Some sample quotes from editorials follow:

"Goodnight, Sweet Prince"

"Barbaro's Death Transcends Sports"

"The Horse Who Captured America's Heart is Dead"

"Legendary Racehorse Barbaro Dies"

Barbaro won the Kentucky Derby in resounding fashion and was a favorite to win the Preakness when his right leg was injured. He waged an eight-month battle for survival. Within twenty-four hours of his breakdown, the entire nation seemed to be caught up in a "Barbaro watch," waiting for any news. The medical center where he was treated was showered with cards, gifts, flowers, and money. Thousands sent get-well e-mail messages.

Write a short essay giving your explanation for this unprecedented outpouring of sympathy. Why do you think so many people got so caught up in the well-being of a horse?

Internet Activities

1. Read the eulogy written by Pulitzer Prize–winning author Jane Smiley titled "Barbaro—the Heart in the Winner's Circle." How does the eulogy make you feel? What reasons does Smiley give for mourning the loss of Barbaro? Locate the eulogy at the following website:

   www.washingtonpost.com

2. Racetracks make money from people betting on horse races, sometimes from gamblers who have become addicted to betting. To learn more about betting addictions, visit the website of Gamblers Anonymous at

   www.gamblersanonymous.org

   Take their twenty-question test to determine whether you have a gambling problem.

3. To listen to radio broadcasts of some of Seabiscuit's races, check out the following PBS website:

   www.pbs.org/wgbh/amex/seabiscuit

SELECTION

"The idea for the sculpture first came to Sardonis
in a dream— . . ."

GETTING THE PICTURE

"The Whale Tails," as the sculpture is commonly called, has an unusual location—a sea of grass in the land-locked state of Vermont. In his sculptures, Jim Sardonis seeks to emphasize "the interconnectedness of all living things and the importance of the survival of each of them." His inspiration comes from natural forms.

Jim Sardonis's *Reverence* in Progress, 1988–1989

© Jim Sardonis/www.sardonis.com

BIO-SKETCH

Henry Sayre, a professor of art at Oregon State University, has won many awards for his teaching. He is the author of six books and has published widely in national and international journals.

BRUSHING UP ON VOCABULARY

naturalist a person who studies nature, especially plants and animals.

beluga whale (white whale) a small northern whale. The beluga may reach a length of 19 feet and a weight of 4,400 pounds. It has a small, round head with a short, broad snout. It produces a variety of noises and is sometimes called a sea canary. The young are born with dark fur but become almost pure white when they mature. Belugas spend the winter in the Arctic Ocean, feeding upon crustaceans, fish, and squid. They are often found in groups of several hundred.

flukes either of the two horizontally flattened divisions of the tail of a whale.

Excerpt from
A WORLD OF ART
by Henry M. Sayre

Reverence

1   Stone is a symbol of permanence, and of all stones, black granite is one of the hardest and most durable. Thus, in 1998, when sculptor Jim Sardonis chose the stone out of which to carve his tribute to the whale, *Reverence*, black granite seemed the most suitable medium. Not only was its color close to that of the whales themselves, but the permanence of the stone stood in stark contrast to the species' threatened survival. Sardonis wanted the work to have a positive impact. He wanted it to help raise the national consciousness about the plight of the whale, and he wanted to use the piece as a means to raise funds for both the Environmental Law Foundation and the National Wildlife Federation, both of which actively engage in wildlife conservation efforts.

"Art is an expression of an enormous preference."

—Wyndham Lewis

2   The idea for the sculpture first came to Sardonis in a dream—two whale tails rising out of the sea. When he woke he saw the sculpture as rising out of the land, as if the land was an imaginary ocean surface. And, surprisingly, whales were not unknown to the area. In 1849, while constructing the first railroad between Rutland and Burlington, Vermont, workers unearthed a mysterious set of bones near the town of Charlotte. Buried nearly ten feet below the surface in a thick blue clay, they were ultimately determined to be the bones of a "beluga" or "white" whale, an animal that inhabits arctic and subarctic marine waters. Because Charlotte is far inland (over 150 miles from the nearest ocean), early naturalists were at a loss to explain the bones of a marine whale buried beneath the fields of rural Vermont. But the Charlotte whale was preserved in the sediments of the Champlain Sea, an arm of the ocean that extended into the Champlain Valley for 2,500 years following the retreat of the glaciers 12,500 years ago.

3   Sculptures of the size that Sardonis envisioned are not easily realized without financial backing. A local developer, who envisioned the piece installed at the entrance of a planned motel and conference center, supported the idea, and Sardonis was able to begin. The piece would require more space, and more complicated equipment, than Sardonis had available in his own studio, so he arranged to work at Granite Importers, an operation in Barre, Vermont, that could move stones weighing twenty-two and fourteen tons respectively and that possessed diamond saws as large as eleven feet for cutting the stones.

4   Sardonis recognized that it would be easier to carve each tail in two pieces, a tall vertical piece and the horizontal flukes, so he began by having each of the two stones cut in half by the eleven-foot saw. Large saws roughed out the shapes, and then Sardonis began to work on the four individual pieces by hand. As a mass, such granite is extremely hard, but in thin slabs, it is relatively easy to break away. The sculptor's technique is to saw the stone, in a series of parallel cuts, down to within two to six inches of the final form, then break each piece out with a hammer. This "cut-and-break" method results in an extremely rough approximation of the final piece that is subsequently realized by means of smaller saws and grinders.

"All animals are equal but some are more equal than others."

—George Orwell

5   When the pieces were finally assembled, they seemed even larger to Sardonis than he had imagined. But as forms, they were just what he wanted: As a pair, they suggest a relationship that extends beyond themselves to the rest of us. The name of the piece, *Reverence*, suggests not only a respect for nature, but a respect tinged with awe, not only for the largest mammals on the planet, but for the responsibility we all share in protecting all of nature. The whale, as the largest creature, becomes a symbol for all species and for the fragility and interconnection of all life on earth.

6   The project had taken almost a year, and by mid-summer 1989, the site at the prospective conference center was being prepared. Though the pair of forms were installed, when funding for the conference center fell through, they were moved to a new site, just south of Burlington, Vermont, on Interstate 89, where they overlook the Champlain Valley.

Source: From Henry M. Sayre, *A World of Art, Revised with CDROM, 4/e.* Copyright © 2005. Reprinted by permission of Pearson Education, Inc., Upper Saddle River, NJ.

✓ COMPREHENSION CHECKUP

Multiple Choice

Write the letter of the correct answer in the space provided.

_____ 1.   Sardonis chose to create his whales out of black granite because
    a. he considers it to be a symbol of permanence
    b. the color of black granite is a good match to the color of whales
    c. both a and b
    d. neither of the above

_____ 2.   We can assume from the selection that Sardonis
    a. is actively concerned about protecting the environment
    b. feels little concern for the well-being of other living creatures
    c. feels that man should rule supreme over lesser beings
    d. recognizes that whales are doomed because of their large size

_d_ 3. The name *Reverence* was chosen for the sculpture because it evokes
    a. a respect for nature and awe for the largest mammal on earth
    b. a sense of responsibility for the preservation of species
    c. a cavalier attitude toward other species
    d. both a and b

_b_ 4. We can assume all of the following about whales *except*
    a. some whales are dark in color
    b. today there are thriving whales in Burlington, Vermont
    c. beluga whales are found in arctic or subarctic waters
    d. whales are a threatened species

_a_ 5. Sardonis was not able to work in his own studio because
    a. his studio did not have enough space available
    b. his saws were too large for the delicate procedures required
    c. his equipment was outdated
    d. he did not have good ventilation

_c_ 6. The construction of the sculpture included all of the following steps *except*
    a. the four smaller pieces were worked on by hand
    b. large saws roughed out the shapes
    c. the pieces were cut down to within ten to twelve inches of the final form
    d. each of the two stones were cut in half

_b_ 7. The sculpture was moved to a new location because
    a. too many visitors wished to visit at one time
    b. the conference center no longer had funding
    c. Sardonis changed his mind
    d. a grassy area closer to the ocean was available

_c_ 8. We can assume from the selection that the area today known as Charlotte, Vermont
    a. has been land-locked throughout geological history
    b. was once home to birdlike dinosaurs and giant wooly mammoths
    c. was once a very different environment than it is today
    d. is currently the capital of Vermont

True or False

Indicate whether the statement is true or false by writing T or F in the space provided.

_F_ 9. The cut-and-break method involves both a saw and a hammer.

_F_ 10. The whale sculpture project took well over a year to complete.

_F_ 11. The sculpture has resided in only one site since its creation.

_T_ 12. Granite Importers had diamond saws capable of cutting through granite.

_F_ 13. Sardonis funded the project all by himself.

_T_ 14. The bones of a whale were buried in blue clay.

_T_ 15. One can infer that Sardonis is a supporter of both the Environmental Law Foundation and the National Wildlife Federation.

Vocabulary in Context

If the italicized words are used correctly in the sentence, write C on the line. If they are used incorrectly, write I.

___C___ 1. The shoes were extremely *durable*; they withstood many years of hard use.

___C___ 2. He lived in a *rural* area noted for its beautiful countryside and dairy farms.

___I___ 3. The top of a table is *vertical*; its legs are *horizontal*.

___C___ 4. Many treasures have been *unearthed* from the tombs of the pharaohs.

_____ 5. I can't imagine a worse *plight* than winning the lottery.

___I___ 6. Many people like to paint the walls in their house colors rather than *stark* white.

_____ 7. Flying a flag at half-mast is meant as a *tribute* to a heroic person.

___F___ 8. Mark and Mike led *parallel* lives. Mark was a priest and Mike was a captain in the Air Force.

_____ 9. The Carter House, at well over 250 years old, has already demonstrated some *permanence*.

___F___ 10. The same clothes that a teenager wears would be *suitable* for an eighty-year-old woman.

Vocabulary Practice

Write a sentence using each of the following words correctly according to the part of speech given in parentheses. (Answers will vary.)

1. reverence (noun) _____

_____

2. ultimately (adverb) _____

_____

3. envisioned (verb) _____

_____

4. awe (noun) _____

_____

5. fragility (noun) _____

_____

In Your Own Words

1. What do you think the ocean is likely to look like in the future? Will the big mammals and fish still be there?

2. Do you think there will be a rise in sea levels because of global warming?

3. What measures can we as individuals take to stop polluting the oceans?

The Art of Writing

Do some research on the status and estimated numbers of great whales. Try to determine how many whale species are currently listed as either endangered or vulnerable. How has whale hunting contributed to the lower numbers? How has the whaling industry responded? Write a few paragraphs describing the results of your research.

Internet Activity

Other sculptures by Sardonis can be found throughout Vermont, as well as in other places such as the New England Aquarium, Yale University, Dartmouth-Hitchcock Medical Center, and Phillips Exeter Academy. Visit one of these sites and write a brief description of Sardonis's sculpture. Compare and contrast the sculpture to *Reverence*.

TEST-TAKING TIP

Creating Review Tools

Following are some tools you might use to improve your test scores:

1. **To-do lists:** Make a list of the items you need to study for your test. Check each item off as you study it.

2. **Flash cards:** Make 3 × 5 flash cards to test yourself. To learn vocabulary, for example, on one side of the card write the word you need to know, and on the other write the definition. Or, to study for a test, on one side write a review question, and on the other write the answer. Carry the cards with you. You will be surprised at the many opportunities you have for studying them, such as when you are standing in line at the bank store.

3. **Summary sheets:** Create summary sheets by going through your lecture notes and text underlinings and jotting down the key points on a piece of paper. Quiz yourself on these key points by asking yourself to recall what is on the sheet.

4. **Question-and-answer sheets:** Create question-and-answer sheets by folding a piece of paper in half or using the front and the back of the paper to create tests for yourself. Then test yourself by trying to come up with the right answer to the question or even the right question for the answer.

Vocabulary   Unit 4

In this unit, we will be working with words having opposite meanings, such as "love" and "hate." We will also introduce you to the word parts *meter*, *equi*, and *a(n)*.

phil(o)—love

bibliophile Since *biblio*- means "book," a *bibliophile* is a person who loves or collects books.

philanderer a man who makes love to a woman he can't or won't marry. *Ander* means "male."

philanthropist a person who shows love for others by donating money or services to help them. Bill and Melinda Gates are both *philanthropists*.

philosopher	a person who offers views and theories on profound questions; "a lover of wisdom." Socrates, Plato, and Aristotle were ancient Greek *philosophers*.
philharmonic	loving music; a symphony or orchestra. The *Philharmonic* Orchestra performs once a month.
philately	the collection and study of postage stamps and postmarks

mis—hate; bad(ly)

misanthrope	a person who hates or distrusts people. Ebenezer Scrooge, a character in *A Christmas Carol* by Charles Dickens, was the town *misanthrope*.
misogynist	Since *-gyn-* means "woman," a *misogynist* is a person who hates or is hostile toward women.
miscreant	a vicious or depraved person
misconstrue	to think of in a wrong way, to misunderstand. Taryn *misconstrued* Brad's response because to her a grunt indicates a sign of displeasure.
misnomer	a wrong name; an error in naming a person or thing. It is a *misnomer* to call a whale a fish.

eu—good or well; dys—bad, abnormal, difficult

eulogy	a speech or composition praising a person or thing, especially a person who has just died.
euphemism	a word or phrase that is used in place of another that is considered to be offensive. "Adult entertainment" is a *euphemism* for "pornography."
euphoria	a feeling of great joy or excitement
euthanasia	the act of putting someone to death painlessly or allowing him or her to die by withholding medical assistance. *To euthanize* means to subject to *euthanasia*.
dysentery	infectious disease of the large intestine marked by diarrhea. *Dysentery* literally means "bad bowel."
dyslexia	any of a variety of reading disorders

meter—measure

speedometer	an instrument to measure the rate of travel in miles or kilometers.
odometer	an instrument for measuring distance traveled, as in a car.
pedometer	an instrument that measures the distance walked or run by recording the number of steps taken
barometer	an instrument that measures atmospheric pressure.

macro—large or long; micro—small

macrocosm	the universe considered as a whole. *Cosmo* means "universe."
microcosm	a little world, a world in miniature; a group thought of as representing a larger group. The 100 representatives to Boys' State were a *microcosm* of the U.S. high school population.
microbe	a disease-causing bacterium; a small bit of life
microfilm	film bearing a miniature photographic copy of graphic or textual material

equi—equal

Don't confuse *equi* with *equus,* which means "horse." (An *equestrian* competition involves horse riding.)

equity	fairness; justice. Also the value of a piece of property after subtracting the amount owed on it in mortgages and liens. How much *equity* do you have in your home?
equitable	fair or just. Maria's will made sure that her assets were distributed in an *equitable* fashion among her three sons.
equivalent	equal in value, measure, force, or significance. Eat five servings of fresh fruits and vegetables or their *equivalent* every day.

a(n)—not, without

atypical	not typical; irregular; abnormal
amoral	without a sense of moral responsibility
aseptic	free from the living germs of disease
atrophy	a wasting away or a shrinking up of a part of the body. Muscles can *atrophy* from lack of use. Can the mind also *atrophy* from lack of use?
anomaly	not following the usual rule or pattern; abnormal. The penguin, which cannot fly, is an *anomaly* among birds.
amorphous	without a definite shape or form. When Carlos examined the amoeba through the microscope, he discovered that it had an *amorphous* shape.
anemia	a condition in which a person's blood does not have enough red blood cells
asymmetrical	having or showing a lack of symmetry; not balanced. Because the design in the painting was *asymmetrical*, it was not pleasing to the eye.

poly—many

polychromatic	having or exhibiting many colors
polysyllabic	consisting of four or more syllables. *Pol-y-syl-lab-ic* has five syllables.
polytechnic	pertaining to or offering instruction in a variety of industrial arts, applied sciences, or technical subjects

Completing Verbal Analogies

Analogy questions involving antonyms (opposites) can be expressed as "A means the opposite of B; C means the opposite of D." An example is shown below.

      A   B   C   D

_____ early : late : : ahead : _____
   a. before
   b. prior
   c. behind
   d. never

You must first look at the relationship between A and B. Since the relationship between A and B is one of opposition, the relationship between C and D must also be one of opposition. *Behind* is the opposite of *ahead*. Therefore, *behind*, which is choice c, is the correct answer.

Complete the following analogies.

_____ 1. asymmetrical : symmetrical : : unbalanced : _____
   a. abnormal
   b. paranormal
   c. unequal
   d. balanced

_____ 2. typical : atypical : : regular : _____
   a. normal
   b. equal
   c. irregular
   d. equitable

_____ 3. macrocosm : microcosm : : whole : _____
   a. measure
   b. universe
   c. world
   d. part

_____ 4. equitable : arbitrary : : just : _____
   a. authentic
   b. unjust
   c. fair
   d. considerate

_____ 5. septic : aseptic : : dirty : _____
   a. putrid
   b. clean
   c. rotted
   d. free

_____ 6. polychromatic : monochromatic : : many : _____
   a. color
   b. one
   c. two
   d. varied

Now that you have studied the vocabulary in Unit 4, practice your new knowledge by completing the crossword puzzle on the following page.

Vocabulary 4

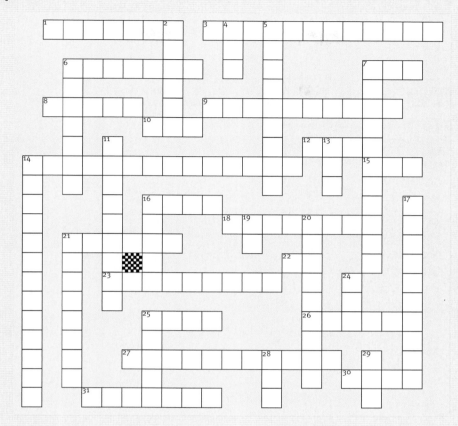

ACROSS CLUES

1. Pneumonia and strep throat are caused by a _____.
3. Her features were not perfectly aligned. Instead they were_____.
6. The roadrunner is an_____ among birds because it rarely flies.
7. A word part meaning "hate or bad."
8. A word part meaning "measure."
9. A confirmed _____ will probably not enjoy the company of women.
10. A word part meaning "bad or difficult."
12. A word part meaning "one."*
14. The _____ made a large monetary contribution to the new science building.
15. The abbreviation for what was once the ninth month.*
16. A word part meaning "four."*
18. An instrument measuring how many miles you have traveled in your car.
21. Condition when a person is lacking sufficient red blood cells.
22. A word part meaning "good or well."
23. The vet said that our dog Bandit was so sick that we should _____ him.
25. A word part meaning "many."
26. A person who lacks moral standards is _____.
27. Thomas Jefferson, a true _____, had over 6,000 volumes of books in his private collection.
30. A word part meaning "five."*
31. A muscle can _____ from lack of use.

DOWN CLUES

2. After Pat's mother died, he delivered a stirring _____ at her memorial service.
4. A word part meaning "six."*
5. A world in miniature is a _____.
6. Surgical instruments must be maintained in _____ condition.
7. Did the reporter _____ the president's remarks or did he quote him accurately?
11. A _____ is used to forecast changes in the weather.
13. The abbreviation for what was once the eighth month.*
14. According to the Bible, Jacob gave his son Joseph a coat of many colors, or a _____ garment.
16. A word part meaning "five."*
17. A liter is almost _____ to a quart.
19. A word part meaning "two."*
20. The judge rendered a decision considered to be _____ by both parties to the dispute.
21. It would be _____ for an *A* student to fail a test.
24. A word part for two.*
25. A word part meaning "love."
28. A word part meaning "six."*
29. An abbreviation for what was once the tenth month.*

*From a previous unit.

Figurative Language

Frida and Diego Rivera, (1931) FRIDA KAHLO

"I never painted dreams. . . . I painted my own reality."—Frida Kahlo

View and Reflect

Frida Kahlo is known for her highly personal paintings. She often made use of symbolism to represent her physical pain and her relationship with her husband, muralist Diego Rivera. This portrait was completed two years after their marriage.

1. Compare and contrast the two images. How is each dressed? Although both are artists, why is only Rivera depicted with an artist's palette and brushes?
2. Which of the two dominates the painting? Why did Kahlo paint it this way?
3. What details in the painting portray the artist as an adoring, subservient wife?
4. In your journal, consider the sense in which this painting reflects Kahlo's "own reality."

TYPES OF FIGURATIVE LANGUAGE

Figurative language (or figures of speech) compares two or more unlike things. **Similes** use *like, as,* or *as if* to make the comparison. Look at the following example and see if you can identify the simile:

> Silence fell while we both cooled down. I knew we would, we always did. Coming apart and coming together, like pigeons fussing on a street corner. It had been like this for as long as I could remember. He had raised me himself, in this shop.

Excerpt from Lisa Scottoline, *Running from the Law,* Harpertorch, 1996 p. 24. Copyright © 1996 by Lisa Scottoline.

In this example, the settling of disagreements is compared to the actions of a flock of pigeons. The differences between the two things are readily apparent, but the similarities between the two enable the reader to come to a better understanding of the situation being described. Most of us have seen how pigeons interact. While they may separate momentarily, they soon come back together again. With a little imagination, the reader now better understands how the two individuals in the example respond to each other.

A **metaphor** compares two unlike things without using *like, as,* or *as if*. In a metaphor, one thing is spoken of as though it were something else. Look at the following example of a metaphor:

> At 81, he is a prune—old, dried up, and wrinkly, but still sweet in the middle.

In this case, an old man is being directly compared to a prune.

Personification is figurative language that assigns human attributes or feelings to a nonhuman object. Authors use personification to make their writing clearer or more vivid. Look at the following example:

> In a hurry to get to California, Marcus set his speedometer at 85, and the car *gobbled* up the road before him.

A car is incapable of gobbling. This use of personification tells us that the car is moving very quickly.

Read the following example and locate the figures of speech:

> [W]hen I spotted the Hamiltons, they struck me as the king, queen, and jack of diamonds. Satisfied and privileged, face cards all, nestled in a corner of this exclusive Main Line restaurant.

"[W]hen I spotted the Hamiltons . . . " Scottoline, *Running from the Law,* p. 43.

The Far Side® by Gary Larson

© 1983 FarWorks, Inc. All Rights Reserved/Dist. by Creators Syndicate

The Far Side® by Gary Larson © 1983 FarWorks, Inc. All Rights Reserved. The Far Side® and the Larson® signature are registered trademarks of FarWorks, Inc. Used with permission.

"Hang him, you idiots! Hang him! ... 'String him up' is a figure of speech!"

1. In the sentences above, what are the Hamiltons being compared to?

    _____

2. What are the similarities between the two things being compared?

    _____

3. What implications can be drawn about the Hamiltons from this comparison?

    _____

4. What are the author's likely feelings toward the Hamiltons?

    _____

Exercise 1: Identifying Similes, Metaphors, and Personification

Directions: Indicate whether the comparison being made uses a simile, metaphor, or personification by writing S, M, or P in the blank provided.

_____ 1. "My life is like a broken bowl." (Christina Rossetti)

_____ 2. "'Hope' is the thing with feathers that perches in the soul." (Emily Dickinson)

_____ 3. "I'm a riddle in nine syllables." (Sylvia Plath)

_____ 4. "A's had once come running." (William Goldman)

_____ 5. "To the north is the Gila River, small and timid most of the year." (Sandra Day O'Connor)

_____ 6. "The world is a glass overflowing with water." (Pablo Neruda)

_____ 7. "The sea awoke at midnight from its sleep." (Henry Wadsworth Longfellow)

_____ 8. "Oh my love is like the melody that's sweetly played in tune." (Robert Burns)

_____ 9. "The rain plays a little sleep-song on our roof at night." (Langston Hughes)

_____ 10. "The alarm clock meddling in somebody's sleep." (Gwendolyn Brooks)

_____ 11. "Papa's hair is like a broom, all up in the air." (Sandra Cisneros)

_____ 12. "But when the trees bow down their heads, the wind is passing by." (Christina Rossetti)

_____ 13. "They don't walk like ordinary dogs, but leap and somersault like an apostrophe and comma." (Sandra Cisneros)

_____ 14. "As my mother taught me, life is a marathon." (Maria Shriver)

_____ 15. "The car as he drives, drifts from lane to lane like a raft on a river." (Joan Aleshire)

_____ 16. "When the stars threw down their spears and water'd heaven with their tears." (William Blake)

Exercise 2: Interpreting Figurative Language

Directions: Read the passages below, and answer the questions that follow. (The similes and metaphors are set in italics.)

The fog spread over the forest *like a soft veil* shrouding everything. The air was *as dense as chocolate cake,* and Mike's breathing sounded laborious to his ears. He had been walking the serpentine path for what seemed like hours caught *like a rat in a maze.* He prayed he was still headed in the right direction. Pictures of food filled his mind, and he was as ravenous *as a bear awakening after the long winter's hibernation.* He knew he could sleep for a week.

In the fog, the trees loomed above him *as shadowy monsters ready to pounce.* Tree roots *like hidden traps* clutched and clawed at his feet as he stumbled along. *As frightening as a muffled scream,* a night owl's sudden cry pierced the air, causing him to tremble uncontrollably. The forest *was a labyrinth* from which he might never escape.

Suddenly, a light beckoned to him from afar. It shimmered in the distance *like the beams from a lighthouse on a dark sea.* The light flickered closer and closer until Monica emerged out of the blackness *like some ghostly apparition.* "Hi," she said. "When Monty came back alone I thought you might be in some sort of trouble."

1. If the fog covering the forest is like a veil, how good is the visibility? _____
2. What might the air have in common with chocolate cake? _____
3. What does being caught *like a rat in a maze* indicate about his ability to escape? _____ Think of a more original comparison of your own. _____

   _____

4. In what way is the forest a labyrinth? Why is Mike afraid of parts of the

   forest? _____

5. How do we know the beams of the flashlight were a welcome sight to

   Mike? _____

6. Monty is most probably a _____

Exercise 3: Identifying and Interpreting Figurative Comparisons

Directions: Each of the sentences below contains a figurative comparison. In the space provided, identify the real subject, indicate what it is being compared to, and explain the meaning of the sentence. Number 1 has been completed as an example.

1. Flattery is like cologne water, to be smelt of, not swallowed.
   Subject: flattery _____

   Compared to: cologne water _____

   Meaning: Flattery is not to be taken seriously. _____

2. "In matters of style, swim with the current; in matters of principle, stand like a rock." (Thomas Jefferson)

Subject: _____

Compared to: _____

Meaning: _____

_____

3. A good laugh is sunshine in a house.

Subject: _____

Compared to: _____

Meaning: _____

4. "Wealth is like seawater; the more we drink, the thirstier we become." (Arthur Schopenhauer)

Subject: _____

Compared to: _____

Meaning: _____

5. "Life is a great big canvas, and you should throw all the paint on it you can." (Danny Kaye)

Subject: _____

Compared to: _____

Meaning: _____

6. "Some books are to be tasted; others to be swallowed; and some few to be chewed and digested." (Francis Bacon)

Subject: _____

Compared to: _____

Meaning: _____

7. "How sharper than a serpent's tooth it is to have a thankless child!" (Shakespeare)

Subject: _____

Compared to: _____

Meaning: _____

8. Success is a ladder that cannot be climbed with your hands in your pockets.

Subject: _____

Compared to: _____

Meaning: _____

9. "Marriage is like life in this—that it is a field of battle, and not a bed of roses." (Robert Louis Stevenson)

Subject: _____

Compared to: _____

Meaning: _____

10. Friendship is like a bank account. You can't continue to draw on it without making deposits.

   Subject: _____

   Compared to: _____

   Meaning: _____

ANALYZING FIGURATIVE LANGUAGE IN POETRY

BIO-SKETCH

Paul Muldoon, winner of the 2003 Pulitzer Prize for Poetry, is an Irish poet known for his "puckish wit." He is currently a professor at Princeton University where he heads the creative writing program. The poem that follows is a "nonsense" poem that plays on proverbs.

Symposium

BY PAUL MULDOON

You can lead a horse to water but you can't make it hold
its nose to the grindstone and hunt with the hounds.
Every dog has a stitch in time. Two heads? You've been sold
one good turn. One good turn deserves a bird in the hand.

A bird in the hand is better than no bread.
To have your cake is to pay Paul.
Make hay while you can still hit the nail on the head.
For want of a nail the sky might fall.

People in glass houses can't see the wood
for the new broom. Rome wasn't built between two stools.
Empty vessels wait for no man.

A hair of the dog is a friend indeed.
There's no fool like the fool
who's shot his bolt. There's no smoke after the horse is gone.

Source: From Paul Muldoon, "Symposium," in *Poems 1968–1998*. Copyright © 2001 by Paul Muldoon. Reprinted by permission of Farrar, Straus & Giroux, Inc.

The proverbs Muldoon "fooled with" are listed below. Try to determine their meaning.

1. You can lead a horse to water but you can't make it drink.

   _____

2. Keep your nose to the grindstone. _____

3. You cannot run with the hare and hunt with the hounds. _____

_____

4. A stitch in time saves nine. _____

5. Two heads are better than one. _____

6. One good turn deserves another. _____

7. A bird in the hand is worth two in the bush. _____

_____

8. You can't have your cake and eat it too. _____

_____

9. Make hay while the sun shines. _____

10. For want of a nail the shoe was lost. _____

11. People who live in glass houses shouldn't throw stones. _____

_____

12. Rome wasn't built in a day. _____

13. Empty vessels make the most sound. _____

_____

14. Time and tide wait for no man. _____

_____

15. A friend in need is a friend indeed. _____

_____

16. There's no fool like an old fool. _____

17. It's too late to shut the stable door after the horse has bolted. _____

_____

18. There's no smoke without fire. _____

Internet Activity

As mentioned in his bio-sketch, Paul Muldoon won the Pulitzer Prize for Poetry in 2003. The Pulitzer Prizes were founded by Joseph Pulitzer. At his death, Pulitzer left money to fund the prizes that bear his name. The first prizes were awarded in 1917. Go to the Pulitzer Prize website to find out who won the prize for poetry or literature in the year you were born. Can you draw any conclusions about the kinds of written materials that were considered exceptional for that year?

www.pulitzer.org

GETTING THE PICTURE

The following poem was inspired by a visit Rita Dove made to her daughter's school. As she visited the classrooms, she realized that many of the children didn't enjoy reading because they were so afraid that they were going to fail. Dove, a voracious reader even as a child, found this very troubling. The poem is an extended metaphor because throughout it Dove compares reading to eating. As a child, she says, she "chewed" her way through many a book. To her, reading provides pleasure in the same way that delicious food does.

BIO-SKETCH

Rita Dove is the youngest person ever appointed to the position of poet laureate in the United States. *Thomas and Beulah*, her book of poetry celebrating the lives of her maternal grandparents, won the Pulitzer Prize in 1987. She is currently a professor at the University of Virginia.

The First Book
BY RITA DOVE

Open it.

Go ahead, it won't bite.
Well . . . maybe a little.

More a nip, like. A tingle.
It's pleasurable, really.

You see it keeps on opening.
You may fall in.

Sure, it's hard to get started;
remember learning to use
knife and fork? dig in
you'll never reach bottom.

It's not like it's the end of the world—
just the world as you think

you know it.

Source: From Rita Dove, "The First Book," in *On the Bus with Rosa Parks,* W. W. Norton and Company. Copyright © 1999 by Rita Dove. Reprinted by permission of the author.

Explain the meaning of the poem in your own words. How are reading and eating similar?

_____

_____

_____

Internet Activity

The Library of Congress website discusses recent poet laureates and gives a brief history of the award and its purposes. Find out who the current poet laureate is and what that person is doing to promote poetry. How have some of the past poet laureates, including Rita Dove, promoted poetry?

www.loc.gov./poetry/laureate.html

SELECTION

"I love people who harness themselves, an ox to a heavy cart, who pull like water buffalo."

GETTING THE PICTURE

As you are reading the poem, think about what work means to you.

BIO-SKETCH

Marge Piercy was born in Detroit, Michigan, to a family she characterizes as working class. She was the first member of her family to attend college. The poem "To Be of Use" is her way of expressing gratitude to those who do physical labor such as growing the food that we eat. Piercy has published fifteen volumes of poetry, including *Colors Passing Through Us* in 2003. In addition, she has published several novels and a play.

BRUSHING UP ON VOCABULARY

amphora a large earthenware storage vessel of Greek and Roman antiquity, having an oval body with two handles extending from below the lip to the shoulder.

To Be of Use

BY MARGE PIERCY

The people I love the best
jump into work head first
without dallying in the shallows
and swim off with sure strokes almost out of sight.
They seem to become natives of that element,
the black sleek heads of seals
bouncing like half-submerged balls.
I love people who harness themselves, an ox to a heavy cart,
who pull like water buffalo, with massive patience,
who strain in the mud and the muck to move things forward,
who do what has to be done, again and again.

"If a man will not work, he will not eat."

—2 Thessalonians 3:10

I want to be with people who submerge
in the task, who go into the fields to harvest
and work in a row and pass the bags along,
who are not parlor generals and field deserters
but move in a common rhythm
when the food must come in or the fire be put out.

The work of the world is common as mud.
Botched, it smears the hands, crumbles to dust.

But the thing worth doing well done
has a shape that satisfies, clean and evident.
Greek amphoras for wine or oil,
Hopi vases that held corn, are put in museums
but you know they were made to be used.
The pitcher cries for water to carry
and a person for work that is real.

Source: "To Be of Use," from *Circles on the Water* by Marge Piercy. Copyright © 1982 by Marge Piercy. Reprinted by permission of Alfred A. Knopf, a division of Random House, Inc.

COMPREHENSION CHECKUP

Multiple Choice

Write the letter of the correct answer in the blank provided.

_____ 1. This poem implies that
   a. a life of leisure is better than a life of work
   b. work that is worth doing has its own intrinsic value
   c. strenuous labor should be avoided
   d. people should begin working when they are young

_____ 2. The speaker of the poem has little respect for people who
   a. direct others from the sidelines
   b. escape doing their fair share
   c. are above doing menial labor
   d. all of the above

_____ 3. A person who "jumps in head first"
   a. avoids difficult labor
   b. is ready and willing to go to work
   c. is reckless
   d. is a slow starter

_____ 4. The phrase "natives of that element" refers to people who
   a. are experiencing something foreign to them
   b. are in their natural environment
   c. make things seem easy
   d. both b and c

_____ 5. The phrase "dallying in the shallows" refers to people who are
   a. unable to swim
   b. prompt and courteous
   c. making only a half effort
   d. having fun

_____ 6. The ox image is used to describe
   a. people who avoid heavy labor
   b. people who need a lot of personal freedom
   c. people who are willing to exert themselves to accomplish something
   d. people who are so slow they can't accomplish anything

_____ 7. The harvest image is used to describe
  a. people who hold back hoping someone else will do it
  b. people who are willing to work for others
  c. people who like to work by themselves
  d. people who are natural leaders

_____ 8. In "To Be of Use" the speaker is describing
  a. a philosophy about the importance of useful work
  b. a close friend
  c. an imaginary world
  d. the importance of taking it easy

_____ 9. The expression "common as mud" means
  a. rare
  b. everywhere
  c. disgusting
  d. lacking in value

_____ 10. The overall feeling of the poem is one of
  a. alarm
  b. high spirits
  c. seriousness
  d. sadness

_____ 11. "The black sleek heads of seals bouncing like half-submerged balls" is
  an example of
  a. simile
  b. metaphor
  c. personification
  d. antonym

_____ 12. "The pitcher cries for water to carry" is an example of
  a. simile
  b. metaphor
  c. literary allusion
  d. personification

Vocabulary Practice

Write a sentence responding to each question.

1. dallying (verb) Do you think it is a good idea to _dally_? Why or why not?

   _____

2. shallows (noun) When would you be better off in the _shallows_? _____

   _____

3. natives (noun) What region are you a _native_ of? _____

   _____

4. element (noun) What is your natural _element_? _____

   _____

5. sleek (adjective) What animal has _sleek_ fur? _____

   _____

6. submerged (verb) A whale can be *submerged* for a half hour. How long can you be *submerged*? _____

_____

7. botched (verb) Can you think of a time when you *botched* a job? _____

_____

In Your Own Words

1. In the poem, what do the references to Greek amphoras and Hopi vases tell us about work?

2. What is the meaning of the last two lines of the poem?

3. What does the author mean when she says, "The work of the world is common as mud"?

The Art of Writing

In a brief essay, discuss what this poem has to say about people and work. Describe a time when you were involved in work that you found very satisfying. When are you willing to do hard work?

Internet Activity

Do you have a career goal? Have you met with a career counselor to explore possible careers? Pull up your college's website and click on career services or counseling. Find out what services are available to you. Does the website contain an interest inventory? If so, take it to help you decide what sorts of careers match your interests and talents.

Check out the website below, and print a want ad for a job that looks appealing to you.

http://www.careerpath.com

ANALYZING FIGURATIVE LANGUAGE IN FICTION

SELECTION

"The ocean bottom is ridged like the roof of a mouth and disappears beneath your feet sometimes when you least expect it."

GETTING THE PICTURE

The following excerpt is about Acapulco, a tourist resort on the west coast of Mexico. The excerpt is from *Caramelo*, a semiautobiographical story of an extended family whose life alternates between Mexico and the United States. As you read "Acapulco," note Cisneros's use of figurative language.

SELECTION *continued*

BIO-SKETCH

Sandra Cisneros was born and raised in Chicago, the daughter of a Mexican father and a Mexican American mother. Cisneros is the recipient of numerous awards for her critically acclaimed poetry and fiction. Her best-known work is *The House on Mango Street*, the story of a young girl growing up in a Hispanic neighborhood in Chicago. Before becoming a full-time writer, Cisneros was a teacher and counselor to high school dropouts.

BRUSHING UP ON VOCABULARY

palapas small, round tables with palm umbrellas, usually located around a pool or on a beach. Tourists often like to sit at *palapas* and sip cold drinks.

Excerpt from

Caramelo

BY SANDRA CISNEROS

ACAPULCO

1 Beyond la Caleta bay, the ring of green mountains dipping and rising like the ocean. And beyond that, sky bluer than water. Tourists yelling in Spanish, and yelling in English, and yelling in languages I don't understand. And the ocean yelling back in another language I don't know.

2 I don't like the ocean. The water frightens me, and the waves are rude. Back home, Lake Michigan is so cold it makes my ankles hurt, even in summer. Here the water's warm, but the waves wash sand inside my bathing suit and scratch my bottom raw. La Caleta is supposed to be the good beach, but I stay out of the water after the ocean tries to take me.

3 The froth of the waves churning and rolling and dragging everything in sight. I make sand houses where the sand is muddy and sucks at my feet, because the dry sand is so hot it burns. The ocean foam like the *babas* of a monkey, little bubbles that turn from green, to pink, and snap to nothing.

4 Candelaria, wearing a shell necklace, weaves a rose for me out of strips of braided palm fronds.

5 "Where did you learn how to do that?"

6 "This? I don't know. My hands taught me."

7 She puts the rose in my hat and runs into the ocean. When she moves into the deep water her skirt billows out around her like a lily pad. She doesn't wear a bathing suit. She wears her street clothes, an old blouse and a skirt gathered up

"Leisure is being allowed to do nothing."

—G. K. Chesterton

and tucked in her waistband, but even like this, bobbing in the water, she looks pretty. Three tourists drinking coconut drinks in the shade of the palm-leaf *palapas* sing a loud Beatles song, "I Saw Her Standing There." Their laughter all across the beach like seagulls.

8   "Cande, watch for sharks!"

9   The ocean bottom is ridged like the roof of a mouth and disappears beneath your feet sometimes when you least expect it. That's why I have to shout to Candelaria to be careful when she wades out in the deeper water. The Acapulco water, salty and hot as soup, stings when it gets in your eyes.

10   "Lalita! Come on in."

11   "No, the water's mean."

12   "Don't be a silly-silly. Come on." Her voice against the roar of ocean, a small chirping.

13   "Noooo!"

14   "And if I throw you in, then what?"

15   We've been to la Roqueta island across the bay on a glass-bottom boat, and on the way there we've seen the underwater statue of la Virgen de Guadalupe all made of gold. We saw the donkey that drinks beer on la Roqueta beach. And we've seen the cliff divers at la Quebrada and the sunset at los Hornos where the ocean is out to get you and comes down slamming hard, like a fist in a game of arm wrestling. And we've had a fish dinner outdoors at a lopsided table set in the sand, and afterward swung in a hammock. Father, in a good mood, bought us all shell necklaces, Mother and me, Aunty and Antoineta Araceli, the grandmother, and even Candelaria.

16   Candelaria wearing her shell necklace and jumping with each wave, is brown as anybody born here, bobbing in the water. Sunlight spangling the skin of water and the drops she splashes. The water shimmering, making everything lighter. You could float away, like sea foam. Over there, just a little beyond reach. Candelaria sparkling like a shiny water bird. The sun so bright it makes her even darker. When she turns her head squinting that squint, it's then I know. Without knowing I know.

17   This all in one second.

18   Before the ocean opens its big mouth and swallows.

Source: "Acapulco," from Sandra Cisneros, "Un Recuerdo," in *Caramelo,* New York: Alfred A. Knopf, 2002, pp. 76–78. Copyright © 2002 by Sandra Cisneros. Published by Vintage Books in paperback in 2003 and originally in hardcover by Alfred A. Knopf, Inc. Reprinted by permission of Susan Bergholz Literary Services, New York, NY. All right reserved.

Identify the figurative language that Cisnernos uses to describe the ocean. What is the overall effect of her description? What human attributes does Cisneros attribute to the ocean?

_____

_____

_____

_____

ANALYZING FIGURATIVE LANGUAGE IN NONFICTION

SELECTION

"Sunlight rules most living things with its golden edicts. When the days begin to shorten . . . a tree reconsiders its leaves."

GETTING THE PICTURE

A **literary allusion** is a reference to an event or person appearing in another literary work. Writers use allusions to quickly express complex thoughts or evoke images or reactions. In this sense, they are much like symbols. To fully understand a literary work containing allusions, you need to be able to recognize the allusions that appear in it. Sometimes, research must be done to discover the meaning of an allusion. In the excerpt below, Diane Ackerman makes a literary allusion when she refers to Adam and Eve, the first man and woman on earth according to the Bible.

BIO-SKETCH

Ackerman's writing style is unique for its mixture of scientific concepts and poetic imagery. This style reflects her educational background. An English major as an undergraduate, she went on to complete an M.A. and a Ph.D. at Cornell University in science-related subjects. In 1991, she published *A Natural History of the Senses*. This was followed by the *Natural History of Love* in 1994, *A Slender Thread: Rediscovering Hope at the Heart of Crisis* in 1997, and *Cultivating Delight* in 2001. Ackerman is presently a professor of English at Cornell University.

BRUSHING UP ON VOCABULARY

stealth secret, hidden; sly, sneaky.

macabre gruesome and horrible. The *danse macabre* is an allegorical story in which Death leads humankind in a dance to the grave.

edict a command or order.

petiole the stalk that connects the leaf of a flowering plant to the plant stem.

photosynthesis the process by which green plants (those containing chlorophyll) use the energy in sunlight to synthesize sugars and other organic molecules from carbon dioxide and water. Photosynthesis releases oxygen as a by-product. *Photo* means "light," and *synthesis* means "put together or combine."

xylem conducting tissue that transports water in plants.

carnal of the flesh, natural; material or worldly.

mute silent.

capricious tending to change abruptly without apparent reason; unpredictable.

Why Leaves Turn Color in the Fall

BY DIANE ACKERMAN

1 THE STEALTH OF AUTUMN CATCHES ONE UNAWARE. Was that a goldfinch perching in the early September woods, or just the first turning leaf? A red-winged blackbird or a sugar maple closing up shop for the winter? Keen-eyed as leopards, we stand still and squint hard, looking for signs of movement. Early-morning frost sits heavily on the grass, and turns barbed wire into a string of stars. On a distant hill, a small square of yellow appears to be a lighted stage. At last the truth dawns on us: Fall is staggering in, right on schedule, with its baggage of chilly nights, macabre holidays, and spectacular, heart-stoppingly beautiful leaves. Soon the leaves will start cringing on the trees, and roll up in clenched fists before they actually fall off. Dry seed pods will rattle like tiny gourds. But first there will be weeks of gushing color so bright, so pastel, so confettilike, that people will travel up and down the East Coast just to stare at it—a whole season of leaves.

2 Where do the colors come from? Sunlight rules most living things with its golden edicts. When the days begin to shorten, soon after the summer solstice on June 21, a tree reconsiders its leaves. All summer it feeds them so they can process sunlight, but in the dog days of summer the tree begins pulling nutrients back into its trunk and roots, pares down, and gradually chokes off its leaves. A corky layer of cells forms at the leaves' slender petioles, then scars over. Undernourished, the leaves stop producing the pigment chlorophyll, and photosynthesis ceases. Animals can migrate, hibernate, or store food to prepare for winter. But where can a tree go? It survives by dropping its leaves, and by the end of autumn only a few fragile threads of fluid-carrying xylem hold leaves to their stems.

3 A turning leaf stays partly green at first, then reveals splotches of yellow and red as the chlorophyll gradually breaks down. Dark green seems to stay longest in the veins, outlining and defining them. During the summer, chlorophyll dissolves in the heat and light, but it is also being steadily replaced. In the fall, on the other hand, no new pigment is produced, and so we notice the other colors that were always there, right in the leaf, although chlorophyll's shocking green hid them from view. With their camouflage gone, we see these colors for the first time all year, and marvel, but they were always there, hidden like a vivid secret beneath the hot glowing greens of summer.

4 An odd feature of the colors is that they don't seem to have any special purpose. Animals and flowers color for a reason—adaptation to their environment—but there is no adaptive reason for leaves to color so beautifully in the fall any more than there is for the sky or ocean to be blue. It's just one of the haphazard marvels the planet bestows every year. We find the sizzling colors thrilling, and in a sense they dupe us. Colored like living things, they signal death and disintegration. In time, they will become fragile and, like the body, return to dust. They are as we hope our own fate will be when we die: not to vanish, just to

sublime from one beautiful state into another. Though leaves lose their green life, they bloom with urgent colors, as the woods grow mummified day by day, and Nature becomes more carnal, mute, and radiant.

5   We call this season "fall," from the Old English *feallan*, to fall, which leads back through time to the Indo-European *phol*, which also means to fall. So the word and the idea are both extremely ancient, and haven't really changed since the first of our kind needed a name for fall's leafy abundance. Fall is the time when leaves fall from the trees, just as spring is when flowers spring up, summer is when we simmer, and winter is when we whine from the cold.

6   Children love to play in piles of leaves, hurling them into the air like confetti, leaping into soft unruly mattresses of them. For children, leaf fall is just one of the odder figments of Nature, like hailstones or snowflakes. Walk down a lane overhung with trees in the never-never land of autumn, and you will forget about time and death, lost in the sheer delicious spill of color. Adam and Eve concealed their nakedness with leaves, remember? Leaves have always hidden our awkward secrets.

7   But how do the colored leaves fall? As a leaf ages, the growth hormone, auxin, fades, and cells at the base of the petiole divide. Two or three rows of small cells, lying at right angles to the axis of the petiole, react with water, then come apart, leaving the petioles hanging on by only a few threads of xylem. A light breeze, and the leaves are airborne. They glide and swoop, rocking in invisible cradles. They are all wing and may flutter from yard to yard on small whirlwinds or updrafts, swiveling as they go. Firmly tethered to earth, we love to see things rise up and fly—soap bubbles, balloons, birds, fall leaves. They remind us that the end of a season is capricious, as is the end of life.

Source: "Why Leaves Turn Color in the Fall," from Diane Ackerman, from *The Natural History of the Senses.* Copyright © 2003 by Diane Ackerman. Used by permission of Random House, Inc.

 COMPREHENSION CHECKUP

Figurative Language

Drawing on what you have learned in the chapter, answer the following questions.

1. In the first paragraph, to what is barbed wire compared? _____

    To what is our vision compared? _____

    To what are dry seed pods compared? _____

2. Throughout the first paragraph, Ackerman uses personification to describe the coming fall. List at least five examples. _____

    _____

    _____

3. Look at Ackerman's use of personification in paragraph 2. Taken together, what do these images convey about nature? _____

    _____

4. To what is Ackerman referring when she speaks of a "vivid secret"?

    _____

    _____

5. How do the "sizzling" colors "dupe" us? What do the colors actually represent?

    _____

6. What figurative expressions does the author use to depict the falling leaves?

    _____

7. How can the end of a season and the end of life both be "capricious"?

    _____

Vocabulary Practice

Find and circle each vocabulary word. Then use each word in a sentence. (Hint: Words can be horizontal or vertical.)

bestows	gravity	squint
camouflage	haphazard	unruly
clench	pares	urgent
dupe	perching	vivid

```
G  S  P  E  R  C  H  I  N  G  T  U

R  Q  W  A  T  A  Z  O  B  P  L  N

A  U  T  S  V  M  P  B  I  R  S  R

V  I  V  I  D  O  S  Z  P  T  A  U

I  N  T  E  D  U  P  E  H  F  S  L

T  T  Q  P  R  F  W  P  D  A  L  Y

Y  V  P  L  C  L  E  N  C  H  F  A

T  H  A  P  H  A  Z  A  R  D  X  T

E  N  I  S  P  G  M  I  S  K  Y  O

L  E  U  G  B  E  S  T  O  W  S  I

D  O  U  R  G  E  N  T  M  V  L  T

P  A  R  E  S  O  B  K  G  E  A  L
```

The Art of Writing

In what way does the cartoon below reinforce a key point made in the reading selection by Diane Ackerman? In what paragraph in the reading does Ackerman come to the same conclusion as expressed in the B.C. cartoon? State that same idea in your own words.

Copyright © 2006. By permission of John L. Hart FLP and Creators Syndicate, Inc.

Internet Activity

Fall colors provide us with one of nature's most beautiful displays. For information about the best time to see the colored leaves in your area, visit the USDA Forest Service website at

www.fs.fed.us/news/fallcolors/

THE USE OF SYMBOLS

A **symbol** is a person, object, or event that stands for something beyond its literal meaning. A good symbol captures in a simple form a more complicated reality. For example, a white dove symbolizes peace, a skull symbolizes death, a flag symbolizes a country's values and aspirations, and a black cat crossing our path symbolizes bad luck. Writers use symbols to create a mood, to reinforce a theme, or to communicate an idea.

See if you can identify the following symbols or icons. What does each icon symbolize?

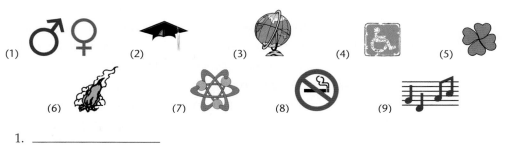

1. _____

2. _____

3. _____

4. _____

5. _____

6. _____

7. _____

8. _____

9. _____

Signs and Symbols

Symbols convey information or embody ideas. Some are so common that we find it difficult to believe they didn't always exist. Who, for example, first used arrows to indicate directions? We follow them instinctively now, but at some point they were new and had to be explained. Other symbols embody more complex ideas and associations. Two well-known and ancient symbols are the yin-yang symbol and the swastika.

The yin-yang symbol, also known as the taiji (or tai chi) diagram, embodies the worldview expressed in ancient Chinese philosophy. It gives elegant visual forms to ideas about the dynamic balance of opposites that are believed to make up the universe and explain existence: male (yang) and female (yin), being and nonbeing, light and dark, action and inaction, and so on. The symbol makes it clear that these opposites are mutually interdependent, that as one increases the other decreases, that a portion of each is in the other, that they are defined by each other, that both are necessary to make the whole.

The swastika has an important lesson to teach about symbols, which is that they have no meaning in themselves but are given a meaning by a society or culture. The swastika was first used as a symbol in India and Central Asia, possibly as early as 3000 B.C.E. It takes its name from the Sanskrit word *svastika*, meaning "good luck" or "good fortune." (Sanskrit was the most important language of ancient India.) In Asia, the swastika is still widely used as an auspicious symbol, even on commercial products. Until the 1930s, the swastika was a popular good-luck symbol in the West as well. Today, however, it is so thoroughly associated with the Nazis, who adopted it as their emblem, that it has become for us a symbol of fascism, racial hatred, and the unspeakable atrocities of the concentration camps. Our instinctive recoil from the swastika underscores not only the power of symbols to serve as repositories for ideas and associations, but also the ability of those ideas and associations to change, sometimes radically.

Among the most pervasive symbols in our visual environment today are logos and trademarks, which are symbols of an organization or product. An impressive number of these are the work of Paul Rand, one of the most influential of all American graphic designers. Simple, clear, distinctive, and memorable, each of these corporate logos has become familiar to millions of people around the world, instantly calling to mind the company and its products or services. As with any symbol, a logo means nothing in itself. It is up to an organization to make its logo familiar and to convince people through sound business practices to associate it with such virtues as service, quality, and dependability.

Source: Signs and Symbols from Mark Getlein, *Living with Art,* 7/e, pp. 239–242. Copyright © McGraw-Hill Companies, Inc. Used with permission.

Symbolic Use of Color

When you're in debt, you speak of being "in the red"; when you make a profit, you're "in the black." When you're sad, you're "blue"; when you're healthy, you're "in the pink"; and when you're jealous, you're "green with envy." To be a coward is to be "yellow" and to be inexperienced is to be "green." When you talk a great deal, you talk "a blue streak"; and when you are angry, you "see red." As revealed through these timeworn clichés, language abounds in color symbolism.

"Languages are the pedigree of nations."

—Samuel Johnson

Colors vary greatly in their meanings from one culture to another. Think about the meanings your own culture gives to such colors as red, black, white, blue, yellow, and purple.

COLOR	CULTURAL MEANINGS AND COMMENTS
Red	In China, red symbolizes prosperity and rebirth and is used for festive and joyous occasions; in France and the United Kingdom, masculinity; in many African countries, blasphemy or death; and in Japan, anger and danger. Red ink, especially among Korean Buddhists, is used only to write a person's name at the time of death or on the anniversary of the person's death, and so problems result when American teachers use red ink to mark the homework of Korean Buddhists.
Green	In the United States, green symbolizes capitalism, initiative, and envy; in Ireland, patriotism; among some Native Americans, femininity; to the Egyptians, fertility and strength; and to the Japanese, youth and energy.
Black	In Thailand, black symbolizes old age; in parts of Malaysia, courage; and in much of Europe and North America, death.
White	In Thailand, white symbolizes purity; in many Muslim and Hindu cultures, purity and peace; and in Japan and other Asian countries, death and mourning.
Blue	In Iran, blue symbolizes something negative; in Egypt, virtue and truth; in Ghana, joy; among the Cherokee, defeat.
Yellow	In China, yellow symbolizes wealth and authority; in the United States, caution and cowardice; in Egypt, happiness and prosperity, and in many countries throughout the world, femininity.
Purple	In Latin America, purple symbolizes death; in Europe, royalty; in Egypt, virtue and faith; in Japan, grace and nobility; and in China, barbarism.

There is some evidence that colors affect us physiologically. For example, respiratory movements increase in the presence of red light and decrease in the presence of blue light. Similarly, eye blinks increase in frequency when eyes are exposed to red light and decrease when exposed to blue. This seems consistent with our intuitive feelings that blue is more soothing and red more provocative. After changing a school's walls from orange and white to blue, the students' blood pressures decreased and their academic performance improved.

Colors surely influence our perceptions and behaviors. People's acceptance of a product, for example, is largely determined by its package. For example, among consumers in the United States the very same coffee taken from a yellow can was described as weak, from a dark brown can it was described as too strong, from a red can it was described as rich, and from a blue can it was described as mild. Even our acceptance of a person may depend on the colors worn. Consider, for example, the comments of one color expert: "If you have to pick the wardrobe for your defense lawyer heading into court and choose anything but blue, you deserve to lose the case. . . ." Black is so powerful that it can work against the lawyer with the jury. Brown lacks sufficient authority. Green will probably elicit a negative response.

Source: "Color Communication," from Joseph A. DeVito, in *Essentials of Human Communication,* 3rd ed. Published by Allyn and Bacon, Boston, MA. Copyright © 1999 by Pearson Education. Reprinted by permission of the publisher.

"Language is the inventory of human experience."

—L. W. Lockhart

See how many of the following phrases you can complete with the appropriate color word below. (Some color words will be used more than once.)

black	brown	gray	pink	rose
blue	gold	green	red	silver

1. He is in a _____ mood.
2. The little boy was good as _____.
3. Mike is true _____.
4. The movie star got the _____-carpet treatment.
5. Every cloud has a _____ lining.
6. People who drink too much are said to see _____ elephants.
7. He looks at the world through _____-colored glasses.
8. Nora is a good gardener. She has a _____ thumb.
9. Silence is _____ en.
10. I'm going to _____-bag my lunch.
11. The police caught him _____-handed.
12. Jeff is the _____ sheep of the family.
13. He was beaten _____ and _____.
14. Play some more of those _____ en oldies.
15. He's very smart. He has lots of _____ matter.
16. There's too much _____ tape involved.

IMAGERY

In addition to the figures of speech discussed earlier, writers use **imagery** to create word pictures. Imagery is language that has a sensory quality. It can appeal to any of the five senses—sight, sound, taste, touch, and smell. A good reader must not only be able to recognize imagery but also understand the author's intent in presenting it.

ANALYZING IMAGERY

SELECTION

"At the end of the island I noticed a small green frog. He was exactly half in and half out of the water, looking like a schematic diagram of an amphibian, and he didn't jump."

GETTING THE PICTURE

Identify the instances of imagery in the following paragraphs. What senses do they primarily appeal to? What overall effect does the imagery evoke? Also pay attention to Dillard's use of figurative language—what similes and metaphors does she use?

BIO-SKETCH

Annie Dillard was born in 1945 in Pittsburgh, Pennsylvania, and received her B.A. and M.A. degrees from Hollins College in Roanoke, Virginia. She has received numerous awards for her writings, which include essays, poetry, memoirs, literary criticism, and even a western novel. The following selection is taken from *Pilgrim at Tinker Creek*, for which she received the 1975 Pulitzer Prize for General Nonfiction. This book was the result of Dillard's stay on Tinker Creek in Virginia's Roanoke Valley, where she observed the natural world while exploring the subjects of theology, philosophy, and science. Many have compared this work to Thoreau's *Walden*.

BRUSHING UP ON VOCABULARY

ruck fold, wrinkle, or crease.

enzymes proteins originating from body cells that produce chemical changes such as paralysis.

Excerpt from

Pilgrim at Tinker Creek

BY ANNIE DILLARD

HEAVEN AND EARTH IN JEST

1   A couple of summers ago I was walking along the edge of the island to see what I could see in the water, and mainly to scare frogs. Frogs have an inelegant way of taking off from invisible positions on the bank just ahead of your feet, in dire panic, emitting a froggy "Yike!" and splashing into the water. Incredibly, this

amused me, and, incredibly, it amuses me still. As I walked along the grassy edge of the island, I got better and better at seeing frogs both in and out of the water. I learned to recognize, slowing down, the difference in texture of the light reflected from mudbank, water, grass, or frog. Frogs were flying all around me. At the end of the island I noticed a small green frog. He was exactly half in and half out of the water, looking like a schematic diagram of an amphibian, and he didn't jump.

2   He didn't jump; I crept closer. At last I knelt on the island's winterkilled grass, lost, dumbstruck, staring at the frog in the creek just four feet away. He was a very small frog with wide, dull eyes. And just as I looked at him, he slowly crumpled and began to sag. The spirit vanished from his eyes as if snuffed. His skin emptied and drooped; his very skull seemed to collapse and settle like a kicked tent. He was shrinking before my eyes like a deflating football. I watched the taut, glistening skin on his shoulders ruck, and rumple, and fall. Soon, part of his skin, formless as a pricked balloon, lay in floating folds like bright scum on top of the water: it was a monstrous and terrifying thing. I gaped bewildered, appalled. An oval shadow hung in the water behind the drained frog; then the shadow glided away. The frog skin bag started to sink.

3   I had read about the giant water bug, but never seen one. "Giant water bug" is really the name of the creature, which is an enormous, heavy-bodied brown beetle. It eats insects, tadpoles, fish, and frogs. Its grasping forelegs are mighty and hooked inward. It seizes a victim with these legs, hugs it tight, and paralyzes it with enzymes injected during a vicious bite. That one bite is the only bite it ever takes. Through the puncture shoot the poisons that dissolve the victim's muscles and bones and organs—all but the skin—and through it the giant water bug sucks out the victim's body, reduced to a juice. This event is quite common in warm fresh water. The frog I saw was being sucked by a giant water bug. I had been kneeling on the island grass; when the unrecognizable flap of frog skin settled on the creek bottom, swaying. I stood up and brushed the knees of my pants. I couldn't catch my breath.

Source: PP. 5–6 from "Heaven and Earth in Jest," by Annie Dillard. Copyright © 1974 by Annie Dillard. Reprinted by permission of HarperCollins Publishers, Inc.

> *"The whole of nature is a conjugation of the verb to eat in the active and the passive."*
>
> —Dean William R. Inge

 ## COMPREHENSION CHECKUP

Figurative Language

Drawing on what you learned from the selection, answer the following questions.

1. To what does Dillard compare the frog's collapse in the second paragraph?

   A kicked tent/ball.

2. What overall image is created by Dillard's figures of speech? _____

   Her passion for nature.

3. What does Dillard mean when she describes the frog as looking like "the schematic drawing of an amphibian"? *The frog look like a drawing on a piece of paper.*

4. At the end of her encounter with the giant water bug, why was Dillard unable to catch her breath?
She was in disbelief to have experienced a frog being sucked up by a giant water bug.

Vocabulary in Context

Look through the paragraph indicated in parentheses to find a word that matches the definition below.

1. terrible; desperate (paragraph 1) *dire*
2. uttering (1) *emitting*
3. tightly drawn, not slack (2) *taut*
4. stared with open mouth as in wonder (2) *gaped – dumbstruck*

In Your Own Words

1. What do you suppose Dillard means to imply by the title "Heaven and Earth in Jest"? The word "jest" usually implies a prank, a joke, or something fun. Is this the meaning that Dillard is using?

2. Are you surprised that Dillard, a naturalist, likes to scare frogs? Is *she* surprised by her actions?

The Art of Writing

Have you ever witnessed something so completely unexpected that it literally took your breath away? If so, write a brief description of your experience.

Internet Activity

Visit the website below to learn more about the giant water bug described above and see a picture of one.

www.insects.org/entophiles/hemiptera/hemi_005.html

In what culture are these bugs considered to be a delicacy?

SELECTION

"A long finger of smoke curled around the corner toward me."

GETTING THE PICTURE

In the following excerpt, Kinsey Millhone, private investigator, finds herself trying to escape from a hotel fire started by the murderer she is trying to apprehend. Notice how the use of sensory images involves the reader in Millhone's distress. These images were chosen by the author to heighten the sense of excitement and danger.

SELECTION *continued*

BIO-SKETCH

Sue Grafton, Edgar Award nominee, helped usher in the era of the modern, female, hard-boiled private eye. Grafton's mysteries, which are titled after letters of the alphabet (*A Is for Alibi, B Is for Burglar,* etc.), are considered to be "humorous" in the sense that they exhibit the wit of her female detective, Kinsey Millhone. According to the author, Millhone is partially based on Grafton herself, but is younger and feistier. Grafton's first mystery, *A Is for Alibi,* was selected by the Mystery Writers of America as one of the top 100 mystery novels of all time.

BRUSHING UP ON VOCABULARY

abyss a bottomless pit.

tawny tan. The word is associated with the brownish-yellow of tanned leather.

catwalk a narrow walkway high above the surrounding area.

blindman's bluff a game in which a blindfolded player tries to catch and identify one of the other players.

Excerpt from

L Is for Lawless

BY SUE GRAFTON

1   BLINDLY, I measured the width of the catwalk, sensing the cavernous abyss on my left where my hand plunged suddenly into nothingness.

2   The entire area was pitch black, but I could hear an ominous crackling noise. A blistering wind blew, sending a shower of sparks in my direction. I could smell hot, dry wood, undercut by the acrid odor of petroleum-based products changing chemical states. I inched my way forward. Ahead, I could now discern a soft reddish glow defining the wall where the corridor curved left. A long finger of smoke curled around the corner toward me. If the fire caught me on the catwalk, it would probably sweep right past, but the rising cloud of toxic fumes would snuff me out as effectively as the flames.

3   While the water from the sprinkler system hissed steadily, it seemed to have no effect on the fire that I could see. The play of tawny light on the walls began to expand and dance, pushing fine ash and black smoke ahead of it, gobbling up all the available oxygen. The metal catwalk was slippery, the chain railing swinging wildly as I propelled myself onward. The public address system came to life again. The same announcement was repeated, a garbled blend of consonants. I reached the top of the ladder. I was afraid to turn my back on the encroaching

fire, but I had no choice. With my right foot, I felt for the first rung, gauging the distance as I moved down from rung to rung. I began descending with care, my hands sliding on the wet metal side rail. Hanging lengths of chain turned gold in the light, sparks flying up, winking out like intermittent fireflies on a hot summer night. By now, the fire was providing sufficient illumination to see the air turn gray as smoke accumulated.

4   I reached the bottom of the ladder and moved to my left. The fire was heating the air to an uncomfortable degree. I could hear a snapping sound, glass shattering; the merry rustle of destruction as the flames roared toward me. Despite the liberal use of concrete, the hotel had sufficient combustible material to feed the swiftly spreading blaze. I heard the dull boom of thunder as something behind me gave way and collapsed. This entire portion of the hotel had apparently been engulfed. I spotted a door on my left. I tried the knob, which was cool to the touch. I turned it and pushed through, spilling abruptly into a second-floor hall.

5   Here the air was much cooler. The rain birds in the ceiling showered the deserted corridor with irregular sprays. I was getting used to the dark, which now seemed less dense, a chalky gloom instead of the impenetrable black of the inner corridor. The carpet was saturated, slapping wetly beneath my feet as I stumbled down the darkened hallway. Afraid to trust my eyes, I held my arms out stiffly, waving my hands in front of me like a game of blindman's bluff. The fire alarm continued its monotonous clanging, a secondary horn bleating gutturally. In a submarine movie, we'd be diving by now. I felt my way across another door frame. Again, the knob seemed cool to the touch; suggesting that, for the time being, the fire wasn't raging on the other side. I turned the knob, pushing the door open in front of me. I found myself on the fire stairs, which I knew intimately by now. I went down through the blackness, reassured by the familiarity of the stairwell. The air was cold and smelled clean.

Source: Excerpt from *L is for Lawless* by Sue Grafton.

 COMPREHENSION CHECKUP

Figurative Language

1. Identify all similes, metaphors, and personification, and explain their meaning.

    _____

    _____

    _____

    _____

    _____

    _____

2. Make a chart with each one of the senses as a category. On your chart, place each relevant detail from the excerpt under the appropriate category.

3. The excerpt provides a word picture of the scene where the action is taking place. From the images, you can imagine the layout of the place as if you were there yourself. Make a sketch of Millhone's actions as she tries to escape the encroaching fire. Label the details of your drawing.

Vocabulary in Context

Look through the paragraphs indicated, and find the words that correctly match each of the definitions given below.

1. threatening (paragraph 2) _____
2. sharp or bitter to the taste or smell (2) _____
3. poisonous (2) _____
4. stopping and starting again at intervals; periodic (3) _____
5. distorted or confused (3) _____
6. generous (4) _____
7. flammable (4) _____
8. thoroughly soaked (5) _____
9. going on and on in the same tone (5) _____
10. closely, familiarly (5) _____

In Your Own Words

1. In stressful situations, many people fall apart, while others become more calm. How do you handle yourself in tense situations?

2. Have you ever been in a situation in which your life was in danger? If so, what did you do?

3. Many accidents occur when children play with matches. What can parents do to teach children the danger of fire?

4. Does your family have a plan for responding to a fire in your home? If so, what kind of plan have you devised?

5. What are some things people can do to help prevent a fire from occuring at home?

6. Many fires occur on major holidays. Why do you think fires are more likely to occur then?

The Art of Writing

Write a metaphor about fire. First, choose a characteristic of fire that you wish to describe or emphasize. Next, select something else that possesses the same characteristic as fire. Finally, put it all together by comparing the two subjects.

Example: Subject: fire
Characteristic: shine
Second subject: gold
Metaphor: Fire is gold, shining ever bright.

Internet Activities

1. Consult Sue Grafton's official website to see what she's working on now.

   http://www.suegrafton.com

2. Consult the following site to get a brief biographical sketch of the author.

   http://www.who-dunnit.com/authors

REVIEW TEST: *Main Ideas and Supporting Details, Transition Words, Vocabulary in Context, and Imagery*

SELECTION

> *"But among the iron rods of the train, the handrail broke and went through Frida from one side to the other at the level of the pelvis."*

GETTING THE PICTURE

This excerpt from Hayden Herrera's biography of the artist Frida Kahlo (see p. 263) gives both Kahlo's and her friend Alejandro Gomez Arias's accounts of the accident that changed her life. She spent over a month in the hospital and endured many operations. Doctors were amazed that she survived. As Kahlo told Arias, "Death dances over my bed at night." Bedridden for over three months, she learned to paint when her mother attached a portable easel and a mirror to her bed so that she could be her own model.

BIO-SKETCH

Biographer/historian Hayden Herrera has lectured widely, curated several exhibitions of art, taught Latin American art at New York University, and been awarded a Guggenheim Fellowship. She is the author of numerous articles and reviews for such publications as *The New York Times.* In addition to *Frida,* her books include *Frida Kahlo: The Paintings, Mary Frank,* and *Matisse: A Portrait.* Frida Kahlo's life story is depicted in the movie *Frida,* starring Salma Hayek as the artist and Alfred Molina as her husband, the renowned Mexican muralist Diego Rivera. The movie, released in 2002, is based on Hayden Herrera's biography of Frida Kahlo.

BRUSHING UP ON VOCABULARY

toreador a term for a bullfighter or matador; the term *toreador* (from the Spanish *torear,* "to bait a bull") was first used by the French composer Georges Bizet in his opera *Carmen.*

lesion an injury to the body tending to result in impairment or loss of function.

contusion a bruise; an injury to the underlying tissue without the skin being broken.

Excerpt from

Frida

BY HAYDEN HERRERA

ACCIDENT AND AFTERMATH

1   It was one of those accidents that make a person, even one separated by years from the actual fact, wince with horror. It involved a trolley car that plowed into a flimsy wooden bus, and it transformed Frida Kahlo's life.

2   Far from being a unique piece of bad luck, such accidents were common enough in those days in Mexico City to be depicted in numerous *retablos* (small votive paintings offering thanks to a holy being, usually the Virgin, for misfortunes escaped). Buses were relatively new to the city, and because of their novelty they were jammed with people while trolley cars went empty. Then, as now, they were driven with toreador bravado, as if the image of the Virgin of Guadalupe dangling near the front window made the driver invincible. The bus in which Frida was riding was new, and its fresh coat of paint made it look especially jaunty.

3   The accident occurred late in the afternoon on September 17, 1925, the day after Mexico had celebrated the anniversary of its independence from Spain. A light rain had just stopped; the grand gray government buildings that border the Zocalo looked even grayer and more severe than usual. The bus to Coyoacan was nearly full, but Alejandro and Frida found seats together in the back. When they reached the corner of Cuahutemotzin and 5 de Mayo and were about to turn onto Calzada de Tlalpan, a trolley from Xochimilco approached. It was moving slowly but kept coming as if it had no brakes, as if it were purposely aiming at a crash. Frida remembered:

> *"Although the world is full of suffering, it is full also of overcoming it."*
>
> —Helen Keller

4   A little while after we got on the bus the collision began. Before that we had taken another bus, but since I had lost a little parasol, we got off to look for it and that was how we happened to get on the bus that destroyed me. The accident took place on a corner in front of the San Juan market, exactly in front. The streetcar went slowly, but our bus driver was a very nervous young man. When the trolley went around the corner the bus was pushed against the wall.

5   I was an intelligent young girl, but impractical, in spite of all the freedom I had won. Perhaps for this reason, I did not assess the situation nor did I guess the kind of wounds I had. The first thing I thought of was a *ballero* [Mexican toy] with pretty colors that I had bought that day and that I was carrying with me. I tried to look for it, thinking that what had happened would not have major consequences.

6   It is a lie that one is aware of the crash, a lie that one cries. In me there were no tears. The crash bounced us forward and a handrail pierced me the way a sword pierces a bull. A man saw me having a tremendous hemorrhage. He carried me and put me on a billiard table until the Red Cross came for me.

7   When Alejandro Gomez Arias describes the accident, his voice constricts to an almost inaudible monotone, as if he could avoid reliving the memory by speaking of it quietly:

8   The electric train with two cars approached the bus slowly. It hit the bus in the middle. Slowly the train pushed the bus. The bus had a strange elasticity. It bent more and more, but for a time it did not break. It was a bus with long benches on either side. I remember that at one moment my knees touched the knees of the person sitting opposite me, I was sitting next to Frida. When the bus reached its maximal flexibility it burst into a thousand pieces, and the train kept moving. It ran over many people.

9   I remained under the train. Not Frida. But among the iron rods of the train, the handrail broke and went through Frida from one side to the other at the level of the pelvis. When I was able to stand up I got out from under the train. I had no lesions, only contusions. Naturally the first thing I did was to look for Frida.

10   Something strange had happened. Frida was totally nude. The collision had unfastened her clothes. Someone in the bus, probably a house painter, had been carrying a packet of powdered gold. This package broke, and the gold fell all over the bleeding body of Frida. When people saw her they cried, *'La bailarina, la bailarina!'* With the gold on her red, bloody body, they thought she was a dancer.

11   I picked her up—in those days I was a strong boy—and then I noticed with horror that Frida had a piece of iron in her body. A man said, 'We have to take it out!' He put his knee on Frida's body, and said 'Let's take it out.' When he pulled it out, Frida screamed so loud that when the ambulance from the Red Cross arrived, her screaming was louder than the siren. Before the ambulance came, I picked up Frida and put her in the display window of a billiard room. I took off my coat and put it over her. I thought she was going to die. Two or three people did die at the scene of the accident, others died later.

12   The ambulance came and took her to the Red Cross Hospital, which in those days was on San Jeronimo Street, a few blocks from where the accident took place. Frida's condition was so grave that the doctors did not think they could save her. They thought she would die on the operating table.

13   Frida was operated on for the first time. During the first month it was not certain that she would live.

14   The girl whose wild dash through school corridors resembled a bird's flight, who jumped on and off streetcars and buses, preferably when they were moving, was now immobilized and enclosed in a series of plaster casts and other contraptions. "It was a strange collision," Frida said. "It was not violent but rather silent, slow, and it harmed everybody. And me most of all."

15   Her spinal column was broken in three places in the lumbar region. Her collarbone was broken, and her third and fourth ribs. Her right leg had eleven fractures and her right foot was dislocated and crushed. Her left shoulder was out of joint, her pelvis broken in three places. The steel handrail had literally skewered her body at the level of the abdomen.

Source: Pages 47–48 from *Frida: A Biography of Frida Kahlo* by Hayden Herrera. Copyright © 1983 by Hayden Herrera. Reprinted by permission of HarperCollins Publishers.

COMPREHENSION CHECKUP

Multiple Choice

Write the letter of the correct answer in the blank provided.

_____ 1. Which of the following statements best expresses the main idea of the selection?
   a. Frida rode a bus.
   b. A handrail broke and went through the pelvis of Frida.
   c. Frida sustained severe injuries in a terrible bus accident but survived.
   d. Frida's spinal column was broken.

_____ 2. The author's main purpose is to
   a. inform
   b. entertain
   c. persuade

_____ 3. The main pattern of organization of paragraph 3 is
   a. example
   b. listing
   c. cause and effect
   d. chronological order

_____ 4. All of the following statements about the bus are true *except*
   a. the bus was new
   b. the bus was fairly empty
   c. the bus was made of wood
   d. the bus was headed to Cayoacan

True or False

Indicate whether the statement is true or false by writing T or F in the blank provided.

_____ 5. Mexican Independence Day is September 17.

_____ 6. The bus driver was an anxious older man.

_____ 7. The trolley was electric with two cars.

_____ 8. The doctors were confident that they could save Frida's life.

_____ 9. Frida's right leg and right foot were injured in the accident.

_____ 10. The rods that pierced Frida were part of the bus.

Sequence

Number the events in the order in which they occurred in the reading selection.

_____ a. Frida gets off a bus to look for her parasol.

_____ b. The trolley car plows into Frida's bus.

_____ c. Frida is operated on.

_____ d. Frida begins to hemorrhage.

_____ e. The ambulance comes and picks up Frida.

_____ f. The handrail pierces Frida.

_____ g. Frida is laid out on the billiard table.

Vocabulary in Context

Each item below includes a sentence from the selection. Using the context clues provided, write a preliminary definition for the italicized word. Then look up the word in a dictionary and write the appropriate definition.

1. "It was one of those accidents that make a person, even one separated by years from the actual fact, *wince* with horror." (paragraph 1)

   Your definition: _____

   Dictionary definition: _____

2. "Far from being a *unique* piece of bad luck, such accidents were common enough in those days in Mexico City to be *depicted* in numerous retablos (small votive paintings offering thanks to a holy being, usually the Virgin, for misfortunes escaped)." (2)

   Your definition: _____

   Dictionary definition: _____

   Your definition: _____

   Dictionary definition: _____

3. "The bus in which Frida was riding was new, and its fresh coat of paint made it look especially *jaunty*." (2)

   Your definition: _____

   Dictionary definition: _____

4. "When Alejandro Gomez Arias describes the accident, his voice *constricts* to an almost *inaudible monotone,* as if he could avoid reliving the memory by speaking of it quietly:" (7)

   Your definition: _____

   Dictionary definition: _____

   Your definition: _____

   Dictionary definition: _____

5. "The bus had a strange *elasticity*." (8)

   Your definition: _____

   Dictionary definition: _____

6. "Frida's condition was so *grave* that the doctors did not think they could save her." (12)

   Your definition: _____

   Dictionary definition: _____

In Your Own Words

1. What is the overall impression created by this excerpt? What specific images contribute to this impression?

2. What details of the accident scene are clearly depicted? Why are these images particularly sharp or vivid?

The Art of Writing

Write a short essay discussing one of the following quotations attributed to Frida Kahlo.

1. "In this hospital, death dances around my bed at night." (said shortly after her accident)

2. "I was a child who went about in a world of colors. My friends, my companions, became women slowly. I became old in instants." (said during her long recovery at home)

Internet Activity

For additional information about Frida Kahlo, explore the following websites:

www.sfmoma.org/msoma/artworks/3825.html

www.eyeconart.net/history/frida-y-diego.htm

The first is an interactive website sponsored by the San Francisco Museum of Modern Art. The painting *Frieda and Diego Rivera* (1931) is in the museum's permanent collection. Study the painting carefully. What do you think Kahlo was trying to express about the couple's relationship in the painting? Did she use any symbols?

The second website shows many pictures and self-portraits by Kahlo. Summarize what you learn from the website about Kahlo.

TEST-TAKING TIP

Taking Multiple-Choice Tests (1)

On your next multiple-choice test, try applying these tips:

1. Pay close attention to oral and written directions.

2. Don't spend too much time on any one question. Leave a difficult question blank, put a mark beside it, and then come back to it if time permits.

3. For each question, read through all of the answers before choosing one.

4. Don't change an answer unless you are quite sure you have found a better one.

5. If one of your choices is a combination of two or more answers (such as *both A and B*), remember that both parts of the answer must be correct.

6. Be aware that a longer answer is more likely to be correct than a shorter answer. It often takes more words to write a correct answer because it may need qualifying phrases to make it correct.

7. Avoid answers with all-inclusive words like *all, always, everyone, none,* and *nobody* because they are likely to be wrong. Any exception makes the answer wrong.

VOCABULARY Unit 5

In Unit 5, you will be introduced to word parts related to direction and motion.

vert—turn; con—with; in—not, opposite, into, within

avert	*a-* means "from," and *-vert* means "turn," so the literal meaning of *avert* is "to turn from." Martha *averted* her eyes during the violent parts of the movie *Road to Perdition*. *Avert* also means "prevent," as in she narrowly *averted* an accident.
invert	Here *in-* means "opposite," so when you *invert* something you are turning it upside down. She could tell that Marco did not know how to read because he had the newspaper *inverted*.
vertigo	a dizzy feeling, especially the feeling that everything is spinning around. After Katrinka got off the merry-go-round, she experienced a bout of *vertigo*.
subvert	to overturn or undermine something established. In the 1950s and 1960s, rock 'n' roll was thought likely to *subvert* the wholesome values of American teenagers.
convert	to turn from one form, use, or belief to another. Missionaries around the world try to *convert* people to Christianity. As a noun, *convert* (pronounced con-vert, with the stress on the first syllable) means a person who has changed from one belief or religion to another.
divert	to turn aside. Trapped by the Doberman, Alicia tried to *divert* the dog's attention by throwing a bone across the yard.
versatile	able to turn with ease from one thing to another. The basketball player was very *versatile* in that he could play many positions.
vertebra(e)	any one of the bones that make up the spinal column, or backbone. The backbone enables us to turn our bodies.

mis, mit—send; re—back, again; dis—apart, away; ad—toward

mission	a special duty or errand that a person or group is sent to do by a church, government, or other entity. Also, a place where a group of missionaries or diplomats live and work. The diplomatic *mission's* goal was to facilitate peace in the Middle East. *Mission* Santa Clara is marked by a California state historical marker.
admit	*ad-* means "toward," so the literal meaning of *admit* is "to send toward, or to let go." When you buy a ticket to a movie, you are *admitted* to the theater. Carol *admitted* that she had not told the truth to Rob.
submissive	willing to give in or obey another; humble or obedient. For years, Shawna had been *submissive* to her husband; finally, after too much abuse, she decided to file for divorce.
remit (remission)	*Re-* means "back" or "again." *Remit* means "to send back," or "to let go." Mark needs to *remit* his car payment by the first of each month. Cerise's breast cancer is currently in *remission*.
intermission	stopping for a time; an interruption. There is a twenty-minute *intermission* between Act I and Act II of the play. The original meaning of the word was "to send between."

intermittent	stopping and starting again from time to time. During a baby's first year of life, pediatricians recommend *intermittent* checkups or well-baby visits.
dismiss	*Dis-* means "away," so the literal meaning of *dismiss* is "to send away," or "to tell or allow to leave." He was *dismissed* from the army after failing to report for duty.
emissary	A person sent on a special mission. The *emissary* was sent to Cuba to arrange a meeting with the president.
emit	to send out or give forth. The owl *emitted* a shrill screech before attacking its prey. Motor vehicles *emit* toxic fumes that contribute to air pollution.

ven—come; circum—around

prevent	to keep from happening, to stop. The literal meaning is "to come before" or "to act in anticipation of." Vaccinations *prevent* the spread of disease.
convention	a meeting of members or delegates from various places. The literal meaning is "coming with." The Republican Party held its *convention* in New York in 2004.
circumvent	to get around, often by using sly or tricky methods. Warren thought we should deal with the problem directly; Sylvia thought we should try to *circumvent* it.

se—apart, away from

separate	to keep or put apart. Tina's job at the cannery required her to *separate* the good peaches from the bad ones.
seclude	to keep away from others; to remove from social contact. *-clude* is derived from *claudere*, meaning "to shut, or close." The literal meaning of *seclude* is "to close away from."
segregation	the practice of keeping people of different religious, racial, or ethnic groups apart from each other.

sequ (secut)—following

consecutive	following in a regular order without a break. In Phoenix, Arizona, it is unusual to have rain for two *consecutive* days.
sequence	one thing following after another. A bizarre *sequence* of events led to his apprehension and arrest.
sequel	a literary or film work that takes up and continues the narrative of a preceding work. The *sequel* to the movie *Star Wars* is *The Empire Strikes Back*.
consequence	the effect, result, or outcome of something occurring earlier. When you are under oath in a court of law, you must tell the truth or face the *consequences*.

dia—through, across, apart, thoroughly; pro—forward; log(ue)—speech, word

diagonal	*-gonia* means "angle," so *diagonal* means "connecting two nonadjacent angles." It also means "slanting." Martina's dress had *diagonal* stripes.

dialect	a form of language that is used only in a certain place or with a certain group. *-lect* means "to speak," so the literal meaning is "to speak across." Because of television, regional *dialects* in the United States are in danger of disappearing.
dialog(ue)	conversation between two or more persons; an exchange of ideas or opinions on a particular issue with a view to reaching a friendly agreement.
diagnosis	*-gnosis* means "to know," so a *diagnosis* means "a thorough examination or learning of all the facts in order to determine the nature of a disease." The doctor's *diagnosis* was that the patient suffered from heat exhaustion.
prognosis	*pro-* is a prefix meaning "forward," so a *prognosis* is a forecast or prediction of how a disease will develop in a person and what the chances are that the person will get well. After undergoing radiation treatments for prostate cancer, his *prognosis* for a full recovery was excellent.
progressive	moving forward. His *progressive* improvement in math is impressive.

duc—lead; in—into

reduce	to lead back; to decrease. Kristin wanted to *reduce* her intake of caffeinated drinks.
abduct	to take someone away forceably; to kidnap. The literal meaning is "to lead away." Most missing children are *abducted* by a parent in a custody dispute.
conduct	to lead or guide. The meeting was *conducted* by the vice president.
conducive	helping to bring about; contributing. The quiet in the library is *conducive* to studying.
seduce	to lead away, lead astray. In the *Star Wars* movies, Darth Vader was *seduced* by the dark side of the Force.
deduct	to lead away; subtract. If I save my receipt, the store will *deduct* 10 percent from the price of a new pair of shoes.
induce	to lead or move by persuasion or influence; to bring about or cause. Can't I *induce* you to stay a little longer?

Completing Verbal Analogies

The following verbal analogies include antonyms and synonyms. Consider the relationship between the first pair carefully before selecting your answer.

Complete the following analogies.

_____ 1. prevent : avert : : allow : _____
   a. prevail
   b. observe
   c. harm
   d. permit

_____ 2. include : seclude : : integration : _____
   a. intermission
   b. segregation
   c. conducive
   d. progressive

_____ 3. submissive : obedient : : prevent : _____
   a. delegate
   b. send toward
   c. hinder
   d. allow

_____ 4. reduce : decrease : : conduct : _____
   a. abandon
   b. overturn
   c. subtract
   d. lead

_____ 5. dismiss : discharge : : admit : _____
   a. allow
   b. renew
   c. turn
   d. send

_____ 6. intermittent : constant : : off-and-on : _____
   a. tentative
   b. concerned
   c. permanent
   d. timely

Now that you have studied the vocabulary in Unit 5, practice your new knowledge by completing the crossword puzzle on the following page.

Vocabulary 5

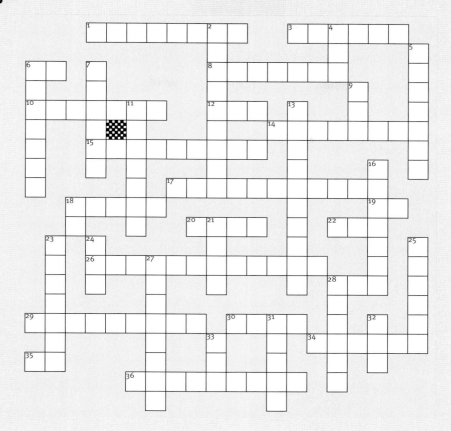

ACROSS CLUES

1. A line slanting from one corner to the opposite corner of a rectangle is a _____ line.
3. If I trade in my old camera, the store will _____ $25 from the price of a new one.
6. A word part meaning "away from."
8. The power failure at the college caused instructors to _____ classes early.
10. It had been his lifelong dream to _____ an orchestra.
12. A word part meaning "with."
14. The two parties were brought together in the hope that they could resolve the dispute with a civil _____.
15. For many students, talking by other students is not _____ to taking a quiz.
17. The _____ of taking drugs could be addiction.
18. A peace agreement was signed between the two countries to _____ further hostilities.
19. A word part meaning "back or again."
20. A word part meaning "following."
22. A word part meaning "send."
26. There was _____ rainfall every few hours all afternoon.

28. A word part for two.*
29. The doctor's _____ was that Ray had chicken pox.
30. A word part meaning "turn."
34. Should you _____ the number of hours that you work so that you can concentrate on your classes?
35. A word part meaning "into."
36. The doctor said that Anna had a good _____ for a complete recovery.

DOWN CLUES

2. The _____ and murder of Charles Lindbergh's son in 1932 led to stronger federal laws against kidnapping.
4. A word part meaning "apart or away."
5. The actress Reese Witherspoon had to speak in a southern _____ for her role in *Sweet Home Alabama*.
6. If you have a contagious disease, it might be necessary to _____ you from others.
7. After her child swallowed a strange pill, the doctor told the mother to _____ vomiting immediately.
9. A word part meaning "forward."

11. When Taryn married Mike, she agreed to _____ to his religion.
13. Have you ever tried to _____ a rule by finding a way to get around it?
16. Christina's ear infection caused her to lose her balance and experience feelings of _____.
18. A word part meaning "toward."
21. Cars _____ carbon monoxide and other harmful gases.
23. A group of doctors were sent on a humanitarian _____ to help with a medical crisis.
24. A word part meaning "across."
25. In *The Lord of the Rings*, the Hobbit Frodo must fight against the power of the "one ring" to _____ him.
27. Former president Jimmy Carter has been an active _____ for peace around the globe.
28. The police were trying to _____ traffic away from the scene of the accident.
31. Please _____ your payment no later than the fifteenth of each month.
32. A word part meaning "lead."
33. A word part meaning "come."

*From a previous unit.

Tone

Mona Lisa (1503) BY LEONARDO DA VINCI

Photo: R.G. Ojeda. Louvre, Paris. Inv.: 779. Réunion des Musées Nationaux/
Art Resource, NY

View and Reflect

1. Some experts believe that it is the *Mona Lisa's* enigmatic smile that fascinates viewers. Others contend that her amazing eye contact—her gaze seems to follow the viewer across the room—is the painting's special allure. What do you think makes so many long to see the *Mona Lisa?*
2. Why do you think da Vinci was so attached to this painting?
3. What is your opinion of this famous work of art?

TONE

Tone refers to the emotional quality of a piece of writing. Just as a speaker's voice can convey a wide range of tones, so can a writer's voice. We infer a speaker's tone by paying attention to such things as word choice, voice volume, and facial expressions. The available clues are more limited when we are trying to infer the tone of a writer's voice. An essay does not speak loudly or softly; it can't frown or smile. If we want to identify the tone of a written work, we can only look at what the author has written. Word choice, phrasing, and subject matter all contribute to the tone of a piece of writing. When you're reading something, it's important for you to be aware of the author's tone. Is the author being humorous or argumentative, or both? Is the author expressing outrage or giving praise? Is the author being ironic or earnest? Understanding the tone of a piece of writing is important to understanding its meaning.

A piece of writing can express one or more of a great variety of possible tones. You need to be familiar with some of the more common possibilities. We will begin by identifying the tones of particular statements taken from pieces of writing. These exercises will help you understand tone and will familiarize you with some of the many ways of describing tone. Then we will work on identifying and describing the overall tone of a piece of writing.

The words mentioned below are useful for describing tone. Words on the same line have the same or a similar meaning.

1. excited, stirred up, impassioned
2. loving, affectionate, fond
3. surprised, astonished, amazed, incredulous
4. mournful, sorrowful
5. cruel, brutal, vicious
6. angry, outraged, offended
7. bitter, resentful
8. formal, stiff
9. patronizing, condescending, supercilious
10. cheerful, glad, joyful, ecstatic, elated
11. humorous, funny, amusing, comical, entertaining
12. arrogant, haughty, contemptuous
13. cynical, negative, pessimistic
14. optimistic, positive, encouraging
15. whining, complaining, querulous
16. witty, clever
17. peevish, cross, irritable
18. charming, pleasing, attractive, delightful
19. flattering, fawning, obsequious
20. skeptical, doubtful, questioning

21. scolding, chiding
22. sad, glum
23. dictatorial, domineering, overbearing, tyrannical
24. rude, churlish, boorish
25. compassionate, caring, solicitous
26. self-pitying, self-indulgent
27. alarmed, fearful, anxious
28. critical, disapproving
29. depressed, gloomy, discouraged
30. solemn, grave, somber
31. informal, casual, relaxed
32. objective, neutral, matter-of-fact
33. evasive, secretive, furtive
34. remorseful, regretful
35. scornful, derisive, contemptuous
36. vindictive, vengeful
37. serious, earnest, sober
38. befuddled, confused
39. sarcastic, mocking, sneering
40. admiring, appreciative
41. playful, lively
42. irreverent, disrespectful, impertinent
43. disgusted, offended
44. appreciative, thankful, grateful
45. nostalgic, sentimental, wistful
46. perplexed, puzzled, bewildered
47. contemptuous, disdainful, scornful
48. ambivalent, conflicted, wavering
49. informative, instructive
50. sincere, honest, frank
51. satiric, mocking
52. ironic, tongue-in-cheek

Exercise 1: Identifying Tone

Directions: Read the following dialog between a police officer and a speeding motorist. After reading each statement, indicate which word best describes the speaker's tone by writing the appropriate letter in the blank provided.

The Traffic Ticket

_____ 1. Officer: "Lady, what's the matter with you? What took you so long to stop?"

      a. casual

      b. cross

      c. pessimistic

_____ 2. Driver: "Officer, I didn't hear the siren. What's your problem? I know I didn't do anything wrong."

      a. sincere

      b. vicious

      c. disdainful

_____ 3. Officer: "You were speeding."

      a. clever

      b. matter-of-fact

      c. appreciative

_____ 4. Driver: "Me? Speeding? Are you sure?"

      a. chiding

      b. charming

      c. doubting

_____ 5. Officer: "Ma'am, what's wrong with you? Do you have any idea at all how fast you were going?"

      a. annoyed

      b. vicious

      c. appreciative

_____ 6. Driver: "Oh my goodness! How fast _was_ I going?"

      a. ambivalent

      b. alarmed

      c. vengeful

_____ 7. Officer: "I have you on the radar gun going 50 miles an hour in a 15-mile-an-hour school zone."

      a. admiring

      b. playful

      c. informative

_____ 8. Driver: "Are you sure, Officer? How can that be? I was watching my speedometer."

      a. thankful

      b. perplexed

      c. sneering

_____ 9. Officer: "No doubt about it, lady! Our radar is very accurate."

      a. assertive

      b. sentimental

      c. wavering

———— 10. Driver: "I'm so sorry, Officer I'm really sorry. I'll be more careful next time."

    a. wistful

    b. contemptuous

    c. remorseful

———— 11. Officer: "Hand me your driver's license and your registration."

    a. ambivalent

    b. demanding

    c. fawning

———— 12. Driver: "Yes. Oh my! I can't believe it. I can't find them. I was in such a hurry I must have left them at home."

    a. bored

    b. cruel

    c. bewildered

Traffic School: Some random comments by the officer teaching traffic school two weeks later.

———— 13. Officer: "Good morning class. Apparently you all couldn't think of anything else to do today, right?"

    a. angry

    b. humorous

    c. elated

———— 14. Officer: "I want to give you some sobering statistics. Every year traffic accidents kill 43,000 people, injure 2.6 million, and cause 130 billion dollars in damage."

    a. self-indulgent

    b. grave

    c. churlish

———— 15. Officer: "We *can't* control other drivers, but we *can* control our own behavior."

    a. impassioned

    b. witty

    c. haughty

———— 16. Officer: "For your safety and the safety of other motorists, *please* think about the consequences of your actions."

    a. boorish

    b. disapproving

    c. imploring

Exercise 2: Identifying Tone in Textbook Material

Directions: Read the passages below and choose the word that best describes the speaker's tone by writing the appropriate letter in the blank provided.

"Hurt not the earth, neither the sea, nor the trees."

—Revelations 7:3

_____ 1. Our impact on the health of the oceans is much more profound than we often assume. You can do a lot to help save the oceans. First of all, take care of the environment. If you go to the seashore or go snorkeling or diving, do not disturb in any way the environment. Return any overturned rocks to their original positions. Leave all forms of life where they are. If you go fishing, know the regulations and take only what you really need for food. Return undersized fish. Corals and shells should be left alone, and alive, in their natural home. Be sure to tell merchants you object to their sale of shells, corals, sand dollars, and other marine life, which were most probably collected alive and killed for sale. Don't buy the yellowfin tuna that is caught in nets that trap dolphins. Look for the "dolphin-safe" seal on the label.

Paragraph from Peter Castro, *Marine Biology,* 6th ed., New York: McGraw-Hill, 2003, p. 421. Copyright © 2007 McGraw-Hill. Reprinted by permission of The McGraw-Hill Companies, Inc.

a. cynical
b. serious
c. arrogant
d. outraged

"The battle for women's rights has been largely won."

—Margaret Thatcher

_____ 2. Remember the *Leave It to Beaver* reruns on television? Mother would spend the day whisking around the house in a stylish outfit protected by an apron, tidying and scrubbing and fixing a delicious dinner, and greet Father warmly when he returned from his day at work. Well, times have changed. Or have they? More than 61 percent of married American women are part of the workforce today. But guess who is still tidying and scrubbing and fixing delicious dinners in American homes? Women. And—here's the kicker—*most women seem to think this is fair!*

Paragraph from Michael Hughes in *Sociology: The Core,* 7th ed., New York: McGraw-Hill, 2005, p. 267. Copyright © 2005 McGraw-Hill. Reprinted by permission of The McGraw-Hill Companies, Inc.

a. rueful
b. nostalgic
c. amazed
d. scolding

_____ 3. We have seen that anorexia is a serious disease with deep-seated causes and devastating, potentially fatal effects. Julie was one of those who couldn't beat anorexia. She died when she was only 17. We will never go to college together and share a dorm room. She will never fulfill her dream of becoming a nurse. And we will never grow old living beside each other and watching our kids grow up together. Anorexia killed my beautiful vibrant friend.

Paragraph from Stephen E. Lucas in *The Art of Public Speaking,* 7th ed., New York: McGraw-Hill, 2001, p. 358. Copyright © 2001 McGraw-Hill. Reprinted by permission of The McGraw-Hill Companies, Inc.

a. sorrowful
b. angry
c. loving
d. whining

_____ 4. Our math classroom is on the third floor of a building that overlooks the top floor of a parking ramp. At most three or four cars are parked up there, although it contains enough space for at least fifty cars. The lower levels of the ramp are also fairly empty. The ramp is only for the use of faculty. We students have to park some distance from campus and even then we have to get to school by 7:30 in the morning if we are to find a parking space. . . . I think the current situation is disgusting. The faculty already enjoy many privileges, including "faculty restrooms," which are distinctive from those simply labeled "restroom." Enough is enough!

Paragraph from Michael Hughes in _Sociolgy: The Core,_ 7th ed., New York: McGraw-Hill, 2005, p. 177. Copyright © 2005 McGraw-Hill. Reprinted by permission of The McGraw-Hill Companies, Inc.

a. outraged
b. vindictive
c. pessimistic
d. alarmed

_____ 5. If you are beginning to think that being computer illiterate may be occupational suicide, you are getting the point. Workers in every industry come in contact with computers to some degree. Even fast-food workers read orders on computer screens. Nearly 80 percent of the respondents to a survey said that they believe it is impossible to succeed in the job market without a working knowledge of technology. Respondents who earned $45,000 a year or more were three times more likely to use a computer than those who earned less. As information technology eliminates old jobs while creating new ones, it is up to you to learn the skills you need to be certain you aren't left behind.

Paragraph from William G. Nickels, _Understanding Business,_ 8th ed., New York: McGraw-Hill 2008, p. 613. Copyright © 2008 McGraw-Hill. Reprinted by permission of The McGraw-Hill Companies, Inc.

a. excited
b. bitter
c. cautious
d. serious

_____ 6. I honestly feel Robert can contribute more than I can. He's better educated. He's just plain smarter. He's genuinely gifted, and when he's able to apply himself, he can really accomplish something, can make a name for himself.

Paragraph from Gloria Bird, _Families and Intimate Relationships,_ New York: McGraw-Hill, 1994, p. 76.

a. critical
b. sympathetic
c. candid
d. sentimental

_____ 7. "Anna, I told you to stop talking. If I've told you once, I've told you 100 times. I told you yesterday and the day before that. The way things are going, I'll be telling it to you all year, and, believe me, I'm getting pretty tired of it. And another thing, young lady . . ."

Paragraph from Myra Pollack Sadker and David Miller Sadker in *Teachers, Schools, and Society,* 5th ed., New York: McGraw-Hill, 2000, p. 58. Copyright © 2000 McGraw-Hill. Reprinted by permission of The McGraw-Hill Companies, Inc.

  a. ironic
  b. sorrowful
  c. scolding
  d. playful

_____ 8. Ever wonder how schools get their names—and which names are the most popular? The National Education Resource Center researched the most popular proper names for U.S. high schools: Washington, Lincoln, Kennedy, Jefferson, Roosevelt (both Franklin and Teddy), and Wilson. (Presidents do well.) (To date, no school has chosen Richard M. Nixon as a namesake.) But proper names are not the most common high school names. Directions dominate: Northeastern, South, and Central High School are right up there. While creativity obviously is not a criterion, politics is. Citizens fight over whether schools should be named after George Washington and Thomas Jefferson—who, after all, were slaveholders. And, considering how many women are educators, it is amazing that so few schools are named to honor women. Some schools have honored writers or reflect local leaders and culture. In Las Vegas, you will find schools named Durango, Silverado, and Bonanza, which some complain sound more like casinos than western culture.

Paragraph from Myra Pollack Sadker and David Miller Sadker in *Teachers, Schools, and Society,* 5th ed., New York: McGraw-Hill, 2000, p. 148. Copyright © 2000 McGraw-Hill. Reprinted by permission of The McGraw-Hill Companies, Inc.

  a. affectionate
  b. flippant
  c. optimistic
  d. outraged

_____ 9. It's Saturday morning, and you are helping clean out your grandmother's attic. After working a while, you stumble upon a trunk, open it, and discover inside hundreds of old postcards. Thinking about getting to the football game on time, you start tossing the cards into the trash can. Congratulations! You have just thrown away a year's tuition.

Paragraph from Stephen E. Lucas, *The Art of Public Speaking,* 7th ed., New York: McGraw-Hill, 2001, p. 215.

  a. elated
  b. regretful
  c. sarcastic
  d. demanding

_____ 10. When the expectant mother drinks, alcohol is absorbed into her bloodstream and distributed throughout her entire body. . . . The fetus is surrounded by the same alcoholic content as its mother had. After being drowned in alcohol, the fetus begins to feel the effect. But it can't sober up. It can't grab a cup of coffee. It can't grab a couple of aspirin. For the fetus's liver, the key organ in removing alcohol from the blood, is just not developed. The fetus is literally pickled in alcohol.

Paragraph from Stephen E. Lucas in *The Art of Public Speaking,* 7th ed., New York: McGraw-Hill, 2001, p. 263. Copyright © 2001 McGraw-Hill. Reprinted by permission of The McGraw-Hill Companies, Inc.

a. carefree
b. aghast
c. casual
d. congratulatory

Exercise 3: Determining Tone in Literature

Directions: Read the following excerpts and indicate the tone of the passage. (You may refer to the list of words at the beginning of the chapter.)

1. I could've been somebody, you know? my mother says and sighs. She has lived in this city her whole life. She can speak two languages. She can sing an opera. She knows how to fix a TV. But she doesn't know which subway train to take to get downtown. I hold her hand very tight while we wait for the right train to arrive.

   She used to draw when she had time. Now she draws with a needle and thread, little knotted rosebuds, tulips made of silk thread. Someday she would like to go to the ballet. Someday she would like to see a play. She borrows opera records from the public library and sings with velvety lungs powerful as morning glories.

   Today while cooking oatmeal she is Madame Butterfly until she sighs and points the wooden spoon at me. I could've been somebody, you know? Esperanza, you go to school. Study hard. That Madame Butterfly was a fool. She stirs the oatmeal. Look at my *comadres*. She means Izaura, whose husband left, and Yolanda, whose husband is dead. Got to take care all your own, she says shaking her head.

   Then out of nowhere:

   Shame is a bad thing, you know. It keeps you down. You want to know why I quit school? Because I didn't have nice clothes. No clothes, but I had brains.

   Yup, she says disgusted, stirring again. I was a smart cookie then.

   From Sandra Cisneros, *The House on Mango Street.* Copyright © 1984 by Sandra Cisneros, pp. 90–91. Published by Vintage Books, a division of Random House, Inc., and in hardcover by Alfred A. Knopf in 1994. Reprinted by permission of Susan Bergholz Literary Services, New York. All rights reserved.

   The tone is _____

   What clues did you use to determine the tone? _____

2. My Rules

   If you want to marry me, here's what you'll have to do
   You must learn how to make a perfect chicken dumpling stew
   And you must sew my holey socks and you must soothe my
   troubled mind
   And develop the knack for scratching my back
   And keep my shoes spotlessly shined
   And while I rest you must rake up the leaves

> And when it is hailing and snowing
> You must shovel the walk, and be still when I talk
> And—hey, where are you going?

From Shel Silverstein, "My Rules," in *Where the Sidewalk Ends,* p. 74. Copyright © 2003 Evil Eye Music, Inc. Reprinted by permission of HarperCollins Publishers.

The tone is _____

What clues did you use to determine the tone? _____

3. I was glad enough when I reached my room and locked out the mold and the darkness. A cheery fire was burning in the grate, and I sat down before it with a comforting sense of relief. For two hours I sat there, thinking of bygone times; recalling old scenes, and summoning half-forgotten faces out of the mists of the past; listening, in fancy, to voices that long ago grew silent for all time, and to once familiar songs that nobody sings now.

   I slept profoundly, but how long I do not know. All at once I found myself awake, and filled with a shuddering expectancy. All was still. All but my own heart—I could hear it beat. Presently the bedclothes began to slip away slowly toward the foot of the bed, as if someone were pulling them! I could not stir; I could not speak.

   From Mark Twain, "A Ghost Story," by Mark Twain.

The tone is _____

What clues did you use to determine the tone? _____

"There is only one way to degrade mankind permanently and that is to destroy language."

—David Hare

4. Attention, techno-weenies. Stop littering the info highway. Don't call a grammatical time-out when you log on. English is English, whether it comes over the phone, via the Postal Service (excuse me, "snail mail"), or on the Internet.

   Let's clean up cyberspace, gang. You wouldn't use *pls* for *please, yr* for *your*, or *thnx* for *thanks* in a courteous letter. So why do it on the Net? You don't shout or whisper on the telephone. So why use ALL CAPITAL or all lowercase letters in your e-mail? Making yourself hard to read is bad "netiquette."

   And another thing. IMHO (in my humble opinion), those abbreviations like CUL (see you later) and BTW (by the way) are overused. You're too busy for full sentences? So what are you doing with the time you're saving by using cute shortcuts? Volunteering at your local hospital? Sure. I'm ROFL (rolling on floor laughing).

   You digerati can speak E-lingo among yourselves, but try real English if you want the cyber-impaired to get it. Next time you log on, remember there's a person at the other end, not a motherboard. Use appropriate grammar and punctuation. Be clear and to the point. And consider phoning once in a while.

   From Patricia T. O'Connor, *Woe Is I,* New York: Riverhead Books, 1996, p. 126.

The tone is _____

What clues did you use to determine the tone? _____

5. At precisely 5:30 in the morning, a bearded man in khaki trousers, a flannel shirt, and a string tie strode to the end of the dock and announced through a

megaphone: "Bass anglers, prepare for the blast-off!" In unison, the fishermen turned their ignitions, and Lake Maurepas boiled and rumbled and swelled. Blue smoke from the big outboards curled skyward and collected in an acrid foreign cloud over the marsh. The boats inched away from the crowded ramp and crept out toward where the pass opened its mouth to the lake. The procession came to a stop at a lighted buoy.

"Now the fun starts," said a young woman standing next to R.J. Decker. She was holding two sleeping babies.

The starter raised a pistol and fired into the air. Instantly a wall of noise rose off Maurepas: the race was on. The bass boats hiccuped and growled and then whined, pushing for more speed. With the throttles hammered down, the sterns dug ferociously and the bows popped up at such alarming angles that Decker was certain some of the boats would flip over in midair. Yet somehow they planed off perfectly, gliding flat and barely creasing the crystal texture of the lake. The song of the big engines was that of a million furious bees; it tore the dawn all to hell.

It was one of the most remarkable moments Decker had ever seen, almost military in its high-tech absurdity: forty boats rocketing the same direction at sixty miles per hour. In darkness.

Most of the spectators applauded heartily.

"Doesn't anyone ever get hurt?" Decker asked the woman with the two babies, who were now yowling.

"Hurt?" she said. "No, sir. At that speed you just flat-out die."

From Carl Hiaasen, *Double Whammy*, p. 129. Copyright © 1987 by Carl Hiaasen. Used by permission of G.P. Putnam's Sons, a division of Penguin Group (USA) Inc.

In the passage above, the term *blast-off* is used to convey the seriousness of this sport. Normally, the term is associated with what Florida activity? _____

_____

What kind of figurative language is the author using when he says the boats "hiccuped, growled, and whined"? _____

What kind of figurative language is the author using when he likens the sound of the boats to bees? _____

Why does the start of the race seem like a military operation? _____

_____

What can you infer about the author's feelings toward this sport? _____

_____

_____

Exercise 4: Detecting Tone

GETTING THE PICTURE

In this particular article, Art Buchwald writes about an issue of propriety or morality that sometimes arises between parents and their college-age children.

BIO-SKETCH

Buchwald was one of the foremost humorists in the United States. His job, as he saw it, was to expose us to our failings as human beings and members of society. Buchwald wrote numerous books and was a syndicated newspaper columnist. He was also the recipient of the Pulitzer Prize. A resident of Washington, D.C., he frequently poked fun at the activities on Capitol Hill. Art Buchwald passed away in 2007.

BRUSHING UP ON VOCABULARY

separate but equal refers to keeping one group apart from another but giving both groups equal opportunities or resources. In 1954, in the famous case of *Brown* v. *Board of Education,* the U.S. Supreme Court declared that states may not maintain a system of separate but equal schools for whites and African Americans.

Directions: Read each item and then choose the word that best describes the tone of each speaker.

Daughter's "Friend" Is a Boy

by ART BUCHWALD

In the good old days, when your daughter said she was bringing home a friend for the weekend, it meant she was bringing home a girlfriend—and when your son said he was bringing home a friend for the weekend, it was a boy. This is not the case anymore, and it is causing houseguest problems throughout the country.

I was over at Ripley's house the other evening, when his daughter, Joan, arrived home for the weekend with her "friend," a tall strapping fellow named Mickey.

_____ 1. "Oh, my goodness! Oh, my goodness! said Mrs. Ripley. "Well, Mickey, I guess you want to put your things away."

    a. detached
    b. flustered
    c. pessimistic

_____ 2. Joan, pointing down the hallway, instructed, "Put them in my room."

    a. evasive
    b. diplomatic
    c. dictatorial

_____ 3. "M-m-m-Mickey can s-s-sleep in the attic," said Mrs. Ripley.

    a. distressed
    b. prayerful
    c. sentimental

_____ 4. Joan's mouth fell open. "Why can't he sleep in my room?"

   a. cheerful
   b. loving
   c. astonished

_____ 5. Mr. Ripley blew up. "Because I know he'd rather sleep in the attic."

   a. joyful
   b. angry
   c. evasive

_____ 6. Mickey: "Thank you very much. That's really very nice of you, but Joan's room is fine with me."

   a. elated
   b. polite
   c. alarmed

_____ 7. Mr. Ripley snarled, "Well, it isn't fine with me! Listen here Mickey. We need to talk to Joan alone."

   a. gentle
   b. conciliatory
   c. harsh

_____ 8. Joan began crying. "How could you humiliate me in front of my friend?"

   a. sorrowful
   b. resigned
   c. apathetic

_____ 9. Mrs. Ripley said solicitously, "How did we humiliate you, honey?"

   a. excited
   b. bored
   c. concerned

_____ 10. Joan: "By asking Mickey to sleep in the attic when you know perfectly well there are two beds in my room."

   a. cheerful
   b. evasive
   c. matter-of-fact

_____ 11. "My dear girl," Mr. Ripley huffed, "it's not a question of the number of beds. Perhaps you don't realize, but there's a certain propriety about people sharing rooms when they're not married."

   a. outraged
   b. amused
   c. wry

_____ 12. Joan looked blankly at them and said, "What propriety could there possibly be?"

    a. baffled
    b. puzzled
    c. both a and b

_____ 13. Mrs. Ripley: "Sweetheart, calm down. I know we're old-fashioned and out-of-date, but your father and I get very nervous when we know two unmarried people of the opposite sex are in the same room under our roof."

    a. mocking
    b. placating
    c. accusatory

_____ 14. "This is ridiculous! Mickey and I aren't strangers," Joan said scornfully. "Where do you think we live in Cambridge?"

    a. light-hearted
    b. bantering
    c. derisive

_____ 15. "I don't want to know where you live in Cambridge! You're not in Cambridge this weekend! You're in our house!" Mr. Ripley yelled.

    a. indignant
    b. embarrassed
    c. patient

_____ 16. Joan: "Well, excuse me. I guess I was mistaken. I thought it was my house, too."

    a. diplomatic
    b. sarcastic
    c. pleading

_____ 17. Mrs. Ripley: "Sweetie, please listen to reason. It is your house—but it's not Mickey's house. After all it would seem to me you would enjoy one weekend sleeping alone in your own room."

    a. imploring
    b. resigned
    c. furious

_____ 18. "If I'd known this was going to be such a big deal, I wouldn't have come home," Joan pouted.

    a. forgiving
    b. sulking
    c. apathetic

_____ 19. "It's not a big deal," said Mr. Ripley seriously. "It's a simple question of moral standards. Ours seem to be different from yours. They may not be better but they are different."

    a. belligerent

    b. earnest

    c. accusatory

_____ 20. Joan's mouth hung open, "And that's why you want to ruin our weekend?"

    a. incredulous

    b. amused

    c. pleased

_____ 21. Mrs. Ripley chuckled: "We're not trying to ruin your weekend, dear. What we're offering you are separate but equal accommodations. . . ."

    a. demanding

    b. scolding

    c. humorous

_____ 22. "That's very funny, Mom," said Joan caustically. "But all the way down in the car Mickey was counting on sleeping in my room. He wouldn't have come if he had known he had to sleep in the attic."

    a. satisfied

    b. bitter

    c. sympathetic

_____ 23. "He'll sleep in your room over my dead body," screeched Mr. Ripley.

    a. detached

    b. incensed

    c. resigned

I decided to intercede. "I have a suggestion. Since Mickey was counting on sleeping in Joan's room, why don't you let him sleep there and have Joan sleep in the attic?"

All three looked at me.

Then Mr. Ripley said, "Wait a minute. Suppose Joan decides to come down from the attic in the middle of the night?"

"It's simple," I said. "Make Mickey promise to lock his door."

Source: Art Buchwald, "Daughter's 'Friend' is a boy." Copyright © 1977 Tribune Media Services, Inc. Reprinted with permission.

In Your Own Words

What is humorous about Buchwald's solution to the problem? What is the solution meant to illustrate?

Internet Activity

You can find Art Buchwald's newspaper column at

www.washingtonpost.com

Type in Buchwald's name and select a column that interests you. What is the overall tone of the column? (You can refer to the list at the beginning of the chapter.) List specific statements from the column that support your choice.

IRONY AND SATIRE

Irony refers to a contrast between what people say and what they actually mean. An ironic comment intends a meaning that is contrary to its stated meaning. The intended meaning is often the opposite of the stated meaning. For instance, if someone backs into your car, you might say, "That's just great!" Your intended meaning is that something bad just happened, but your words say that something good just happened. Since the meaning of an ironic statement is often expressed indirectly, you must use inference to discover it.

Satire refers to comments that exaggerate flaws or failings for the purpose of making them seem ridiculous. Because satire relies on distortion, it is often humorous. Almost anything can be satirized, including people, institutions, and ideas.

Exercise: Identifying Irony and Satire

GETTING THE PICTURE
In the following poem, Wislawa Szymborska pokes fun at bodybuilders.

BIO-SKETCH
The Polish poet Wislawa Szymborska (1923–) won the Nobel Prize for Literature in 1996. The Nobel committee praised her for the "ironic precision" of her poetry.

Bodybuilders' Contest
BY WISLAWA SZYMBORSKA

From scalp to sole, all muscles in slow motion.
The ocean of his torso drips with lotion.
The king of all is he who preens and wrestles

with sinews twisted into monstrous pretzels.
Onstage he grapples with a grizzly bear
the deadlier for not really being there.
Three unseen panthers are in turn laid low,
each with one smoothly choreographed blow.

He grunts while showing his poses and paces.
His back alone has twenty different faces.
The mammoth fist he raises as he wins
is tribute to the force of vitamins.

Source: Wislawa Szymborska, "Bodybuilders' Contest," in *View with a Grain of Sand*, p. 25. Copyright © 1993 by Wislawa Szymborska, English translation by Stanislaw Baranczak and Clare Cavanagh. Copyright © 1995 by Harcourt Inc. Reprinted by permission of the publisher.

In Your Own Words

1. What is the tone of this poem?

2. How can we tell that the poet is making fun of bodybuilders? Exactly what in the poem makes her feelings clear?

3. How many of the senses are represented in this poem? What is the overall image of the bodybuilder?

4. What metaphors does Szymborska use? What is she trying to convey with each of these metaphors?

The Art of Writing

Write a paraphrase of the poem, being careful to include the implied main idea.

SELECTION

"Standing in line is so important, it's the first thing they teach you how to do at school."

GETTING THE PICTURE

In the following satire, Tom Mather humorously talks about standing in line.

BIO-SKETCH

Tom Mather is a former humor columnist for the *BGNews* at Bowling Green State University in Bowling Green, Ohio. He published his first book, *The Cheeseburger Philosophy*, at the age of 21. Below is an excerpt from his second book, *Voyages in the Toilet Dimension*, which was published in 1999.

BRUSHING UP ON VOCABULARY

admonish to reprove or scold in a mild-mannered way. The word *admonish* derives from the Latin *ad*, meaning "to," and *monere*, meaning "advise or warn."

out of line behaving improperly.

Waiting in Life's Long Lines

BY TOM MATHER

1   IT'S TIME TO DISCUSS The Great American Pastime. And I'm not talking about baseball.

2   No, America's new pastime is standing in line.

3   Standing in line is so important, it's the first thing they teach you how to do at school:

4   "As soon as you're finished, everyone get in line."

5   "We're not leaving until everyone gets in line."

6   They continually admonish bad kids by telling them that they are "out of line."

7   It seems that for practically everything we do today, we have to wait in line. Whether it's to see the new baby, or pay our respects to the dead, we wait in line.

8   We stand in line so much, we even wait when we're not working. What happens when you get fired? You go wait in the unemployment line. The government figures, "They don't have anything else to do. They might as well stand in line."

9   To be fair, people in other countries stand in line too. It's just a little different when they do it. For example, you probably have heard how in many countries the people wait hours in long lines for food. You might not realize that Americans wait hours in long lines for fun.

10   Yes, that's right. It's gotten so bad there are even parks designed specifically for standing in line. Some of the more famous ones are Disneyland, Disney World, and Six Flags. Have you been to any of these? Whoever said, "The shortest distance between two points is a line," never went to an amusement park. They have designed rides that allow you to stand in line for up to three hours, so that you can go down hills and through turns at 70 miles per hour. Never mind that most people did that on the trip there, because they wanted to get there as early as possible, to avoid the lines.

11   So if being in a line can be so much "fun," then how come we hate it so much? I think it's not so much the actual standing in line that we hate. The problem is that one line always moves faster than the other. And it's always the line you're not in. If you get in the short line, there is inevitably some crazy event that holds up the line. You know you're going to be in trouble when you hear one of the following:

"Price check on lane fourteen, price check on lane fourteen."
"What do you mean you don't take VISA?" or
"I could've *sworn* I brought my checkbook."

12   And no place is more annoying about lines than banks. There will be 30 people in line, and one teller. But that kind of thing you're used to. What the banks like to do, in addition, is to have five other tellers working at the same time

> "When you sit with a nice girl for two hours, you think it's only a minute. But when you sit on a hot stove for a minute, you think it's two hours."
> —Albert Einstein

> "The passing minute is every man's possession, but what has once gone by is not ours."
> —Marcus Aurelius

on other projects. They each sit at their own window, watching to see how long the line can get, counting pennies. This in turn leads to a lot of bank robberies, because some people get so mad at those holding up the line, they decide it's just easier and quicker to hold up the line.

13   Lines aren't simply long, they can be confusing too. There's the line to get tickets, the line to get food, the line to get in, and the line to get out. Half of the problem is figuring out which line is the one you want to be in.

14   "Is this the line to buy tickets?"

15   "Tickets? I thought this was the line for the women's bathroom."

Source: "Waiting in Life's Long Lines," from Tom Mather, *The BG News,* Bowling Green State University, August 6, 1997. Reprinted courtesy of The BG News. Article first published 8/06/97.

 COMPREHENSION CHECKUP

Multiple Choice

Write the letter of the correct answer in the blank provided.

_____ 1. The topic of this article is
   a. baseball
   b. standing in line at banks
   c. standing in line
   d. waiting in line at theme parks

_____ 2. The author mentions that Americans stand in line for all of the following *except*
   a. to visit a new baby
   b. to pay our respects to the dead
   c. to see a teller at a bank
   d. to visit Santa Claus and his elves

_____ 3. The author's purpose in writing this selection is to
   a. inform us of ways to foil bank robberies
   b. entertain us with examples of where and when Americans stand in line
   c. persuade us to abandon the time-wasting custom of standing in line
   d. explain how the custom of standing in line differs in the United States from other countries

_____ 4. The tone of this article could best be described as
   a. sentimental and sad
   b. humorous and ironic
   c. angry and vindictive
   d. cautious and logical

_____ 5. You can infer from the article that the author believes that
   a. standing in line has gotten out of hand
   b. people had better learn to cope with the irritation of standing in line
   c. standing in line is fun
   d. people should learn to talk to each other while standing in line to relieve the boredom

_____ 6. The statement "some people get so mad at those holding up the line, they decide it's just easier and quicker to hold up the line" is an example of
   a. a play on words
   b. a literary allusion
   c. an ironic exaggeration
   d. both a and c

_____ 7. The main intention of the writer is to
   a. describe rude persons who hold up lines
   b. expose the rudeness of bank tellers
   c. comment on the problems inherent in standing in lines
   d. extol the virtues of a system in which lines don't exist and it's every person for her- or himself

_____ 8. The author of this selection says that schools
   a. encourage students to stand in line
   b. disparage students by telling them that they are out of line
   c. both a and b
   d. none of the above

_____ 9. The author would agree that
   a. Americans wait hours in lines for food
   b. children should not be forced to stand in line
   c. lines are lots of fun if you have the right attitude
   d. lines can be confusing at times

_____ 10. The author ends the selection with an illustration of
   a. the difficulty in figuring out the correct line to stand in
   b. the irritation people feel when standing in a lengthy line
   c. the differences between the employed and the unemployed
   d. the differences between U.S. citizens and Europeans

SELECTION

"These last ten years of coming to terms with my disease would turn out to be the best ten years of my life—not in spite of the illness, but because of it."

GETTING THE PICTURE

The following excerpt from Michael J. Fox's book, titled *Lucky Man*, expresses Fox's optimistic spirit after being diagnosed with Parkinson's disease. The book, published in 2002, describes how he learned to cope with Parkinson's disease and how he accepted the illness as a challenge and a positive factor in his life. Fox is an example of a person who sees a glass as being half-full rather than as half-empty.

BIO-SKETCH

Born Michael Andrew Fox in 1961 in Edmonton, Canada, Fox later added the "J" to his name in honor of actor Michael J. Pollard. Fox grew up loving hockey and even had dreams of one day playing in the National Hockey League. Later, though, after experimenting with writing, art, and playing guitar in rock-and-roll bands, he came to realize that he loved acting.

His first paid acting job was costarring in a sit-com for the Canadian Broadcasting Corporation. At 18, he moved to Los Angeles and took a series of bit parts before winning the role of Alex P. Keaton on *Family Ties* in 1981. He earned three Emmy Awards and a Golden Globe for his performances in that role. Although diagnosed with Parkinson's Disease in 1991, Fox continued his acting career, starring in the TV show *Spin City* as well as in several films, including *Back to the Future, Doc Hollywood*, and *The American President*. He disclosed his condition in 1998 and retired from *Spin City* in 2000.

Although still strongly committed to acting, Fox has shifted most of his energies to the Michael J. Fox Foundation for Parkinson's Research, which he founded in 2000. He hopes the foundation can discover the cause and find a cure for Parkinson's disease.

BRUSHING UP ON VOCABULARY

Parkinson's disease According to the Michael J. Fox Foundation's website, Parkinson's is a "chronic, progressive disorder of the central nervous system. . . . Parkinson's disease has been known since ancient times. An English doctor, James Parkinson, first described it extensively in 1817. Symptoms of Parkinson's may include tremors or trembling, difficulty maintaining balance and gait, rigidity or stiffness of the limbs and trunk, and general slowness of movement." The cause of the disease is still unknown, as is the ability to predict who will get it.

missive a written message or letter, originally from the Latin *missus*, meaning "send."

geek a strange or eccentric person, probably from the Scottish word *geck*, meaning "fool."

Excerpt from

Lucky Man

BY MICHAEL J. FOX

A WAKE UP CALL

Gainesville, Florida—November 1990

1   I woke up to find the message in my left hand. It had me trembling. It wasn't a fax, telegram, memo, or the usual sort of missive bringing disturbing news. In fact, my hand held nothing at all. The trembling was the message.

2   I was feeling a little disoriented. I'd only been shooting the movie in Florida for a week or so, and the massive, pink-lacquered, four-poster bed surrounded by the pastel hues of the University Center Hotel's Presidential Suite still came as a bit of a shock each morning. Oh yeah: and I had a ferocious hangover. That was less shocking.

3   Even with the lights off, blinds down, and drapes pulled, an offensive amount of light still filtered into the room. Eyes clenched shut, I placed the palm of my left hand across the bridge of my nose in a weak attempt to block the glare. A moth's wing—or so I thought—fluttered against my right cheek. I opened my eyes, keeping my hand suspended an inch or two in front of my face so I could finger-flick the little beastie across the room. That's when I noticed my pinkie. It was trembling, twitching, auto-animated. How long this had been going on I wasn't exactly sure. But now that I noticed it, I was surprised to discover that I couldn't stop it.

4   *Weird—maybe I slept on it funny.* Five or six times in rapid succession I pumped my left hand into a fist, followed by a vigorous shaking out. Interlocking the fingers of each hand steeple-style with their opposite number, I lifted them up and over behind my head and pinned them to the pillow.

5   Tap. Tap. Tap. Like a moisture-free Chinese water torture, I could feel a gentle drumming at the back of my skull. If it was trying to get my attention, it had succeeded. I withdrew my left hand from behind my head and held it in front of my face, steadily, with fingers splayed—like the bespectacled X-ray glasses geek in the old comic book ad. I didn't have to see the underlying skeletal structure; the information I was looking for was right there in the flesh: a thumb, three stock-still fingers, and out there on the lunatic fringe, a spastic pinkie.

6   It occurred to me that this might have something to do with my hangover, or more precisely with alcohol. I'd put away a lot of beers in my time, but had never woken up with the shakes; maybe this was what they called delirium tremens? I was pretty sure they would manifest themselves in a more impressive way—I mean, who gets the d.t.'s in one finger? Whatever this was, it wasn't alcoholic deterioration.

7   Now I did a little experimentation. I found that if I grabbed my finger with my right hand, it would stop moving. Released, it would keep still for four or five seconds, and then, like a cheap wind-up toy, it would whir back to life again. *Hmmm.* What had begun as a curiosity was now blossoming into full-fledge worry. The trembling had been going on for a few minutes with no sign of quitting and my brain, fuzzy as it was, scrambled to come up with an explanation. Had I hit my head, injured myself in some way? The tape of the previous night's events was grainy at best. But I didn't feel any bumps. Any pain in my head was from boozing, not bruising.

IRRECONCILABLE DIFFERENCES

8   Throughout the course of the morning, the twitching would intensify, as would my search for a cause—not just for the rest of that day, but for months to follow. The true answer was elusive, and in fact wouldn't reveal itself for another full year. The trembling was indeed the message, and this is what it was telling me:

9   That morning—November 13, 1990—my brain was serving notice: it had initiated a divorce from my mind. Efforts to contest or reconcile would be futile; eighty percent of the process, I would later learn, was already complete. No grounds were given, and the petition was irrevocable. Further, my brain was demanding, and incrementally seizing, custody of my body, beginning with the baby: the outermost finger of my left hand.

10   Ten years later, knowing what I do now, this mind–body divorce strikes me as a serviceable metaphor—though at the time it was a concept well beyond my grasp. I had no idea there were even problems in the relationship—just assumed things were pretty good between the old gray matter and me. This was a false assumption. Unbeknownst to me, things had been deteriorating long before the morning of the pinkie rebellion. But by declaring its dysfunction in such an arresting manner, my brain now had my mind's full attention.

11   It would be a year of questions and false answers that would satisfy me for a time, fueling my denial and forestalling the sort of determined investigation that would ultimately provide the answer. That answer came from a doctor who would inform me that I had a progressive, degenerative, and incurable neurological disorder; one that I may have been living with for as long as a decade before suspecting there might be anything wrong. This doctor would also tell me that I could probably continue acting for another "ten good years," and he would be right about that, almost to the day. What he did not tell me—what no one could—is that these last ten years of coming to terms with my disease would turn out to be the best ten years of my life—not in spite of my illness, but because of it.

12   I have referred to it in interviews as a *gift*—something for which others with this affliction have taken me to task. I was only speaking from my own experience, of course, but I stand partially corrected: if it is a gift, it's the gift that just keeps on taking.

13   Coping with this relentless assault and the accumulating damage is not easy. Nobody would ever choose to have this visited upon them. Still, this unexpected crisis forced a fundamental life decision: adopt a siege mentality—or embark upon a journey. Whatever it was—courage? acceptance? wisdom?—that finally allowed me to go down the second road (after spending a few disastrous years on the first) was unquestionably a gift—and absent this neurophysiological catastrophe, I would never have opened it, or been so profoundly enriched. That's why I consider myself a lucky man.

Source: Michael J. Fox, *Lucky Man,* pp. 1–5.

> *"Be willing to have it so; acceptance of what has happened is the first step in overcoming the consequences of any misfortune."*
> —William James

COMPREHENSION CHECKUP

Multiple-Choice

Write the letter of the correct answer in the blank.

_____ 1. The reader may conclude that Michael J. Fox
     a. knew immediately that he had Parkinson's disease
     b. initially thought that he might have slept on his finger in an awkward position
     c. thought that his finger was trembling because he had been drinking alcohol to excess
     d. both b and c

_____ 2. Which of the following is true about what doctors told Fox?
    a. He would only be able to continue acting for a few more months.
    b. He had just ten years to live.
    c. He had an incurable neurological disorder.
    d. None of the above

_____ 3. Which of the following is true about Fox's reaction to his disease?
    a. He quickly adopted a siege mentality that has stayed with him for ten years.
    b. He has always been cheerful about his disease.
    c. He now views his disease as a complete catastrophe.
    d. He now sees his disease as a special sort of gift.

_____ 4. What does Fox mean when he says, "I woke up to find the message in my left hand"?
    a. A friend had placed a letter in his left hand while he was sleeping.
    b. He awoke to find his left hand clutching a beer bottle.
    c. The trembling finger of his left hand was telling him something.
    d. His left hand was swollen from an unknown trauma that must have happened the night before.

_____ 5. What does Fox mean when he says, "my brain was demanding and incrementally seizing custody of my body"?
    a. His brain was starting to do things to his body that he could not stop.
    b. His brain was no longer obeying his wishes and demands.
    c. His condition was gradually getting worse.
    d. All of the above.

_____ 6. When Fox states that "efforts to contest or reconcile would be futile," he means that
    a. there is nothing he can do about the situation
    b. the situation is shocking
    c. given time and work the situation can be ameliorated
    d. Both a and b

_____ 7. The overall feeling expressed in this selection could best be described as
    a. acceptance
    b. puzzlement
    c. bitterness
    d. despair

_____ 8. Which of the following proverbs best expresses the main idea of the selection?
    a. The bigger they are the harder they fall.
    b. Blood is thicker than water.
    c. When the cat's away the mice will play.
    d. Every cloud has a silver lining.

_____ 9. What does Fox do directly after he discovers his twitching little finger?
    a. makes a fist and then shakes out his fingers
    b. places his fingers behind his head
    c. spreads his fingers out in front of his face
    d. grabs his left finger with his right hand

_____ 10. Which of the following expresses how the author feels?
- a. Too much light was coming into the room.
- b. The unfamiliar surroundings were making him confused.
- c. Coming to terms with his disease has been a positive in his life.
- d. All of the above.

_____ 11. What implications does the phrase "mind-brain divorce" have for Fox?
- a. The mind is something different from the brain.
- b. His mind and brain had once cooperated well, but now were no longer doing so.
- c. When his mind tells his brain to make his body stop shaking, his brain does not obey.
- d. All of the above.

_____ 12. What are some of the things that Fox means when he calls his disease a "gift"?
- a. He means that it has brought only happiness in his life.
- b. He means that from his personal perspective it has been a gift.
- c. He means that it gave him the opportunity to begin a journey that has enriched his life.
- d. Both b and c

True or False

Indicate whether the statement is true or false by writing T or F in the blank provided.

____T____ 13. A doctor felt that Fox may have had Parkinson's disease for ten years prior to its discovery.

____F____ 14. Fox discovered his trembling when he was in the University Center Hospital.

____F____ 15. Fox's finger kept moving when he held it.

____F____ 16. Fox often woke up shaking after drinking.

____T____ 17. Fox searched for a cause for his dysfunction for many months.

Vocabulary in Context

Determine the meaning of the follwing words from the context wihout using a dictionary. (The paragraph in which the word appears in the reading selection is indicated in parentheses.) Write your answers in your own words in the space provided.

1. offensive (paragraph 3) _____

2. pinkie (3) _____

3. auto-animated (3) _____

4. fuzzy (7) _____

5. dysfunction (10) _____

6. arresting (10) _____

7. affliction (12) _____

Vocabulary Puzzle

Directions: Look through the paragraphs indicated in parentheses to find words that match the definitions below. Then write these words in the puzzle.

ACROSS CLUES

8. unyielding; severe, strict, or harsh (paragraph 13)
9. hard to comprehend (8)
10. any prolonged effort to overcome resistance (13)
13. gradations or varieties of colors; tints (2)
14. to cause a person to accept something not desired (9)
16. spread out (5)
17. the act of making worse (6)
18. lying under or beneath (5)
19. extreme or intense (2)

DOWN CLUES

1. closed tightly (paragraph 3)
2. written message; letter (1)
3. not to be recalled; unalterable (9)
4. a great, often sudden calamity (13)
5. preventing or hindering by action in advance (11)
6. declining in physical qualities (11)
7. flapped about (3)
11. not successful; useless (9)
12. to make clear or evident to the eye (6)
15. to start on a trip (13)

In Your Own Words

Psychotherapist Alan McGinnis, author of *Power of Optimism*, says that optimists see themselves as "problem solvers and trouble shooters." According to McGinnis, the following qualities help optimists maintain a positive attitude while still being realistic:

- They look for partial solutions.
- They believe they have control over their future.
- They interrupt their negative trains of thought.
- They heighten their powers of appreciation.
- They are cheerful even when they can't be happy.
- They accept what cannot be changed.

In what ways has Michael J. Fox demonstrated the characteristics of an optimist?

The Art of Writing

In a brief essay, respond to one of the following quotes:

1. "Courage is resistance to fear, mastery of fear—not absence of fear." (Mark Twain)

2. "Courage is the price that life exacts for granting peace. The soul that knows it not, knows no release." (Amelia Earhart)

What do you think the author means? Do you agree? Why or why not? How does the quote apply to the situation that Michael J. Fox faced?

Internet Activities

1. For information about Parkinson's disease and the Michael J. Fox Foundation for Parkinson's Research, go to its website:

   www.michaeljfox.org

   Based on what you read there, write a paragraph about what's new in Parkinson's research.

2. Two other organizations dealing with Parkinson's are

   - The Parkinson's Disease Foundation, www.pdf.org
   - The National Parkinson Foundation, www.parkinson.org

   Go to the website of one of these organizations, and write a paragraph about its mission and activities.

SELECTION

*"All clues, however far-fetched, were followed up, but
no trace of Mona Lisa could be found."*

GETTING THE PICTURE

The article below describes the theft of Leonardo da Vinci's *Mona Lisa,* one of the most famous paintings in the world. Da Vinci (1452–1519) was an Italian artist, scientist, and inventor. Because of his widely varied interests, he created few paintings in his lifetime. The *Mona Lisa* was probably commissioned by a local merchant who wanted a portrait of his young wife. By portraying the young woman in a relaxed, informal way, the painting broke many of the stylistic barriers of the time. Da Vinci, who studied anatomy, created especially lifelike hands. But the eyes of the *Mona Lisa* and the enigmatic half-smile are the painting's best-known features. The *Mona Lisa* hung in Napoleon's bedroom until it was transferred to the Louvre in 1804.

BRUSHING UP ON VOCABULARY

enigmatic perplexing or mysterious. It is derived from the Greek words *ainigma* and *ainissesthai,* meaning "to speak in riddles." To the ancient Greeks, riddles were a serious business: If you were unable to answer one correctly, you might be handed over to the poser of the riddle for a lifetime of servitude.

patriotism devoted love, and support for and defense of one's country. This word comes from the Greek words *pater,* meaning "father," and *patrios,* meaning "founded by the forefathers." The word *patriotism* referred to someone who was so devoted to his family that he would defend them and the land that his "fathers" founded at great cost.

Excerpt from
GILBERT'S LIVING WITH ART
by Mark Getlein

Vincenzo Perugia

1   At 7:20 on the morning of August 21, 1911, three members of the maintenance staff at the Louvre paused briefly in front of the *Mona Lisa.* The chief of maintenance remarked to his workers, "This is the most valuable picture in the world." Just over an hour later the three men again passed through the Salon Carré, where Leonardo's masterpiece hung, and saw that the painting was no longer in its place. The maintenance chief joked that museum officials had removed the picture for fear he and his

crew would steal it. The joke soon proved to be an uncomfortably hollow one. *Mona Lisa* was gone.

2   Thus begins the story of the most famous art theft in history, of the most famous painting in the world, and of the man who would inevitably become the most famous art thief of all time: Vincenzo Perugia.

3   French newspapers announced the catastrophe under the banner headline "Unimaginable!" All during the weeks that followed, rumors abounded. A man carrying a blanket-covered parcel had been seen jumping onto the train for Bordeaux. A mysterious draped package had been spotted on a ship to New York, a ship to South America, a ship to Italy. The painting had been scarred with acid, had been dumped in the sea. All clues, however far-fetched, were followed up, but no trace of the *Mona Lisa* could be found.

4   More than two years would pass before the thief surfaced. Then, in November of 1913, an art dealer in Italy received a letter from a man who signed himself "Leonard." Would the dealer like to have the *Mona Lisa?* Would he. Of course it was a joke. But was it? The dealer arranged to meet "Leonard" in a hotel room in Florence. "Leonard" produced a wooden box filled with junk. The junk was removed, a false bottom came out of the box, and there, wrapped in red silk and perfectly preserved, was the smiling face of *Mona Lisa.* The dealer swallowed his shock and phoned for the police.

5   "Leonard" was actually an Italian named Vincenzo Perugia—a house painter who had once done some contract work in the Louvre. As he told the story of the theft, it was amazingly simple. On the morning in question Perugia, dressed in a workman's smock, walked into the museum, nodded to several of the other workers, and chose a moment when no one else was in the Salon Carré to unhook the painting from the wall. Then he slipped into a stairwell, removed the picture from its frame, stuck it under his smock, and walked out. Stories that Perugia had accomplices have never been proved.

6   What were the thief's motives? And why, after pulling off what can only be described as the heist of the century, did he so naively offer the painting to the Italian dealer? Perugia claimed he was motivated by patriotism. *Mona Lisa* was an Italian painting by an Italian artist. Believing (mistakenly) that it had been stolen by Napoleon to hang in France, he wanted to restore it to its rightful home. At the same time, however, he expected to be "rewarded" by the Italian government for his heroic act and thought $100,000 would be a good amount. No one shared this point of view.

7   Perugia was tried, convicted, and sentenced to a year in prison. After his release he served in the army, married, settled in Paris, and operated a paint store. Soon Perugia, who had so briefly captured the world's headlines, settled back into the obscurity from which he had emerged.

8   And *Mona Lisa.* After a triumphal tour of several Italian museums, she was returned to France. She hangs—at least as of this writing—safely in the Louvre. Romantics say her smile is even more enigmatic than before.

Source: "Vincenzo Perugia," from Mark Getlein, *Gilbert's Living with Art,* 6th ed., New York: McGraw-Hill, 2002, p. 387. Copyright © 2002 McGraw-Hill. Reprinted by permission of The McGraw-Hill Companies, Inc.

COMPREHENSION CHECKUP

True or False

Indicate whether the statement is true or false by writing T or F in the blank provided.

T 1. The man calling himself "Leonard" was actually Vincenzo Perugia.

T 2. The author implies that Perugia was not motivated solely by patriotism.

F 3. A *naive* individual is sophisticated and worldly.

F 4. The French police immediately settled on Perugia as the most likely culprit.

F 5. The painting was finally recovered in Rome, Italy.

Multiple Choice

Write the letter of the correct answer in the blank provided.

_____ 6. Perugia was able to steal the *Mona Lisa* successfully because
   a. he had previously worked at the Louvre and thus did not seem out of place
   b. he was wearing clothing that was loose enough to conceal a painting
   c. he was able to steal the painting when no one was looking
   d. all of the above

_____ 7. Perugia was under the impression that
   a. he was engaging in a patriotic gesture
   b. he would be richly rewarded for his services by the Italian government
   c. he would easily be able to sell the painting for millions of dollars
   d. both a and b

_____ 8. We can assume that
   a. Perugia was no longer welcome in his native Italy
   b. the government of France forgave Perugia once his debt to society had been paid
   c. Perugia continued to enjoy his status as a celebrity
   d. the *Mona Lisa* is back in Italy where it belongs

_____ 9. The reader can conclude that
   a. the *Mona Lisa* was seriously damaged by Perugia's theft
   b. Perugia had thought about how to conceal the *Mona Lisa*
   c. Perugia had no intention of parting with the *Mona Lisa*
   d. the chief of maintenance was behind the scheme to steal the painting

_____ 10. The reader can conclude that
   a. the *Mona Lisa* is more carefully protected today
   b. the Italian government determined that the *Mona Lisa* belongs in Italy
   c. the rumors that the painting had been defaced proved to be correct
   d. many hours went by before the painting was discovered to be missing

Vocabulary Puzzle

Directions: Use the vocabulary words to complete the puzzle.

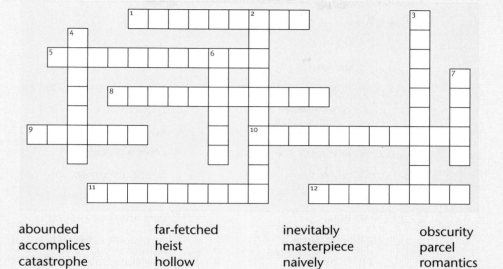

abounded	far-fetched	inevitably	obscurity
accomplices	heist	masterpiece	parcel
catastrophe	hollow	naively	romantics

ACROSS CLUES

1. people preoccupied with love
5. a momentous tragic event
8. a supreme artistic achievement
9. false or meaningless
10. people who knowingly help another in a crime or wrongdoing
11. having little or no prominence or distinction
12. occurred in great quantities

DOWN CLUES

2. has to be expected
3. improbable (omit hyphen)
4. showing a lack of judgment or information
6. package
7. robbery or hold-up

Vocabulary Matching

Match the vocabulary words in Column A with their synonyms in Column B. Place the correct letter in the space provided.

Column A	Column B
_____ 1. inevitably	a. fiasco; disaster
_____ 2. hollow	b. improbable; unlikely
_____ 3. famous	c. protected; unchanged
_____ 4. catastrophe	d. renowned; celebrated
_____ 5. far-fetched	e. empty; false
_____ 6. surfaced	f. robbery; burglary
_____ 7. preserved	g. being unknown
_____ 8. naively	h. joyful; celebratory
_____ 9. heist	i. certainly; unavoidably
_____ 10. obscurity	j. appeared; emerged
_____ 11. triumphal	k. puzzling; mysterious
_____ 12. enigmatic	l. artlessly; credulously

In Your Own Words

1. Perugia was sentenced to a year and two weeks in prison for the theft of the *Mona Lisa,* a surprisingly brief term considering the magnitude of the crime. Why do you suppose he got such a light sentence?

2. Do you think Perugia's sentence was lengthy enough to serve as a deterrent to future art thieves?

3. Have you noticed that many art museums appear to have relatively lax security measures in place? What steps do the museums you have visited take to safeguard their paintings from theft or vandalism?

4. Many museums safeguard valuable paintings by putting them inside glass or plastic viewing boxes. In fact, Perugia himself built *Mona Lisa's* viewing box. How do you feel about viewing paintings through "glass"?

5. In this case, do the ends justify the means?

The Art of Writing

1. Perugia claims he stole the *Mona Lisa* because she was so beautiful and had bewitched him. How do you account for the painting's universal appeal? Write a short essay giving your opinion.

2. Initially, Perugia was a hero to Italians because of his desire to relocate the *Mona Lisa* to Italy. How do you feel about turning a thief into a hero? Are we still likely to do that today? Can you think of any recent instances?

Internet Activities

1. Consult the following website to learn more about other famous art thefts including Sweden's National Museum heist, the stolen *Scream,* the Manchester

robbery, the Van Gogh Museum robbery, and the biggest U.S. art theft. Briefly summarize your findings.

www.crimelibrary.com/gangsters_outlaws/outlaws/
major_art_thefts/index.html

2. Art theft continues to be a worldwide problem. In 1986, a gang of Irish thieves broke into an estate in Ireland and made off with eleven paintings, including works by Goya, Rubens, Gainsborough, and Vermeer. So far, none have been recovered. To find out about works of art stolen recently, go to the following website and click on "Update."

www.saztv.com

3. Find an article about a recent art theft, and write a description of a stolen painting. What is the overall tone of the painting that was stolen?

TEST-TAKING TIP

Taking Multiple-Choice Tests (2)

Here are some more tips for taking multiple-choice tests:

1. When the question asks you to pick a missing word, look for grammatical clues such as *a* and *an*. *A* goes before words beginning with consonants, and *an* goes before words beginning with vowels.

2. When one of the answers is *all of the above*, and you are pretty sure that two of the three answers are correct but are unsure about the third answer, go with *all of the above*.

3. Be aware that two questions on the test may be similar. Use the correct answer for one question to help you find the correct answer for the other.

4. If there is no penalty for guessing, make an educated guess rather than leaving a question blank.

5. If you are using a computerized scoring sheet, be sure to eliminate any stray marks.

VOCABULARY   Unit 6

This unit begins with the word parts *inter-* and *intra-*, *-medius*, *ped-*, *-capt* and *-cept*, and *cap-* and *corp-*. It concludes with word parts for blood relations and the suffix *-cide*.

inter—between, among; intra—within, inside; medius—middle

interpersonal	between persons. In hopes of bettering his relationships with his peers, he is taking a class called *Interpersonal* Communication.
intrapersonal	self-knowledge, as in *intrapersonal* intelligence
interloper	a person who intrudes into the affairs or business of others
interlude	an intervening episode; an interval in the course of action. There was a brief *interlude* of good weather between the two storms.
interject	to interrupt with; to insert. Class is much more interesting when students *interject* questions or comments during the lecture.
intercede	to come between or plead on another's behalf. Because the mother was unable to refrain from taking drugs, the state *interceded* and placed the young child in foster care.

intervene	to come between. When the two boys got into a fight, the teacher *intervened* to settle the dispute.
intermediate	coming between two other things or events; in the middle. Adolescence is an *intermediate* stage that comes between childhood and adulthood.
intermediary	*medius* means "middle." An *intermediary* is a go-between or mediator. The airline hired an *intermediary* to write a contract acceptable to both labor and management.

ped—child

The Latin prefix *ped-* also means "foot," as in *pedal* and *pedestrian*. Don't get the two meanings confused.

pediatrician	a doctor who takes care of babies and children
pedagogy	comes from the Greek word *paidos,* meaning "child," and *agogos,* meaning "leader." In Latin, a *pedagogue* was a slave who escorted children to school and then was responsible for supervising them. Later the term came to refer to a teacher. Today, the word refers to teaching or the study of teaching.
pedophile	an adult who has a sexual desire for a child. In California, a suspected *pedophile* was charged in the rape and murder of a five-year-old girl.
pedantic	showing off learning in a boring way or attending too closely to the minute details of a subject. The term originally referred to a schoolmaster.

capt, cept—hold, seize, take

captivity	the condition of being held by force. There are very few giant pandas held in *captivity*.
capability	the power to do something
capacious	able to hold much. The best features of the house were the *capacious* walk-in closets.
deception	If we practice *deception*, we are "taking" something from someone by fraud.
intercept	to take or seize on the way (between). He *intercepted* the quarterback's pass and ran 30 yards for the touchdown.

cap—head; corp—body

decapitate	to cut off the head. During the French Revolution, people were *decapitated* by the guillotine.
caption	a title at the head of an article or below a photo in a newspaper or magazine. Sonia quickly scanned the *captions* to determine whether the articles were relevant to her research paper.
capital punishment	the killing of someone by law as punishment for a crime
corporal punishment	physical punishment (of the body), as in whipping or spanking

corpulent	fat and fleshy; stout body build
corporation	a business, city, college, or other body of persons having a government charter, which gives it some of the legal powers and rights of a person.
corps	a group of people joined together in some work; a section or special branch of the military. *Corps* has the same pronunciation as apple "core." After graduation from college, Jeremy joined the Peace *Corps*. At age fifty-five, Kirk retired from the Marine *Corps*.
corpse	the dead body of a person

mater, matri—mother; pater, patri—father; soror—sister; frater, fratri—brother; homo—man; genus—birth, begin, race; cide—kill

This section discusses "blood" relations and the suffix -*cide*, which means "kill."

maternal	relating to a mother. The *maternal* instincts of a lioness make it dangerous to get caught playing with the cubs.
maternity	the state of being a mother. The new mothers were in the *maternity* ward of the hospital.
matricide	The suffix -*cide*, as in insecti*cide* and pesti*cide*, means "kill," so *matricide* means murdering one's mother.
paternal	relating to a father. Your father's father is your *paternal* grandfather.
paternity	the state of being a father. The mother brought a *paternity* suit against her child's father.
patricide	murdering one's father
fraternity	a brotherhood. College *fraternities* are groups of young men who live together like brothers.
fratricide	murdering one's brother
sorority	a sisterhood. College *sororities* are groups of young women who live together like sisters.
sororicide	murdering one's sister
homicide	the murder of one human being by another. *Homo-* means "same," but *homo-* also has a second meaning of "man," which is the meaning that applies to the word *homicide* and other words. The *homo-* meaning "same" has a different derivation than the *homo-* meaning "man."
Homo sapiens	mankind; human beings. *Sapiens* means "wisdom," so *Homo sapiens* are humans with wisdom. This is the scientific term for all human beings.
genius	A *genius* is a person with very high intelligence. The word *genius* has an interesting etymology. It comes from *genus*, meaning "birth." The ancient Romans believed that each person was assigned a guardian spirit at birth.
genocide	the systematic killing of a national or ethnic group. The word *genocide* was first applied to the attempted extermination of the Jews by the Nazis.

Genesis   the beginning; the origin. The first book of the Bible is called *Genesis* because it gives an account of the Creation.

genealogy   a history of a person's descent from ancestors. Your "family tree" or birth history shows your *genealogy*.

Completing Verbal Analogies

Another common type of analogy can be expressed as "A is by definition a person who does B or has characteristics of B or is B; C is by definition a person who does D or has characteristics of D or is D." An example is shown below.

```
        A      B      C          D
_____ thief : steals : : spectator : _____
        a. thinks
        b. observes
        c. mediates
        d. whines
```

The answer is (b). A *spectator* is by definition someone who *observes*, just as a *thief* is by definition someone who *steals*.

Complete the following analogies.

_____ 1. pedagogue : teaches : : intermediary : _____
    a. punishes
    b. deceives
    c. mediates
    d. flatters

_____ 2. interloper : intrudes : : interceptor : _____
    a. cuts off
    b. mediates
    c. seizes
    d. hires

_____ 3. homicide : killing a human : : genocide : _____
    a. sororicide
    b. killing an ethnic group
    c. killing one's brother
    d. killing one's mother

_____ 4. father : paternal : : mother : _____
    a. authentic
    b. maternal
    c. fair
    d. considerate

_____ 5. fraternity : brotherhood : : sorority : _____
    a. motherhood
    b. fatherhood
    c. sisterhood
    d. adulthood

Now that you have studied the vocabulary in Unit 6, practice your new knowledge by completing the crossword puzzle on the next page.

Vocabulary 6

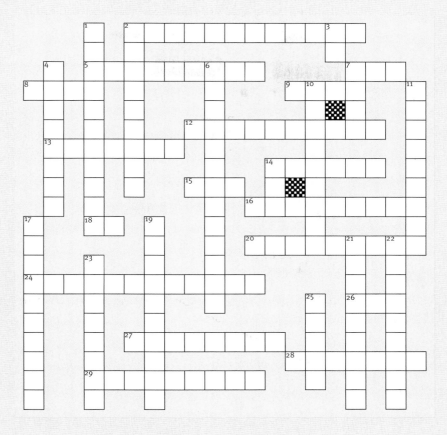

ACROSS CLUES

2. Roberta's _____ advises going easy in toilet-training toddlers.
5. An act of _____ has a mother as a victim.
7. A word part meaning "head."
8. A word part meaning "man."
9. A word part meaning "kill."
12. Kill by beheading.
13. The newspaper issued a retraction because the _____ had mistakenly identified the wrong person as the arsonist.
14. A dead body.
15. A word part meaning "child."
16. There was a brief musical _____ between the first and second acts of the play.
18. A word part meaning "apart."*
20. The defensive back tried to _____ the pass.
24. The school board hired an _____ to work on conflicts between parents and faculty.

26. A word part meaning "forward."*
27. I was pleased to receive stationery with my_____ .*
28. The first book of the Bible.
29. Virginia, who traces her family history back to the *Mayflower,* is an expert in _____.

DOWN CLUES

1. "Humans with wisdom." (Don't leave a space between the two words.)
2. DNA tests were conducted to determine the child's_____ .
3. A word part meaning "toward."*
4. If his victim dies, he will be charged with _____ .
6. Conflict management and assertiveness are _____ skills that can help you become a more effective person.
7. A word part meaning "seize."
10. The U.S. decided to _____ in the dispute between the two

nations in the hope of preventing a war.
11. Bob raised his hand to _____ a question, but the teacher ignored him.
14. A word part meaning "with."*
17. A 3-ounce bourbon and soda and a 12-ounce light beer have an _____ amount of alcohol.*
19. Is Marie Barone on *Everybody Loves Raymond* an _____ because she meddles in Ray and Debra's life without being asked?
21. The doctor told the _____ man that he needed to go on a diet.
22. The _____ was sentenced to life in prison for the rape and murder of the young child.
23. Students who major in education take classes in _____ .
25. A word part meaning "between."

*From a previous unit.

Reading Critically

CHAPTERS IN PART 4

Sugar Cane (1931)
BY DIEGO RIVERA

Philadelphia Museum of Art,
Philadelphia, Pennsylvania, U.S.A.
Photo: The Philadelphia Museum of
Art/Art Resource, NY. © Banco de
México Trust.

Fact and Opinion

The Starry Night (1889) BY VINCENT VAN GOGH

Acquired through the Lillie P. Bliss Bequest (472.1941). Digital Image
© The Museum of Modern Art/Licensed by SCALA/Art Resource, NY.
The Museum of Modern Art, NY, U.S.A.

View and Reflect

1. How many stars are in the painting?
2. What is the structure on the left side of the painting?
   The topic of this chapter is fact and opinion. The answer to the first question is factual because it can be verified. The answer to the second question is an opinion. Many people have different ideas about the structure on the left—some think it's a mountain or a bush, and others think it represents van Gogh's inner turmoil because it was completed while van Gogh was in a mental asylum.
3. What is the tallest building in the town? Is your answer fact or opinion?

INTRODUCTION TO FACT AND OPINION

In order to be a critical reader, you must be able to tell the difference between fact and opinion. Writers sometimes present opinions as though they were facts. You need to be able to know when this is happening.

A **fact** is a statement whose truth or falsity can be proved in some objective way. Statements of fact can be verified or disproved by records, tests, historical or scientific documents, or personal experience. A statement of fact offers neither judgment nor evaluation. Factual statements present information without interpreting it. Statements of fact often rely on concrete data or measurements. Here are some examples of statements of fact and how they can be proved.

Statement	Type of Proof
George Washington was our first president.	Historical records
I have seven french fries left on my plate.	Counting
It's sunny outside.	Observation
He's six feet tall.	Measurement

An **opinion** expresses a personal preference or value judgment. Statements of opinion cannot be proved to be true or false. Here are some examples of opinions. The words that express a preference or value judgment are underlined.

George Washington was a <u>great</u> president.

These french fries are <u>delicious</u>.

It is a <u>lovely</u>, sunny day.

He is <u>very</u> tall.

Statements of future events or probabilities are often opinions no matter how reasonable or likely they seem.

By the year 2015, 90 percent of Americans will be online.

In 2015, water will be rationed.

Statements of fact can sometimes be false. Both of the following statements are factual, but only one of them is correct.

George Washington was 67 years old when he died.

George Washington was 66 years old when he died.

Exercise 1: Identifying Facts and Opinions

Directions: Study the painting of the *Mona Lisa* on page 303. Indicate whether each statement below contains a fact or an opinion by writing F or O in the space provided. (Note that not all factual statements will be true.)

_____ 1. The *Mona Lisa* measures 30 × 21 inches (or approximately 77 × 53 centimeters).

_____ 2. The *Mona Lisa* has been a part of France's royal collection since the early sixteenth century.

_____ 3. The painting of the polite lady with the self-satisfied expression is perhaps the most recognized work of art in the world.

_____ 4. The otherworldly landscape in the background seems at odds with *Mona Lisa's* maternal image in the foreground.

_____ 5. Leonardo painted the *Mona Lisa* with oils on a poplar wooden panel.

_____ 6. The *Mona Lisa* is encased in a 157 × 98-inch box of triplex glass, a gift from the Japanese on the occasion of the painting's 1974 trip to Japan—the last time it left the Louvre.

_____ 7. This bullet-proof box is kept at a constant 68 degrees Fahrenheit and 55 percent humidity, which is maintained by a built-in air conditioner and nine pounds of silica gel.

_____ 8. *Mona Lisa* seems like a goddess or a saint.

_____ 9. The painting's magic might derive from our desire to know whether the lady is smiling, and if she is, why?

_____ 10. In 2003, the *Mona Lisa* received a checkup in which the box surrounding it was opened and the climatic conditions as well as the painting's condition were examined.

Exercise 2: Identifying Facts and Opinions

Directions: First, study the illustrations on the following page. Then indicate whether each statement contains a fact or an opinion by writing F or O in the space provided. (Remember that a statement may state a fact, even if it is false.)

_____ 1. Your future life depends on the position of the stars and planets on the date of your birth.

_____ 2. The Western system of astrology is based on month and day of birth.

_____ 3. The Eastern system of astrology is based on year of birth.

_____ 4. A child born on March 15, 2003, is a "Pisces" in Western astrology.

_____ 5. In the Eastern system, a child born in 2003 is a "goat."

_____ 6. In the Western system of astrology, the symbol for Capricorn is a goat.

_____ 7. In the Eastern system, a "rabbit" seeks tranquility.

_____ 8. Except for the scales of Libra, the twelve signs of the zodiac are symbolized by living creatures.

Eastern (Chinese)

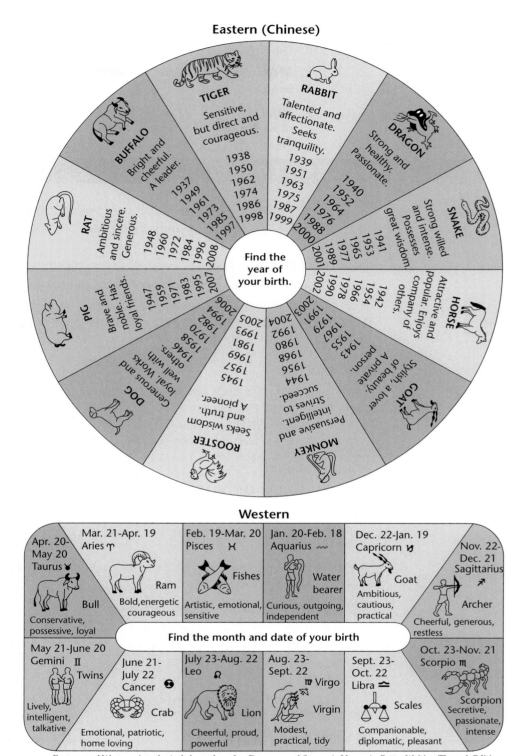

Western

Eastern and Western Astrological charts from Jon Peterson and Stacey A. Hagen in *Better Writing Through Editing*, New York: McGraw-Hill, 1999, p. 56. Copyright © 1999 McGraw-Hill. Reprinted by permission of The McGraw-Hill Companies, Inc.

_____ 9. The symbols of the Eastern zodiac are all animals.

_____ 10. The zodiac has an amazing influence on our lives.

_____ 11. According to the Western zodiac, a Libra is compassionate, diplomatic, and pleasant.

_____ 12. Virgo is the only female in the Western zodiac; the other three human signs are all male.

SELECTION

"Early astronomers had very practical reasons for studying the sky."

GETTING THE PICTURE

The topic of the next two selections is astronomy and astrology. These selections continue our work with fact and opinion. The first selection, from an astronomy textbook, gives an overview of the constellations. The second selection, from a psychology textbook, discusses astrology as a pseudoscience.

BIO-SKETCH

Eric Chaisson holds a doctorate in astrophysics from Harvard University, where he spent ten years on the Faculty of Arts and Sciences. He is now professor of physics and education and director of the Wright Center for Innovative Science Education at Tufts University. He has written books on astronomy and has published many scientific papers in professional journals.

BRUSHING UP ON VOCABULARY

constellations a group of stars seen as making a figure or design. Many constellations take their names from classical mythology and various common animals and objects.

mythological deriving from traditional stories; lacking factual basis or historical validity; of or relating to mythology.

Stonehenge a group of standing stones on Salisbury Plain in southern England. Dating to c. 2000–1800 B.C., these megaliths are surrounded by a ditch and embankment that may date to c. 2800 B.C. The arrangement of the stones suggests that Stonehenge may have served as a religious center and also as an astronomical observatory.

Excerpt from
ASTRONOMY TODAY
by Eric Chaisson

Charting the Heavens

1   Between sunset and sunrise on a clear night, we can see about 3,000 points of light. If we include the view from the opposite side of Earth, nearly 6,000 stars are visible to the unaided eye. A natural human tendency is to see patterns and relationships

"The sky is filled with stars, invisible by day."

—Henry Wadsworth Longfellow

among objects even when no true connection exists. People long ago connected the brightest stars into configurations called *constellations,* which ancient astronomers named after mythological beings, heroes, and animals—whatever was important to them. Figure 1 shows a constellation especially prominent in the nighttime sky from October to March: the hunter named Orion. Orion was a mythical Greek hero famed, among other things, for his amorous pursuit of the Pleiades, the seven daughters of the giant Atlas. According to Greek mythology, to protect the Pleiades from Orion, the gods placed them among the stars, where Orion nightly stalks them across the sky. Many constellations have similarly fabulous connections with ancient lore.

2   Perhaps not surprisingly, the patterns have a strong cultural bias. The astronomers of ancient China saw mythical figures different from those seen by the ancient Greeks, the Babylonians, and the people of other cultures, even though they were all looking at the same stars in the night sky. Interestingly, different cultures often made the same basic groupings of stars, despite widely varying interpretations of what they saw. For example, the group of seven stars usually known in North America as "the Dipper" is known as "the Wagon" or "the Plough" in Western Europe. The ancient Greeks regarded these same stars as the tail of "the Great Bear," the Egyptians saw them as the leg of an ox, the Siberians as a stag, and some Native Americans as a funeral procession.

3   Early astronomers had very practical reasons for studying the sky. Seafarers needed to navigate their vessels and some constellations served as navigational guides. The star Polaris, which is part of the Little Dipper, indicates north. The near constancy of its location in the sky, from hour to hour and night to night, has aided travelers for centuries. Other constellations served as primitive calendars to predict planting and harvesting seasons. For example, many cultures knew that the appearance of certain stars on the horizon just before daybreak signaled the beginning of spring and the end of winter.

"The sun, moon, and stars are there to guide us."

—Dennis Banks

4   The realization that these patterns returned to the night sky at the same time each year met the need for a practical means of tracking the seasons. Widely separated cultures all over the world built elaborate structures, to serve, at least in part, as primitive calendars. Often the keepers of the secrets of the sky enshrined their knowledge in myth and ritual, and these astronomical sites were also used for religious ceremonies.

5   Perhaps the best known such site is *Stonehenge,* located on Salisbury Plain in England, and shown in Figure 2. This ancient stone circle, which today is one of the most popular tourist attractions in Britain, dates from the Stone Age. Researchers believe it was a kind of three-dimensional calendar or almanac, enabling its builders and their descendants to identify important dates by means

Fig. 1 Orion Constellation

Fig. 2 Stonehenge

© John Wang/Getty Images

of specific celestial events. Its construction apparently spanned a period of about 17 centuries, beginning around 2800 B.C. Additions and modifications continued to about 1100 B.C., indicating its ongoing importance to the Stone Age and, later, Bronze Age people who built, maintained, and used Stonehenge. The largest stones weigh up to 50 tons and were transported from quarries miles away.

6   Many of the stones are aligned so that they point toward important astronomical events. For example, the line joining the center of the inner circle to the so-called heel stone, set off some distance from the rest of the structure, points in the direction of the rising Sun on the summer solstice. While some of Stonehenge's purposes remain uncertain and controversial, the site's function as an astronomical almanac seems well established. Although Stonehenge is the most impressive and the best preserved, other stone circles, found all over Europe, are believed to have performed similar functions.

7   In many societies, people came to believe that there were other benefits in being able to trace the regularly changing positions of heavenly bodies. The relative positions of stars and planets at a person's birth were carefully studied by *astrologers,* who used the data to make predictions about that person's destiny. Thus, in a sense, astronomy and astrology arose from the same basic impulse—the desire to "see" into the future—and, indeed, for a long time they were indistinguishable from one another. Today, most people recognize that astrology is nothing more than an amusing diversion. However, millions still study their horoscope in the newspaper every morning! Nevertheless, the ancient astrological terminology—the names of the constellations and many terms used to describe the locations and motions of the planets—is still used throughout the astronomical world.

8   Generally speaking, the stars that make up any particular constellation are not actually close to one another in space, even by astronomical standards. They merely are bright enough to observe with the naked eye and happen to lie in roughly the

same direction in the sky as seen from Earth. Still, the constellations provide a convenient means for astronomers to specify large areas of the sky. This is similar to the way geologists use continents or politicians use voting precincts to identify certain localities on planet Earth. In all, there are 88 constellations, most of them visible from North America at some time during the year.

Source: "Charting the Heavens" from Eric Chaisson and Steve McMillan, *Astronomy Today,* 5/e, pp. 8–9, 34.

COMPREHENSION CHECKUP

Fact or Opinion

Indicate whether the statement is a fact or an opinion by writing F or O in the blank provided.

_____ 1. Between sunset and sunrise on a clear night, we can see about 3,000 points of light.

_____ 2. If we include the view from the opposite side of Earth, nearly 6,000 stars are visible to the unaided eye.

_____ 3. A natural human tendency is to see patterns and relationships among objects even when no true connection exists.

_____ 4. According to Greek mythology, to protect the Pleiades from Orion, the gods placed them among the stars, where Orion nightly stalks them across the sky.

_____ 5. Many constellations have similarly fabulous connections with ancient lore.

_____ 6. Perhaps not surprisingly, the patterns have a strong cultural bias.

_____ 7. The astronomers of ancient China saw mythical figures different from those seen by the ancient Greeks, the Babylonians, and the people of other cultures, even though they were all looking at the same stars in the night sky.

_____ 8. For example, the group of seven stars usually known in North America as "the Dipper" is known as "the Wagon" or "the Plough" in Western Europe.

_____ 9. Early astronomers had very practical reasons for studying the sky.

_____ 10. The star Polaris, which is part of the Little Dipper, indicates north.

_____ 11. The largest stones weigh up to 50 tons and were transported from quarries miles away.

_____ 12. For example, the line joining the center of the inner circle to the so-called heel stone, set off some distance from the rest of the structure, points in the direction of the rising Sun on the summer solstice.

_____ 13. Today, most people recognize that astrology is nothing more than an amusing diversion.

———— 14. Nevertheless, the ancient astrological terminology—the names of the constellations and many terms used to describe the locations and motions of the planets—is still used throughout the astronomical world.

———— 15. Still, the constellations provide a convenient means for astronomers to specify large areas of the sky.

———— 16. In all, there are 88 constellations, most of them visible from North America at some time during the year.

Vocabulary in Context

In the paragraphs indicated, find a word that matches the definition given, and write the word in the space provided.

Paragraph 1

1. ———————— standing out so as to be seen easily; conspicuous
2. ———————— inclined or disposed to love
3. ———————— pursues stealthily
4. ———————— knowledge or learning of a traditional nature

Paragraph 3

1. ———————— early; simple

Paragraph 4

1. ———————— detailed; painstaking

Paragraph 5

1. ———————— offspring
2. ———————— heavenly
3. ———————— excavations or pits from which stone is obtained

Paragraph 6

1. ———————— when the sun is at its greatest distance from the celestial equator, about June 21
2. ———————— disputed; contentious

Paragraph 7

1. ———————— a person's fate
2. ———————— distraction

In Your Own Words

1. How did people in earlier times make use of the constellations?
2. What importance do the constellations have today?
3. How do you explain the fact that both the early Egyptians and the early Greeks organized the stars in similar ways?
4. What is the attraction of astrology?

The Art of Writing

1. Try your hand at creating a myth or story that accounts for a constellation such as Orion. Make your story as detailed and descriptive as possible.

2. Research a zodiac sign such as Scorpio. What did the sign represent or commemorate to the ancient Greeks? To other cultural groups?

Internet Activities

1. Find out some "facts" about the constellation Orion. What are Orion's brightest stars? What star marks his sword? What star marks Orion's left leg? Type in "facts about the constellation Orion" and see what you get.

2. What are the latest research findings or theories on Stonehenge?

SELECTION

"Astrology's popularity shows the difficulty many people have separating valid psychology from systems that seem valid but are not."

GETTING THE PICTURE

Many newspapers and magazines around the country carry daily horoscopes, and millions of readers consult them. Some consult their horoscopes just "for the fun of it." Others, however, take horoscopes very seriously, using them to guide their daily activities and plan their futures. How do you feel about horoscopes? If you still take them seriously after the previous selection, perhaps the following selection will change your mind.

BRUSHING UP ON VOCABULARY

nitpicking being critical of inconsequential information or data.

horoscopes predictions or advice based on the position of the planets and signs of the zodiac at the time of your birth. *Horoscope* comes from the Greek words *hora,* meaning "hour," and *skopos,* meaning "watching." Most newspapers publish daily horoscopes that attempt to predict what is going to happen to you on a particular day and to advise you how to act according to those predictions.

Excerpt from
INTRODUCTION TO PSYCHOLOGY
by Dennis Coon

Pseudopsychology—Astrology

1 A **pseudopsychology** *is any unfounded system that resembles psychology*. Many pseudopsychologies offer elaborate schemes that give the appearance of science, but are actually false. (*Pseudo* means "false.") Pseudopsychologies change little over time

because their followers do not seek new data. In fact, pseudopsychologists often go to great lengths to avoid evidence that contradicts their beliefs. Scientists, in contrast, actively look for contradictions as a way to advance knowledge. They must be skeptical critics of their own theories.

2   If pseudopsychologies have no scientific basis, how do they survive and why are they so popular? There are several reasons, all of which can be demonstrated by a critique of astrology.

3   **Problems in the Stars**   Astrology is probably the most popular pseudopsychology. Astrology *holds that the position of the stars and planets at the time of one's birth determines personality traits and affect behavior.* Like other pseudopsychologies, astrology has repeatedly been shown to have no scientific validity.

4   The objections to astrology are numerous and devastating:

5   1. The zodiac has shifted by one full constellation since astrology was first set up. However, most astrologers simply ignore this shift. (In other words, if astrology calls you a Scorpio you are really a Libra and so forth.)

6   2. There is no connection between the "compatibility" of couples' astrological signs and their marriage and divorce rates.

7   3. Studies have found no connection between astrological signs and leadership, physical characteristics, career choices, or personality traits.

8   4. The force of gravity exerted by the physician's body at the moment of birth is greater than that exerted by the stars. Also, astrologers have failed to explain why the moment of birth should be more important than the moment of conception.

9   5. A study of over 3,000 predictions by famous astrologers found that only a small percentage were fulfilled. These "successful" predictions tended to be vague ("There will be a tragedy somewhere in the east in the spring.") or easily guessed from current events.

10   6. If astrologers are asked to match people with their horoscopes, they do no better than would be expected by chance.

11   7. A few astrologers have tried to test astrology. Their results have been just as negative as those obtained by critics.

12   In short, astrology doesn't work.

13   *Then why does astrology often seem to work?*

14   The following discussion tells why.

15   **Uncritical Acceptance**   If you have ever had your astrological chart done, you may have been impressed with its apparent accuracy. However, such perceptions are typically based on **uncritical acceptance** (*the tendency to believe positive or flattering descriptions of yourself*). Many astrological charts are made up of mostly flattering traits. Naturally, when your personality is described in *desirable* terms, it is hard to deny that the description has the "ring of truth." How much acceptance would astrology receive if the characteristics of a birth sign read like this:

16   **Virgo:** You are the logical type and hate disorder. Your nitpicking is unbearable to your friends. You are cold, unemotional, and usually fall asleep while making love. Virgos make good doorstops.

"When I want your opinion, I'll give it to you."
—Lawrence J. Peter

17   **Positive Instances**   Even when an astrological description contains a mixture of good and bad traits, it may seem accurate. To find out why, read the following personality description.

Your Personality Profile

18   You have a strong need for other people to like you and for them to admire you. You have a tendency to be critical of yourself. You have a great deal of unused energy which you have not turned to your advantage. While you have some personality weaknesses, you are generally able to compensate for them. Your sexual adjustment has presented some problems for you. Disciplined and controlled on the outside, you tend to be worrisome and insecure inside. At times you have serious doubts as to whether you have made the right decision or done the right thing. You prefer a certain amount of change and variety and become dissatisfied when hemmed in by restrictions and limitations. You pride yourself on being an independent thinker and do not accept other opinions without satisfactory proof. You have found it unwise to be too frank in revealing yourself to others. At times you are extroverted, affable, sociable, while at other times you are introverted, wary, and reserved. Some of your aspirations tend to be pretty unrealistic.

"Too often we enjoy the comfort of opinion without the discomfort of thought."

—John F. Kennedy

19   Does this describe your personality? A psychologist read this summary individually to college students who had taken a personality test. Only 5 students out of 79 felt that the description failed to capture their personalities. Another study found that people rated this "personality profile" as more accurate than their actual horoscopes.

20   Reread the description and you will see that it contains both sides of several personality dimensions ("At times you are extroverted . . . while at other times you are introverted . . ."). Its apparent accuracy is an illusion based on the **fallacy of positive instances,** *in which we remember or notice things that confirm our expectations and forget the rest.* The pseudopsychologies thrive on this effect. For example, you can always find "Leo characteristics" in a Leo. If you looked, however, you could also find "Gemini characteristics," "Scorpio characteristics," or whatever.

21   The fallacy of positive instances is used by various "psychic mediums" who pretend to communicate with the deceased friends and relatives of audience members. An analysis of their performances shows that the number of "hits" (correct statements) made by these fakes tends to be very low. Nevertheless, many viewers are impressed because of the natural tendency to remember apparent hits and ignore misses. Also, embarrassing misses are edited out before the shows appear on television.

22   **The Barnum Effect**   Pseudopsychologies also take advantage of the **Barnum effect,** *which is a tendency to consider personal descriptions accurate if they are stated in very general terms.* P. T. Barnum, the famed circus showman, had a formula for success: "Always have a little something for everybody." Like the all-purpose personality profile, palm readings, fortunes, horoscopes, and other products of pseudopsychology are stated in such general terms that they can hardly miss. There is always "a little something for everybody." To observe the Barnum effect, read *all* 12 of the daily horoscopes found in newspapers for several days. You will find that predictions for other signs fit events as well as those for your own sign do.

23   Astrology's popularity shows the difficulty many people have separating valid psychology from systems that seem valid but are not. The goal of this discussion, then, has been to make you a more critical observer of human behavior and to clarify what is, and what is not, psychology. In the meantime, here is what the "stars" say about your future:

24   Emphasis now on education and personal improvement. A learning experience of lasting value awaits you. Take care of scholastic responsibilities before engaging in recreation. The word *reading* figures prominently in your future.

25   Pseudopsychologies may seem like no more than a nuisance, but they can do harm. For instance, people seeking treatment for psychological disorders may become the victims of self-appointed "experts" who offer ineffective, pseudoscientific "therapies." Valid psychological principles are based on observation and evidence, not fads, opinions, or wishful thinking.

Source: Excerpt "Pseudopsychology—Astrology," from Dennis Coon, *Introduction to Psychology: A Modular Approach to Mind and Behavior,* 10th ed., pp. 46–47. Copyright © Thomson Learning. Reprinted with permission of Wadsworth, a division of Thomson Learning: www.thomsonrights .com. Fax 800-730-2215.

 COMPREHENSION CHECKUP

True or False

Indicate whether the statement is true or false by writing T or F in the blank provided.

___F___ 1. Pseudopsychologists look for examples that contradict their beliefs.

___F___ 2. Pseudopsychologies are always changing and improving.

___F___ 3. Astrology has been shown to have scientific validity.

___T___ 4. A person who *aspires* to be a doctor seeks to become one.

___F___ 5. Scorpios always display Scorpio characteristics.

Multiple Choice

Write the letter of the correct answer in the blank provided.

_____ 6. A pseudopsychology is a _____ system that purports to be a valid psychology.
   a. valid
   b. current
   c. false
   d. common sense

_____ 7. Pseudopsychologies state personality descriptions in general terms and so provide "a little something for everybody." They do this to take advantage of
   a. the force of gravity
   b. uncritical acceptance
   c. the fallacy of positive instances
   d. the Barnum effect

_____ 8. So-called psychic hotlines typically dispense lots of flattering information to callers. The "psychics" are relying on _____ to create an illusion of accuracy.
   a. analysis of the zodiac
   b. uncritical acceptance
   c. the Barnum effect
   d. the fallacy of positive instances

_____ 9. Each New Year's Day, "psychics" make predictions about events that will occur during the coming year. The vast majority of these predictions are wrong, but the practice continues each year. The _____ helps to explain why people only remember predictions that seemed to come true and forget all of the errors.
   a. pattern of uncritical acceptance
   b. fallacy of positive instances
   c. Barnum effect
   d. Virgo effect

_____ 10. Other kinds of pseudopsychology mentioned in the essay are
   a. palm readings
   b. personality profiles
   c. fortunes
   d. all of the above

Fact or Opinion

Indicate whether the statement is a fact or an opinion by writing F or O in the blank provided.

_F_ 1. The zodiac has shifted by one full constellation since astrology was first set up.

_O_ 2. Many astrological charts are made up of mostly flattering traits.

_F_ 3. Only 5 students out of 79 felt that the description failed to capture their personalities.

_F_ 4. Studies have found no connection between astrological signs and leadership . . . .

_F_ 5. *Pseudo* means "false."

Vocabulary

Answer each of the following questions with a complete sentence.

1. elaborate (adjective) Have you ever created anything *elaborate*? _____

_____

2. devastating (adjective) Have you recently heard about a *devastating* event? _____

_____

3. exert (verb) What subject do you have to *exert* yourself the most in?

_____

4. hemmed in (verb) What makes you feel *hemmed in* or surrounded? _____

_____

5. affable (adjective) Is there somebody you know who is especially *affable* and pleasant? _____

_____

6. reserved (adjective) Are there certain people you tend to be *reserved* around?

_____

7. valid (adjective) Under the law, what needs to be *valid* or binding? _____

_____

In Your Own Words

1. Why do you think the author includes the warning paragraph at the end of the selection?

2. Do you know anybody who has been duped by unscrupulous astrologers? Why were they willing to consult them in the first place?

3. Can you explain the popularity of the TV show *Medium* starring Patricia Arquette as Allison DuBois, a self-proclaimed psychic?

4. The real Allison DuBois is a Phoenix resident who states on her website: "I can contact the deceased, I can profile the living, and I predict future events. Readings can be conducted on the phone and by e-mail." *The Arizona Republic* reported that the charge for such a reading was $250 per hour. Is this a legitimate business enterprise? Or do you think DuBois should have to prove her credibility before she takes people's money? Do you think that the law should do anything about people who make these kinds of claims?

The Art of Writing

1. Read the daily horoscope in your local newspaper. Does the horoscope for your astrological sign seem to apply to you? Read what is written for people with other astrological signs. Does this information seem to apply equally as well to you as to them? Does this lead you to any conclusions about astrological forecasts? Write a few paragraphs summarizing your findings.

2. In what way does the following cartoon reinforce the author's main ideas in the reading selection?

NON-SEQUITUR © 1993. Reprinted by permission of Universal Press Syndicate. All rights reserved.

Internet Activity

Consult the website below. Scroll down to DuBois's professed abilities and criticism. Assuming that the information is accurate, which viewpoint do you find most persuasive?

www.answers.com/topic/Allison-dubois

SELECTION

*"Artists working in Paleolithic caves used a wide
variety of techniques . . ."*

GETTING THE PICTURE

Altamira, the cave described in the following selection, was shut down in 2002 as a preventive measure after nearby Lascaux (in southwestern France) was devastated by a fungal infection. Instead of viewing the actual cave, most visitors to Altamira can tour a replica of part of the cave. Such restrictions are necessary because visitors introduce fungi and bacteria to the cave. With the high humidity inside the cave, moldlike conditions develop rapidly, threatening the wall paintings within.

BIO-SKETCH

Penelope J. E. Davies is an associate professor of Roman art and architecture at the University of Texas at Austin. She is a recent winner of the Vasari Award, given annually for the outstanding publication by an art historian.

BRUSHING UP ON VOCABULARY

flint a chunk of hard stone.

bison a buffalo.

radiocarbon dating determination of the age of objects of organic origin by measurement of their radiocarbon content.

Excerpt from
JANSON'S HISTORY OF ART
by Penelope J. E. Davies

Prehistoric Art

1 Prehistoric paintings were first recognized in 1878 in a cave named Altamira, in the village of Santillana del Mar in northern Spain. Accompanying her father, Count Don Marcelino Sanz de Sautuola, as he scoured the ground for flints and animal bones, 12-year-old Maria looked up to spy bison, painted in bold black outline and filled with bright earth colors on the ceiling of the cave. There, and in other more recently discovered caves, the painted and engraved images depict animals as the dominant subject.

© AAAC/Topham/The Image Works

"Art is a delayed echo."
—George Santayana

2   When they first assessed the Altamira paintings toward the end of the nineteenth century, experts declared them too advanced to be authentic and dismissed them as a hoax. Indeed, though cave art represents the dawn of art as we know it, it is often highly sophisticated. The bison of Altamira were painted from memory, yet their forms demonstrate the painters' acute powers of observation, and an equal skill in translating memory into image. Standing at rest, or bellowing, or rolling on the ground, the bison behave in these paintings as they do in the wild.

3   Initially, scholars assigned relative dates to cave paintings by dating them according to the degree of naturalism they displayed, that is, how closely the image resembled the actual subject in nature. As naturalism was considered at that time the most advanced form of representation, the more naturalistic the image, the more evolved and, therefore, the more recent it was considered to be. Radiocarbon dating exposed the flaws in this approach.

Cave Painting

4   Artists working in Paleolithic caves used a wide variety of techniques to achieve the images that have survived. Often working far from cave entrances, they illuminated the darkness using lamps carved out of stone and filled with fat or marrow. Archaeologists have found several of these lamps at a cave in Lascaux, France, and elsewhere. Sometimes, when the area of rock to be painted was high above ground level, they may have built scaffolds of wood, stabilized against the wall by driving the poles into the limestone surface.

5   They prepared the surface by scraping the limestone with stone tools, bringing out its chalky whiteness as a background. Some images were then engraved on the wall, with a finger if the limestone was soft enough, or, where it was harder, with a sharp flint. Sometimes they combined this technique with the application of color. Black was

created using vegetal charcoal and perhaps charred bones. Ochre, a natural iron ore, provided a range of vivid reds, browns, and yellows. For drawing—outlines of animals, for instance—the charcoal and ochre were deployed in chunks, like a crayon; to generate paint, they ground the minerals into powder on a large flat stone. By heating them to extremely high temperatures, they could also vary the shades of red and yellow.

6   To fill in animal or human outlines with paint, they mixed the powders with blenders, which consisted of cave water, saliva, egg white, vegetal or animal fat, or blood; they then applied the colors to the limestone surface, using pads of moss or fur, and brushes made of fur, feather, or chewed stick. Pigment was also often chewed up in the mouth and then blown through animal bones or reeds, or spit directly onto the walls to form images. In some cases, paint was applied in dots. An analysis of the paintings indicates that women and adolescents were painters as well as men.

Interpreting Prehistoric Painting

7   As majestic as these paintings can be, they are also profoundly enigmatic: what purpose do they serve? The simplest view, that they were merely decorative—"art for art's sake"—is highly unlikely. Most of the existing paintings and engravings are readily accessible, and many more that once embellished caves that open directly to the outside have probably perished. But some lie deep inside extended cave systems, remote from habitation areas and difficult to reach. In these cases, the power of the image may have resided in its making, rather than in its viewing. According to some historians who have attempted to interpret these images, the act of painting or incising the image may have served some ritual or religious purpose.

"The object of art is   8   Perhaps early humans perceived an image as equivalent to the animal it repre-
to give life a shape."   sented, and therefore, to create or perceive the image was to exert power over what it
                                    portrayed. Image making could have been considered as a force of sympathetic magic,
—Jean Anouilh   which might improve the success of a hunt. Gouge marks on cave walls indicate that in some cases spears were cast at the images. Similarly, artists may have hoped to stimulate fertility in the wild—ensuring a continuous food supply—by depicting pregnant animals. A magical-religious interpretation might explain the choice to make animals appear lifelike. Some scholars have cast the paintings in a central role in early religion, as images for worship. Most important, recent interpretations have acknowledged that one explanation may not suffice for all times and places.

Source: From Penelope J. E. Davies, et al., *Jansen's History of Art: Western Tradition, 7/e.* Copyright © 2007. Reprinted by permission of Pearson Education, Inc., Upper Saddle River, NJ.

 COMPREHENSION CHECKUP

True or False

Indicate whether the statement is true or false by writing T or F in the space provided.

_____T_____ 1. Cave paintings represent the earliest works of art known to man.

_____T_____ 2. Images of animals were incised or painted on the surfaces of cave walls.

___T___ 3. Many cave paintings exhibit a sense of refinement.

___F___ 4. The paintings on the walls show little sense of observation by the painter.

___F___ 5. The majority of the paintings are located near the mouth of the cave.

___T___ 6. The paintings may have been produced as part of a magic ritual to ensure a good hunt.

___F___ 7. The word *prehistoric* implies after written history.

___T___ 8. The cave paintings in Altamira, Spain, were the first to be discovered in modern times.

___F___ 9. The cave paintings were always thought to be genuine.

___T___ 10. Because the caves were dark, the artists used stone lamps to illuminate the area.

___F___ 11. The black paint was probably made from tar.

___T___ 12. The cave paintings were originally discovered by accident.

Multiple Choice

Write the letter of the correct answer in the space provided.

_____ 13. The cave painters might have created the paintings
  a. to ensure a successful hunt
  b. to ensure the successful propagation of the animals they hunted
  c. as a form of ritualistic magic
  (d.) all of the above

_____ 14. Cave paintings were initially believed to be hoaxes because they
  (a.) appeared to be an advanced form of art
  b. were painted from photographs
  c. had a modern color palette
  d. were created with oil-based pigments

_____ 15. According to the selection, cave paintings depicted animals as all of the following *except*
  a. as behaving as they do in the wild
  b. as the dominant subject matter
  (c.) as domesticated animals
  d. as pregnant

_____ 16. To create a painting on the ceiling of a cave, the artist would likely have needed
  a. light from a torch or lamp
  b. some form of scaffolding
  c. neither a nor b
  (d.) both a and b

_____ 17. According to the selection, paint was created from all of the following *except*
  a. charcoal and charred bones
  b. natural iron ore
  (c.) leaves and roots
  d. blood and saliva

_____ 18. According to the selection, paint was applied to the walls by all of the
following means *except*
   a. by pads of moss or fur
   b. by trowel
   c. by brushes made of feathers
   d. by blowing through animal bones

Vocabulary in Context

Fill in the blanks using words from the following list. Not all words will be used.

accessible	embellished	profoundly	suffice
acute	enigmatic	remote	vivid
depicted	equivalent	resided	
deployed	hoax	scoured	
dominant	perished	stabilized	

1. Volunteers _____scoured_____ the mountains for the missing climbers.
2. Rembrandt _____depicted_____ many of his subjects in drab colors.
3. The United States is the _____dominant_____ power in the world today.
4. Many of van Gogh's paintings featured _____vivid_____ colors.
5. More troops were recently _____deployed_____ to Iraq.
6. *Mona Lisa*'s _____enigmatic_____ smile has fascinated millions of visitors to the
Louvre in Paris.
7. Many colleges across the country are trying to make the campus more
_____accessible_____ to the disabled.
8. Entire families _____perished_____ in the latest tornado.
9. I don't think I'll be seeing much of my friend Ann since she and her husband
relocated to a _____remote_____ part of the world.
10. His hearing was so _____acute_____ that he could almost hear a pin drop in the
next room.
11. The seamstress _____embellished_____ the wedding dress with seed pearls, sequins,
and lace.
12. Albert Einstein, having a genius-level IQ, was considered to be _____profoundly_____
intelligent.

Fact or Opinion

Indicate whether the statement is fact or opinion by writing F or O in the blank
provided.

___F___ 1. Prehistoric paintings were first recognized in 1878 in a cave named
Altamira, in the village of Santillana del Mar in northern Spain.

___F___ 2. When they first assessed the Altamira paintings toward the end of the
nineteenth century, experts declared them too advanced to be authentic
and dismissed them as a hoax.

_____F_____ 3. Archaeologists have found several of these lamps at a cave in Lascaux, France, and elsewhere.

_____F_____ 4. In some cases, paint was applied in dots.

_____F_____ 5. An analysis of the paintings indicates that women and adolescents were painters as well as men.

_____O_____ 6. As majestic as these paintings can be, they are also profoundly enigmatic: what purpose do they serve?

_____O_____ 7. The simplest view, that they were merely decorative—"art for art's sake"—is highly unlikely.

_____O_____ 8. In these cases, the power of the image may have resided in its making, rather than in its viewing.

In Your Own Words

1. Most art today is created to be viewed by relatively large numbers of people. Cave art, on the other hand, is not readily accessible. Why do you think it was created in the deep recesses of caves?

2. It appears that both men and women were cave artists. However, as time progressed, women were excluded from creating art. Why do you think that happened?

3. Why do you think cave painters primarily painted large animals such as bison and bears, rather than the smaller animals that must have existed at the same time?

4. Do you think the desire to produce art is universal?

5. Do you think cave art has some hidden meaning? Or is it just "art for art's sake"?

The Art of Writing

What do you think the cave paintings mean? Do you think the selection of caves' relatively permanent places, was deliberate? Why do you think early humans painted primarily animal images rather than human images? Write a short essay giving your interpretation.

Internet Activity

Visit the Altamira, Lascaux, or Chauvet website. Choose a cave painting and write a few paragraphs describing it. What kind of feeling does it evoke in you?

The next three selections on fact and opinion focus on the topic of food and health. What these selections have to say about food may surprise you.

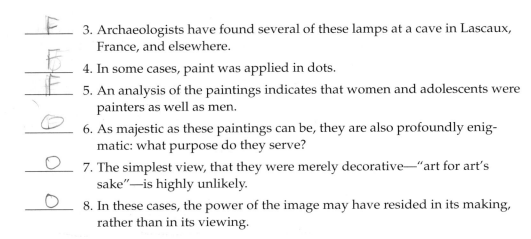

SELECTION

"What do these insects that we are eating every day taste like?"

GETTING THE PICTURE

Do you know how many insect body parts are allowed in your Fig Newton? Quite a lot, actually. The FDA has published a booklet titled *Food Defect Action Levels* that specifies exactly how many are allowed. According to a University of Ohio study, we eat one

SELECTION *continued*

to two pounds of insects each year without knowing it. Is this necessarily bad for us? Apparently not. In fact, in many cultures, insects are deliberately consumed as either a staple to the diet (they're high in protein) or as a delicacy. To find out more about detecting "filth" in food, read the following selection by Mary Roach.

BIO-SKETCH

Mary Roach's humorous science articles have appeared in *Salon, Discover, Vogue, The New York Times Magazine,* and *Outside.* She has a monthly column titled "My Planet" in *Reader's Digest* and is a contributing editor at *Health* magazine. Recent books include *Stiff: The Curious Life of Human Cadavers* and *Spook: Science Tackles the Afterlife.*

BRUSHING UP ON VOCABULARY

thrip tiny sucking insects.

aesthetic pertaining to a sense of beauty.

esoteric understood by only a select few who have special knowledge.

entomophagous feeding on insects.

angora yarn or fabric made from the hair of an Angora rabbit or an Angora goat.

Bug Heads, Rat Hairs—Bon App*tit!

by MARY ROACH

1 IF YOU MADE FIG NEWTONS for a living and you wanted to know how many insects could get into your Newtons without your getting into hot water with the FDA, you could look it up on the U.S. Food and Drug Administration's Food Defect Action Levels Web site. Here you would learn that fig paste is allowed to have up to 13 insect heads per 100 grams.

2 You would then become sidetracked and further learn that approximately four rodent hairs are allowed in a jar of peanut butter, that an average of 60 thrips are allowed in 100 grams of frozen broccoli, that 10 grams of hops are allowed to contain 2,500 aphids, and that 5 milligrams of rat excreta in a pound of sesame seeds is A-OK with the FDA.

3 What you would not learn is why the FDA might put a limit on insects' heads and not other parts of their anatomy, what rat excreta tastes like, and what sort of person takes a job that entails searching for insect heads in fig cookie innards. To find these things out, you would have to pay a visit to one of the FDA's regional filth labs. You would, but now you don't have to, because I'm doing it for you.

4 I have arranged to meet with an entomologist named Dana Ludwig, who works in the FDA's Alameda, Calif., Filth Lab, which analyzes thousands of samples of foods, most imported from the Pacific Rim, each year. In a moment of social ineptitude, I have asked Ludwig if the ludwig is a relative of the

earwig. Straight off the bat, I have my foot in my mouth. I should be used to having feet in my mouth, for humans are eating insect parts all the time without knowing it. According to an Ohio State University Extension fact sheet, most Americans unintentionally swallow 1 to 2 pounds of insects and insect pieces each year. Insects are very lightweight. If you think about how many of them it would take to make 2 pounds (and I advise you not to), you will begin to appreciate the somewhat shocking dimensions of our entomophagous intake.

5   The Alameda Filth Lab employs several analytical entomologists. Ludwig refers to them collectively as "filth people." Just inside the lab doorway, we stop to go over our clothing with a lint roller. A sign on the wall says, "Pet-Hair Free Zone." Ludwig is looking at my shirt. The look says that there's a name for me too, somewhere in the neighborhood of "filth person."

"Reason, observation, and experience—the Holy Trinity of Science."
—Robert G. Ingersoll

6   "There's a lot of hair on your shirt," says Ludwig as nicely as she can. The problem turns out to be my pet angora sweater. Ludwig covers me up with a lab coat. If my sweater were to shed into a food sample, some hapless Third World manufacturer might be cited for an infestation of lavender angora rabbits.

7   For demonstration purposes, Ludwig has set aside a bag of imported black bean wafers. Earlier in the morning, she measured out a sample of the wafers and put them in a beaker with boiling hydrochloric acid. Two hours later, the acid has digested the black bean wafer ingredients, leaving nothing solid behind but "the filth." Ludwig sieves the liquid to isolate the filth, which looks but probably does not taste like a teaspoon of melted coffee ice cream. She then

scrapes it onto a "filth plate," which she slides under her microscope.

8   Ludwig shows me the head of a book louse, a mite fragment, a confused flour beetle underwing fragment, assorted hairs, and an ant head. The magnified ant head is beautiful, a fragment of translucent amber, like what's left on your tongue in the morning when you fall asleep with a Ricola in your mouth. I ask Ludwig why there are so many more heads than bodies. I am trying to imagine the scenario that would result in an ant's head winding up in the flour sack while the rest of its body continues along its merry way. I am one confused flour beetle.

9   Ludwig explains that insects' "head capsules" are often more durable than their bodies. "This is especially common with larvae and caterpillars, where the body parts are soft and really get messed up" in the milling process. In other words, the bodies are in the food too; they're just not countable.

10   What do these insects that we are eating every day taste like? FDA entomologist Steve Anghold told me that if you have enough aphids ground up in a batch of hops, it might conceivably make the beer taste sweeter, because aphids secrete a sweet fluid. In fact, he went on to say, ants "herd aphids like cattle and milk 'em," feeding the sweet fluid to their ant infants. "That's why aphids are called ant cows," he said. It was one of those unsettling journalistic moments where you wonder whether your source has been having an especially dull afternoon and is having you on for the fun of it.

11   I ask Ludwig if a couple dozen beetle larvae would change the taste of a food. She says the insects she typically deals with wouldn't impart much flavor, but that "their metabolic byproducts probably

don't taste very good." I ask her what exactly she means by "metabolic byproducts." She says, "Their waste materials." She isn't talking about coffee grounds and recyclables. Not only do you have to put up with thrips in your broccoli, you have to put up with thrip excreta.

12   If it makes you feel any better, none of this filth is bad for you. With the exception of the dermested beetle larvae, which have hook-shaped hairs that become embedded in your intestines and prompt all manner of gastroenterological sturm und drang, the insects encompassed in the FDA's Food Defect Action Levels are objectionable either on a purely aesthetic level, or as an indicator of unsanitary warehouse conditions.

13   On the contrary, meals made from "microlivestock," as edible insects are called by those who enjoy eating them, are good for you. According to the Ohio State fact sheet, caterpillars have as much protein as beef, a fraction of the fat, 10 times the iron and way more riboflavin and thiamine. Plus the ranches take up much less room and can be staffed by cowboy ants hired away from low-paying aphid-herding jobs.

14   Ludwig's area of expertise is filth hair identification. On her desk between the copy of "World of Moths" and an 8-by-10 color photograph of Colorado potato beetles mating, is a diploma in hair and fiber microscopy. The more common filth hairs—rats, dogs, cats, mice—she can identify under the microscope by sight. For less common specimens she consults highly esoteric reference books and a cabinet of "authentics": sample animal hairs culled from zoos.

15   She opens a drawer and shows me a glass slide with a mongoose hair fixed to it, and another from a ring-tailed cat. While Ludwig is off attending to a sample of chili paste, I pull open another drawer. This one contains human hairs of various ethnicities. "Japanese arm hair," says one label. There are Chinese hairs, Caucasian hairs, Filipino hairs, knuckle hairs, eyelashes, eyebrow hairs. Without saying a word, Ludwig reaches in front of me and slides the drawer shut, leading me to wonder whether somewhere in that collection is an authentic human pubic hair.

16   Ludwig and her colleagues also make use of excreta "authentics," glass vials of teeny tiny sample turds. I notice one labeled "caterpillar excreta." Each unit in the vial is as small as a cake crumb.

17   One more reason to ranch caterpillars and not cows.

Source: "Bug Heads, Rat Hairs—Bon App*tit" Mary Roach, 1/14/00.

COMPREHENSION CHECKUP

Fact or Opinion

Underline the factual part of each statement.

1. In a moment of social ineptitude, I have asked Ludwig if the ludwig is a relative of the earwig.

2. Ludwig sieves the liquid to isolate the filth, which looks but probably does not taste like a teaspoon of melted coffee ice cream.

3. A sign on the wall says, "Pet-Hair Free Zone."

Indicate whether the statement is fact or opinion by writing F or O in the blank provided.

_____O_____ 4. Straight off the bat, I have my foot in my mouth.

_____F_____ 5. According to an Ohio State University Extension fact sheet, most Americans unintentionally swallow 1 to 2 pounds of insects and insect pieces each year.

_____F_____ 6. The Alameda Filth Lab employs several analytical entomologists.

_____F_____ 7. Ludwig refers to them collectively as "filth people."

_____O_____ 8. If my sweater were to shed into a food sample, some hapless Third World manufacturer might be cited for an infestation of lavender angora rabbits.

Multiple Choice

Write the letter of the correct answer in the blank provided.

_____ 1. The topic of this selection is
   a. Fig Newtons
   b. laboratory conditions
   c. insect parts in food
   d. the nutritional value of insects

_____ 2. The author's purpose in writing this selection is to
   a. entertain the reader with an amusing account of a visit to a "filth" lab
   b. persuade the reader to lobby the FDA for more stringent food safety guidelines
   c. inform the public about insect parts in food
   d. both a and c

_____ 3. The tone of this selection could best be described as
   a. sentimental and somber
   b. mean-spirited and critical
   c. lightly humorous and witty
   d. respectful and thoughtful

_____ 4. When the author speculates that "some hapless Third World manufacturer might be cited for an infestation of lavender angora rabbits," she is being
   a. maudlin
   b. serious
   c. facetious
   d. compassionate

_____ 5. The statement "the ranches take up much less room and can be staffed by cowboy ants hired away from the low-paying aphid-herding jobs," is an example of
   a. humor by exaggeration
   b. literary allusion
   c. figurative language
   d. transition words

_____ 6. The use of the word *microlivestock* (paragraph 13) to refer to edible insects is a(n)
   a. understatement
   b. euphemism
   c. simile
   d. inference

_____ 7. From the selection as a whole, we can infer that the author
   a. no longer eats foods imported from the Pacific Rim.
   b. is amazed at how many bug parts are consumed unintentionally in the American diet
   c. believes that insect by-products in food are bad for us.
   d. wishes everyone could visit a "filth" lab

_____ 8. The term *metabolic byproducts* (paragraph 11) is a
   a. figurative expression
   b. reference to waste material
   c. joke
   d. scientific term referring to photosynthesis

_____ 9. Synonyms for *sturm and drang* (paragraph 12) are all of the following *except*
   a. storm and stress
   b. turmoil and upheaval
   c. calmness and placidity
   d. tumultuousness

_____ 10. "As small as a cake crumb" is a
   a. simile
   b. metaphor
   c. personification
   d. literary allusion

_____ 11. Throughout the selection, the author uses the pronoun *you*, which makes her style
   a. formal and serious
   b. informal and chatty
   c. objective and neutral
   d. serious and somber

_____ 12. When the author writes in the last sentence of paragraph 8, "I am one confused flour beetle," she is being
   a. formal
   b. humorous
   c. charming
   d. flattering

True or False

Indicate whether the statement is true or false by writing T or F in the blank provided.

___T___ 13. Under FDA guidelines, a certain amount of insect parts are permissible in food products.

___T___ 14. The dermested beetle larvae can cause intestinal distress.

_____F_____ 15. The average American unknowingly ingests at least six pounds of insects or insect parts yearly.

_____I_____ 16. A caterpillar head capsule is more durable than its body.

_____F_____ 17. Aphids secrete a sour fluid.

_____F_____ 18. Caterpillars have as much protein as chicken.

_____I_____ 19. Ludwig is an expert in identifying filth hair.

_____F_____ 20. "Authentics" are sample hairs gathered from zoos.

_____I_____ 21. Excreta "authentics" are waste products.

_____T_____ 22. An entomologist studies insects.

Vocabulary Practice

Write the meanings of the following words or phrases.

1. getting into hot water (paragraph 1) _____

2. sidetracked (2) _____

3. A-OK (2) _____

4. straight off the bat (4) _____

5. foot in my mouth (4) _____

Vocabulary in Context

Choose one of the following words to complete each of the sentences below. Use each word only once. Be sure to pay close attention to the context clues provided.

durable	impart
embedded	ineptitude
encompasses	infestation
fragments	innards
hapless	translucent

1. The _____ student couldn't seem to remember to bring all of his supplies to class each day.

2. After Wanda broke the pitcher, tiny _____ of glass were found for days.

3. The stained glass window in the church was _____.

4. That dress has proved to be especially _____; I have worn it for over ten years.

5. _____ in the limestone were several valuable pieces of pottery.

6. For most home owners, an _____ of termites is cause for alarm.

7. I like to eat freshly caught fish, but I don't like to clean out the _____.

8. His _____ as a mechanic is well known; as a result, he should probably choose another profession.

9. I'd like to _____ some advice: Most people are about as happy as they make up their minds to be.

10. An unabridged dictionary _____ far more information than an abridged one.

In Your Own Words

1. What does the title of the selection mean? How does the title indicate the author's point of view?

2. Do you think food products should be more carefully regulated by the FDA?

3. Would you be willing to pay more for food that is certified as "pure"?

4. Recent research indicates that dirt might actually be good for us. For instance, children who are allowed to play in dirt and mud appear to have stronger immune systems than children who are kept scrupulously clean. Do you think the same thing is true about food? The FDA assures us that a small amount of contamination causes no harm, but do you think there is also a benefit to eating food that contains a small amount of insect parts?

5. Have you ever eaten insects? How did they taste? Would you advise others to try them?

The Art of Writing

1. In your opinion, what are the best kinds of food for good health? How much of each of these foods should a person eat every day? Describe the optimum diet for a young child, young adult, and senior citizen.

2. Are you an "eat to live" or "live to eat" kind of person? Write a few paragraphs describing the difference between the two "food" philosophies.

Internet Activity

Read one of the following interviews with Mary Roach:

www.identitytheory.com/interviews/roach_interview.html

www.bookbrowse.com/biographies/index.cfm?author_number=89B

Mary Roach interviewed by Ralph Spinelli, spring 2005, *A Journal of New Writing*

Summarize what you learned about her former and present jobs and how she got her start as a writer. What advice for others does she share?

SELECTION

"The heart of the flavor industry lies between Exit 4 and Exit 19 of the New Jersey Turnpike."

GETTING THE PICTURE

The following excerpt from *Fast Food Nation* was included in *Best Science Writing* of 2001. In it, author Eric Schlosser describes how fast-food products acquire their particular tastes.

BIO-SKETCH

Eric Schlosser has received numerous awards for his investigative journalism, including a National Magazine Award. His first book, *Fast Food Nation,* has been a national best-seller since its initial publication in 2001. A correspondent for the *Atlantic Monthly,* Schlosser set out to explore "the dark side of the American meal."

SELECTION *continued*

BRUSHING UP ON VOCABULARY

barrage a sudden outpouring. The original *barrage* was a dam designed to contain large amounts of water. It comes from the French *barrage*, meaning "barrier," and had an opposite meaning from its present one.

innocuous not harmful or injurious; harmless. Derived from the Latin word part *in*, meaning "not," and *nocuus*, meaning "hurtful."

palatable acceptable or agreeable to the palette or taste; appetizing. Comes directly from the Latin word *palatum*, meaning "roof of the mouth."

Excerpt from

Fast Food Nation

BY ERIC SCHLOSSER

FOOD PRODUCT DESIGN

"It requires a certain kind of mind to see beauty in a hamburger bun."

—Ray Kroc

1   The taste of McDonald's French fries has long been praised by customers, competitors, and even food critics. Their distinctive taste does not stem from the type of potatoes that McDonald's buys, the technology that processes them, or the restaurant equipment that fries them. Other chains buy their French fries from the same large processing companies, use Russet Burbanks, and have similar fryers in their restaurant kitchens. The taste of a fast food fry is largely determined by the cooking oil. For decades, McDonald's cooked its French fries in a mixture of about 7 percent soy oil and 93 percent beef fat. The mix gave the fries their unique flavor—and more saturated beef fat per ounce than a McDonald's hamburger.

2   Amid a barrage of criticism over the amount of cholesterol in their fries, McDonald's switched to pure vegetable oil in 1990. The switch presented the company with an enormous challenge: how to make fries that subtly taste like beef without cooking them in beef fat. A look at the ingredients now used in the preparation of French fries suggests how the problem was solved. At the end of the list is a seemingly innocuous, yet oddly mysterious phrase: "natural flavor." The frozen potatoes and the cooking oil at McDonald's both contain "natural flavor." That fact helps to explain not only why the fries taste so good, but also why most fast food—indeed, most of the food Americans eat today—tastes the way it does.

3   Open your refrigerator, your freezer, your kitchen cupboards, and look at the labels on your food. You'll find "natural flavor" or "artificial flavor" in just about every list of ingredients. The similarities between these two broad categories of flavor are far more significant than their differences. Both are man-made additives that give most processed food its taste. The initial purchase of a food

item may be driven by its packaging or appearance, but subsequent purchases are determined mainly by its taste. Americans now spend more than $1 trillion on food every year—and more than 90 percent of that money is spent on processed food. But the canning, freezing, and dehydrating techniques used to process food destroy most of its flavor. Since the end of World War II, a vast industry has arisen in the United States to make processed food palatable. Without this flavor industry, today's fast food industry could not exist. The names of the leading American fast food chains and their best-selling menu items have become famous worldwide, embedded in our popular culture. Few people, however, can name the companies that manufacture fast food's taste.

4   The flavor industry is highly secretive. Its leading companies will not divulge the precise formulas of flavor compounds or the identities of clients. The secrecy is deemed essential for protecting the reputation of beloved brands. The fast food chains, understandably, would like the public to believe that the flavors of their food somehow originate in their restaurant kitchens, not in distant factories run by other firms.

5   The heart of the flavor industry lies between Exit 4 and Exit 19 of the New Jersey Turnpike. More than fifty companies manufacture flavors along that stretch of the Turnpike. Indeed, the state produces about two thirds of the flavor additives sold in the United States.

6   International Flavors & Fragrances (IFF), the world's largest flavor company, has a manufacturing facility off Exit 8A in Dayton, New Jersey. A tour of the IFF plant is the closest thing in real life to visiting Willy Wonka's chocolate factory. Wonderful smells drift through the hallways, men and women in neat white lab coats cheerfully go about their work, and hundreds of little glass bottles sit on laboratory tables and shelves. The bottles contain powerful but fragile flavor chemicals. The long chemical names on the little white labels seem like a strange foreign language. The chemicals are mixed and poured and turned into new substances, just like magic potions.

7   IFF's snack and savory lab is responsible for the flavor of potato chips, corn chips, breads, crackers, breakfast cereals, and pet food. The confectionary lab devises the flavor for ice cream, cookies, candies, toothpastes, mouthwashes, and antacids. The beverage lab creates the flavors for popular soft drinks, sports drinks, bottled teas, wine coolers, and for all-natural juice drinks, organic soy drinks, and malt liquors.

8   In addition to being the world's largest flavor company, IFF makes the smell of household products such as deodorant, dishwashing detergent, bath soap, shampoo, furniture polish, and floor wax. All of these aromas are made through the same basic process: mixing different chemicals to create a particular smell. The basic science behind the scent of your shaving cream is the same as that governing the flavor of your TV dinner.

9   The aroma of the food can be responsible for as much as 90 percent of its flavor. Scientists now believe that human beings acquired the sense of taste as a way to avoid being poisoned. Edible plants generally taste sweet; deadly ones, bitter. Taste is supposed to help us differentiate food that's good for us from food that's not. The taste buds on our tongues can detect the presence of half a dozen or so basic tastes, including sweet, sour, bitter, salty, and astringent. Taste buds offer

a relatively limited means of detection, however, compared to the human olfactory system, which can perceive thousands of different chemical aromas. Indeed "flavor" is primarily the smell of gases being released by the chemicals you've just put in your mouth.

10   The act of drinking, sucking, or chewing a substance releases its volatile gases. They flow out of your mouth and up your nostrils, or up the passageway in the back of your mouth, to a thin layer of nerve cells called the olfactory epithelium, located at the base of your nose, right between the eyes. The brain combines the complex smell signals from the epithelium with the simple taste signals from the tongue, assigns a flavor to what's in your mouth, and decides if it's something you want to eat.

11   The Food and Drug Administration does not require flavor companies to disclose the ingredients of their additives, so long as all the chemicals are considered by the agency to be GRAS (Generally Regarded As Safe). This lack of public disclosure enables the companies to maintain the secrecy of their formulas. It also hides the fact that flavor compounds sometimes contain more ingredients than the foods being given their taste. The ubiquitous phrase "artificial strawberry flavor" gives little hint of the chemical wizardry and manufacturing skill that can make a highly processed food taste like a strawberry.

"Chemicals—noxious substances from which modern food is made."
—Unknown

12   A typical artificial strawberry flavor, like the kind found in a Burger King strawberry milk shake, contains the following ingredients: amyl acetate, amyl butyrate, amyl valerate, anethol, anisyl formate, benzyl acetate, benzyl isobutyrate, butyric acid, cinnamyl isobutyrate, cinnamyl valerate, cognac essential oil, diacetyl, dipropyl ketone, ethyl butyrate, ethyl cinnamate, ethyl heptanoate, ethyl heptylate, ethyl lactate, ethyl methylphenylglycidate, ethyl nitrate, ethyl propionate, ethyl valerate, heliotropin, hydroxyphrenyl-2-butanone (10 percent solution in alcohol), a-ionone, isobutyl anthranilate, isobutyl butyrate, lemon essential oil, maltol, 4-methylacetopphenone, methyl anthranilate, methyl benzoate, methyl cinnamate, methyl heptine carbonate, methyl naphthyl ketone, methyl salicylate, mint essential oil, neroli essential oil, nerolin, neryl isobutyrate, orris butter, phenethyl alcohol, rose, rum ether, y-undecalactone, vanillin, and solvent.

13   The 1960s were the heyday of artificial flavors. For the past twenty years food processors have tried hard to use only "natural flavors" in their products. However, natural flavors and artificial flavors sometimes contain exactly the same chemicals, produced through different methods. A natural flavor is not necessarily purer or healthier than an artificial one. Natural and artificial flavors are now manufactured at the same chemical plants, places that few people would associate with Mother Nature. Calling any of these flavors "natural" requires a flexible attitude toward the English language and a fair amount of irony.

14   In addition to flavor additives, most processed food has color additives, which are used to make processed foods look good. Food coloring serves much the same purpose as women's makeup, and it's often made from the same basic ingredients. Titanium dioxide, for example, is a mineral with

many different uses. It can give candies, frosting, and icing their bright white colors. It is used as a coloring in makeup. And it is also commonly used in white house paints. So you can use titanium dioxide to ice your cake—or paint your house. At Burger King, Wendy's, and McDonald's, color additives can be found in many of the sodas, salad dressings, cookies, chicken dishes, and even sandwich buns.

15   One of the most widely used color additives comes from an unexpected source. Cochineal extract (also known as carmine or carminic acid) is made from the dead bodies of small bugs harvested mainly in Peru and the Canary Islands. The little bugs are collected, dried, and ground into a coloring additive. It takes about 70,000 of the insects to make a pound of carmine, which is used to make processed foods look pink, red, or purple. Dannon strawberry yogurt gets its color from carmine, as do many candies, frozen fruit bars, fruit fillings, and Ocean Spray pink grapefruit juice drink.

16   The U.S. government claims that the color and flavor additives widely used in processed foods are safe. That may not always be the case. Carmine can cause allergic reactions in some people. Tartrazine, a yellow food coloring, can cause hyperactivity, headaches, rashes, and an increased risk of asthma in some children. It has been banned in Norway, Finland, and Austria, but is still used by food companies in the United States and Great Britain. Tartrazine can be found in British and American sodas, candies, chewing gum, Jell-O, and butterscotch pudding mixes, among other things.

17   A number of scientists now worry that eating so many different chemicals in processed foods may not be good for young children. While each of the widely used chemical additives may be safe to eat by itself, the safety of eating a large combination of additives at every meal remains unknown. "We assume that because these things do not make us drop dead, they're safe," says Dr. Vyvyan Howard, a leading expert on toxic substances at the University of Liverpool in England. "It's not true. In my opinion, I would recommend that kids just stay away from them."

Source: "Food Product Design" from Eric Schlosser, *Fast Food Nation,* pp. 120–123, 125–127. Copyright © 2001 by Eric Schlosser. Reprinted by permission of Houghton Mifflin Company. All rights reserved. Eric Schlosser, *Chew on This: Everything You Didn't Want to Know about Fast Food,* pp. 121–124. Text copyright © 2006 by Eric Schlosser. Reprinted by permission of Houghton Mifflin Company. All rights reserved.

✓ COMPREHENSION CHECKUP

Multiple Choice

Write the letter of the correct answer in the blank provided.

_____ 1. The main idea of the selection is that
   a. the fast food we eat every day contains many interesting ingredients
   b. the production of McDonald's French fries is a complicated process
   c. if teenagers really knew what was in fast food, they'd stop eating it
   d. flavor and color additives have transformed the foods Americans eat

_____ 2. The author's purpose in writing this selection is to
    a. criticize the flavor industry
    b. inform the public about what fast food is made of
    c. describe how a strawberry milkshake is made
    d. persuade readers to abandon McDonald's take-out

_____ 3. According to Schlosser, the ingredient that makes McDonald's French fries taste so good is
    a. salt
    b. monosodium glutamate
    c. natural flavor
    d. peanut oil

_____ 4. Titanium dioxide is used in all of the following _except_
    a. dishwashing detergent
    b. cake frosting
    c. house paint
    d. makeup

_____ 5. All of the following get their color from carmine _except_
    a. Dannon strawberry yogurt
    b. Ocean spray pink grapefruit juice drink
    c. orange marmalade
    d. raspberry fruit fillings

_____ 6. From paragraph 13, we can infer that a natural flavor
    a. comes directly from nature
    b. has little to do with nature
    c. is very fattening
    d. is extremely expensive

_____ 7. Tartrazine, a yellow food coloring
    a. has been banned in Norway and Finland
    b. can cause headaches and rashes
    c. is found in Jell-O and butterscotch pudding mixes
    d. all of the above

_____ 8. All of the following conclusions can be drawn from the selection _except_
    a. McDonald's bowed to pressure and changed the cooking method of its French fries
    b. the author of the selection does not believe that color additives in processed food are always safe
    c. brightly colored foods taste better than bland-looking ones
    d. color additives are important in making processed food look good

_____ 9. After reading the selection, we can conclude that
    a. a strawberry milkshake made at home is likely to contain fewer flavor additives than one purchased at Burger King
    b. companies are willing to share their flavor formulas
    c. Pop-Tarts are unlikely to contain color and flavor additives
    d. both a and c

_____ 10. In paragraph 3, the transition word _both_ is used to show
    a. chronological order
    b. comparison
    c. steps in a process
    d. none of the above

_____ 11. In paragraph 1, the words *distinctive* and *unique* are
 a. antonyms
 b. homonyms
 c. synonyms
 d. similes

_____ 12. The author of the selection concludes with
 a. a warning about the dangers of chemical additives for children
 b. an opinion from an expert in toxic substances
 c. U.S. government facts and statistics
 d. both a and b

Fact or Opinion

For each of the following statements, write F if the statement is primarily factual or O if the statement represents an opinion.

_____F____ 1. For decades, McDonald's cooked its French fries in a mixture of about 7 percent soy oil and 93 percent beef fat.

_____F____ 2. The frozen potatoes and the cooking oil at McDonald's both contain "natural flavor."

_____O____ 3. The similarities between natural and artificial flavors are far more significant than their differences.

_____F____ 4. Americans now spend more than $1 trillion on food every year—and more than 90 percent of that money is spent on processed food.

_____F____ 5. Indeed, New Jersey produces about two thirds of the flavor additives sold in the United States.

_____F____ 6. International Flavors & Fragrances (IFF), the world's largest flavor company, has a manufacturing facility off Exit 8A in Dayton, New Jersey.

_____O____ 7. A tour of the IFF plant is the closest thing in real life to visiting Willy Wonka's chocolate factory.

_____O____ 8. The long chemical names on the little white labels seem like a strange foreign language.

_____F____ 9. Edible plants generally taste sweet; deadly ones, bitter.

_____F____ 10. The Food and Drug Administration does not require flavor companies to disclose the ingredients of their additives, so long as all the chemicals are classified as GRAS (Generally Regarded As Safe).

Vocabulary in Context

Look through the paragraphs listed below to find a word that matches each of the definitions. Write the words on the lines provided.

1. not harmful or injurious; harmless (paragraph 2) _____

2. pleasing to the taste (3) _____

3. disclose; reveal (4) _____

4. the innermost or central part (5) _____

5. easily damaged (6) _____

6. omnipresent (11) _____

7. prime; period of greatest success (13) _____

8. prohibited; forbidden (16) _____

In Your Own Words

1. For some people, McDonald's and other fast-food restaurants represent "comfort food." They associate cheeseburgers, French fries, and milkshakes with fond childhood memories. And, of course, some people just like the taste of foods such as the Big Mac. Former president Bill Clinton was a notorious example. What can nutritionists and other concerned individuals do to get children and adults to eat fewer highly processed foods?

2. Part of the appeal of a "Happy Meal" is the free toy. Do you think pressure should be exerted to get fast-food restaurants to stop making direct appeals to children?

3. Did the selection change your mind about eating highly processed foods? Or do you still think they can be part of an overall healthy diet?

4. Throughout the United States, meals in school cafeterias have come to resemble the meals at fast-food restaurants. Indeed, some schools have gone so far as to allow Subway or Pizza Hut to sell their products *in* the school cafeteria. Is this a good idea? Why or why not?

5. Many children badger their parents to take them to fast-food restaurants because they see these places advertised on TV. Do you think Congress should limit food advertisements aimed specifically at children?

The Art of Writing

1. What does your current diet look like? Keep track of the foods you eat for one week. If you are eating highly processed foods, what can you do to substitute more nutritious food products? Can you think of two dietary changes you should be making?

2. Healthy eating can be a real challenge today with all of the fast foods available and the cautions expressed about other food choices (beef, tuna, lettuce, peanut butter). How do you personally cope with all of the dietary guidelines and warnings?

Internet Activities

1. The United States Department of Agriculture (USDA) has determined that diet should no longer be a "one size fits all" concept. As a result, there is a new approach to the traditional food pyramid. A healthy diet is now based on age, sex, and level of activity. To determine your appropriate food choices, log on to

   www.mypyramid.gov

   Write a paragraph or two about the dietary selections that are appropriate for you.

2. To learn more about food safety and preventing food-borne illnesses, visit one of the following websites:

www.cfsan.fda.gov/

www.foodsafety.gov

Make a list of the prevention tips most valuable to you.

SELECTION

"With so much at stake, it's not surprising that the debate over herbal supplements is fierce."

GETTING THE PICTURE

Today over 60 million Americans are using a great variety of vitamins, minerals, and other supplements in a quest for improved health. These products are being consumed in record quantities despite the fact that they are not subjected to the same level of testing and regulation as prescription medications. As a result, many health professionals worry that consumers are throwing away money on "unproven, useless, or even harmful" health products.

BIO-SKETCH

Cecie Starr is a best-selling author of biology textbooks. She is noted for her clear and lucid writing style.

BRUSHING UP ON VOCABULARY

ephedra an herbal supplement taken to lose weight that has been blamed for several deaths.

St. John's wort *Hypericum perforatum*, a flowering plant from which an over-the-counter herbal supplement is derived, for use in the treatment of depression. St. John's wort has been thought to have curative properties since the time of Hippocrates in ancient Greece. There are approximately 7.5 million users of St. John's wort.

Excerpt from
HUMAN BIOLOGY
by Cecie Starr

What Is the Truth About Herbal Food Supplements?

"First do no harm."
—Hippocrates

1 Each year Americans spend more than $4 billion on herbal food supplements to ward off ailments ranging from the common cold and forgetfulness to depression, stress, and high cholesterol. Until recently one of the biggest sellers was ephedra, which recently came under heavy scrutiny after a spate of deaths due to stroke and heart attacks in people using it as a weight-loss "metabolism booster." Ephedra marketers denied any link between their product and the deaths, but the incidents led to a federal ban.

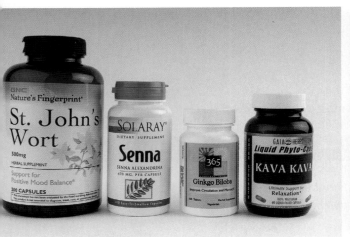

Herbal food supplements are a $4-billion-plus industry in the United States.
© The McGraw-Hill Companies, Inc./Jill Braaten

Ephedra plant in the wild.
© Zach Holmes/Alamy

"The desire to take medicine is perhaps the greatest feature which distinguishes man from animals."

—William Osler

2　Controversy has swirled around several other herbal supplements as well. When people using the stress-relief supplement kava began being diagnosed with liver damage, the Food and Drug Administration issued a consumer warning and the American Medical Association called for an outright ban. Regulators in Germany, Canada, and Singapore did just that. In 2000 a study of echinacea's effectiveness in warding off colds found "no significant effect on either the occurrence of infection or the severity of illness." In 2002 research on St. John's wort, an herb touted for soothing depression, no biological effect was detected either. And in a recent investigation of the "memory aid" gingko biloba, the research team found that the gingko did nothing to improve users' memory functions. Even gingko biloba supporters did not dispute the finding.

3　With so much at stake, it's not surprising that the debate over herbal supplements is fierce. Advocates on both sides point to conflicting experience and research results. In the case of ephedra, for example, companies that sell the supplements point to several studies they say support its safety and usefulness. Critics respond that the cited research was flawed on several counts. For instance, the subjects were pre-screened to weed out those with risky health histories (such as heart problems); unlike home users, they were monitored by physicians throughout the study; and only a small sample, about 80 subjects, was tested.

4　As the battle goes on, alert consumers are likely to be the ultimate winners. Recognizing that millions of people are buying and using herbal supplements, the National Institutes of Health has stepped up its support for scientifically rigorous testing of various herbal products. These controlled trials are designed to meet the highest research standards, and their results will probably be headline news.

5　In the meantime, the American Medical Association recommends that anyone who uses herbal supplements check with a physician to ensure that the herb in question hasn't been associated with harmful side effects. Consumers can also get reliable updates from the National Institutes of Health Web site at www.nih.gov.

Source: From STARR/MCMILLAN. *Human Biology (with CD-ROM and InfoTrac),* 6E. © 2005 Brooks/Cole, a part of Cengage Learning, Inc. Reproduced by permission. www.cengage.com/permissions.

COMPREHENSION CHECKUP

Fact or Opinion

Indicate whether each statement is a fact or an opinion by writing F or O in the blank provided.

_F_ 1. Ephedra marketers denied any link between their product and the deaths, but the incidents led to a federal ban.

_O_ 2. Controversy has swirled around several other herbal supplements as well.

_F_ 3. When people using the stress-relief supplement kava began being diagnosed with liver damage, the Food and Drug Administration issued a consumer warning and the American Medical Association called for an outright ban.

_F_ 4. Regulators in Germany, Canada, and Singapore did just that [banned them].

_F_ 5. In 2000 a study of echinacea's effectiveness in warding off colds found "no significant effect on either the occurrence of infection or the severity of illness."

_F_ 6. And in a recent investigation of the "memory aid" gingko biloba, the research team found that the gingko did nothing to improve users' memory functions.

_F_ 7. Even gingko biloba supporters did not dispute the finding.

_O_ 8. With so much at stake, it's not surprising that the debate over herbal supplements is fierce.

_O_ 9. As the battle goes on, alert consumers are likely to be the ultimate winners.

Vocabulary Practice

Match the words in Column A with their definitions in Column B, and write the appropriate answer letter in the space provided.

Column A	Column B
_J_ 1. scrutiny	a. dangerous
_C_ 2. spate	b. primary
_I_ 3. ban	c. unusually large outpouring
_L_ 4. touted	d. in error; defective
_G_ 5. dispute	e. watched in order to check up on
_K_ 6. advocates	f. watchful; vigilant; attentive
_D_ 7. flawed	g. contest; quarrel with
_A_ 8. risky	h. precise; thorough
_E_ 9. monitored	i. official order forbidding something
_F_ 10. alert	j. close examination
_B_ 11. ultimate	k. supporters
_H_ 12. rigorous	l. praised extravagantly

Vocabulary Practice

Without consulting a dictionary, write a definition in the blank provided for each of the following

1. ward off (paragraph 1) _____

2. weed out (3) _____

3. prescreened (3) _____

4. stepped up (4) _____

In Your Own Words

1. On popular radio shows, disc jockeys sometimes recommend a specific diet or dietary supplement that worked for them. How reliable do you think such recommendations are? If you were serious about researching such a product, what resources would you consult?

2. Commissioner Mark McClellan of the FDA calls the supplement industry a "buyer-beware market." He says that there are currently more than 1,000 manufacturers of dietary supplements, and all are exempt from most safety oversight, thereby creating a potentially dangerous situation. Should any products sold to consumers fall into a buyer-beware category? Or does the public have the right to expect some protection from the FDA?

3. Do you think more funds should be allocated to investigate herbal remedies?

The Art of Writing

What advice would you give a person who is choosing to self-medicate using herbs?

Internet Activity

Check out the National Institutes of Health website at

www.nih.gov

Print out the latest information about a dietary supplement.

EVALUATING HEALTH NEWS

Health-related research is now described in popular newspapers and magazines instead of only medical journals, and so more and more people have access to the information. Greater access is certainly a plus, but news reports of research studies may oversimplify both the results and what those results mean to the average person. Researchers do not set out to mislead people, but they must often strike a balance between reporting promising preliminary findings to the public, thereby allowing people to act on them, and waiting 10–20 years until long-term studies confirm or disprove a particular theory.

All of this can leave you in a difficult position. You cannot become an expert on all subjects, capable of effectively evaluating all the available health news. However, the following questions should help you better assess health advice appearing in the popular media:

1. *Is the report based on research or on an anecdote?* Advice based on carefully designed research studies has more validity than advice that relies on testimonials or stories.

2. *What is the source of the information?* A study published in a respected peer-reviewed journal has been examined by editors and other researchers in the field, people who are in a position to evaluate the merits of the study and its results. Research presented at medical meetings should be considered very preliminary because the results have not yet undergone a thorough prepublication review. It is also wise to ask who funded a study to determine whether there is any potential for bias. Information from government agencies and national research organizations is usually considered fairly reliable.

3. *How big was the study?* A study that involves many subjects is more likely to yield reliable results than a study involving only a few people. Another important indication that a finding is meaningful is if several different studies yield the same results.

4. *Who were the participants involved in the study?* Research findings are more likely to apply to you if you share important characteristics with the participants in the study. For example, the results of a study on men over 50 who smoke may not be particularly meaningful for a 30-year-old nonsmoking woman. Even less applicable are studies done in test tubes or on animals. Such research should be considered very preliminary in terms of its applicability to humans. Promising results from laboratory or animal research frequently cannot be replicated in human study subjects.

5. *What kind of study was it?* Epidemiological studies rely on observation or interviews to trace the relationship among lifestyle, physical characteristics, and diseases. While epidemiological studies can suggest links, they cannot establish cause-and-effect relationships. Clinical or interventional studies or trials involve testing the effects of different treatments on groups of people who have similar lifestyles and characteristics. They are more likely to provide conclusive evidence of a cause-and-effect relationship. The best interventional studies share the following characteristics:

   - *Controlled*: A group of people who receive the treatment is compared with a matched group who does not receive the treatment.

   - *Randomized*: The treatment and control groups are selected randomly.

   - *Double-blind*: Researchers and participants are unaware of who is receiving the treatment.

   - *Multicentered*: The experiment is performed at more than one institution.

6. *What do statistics really say?* First, are the results described as "statistically significant"? If a study is large and well designed, its results can be deemed statistically significant, meaning there is less than a 5 percent chance that the findings resulted from chance.

7. *Is new health advice being offered?* If the media report new guidelines for health behavior or medical treatment, examine the source. Government agencies and national research foundations usually consider a great deal of evidence before offering health advice. Above all, use common sense, and check with your physician before making a major change in your health habits based on news reports.

"The placebo cures 30 percent of the patients—no matter what they have."

—David Kline

"Common sense is in medicine the master workman."

—Peter Latham

Internet Activity

The importance of evaluating health care supplements and health-related research carefully cannot be overstated, especially if this information comes to you over the Internet. Using any search engine, type in "health supplements," and select a website to evaluate. After answering the questions below, write a paragraph summarizing your conclusions about the website.

Name of site:

_____

Web address:

_____

Type of information provided:

_____

_____

Organization or person responsible for information:

_____

_____

Place an X on the line if the statement is true for the site you are evaluating. Total the number of Xs. The more Xs, the more likely the site is reputable.

_____ 1. The site does not sell products associated with the information provided.

_____ 2. The provider is a person, an organization (org), or a governmental agency (gov) with a sound reputation.

_____ 3. The site does not try to discredit well-established organizations or government agencies.

_____ 4. The site does not rely on testimonials, celebrities, or people with unknown credentials.

_____ 5. The site is well-regarded by experts, and has a high rating at navigator.tufts.edu.

_____ 6. The site has a history of providing good information.

_____ 7. The site provides complete information that is documented by research.

_____ 8. No claims of quick cures or miracle results are made.

_____ 9. The site provides information consistent with health textbooks or medical encyclopedias.

Source: Information from Charles B. Corbin, *Concepts of Fitness and Wellness,* 4th ed. New York: McGraw-Hill, 2002, pp. 453–458.

What main idea from the previous selections does this cartoon reinforce?

WARNING: Patient will be charged extra for annoying the doctor with any self-diagnosis gotten off the Internet.

K. LEMIEUX 1-3

SIX CHIX: © Katherine Lemieux. King Features Syndicate.

TEST-TAKING TIP

Improving Your Performance on Essay Tests (1)

BEFORE THE TEST

There is no substitute for simply knowing the course material well. But that can be a big task, and realistically, some parts of the material are probably more important, and more likely to appear on an essay test, than others.

One way to give your preparation some focus is to try to think of questions that might appear on the test:

1. Ask yourself what questions you think your teacher might ask.

2. Look at your returned test papers. You can learn a lot by reading the instructor's comments and correcting the answers as needed.

3. Review your class notes and any handouts to see what the teacher emphasized in the course. What topics did the teacher spend the most time on? What topics did the teacher seem to care the most about?

Keep in mind that an essay question may ask for information on a specific topic, or it may be directed at a general understanding of the course material. You need to prepare yourself for both kinds of questions.

General or "big picture" essay questions often deal with relationships among topics or concepts. A good way to prepare for these questions is to:

1. Make an outline or map of the course material.

2. Look at your class notes, handouts, and textbook, and organize this material into an outline. If your teacher has closely followed a textbook, the book's table of contents should give you a good start on making your outline.

3. Prepare answers to your possible questions. You may even want to practice writing out answers.

Point of View

Vietnam Veterans Memorial (1981–1983) BY MAYA YING LIN

View and Reflect

"It is the name of the deceased, rather than the image or likeness, that conveys immortality."

1. What do you think this quote means?
2. What is your point of view about war? About the war in Vietnam?

INTRODUCTION TO POINT OF VIEW

Point of view is defined as a mental attitude from which a person views or judges something. Other terms for point of view are *perspective* and *standpoint*. A point of view can be favorable, unfavorable, or neutral. A writer's point of view leads to opinions and beliefs.

View I

View II

View III

In the best-selling book *The 7 Habits of Highly Effective People*, Stephen R. Covey describes an experiment that took place at Harvard University. Professors showed one group of students the drawing at top left of a toothless old woman with a large nose and chin buried in her dark collar. Another group of students was shown the drawing at upper right of a profile of a young woman. Each group studied their assigned drawing for about ten seconds. When ten seconds had elapsed, both groups were shown the third picture, at top center. When the groups were asked to describe what they now saw, each group strongly tended to describe the picture it had previously studied for ten seconds. But when particular features of either the old woman or the young lady were pointed out to the group as a whole, the students momentarily saw the other point of view expressed in the other picture. However, when they looked away for a brief interval, they again immediately saw the picture they had been conditioned to see.

All of us have points of view on many topics. Our particular backgrounds and experiences shape our points of view. It took the Harvard students only ten seconds to become conditioned to see only one image. Our family, friends, school experiences, religion, and the media among other influences have conditioned us over a lifetime to have particular points of view and to see things in certain ways.

The cartoon on the next page illustrates how point of view is relative to our experiences.

A critical reader must be able to recognize and understand an author's point of view. While you may not agree with the author on a particular subject, it is important to maintain an open and questioning attitude.

"It's all according to your point of view. To me, you're a monster."

Handelsman Cartoon"It's all according to your point of view… © 2007 J.B. Handelsman from cartoonbank.com.
All rights reserved.

Exercise 1: Identifying Point of View

Directions: To better understand point of view, select one of the following fairy tales, and retell it from the point of view of the character mentioned.

1. *Cinderella* from the point of view of one of her stepsisters

2. *Little Red Riding Hood* from the point of view of the wolf

3. *Snow White and the Seven Dwarfs* from the point of view of the queen

Exercise 2: Identifying an Author's Point of View in Textbook Material

Directions: Read each of the following selections from textbooks, and indicate the author's point of view in your own words.

EXAMPLE

Many people are concerned that art be "pretty." These people often remark, for example, "I only want to look at pleasant things" or "There's already too much ugliness in this world" or "Isn't that cute! It's darling!" They want only happy endings at the movies; they want only to be entertained. The problem with insisting that all art be pretty is that doing so limits art to one kind of expression. Because human experience is much richer than the cute and pleasant, art should be free to reflect life in all its richness. It would be nice if everything in life were pleasing, but some of the most important things are not so nice. Birth and death can be rather painful; so can falling in or out of love. Who is to stop an artist from saying something truthful about these or any other aspects of life that she or he finds meaningful?

Paragraph from Thomas Buser, *Experiencing Art Around Us,* St. Paul, MN: West Publishing, 1995, p. 18.

Author's point of view: _____

_____

1. Stress is not always harmful. In fact, a lack of stress, sometimes called "rust out," can lead to boredom, apathy, and less than optimal health. Moderate stress may enhance behavioral adaptation and is necessary for maturation and health. Stress stimulates psychological growth. It has been said that "freedom from stress is death" and "stress is the spice of life."

Paragraph from Charles B. Corbin, *Concepts of Fitness and Wellness,* 4th ed., New York: McGraw-Hill, 2002, p. 348.

Author's point of view: _____

_____

2. If you want to get ahead in an organization, it is important to do a good job. But it is also important that people like you. If people like you, they will forgive just about anything you do wrong. If they don't like you, you can do everything right and it will not matter. Many hardworking talented people have been bypassed for promotion and fired simply because their boss or some other high-level manager didn't like them. In fact, when Henry Ford fired Lee Iacocca, he used only four words to explain his decision: "I don't like you."

Paragraph from Robert N. Lussier, *Human Relations in Organizations,* 4th ed., New York: McGraw-Hill, 1999, p. 16.

Author's point of view: _____

_____

3. Smoking interferes with your studying and your concentration: It's a disaster for your lungs, all of your body systems, your skin and your other organs, your immune system, and your brain. It's an insult you commit against yourself. (You already know the specific health risks, so I won't bore you with those. And I won't even mention chewing tobacco and its carcinogenic effects on the mouth, the throat, and the rest of the body.) If you don't smoke, that's terrific. Keep on *not* smoking. If you do smoke, make the decision to quit. I know it's a tough habit to break. Cigarette smoking is considered more addictive than cocaine, but if you want to quit, you can. Do you really want to go through life with cigarettes controlling you?

Paragraph from Janet Elder, *Exercise Your College Reading Skills,* 1st ed., New York: McGraw-Hill, 2004, p. S-12.

Author's point of view: _____

_____

4. The educational practice known as *tracking,* or grouping students by abilities, may contribute to failure. Students placed in low-track classes lack the stimulation of higher-ability peers and often get poorer teaching. They rarely move up to higher tracks, and many lose interest in trying to do better. Furthermore, since school failure and contact with antisocial peers are often related

to antisocial behavior, grouping poor achievers together may solidify problem behaviors.

Paragraph from Diane E. Papalia, *Human Development,* 8th ed., New York: McGraw-Hill, 2001, p. 439.

Author's point of view: _____

_____

5. Jennifer unlocked her door quickly, raced inside, and shut it loudly behind her. She fastened the lock, threw the bolt, dropped her books on the floor, and made her way to the kitchen for her usual snack. Within a few minutes Jennifer was ensconced on the sofa, the television on and her stuffed animals clutched firmly in her hand. She decided to do her homework later. Her parents would be home then, and she tried not to spend too much time thinking about being lonely. She turned her attention to the television, to spend the next few hours watching talk shows. Jennifer is a latchkey kid. More than one in five children between 5 and 13, like Jennifer, are left to care for themselves after school. Although the average latchkey child is left alone two and a half hours per day, a significant number are alone much longer, more than thirty-six hours per week. Some latchkey children adjust to their situations. But, for others, problems do develop, and sad to say there are few educational or social agencies to respond to their needs.

From David Sadker, *Teachers, Schools, and Society,* 8th ed., New York: McGraw-Hill, 2008, p. 192. Copyright © 2008 McGraw-Hill Companies, Inc. Used with permission.

Author's point of view: _____

_____

6. Lamar was finishing junior high school with resignation and despair. He had just managed to squeak through Beaton Junior High with poor grades and no understanding of how this frustrating experience would help him. He wasn't good at schoolwork and felt that the classes he had to sit through were a waste of time. Lamar's father had left school after eighth grade to go to work. Although he did not make much money, he had a car and seemed to be getting along okay. Lamar's mother had left high school when she became pregnant and had never returned. Neither of Lamar's parents thought school was critical, although both wanted Lamar to finish. But Lamar's patience was wearing thin. He wanted to end these long, boring days, get a job, and get a car. He'd had enough of school. Unfortunately, Lamar is a good candidate to join the nation's dropouts. Today, roughly one out of every nine students does not graduate from high school. This represents not only a loss of human potential but also increased costs in welfare, unemployment benefits, and potential criminal activity. And that is a national tragedy.

From Myra Pollack Sadker and David Miller Sadker, *Teachers, Schools, and Society,* 8th ed., New York: McGraw-Hill, 2008, pp. 196–197. Copyright © McGraw-Hill. Reprinted by permission of The McGraw-Hill Companies, Inc.

Author's point of view: _____

_____

7. The first step to improvement is always self-awareness. Analyze your shortcomings as a listener and commit yourself to overcoming them. Good listeners are not born that way. They have *worked* at learning how to listen effectively. Good listening does not go hand in hand with intelligence, education, or social

standing. Like any other skill, it comes from practice and self-discipline. Begin to think of listening as an active process. So many aspects of modern life encourage us to listen passively. We "listen" to the CD while studying or "listen" to the television while moving about from room to room. This type of passive listening is a habit—but so is active listening. We can learn to identify those situations in which active listening is important. If you work seriously at becoming a more efficient listener, you will reap rewards in your schoolwork, in your personal and family relations, and in your career.

From Stephen E. Lucas, *The Art of Public Speaking,* 9th ed., New York: McGraw-Hill, pp. 62, 64. Copyright © 2007 McGraw-Hill. Reprinted by permission of The McGraw-Hill Companies, Inc.

Author's point of view: _____

_____

8. Littleton, Colorado; Jonesboro, Arkansas; West Paducah, Kentucky; Peal, Mississippi; Edinboro, Pennsylvania; Springfield, Oregon—these are now more than just names of small and medium-size cities. They resonate with the sound of gunshots of kids killing other kids on school grounds. Each town was the scene of schoolhouse murders. As a result, people no longer perceive schools as safe havens but as another extension of the harsh reality of violence in society. But how accurate is that impression? Statistics demonstrate that a child has a one in a million chance of being killed at school. According to the Center for Disease Control, 99 percent of violent deaths of school-aged children occurred *outside* school grounds. Twenty-three times more children are killed in gun *accidents* than in school killings. Schools, then, are *safer* than their neighborhoods, but people still are unnerved by a perception of an alarming rise in schoolyard violence, perhaps generated by heavy media coverage of the recent incidents.

From Richard Schaefer, *Sociology,* 10th ed., New York: McGraw-Hill, p. 349. Copyright 2007 McGraw-Hill. Reprinted by permission of The McGraw-Hill Companies, Inc.

Author's point of view: _____

_____

SELECTION

"He crowded her into the wall then, trying to break her grip. He held on to the baby and pushed with all his weight."

GETTING THE PICTURE

As you are reading "Popular Mechanics" by Raymond Carver, think about the point of view of each character. Where should your sympathies lie—with the wife, the husband, or the baby?

BIO-SKETCH

Raymond Carver is considered by many to be one of the great short story writers of the twentieth century. The language of his stories is deceptively simple and, as in this

SELECTION *continued*

short story, is meant to mirror the language used by the working poor. Carver based his realistic portrayals on what he knew best. Married at 19, and a father soon afterward, Carver, with no marketable skills, was forced to work at a series of odd jobs to support his family. Unfortunately, the strains proved to be too much, and his first marriage ended in divorce. Eventually, he received his B.A. from what is now California State University–Humboldt and began a career as an English and creative writing instructor.

In his over twenty-year career, his writings have received many honors, including nominations for a Pulitzer Prize, three O' Henry Awards, two grants from the National Endowment for the Arts, and a Guggenheim Fellowship. Mr. Carver died in 1988 of lung cancer, and his second wife, the poet Tess Gallagher, collaborated with director Robert Altman to create the critically acclaimed movie *Short Cuts,* based on a collection of Carver short stories. Interestingly, the short story below has also been published under the title "Little Things." What do you suppose, given Carver's personal history, he meant to imply by the change in the title?

Popular Mechanics

BY RAYMOND CARVER

1   EARLY THAT DAY THE WEATHER TURNED AND THE snow was melting into dirty water. Streaks of it ran down from the little shoulder-high window that faced the backyard. Cars slushed by on the street outside, where it was getting dark. But it was getting dark on the inside too.

2   He was in the bedroom pushing clothes into a suitcase when she came to the door.

3   "I'm glad you're leaving! I'm glad you're leaving!" she said. "Do you hear?"

4   He kept on putting his things into the suitcase.

5   "I'm so glad you're leaving!" She began to cry. "You can't even look me in the face, can you?"

6   Then she noticed the baby's picture on the bed and picked it up.

7   He looked at her and she wiped her eyes and stared at him before turning and going back to the living room.

8   "Bring that back," he said.

9   "Just get your things and get out," she said.

10   He did not answer. He fastened the suitcase, put on his coat, looked around the bedroom before turning off the light. Then he went out to the living room.

11   She stood in the doorway of the little kitchen, holding the baby.

12   "I want the baby," he said.

13   "Are you crazy?"

14   "No, but I want the baby. I'll get someone to come by for his things."

15   "You're not touching this baby," she said.

16   The baby had begun to cry and she uncovered the blanket from around his head.

17   "Oh, oh," she said, looking at the baby.

18   He moved toward her.

19   "For God's sake!" she said. She took a step back into the kitchen.

20   "I want the baby."

21   "Get out of here!"

22   She turned and tried to hold the baby over in a corner behind the stove.

23   But he came up. He reached across the stove and tightened his hands on the baby.

24   "Let go of him," he said.

25   "Get away, get away!" she cried.

26   The baby was red-faced and screaming. In the scuffle they knocked down a flowerpot that hung behind the stove.

27   He crowded her into the wall then, trying to break her grip. He held on to the baby and pushed with all his weight.

28   "Let go of him," he said.

29   "Don't," she said. "You're hurting the baby," she said.

30   "I'm not hurting the baby," he said.

31   The kitchen window gave no light. In the near-dark he worked on her fisted fingers with one hand and with the other hand he gripped the screaming baby up under an arm near the shoulder.

32   She felt her fingers being forced open. She felt the baby going from her.

33   "No!" she screamed just as her hands came loose.

34   She would have it, this baby. She grabbed for the baby's other arm. She caught the baby around the wrist and leaned back.

35   But he would not let go. He felt the baby slipping out of his hands and he pulled back very hard.

36   In this manner, the issue was decided.

Source: "Popular Mechanics," from Raymond Carver, *What We Talk About When We Talk about Love,* pp. 123–125. Copyright © 1974, 1976, 1978, 1980, 1981 by Raymond Carver. Used by permission of Alfred A. Knopf, a division of Random House, Inc.

 COMPREHENSION CHECKUP

Fact Check

Answer the following factual questions.

1. At what time of day does the story occur? _____

2. Where is the baby's picture? _____

3. Is the baby a boy or a girl? _____

4. Where was the flowerpot hanging? _____

5. What is the baby wrapped in? _____

Vocabulary Practice

1. How many times is the word *little* used? _____ To what does it refer?

   _____

2. In the story, where does the author refer to "light" and "dark"? What does he mean to imply by each of these references?

   _____

   _____

   _____

   _____

In Your Own Words

1. In the beginning of the story, concrete details set the scene for the reader. What is the overall tone of the first paragraph?

2. When did the man decide he wanted the baby?

3. What is the man's likely reason for wanting the baby?

4. Is the baby in any actual physical danger?

5. What is meant by the last line of the story? What has been decided? What has happened to the baby?

6. In what way is the baby symbolic of the couple's relationship?

7. Why don't the characters have names? Why are they only referred to as *he* and *she*?

The Art of Writing

In a brief essay, respond to one of the items below.

1. The story illustrates how parents can harm their child. In what ways can parents psychologically or emotionally damage their children? In your opinion, which type of abuse is worse?

2. In the story, the parents are behaving in an immature manner, like children fighting over a toy. What attributes do adults need to possess to be able to rear a child successfully? What attributes should they possess in order to have a healthy marriage?

3. Do you think "Popular Mechanics" is true to the way most relationships end today? What can people do to end a relationship on a positive note?

Internet Activity

Use a search engine such as Google www.google.com to find out more information about the magazine *Popular Mechanics*. Why do you suppose Carver chose the name of the magazine for the title of his short story?

SELECTION

*"Now the point of the story is this: Did the tiger come
out of the door, or did the lady?"*

GETTING THE PICTURE

Ralph Waldo Emerson once wrote: "As a man thinketh so is he, and as a man chooseth
so is he." The princess described in this classic short story faces a clear dilemma. She
must choose the fate of her lover and in the process reveal what sort of person she is.
As you are reading the story, keep the quotation in mind. When you finish, explain the
meaning of the quotation as it applies to the princess.

BIO-SKETCH

Frank Stockton (1834–1902) was born in Philadelphia. He was a wood engraver by
trade but spent much of his time writing stories. His earliest stories were for children,
but later he began writing for adults. Stockton's most famous story, "The Lady or the
Tiger?" appeared in 1882 in the *Century Magazine.* It caused a great outcry, and
debates were held all over the country to decide the ending.

BRUSHING UP ON VOCABULARY

epithalamic measure   marriage dance.

barbaric   lacking civilizing influences; primitive. It comes from the Latin word *barbari-
cus,* meaning "foreign or rude." It is often used to describe someone who is uncultured and ignorant.

The Lady or the Tiger?

BY FRANK R. STOCKTON

1   IN THE VERY OLDEN TIME, there lived a semibarbaric king, whose ideas,
though somewhat polished and sharpened by the progressiveness of distant
Latin neighbors, were still large, florid, and untrammeled, as became the half
of him which was barbaric. He was a man of exuberant fancy, and, withal, of
an authority so irresistible that, at his will, he turned his varied fancies into
facts. He was greatly given to self-communing; and when he and himself
agreed upon any thing, the thing was done. When every member of his domestic and political systems moved smoothly in its appointed course, his nature was bland and genial; but whenever there was a little hitch, and some of
his orbs got out of their orbits, he was blander and more genial still, for nothing pleased him so much as to make the crooked straight and crush down
uneven places.

2   Among the borrowed notions by which his barbarism had become semified was that of the public arena, in which, by exhibitions of manly and beastly valor, the minds of his subjects were refined and cultured.

3   But even here the exuberant and barbaric fancy exerted itself. The arena of the king was built, not to give the people an opportunity of hearing the rhapsodies of dying gladiators, nor to enable them to view the inevitable conclusion of a conflict between religious opinions and hungry jaws, but for purposes far better adapted to widen and develop the mental energies of the people. This vast amphitheater, with its encircling galleries, its mysterious vaults, and its unseen passages, was an agent of poetic justice, in which crime was punished, or virtue rewarded, by the decrees of an impartial and incorruptible chance.

4   When a subject was accused of a crime of sufficient importance to interest the king, public notice was given that on an appointed day the fate of the accused person would be decided in the king's arena—a structure which well deserved its name; for although its form and plan were borrowed from afar, its purpose emanated solely from the brain of this man, who, every barleycorn a king, knew no tradition to which he owed more allegiance than pleased his fancy, and who ingrafted on every adopted form of human thought and action the rich growth of his barbaric idealism.

5   When all the people had assembled in the galleries, and the king, surrounded by his court, sat high up on his throne of royal state on one side of the arena, he gave a signal, a door beneath him opened, and the accused subject stepped out into the amphitheater. Directly opposite him, on the other side of the enclosed space, were two doors, exactly alike and side by side. It was the duty and the privilege of the person on trial to walk directly to these doors and open one of them. He could open either door he pleased. He was subject to no guidance or influence but that of the aforementioned impartial and incorruptible chance. If he opened the one, there came out of it a hungry tiger, the fiercest and most cruel that could be procured, which immediately sprang upon him and tore him to pieces as a punishment for his guilt. The moment that the case of the criminal was thus decided, doleful iron bells were clanged, great wails went up from the hired mourners posted on the outer rim of the arena, and the vast audience, with bowed heads and downcast hearts, wended slowly their homeward way, mourning greatly that one so young and fair, or so old and respected, should have merited so dire a fate.

6   But if the accused person opened the other door, there came forth from it a lady, the most suitable to his years and station that his majesty could select among his fair subjects, and to this lady he was immediately married as a reward of his innocence. It mattered not that he might already possess a wife and family, or that his affections might be engaged upon an object of his own selection. The king allowed no such subordinate arrangements to interfere with his great scheme of retribution and reward. The exercises, as in the other instance, took place immediately, and in the arena. Another door opened beneath the king, and a priest, followed by a band of choristers and dancing maidens blowing joyous

airs on golden horns and treading an epithalamic measure, advanced to where the pair stood, side by side; and the wedding was promptly and cheerily solemnized. Then the brass bells rang forth their merry peals, the people shouted glad hurrahs, and the innocent man, preceded by children strewing flowers on his path, led his bride to his home.

7   This was the king's semibarbaric method of administering justice. Its perfect fairness is obvious. The criminal could not know out of which door would come the lady. He opened either he pleased, without having the slightest idea whether, in the next instant, he was to be devoured or married. On some occasions the tiger came out of one door, and on some out of the other. The decisions of this tribunal were not only fair, they were positively determinate. The accused person was instantly punished if he found himself guilty; and if innocent, he was rewarded on the spot, whether he liked it or not. There was no escape from the judgments of the king's arena.

8   The institution was a very popular one. When the people gathered together on one of the great trial days, they never knew whether they were to witness a bloody slaughter or a hilarious wedding. This element of uncertainty lent an interest to the occasion which it could not otherwise have attained. Thus, the masses were entertained and pleased, and the thinking part of the community could bring no charge of unfairness against this plan; for did not the accused person have the whole matter in his own hands?

9   This semibarbaric king had a daughter as blooming as his most florid fancies and with a soul as fervent and imperious as his own. As is usual in such cases, she was the apple of his eye and was loved by him above all humanity. Among his courtiers was a young man of that fineness of blood and lowness of station common to the conventional heroes of romance who love royal maidens. This royal maiden was well satisfied with her lover, for he was handsome and brave to a degree unsurpassed in all this kingdom; and she loved him with an ardor that had enough of barbarism in it to make it exceedingly warm and strong. This love affair moved on happily for many months until one day the king happened to discover its existence. He did not hesitate nor waver in regard to his duty in the premises. The youth was immediately cast into prison, and a day was appointed for his trial in the king's arena. This, of course, was an especially important occasion; and his majesty, as well as all the people, was greatly interested in the workings and development of this trial. Never before had such a case occurred; never before had a subject dared to love the daughter of a king. In after-years such things became commonplace enough; but then they were, in no slight degree, novel and startling.

10   The tiger cages of the kingdom were searched for the most savage and relentless beasts, from which the fiercest monster might be selected for the arena; and the ranks of maiden youth and beauty throughout the land were carefully surveyed by competent judges in order that the young man might have a fitting bride in case fate did not determine for him a different destiny. Of course, everybody knew that the deed with which the accused was charged had been done. He had loved the princess, and neither he, nor she, nor anyone else

thought of denying the fact; but the king would not think of allowing any fact of this kind to interfere with the workings of the tribunal, in which he took such delight and satisfaction. No matter how the affair turned out, the youth would be disposed of; and the king would take an aesthetic pleasure in watching the course of events which would determine whether or not the young man had done wrong in allowing himself to love the princess.

11   The appointed day arrived. From far and near the people gathered and thronged the great galleries of the arena; and crowds, unable to gain admittance, massed themselves against its outside walls. The king and his court were in their places, opposite the twin doors—those fateful portals, so terrible in their similarity!

12   All was ready. The signal was given. A door beneath the royal party opened, and the lover of the princess walked into the arena. Tall, beautiful, fair, his appearance was greeted with a low hum of admiration and anxiety. Half the audience had not known so grand a youth had lived among them. No wonder the princess loved him! What a terrible thing for him to be there!

13   As the youth advanced into the arena, he turned, as the custom was, to bow to the king. But he did not think at all of that royal personage; his eyes were fixed upon the princess, who sat to the right of her father. Had it not been for the moiety of barbarism in her nature, it is probable that lady would not have been there; but her intense and fervid soul would not allow her to be absent on an occasion in which she was so terribly interested. From the moment that the decree had gone forth that her lover should decide his fate in the king's arena, she had thought of nothing, night or day, but this great event and the various subjects connected with it. Possessed of more power, influence, and force of character than anyone who had ever before been interested in such a case, she had done what no other person had done—she had possessed herself of the secret of the doors. She knew in which of the two rooms that lay behind those doors stood the cage of the tiger, with its open front, and in which waited the lady. Through these thick doors, heavily curtained with skins on the inside, it was impossible that any noise or suggestion should come from within to the person who should approach to raise the latch of one of them. But gold—and the power of a woman's will—had brought the secret to the princess.

14   And not only did she know in which room stood the lady ready to emerge, all blushing and radiant, should her door be opened, but she knew who the lady was. It was one of the fairest and loveliest of the damsels of the court who had been selected as the reward of the accused youth, should he be proved innocent of the crime of aspiring to one so far above him; and the princess hated her. Often had she seen, or imagined that she had seen, this fair creature throwing glances of admiration upon the person of her lover, and sometimes she thought these glances were perceived and even returned. Now and then she had seen them talking together; it was but for a moment or two, but much can be said in a brief space. It may have been on most unimportant topics, but how could she know that? The girl was lovely, but she had dared to raise her eyes to the loved

one of the princess; and with all the intensity of the savage blood transmitted to her through long lines of wholly barbaric ancestors, she hated the woman who blushed and trembled behind that silent door.

15   When her lover turned and looked at her, and his eye met hers as she sat there paler and whiter than anyone in the vast ocean of anxious faces about her, he saw, by the power of quick perception which is given to those whose souls are one, that she knew behind which door crouched the tiger, and behind which stood the lady. He had expected her to know it. He understood her nature, and his soul was assured that she would never rest until she had made plain to herself this thing, hidden to all other lookers-on, even to the king. The only hope for the youth in which there was any element of certainty was based upon the success of the princess in discovering this mystery; and the moment he looked upon her, he saw she had succeeded, as in his soul he knew she would succeed.

16   Then it was that his quick and anxious glance asked the question: "Which?" It was as plain to her as if he shouted it from where he stood. There was not an instant to be lost. The question was asked in a flash; it must be answered in another.

17   Her right arm lay on the cushioned parapet before her. She raised her hand and made a slight, quick movement toward the right. No one but her lover saw her. Every eye but his was fixed on the man in the arena.

"He who reflects too much will achieve little."

—J.C.F. von Schiller

18   He turned, and with a firm and rapid step he walked across the empty space. Every heart stopped beating, every breath was held, every eye was fixed immovably upon that man. Without the slightest hesitation he went to the door on the right and opened it.

* * * *

19   Now, the point of the story is this: Did the tiger come out of the door, or did the lady?

20   The more we reflect upon this question, the harder it is to answer. It involves a study of the human heart which leads us through devious mazes of passion, out of which it is difficult to find our way. Think of it, fair reader, not as if the decision of the question depended upon yourself, but upon that hot-blooded semibarbaric princess, her soul at white heat beneath the combined fires of despair and jealousy. She had lost him, but who should have him?

21   How often, in her waking hours and in her dreams, had she started in wild horror and covered her face with her hands as she thought of her lover opening the door on the other side of which waited the cruel fangs of the tiger!

22   But how much oftener had she seen him at the other door! How in her grievous reveries had she gnashed her teeth and torn her hair when she saw his start of rapturous delight as he opened the door of the lady! How her soul had burned in agony when she had seen him rush to meet that woman, with her flushing cheek and sparkling eye of triumph; when she had seen him lead her forth, his whole frame kindled with the joy of recovered life; when she had heard the glad shouts from the multitude and the wild ringing of the happy bells; when she had seen the priest, with his joyous followers, advance to the

couple and make them man and wife before her very eyes; and when she had seen them walk away together upon their path of flowers, followed by the tremendous shouts of the hilarious multitude, in which her one despairing shriek was lost and drowned!

23   Would it not be better for him to die at once and go to wait for her in the blessed regions of semibarbaric futurity?

24   And yet, that awful tiger, those shrieks, that blood!

25   Her decision had been indicated in an instant, but it had been made after days and nights of anguished deliberation. She had known she would be asked, she had decided what she would answer, and without the slightest hesitation she had moved her hand to the right.

26   The question of her decision is one not to be lightly considered, and it is not for me to presume to set myself up as the one person able to answer it. And so I leave it with all of you: Which came out of the opened door—the lady or the tiger?

Source: Frank R. Stockton, "The Lady or the Tiger?" first published 1882.

 ## COMPREHENSION CHECKUP

Multiple Choice

Write the letter of the correct answer in the blank provided.

_____ 1. The king is described as possessing all of the following character traits except that of being
 a. semibarbaric
 b. tyrannical
 c. generous and forgiving
 d. self-absorbed

_____ 2. Given the similarity of the princess to her father, we can assume that she is
 a. timid
 b. semibarbaric
 c. fervid
 d. both b and c

_____ 3. The narrator calls the king's system of deciding the fate of the accused "poetic justice." This is an example of
 a. literary allusion
 b. irony
 c. patterns of organization
 d. summary

_____ 4. The princess's lover is lacking
 a. good looks
 b. high social standing
 c. bravery
 d. height

_____ 5. The tiger chosen for the trial of the princess's lover is all of the following *except*
   a. savage
   b. relentless
   c. meek
   d. fierce

_____ 6. The maiden chosen for the princess's lover is
   a. fair and lovely
   b. blushing and radiant
   c. rich and powerful
   d. both a and b

_____ 7. The guilt or innocence of the accused is determined by
   a. a confession
   b. a court of law
   c. the appearance of a tiger or a lady
   d. the king's subjects

_____ 8. "She was the apple of his eye" is a figurative expression meaning that
   a. the king considered the princess to be expendable
   b. the king was very fond of the princess
   c. the princess was the king's favorite person
   d. both b and c

_____ 9. The king's system of dispensing justice is
   a. arbitrary and capricious
   b. fair to all concerned
   c. unpopular with his subjects
   d. civilized

_____ 10. The author states that the reader must look to the character of the princess to determine
   a. whether the princess's lover will live or die
   b. whether love or jealousy will win out
   c. how the story will end
   d. all of the above

True or False

Indicate whether the statement is true or false by writing T or F in the blank provided.

_____ 11. The king's daughter has a fervent soul.

_____ 12. The king places a high value on human life.

_____ 13. The king approves of his daughter's love affair.

_____ 14. Both the king and the princess are present at the arena.

_____ 15. The princess is fond of the maiden behind the door.

_____ 16. The princess points to the door on the left.

_____ 17. The princess's lover unhesitatingly follows the princess's signal to go to the right.

_____ 18. The princess's lover expects the princess to know the secret of the doors.

_____ 19. When the princess's lover turns toward the king, his attention is focused on the princess.

_____ 20. Of all the onlookers, the king alone knows the secret of what is behind each door.

Vocabulary in Context

Using the context clues below, write a definition for the italicized word.

1. "... by the decrees of an *impartial* and incorruptible chance."

   Definition: _____

2. "... with bowed heads and *downcast* hearts ..."

   Definition: _____

3. "He did not hesitate nor *waver* in regard to his duty in the premises."

   Definition: _____

4. "... opposite the twin doors—those fateful *portals* ..."

   Definition: _____

5. "... but her intense and *fervid* soul would not allow her to be absent ..."

   Definition: _____

6. "... which leads us through devious *mazes* of passion, out of which it is difficult to find our way."

   Definition: _____

Vocabulary Practice

Look through the paragraph indicated in parentheses to find a word that matches the definition below.

1. pleasantly gentle or agreeable (paragraph 1) _____

2. ecstatically expressing feelings or enthusiasm (3) _____

3. issued forth; originated (4) _____

4. proceeded or went; traveled (5) _____

5. pertaining to a sense of beauty (10) _____

6. an indefinite portion, part, or share (13) _____

7. daydreams (22) _____

Vocabulary in Context

Match the word in Column A with the definition in Column B.

Column A	**Column B**
_____ 1. florid	a. zeal; fervor
_____ 2. untrammeled	b. maiden
_____ 3. barbaric	c. ordinary
_____ 4. bland	d. ornate; showy
_____ 5. valor	e. shifty; underhand

_____ 6. doleful	f. court of justice
_____ 7. dire	g. loud, sustained sound
_____ 8. retribution	h. properly qualified
_____ 9. peals	i. unrestrained
_____ 10. tribunal	j. sorrowful; mournful
_____ 11. damsel	k. crowded
_____ 12. imperious	l. crude; primitive
_____ 13. unsurpassed	m. terrible
_____ 14. ardor	n. pleasantly gentle or agreeable
_____ 15. commonplace	o. punishment for a wrong act
_____ 16. competent	p. not exceeded
_____ 17. thronged	q. courage or bravery
_____ 18. devious	r. dictatorial; domineering

In Your Own Words

1. Describe the nature of the princess in your own words. How might these qualities influence her decision?

2. From what you know of the princess, which door do you think she pointed to: the one hiding the lady or the one hiding the tiger? State your reasons.

3. The princess's lover goes to the door on the right "without the slightest hesitation." If you were the young man, would you follow the princess's direction? Explain your answer.

The Art of Writing

In a brief essay, write your own ending, telling what happens when the young man opens the door. Describe the princess's reaction as the door opens. Describe the young man's reaction to what he finds.

Internet Activity

In the short story "The Lady or the Tiger?" the princess must choose between two unpleasant alternatives. The Institute for Global Ethics addresses ethical dilemmas. In particular, they focus on "tough choices" or those that "pit one right value against another." Visit their website at

www.globalethics.org/pub/toughchoices.html

The website includes the first chapter of Rushworth Kidder's book *How Good People Make Tough Choices.* Skim the introductory material and then carefully read the ethical dilemma that a librarian working at the reference desk at a public library recently faced. What do you think the librarian decided to do? If you were in a similar situation, what would you do?

SELECTION

*"By mid-1967, in fact, more than 400,000 Americans were
fighting in Vietnam. As many as 300 died each week."*

GETTING THE PICTURE

The following selection from the history textbook *America Past and Present* discusses the Vietnam War. Fought in the 1960s and 1970s, the war was highly divisive within the United States. In the 1960s, the war became increasingly controversial. Initially, Presidents Eisenhower and Kennedy sent military advisers to aid the noncommunist South Vietnamese in resisting the communist North Vietnamese. Under President Johnson, the U.S. involvement deepened to the point at which half a million U.S. troops became involved in the conflict. In 1973, President Nixon negotiated a cease-fire with North Vietnam, and soon all U.S. troops returned home. In 1982, the Vietnam Veterans Memorial was dedicated to the American soldiers who were killed or missing in action in Vietnam.

BIO-SKETCH

Robert A. Divine is the George W. Littlefield Professor (Emeritus) at the University of Texas at Austin. An award-winning teacher, he taught diplomatic history for 42 years. His primary interest is recent political and diplomatic history, with an emphasis on presidents from Franklin Roosevelt to George W. Bush. His book *Perpetual War for Perpetual Peace* (2000) is an analysis of U.S. involvement in the wars of the twentieth century.

BRUSHING UP ON VOCABULARY

Tet   the first day of the Vietnamese New Year. On January 30, 1968, Communist forces struck civilian and military sites without warning throughout South Vietnam, including the U.S. embassy in Saigon.

Excerpt from
AMERICA PAST AND PRESENT
by Robert A. Divine

Surviving Vietnam

1   Vietnam ranks after World War II as America's second most expensive war. Between 1950 and 1975, the United States spent $123 billion on combat in Southeast Asia. More importantly, Vietnam ranks—after our Civil War and World Wars I and II—as the nation's fourth deadliest war, with 57,661 Americans killed in action.

2   Yet, when the last U.S. helicopter left Saigon, Americans suffered what historian George Herring terms "collective amnesia." Everyone, even those who had fought in 'Nam, seemed to want to forget Southeast Asia. It took nearly ten years for the nation to erect a national monument to honor those who died in Vietnam. The Vietnam Veterans Memorial in Washington, D.C., was dedicated in November 1982; on its polished black granite walls are carved the names of the dead and missing in action. And only in 1981 did collections of oral histories of some of those who served in Vietnam begin to appear: Al Santoli's well-documented *Everything We Had: An Oral History of the Vietnam War by Thirty-three American Soldiers Who Fought It* and Mark Baker's *Nam: The Vietnam War in the Words of the Men and Women Who Fought There*. Both books demonstrate that in the steaming jungles of Vietnam one thing mattered most: survival.

"Above all, Vietnam was a war that asked everything of a few and nothing of most of America."

—Myron McPherson

3   One Vietnam veteran expressed the general feeling of men in combat: "War is not killing. Killing is the easiest part. . . . Sweating twenty-four hours a day, seeing guys drop all around you from heatstroke, not having food, not having water, sleeping only three hours a night for weeks at a time, that's what war is. Survival."

4   During his term President Kennedy ordered a more than tenfold increase in the number of U.S. advisers in Vietnam. Yet, for the ten to twelve thousand predominantly career soldiers there by December of 1962, Vietnam seemed a nice little nine-to-five war. Recalls radio technician Jan Barry of the army's 18th Aviation Company, "If we wanted to go out and chase people around and shoot at them . . . we had a war going. If we didn't . . . they left us alone." In those early days, even the Special Forces Green Berets "used to stop at four-thirty and have a happy hour and get drunk," says Barry, adding that "there was no war after four-thirty. On Saturdays, no war. On Sundays, no war. On holidays, no war. That's right, a nine-to-five war."

5   Within two years, however, the Joint Chiefs of Staff and President Johnson committed 50,000 American troops to combat in Vietnam, and the nice little war turned grim. By mid-1967, in fact, more than 400,000 Americans were fighting in Vietnam. As many as 300 died each week. Combat, recalls 26th Marine division scout-sniper James Hebron, turned out "totally different" from what he had expected when he had joined the corps at age seventeen early in 1967. "There was no romance at all," says Hebron. During one combat period, Hebron's Bravo Company went without a hot meal for seven months. During that same operation, he notes, "I didn't brush my teeth for two months," explaining that "they sent toothbrushes . . . we had to use them to clean our rifles."

6   The Screaming Eagles of the elite 101st Airborne Division arrived in Vietnam shortly before the Tet offensive of January 1968. Lieutenant Robert Santos, destined to become one of the division's most decorated men, told his platoon, "Two things can happen to you. You can get wounded and go home early. Or you can die." He added that the "best way to go home is whole. If you stick with me . . . and learn from the [more experienced men] you won't get wounded. You won't die." Santos and his men earned a basketful of medals for valor in combat. Lieutenant Santos explains those medals in grim terms: "My responsibility was to kill and in the process of killing to be so good at it that I indirectly saved my men's lives." So, notes Santos, "You come home with the high body count, high kill ratio," but, he concludes, "there's nothing, nothing, that's very satisfying about that."

"The object of war is to survive it."

—John Irving

7   Few who served in Vietnam survived unscathed, whether psychologically or physically. One of the 303,600 Americans wounded during the long war was 101st Airborne platoon leader James Bombard, first shot and then blown up by a mortar round during the bitter Tet fighting at Hue in February 1968. He describes his traumatic experience as

8   feeling the bullet rip into your flesh, the shrapnel tear the flesh from your bones and the blood run down your leg. . . . To put your hand on your chest and to come away with your hand red with your own blood, and to feel it running out of your eyes and out of your mouth, and seeing it spurt out of your guts, realizing you were dying. . . . I was ripped open from the top of my head to the tip of my toes. I had forty-five holes in me.

9   Somehow Bombard survived Vietnam.

10   The fighting continued for four years after President Nixon took office. Robert Rawls served as a rifleman with the 1st Cavalry Division from early 1969 to 1970. He recalls:

11   We got fire fights after fire fights. My first taste of death. After fire fights you could smell it. They brought the [dead men] back wrapped in ponchos. . . . [T]hey just threw them up on the helicopter and [piled empty, reusable supply cases] on top of them. You could see the guys' feet hanging out. . . . I had nightmares. . . . I can still see those guys.

12   As the war dragged on, pacifist frustration at home paralleled the bitterness of those who had fought in Vietnam. John Muir's experience is typical. Early in the war, Muir had served as a rifleman with the 1st Marine Division during the battle of Dong Ha. Muir's single company fought continuously for four days and four nights, frequently in hand-to-hand combat, against two divisions of the North Vietnamese Army. When the marines were relieved, only ninety-one men—all wounded—were still able to fight at all. Muir's squad, however, had been wiped out: He had ended up throwing rocks at his attackers.

13   "It was a major battle," recalls Muir. "We did a fine job there. If it had happened in World War II, they still would be telling stories about it. But it happened in Vietnam, so nobody knows about it."

14   Withdrawing U.S. forces from Vietnam ended only the combat. Returning veterans fought government disclaimers concerning the toxicity of the defoliant Agent Orange. VA hospitals across the nation still contain thousands of para- and quadriplegic Vietnam veterans, as well as the maimed from earlier wars. Throughout America the "walking wounded" find themselves still embroiled in the psychological aftermath of Vietnam. To this day, says former 1st Infantry Division combat medic David Ross, "If I'm walking someplace and there's grass, I find myself sometimes doing a shuffle and looking down at the ground. . . . I'm looking for a wire or a piece of vine that looks too straight, might be a [land mine] trip wire. Some of the survival habits you pick up stay residual for a long time."

Source: "Surviving Vietnam," from Robert Divine et al., *America Past and Present,* 5th ed., pp. 954–955. Copyright © 1999 by Addison Wesley Educational Publishers, Inc. Reprinted by permission of Pearson Education, Inc.

COMPREHENSION CHECKUP

True or False

Indicate whether the statement is true or false by writing T or F in the blank provided.

_____ 1. The Vietnam War was the deadliest war in U.S. history.

_____ 2. Collections of oral histories of Vietnam veterans did not begin appearing until after the conflict was over.

_____ 3. Many U.S. soldiers in Vietnam made surviving their foremost goal.

_____ 4. President Kennedy reduced the number of Americans serving as military advisers to the South Vietnamese.

_____ 5. Under President Kennedy, soldiers stationed in Vietnam were mostly persons who had chosen to make the military their careers.

_____ 6. Some soldiers who arrived in Vietnam were disillusioned to discover that the war did not have a romantic side.

_____ 7. Once the conflict escalated in the early 1960s, U.S. soldiers faced many hardships.

_____ 8. The Tet offensive occurred in 1978.

_____ 9. Robert Santos and his division earned many medals.

_____ 10. James Bombard was lucky to be able to return home unscathed by his Vietnam experience.

Multiple Choice

Write the letter of the correct answer in the blank provided.

_____ 11. *Collective amnesia* refers to
  a. a desire to remember and celebrate an event
  b. a desire to forget an event or put it out of mind
  c. a desire to reminisce about the past
  d. a desire to commiserate over past sorrows

_____ 12. Jan Barry's reference to a "nine-to-five" war implies that
  a. soldiers fought around the clock in stressful circumstances
  b. soldiers could fight when they wanted to
  c. soldiers were unlikely to be waging war on the weekends
  d. both b and c

_____ 13. Lieutenant Robert Santos was
  a. unsuccessful at killing the enemy
  b. not recognized by his superiors for bravery
  c. conflicted about achieving a high kill ratio
  d. a member of the Screaming Hawks

_____ 14. A *traumatic* experience is one that has
  a. no effect on a person
  b. a slight effect on a person
  c. a great effect on a person
  d. a relaxing effect on a person

_____ 15. After President Nixon was elected to office,
   a. the fighting in Vietnam ceased immediately
   b. the fighting continued for two more years
   c. an immediate cease-fire was negotiated
   d. the fighting continued for an additional four years

_____ 16. In Vietnam, the dead American soldiers were
   a. handled with dignity and respect
   b. wrapped in ponchos
   c. evacuated by helicopter
   d. both b and c

_____ 17. A *pacifist* is someone who
   a. subjugates others
   b. advocates going to war
   c. opposes war or violence to settle disputes
   d. has a calm disposition

_____ 18. *Hand-to-hand* combat implies
   a. direct physical contact with the enemy
   b. dropping bombs from a great distance
   c. overwhelming the enemy with tanks and mobile units
   d. none of the above

_____ 19. When the author says that the squad was *wiped out,* he means that its members
   a. were completely exhausted
   b. were nearly all killed
   c. were intoxicated
   d. were discharged from the armed services

_____ 20. Soldiers who returned home after the war
   a. were treated as heroes
   b. suffered few ill effects of their experiences
   c. had to contend with the aftereffects of exposure to Agent Orange
   d. made an easy transition to civilian life

Vocabulary Practice

Fill in the blanks with a word from the list below. Not all of the words will be used.

amnesia	disclaimer	maimed	predominantly	toxicity
combat	elite	offensive	residual	traumatic
dedicated	embroiled	paralleled	shuffled	unscathed
destined	grim	paraplegic	spurt	valor

1. Mara _____ her book to a very close personal friend.

2. Luckily, we came out of the accident completely _____.

3. The soldier received a medal for courage and _____ beyond the call of duty.

4. The _____ of many new drugs has not yet been determined.

5. Bill Gates's teachers recognized at an early age that Bill Gates was _____ for greatness.

6. For many young boys, a growth _____ occurs around age twelve.

7. Persons attending the politician's $500-a-plate dinner were _____ wealthy.

8. Michael and Jennie are _____ in a very nasty divorce.

9. I felt a special closeness to him because his situation at school so closely

   _____ mine.

10. Sarah pulled herself out of bed and with the aid of a walker _____ off to get breakfast.

In Your Own Words

1. What is the main idea of this selection?

2. What do you think the author's point of view is toward the Vietnam War? Does he give us any clues to his point of view? In general, are the quotations he provides throughout the selection positive or negative about the war?

3. If you had been a young person growing up in the 1960s, what do you think your response would have been to the Vietnam conflict? Would you have supported it or opposed it?

4. Do you think that people who protested against the war at home showed a lack of respect for the soldiers doing the fighting? Do you think that the protestors were patriotic or unpatriotic?

The Art of Writing

In a brief essay, respond to the item below.

In 1967, naval aviator John McCain was shot down over Hanoi. Severely injured, he was held as a prisoner-of-war for five and a half years. At times, he was tortured and held in solitary confinement. Despite such harsh treatment, he not only survived, but returned to serve first in the House of Representatives and then in the Senate. What qualities do you think an individual must possess to be able to survive and overcome such an ordeal.

VIETNAM WAR MEMORIAL: MULTIPLE POINTS OF VIEW

GETTING THE PICTURE

The Vietnam Veterans Memorial, located on the mall in Washington, D.C., receives about 3.5 million visitors annually. Designed to help promote national reconciliation, it has become America's best-known public art work. Although initial reaction to the memorial design was positive, many veterans came to feel that it had a tone of "defeat." As a result, a flag and *The Face of Honor* sculpture were added.

Presented below is a sample of different points of view about the memorial from a variety of sources. These viewpoints are given in chronological order starting from 1982 and ending in 2000.

What's in A Name

1   The Vietnam War Memorial is on hallowed ground—two acres of land near the Lincoln Memorial and the Washington Monument. The controversial

design follows a controversial war that cost almost 58,000 lives. The war was a 25-year struggle to contain communism, a war that U.S. presidents could not afford to lose and were afraid to win. It ended in the final eerie days of spring 1975, when South Vietnam slowly collapsed like a building going down under demolition charges and the last of the besieged Americans lifted off a rooftop in a helicopter.

2   How do you have a memorial for this sort of thing? Seven-million dollars were raised for it and the winning design was that of Maya Ying Lin, a young Yale architecture student. The contestants were instructed only that their entries display the names of the fallen "without political or military content." I think it is one of the most impressive memorials I ever saw.

3   It is an outdoor affair. As you approach the monument, you come up a walk bent to make a long V, each side of which is two hundred and fifty feet long. The meadow is on one side, and the polished granite slabs on the other. The slabs have names on them; they are sunk into a gentle hill. It is the names that do it. They are not listed by rank or alphabet, but in the order of their deaths. These were eager young men fighting in the jungles. Sometimes they thought they knew what they were doing; often they were confused. Now the names are there—Leland G. Deeds, Imlay S. Swiddeson, Richard M. Seng—but take your eye off the cluster and you can't find the place again. It's just names, people, you and me and our sons. There are no inscriptions to tell you what to think; there are no heroic utterances. It is stark. Each name is a special boy who never came home. It is all left to the observer. The dark, shining slabs of granite are as hard and polished as a mirror, and you can see your image reflected over the names as you lean forward. My eyes moistened. In the crowd we looked at each other, deeply moved.

4   The austere jumble is extraordinarily personal, it appears, judging by the first week's experience. In a bold, slow tone, the individual names were read in a chapel in Washington's National Cathedral, one of the ceremonies that took place to honor those who served in Vietnam. It took three days, one thousand names an hour, with only a few hours off each morning. At the memorial itself, volunteers have books telling where individual names can be located. Small flags flutter at the base; at some spots a family has placed a wreath. One reads, "SP/4 Peter Lopez, A True American Hero, Eddie, Danny, Rosie, Lizbel, Mable, Mom and Dad: We miss you."

5   One man points at the name of Jose P. Ramos and his friend takes the picture. There is a search for names, and it will be hard to keep the place clear of trivia all saying the same thing: This is not a name, it is a person.

6   Some have said they think the memorial is too negative; perhaps they have spoken before seeing its powerful effect on visitors. Crowds increased each day at the memorial ceremonies. Officials agreed to add a conventional sculpture of three soldiers next year. They can do nothing, I think, to increase its impressiveness.

Source: From Paul Fussell, "What's in a Name," *The New Republic,* 12/6/82, pp. 6, 39. Copyright © 1982 Paul Fussell. Reprinted by permission.

COMPREHENSION CHECKUP

Multiple Choice

Write the letter of the correct answer in the blank provided.

_____ 1.   "... South Vietnam slowly collapsed like a building going down under demolition charges ..." is an example of a
   a. simile
   b. metaphor
   c. personification
   d. literary allusion

_____ 2.   Which of the following statements is an opinion?
   a. At the memorial itself, volunteers have books telling where individual names can be located.
   b. They can do nothing, I think, to increase its impressiveness.
   c. They are not listed by rank or alphabet, but in the order of their deaths.
   d. One man points at the name of Jose P. Ramos, and his friend takes the picture.

_____ 3.   The writer states that the Vietnam War was
   a. controversial
   b. fought to contain communism
   c. too long
   d. both a and b

_____ 4.   We can assume that the writer feels that
   a. $7 million was too much money to spend for a memorial
   b. the memorial is too stark without the addition of a conventional piece of sculpture
   c. the memorial needs no further embellishment
   d. the memorial would be more effective if no names were inscribed on the granite slabs

Vietnam Memorial Wall

1   Maya Ying Lin was 13 in January 1973, when the cease-fire between the United States and North Vietnam was declared. In 1981, the Ohio-born Lin—by then a 21-year-old senior majoring in architecture at Yale University—produced the winning proposal in the design competition for a memorial to Vietnam veterans to be located on the mall in Washington, D.C. It called for two 200-foot-long walls (later expanded to 250 feet) of polished black granite to be set into a gradual rise in the landscape of Constitution Gardens, meeting at a 136-degree angle at the point where the walls and slope would be at their highest (10 feet). The names of the war dead, chronologically arranged in the order in which the servicemen fell, were to be incised in the stone, with only the dates of the first and last deaths, 1959 and 1975, to be recorded.

2   A year and a half later, the memorial was dedicated during Veterans' Day celebrations last November. Sometime later this year, the memorial's

"modifications"—a flagpole and a realistic sculpture of three infantrymen, which were not in the original design—will be added near the memorial's entrance. Like so much about the Vietnam War, the memorial and its additions became the source of controversy—and finally of a compromise that would not have been as likely in the days during the war.

3   What had happened? Lin's proposal followed the guidelines set forth by the Vietnam Veterans Memorial committee, which included the stipulations that "the emphasis is to be on those who died," that the memorial be "without political or military content," and that it include the "suitable display of the names of the 57,692 Americans who died in Vietnam." The jury that chose Lin was made up primarily of architects, landscape designers, and artists. Charles Atherton, an architect and secretary of the federal Fine Arts Commission, which rules on the building of new structures on federal land, says that the commission was particularly pleased with the jury's choice of a design that had "great respect for the environment." Lin used no vertical lines, nothing to "disturb" the integrity of the location, an area roughly between the Lincoln and Washington monuments.

4   The designer—now in her first year of the graduate architecture program at the Harvard School of Design—sees her age as having been a boon, since she was too young to be involved in the politics of the Vietnam era. "It's a memorial to other human beings; to the people who served, to those who died, and to those who lost people," she says. She cites as primary models European memorials constructed after the First World War, especially one in France designed by the British architect Edwin Lutyens, where the experience of walking into or through the memorial provides the stimulus for reflection.

5   Not everyone thought this was enough, it turned out. Atherton recalls no opposition to the design during the first meeting on implementation. At the second one, though, a statement was made on behalf of surviving veterans to the effect that they were neither represented nor honored by the monument. Various veterans groups, which have provided much of the approximately $7 million funding for the monument and which originally supported the Lin design, got behind the movement to propose changes. The memorial fund proceeded to create a second jury made up of Vietnam veterans to decide on an appropriate additional memorial. The jury chose sculptor Frederick Hart, who had been on the third-place design team in the original competition. His eight-foot sculpture of the three soldiers was to be featured prominently toward the apex of Lin's design, with the 59-foot flagpole in the near distance.

6   In March 1982, Secretary of the Interior James Watt proposed this change, and the Fine Arts Commission voiced opposition, suggesting a compromise that would separate the sculpture from the memorial structure. By that time, the American Institute of Architects had entered the fray, objecting to the undercutting of the original competition process. As the final granite slabs were being put in place on the monument, the Fine Arts Commission set an open hearing in October on the fate of the Hart sculpture. It was an emotional hearing, especially

on the part of various veterans, who pleaded in favor of the statue as a literal representation to which the survivors could relate. Says Atherton, "You had to recognize the enormously strong feelings aroused, the compelling evidence by those in support of the flag and the statue. That couldn't be ignored on purely esthetic grounds." Lin appealed to the commission to protect the integrity of the design, voicing fears that the additions, if placed centrally, would turn it into "no more than an architectural backdrop."

7   At the end of the hearing, J. Carter Brown, chairman of the Fine Arts Commission and director of the National Gallery of Art, announced the commission's approval of the flagpole and statue, and its intention to see that these elements be placed near one another at the entrance to the memorial area. There the sculpture could strike "a chord of recognition" for many, while preserving the feeling of the original design, about which he said: "I think the litany of those names is enough to bring enormous emotions to everyone's heart." Brown referred his listeners to the abstract nature of the Washington monument, which has no statues of "George crossing the Delaware." As for the sculpture, Brown says it is a credit to Hart. "The three soldiers act as a kind of Greek chorus, facing the monument, commenting on its meaning. We were lucky with the statue; it could have been kitschy, but it isn't."

8   The commission's compromise decision was hailed by the American Institute of Architects, the Vietnam Veterans Memorial Committee, the Interior Department, and designer Lin. "I feel relief," she says, at the decision "not to let the sculpture destroy the quiet and simplicity" of the original design. The finished memorial is, she says, "so close to what I had envisioned that it's scary. Now that it's completed, it's got a life of its own. I feel like just another visitor."

Source: "Vietnam Memorial Wall," from "The 'Vasari' Diary," pp. 11–12. Copyright © 1983 ARTnews, LLC, January. Reprinted with permission.

COMPREHENSION CHECKUP

Multiple Choice

Write the letter of the correct answer in the blank provided.

_____ 1. The writer encloses the word *modifications* in quotes to indicate
   a. that in a sense the flagpole and the sculpture of the three infantrymen did not modify the original design
   b. that Lin's design failed to maintain the integrity of the location
   c. that Lin failed to follow the rules of the competition
   d. acceptance of Lin's original design

_____ 2. As the designer of the memorial, Maya Ying Lin viewed her age at the time of the cease-fire as
   a. a handicap
   b. a benefit
   c. of no great importance
   d. a slight consideration

_____ 3. When Brown refers to Hart's sculpture "as a kind of Greek chorus," he is using a
   a. literary allusion
   b. caricature
   c. euphemism
   d. satire

_____ 4. The commission's compromise entailed
   a. abandoning the idea of a sculpture and a flagpole
   b. moving the Hart sculpture from the highest point of the Wall to the entrance of the memorial
   c. asking Lin to redesign the memorial to accommodate the additions
   d. relinquishing control of the memorial to the Vietnam veterans

What Happens When a Woman Designs a War Monument?

1   A few days before the official dedication, I went to have a look at the Vietnam Memorial. I was prepared for an ambivalent experience. Like all monuments, it proposes a place in history for its subject. In this case, though, the task of interpretation was full of risk: memories of Vietnam are divided, in conflict. Even the idea of remembrance is charged. Until a group of veterans organized this project, America's official preference had been amnesia.

2   The design for a memorial was selected in a national competition won unanimously by Maya Ying Lin, an architectural student at Yale University. From the outburst of vituperation that greeted Maya Lin's project one might have thought she proposed to erect a statue of Ho Chi Minh. Judgments ranged from "a tribute to Jane Fonda" to "a black hole" to "a wailing wall for Draft Dodgers and New Lefters of the future."

3   The object of this vehemence—I discovered on my visit—is a serene and beautiful place. It's a place with a rare capacity to move. On the day I was there, I saw flowers and personal mementos leaning against the sides of the walls, messages taped to them. Instinctively, visitors reached out to touch the names of relations and comrades, their hands reflected in the polished surface so that another hand appeared to be reaching out from within.

4   At about the same time I was observing all of this, the Washington Fine Arts Commission was voting to make certain modifications to the memorial. These will include a large flagpole with the emblems of the five military services carved into its base and a realistic statue of three soldiers (two white and one black) in full battle regalia. But why should this be necessary? Where does Maya Lin's compelling work "fail"?

5   It seems to me that Maya Lin's monument is being assaulted because it is out of character. It is not the kind of war memorial that is a memorial to war—no charging GIs with bayonets fixed here. Vietnam veterans wanted to build a memorial precisely to establish a connection with veterans of other wars whose monuments abound. Most people can scarcely imagine a monument without statues and classical decor. To build one outside this area of convention seems a provocation. Many Vietnam veterans were especially sensitive to the fact that

the memorial is an exception. What is being said, in essence, is that abstract art cannot evoke abstract ideas like "courage," "honor," or "sacrifice."

6   The final reason that had Maya Lin's (male) critics in such a dither was that the source of this seditious modernism was not simply a student, not simply an Asian, but worst of all a woman. That a woman should have won the commission was the final affront, absolute confirmation that the war was to be remembered differently, a monument emasculated.

Source: From Michael Sorkin, "What Happens When a Woman Designs a War Monument?" *in Vogue,* May 1983, pp. 120, 122. Reprinted by permission of the author.

COMPREHENSION CHECKUP

Multiple Choice

Write the letter of the correct answer in the blank provided.

_____ 1.   We can assume that the writer thinks Maya Lin's monument
   a. glorifies war
   b. will not be complete even with modifications
   c. has a rare capacity to move individuals
   d. insults veterans

_____ 2.   The writer feels that the memorial has been criticized for all of the following reasons *except*
   a. it was designed by a woman
   b. it represents an abstract architectural design
   c. it is unlike other war memorials
   d. it touches people emotionally

_____ 3.   When the writer describes the memorial as a "serene and beautiful place," we can assume the writer's point of view is
   a. positive
   b. negative

_____ 4.   The words *outburst of vituperation* imply
   a. condemnation
   b. castigation
   c. denunciation
   d. all of the above

Vietnam Memorial

1   In 1982, a group of Vietnam veterans had just obtained Congressional approval for a memorial that would pay long-delayed tribute to those who had fought in Vietnam with honor and courage in a lost and highly unpopular cause. They had chosen a jury of architects and art worldlings to make a blind selection in an open competition; that is, anyone could enter, and no one could put his name on his entry. Every proposal had to include something—a wall, a column—on which a hired engraver could inscribe the names of all 57,000-plus members of the American military who had died in Vietnam. Nine of the top 10 choices were

abstract designs that could be executed without resorting to that devious and accursed bit of trickery: skill. Only the No. 3 choice was representational. Up on one end of a semicircular wall bearing the 57,000 names was an infantryman on his knees beside a fallen comrade, looking about for help. At the other end, a third infantryman had begun to run along the top of the wall toward them. The sculptor was Frederick Hart.

2   The winning entry was by a young Yale undergraduate architectural student named Maya Lin. Her proposal was a V-shaped wall, period, a wall of polished black granite inscribed only with the names; no mention of honor, courage, or gratitude; not even a flag. Absolutely skillproof, it was.

3   Many veterans were furious. They regarded her wall as a gigantic pitiless tombstone that said, "Your so-called service was an absolutely pointless disaster." They made so much noise that a compromise was struck. An American flag and statue would be added to the site. Hart was chosen to do the statue. He came up with a group of three soldiers, realistic down to the aglets of their boot strings, who appear to have just emerged from the jungle into a clearing, where they are startled to see Lin's V-shaped black wall bearing the names of their dead comrades.

4   Naturally enough, Lin was miffed at the intrusion, and so a make-peace get-together was arranged in Plainview, New York, where the foundry had just completed casting the soldiers. Doing her best to play the part, Lin asked Hart—as Hart recounted it—if the young men used as models for the three soldiers had complained of any pain when the plaster casts were removed from their faces and arms. Hart couldn't imagine what she was talking about. Then it dawned on him. She assumed that he had covered the model's body in wet plaster and removed it when it began to harden. No artist of her generation (she was 21) could even conceive of a sculptor starting out solely with a picture in his head, a stylus, a brick of moist clay, and some armature wire. No artist of her generation dared even speculate about . . . skill.

Source: From Tom Wolfe "The Invisible Artist" in *Hooking Up.* Copyright © 2000 by Tom Wolfe. Reprinted by permission of Farrar, Straus and Giroux, LLC.

 COMPREHENSION CHECKUP

Multiple Choice

Write the letter of the correct answer in the blank provided.

_____ 1. We can assume that a blind selection was used to
   a. allow those who were well known in the art world to have a better chance of being chosen
   b. give each entry an equal chance to be chosen
   c. keep the press from knowing the results too early in the process
   d. keep the public from voicing opinions prematurely

_____ 2. Which of the following value assumptions does the writer seem to make?
   a. A person as young as Lin could not possibly understand the concept of skill.
   b. A representational design embodying skill is superior to a design that is abstract.
   c. The veterans were justifiably angry about Lin's design.
   d. All of the above

_____ 3. The expression "miffed at the intrusion" implies
   a. acceptance
   b. displeasure
   c. annoyance
   d. both b and c

_____ 4. The tone of the writer toward Maya Lin is
   a. indifferent
   b. sympathetic
   c. contemptuous
   d. neutral

Boundaries

1   I wanted to create a memorial that everyone would be able to respond to, regardless of whether one thought our country should or should not have participated in the war. On a personal level, I wanted to focus on the nature of accepting and coming to terms with a loved one's death. Simple as it may seem, I remember feeling that accepting a person's death is the first step in being able to overcome that loss.

2   I felt that as a culture we were extremely youth-oriented and not willing or able to accept death or dying as a part of life. The rites of mourning, which in more primitive and older cultures were very much a part of life, have been suppressed in our modern times. In the design of the memorial, a fundamental goal was to be honest about death, since we must accept that loss in order to begin to overcome it. The pain of the loss will always be there, it will always hurt, but we must acknowledge the death in order to move on.

3   What then would bring back the memory of a person? A specific object or image would be limiting. A realistic sculpture would be only one interpretation of that time. I wanted something that all people could relate to on a personal level. At this time I had as yet no form, no specific artistic image.

4   Then someone in my class received the design program, which stated the basic philosophy of the memorial's design and also its requirements: all the names of those missing and killed (57,000) must be a part of the memorial; the design must be apolitical, harmonious with the site, and conciliatory.

5   These were all the thoughts that were in my mind before I went to see the site.

6   Without having seen it, I couldn't design the memorial, so a few of us traveled to Washington, D.C., and it was at the site that the idea for the design took shape. The site was a beautiful park surrounded by trees, with traffic and noise coming from one side—Constitution Avenue.

7   I had a sudden impulse to cut into the earth.

8   I imagined taking a knife and cutting into the earth, opening it up, an initial violence and pain that in time would heal. The grass would grow back, but the initial cut would remain a pure flat surface in the earth with a polished, mirrored surface, much like the surface on a geode when you cut it and polish the edge. The need for the names to be on the memorial would be the memorial; there was no need to embellish the design further. The people and their names would allow everyone to respond and remember.

9   It would be an interface, between our world and the quieter, darker, more peaceful world beyond. I chose black granite in order to make the surface reflective and peaceful. I never looked at the memorial as a wall, an object, but as an edge to the earth, an opened side. The mirrored effect would double the size of the park, creating two worlds, one we are a part of and one we cannot enter. The two walls were positioned so that one pointed to the Lincoln Memorial and the other pointed to the Washington Monument. By linking these two strong symbols for the country, I wanted to create a unity between the nation's past and present.

10   On our return to Yale, I quickly sketched my idea up, and it almost seemed too simple, too little. But the image was so simple that anything added to it began to detract from it.

11   I always wanted the names to be chronological, to make it so that those who served and returned from the war could find their place in the memorial.

12   As far as all the controversy, I really never wanted to go into it too much. The memorial's starkness, its being below grade, being black, and how my age, gender, and race played a part in the controversy, we'll never quite know. I think it is actually a miracle that the piece ever got built. From the beginning I often wondered, if it had not been an anonymous entry 1026 but rather an entry by Maya Lin, would I have been selected?

Source: From Maya Lin, *Boundaries,* pp. 410–11. Copyright © 2000 by Maya Lin Studio, Inc. Reprinted by permission of Simon & Schuster Adult Publishing Group (pp. 329–30).

 COMPREHENSION CHECKUP

Multiple Choice

Write the letter of the correct answer in the blank provided.

_____ 1.   Which one of the following statements best reveals the writer's attitude toward the memorial?
   a. A memorial is not the place for personal reflection.
   b. A war memorial must include a heroic statue.
   c. A realistic sculpture would have been too limiting.
   d. A black memorial is more appropriate for a losing war effort.

_____ 2.   A key point the writer makes is that
   a. in light of the many controversies, it's surprising that the memorial was ever built
   b. the site did not influence the design
   c. the reflective property of black granite was an unexpected dividend
   d. it was important that the names of those who died be listed on the memorial in alphabetical order

_____ 3.   The writer would agree with which of the following statements?
   a. Black granite was chosen to indicate deep sadness and shame.
   b. The names are the memorial; no further embellishment is required.
   c. It was important to link the Vietnam Memorial to the Washington Monument and the Jefferson Memorial.
   d. A memorial should make a political statement.

_____ 4.   What can we infer about the values of the writer?
   a. She feels that the first step toward overcoming a loved one's death is acceptance of the loss.
   b. She believes that American culture focuses too much on the problems of the elderly.
   c. She feels that death and dying should be a part of life.
   d. Both a and c

A Quiet Place for Personal Reflection

1   Snow and ice carpet the ground, making walking especially hazardous. Yet thousands have come on this cold January day to see the Vietnam Veterans Memorial.

2   Each year, more than 2.5 million people visit the site, located just north of the Lincoln Memorial, ranking it among the most popular tourist attractions in Washington.

3   For many, the monument's shimmering black panels—containing the names of the more than 58,000 American men and women who died in Vietnam—symbolize the nation's effort to come to grips with one of the most divisive chapters in its history.

4   "This place is an important national symbol, like the Statue of Liberty," says John R. Gifford, 43, a Westport, Massachusetts, police officer who was making his second visit to the memorial.

5   But, Gifford says, the "Wall" is more than just a symbol. It has deep personal meaning for those who lived during the Vietnam era—especially those who fought or lost a loved one in the war. "You can see how hard it is when folks who have lost someone near and dear to them in Vietnam come here," he says.

6   The monument contains 140 slabs of black granite quarried in India. The names are inscribed in chronological order, beginning with the first American casualty in 1959 and ending with those who died in 1975, the year South Vietnam fell.

7   The Wall consists of two sections, each 246 feet long, that meet at a 125-degree angle, forming a wide V. The height of the wall rises from just a foot, at each end, to about 10 feet at the point where the sections meet.

8   The design by Maya Lin, a young architecture student, was controversial when she proposed it almost two decades ago. Many veterans wanted a more traditional war monument—with statues of soldiers. But Lin wanted the memorial to be "a quiet place, meant for personal reflection and private reckoning." When submitting her design in 1981, she wrote, "The actual area is wide and shallow, allowing for a sense of privacy, and the sunlight from the memorial's

southern exposure, along with the grassy park surrounding and within its walls, contribute to the serenity of the area. Thus, the memorial is for those who have died, and for us to remember them."

9   To mollify the critics, the Vietnam Veterans Memorial Fund (VVMF) in 1982 commissioned the late Frederick Hart, a noted Washington, D.C., sculptor, to create a traditional statue to accompany Lin's design. Sited just a few feet from the Wall, it depicts three rifle-carrying infantryman—a white, a black, and a Hispanic.

10   Judging by the streams of visitors to the Wall, and the solemnity that envelops it, Lin's concept was sound. "This is such a solemn place," says Mark Yanick, a 37-year-old human resources trainer from Washington, D.C., who had brought an out-of-town friend to see the Wall. "This is the only monument I've ever been to where there is total silence, even when it's crowded."

11   The memorial is the brainchild of Jan C. Scruggs, an infantryman who was wounded in Vietnam. Scruggs conceived of the idea for a memorial after watching Michael Chamino's *The Deer Hunter,* a troubling 1979 film about the tortured lives of a group of returning Vietnam vets. "After I made the decision that we needed something like this, I became obsessed with it," he says.

12   Along with other veterans from "Nam," Scruggs formed the VVMF in 1979 to raise money and find a location and design for the memorial. The project came together with remarkable speed. Within a few years, they had raised more than $8 million from private sources, including more than 275,000 individuals. In 1980, Congress provided two acres on the Mall for the memorial.

13   That year, the VVMF held a design competition. Lin, then a 21-year-old student at Yale University, bested the 1,421 entries submitted, many by some of the world's leading architects. Construction began in March 1982, and in November the memorial was dedicated.

14   "We figured that a lot of people would come the first year because it would be a novelty, but after that it would just be something for the vets," Scruggs says. "Now it's a symbol to the nation, much like the Eiffel Tower is the symbol of France."

Source: "A Quiet Place for Personal Reflection," in *Congressional Quarterly* by Congressional Quarterly on the Web. Copyright © 2000 by Congressional Quarterly Inc. Reproduced with permission of the Congressional Quarterly, Inc.

 COMPREHENSION CHECKUP

Multiple Choice

Write the letter of the correct answer in the blank provided.

_____ 1. The phrase *to mollify* as used in paragraph 9 means
   a. to annoy
   b. to appease
   c. to embroil
   d. to mislead

_____ 2.   It is amazing that
   a. it took so long to raise enough money to build the monument
   b. visitors to the memorial become so loud and excited
   c. the memorial grounds remain quiet even when they are crowded
   d. such a small number of people submitted design proposals

_____ 3.   We can assume that
   a. the Wall has become a national symbol that has little personal mean-
       ing for people who visit it
   b. the memorial depicts the passing of time from the first fatality to the last
   c. Lin's design proposal was popular right from the start
   d. the memorial is located far from other monuments in Washington, D.C.

_____ 4.   It is ironic that
   a. a wall has come to symbolize a nation's coming to terms with a dif-
       ficult chapter in its history
   b. the controversial memorial has endured as a popular tourist attraction
   c. the design submitted by a young architecture student was chosen
       over designs submitted by world famous architects
   d. all of the above

Some Facts About the Vietnam Wall

Drawing on what you learned from the previous selections, insert the missing information in the blanks.

1. The Vietnam Memorial was designed by _____, an architecture student

    at _____ University.

2. Out of _____ entries submitted in the competition to design the Viet-

    nam Memorial, the winning entry was number _____.

3. The Vietnam Memorial is located near the _____ Monument and the

    _____ Memorial.

4. The names of more than _____ soldiers missing or killed in action are
    carved into the memorial. (Use the most recent count.)

5. The memorial is made of _____ (number) polished black _____
    slabs.

6. The first American casualty in the Vietnam War occurred in _____.

7. In 1982, a sculpture of three infantrymen by _____ was commissioned.

8. The Vietnam Memorial was the idea of _____, an infantryman
    wounded in Vietnam.

9. The memorial was dedicated on _____ Day.

Who Said It?

Match the quotation with the speaker. Write the letter of the speaker in the appropriate blank.

   a. Charles Atherton
   b. J. Carter Brown
   c. John R. Gifford
   d. Maya Lin

   e. Jan C. Scruggs
   f. Tom Wolfe
   g. Mark Yanick

_____ 1. "I think the litany of those names is enough to bring enormous emotions to everyone's heart."

_____ 2. "Thus the memorial is for those who have died, and for us to remember them."

_____ 3. "Now it's a symbol to the nation, much like the Eiffel Tower is the symbol of France."

_____ 4. "You had to recognize the enormously strong feelings aroused, the compelling evidence by those in support of the flag and the statue."

_____ 5. "No artist of her generation dared even speculate about . . . skill."

_____ 6. "This place is an important national symbol, like the Statue of Liberty."

_____ 7. "This is the only monument I've ever been to where there is total silence, even when it's crowded."

Determining Point of View

Below is a list of the selections you have just read. For each one, indicate whether the author's point of view about the Vietnam Memorial is primarily positive, negative, or neutral.

1. "What's in a Name" _____

2. "Vietnam Memorial War" _____

3. "What Happens When a Woman Designs a War Monument?" _____

4. "Vietnam Memorial" _____

5. "Boundaries" _____

6. "A Quiet Place for Personal Reflection" _____

In Your Own Words

1. Over the last twenty years, the National Park Service has collected more than 65,000 objects left at the Vietnam Memorial by visitors, including service medals, combat boots, flowers, poems, and photographs. Some visitors to the memorial place a piece of paper over a name and then draw back and forth with a pencil to make a "rubbing" of it. Why do you think many visitors are so expressive when they visit the memorial?

2. Paul Spreiregen, a Washington-based architect who organized the competition and helped select the judging panel, views Lin's design as an effective symbol: "It's a rift in the earth, as the war was a tear in the fabric of the American experience." Stanley Karrow, author of *Vietnam: A History*, says that the monument "stands as a vivid symbol of both unity and redemption." What do you think the memorial symbolizes?

The Art of Writing

In a brief essay, respond to one of the items below.

1. The Vietnam Memorial is often referred to as "the Wall." There are many idiomatic expressions that have the word *wall* in them, such as the walls have ears, one's back to the wall, beat one's head against the wall, climb the walls, drive someone up the wall, fly on the wall, go to the wall, handwriting on the wall, hole in the

wall, off the wall, and run into a stone wall. Choose one of these expressions, and explain its meaning.

2. Read the poem "Mending Wall" by Robert Frost. What does Frost think should be done with walls? Do you think that "good fences make good neighbors"?

3. Compare and contrast Tom Wolfe's view of the Vietnam Memorial with that of *The New Republic*'s editor. Which view is closest to your own, and why?

Internet Activities

1. Investigate the Virtual Wall at

   www.thevirtualwall.org.

   Write a summary of your findings.

2. Using the World Wide Web, investigate one of the following "walls" and write a summary of your findings.

Wall Street
Hadrian's Wall
Berlin Wall

Wailing Wall
Great Wall of China

Making Connections

A documentary about Maya Ying Lin titled *Maya Lin: A Strong Clear Vision* (produced by Freida Lee Mock and Terry Sanders, 82 minutes) won an Academy Award in 1995. A brief clip from this film can be seen at

www.americanfilmfoundation.com/order/maya_lin.html

SELECTION

"Even though the goals of propaganda may not be evil, some of the techniques used are questionable because they appeal primarily to our emotions rather than to our intellect."

GETTING THE PICTURE

"Propaganda is a daily feature of our popular culture. It is a prime ingredient in political rhetoric and is used extensively in advertising campaigns. For these reasons, it is important for all of us to be familiar with the basic propaganda devices so that we can detect them, ward off their emotional appeal, and analyze the messages intellectually." (*James R. Wilson*)

BIO-SKETCH

James Ross Wilson is a professor of mass communication and journalism at California State University, Fresno. In addition to teaching classes in mass communications, Wilson serves as general manager of the student-run radio station. He has also trained military personnel for work in the Armed Forces Radio and Television Service.

SELECTION *continued*

Stan LeRoy Wilson is professor emeritus of mass communication at the College of the Desert in Palm Desert, California. He has had a 34-year teaching career at California state universities and community colleges. In addition to his teaching career, he served 17 years on the Palm Desert City Council, including four terms as mayor, and presently serves on the Riverside County Board of Supervisors.

BRUSHING UP ON VOCABULARY

egghead an intellectual, but the word is usually used in a derogatory manner.

Excerpt from

MASS MEDIA MASS CULTURE

by James R. Wilson and Stan LeRoy Wilson

Propaganda

1 Webster's dictionary defines **propaganda** as "a systematic effort to promote a particular cause or point of view."

2 Thus by definition, propaganda is not evil or deceptive. However, ever since the British used propaganda to solicit U.S. support for the Allies' war effort against Germany in World War I, the word has taken on undesirable connotations. But even though the goals of propaganda may not be evil, some of the techniques used are questionable because they appeal primarily to our emotions rather than to our intellect.

3 Propaganda was probably used most destructively in the 1930s, when Adolf Hitler used it to take control of Germany and neighboring lands. One of Hitler's first acts when he came to power was to name Joseph Goebbels minister of propaganda. Goebbels immediately took over the German mass media and turned them into propaganda outlets that endorsed Hitler and his reign of terror. While Hitler waged his propaganda campaign, the rest of the world sat back and watched. Yet years earlier, in his 1925 book, *Mein Kampf,* which he wrote in prison, Hitler had spelled out the importance of propaganda and how he planned to use it:

4 The great masses' receptive ability is only very limited, their understanding is small, but their forgetfulness is great. As a consequence of these facts, all effective propaganda has to limit itself only to a very few points and to use them like slogans until even the very last man is able to imagine what is intended by such a word. As soon as one sacrifices this basic principle and tries to become versatile, the effect will fritter away, as the masses are neither able to digest the material offered nor to retain it. Thus the result is weakened and finally eliminated.

5 If this philosophy sounds as if it is alive and well in American advertising today, it is because propaganda techniques are still very much in use. But fortunately the American advertising industry aims only to sell us consumer goods and political

candidates, not the bigotry and totalitarianism of Adolf Hitler. Following are some of the more common forms of propaganda devices used today.

Slogans

6   The slogan is equally effective in advertising and political campaigns. In the latter, it usually takes the form of a chant that can unite large crowds into one common emotion. An example of a political slogan is "Four More Years," chanted by delegates to the 1996 Democratic National Convention. Product slogans include Nike's "Just Do It," "Always Coca-Cola," "It's Miller Time," the U.S. Army's "Be All That You Can Be," and Hallmark's "When You Care Enough to Send the Very Best."

Name-Calling

7   Name-calling is a device used widely in political and ideological battles as well as in commercial advertising campaigns. It tries to make us form a judgment without examining the evidence on which it should be based. Propagandists appeal to our instincts of hate and fear. They do this by giving bad names to those individuals, groups, nations, races, or consumer products that they would like us to condemn or reject. Such names as *communist, capitalist, imperialist, pervert,* and *egghead* are just a few that have been used to discredit the opposition.

8   Not all name-calling is so blatant. Often it can work by inference or association. Presidential candidate Al Smith once used indirect name-calling against President Franklin D. Roosevelt by stating, "There can be only one capital, Washington or Moscow." He was indirectly calling the incumbent president a communist.

9   Most name-calling in advertising uses this indirect approach: "Our painkiller doesn't give you an upset stomach"—implying, of course, that the competition does. Some advertisers actually name a competing brand and charge it with being inferior.

Glittering Generalities

10 Glittering generalities are broad, widely accepted ideals and virtuous words that are used to sell a point of view. Like name-calling, glittering generalities urge us to accept and approve something without examination. Many ads declare the product to be "the best," or "the greatest," or "preferred by more people." Such expressions as "the American way," "it's in the public interest," and "taste America's favorite bran flake cereal" are examples. Words such as *America, truth, freedom, honor, liberty, justice, loyalty, progress, democracy,* and *America's favorite* are all common glittering generalities.

Transfer

11 Some advertisements use symbols of authority, prestige, and respect that arouse emotions to sell a cause, a candidate, or a consumer product through the process of subconscious transfer or association. Typical examples are a political candidate photographed next to the American flag ("She's a good American") and a cigarette smoker by a peaceful lake ("Enjoy the natural taste of this brand of cigarette and you too will feel healthy and calm").

12 Many ads for automobiles feature a physically attractive person in the passenger seat or at the wheel. The point, of course, is to transfer the sexuality of the person to the brand of vehicle. Designer jeans and perfume ads are also effective in transferring sexuality to their products.

13   And who can forget the cough syrup television commercial in which a soap opera actor established his authority as an official spokesperson for the product by looking directly into the camera and declaring "I'm not a doctor, but I play one on TV"?

Testimonial

14   A testimonial is an endorsement of a product or an individual by celebrities or other well-respected persons. When a movie star endorses a particular savings and loan institution, for example, thousands of people may invest there solely on the rationale that if it is good enough for their idol, it's good enough for them. How many sports fans have selected a certain brand of athletic shoe, shaving cream, or deodorant because their favorite professional athlete endorsed it?

Plain Folks

15   The plain-folks device creates the impression that the advertisers or political candidates are just ordinary folks like you and me. In every presidential election, we see candidates doing things such as visiting a coal mine wearing hard hats. They don't actually go down into the coal mine, so obviously they don't wear the hard hats for protection. Instead, the hats are used to give the impression that they are just ordinary folks like the rest of the workers. Similarly, many laundry detergent ads show "ordinary housewives" rather than attractive models promoting the product.

Card Stacking

16   Card stacking is the technique by which facts, illustrations, and statements are carefully selected to make the maximum impact and sometimes give misleading impressions. The cliché that "statistics don't lie, but you can lie with statistics" applies to this technique. For example, a politician may tell his constituents that he votes only for bills that help his district, while neglecting to mention that when special-interest groups have opposed such a bill, he has ducked the issue by not showing up for the vote.

17   An advertisement claiming that "Four out of five dentists surveyed recommend Chewy chewing gum" may certainly be true, but it may also omit the fact that only five dentists were contacted and four of them were paid to give an anonymous endorsement.

Bandwagon

18   The bandwagon device is based on the idea that "if everybody else is doing it, so should you." "Jump on the bandwagon," "follow the crowd," "be the first in your neighborhood," and "don't throw your vote away by voting for a loser" are clichés associated with this device. The psychology behind this technique makes political polling important at election time. The fact that each candidate needs to project the image that he or she is a winner often leads to some conflicting polling results. (Pollsters can skew their results by carefully selecting their samples or using loaded wording in their questions.) Advertisements telling you to join the Pepsi generation ("Generation X") or to have a good time with the crowd when it's "Miller time" are examples of bandwagon.

Sex Appeal

19   We don't ordinarily think of sex as a propaganda device, but it sells products in many ways. In recent years, emotional appeals based on sex have been used more and more in product advertising. How about beer commercials or the aftershave lotion ad that

features a sexy female voice crooning, "My men wear English Leather or they wear nothing at all"? Or the billboard for Canadian Black Velvet whiskey showing a sexy blond in a black velvet dress with the words "Feel the Velvet Canadian?" And don't forget the Calvin Klein ads that feature partially clad and sometimes nude men and women. When it comes to beer commercials, many people believe that you can only drink the product while playing volleyball on the beach with beautiful, bikini-clad women. Sex appeal is used to stimulate emotions and sell consumer products to both sexes.

Music

20   The last device in our list is also seldom thought of as a propaganda device, yet it is one of the most effective techniques in radio and television commercials. Music is an excellent tool for creating specific moods, and it can be used effectively for product identification. Often people will think of a certain product when they hear a tune that has been associated with the product in ads. In past years, songs used in commercials have gone on to become popular songs on the radio and in record sales (e.g., Coca-Cola's "I'd Like to Teach the World to Sing"), and popular songs have been used in commercials (e.g., the Beatles's "Revolution," used in Nike commercials). Other songs have been catchy enough to just run through your mind ("Give Me a Break, Give Me a Break, Break Me Off a Piece of That Kit-Kat Bar").

21   In politics, music is used to stir the crowds, and the president of the United States uses it effectively to generate a mood of respect when making a grand entrance to the strains of "Hail to the Chief," "Happy Days Are Here Again," or catchy political campaign theme songs.

Source: Excerpt from James R. Wilson in *Mass Media Mass Culture*, 5th ed., New York: McGraw-Hill, 2001, pp. 352–357. Copyright © 2001 McGraw-Hill. Reprinted by permission of The McGraw-Hill Companies, Inc.

Internet Activity

We often think of propaganda just in negative terms, but propaganda can also be put to positive uses. One such example was the concerted effort by the U.S. government during World War II to get Americans involved in the war effort. The following website shows a variety of government posters designed to encourage Americans to become involved:

www.library.northwestern.edu/govpub/collections/wwii-posters/

Go to this website, print out three posters, identify any words showing bias, and then discuss the propaganda devices used.

Exercise 3: Identifying Propaganda Devices

Directions: For each passage, identify the propaganda device being used. Use each device only once.

bandwagon	name-calling	testimonial
card stacking	plain folks	transfer
glittering generalities	sex appeal	
music	slogans	

1. Smartnet—the Internet broker with great information, great service, and great people to help you invest your money wisely. _____

2. "I wouldn't think about banking anywhere else than Dollar Bank." —Sarah Brooks, CEO of True Blue Corporation _____

3. Satin Hand Cream is available without a prescription. For pennies a day, it can make your hands beautiful again. Effectively eliminates dryness, scaliness, and embarrassing age spots. _____

4. Janet Hardworker for Governor—just a small-town gal with a big heart

_____

5. A commercial: A driver zooms away in a black Jaguar accompanied by the music "Born to be Wild." _____

6. The president running for reelection: "Don't switch horses in midstream."

_____

7. My opponent is misguided in his support of vouchers for private schools. His foolish, reckless scheme will bankrupt the public schools. Think again before giving him your vote in November. _____

8. A picture of the Statue of Liberty with the following statement below it: Freedom Insurance will protect your family when they need it the most. _____

9. "All trucks on our lot have to go. We need room for the new inventory. Hurry on down. Don't be left out of this once-in-a-lifetime deal. If you don't try us, we both lose." _____

10. Sexy model purrs, "Nothing comes between me and my blue velvet jeans."

_____

What propaganda device does the following cartoon illustrate? _____

_____

"Thank goodness all those negative campaigns are over and done with. Now we can concentrate for the next few years on griping about the winners."

© Steve Benson

TEST-TAKING TIP

Improving Your Performance on Essay Tests (2)

DURING THE TEST

1. Read the question carefully! You might write a wonderful essay, but if it doesn't answer the question, it will not do you much good. Make sure you know what the question is asking, and make sure you consider all parts of the question.

2. Think about how best to answer the question before you start writing! What material from the course will the answer involve? What do you remember about this material. Think of specific examples that will illustrate your points. Make sure you can answer the six question words: *who, what, where, when, why,* and *how.* If you are prepared well for the test, the more you think about this material, the more of it you will remember.

3. Start writing! Remember to write carefully and legibly. Try to avoid erasures, crossed out words, and words written between lines and in the margins. You might want to consider using a pen with erasable ink. And make sure you answer in complete sentences.

4. Proofread your essay before turning it in! Correct as many grammar, spelling, and punctuation errors as you can. Sloppy writing is likely to produce a bad impression.

If you find you do not have time to answer the questions at the end of the test, write some notes in summary form. These will often earn you at least partial credit.

VOCABULARY   Unit 7

This unit begins with word parts relating to law, politics, and power. It then looks at word parts relating to religious beliefs. The last section covers word parts relating to time.

legis—law; demos—people; polis—city; graph—write

legal	of or based on law; lawful. Comes from the Latin *legis* meaning "law." Cynthia needed to see a lawyer to find out if her marriage to Paul was *legal*.
legislature	a group of people who meet together to write and enact laws. The Florida state *legislature* played an active role in the battle for Florida's electoral votes during the presidential race between Al Gore and George W. Bush.
legitimate	allowed by law or custom; being justifiable. He had a *legitimate* claim to ownership of the land.
illegitimate	against the laws or rules
democracy	*Demos* means "the people" in Greek, so *democracy* means "government by the people"

demography	Literally, *demography* means "writing about people." It is the science of vital and social statistics, concerned with such things as the births, deaths, diseases, marriages, and the educational level of a population. A *demographer* gathers data, such as in the census we take every ten years, and then compiles that data into maps and charts. A *demographic* map might show income levels in different areas of a city or county.

The following words come from the Greek word *polis*, which means "city-state." In ancient Greece, each city was a state unto itself because there was no greater political authority.

political	In ancient Greece, each city-state was responsible for its own *political* or governmental affairs. Today, the word also refers to *political* parties, such as Libertarian, Republican, Democratic, or Green.
politician	a person who is active in politics as a career; a seeker or holder of public office

cracy—rule, strength, power; archy—rule; auto—self, by oneself; theo—god

anarchy	the complete absence of government or the rule of law
monarchy	government by one person, usually a king, queen, or emperor. Monaco is an example of a *monarchy*.
autocracy	government in which one person has all the power. *auto-* means "self or by one's self." Germany under Adolf Hitler was an *autocracy*. Hitler was an *autocrat*.
oligarchy	a form of government in which power is vested in a few persons
plutocracy	a government in which the wealthy class rules
patriarchy	an institution or organization in which power is held by males and passed on through males, quite often from father to son
matriarchy	a family, society, or state governed by women or in which a woman is the dominant member of the group. The Navajo nation is a *matriarchy*.
theocracy	*theo-* means "god," so a *theocracy* means "rule by God." A *theocracy* is a government that claims to be based on divine authority.

agogos—lead, bring together, excite; potis—powerful; syn—same

demagog(ue)	according to its word parts, a *demagogue* is a person who leads and excites people, or a person who gains power by arousing people's emotions and prejudices. The word usually has a negative connotation. Hitler was a *demagogue*.
synagogue	a building where Jews gather for worship and religious study. The literal meaning is "a place to which people are brought together or led to." The origin of the word *synagogue* may date back to the sixth century B.C.E. when the Jewish people were in exile in Babylon. Formal worship in a temple was impossible, so the Jewish people began to meet in member's homes. These homes became the first *synagogues*.

potent	having great power; having a strong effect on the body or mind; producing powerful physical or chemical effects. The doctor told the patient that she needed some *potent* medicine.
potential	capable of coming into being but not yet actual. He had the *potential* to become a great swimmer.
potentate	a person having great power; a ruler or monarch. The sultan was a very wealthy *potentate*.

deus—god; sanct—holy; sacri—holy; ology—study of, -ism, doctrine, or theory

theology	the study of God and religious beliefs
atheism	the belief that there is no god
monotheism	the belief that there is only one god. Judaism, Christianity, and Islam are *monotheistic* religions.
polytheism	the belief in more than one god. The ancient Greeks were *polytheists*. Their gods included Zeus, Athena, and Apollo.
deity	a god or goddess. The ancient Greeks and Romans believed in many *deities*.
deify	to make a god of. In ancient Rome, the emperors were often *deified*.
sanctuary	a sacred or holy place; a place of protection, shelter, or refuge. The World Wildlife *Sanctuary* was created to provide a home for animal species in danger of extinction.
sanctify	to make saintly or holy
sanction	approval given by someone in authority. The students formed a club with the *sanction* of the school administration.
sacred	holy or set apart for some religious purpose; not to be broken or ignored. She took a *sacred* vow to become a nun.
sacrament	a sacred ceremony in Christian churches, such as baptism and Holy Communion. A *sacrament* was originally an oath of allegiance taken by a Roman soldier.

chrono—time; temp—time, moderate; ana—back, up, again

chronology	the science or study of measuring time; arranging events in the sequence in which they happened. What was the *chronology* of events for the assassination of President Kennedy?
synchronize	According to its word parts, *synchronize* means "at the same time." We need to *synchronize* our watches so that we can meet at the restaurant at the same time. *Synchronized* swimming is an Olympic event.
anachronism	The literal meaning is "back in time"; anything that is out of its proper time in history is an *anachronism*. Using a horse and buggy for transportation is an *anachronism* in the United States today.
chronicle	to tell or write the story of; a *chronological* record of events; a history. Lewis and Clark *chronicled* their adventures as they made their way to the Pacific Northwest.
chronometer	a device for measuring time; a clock or watch. A stop watch is one kind of *chronometer*.
temporary	lasting or effective for a short time only. She worked at Macy's as *temporary* help during the Christmas holidays.

contemporary   existing or happening in the same period of time; a person living in the same period as another. George W. Bush and Bill Clinton are *contemporaries*.

temper   a mood or state of mind; also, to moderate. He was in a foul *temper* after he wrecked his brand-new car. The passing years *tempered* his rashness.

temperate   neither very hot nor very cold; moderate. Hawaii has a *temperate* climate.

temperance   moderation in one's actions, appetites, or feelings; drinking few, if any, alcoholic beverages. Is a lifestyle that emphasizes *temperance* healthier?

Completing Verbal Analogies

One type of analogy involves examples: "A is an example of B; C is an example of D." Look at the sample below.

A   B   C   D

_____ red : color : : oak : _____
   a. bright
   b. large
   c. tree
   d. clothing

As always, you must first look at the relationship between A and B. *Red* is an example of a color. And *oak* is an example of a tree. Therefore, *tree*, or choice c, is the correct answer.

Complete the following analogies.

_____ 1.   United States : democracy : : Vatican City : _____
   a. god
   b. theocracy
   c. pope
   d. matriarchy

_____ 2.   Hitler : autocrat : : Queen Elizabeth : _____
   a. democrat
   b. politician
   c. monarch
   d. deity

_____ 3.   Navajo nation : matriarchy : : ancient Hebrews : _____
   a. men
   b. women
   c. patriarchy
   d. Arizona

_____ 4.   Islam : monotheism : : ancient Greeks : _____
   a. polytheism
   b. atheism
   c. Christianity
   d. deity

_____ 5. baptism : sacrament : : stop watch : _____
a. chronology
b. chronometer
c. theology
d. sanction

_____ 6. president : executive branch : : Congress : _____
a. judiciary
b. laws
c. legislative branch
d. George W. Bush

Now that you have studied the vocabulary in Unit 7, practice your new knowledge by completing the crossword puzzle on the next page.

Vocabulary 7

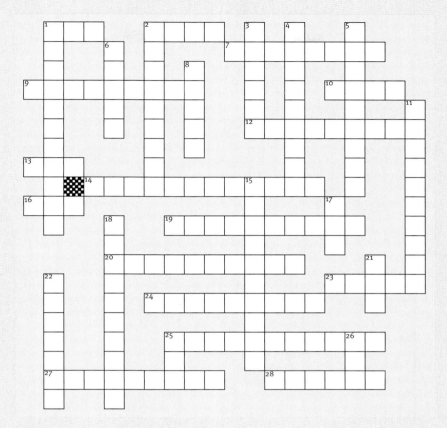

ACROSS CLUES

1. A word part meaning "with."*
2. A word part meaning "god."
7. Rule by one person, usually a king or queen.
9. A person with great power; a ruler.
10. A word part meaning "many."*
12. The climate in Vilcabamba, Ecuador, is a _____ 70 degrees Fahrenheit all year long.
13. A word part meaning "child."*
14. The U.N. considered the dictator's government to be _____ because he seized power from the lawfully elected president.
16. A word part meaning "come."*
19. Alex would like to run for political office. Many people think he would be a good _____.

20. The belief in only one god.
23. To make a god of.
24. A country governed by a few people is an _____.
25. A typewriter is an _____ today.
27. Churches have historically given _____ to those in trouble.
28. A word part meaning "time."

DOWN CLUES

1. A wristwatch is an example of a _____.
2. A person who "leads and excites people."
3. Snow White ate an apple that contained a _____ poison that put her into a deathlike sleep.
4. Zachary received the _____ of baptism when he was two months old.

5. Rule by god.
6. A word part meaning "holy."
8. It is not _____ to park close to a fire hydrant.
11. The literal meaning is "to write about people."
15. Where a woman is the dominant member of the society.
17. A word part meaning "head."*
18. _____ advocates proposed laws that would outlaw the sale of alcohol.
21. A word part meaning "across."*
22. The belief that there is no god.
25. A word part meaning "back."
26. A word part meaning "same."

*From a previous unit.

Bias

The Uprising (L'Emeute) 1848 or later. BY HONORÉ DAUMIER

The Phillips Collection, Washington, D.C.

View and Reflect

This painting depicts a scene from a revolution. According to Duncan Phillips, who purchased the painting in 1931, *Uprising* stands as a "symbol for all pent-up human indignation."

1. What emotion is the man with the raised fist expressing? What is the significance of his casual dress?
2. Is the crowd standing still or advancing? How can you tell?
3. Is there anything in this painting that could relate to the war for American independence?

INTRODUCTION TO BIAS

A **bias** is a strong leaning in either a positive or a negative direction. Bias is very similar to prejudice. Good critical readers must be aware of their own biases and the biases of others.

Sometimes writers simply state their biases; however, most biases are implied by the writer. Subjective material generally places more emphasis on opinions than facts, and it is more likely to display a strong bias.

A critical reader will study the author's line of reasoning, notice whether opinions are supported by facts and reasons, and then decide if the author's bias has hindered the making of a good argument.

Look at the following cartoon. Does the person in the first frame express a bias?

Carlson Cartoon, "I'm sick of all these immigrants . . ." (Art, 1e, p. 337) CARLSON © 2000 Milwaukee Sentinel. Reprinted with permission of Universal Press Syndicate. All rights reserved.

As you are reading textbook material, keep in mind that the authors also have biases. Their biases will influence the way they present the material. Although textbooks primarily deal with factual material, authors must decide what facts to include, omit, and emphasize. Pay attention to the author's tone and choice of words to determine whether he or she is biased. Such caution is especially important when the material deals with a controversial issue.

Two interesting and important personalities in the early history of the United States were John Adams and Alexander Hamilton. In 1789, George Washington was unanimously elected our first president, Adams became our first vice-president, and Hamilton became our first secretary of the treasury. Hamilton resigned from the cabinet in 1795, during Washington's second term. Adams was elected the second president in 1797 and served one term. Adams and Hamilton, both instrumental in the founding of the United States, came to have an increasing dislike for each other. Read the following two quotes from two different history textbooks, and decide which example gives the reader a more negative view of Alexander Hamilton.

Example 1

Hamilton even secretly plotted with certain members of the cabinet against President Adams, who had a conspiracy rather than a cabinet on his hands.

From Thomas A. Bailey, et al., *American Pageant,* Vol. 1: To 1877, 11th ed., Boston: Houghton Mifflin, 1998, p. 201.

Example 2

Although Hamilton had resigned from the Treasury Department in 1795, key members of Adams's cabinet turned to the former secretary for advice.

From James West Davidson, et al., *Nation of Nations,* Vol. 1: To 1877, 4th ed., New York: McGraw-Hill, 2001, p. 248.

The first quote appears to portray Hamilton in a far more sinister way. The words *plotted* and *conspiracy* are examples of words with strong negative feelings.

DENOTATIVE AND CONNOTATIVE LANGUAGE

"Thanks to words we have been able to rise above the brutes; and thanks to words we have often sunk to the level of demons."

—Aldous Huxley

When you look a word up in the dictionary, you are determining its exact meaning, without the suggestions or implications that it may have taken on. This is called the **denotative** meaning of a word. In contrast, the **connotative** meaning of a word refers to the ideas or feelings suggested by the word.

Words that have the same denotative meaning can have much different connotative meanings. The words *cautious* and *timorous,* for example, have similar denotative meanings, but their connotative meanings are very different. *Cautious* has a positive ring. It's good to be "cautious," isn't it? The word *timorous,* however, has a more negative connotative meaning. It suggests fearfulness or reluctance. The words *firm,* *resolute,* and *obstinate* all have similar denotative meanings. Which of these words has the more negative connotation?

Not all words have connotative meanings. The words *pen* and *pencil,* for example, do not evoke strong emotions. Words that are heavily connotative are often referred to as "loaded" or "emotionally charged." Writers who have a particular point of view and want to persuade you to accept that view often make use of loaded words or phrases. Thus, subjective material is more likely to rely on heavily connotative language, and it is more likely to display a strong bias. If a writer approves of a city's monetary policy toward libraries, the word *thrifty* might be used. If the writer disagrees with the policy, the word *cheap,* which calls up negative feelings, might be used instead. The connotation of the words used can tell you a lot about the speaker or writer's opinion.

Exercise 1: Recognizing Connotative Meaning

Which of the following words in each group is the most positive?

1. _____ resolute, stubborn, unyielding

2. _____ timid, wary, cautious

3. _____ bizarre, eccentric, nutty

4. _____ old-fashioned, traditional, out-of-date

5. _____ obnoxious, abrasive, self-assertive

6. _____ thin, slim, scrawny

7. _____ miserly, cheap, thrifty

8. _____ foolhardy, courageous, vainglorious

9. _____ curious, nosy, officious

10. _____ solemn, dignified, glum

Exercise 2: Identifying Connotative Language

What are the three connotative words in the following cartoon? Put these three connotative words in order from the most positive to the most negative.

1. _____

2. _____

3. _____

PEANUTS: © United Feature Syndicate, Inc.

Exercise 3: Using Connotative Language

Well-known linguist S. I. Hayakawa developed the idea of "conjugating irregular verbs" to demonstrate how connotative language works. With Hayakawa's method, an action or a personality trait is "conjugated" to show how it can be viewed either favorably or unfavorably depending on the "spin" we put on it.

For example:

> I'm casual.
>
> You're a little careless.
>
> He's a slob.

Or:

> I'm thrifty.
>
> You're money conscious.
>
> She's a cheapskate.

Try a few of these conjugations yourself.

1. I'm tactful. _____
2. I'm conservative. _____
3. I'm relaxed. _____
4. I'm quiet. _____
5. I'm proud. _____

EUPHEMISM

The word **euphemism** is derived from the Greek word *euphemos*, meaning "to use a good word for an evil or unfavorable word." The Greek prefix *eu* means "good," and *phemi* means "speak."

When someone substitutes an inoffensive word or phrase for one that could be offensive to someone, they are using a euphemism. Most of the time euphemisms are used to be polite or to avoid controversy. The result is often a more positive connotation, such as when a garbage collector is referred to as a "sanitation engineer" or a clerk is referred to as a "junior executive."

Euphemisms can also be used to mislead or to obscure the truth. For example, workers are sometimes fired or dismissed or terminated. A number of euphemisms are available for referring to this process that removes responsibility from employer or employee, and places it, instead, on economic or market forces, such as having a "reduction in force" or "releasing resources." The cartoon below illustrates this point.

STONE SOUP © 2003 Jan Eliot. Reprinted by permission of Universal Press Syndicate. All rights reserved.

Exercise 4: Identifying Euphemisms

Directions: Rewrite the paragraph below by substituting more direct and frank language for the italicized euphemisms.

I was driving down the street in my *preowned vehicle* when I came upon a *pavement deficiency*. As a result I *made contact with* the car in front of me. The other car was being driven by a *senior citizen* who yelled at me angrily. I immediately started to *perspire* because I was afraid I would be late getting to the *memorial park*. When I spoke to the policeman who arrived shortly I *stretched the truth* a little about the speed I was going, but he issued me a ticket anyway. I don't know how I'm going to be able to pay the ticket, because I was recently *terminated* from my job and I am currently *financially embarrassed*. I did, however, arrive in time to see the *deceased,* my pet cat, *laid to rest*. He had *passed on* because a *mixed breed dog* not on a leash had attacked him. I noticed that the *animal control warden* had come to pay his respects. It had been a hard day and so I headed to a *cocktail lounge* to meet friends.

SELECTION

"What, exactly, is adult content?"

GETTING THE PICTURE

What do you think the intent is behind the use of the euphemisms "adult content" and "adult language"? Are they meant to be descriptive? Or are they meant to purposely obscure the truth?

BIO-SKETCH

Bob Greene, a former syndicated columnist for the *Chicago Tribune,* is the best-selling author of *Duty: A Father, His Son, and the Man Who Won the War.*

BRUSHING UP ON VOCABULARY

mayhem random or deliberate violence; rowdy disorder. The word derives from the old French *maim*. In the nineteenth century, the word acquired the meaning of "chaos."

paradoxical a seemingly contradictory statement that expresses a possible truth. The word comes from Greek *paradoxon*, which means "contrary opinion."

sheepish embarrassed or bashful; like a sheep, as in meekness.

Excerpt from

Chevrolet Summers, Dairy Queen Nights

BY BOB GREENE

ADULTS ONLY

1 It's one of the great untruths of our times, and it is so common that it passes without notice.

2 You see it—or some variation of it—on television screens, in movie advertisements, on the labels of recorded music. The wording goes something like this:

3 "Adult content." Or: "Contains adult language."

4 Few people ever stop to think about what this means. What, exactly, is adult content? What words constitute adult language?

5 In our contemporary culture, adult content usually means that people are shown attacking each other with guns, hatchets and blowtorches; that half-naked people are assaulting other people, ripping their clothes off, treating humans like garbage; that people are detonating other people's cars and houses, setting fire to property, bludgeoning and disemboweling and pumping holes in one another. That's adult content; that's how adults behave.

6 Adult language? Adult language, by our current definition, consists of the foulest synonyms for excrement, for sexual activity, for deviant content. Adult language usually consists of four letters; adult language is the kind of language that civilized people are never supposed to use.

7 It makes you wonder what lesson we are sending—not only to children, but to ourselves. If a TV show or motion picture concerned itself with responsible adults treating each other and the people around them with kindness, with consideration, with thoughtfulness, that TV show or movie would never be labeled as containing adult content. If a TV show or movie dealt quietly and responsibly with as many choices of conscience and generosity that adults face every day in the world, it would not warrant an "adult content" rating.

8 Similarly, if a movie featured adults talking with each other civilly, never resorting to gutter language or obscenities, choosing their words with care and precision, no one would ever think to describe the dialogue as "adult." A cable TV show or a music CD in which every word spoken or sung was selected to convey a thought or emotion without resorting to cheap and offensive vulgarities—that TV show or that CD would never be labeled as containing adult language.

9 We seem to be so sheepish about what our culture has become—so reluctant to concede the debasement of society—that we have decided to declare that darkness is light, that down is up, that wrong is right. We are sending a clear signal to young people: The things in our world that are violent, that are crude, that are dull and mean-spirited are the things that are considered "adult." The

words that children are taught not to say because they are ugly and foul are "adult language." As if they are something to strive for, to grow into.

10   What is the solution? Truth in packaging might be a good idea, although it will never happen. No movie studio that has hired a top-money action star to headline in a film that consists of explosions, bloodshed and gore would ever agree to describe the movie truthfully. The lie of "adult content" is acceptable to Hollywood; the true label of "pathetic, moronic content, suitable for imbeciles" will never see the light of day.

11   Language? The movie studios, cable channels, and record labels can live with the inaccurate euphemism of "adult language." To phrase it honestly—"infantile, ignorant, pitiful language"—would remove a certain sheen from a big-budget entertainment project.

12   Ours is becoming a society in which the best ideals of childhood—innocence, kindness, lack of spitefulness, rejection of violence—are qualities toward which adults ought to strive. A paradoxical society in which the things labeled "adult"— lack of restraint, conscienceless mayhem, vulgarity, raw and cynical carnality—are the things that children should be warned against growing up to embrace.

13   So perhaps we should learn to read the current "adult" warning labels in a different way. "Adult content" on a movie or television show should be read as a warning against becoming the kind of adult who welcomes such things into his or her life. The "adult language" label on a TV show or CD should be read as a genuine kind of warning to children about becoming the sort of adult who chooses to speak that way.

14   Then there is "For Mature Audiences Only," but that will have to wait for another day. . . .

Source: "Adults Only" from Bob Green, *Chevrolet Summers, Dairy Queen Nights*, pp. 135–137, 2001.

◤ COMPREHENSION CHECKUP

Multiple Choice

Write the letter of the correct answer in the space provided.

_____   1. We can infer that the writer probably feels that
        a. we are sending the wrong message to our children
        b. entertainment today depicts responsible adults
        c. children might as well get used to hearing obscenities

_____   2. When Greene says, "That's adult content; that's how adults behave" in paragraph 5, he is being
        a. admiring
        b. sarcastic
        c. humorous

_____   3. The dominant tone throughout is
        a. playful
        b. offended
        c. nostalgic

_____ 4. The author's point of view toward the current use of the term "adult content" in labeling contemporary entertainment is
    a. favorable
    b. unfavorable
    c. neutral

_____ 5. We can infer that Greene is not fond of
    a. entertainment that glorifies violence
    b. entertainment that features human beings treating each other with kindness and consideration.
    c. entertainment that features big-budget stars

_____ 6. The words "pathetic, moronic content, suitable for imbeciles" in paragraph 10 have a
    a. positive connotation
    b. negative connotation
    c. neutral meaning

_____ 7. The phrase "never see the light of day" in paragraph 10 means
    a. it will take place at night
    b. it's not going to happen
    c. it might or might not happen

_____ 8. As used in paragraph 11, *sheen* most nearly means
    a. beauty
    b. luster
    c. opulence

_____ 9. Greene feels strongly that the word *adult*
    a. should not be used to describe behavior that is immature, destructive, or degrading
    b. is an apt description of violent or vulgar content
    c. has nothing to do with mass entertainment

_____ 10. Greene in the last paragraph implies that
    a. he prefers to see movies that appeal to mature audiences
    b. he likes to see old classics
    c. the word "mature" is also being used euphemistically

Vocabulary in Context

In the space provided, write the letter for the word or phrase that gives the best definition of the italicized word as used in the selection.

_____ 1. "What words *constitute* adult language?"
    a. restrict
    b. appoint
    c. form; make up
    d. challenge

_____ 2. "In our *contemporary* culture . . ."
    a. simultaneous
    b. recently produced visual art
    c. modern; of the present time
    d. a person at nearly the same age as another

_____ 3. "... it would not _warrant_ an "adult content" rating."
   a. defeat
   b. vouch for
   c. hasten
   d. justify

_____ 4. "... choosing their words with care and _precision_ ..."
   a. scientific exactness
   b. accuracy
   c. strict observance
   d. mechanical exactness

_____ 5. "... was selected to _convey_ a thought or emotion ..."
   a. carry from one place to another
   b. communicate; impart
   c. transport
   d. take away secretly

_____ 6. "The things in our world that are violent, that are _crude_ ..."
   a. in a raw or unrefined state
   b. rudimentary or undeveloped
   c. showing a lack of completeness
   d. vulgar

_____ 7. "As if they are something to _strive for_, to grow into."
   a. make strenuous efforts toward a goal
   b. contend in opposition; compete
   c. struggle vigorously; as in resistance
   d. rival; vie

_____ 8. "... the true label of _pathetic_, moronic content ... "
   a. sad; sorrowful; mournful
   b. causing or evoking pity
   c. pitiful; contemptible
   d. made or liable to suffer

In Your Own Words

1. Do you think adults should have to censor their speech when they are around impressionable children in such public places as stadiums, amusement parks, and schools? Should fines be issued when adults cross the line and utter vulgar words around young kids?

2. Do you think Hollywood has gone too far in its portrayal of "adult" situations? What kind of rating system for movies would you like to see implemented?

3. A proposal has been made to give movies that show actors smoking an "R" rating because smoking in movies is said to encourage children to begin smoking themselves. How do you feel about this proposal?

4. Young children surfing the Internet are sometimes inadvertently exposed to online pornography. Some pornographic websites are only one or two letters different from popular children's sites. What do you think should be done about this?

5. If you have young children, how do you keep them from being exposed to inappropriate material either on TV or on the computer?

6. Many people from other countries are confused about what values or standards American society represents. How would you describe American culture today?

The Art of Writing

Choose one of the following and write a few paragraphs stating your opinion.

1. Do you agree or disagree with Greene's central argument? Write a few paragraphs supporting your point of view.

2. Some professors have suggested that media literacy classes designed to teach children the dangers of media should be a required part of grade school and high school curriculums. What do you think about this idea? Would it help?

3. Do you think the media has primarily a positive or a negative impact on people? How would you characterize this impact?

Internet Activity

1. Do research on the rating system for U.S. movies by accessing the Motion Picture Production Code. Do you think this voluntary system goes too far or not far enough? Write a few paragraphs giving your opinion.

2. Go to the Freedom Forum at

   www.freedomforum.org

   Locate a current research report and briefly discuss its results.

SELECTION

"Perhaps the most fundamental form of bias in instructional materials is the complete or relative exclusion of a particular group or groups . . ."

GETTING THE PICTURE

In the United States, the question of bias in textbooks is increasingly becoming a controversial issue. The excerpt by Myra and David Sadker describes various forms of bias that can appear in textbooks.

BIO-SKETCH

Dr. Myra Sadker was professor of education and dean of the school of education at American University (Washington, D.C.) until her death in 1995 from breast cancer. She and her husband, Dr. David Sadker, also a professor at American University, gained a national reputation for their work in confronting gender bias and sexual harassment. The Sadkers' work has been mentioned in hundreds of newspapers and magazines.

BRUSHING UP ON VOCABULARY

suffrage the right to vote. Originally, *suffrage* meant "intercessory prayers." The term evolved to mean a vote given to support a proposal or in favor of the election of a particular person. The Constitution of the United States declares, "No state shall be deprived of its equal *suffrage* in the Senate."

suffragette a woman seeking the right to vote through organized protest. The *suffragettes* were members of the Women's Suffrage Movement, an organization that combined demonstrations and militant action to campaign for the right to vote in the late nineteenth and early twentieth centuries.

bootlegger a smuggler of liquor. The term, which arose in the late nineteenth century, refers to the smugglers' habit of concealing bottles of liquor in their boots.

Excerpt from
TEACHERS, SCHOOLS, AND SOCIETY
by Myra and David Sadker

Seven Forms of Bias

1   Many Americans are passionate about how various groups are portrayed in textbooks. In the 1970s and 1980s, textbook companies and professional associations, such as the American Psychological Association, issued guidelines for nonracist and nonsexist books; as a result, textbooks became more balanced in their description of underrepresented groups. Today, educators work to detect underrepresentation of those groups.

2   Following is a description of seven forms of bias, which can be used to assess instructional materials. Although this approach has been used to identify bias against females and various racial and ethnic groups, it can also help identify bias against the elderly, people with disabilities, non-English speakers, gays and lesbians, limited English speakers, and other groups.

Invisibility

3   Perhaps the most fundamental form of bias in instructional materials is the complete or relative exclusion of a particular group or groups from representation in text narrative or illustrations. Research suggests, for example, that textbooks published prior to the 1960s largely omitted any consideration of African-Americans within contemporary society and, indeed, rendered them relatively invisible in accounts of or references to the United States after Reconstruction. Latinos, Asian-Americans, and Native Americans were largely absent from most resources as well. Many studies indicate that women, who constitute more than 51 percent of the U.S. population, represented approximately 30 percent of the persons or characters referred to throughout the textbooks in most subject areas.

Stereotyping

4   By assigning rigid roles or characteristics to all members of a group, individual attributes and differences are denied. While stereotypes can be positive, they are more often negative. Some typical stereotypes include

5   • African-Americans as servants, manual workers, professional athletes, or troublemakers

- Asian-Americans as laundry workers, cooks, or scientists
- Mexican-Americans as non-English speakers or migrant workers
- Middle-class Americans in the dominant culture as successful in their professional and personal lives
- Native Americans as "blood-thirsty savages" or "noble sons and daughters of the earth"
- Men in traditional occupational roles and as strong and assertive
- Women as passive and dependent and defined in terms of their home and family roles

Imbalance and Selectivity

6 Curriculum may perpetuate bias by presenting only one interpretation of an issue, a situation, or a group of people. These imbalanced accounts simplify and distort complex issues by omitting different perspectives. Examples include

7 - The origins of European settlers in the New World are emphasized, while the origins and heritage of other racial and ethnic groups are omitted.

- The history of the relations between Native Americans and the federal government is described in terms of treaties and "protection," omitting broken treaties and progressive government appropriation of Native American lands.

- Sources refer to the fact that women were "given" the vote but omit the physical abuse and sacrifices suffered by the leaders of the suffrage movement that "won" the vote.

- Literature is drawn primarily from Western male authors.

- Math and science courses reference only European discoveries and formulas.

Unreality

8 Many researchers have noted the tendency of instructional materials to ignore facts that are unpleasant or that indicate negative positions or actions by individual leaders or the nation as a whole. By ignoring the existence of prejudice, racism, discrimination, exploitation, oppression, sexism, and intergroup conflict and bias, we deny children the information they need to recognize, understand, and perhaps some day conquer the problems that plague society. Examples of unreality may be found in programs that portray

9 - People of color and women as having economic and political equality with white males

- Technology as the resolution of all our persistent social problems

Fragmentation and Isolation

10 Bias through fragmentation or isolation primarily takes two forms. First, content regarding certain groups may be physically or visually fragmented and delivered separately (for example, a chapter on "Bootleggers, Suffragettes, and Other Diversions"). Second, racial and ethnic group members may be depicted as interacting only with persons like themselves, isolated from other cultural communities. Fragmentation

and isolation ignore dynamic group relationships and suggest that nondominant groups are peripheral members of society.

Linguistic Bias

11 Language is a powerful conveyor of bias in instructional materials, in both blatant and subtle forms. Written and verbal communication reflects the discriminatory nature of the dominant language. Linguistic bias issues include race or ethnicity, gender, accents, age disability, and sexual orientation—for example,

12 • Native Americans are frequently referred to as "roaming," "wandering," or "roving" across the land. These terms might be used to apply to buffalo or wolves; they suggest a merely physical relationship to the land, rather than a social or purposeful relation. Such language implicitly justifies the seizure of native lands by "more goal-directed" white Americans who "traveled" or "settled" their way westward.

• Such words as *forefathers, mankind, and businessman* deny the contribution and existence of females.

13 The insistence that we live in an English only, monolingual society creates bias against non-English speakers in this country and abroad. An imbalance of word order ("boys and girls") and a lack of parallel terms ("girls and young men") are also forms of linguistic bias.

Cosmetic Bias

Cosmetic bias offers the appearance of an up-to-date, well-balanced curriculum. The problem is that, beyond the superficial appearance, bias persists. Cosmetic bias emerges in a science textbook that features a glossy pullout of female scientists but includes precious little narrative of the scientific contributions of women. A music book with an eye-catching, multiethnic cover that projects a world of diverse songs and symphonies belies the traditional white male composers lurking behind the cover. This "illusion of equity" is really a marketing strategy directed at potential purchasers who *flip* the pages and might be lured into purchasing books that appear to be current, diverse, and balanced.

Source: Myra Pollack Sadker and David Miller Sadker in *Teachers, Schools, and Society,* 6th ed., New York: McGraw-Hill, 2003, pp. 276–279. Copyright © 2003 McGraw-Hill. Reprinted by permission of The McGraw-Hill Companies, Inc.

▼ COMPREHENSION CHECKUP

Multiple Choice

Write the letter of the correct answer in the blank provided.

_____ 1. The authors' primary purpose is to
   a. argue that bias against nondominant groups should be eliminated from textbook material
   b. describe the destructive effects of stereotyping
    c. describe seven forms of group bias that often appear in textbooks
   d. explain the history of group bias in textbooks

_____ 2. You could infer from this excerpt that the authors favor
     a. exposing students to multiple viewpoints about particular issues
     b. presenting historical facts regardless of their unpleasantness
     c. minimizing the contributions of nondominant groups in textbook material
     d. both a and b

_____ 3. The last sentence of paragraph 3 ("Many studies indicate that women . . .") is a statement of
     a. fact
     b. opinion

_____ 4. Which of the following best expresses the main idea of paragraph 3?
     a. the first sentence
     b. the second sentence
     c. the last sentence
     d. There is no main idea.

_____ 5. In the last paragraph, the authors express a bias against textbooks that
     a. include the contributions of nondominant groups
     b. devalue Western culture
     c. emphasize female accomplishments over male ones
     d. only purport to take into account the contributions of non-dominant groups

_____ 6. A synonym for the word _blatant_ as used in paragraph 11 on linguistic bias is
     a. dominant
     b. obvious
     c. offensive
     d. tasteless

_____ 7. The authors probably feel that stereotyping
     a. cannot be avoided
     b. obscures individual differences

_____ 8. The word _peripheral_ as used in "peripheral members of society" most likely means
     a. dominant
     b. superficial
     c. marginal
     d. essential

_____ 9. As used in the last paragraph, the word _lurking_ has a
     a. negative connotation
     b. positive connotation

_____ 10. In the last paragraph the phrase _illusion of equity_ implies that
     a. the material is balanced and diverse
     b. bias still persists in the material
     c. the material presented is comprehensive and fair
     d. none of the above

In Your Own Words

The Sadkers provide a justification or rationale for bias and sensitivity committees. What justifications do they provide? Do you agree with their views? Why or why not?

The Art of Writing

In a brief essay, respond to the item below.

> When do you think it is appropriate to censor textbooks for material that could be objectionable to some group? Is it important for children to read textbooks that contain controversial or objectionable thoughts or expressions? When children are exposed to so much objectionable and offensive material by the mass media, does it make sense to censor textbooks?

Internet Activity

Go to the American Library Association's website at

www.ala.org

Type in "banned books" to locate a list of the 100 most frequently challenged books. Print a copy of the list, and see which books you recognize. How many have you read? Do you think these books should be banned? Are there ways to respond to objectionable books other than banning them?

SELECTION

> *"[Girls] tend to dominate the landscape*
> *academically right now . . . "*

GETTING THE PICTURE

The National Assessment of Educational Progress (commonly known as the nation's report card) found that the reading skills of twelfth-graders tested in 2005 were significantly worse than those of students tested in 1992. At the same time, the gap between boys and girls grew, with girls' reading skills more than a year ahead of boys'. The test results also showed that the majority of high school seniors have not mastered high-school-level math. Girls scored about as well as boys did on the math assessment. However, boys who had taken advanced math and science courses scored higher than girls who had also taken such courses.

BIO-SKETCH

George S. Morrison is a professor of early childhood education at the University of North Texas. He is the author of many books on early childhood education, child development, curriculum, and teacher education, including *Teaching in America*, from which this excerpt is taken. He also gives advice to public and private agencies about teacher education programs and early childhood education.

BRUSHING UP ON VOCABULARY

gender-fair fair and equitable to both sexes.

gender-fair schools learning environments in which male and female students participate equally and respond to similar high expectations in all subjects.

aptitude innate ability; talent.

advanced placement a college-level course taught at the high school level.

Excerpt from
TEACHING IN AMERICA
by George S. Morrison

How Does Gender Affect Teaching and Learning?

1   In an ideal gender-fair school, teachers would have similar high expectations of all students in all subjects. Male and female students would participate equally in classroom discourse. Students of both genders would receive a similar amount and quality of attention from teachers. Counselors would advise on career choices based on student interest, aptitude, and academic achievement. Administrators would have similar leadership expectations of male and female students.

2   Do you recall any incidents of gender bias toward you or your classmates in school? If you do, please explain. If you do not, what made those teachers gender fair?

_____

_____

_____

_____

Academic Achievement and Gender

3   When we examine how gender and achievement interact, we find on the one hand that it is a complex issue, with very few differences apparent. On the other hand, the differences are rather striking.

4   A review of gender differences in elementary and secondary education achievement reveals the following:

- **Reading.** In grades 4, 8, and 12, females scored higher than males across all racial and ethnic groups, with the gap widening as the student progressed through the school.

- **Writing.** In grades 4, 8, and 12, females scored higher than males across all racial and ethnic groups.

- **Science.** At age 9, there were no statistically significant score differences between males and females in all ethnic groups. At age 17, white males scored higher than white females, and Hispanic males outscored Hispanic females. Other groups exhibited no gender gap.

- **Mathematics.** At grade 4, white males scored higher than white females; there was no gender difference within the other groups. At grades 8 and 12, no group demonstrated a gender gap.

- **Advanced placement.** Over the last decade the gender gap is widening. Across all ethnic groups, more females have taken AP examinations than males.

- **High school completion.** The overall high school completion rate for females was 90 percent; for males, 87 percent.

5   Gender remains a salient factor in school life. Care must be taken to ensure that female and male students are given equitable academic and extracurricular

opportunities in schools. One issue that is in the forefront currently is the question of gender equity for boys. After years of focusing on the needs of girls, many now contend that it's boys who are being short-changed.

The New Gender Gap: Boys Lagging

6   Remember when girls became nurses and not doctors? Stenographers, not CEOs? Teachers, not principals?

7   Well, that's not the way it is anymore. Thirty years after the passage of equal opportunity laws, girls are graduating from high school and college and going into professions and businesses in record numbers.

8   Now, it's the boys who could use a little help in school, where they're falling behind their female counterparts.

9   And if you think it's just boys from the inner cities, think again. It's happening in all segments of society, in all fifty states. That's why more and more educators are calling for a new national effort to put boys on an equal footing with their sisters.

10   At graduation ceremonies last June at Hanover High School in Massachusetts, it was the ninth year in a row that a girl was on the podium as school valedictorian. Girls also took home nearly all the honors, including the science prize, says principal Peter Badalament.

11   "[Girls] tend to dominate the landscape academically right now," he says, even in math and science.

12   The school's advanced placement classes, which admit only the most qualified students, are often 70 percent to 80 percent girls. This includes calculus. And in AP biology, there is not a single boy.

13   According to Badalament, three out of four of the class leadership positions, including the class presidents, are girls. In the National Honor Society, almost all of the officers are girls. The yearbook editor is a girl.

14   "Girls outperform boys in elementary school, middle school, high school, college, and graduate school," says Dr. Michael Thompson, a school psychologist who writes about the academic problems of boys in his book *Raising Cain*. He says that after decades of special attention, girls are soaring, while boys are stagnating.

15   "Girls are being told, 'Go for it, you can do it.' They are getting an immense amount of support," he says. "Boys hear that the way to shine is athletically. And boys get a lot of mixed messages about what it means to be masculine and what it means to be a student. Does being a good student make you a real man? I don't think so . . . It's not cool."

Table 1   National High School Graduation Rates by Race and Gender

RACE/ETHNICITY	NATION	FEMALE	MALE
Native American	51.1	51.4	47.0
Asian/Pacific Islander	76.8	80.0	72.6
Hispanic	53.2	58.5	48.0
Black	50.2	56.2	42.8
White	74.9	77.0	70.8
All students	68.0	72.0	64.1

Single-Sex Schools and Classes

16   Educators, politicians, and the public are constantly seeking new ways to provide opportunities for boys and girls to excel. Single-sex schools, while not new, are now being tested as one way to ensure that boys and girls get the most out of their educational opportunities. Single-sex classrooms and programs in existing middle and high schools are another way. At Arapahoe High School in Littleton, Colorado, Principal Ron Booth comments:

> A lot of people deny the difference between boys and girls. It's denied because who would know what to do with it? It's politically incorrect even to say boys and girls are different.

Single-Sex Schools Stage a Comeback

17   On March 3, 2004, the U.S. Department of Education published new regulations governing single-sex education in public schools. The new regulations allow coeducational public schools (elementary and secondary schools) to offer single-sex classrooms, provided that the schools

   1. Provide a rationale for offering a single-gender class in that subject. A variety of rationales are acceptable (e.g., if very few girls have taken computer science in the past, the school could offer a girls-only computer science class).
   2. Provide a coeducational class in the same subject at the same school.
   3. Conduct periodic reviews to determine whether single-sex classes are still necessary to remedy whatever inequity prompted the school to offer the classes in the first place.

18   Just as important, the new regulations clear the way for single-sex schools—schools that are all girls or all boys. In fact, the new regulations provide some incentive for school districts to offer single-sex schools rather than single-sex classrooms within coed schools. Single-sex schools are specifically exempted from two of the three requirements above. They do not have to provide any rationale for their single-sex format, and they do not have to conduct any periodic review to determine whether single-sex education is "necessary" to remedy some inequity. They will have to offer "substantially equal" courses, services, and facilities at other schools within the same school district, but those other schools can be single-sex or coed. In other words, a school district may offer a single-sex high school for girls without having to offer a single-sex high school for boys. A school district can offer an all-boys elementary school without having to offer an all-girls elementary school.

19   All across the country, from Camden to Denver to Los Angeles, almost one hundred public schools now offer single-sex education. Proponents argue that single-sex classes provide a better learning environment for both boys and girls. Critics argue that such classes undermine civil rights gains and promote discrimination. What do you think? Should boys and girls be educated separately? What reasons can you give?

_____

_____

_____

_____

Summary

20   Boys and girls do not have identical experiences in school. There are many significant differences.

- **Academic achievement and gender.** In many indicators of school success, boys now lag behind girls.

- **Providing a gender-fair education.** Schools should conduct high-quality programs that will help all students graduate from high school.

- **Single-sex schools and classes.** Educators are implementing single-sex schools and single-sex classrooms as two ways of helping ensure that education for boys and girls is gender fair and equal in opportunity. Critics of such programs claim they provide unequal opportunity and undermine advances in civil rights.

Source: "How does gender affect teaching and learning?" from George S. Morrison, *Teaching in America, 4/e,* pp. 136–141. Copyright © 2006 by Pearson Education. Reprinted by permission of Allyn and Bacon, Boston, MA.

 COMPREHENSION CHECKUP

True or False

Indicate whether the statement is true or false by writing T or F in the space provided.

___T___ 1. At grade 12, girls score higher in reading and writing than boys.

___F___ 2. At age 17, Asian males scored higher than Asian females in science.

___F___ 3. More males take AP examinations than females.

___F___ 4. Males continue to graduate from high school in larger numbers than females.

___T___ 5. According to the author, some people feel that academic opportunities in school are not equitable.

___T___ 6. The author feels that boys could benefit from a little more help in school.

___T___ 7. High school principal Peter Badalament notes that the class valedictorian has been a girl nine years in a row.

___F___ 8. The words *soaring* and *stagnating* are synonyms.

___T___ 9. According to Dr. Michael Thompson, boys are encouraged to do well in athletics.

___T___ 10. More Hispanic females graduate from high school than Hispanic males.

___F___ 11. Single-sex schools are a recent innovation in the educational system.

___F___ 12. Principal Ron Booth feels that it is politically incorrect to discuss gender differences between males and females.

___T___ 13. The U. S. Department of Education now allows coed public schools to offer single-sex classrooms if the schools follow certain guidelines.

___F___ 14. Regulations adopted by the U. S. Department of Education in 2004, provide for the eventual implementation of single-sex schools.

___T___ 15. Some public schools already offer single-sex education.

___F___ 16. The words *equality* and *inequity* are synonyms.

Vocabulary in Context

Fill in the blanks with a word from the list below. Not all of the words will be used.

contends	forefront	lag	rationale	undermine
counterparts	gap	landscape	remedy	valedictorian
equitable	implementing	periodic	salient	
exempted	incentive	proponent	segments	

1. The _____ points of the new budget were stated at the beginning of the report to the stockholders.

2. There is a widening _____ between the incomes of the rich and the poor.

3. In the next few years, Ford Motor Company is going to be _____ a variety of changes to increase their market share.

4. Because you have longer legs than I do, I always seem to _____ behind you when we walk together.

5. Whenever Sal came up with a good idea, his older brother seemed to deliberately _____ it.

6. Darlene did not want any special favors, but she did expect to be treated in an _____ manner by her boss.

7. After his accident, Randy was routinely _____ from jury duty.

8. He _____ that he has been sober for the last six months, but a lot of people claim to have seen him drunk.

9. Most teachers are subject to _____ evaluations by students, peers, and administrators.

10. I'm sure you have a good _____ for wanting to get married and drop out of school, but could you please tell me what your reasons are?

11. The promise of a substantial raise is a strong _____ for me to work a lot harder at my job.

12. Are you a _____ of higher or lower taxes?

In Your Own Words

1. Thirty years ago, the number of male undergraduates on college campuses was 58 percent. Today that number is 44 percent. What reasons can you think of that account for the difference?

2. While the sexes start out fairly equal in the amount of time spent reading books in the elementary years, girls are far more likely to read books in the upper grades. How do you account for this discrepancy?

3. Over the past decade, physical education, sports programs, and recesses have been cut from the typical grade school curriculum. On the other hand, the amount of standardized testing has substantially increased. How might this trend in education be detrimental to boys?

4. Michael Thompson, co-author of the book *Raising Cain*, says that school curriculums that place a premium on sitting still and keeping quiet are detrimental to

boys. He says that "girl behavior has become the gold standard and boys are treated like defective girls." What is your opinion of Thompson's claim?

5. Family therapist Michael Gurian, author of *The Minds of Boys,* believes that "an adolescent boy without a father figure is like an explorer without a map." Do you think the number of boys being raised in single-parent families could help account for the school-related problems of boys? Gurian recommends mentoring programs for boys. Do you think a mentoring program could help reduce the high drop-out rate of males from high school?

6. Which of the following positions do you agree with?

Teaching kids in segregated settings by gender can focus on academic needs. Same-gender classes help students focus on academics, not on each other. Girls can get extra encouragement in math and science; boys can get special assistance in reading and arts. (Sadker, p. 73)

Teaching kids together promotes gender equality. Learning and succeeding together in the classroom prepares boys and girls to live and work together as adults. Equitable instruction and curriculum will teach students how to eliminate traditional gender barriers in society.

The Art of Writing

Critics of gender-fair education argue that women's perspectives on issues and events do not differ fundamentally from those of men. Therefore, presenting knowledge with particular attention to women's perspectives is using an "artificial prism" on knowledge. Do you agree or disagree with this position? Explain why.

Internet Activity

Research single-sex schools and classrooms. Do the available data support the implementation of single-sex schools and classrooms?

What's Worth Knowing?

To see how society's notion of what is important can change, try your hand at the following test questions that were used to make certain the eighth-graders in Kansas knew "important information." All of the following questions are from the original examination. See if you would qualify to graduate from elementary school in 1895.

8th Grade Examination Graduation Questions
Saline County, Kansas
April 13, 1895

Grammar

1. Give nine rules for the use of capital letters.
2. Define verse, stanza, and paragraph.
3. What are the principal parts of a verb? Give the principal parts of *do, lie, lay,* and *run.*

Arithmetic

1. District No. 33 has a valuation of $35,000. What is the necessary levy to carry on a school seven months at $50 per month and have $104 (for incidentals)?
2. What is the cost of a square farm at $15 per acre, the distance around which is 640 rods?
3. Write a bank check, a promissory note, and a receipt.

U.S. History

1. Give the epochs into which U.S history is divided.
2. Give a description of the history of Kansas.
3. Describe three of the most prominent battles of the Rebellion.

Geography

1. Name and describe the following: Monrovia, Odessa, Denver, Manitoba, Yukon, St. Helena, Juan Fernandez, Orinoco.
2. Name all the countries of Europe and give the capital of each.
3. Describe the movements of the earth. Give the inclination of the earth.

Physiology

1. Describe the circulatory system.
2. What is the function of the liver? Of the kidneys?
3. Give some general directions that you think would be beneficial to preserve the human body in a state of health.

How did you do? Well, if you bombed it, don't feel too badly; few of today's PhDs would pass. So what does this teach us? Are today's schools far weaker than earlier ones? If we failed are we not truly educated? Or perhaps what we consider "important knowledge" is less enduring than we believe. How much of today's "critical" information will be a curious and unimportant footnote in the years ahead?

What do you think teachers should be teaching? What do you think is worth knowing?

*Note that the exam has been shortened.
Source: "What's Worth Knowing?" from David Miller Sadker, *Teachers, Schools, and Society,* 8/e, p. 241. Copyright © 2008 McGraw-Hill Companies, Inc. Used with permission.

MULTICULTURALISM VERSUS CORE CURRICULUM

The following selection explores the question of multiculturalism versus core curriculum.

SELECTION

"What some call cultural literacy others see as cultural imperialism. 'Whose knowledge is of most worth?' is the question of the day."

GETTING THE PICTURE

"What balance should schools seek between teaching a common core curriculum that binds all Americans together and teaching a curriculum that celebrates the many cultures that have been brought to the United States?" —Myra and David Sadker

BRUSHING UP ON VOCABULARY

George Orwell the pseudonym of the English author Eric Blair (1903–1950). His most famous novels are *Animal Farm* and *Nineteen Eighty-four*.

Aldous Huxley an English author of the twentieth century (1894–1963). His best-known work is *Brave New World*.

Excerpt from
TEACHERS, SCHOOLS AND SOCIETY
by Myra and David Sadker

Cultural Literacy or Cultural Imperialism?

1   Both George Orwell and Aldous Huxley were pessimists about the future. "What Orwell feared were those who would ban books," writes author Neil Postman. "What Huxley feared was that there would be no one who wanted to read one." Perhaps neither of them imagined that the great debate would revolve around neither fear nor apathy but, rather, deciding which books are most worth reading.

2   Proponents of **core knowledge**, also called **cultural literacy**, argue for a common course of study for all students, one that ensures that an educated person knows the basics of our society. Novelist and teacher John Barth laments what ensues without core knowledge:

3   In the same way you can't take for granted that a high school senior or a freshman in college really understands that the Vietnam War came after World War II, you can't take for granted that any one book is common knowledge even among a group of liberal arts or writing majors at a pretty good university.

"One could get a first-class education from a shelf of books five feet long."
—Charles William Eliot (when president of Harvard)

4   Allan Bloom's *The Closing of the American Mind* was one of several books that sounded the call for a curriculum canon. A canon is a term with religious roots, referring to a list of books officially accepted by the church or a religious hierarchy. A curriculum **canon** applies this notion to schools by defining the most useful and valued books in our culture. Those who support a curricular canon believe that all students

should share a common knowledge of our history and the central figures of our culture, an appreciation of the great works of art and music and, particularly, the great works of literature. A shared understanding of our civilization is a way to bind our diverse people.

5   Allan Bloom, professor of social thought at the University of Chicago, took aim at the university curriculum as a series of often unrelated courses lacking a vision of what an educated individual should know, a canonless curriculum. He claimed that his university students were ignorant of music and literature, believing that too many students graduate with a degree but without an education. One of the criticisms of Bloom's vision was that his canon consisted almost exclusively of white, male European culture.

6   E. D. Hirsch, Jr., in his book *Cultural Literacy,* was more successful than Bloom in including the contributions of various ethnic and racial groups, as well as women. This is a rarity among core curriculum proponents. In fact, Hirsch believes that it is the poorer children and children of color who will most benefit from a cultural literacy curriculum. He points out that children from impoverished homes are less likely to become culturally literate. A core curriculum will teach them the names, dates, places, events, and quotes that every literate American needs to know in order to succeed. In 1991, Hirsch published the first volume of the core knowledge series, *What Your First Grader Needs to Know.* Other grades followed in these mass-marketed books directed not only at educators but at parents as well.

7   Not everyone is enamored with the core curriculum idea. A number of educators wonder who gets included in this core, and, just as interesting, who gets to choose? Are Hirsch, Bloom, and others to be members of a very select committee, perhaps a blue-ribbon committee of "Very Smart People"? Why are so many of these curriculum canons so white, so male, so Eurocentric, and so exclusionary?

8   Many call for a more inclusive telling of the American story, one that weaves the contributions of many groups and of women as well as of white males into the textbook tapestry of the American experience. Those who support **multicultural education** say that students of color and females will achieve more, will like learning better, and will have higher self-esteem if they are reflected in the pages of their textbooks. And let's not forget white male students. When they read about people other than themselves in the curriculum, they are more likely to honor and appreciate their diverse peers. Educator and author James Banks calls for increased cultural pluralism:

9   People of color, women, other marginalized groups are demanding that their voices, visions, and perspectives be included in the curriculum. They ask that the debt Western civilization owes to Africa, Asia, and indigenous America be acknowledged. . . . However, these groups must acknowledge that they do not want to eliminate Aristotle and Shakespeare, or Western civilization, from the school curriculum. To reject the West would be to reject important aspects of their own cultural heritages, experiences, and identities.

"A nation is a body of people who have done great things together in the past and hope to do great things together in the future."

—Frank Underhill

Source: "Cultural Literacy or Cultural Imperialism," from Myra Pollack Sadker and David Miller Sadker in *Teachers, Schools, and Society,* 8th ed., New York: McGraw-Hill, pp. 246–248. Copyright © 2008 McGraw-Hill. Reprinted by permission of The McGraw-Hill Companies, Inc.

COMPREHENSION CHECKUP

Core or Multicultural

Indicate whether the statement is representative of the core curriculum or multicultural philosophy of education by writing C or M in the blank provided.

M   1. "Non-Western cultures have rich traditions that any student could and should benefit from. In fact, people steeped only in the art and ideas of Europe cannot consider themselves well educated."

M   2. "We need to prepare students for living in a diverse democracy. Focusing only on the West won't accomplish that."

C   3. "It is important for all Americans to have common cultural connections to preserve national unity and cohesiveness."

M   4. "Students, regardless of their color or ethnicity, cannot properly prepare to live in an increasingly global society without having at least some understanding of a broad range of cultures."

C   5. "Americans, regardless of their heritage, live in the West, with Western traditions, institutions, and culture. Students in the U.S. need a grounding in the Western tradition in order to understand their own society. Notions like equality before the law and democratic institutions come out of the Western tradition."

M   6. "It is undemocratic and just plain narrow-minded to expose students solely or largely to Western culture and a Western point of view."

C   7. "Almost all scientific and political advances have taken place in the West. Even in less quantifiable disciplines, like literature or philosophy, the size and historical impact of the Western canon far outweigh those of, say, Asia or Africa."

M   8. "The notion that the West did it all alone is a fallacy. Take the Greeks, for instance. They were influenced by the rich cultures of the Mediterranean and Africa."

True or False

Indicate whether the statement is true or false by writing T or F in the blank provided.

T   1. John Barth favors a multicultural curriculum.

T   2. Alan Bloom was criticized for excluding ethnic and racial groups from his curriculum canon.

T   3. E. D. Hirsch, Jr., believes that teaching a core curriculum will enable minority students to become more successful.

F   4. Proponents of multicultural education believe that a more inclusive curriculum will boost the self-esteem of females.

F   5. James Banks, a proponent of cultural pluralism, is in favor of eliminating the study of Western civilization from the school curriculum.

T   6. A synonym for *empower* is weaken.

T   7. A plant that is *indigenous* to the United States was brought here from somewhere else.

_____ 8. If someone *laments* the loss of something, they are filled with sorrow or regret.

In Your Own Words

1. Should traditional heroes, sometimes called "DWMs" (dead white males)— such as Washington, Jefferson, and other revered Americans—be the focus of the curriculum, or should the experiences and contributions of other groups, women, and people of color be included?

2. Should history continue to emphasize European roots, or should Afrocentric issues be included? What about the views of other groups? For instance, should a penetrating view of European settlement of the Americas as seen through the eyes of Native Americans and Mexican-Americans be taught to schoolchildren?

3. Should U.S. history tell only a story of victors and triumphs, or should it also relate varied views of social, cultural, and economic issues?

4. Try your hand at identifying some of Hirsch's core curriculum concepts:

Achilles	Pike's Peak
Homer	phylum
Uriah Heep	ukelele
John Bull	Uncle Tom
je ne sais quoi	Emile Zola

5. Study the following cartoon. What is the cartoon's main idea? What main idea from the selection does the cartoon highlight?

NON-SEQUITUR © 1992. Reprinted by permission of Universal Press Syndicate. All rights reserved.

Exercise 5: Identifying Bias in Textbook Material

Directions: Read each paragraph. Then choose the best answer for each item.

A. Elephants, like humans, grieve, cry from frustration and sadness, and help one another. They have a long childhood and remain with their mothers for fifteen years. They are sensitive, intelligent, and affectionate, and they long for social relationships. Now try to imagine one of these magnificent creatures in complete isolation, spending its entire life in either a small cage or the back of a truck, being moved from city to city. Confined, chained, and caged, the elephant quickly learns the futility and brutal repercussion of protesting. Picture this dignified and social animal responding to this isolation and lack of space. Pacing, weaving, rocking, sucking, or chewing on the steel bars of the cage are the animals' response to monotony and loneliness. Many, of course, simply go mad.

From Larry A. Samovar in *Oral Communication: Speaking Across Culture,* 10th ed., New York: McGraw-Hill, 1998, p. 268. Copyright © 1998 McGraw-Hill. Reprinted by permission of the author.

_____ 1. The author is most opposed to which of the following?
   a. depriving an elephant of its mother
   b. moving elephants from city to city
   c. depriving an elephant of companionship and space
   d. depriving an elephant of peanuts

_____ 2. The choice of the words "futility and brutal repercussion of protesting" suggest that
   a. the elephant will be sent to a zoo if it causes trouble
   b. the elephant will be dealt with harshly if it protests
   c. the elephant will not be allowed to socialize with other elephants if it does not behave
   d. elephants will not receive treats if they cause trouble

B.   There it was—the ship from New York bobbing down the Atlantic Coast and through the Caribbean. It was a 3,100-ton barge loaded with unwanted trash. After 41 days and more than 2,000 smelly miles at sea, the barge was still searching for a home. With an end to its odious odyssey nowhere in sight, the scow raised once again the dilemma of a throwaway society, quickly running out of room for all its solid waste.

From Larry A. Samovar in *Oral Communication: Speaking Across Culture,* 10th ed., New York: McGraw-Hill, 1998, p. 130. Copyright © 1998 McGraw-Hill. Reprinted by permission of the author.

_____ 1. In this paragraph, the author expresses disgust for
   a. large barges
   b. a society that does not reuse and recycle materials
   c. smelly trash
   d. New Yorkers

_____ 2. Which phrase best expresses the author's disapproval?
   a. "bobbing down the Atlantic Coast"
   b. "throwaway society, quickly running out of room"
   c. "2,000 smelly miles at sea"
   d. "solid waste"

C.   One of history's most tragic figures, Wolfgang Amadeus Mozart began his performing career as a child prodigy. He played the piano (still something of a novelty in his day), harpsichord, organ, and violin beautifully, and was taken by his father on a number of concert tours through several European countries. The young performer delighted his noble audiences, but was rewarded with flattery and pretty gifts rather than fees. Mercilessly prodded by his self-seeking father, upon whom he remained emotionally dependent most of his life, Mozart constantly sought to please his parent (who was never satisfied), his wife (demanding and ungrateful), his public (appreciative but ungenerous), and finally himself (who never doubted his own genius). Though fun-loving, sociable, and generous to a fault, Mozart never learned the art of getting along with people.

He could not refrain from offering honest but unsolicited criticism; nor could he bring himself to flatter a potential patron. Fiercely independent, he insisted upon managing his own affairs, although he was quite incapable of doing so. Few besides Mozart's great contemporary Haydn appreciated the true worth of this man who wrote such quantities of beautiful music in such a short time. Mozart lived a short and difficult life, and now lies buried in an unmarked grave.

From Jean Ferris in *Music the Art of Listening,* 7th ed., New York: McGraw-Hill, 2008, pp. 173–174.

_____ 1. Which statement best expresses the main point the author is trying to convey about Mozart's life?
   a. [Mozart] was rewarded with flattery and pretty gifts rather than fees."
   b. "Mozart lived a short and difficult life . . ."
   c. "[Mozart] began his performing career as a child prodigy."
   d. "Mozart constantly sought to please his parent . . ."

_____ 2. In this paragraph, the author expresses disapproval of all the following *except*
   a. Mozart's father
   b. Mozart's wife
   c. Mozart's mother
   d. Mozart's public

D. There are hundreds of fad diets and diet books, but such diets are usually unbalanced and may result in serious illness or even death. Fad diets cannot be maintained for long periods; therefore, the individual usually regains any lost weight. Less than 5 percent of people who lose weight maintain the loss for more than a year. Constant losing and gaining, known as the "yo-yo syndrome," may be as harmful as the original overweight condition.

From Charles B. Corbin in *Concepts of Fitness and Wellness,* 7th ed., New York: McGraw-Hill, p. 338. Copyright © 2008.

_____ 1. The author is opposed to
   a. fruits and vegetables
   b. fad diets
   c. constant losing and gaining of weight
   d. both b and c

_____ 2. The author would agree that
   a. fad diets are often popularized by celebrities
   b. fad diets are a good way to maintain a healthy weight
   c. fad diets are likely to be unhealthy
   d. if persons lose weight by means of a fad diet, it is likely they will maintain the weight loss for at least several years

E. You should know that the gap between the earnings of high school graduates and college graduates, which is growing every year, now ranges to more than 80 percent. According to the U.S. Census Bureau, the holders of bachelor's degrees will make an average of $51,206 per year as opposed to just $27,915 for high school graduates. That's a whopping additional $23,291 a year. Thus, what you invest in a college education is likely to pay you back many times. That doesn't mean there aren't good careers available to non-college graduates. It just means that those with an education are more likely to have higher earnings over their lifetime. But the value of a college education is more than just a larger paycheck. Other benefits include increasing your ability to think critically and communicate your ideas to others, improving your ability to use technology, and preparing yourself to live in a diverse world. Knowing you've met your goals and earned a college degree also gives you the self-confidence to continue to strive to meet your future goals.

From William G. Nickels et al., in *Understanding Business,* 8th ed., New York: McGraw-Hill, p. 8. Copyright © 2008 McGraw-Hill. Reprinted by permission of The McGraw-Hill Companies, Inc.

_____ 1. The author would agree that
  a. college is a waste of time for many people
  b. college is a good investment
  c. it is unlikely that in the future there will be an earnings gap between those who choose to attend college and those who do not
  d. students are unlikely to recover their original investment in a college education

_____ 2. The author would disagree with which of the following statements?
  a. A college education is unlikely to develop critical thinking skills.
  b. A college degree is unlikely to contribute to a feeling of self-confidence.
  c. A college education is unlikely to prepare a student to live in a diverse, technical world.
  d. All of the above

F. Let us imagine that you are feeling good as you take a long, deep puff on your cigarette. But let us add a touch of realism to this scene by asking you to also picture what your body is doing with this invisible and sinister chemical as it invades your body. Your gums and teeth are the first recipients of the poisonous chemical. While the smoke pays but a short visit to your mouth it is leaving enough pollution to increase the risk of painful gum diseases and the agony of mouth and throat cancer. But this is just the beginning. As the smoke continues its journey into your unsuspecting lungs, you will soon find that your breathing is shallow and impaired, for now the smoke deposits insidious toxins that, after a period of time, will increase your chances of crippling and deadly cancer. Your stomach too will experience the effects of this corrupt and silent killer. While you cannot see them, small bits of acid are coating your stomach, adding to the chances that you will develop lacerated ulcers. Think about all this the next time you decide that it is okay to take one little puff of this cleverly concealed stick of dynamite.

From Larry A. Samovar in *Oral Communication: Speaking Across Culture,* 10th ed., New York: McGraw-Hill, 1998, p. 268. Copyright © 1998 McGraw-Hill. Reprinted by permission of the author.

_____ 1. Which phrase expresses the author's bias against smoking?
  a. "invisible and sinister chemical"
  b. "agony of mouth and throat cancer"
  c. "corrupt and silent killer"
  d. all of the above

———— 2. The author would agree that
   a. smoking is on the rise with young teens
   b. young girls smoke to keep from gaining weight
   c. smoking is not a healthful activity
   d. smoking is such a pleasurable activity that it is worth the risk of cancer and other diseases

SELECTION

"Why wouldn't I be proud of being a woman?"

GETTING THE PICTURE

Rosa Bonheur (1822–1899), the nineteenth century's leading painter of animals, is the most famous woman artist of her time. She realistically portrayed sheep, cows, tigers, wolves, and other animals. The underlying theme of Bonheur's work is "humanity's union with nature." When someone criticized her by saying, "You are not fond of society," Bonheur replied, "That depends on what you mean by society. I am never tired of my brute friends." Bonheur, the daughter of an artist, began to study at the Louvre at 14 and soon eclipsed her father and her siblings, also artists. Throughout her lengthy career, she received many honors, including the Cross of the French Legion of Honor. Upon presenting this award to Bonheur, the Empress of France declared, "Genius has no sex." Bonheur, a noncomformist, was one of the first advocates of women's rights.

BIO-SKETCH

Patrick Frank, professor of art history at the University of Kansas, first became involved in *Artforms* as an instructor in 1991. A long-time educator and writer, Frank is an expert in Latin American art.

BRUSHING UP ON VOCABULARY

Messiah any expected deliverer or savior.

slaughterhouse a building or place where animals are butchered for food.

Excerpt from
PREBLE'S ARTFORMS

by Patrick Frank

Rosa Bonheur—Flouting Social Conventions

1 The list of awards that Rosa Bonheur earned in her lifetime was impressive by any standard: First Medal at the Paris Salon; Grand Cross of the French Legion of Honor; Commander of the Order of Isabella the Catholic; Member of the Order of King Leopold of Belgium. She was the first woman ever to receive most of these honors. She was also a friend to Queen Victoria of England and the French Emperor Napoleon III. Yet Rosa Bonheur also led an unusual personal life that

showed clearly the difficulties that a woman of her day had to face if she wanted a career.

2   Her most important early influence was her father, Raymond, a drawing instructor. He was a Saint-Simonian Socialist—that is, he believed all wealth should be shared because everybody was equal; girls were as worthy as boys and should be raised the same way. These beliefs are somewhat radical even today, but he took them even further. He believed that a new savior would come to the human race, and that this new Messiah would be a woman. Hence he took special pains to educate his daughters, an unusual step for that period.

3   Rosa Bonheur decided as a teenager to become an artist, and benefited from her father's teaching; in fact, she soon surpassed him. Since the Academy forbade women from studying the nude model, she decided to specialize in painting country scenes with animals. There was a ready market for such works, partly because France was industrializing and people from the country were moving to the city in great numbers. People wanted to remember country life, and Bonheur became their painter. A few Parisian artists had already specialized in this subject, but she soon surpassed them too.

4   The main problem inherent in her career choice was that she would have to do things that women just did not do: spend a lot of time on farms and ranches, become an expert rider, and sketch animal anatomy in slaughterhouses. All of these she did, apparently with pleasure.

5   She found that she could do her work with more ease and comfort if she cut her hair short and wore trousers. Cutting the hair was not a problem, but for a woman to wear trousers in public was illegal. Well, not exactly: She had to get a permit from the local police and renew it every six months. The stack of papers was found among her possessions after she died.

6   How else might a woman forward her career in a male-dominated society? Bonheur always insisted that her only goals were convenience and career advancement: "If, however, you see me dressed as I am, it is not in the least in order to make me into an original, but simply in order to facilitate my work. Consider that, at a certain period in my life, I spent whole days at the slaughterhouse."

7   She never married, regarding it as a hindrance. Rather, she lived most of her life with her friend Natalie Micas in a home filled with pets. The two of them were active in the Society for the Prevention of Cruelty to Animals. Her favorite males, she said, were the bulls that she painted.

8   Meanwhile her work kept selling and gaining honors. She bought a country estate next to the Emperor's family home. When Empress Eugenie arrived at her door to present her with the Legion of Honor, the artist kept Her Majesty waiting while she threw a robe on over her pants.

9   To the end of her life, Bohheur lived the dichotomy of the successful and honored career woman forced into an unconventional personal life. Accused of seeming unfeminine, she defended herself in a way that rings as a call for women's equality:

"The battle for women's rights has largely been won."
—Margaret Thatcher

10   "Why wouldn't I be proud of being a woman? My father, that enthusiastic apostle of humanity, repeated to me many times that a woman's mission was to uplift the human race. I am persuaded that the future belongs to us."

Source: From Patrick Frank, et al., *Preble's Art Forms*, 8/e. Copyright © 2006. Reprinted by permission of Pearson Education, Inc., Upper Saddle River, NJ.

✓ COMPREHENSION CHECKUP

True or False

Indicate whether the statement is true or false by writing T or F in the space provided.

_____ T _____ 1. The selection suggests that Bonheur had a highly successful and lucrative career.

_____ T _____ 2. Despite Bonheur's unconventional lifestyle, she was welcomed by royalty.

_____ T _____ 3. Rosa Bonheur was passionate about art.

_____ F _____ 4. The author believes that Bonheur's fame rests entirely on her ability to depict horses.

_____ F _____ 5. Bonheur's mother and siblings were the most important influences on her life.

_____ F _____ 6. Above all, Bonheur disliked working outdoors.

_____ T _____ 7. As an artist, Bonheur was noted for making studies from nature.

_____ T _____ 8. Bonheur was one of the first advocates of women's rights.

_____ T _____ 9. Bonheur had a police permit to wear trousers.

_____ T _____ 10. To gain an accurate knowledge of anatomy, Bonheur sketched in slaughterhouses.

Vocabulary in Context

Indicate whether the words in italics are used correctly or incorrectly in the following sentences by writing C or I in the blanks provided.

_____ 1. His *unconventional* behavior caused him to be labeled an eccentric.

_____ 2. Karla believed in *equality* of the sexes, so she clearly favored her son over her daughter.

_____ 3. As I aged, he *surpassed* me in youth and vigor.

_____ 4. A good education is generally considered to be a *hindrance* to success.

_____ 5. Giving up his job and retiring at age 40 made for a *radical* change in his life.

_____ 6. Her *inherent* good manners made her an asset at any social gathering.

_____ 7. Unfortunately for Martha, her son *specialized* in getting in trouble.

_____ 8. His training to be a surgeon was *facilitated* by his shaky hands.

_____ 9. She became an *apostle* for change when she began promoting universal health coverage.

_____ 10. In his case, there is a *dichotomy* between his words and his action.

In Your Own Words

1. Why do you think there were so few female artists in the nineteenth century?

2. What can we infer about the character of Rosa Bonheur's father? What type of educational system did he favor?

The Art of Writing

The author mentions some of the difficulties that Bonheur needed to overcome to pursue her chosen career as an artist. Discuss some of these difficulties. How did Bonheur deal with those who were biased against her?

Internet Activity

You can view some of Rosa Bonheur's paintings at the following website:

www.artcyclopedia.com/artists/bonheur_rosa.html

After viewing the paintings, select a favorite. What is it about the painting that appeals to you? Can you infer anything about Bonheur's relationship to either nature or society from this particular work?

Exercise 6: Identifying Bias

Directions: Read the following accounts of a confrontation between women faculty members and the administration of a local college. Circle the biased or loaded words in both accounts, and then write an objective or unbiased account of the event.

1. This past week, 25 female faculty members struck a blow against male dominance and caught the attention of Wellstone College's sexist administration for three hours. The well-justified protest was organized by those hard-working female teachers in the trenches who are forced to cope with degrading working conditions, unfair salary scales, and lack of promotional opportunities. Embarrassed administrators watched in disgrace as the teachers organized a peaceful, orderly picket line in front of the administration building. The teachers carried placards and talked calmly and earnestly to passersby. Many passersby voiced support of the protest. When the media arrived, an apologetic college vice president rushed forward to agree to form a committee to study the group's modest demands and to immediately curtail discriminatory policies. The group's success serves as an inspiration to oppressed female employees everywhere.

2. An outlandish protest was lodged against the administration of Wellstone College on November 15. A group of irate female faculty disgraced themselves by milling about in front of the administration building. They thrust placards in the faces of passersby and railed against supposed inequities in hiring, wages, working conditions, and promotion of female faculty. It required a great deal of patience and diplomacy on the part of the college vice president to maintain control of the disturbance and to soothe the group's hurt feelings. Speaking in a dignified manner, the vice president promised to evaluate the teachers' claims in a calmer, more appropriate setting. Judging from the chorus of boos that were heard, it appears that the ladies have done a grave disservice to themselves and to the college with their immoderate demands and juvenile, attention-seeking behavior.

_____

_____

_____

_____

_____

_____

AN INTRODUCTION TO LOGICAL FALLACIES

Faulty Cause and Effect (*Post Hoc, Ergo Propter Hoc*)

The Latin meaning, "after this, therefore because of this," suggests that because B follows A, A must *cause* B. But just because two events or two sets of data are sequential does not necessarily mean that one caused the other. In the following cartoon, Fred Bassett is guilty of faulty cause-and-effect reasoning. He thinks that because the car washing happened before the rain, the car washing caused the rain.

Non Sequitur ("It Does Not Follow")

A non sequitur applies to any argument in which the conclusion does not follow from the evidence. "She will make a fine governor because she was an excellent attorney" is an example of a non sequitur. There is not a lot of reason to believe that because she was an excellent attorney she will make a fine governor.

Begging the Question

This fallacy occurs when you assume as true what you are trying to prove. This sort of faulty reasoning could occur when a person says, "Stores should be required to carry organic vegetables because organic vegetables are superior to nonorganic vegetables." It may or may not be true that organic vegetables are superior to nonorganic. It is something that reasonable people disagree about.

Circular Logic

In this type of fallacy, the conclusion restates the information presented as evidence. Here's an example: "Al Gore lost Tennessee because he didn't get enough votes."

That Al Gore lost Tennessee and that he didn't get enough votes there say the same thing. Here's another example: "The team is in last place because they have lost more games than the other teams."

Hasty Generalization

In this fallacy, the conclusion is based on too little evidence. Here's an example: "Jane had a very hard time with her first husband and concluded that all men are no good."

Either/Or Fallacy (or False Dilemma)

This is a fallacy of "black-and-white thinking": Only two choices are given; there are no shades of gray. People who exhibit this type of thinking have a "bumper sticker" mentality. They say things like "America—love it or leave it." When we polarize issues, we make it more difficult to find a common ground. In the following cartoon, Hagar's wife is offering only two viewpoints to an issue.

HAGAR: © King Features Syndicate.

False Analogy

In this fallacy, two things that may not really be similar are portrayed as being alike. The store brand of coffee may be packaged to look like the name brand, but are the two the same? We have to ask some questions to determine the answer. Is the coffee of the same quality? Is there as much coffee in the can? In most false analogies, there is simply not enough evidence available to support the comparison.

Ad Hominem Argument (Argument Against the Man)

This fallacy involves an attempt to discredit an argument by attacking the person making it. For instance, saying that Jill is a liar does not disprove Jill's argument that free speech is critical in a democracy.

Ad Populum Argument (Argument to the People)

This kind of argument seeks to win agreement by making an appeal to common prejudices, values, and emotions. It does not rely on facts or reasoning. Take the following example: "Americans are strong, independent, and free, so we need to privatize Social Security." Americans like to think of themselves as being strong, independent, and free. If these values are secured by privatizing Social Security, then many Americans may want to do this. The question to be asked is whether these values have anything to do with privatizing Social Security. A common form of an ad populum argument is an appeal to patriotism, as in the following example: "Support America. Buy American cars." Of course, what is not stated is that many parts of American cars are made outside the United States, and many "foreign" cars are assembled in the United States. At its extreme, ad populum arguments rely on "mob appeal."

Red Herring

This fallacy involves directing attention away from a debatable point to one that most people will quickly agree with. An uncooked herring has a very strong odor. If a herring is dragged across the trail of an animal (or person) that dogs are tracking, the dogs will abandon the original scent and follow the scent of the herring. A red herring argument is meant to distract the listener from the issue at hand. "It is pointless to worry about too much violence on television when thousands are killed by drunk drivers every year" is an example.

Slippery Slope

This fallacy assumes that taking a first step down a path will necessarily lead to later steps. If we let X happen, the next thing you know Y will happen. The image is one of a boulder rolling uncontrollably down a steep hill. The boulder can't be stopped until it reaches the very bottom. Consider this example: "Requiring ratings on record labels will lead to censorship and government control of free speech." When we assume that the first step will inevitably lead to disaster without providing evidence, we are committing the slippery slope fallacy. The following cartoon illustrates slippery slope thinking.

SIX CHIX: © Rina Piccolo. King Features Syndicate.

Exercise 7: Identifying Logical Fallacies

Directions: Indicate the logical fallacies being used in each of the following items.

_____ 1. Central State University has won its first two basketball games, and therefore it's going to win all of its games.
  a. slippery slope
  b. either/or
  c. hasty generalization

_____ 2. I just washed my car, so I know it's going to rain.
   a. begging the question
   b. faulty cause and effect
   c. ad hominem

_____ 3. The Wildcats are in last place because they lost more games than any other team.
   a. ad populum
   b. ad hominem
   c. circular logic

_____ 4. Senator Wealthy wants to change the inheritance tax laws. But he's a notorious womanizer who has a profligate lifestyle. So let's not waste our time with his proposals.
   a. hasty generalization
   b. ad hominem
   c. non sequitur

_____ 5. Either the Democrats will quickly unite behind Gary Goodfellow, or the Republicans will to roll to victory.
   a. faulty cause and effect
   b. red herring
   c. either/or

_____ 6. Don't ever let children have second helpings of dinner. If you do, pretty soon they will be gorging themselves.
   a. red herring
   b. slippery slope
   c. begging the question

_____ 7. Americans are honest, hardworking, and caring. That's why we need to lower taxes.
   a. ad populum
   b. either/or
   c. slippery slope

_____ 8. Phil likes chocolate because he's a caring person.
   a. either/or
   b. non sequitur
   c. ad populum

_____ 9. Araceli did poorly in a bilingual school. Bilingual education must be a failure.
   a. ad hominem
   b. red herring
   c. hasty generalization

_____ 10. To improve education, we can either hire more teachers or build more schools.
   a. either/or
   b. false analogy
   c. slippery slope

_____ 11. All of the following contain fallacies *except:*
   a. We can't adopt Laurie Legislator's proposal. She comes from a long line of chiselers.
   b. The school rules state that after three absences you can be dropped from a class.

c. I'm going to have bad luck for the rest of the year because a black cat crossed my path on New Year's Day.

_____ 12. All of the following contain fallacies *except:*
a. Two of my son's friends got in accidents the day after they got their licenses at 16. Sixteen-year-olds should not be allowed to drive.
b. An Infiniti is a good car because it costs a lot of money.
c. I didn't study for the final exam, and I failed it.

Now look at the illustration below, and consider the strategies it uses to get its message across. Can you identify any propaganda techniques or logical fallacies in the work? Explain your thinking.

We will roll up our sleeves.
We will move forward together.
We will overcome.
We will never forget.

A message from

Courtesy of General Electric Company

_____

_____

_____

_____

TEST-TAKING TIP

Improving Your Performance on Essay Tests (3)

ORGANIZING YOUR ANSWER

Once you have considered the question and re-called the material you need to answer it, you are ready to think about organizing your answer. Organizing your answer clearly—especially for "big picture" essay questions—will show the teacher how well you understand the relationships among ideas and concepts.

A good answer to an essay question typically includes:

- An introduction, with a clear introductory statement (or thesis)
- Three paragraphs of development, including supporting examples, developed in the same order in which the main ideas are mentioned in the introductory statement (each paragraph should develop only one main idea)
- A conclusion

The introductory statement plays a crucial role in organizing an answer on an essay exam, since it drives the development of the body paragraphs. How can you write an effective introductory statement? One way is to turn the essay question itself into your introductory statement. Imagine you encounter the following item on an exam:

> Discuss whether an increase in state financial aid for public education will raise student scores on standardized tests.

You can use this question as the basis of your introductory statement by turning it into a statement

and adding reasons. For example, your introductory statement might start:

> *An increase* in state financial aid for public education will raise student scores on standardized tests because . . . [list three reasons]

Or

> An increase in state financial aid for public education will not raise student scores on standardized tests because . . . [list three reasons]

Once you've devised your introductory statement, you have the outline of your body paragraphs.

SAMPLE INTRODUCTORY STATEMENT

> An increase in state financial aid for public education will raise student scores on standardized tests because *teacher salaries can be increased,* which will attract more talented people into teaching; *more teachers can be hired,* which will reduce class size; and school districts will have *more money available for learning resources and activities.*

Each body paragraph would develop one of the ideas included in the introductory statement:

- Paragraph 1—the role more talented teachers would play in increasing test scores
- Paragraph 2—the role smaller classes would play in increasing test scores
- Paragraph 3—the role more learning resources would play in increasing test scores

Analyzing and Evaluating Arguments

Trial by Jury (1964) BY THOMAS HART BENTON

The Nelson-Atkins Museum of Art, Kansas City, Missouri. Bequest of
the artist F/75-21/11. Photo by Mel McLean. © T.H. Benton and R.P.
Benton Testamentary Trusts/Licensed by VAGA, New York, NY. © T.H.
Benton and R.P. Benton Testamentary Trusts/UMB Bank.

View and Reflect

1. Which figure in the painting is making an argument? Do you think this person is the prosecutor or the defense attorney?
2. How many jurors appear in the painting? What is the composition of the jury in terms of sex and ethnicity?
3. Who do you think the defendant is?
4. Does this scene accurately depict how a courtroom looks? In what ways does it differ? Have you ever served on a jury?

IDENTIFYING ARGUMENTS

The critical reader must be able to evaluate arguments. When you *evaluate* an argument (a claim supported by reasons or evidence), you determine its value or persuasiveness. When an author tries to persuade the reader that something is true or correct by presenting supporting reasons or evidence, an argument is being made.

This means that an argument is different from an assertion. If an author says, "Toughguy makes better trucks than Strongman," that's an assertion, not an argument, because no reasons or evidence is given. But if an author says, "Toughguy makes better trucks than Strongman because Toughguy trucks are more reliable and last longer," then an argument is being made. The author is stating a claim (Toughguy trucks are better than Strongman trucks) and is backing up this claim with reasons (Toughguy trucks last longer and hold up better).

Arguments can be broken down into their parts. An argument is made up of assumptions, premises, and a conclusion.

The **assumptions** of an argument support the conclusion but are not stated in the argument. Assumptions tie the premises to the conclusions. They are claims that lie in the background of the argument that make the argument work. Our sample argument assumes that trucks that are more reliable and last longer are better than trucks that are less reliable and do not last as long. That's an assumption that many would agree with. But what about someone who cares more about the appearance or style of a truck than how reliable it is or how long it lasts? Our argument assumes that appearance is not all that important. Our argument only works if its assumptions are true. To find the assumptions underlying an argument, ask yourself what is left unstated in the argument that must be true for it to work.

The **premises** of an argument are the reasons or evidence that the author presents to support the conclusion. Our example has two premises: Toughguy trucks are more reliable, and Toughguy trucks last longer. The premises of an argument are often introduced by words such as *since* or *because*.

The **conclusion** of an argument is the claim that is the point of the argument. When an author makes an argument, it's the conclusion that the author is trying to persuade the reader to accept as true. The premises and assumptions in an argument are there to support the conclusion. Going back to our example, the conclusion of our argument is that "Toughguy makes better trucks than Strongman." The conclusion of an argument is often introduced by words such as *accordingly, consequently,* or *thus*.

EVALUATING ARGUMENTS

Now that we know what an argument is and how it is put together, let's talk about how to evaluate an argument. To evaluate an argument, you need to analyze it. When you *analyze* an argument, you break it down into its parts and examine them by themselves and in relation to the other parts of the argument. Here are the steps for analyzing an argument:

1. Identify the argument's conclusion (claim). What is the conclusion the author is trying to persuade the reader to accept as true? What is the point of the argument?

2. Identify the assumptions that the argument makes.

3. Identify the premises (reasons or evidence) that the author puts forth in support of the conclusion.

4. Think critically and skeptically about the premises (reasons or evidence) that the argument presents and the assumptions that the argument makes. Are the premises true? Do the assumptions defeat or weaken the argument? Take our example. Is it true that Toughguy trucks are more reliable than Strongman trucks? Is it true that Toughguy trucks last longer than Strongman trucks? How important is appearance? If toughguy trucks are more reliable and last longer than Strongman trucks, but Strongman trucks are better looking, are Toughguy trucks really superior to Strongman trucks?

5. Ask yourself how well the premises and assumptions support the conclusion. If the assumptions are not shared by the reader or if the premises are weak or false, then the argument will be unpersuasive or even unsound.

Exercise 1: Identifying Arguments

Directions: Identify the conclusion (or central issue) and the supporting reasons in each of the following excerpts. Where indicated, also list the logical fallacies used.

A. A Fair Share of Resources?

The affluent lifestyle that many of us in the richer countries enjoy consumes an inordinate share of the world's natural resources and produces a shockingly high proportion of pollutants and wastes. The United States, for instance, with less than 5 percent of the total population, consumes about one-quarter of most commercially traded commodities and produces a quarter to half of most industrial wastes.

To get an average American through the day takes about 450 kg (nearly 1,000 lbs) of raw materials, including 18 kg (40 lbs) of fossil fuels, 13 kg (29 lbs) of other minerals, 12 kg (26 lbs) of farm products, 10 kg (22 lbs) of wood and paper, and 450 liters (119 gal) of water. Every year we throw away some 160 million tons of garbage, including 50 million tons of paper, 67 billion cans and bottles, 25 billion styrofoam cups, 18 billion disposable diapers, and 2 billion disposable razors.

This profligate resource consumption and waste disposal strains the life-support system of the Earth on which we depend. If everyone in the world tried to live at consumption levels approaching ours, the results would be disastrous. Unless we find ways to curb our desires and produce the things we truly need in less destructive ways, the sustainability of human life on our planet is questionable.

From William Cunningham & Barbara Saigo in *Environmental Science*, 6th ed., New York: McGraw-Hill, 2001, p. 27. Copyright © 2001.

1. What is the central issue that is being argued? _____

_____

2. List the author's support for the argument.

a. _____

b. _____

c. _____

B. Inside Job

Roughly four or five fast-food workers are now murdered on the job every month, usually during the course of a robbery. Although most fast-food robberies end without bloodshed, the level of violent crime in the industry is surprisingly high. In 1998, more restaurant workers were murdered on the job in the United States than police officers.

America's fast-food restaurants are now more attractive to armed robbers than convenience stores, gas stations, or banks. Other retail businesses increasingly rely upon credit card transactions, but fast-food restaurants still do almost all of their business in cash. While convenience store chains have worked hard to reduce the amount of money in the till (at 7-Eleven stores the average robbery results in a loss of about thirty-seven dollars), fast-food restaurants often have thousands of dollars on the premises. Gas stations and banks now routinely shield employees behind bullet-resistant barriers, a security measure that would be impractical at most fast-food restaurants. And the same features that make these restaurants so convenient—their location near intersections and highway off-ramps, even their drive-through windows—facilitate a speedy getaway.

The same demographic groups widely employed at fast-food restaurants—the young and the poor—are also responsible for much of the nation's violent crime. According to industry studies, about two-thirds of the robberies at fast-food restaurants involve current or former employees. The combination of low pay, high turnover, and ample cash in the restaurant often leads to crime. A 1999 survey by the National Food Service Security Council, a group funded by the large chains, found that about half of all restaurant workers engaged in some form of cash or property theft—not including the theft of food. The typical employee stole about $218 a year; new employees stole almost $100 more.

Studies conducted by Jerald Greenberg, a professor of management at the University of Ohio and an expert on workplace crime, have found that when people are treated with dignity and respect, they're less likely to steal from their employer. "It may be common sense," Greenberg says, "but it's obviously not common practice." The same anger that causes most petty theft, the same desire to strike back at an employer perceived as unfair, can escalate to armed robbery. Restaurant managers are usually, but not always, the victims of fast-food crimes. Not long ago, the day manager of a McDonald's in Moorpark, California, recognized the masked gunman emptying the safe. It was the night manager.

The leading fast-food chains have tried to reduce violent crime by spending millions on new security measures—video cameras, panic buttons, burglar alarms, additional lighting. But even the most heavily guarded fast-food restaurants remain vulnerable. In April of 2000, a Burger King on the grounds of Offut Air Force Base in Nebraska was robbed by two men in ski masks carrying shotguns. They were wearing purple Burger King shirts and got away with more than $7,000. Joseph A. Kinney, the president of the National Safe Workplace Institute, argues that the fast-food industry needs to make fundamental changes in its labor relations. Raising wages and making a real commitment to workers will do more to cut crime than investing in hidden cameras. "No other American industry," Kinney notes, "is robbed so frequently by its own employees."

From Eric Schlosser, *Fast-Food Nation: The Dark Side of the All-American Meal*, pp. 83–85. Copyright © 2001 by Eric Schlosser. Reprinted by permission of the Houghton Mifflin Company. All rights reserved.

1. What is the central issue that is being argued? _____

   _____

   _____

   _____

   _____

2. List the author's support for the argument.

   a. _____

   b. _____

   c. _____

C. Come Together . . . Right Now!

Small children play with cyberpets while old women stare out their windows at empty streets. Grandparents feel lonely and useless while, a thousand miles away, their grandchildren do not get the love and attention they desperately need. What's wrong with this picture? A lot.

In our society today, we practice a particularly virulent form of segregation—we separate people by age. We put our 3-year-olds together in preschools or day care centers, our 14-year-olds together in high schools, and our 80-year-olds in nursing homes—institutions that Betty Friedan, in *The Fountain of Age*, vividly labels "playpens for adults."

Segregating the generations in this way means that people of all ages lose out: Older people are deprived of the energy and joy of children, and our kids end up learning their ideas about the world from each other or from television instead of through that most time-honored of traditions: being socialized by their elders.

But age segregation is more than just one of those regrettable casualties of changing times. It is a dangerous pattern that leads to all sorts of other social breakdowns. When our elders have no regular, everyday contact with young people, they rarely have the same emotional stake in the fate of their communities. They are less likely to care about the environment and to invest in green spaces and playgrounds. An older person who never mingles with children and no longer feels a sense of common cause with the young may not vote in favor of school referendums, child-health laws, or funding for teen programs. To put it bluntly, he may simply fail to see what a good school system has to do with him and his well-being. By the same token, a child who has no contact with old people is more likely to look the other way when one of them needs assistance or to become impatient when they share a joke or story. Age segregation fosters short-term selfish planning by the old and less empathy and respect from the young.

Because they don't get to know each other as people, old and young alike tend to think in negative stereotypes (often, alas, generated by the media). This breeds misunderstanding and fear. How many times do older people freeze up when they see a rambunctious group of young people approaching? Or hold back from nurturing or correcting other people's kids for fear of being misinterpreted? For their part, children often see older people as hopelessly out of it, if not downright weird, with nothing to contribute to their lives.

Yet society cannot hold together when old people are afraid of children and children are afraid of old people. Every culture is just one generation away from anarchy: It is the socialization of the young by the elders that allows the next generation to come of age civilized. A society in which this torch no longer gets passed is a society in trouble.

Each generation has its own wisdom and ways of loving. When we bring them together, we create a kind of social wealth that enriches us all.

From Mary Pipher, "Come Together . . . Right Now!" in *Parents*, December 1999, p. 100. Copyright © 1999 Gruner & Jahr USA. Reprinted with permission.

1. What is the central issue that is being argued? _____

_____

_____

2. List the author's support for the argument.

    a. _____

    _____

    b. _____

    c. _____

D. Yes, Let's Pay for Organs

Pennsylvania plans to begin paying the relatives of organ donors $300 toward funeral expenses. Already there are voices opposing the very idea of pricing a kidney.

It is odd that with 62,000 Americans desperately awaiting organ transplantation to save their life, no authority had yet dared to offer money for the organs of the dead in order to increase the supply for the living. If we can do anything to alleviate the catastrophic shortage of donated organs, should we not?

One objection is that Pennsylvania's idea will disproportionately affect the poor. The rich, it is argued, will not be moved by a $300 reward; it will be the poor who will succumb to the incentive and provide organs.

So what? Where is the harm? What is wrong with rewarding people, poor or not, for a dead relative's organ? True, auctioning off organs in the market so that the poor could not afford to get them would be offensive. But this program does not restrict supply to the rich. It seeks to increase supply for all.

Moreover, everything in life that is dangerous, risky, or bad disproportionately affects the poor: slum housing, street crime, small cars, hazardous jobs. By this logic, coal mining should be outlawed because the misery and risk and diseases of coal mining disproportionately fall on people who need the money.

No, the real objection to the Pennsylvania program is this: It crosses a fateful ethical line regarding human beings and their parts. Until now we have upheld the principle that one must not pay for human organs because doing so turns the human body—and human life—into a commodity. Violating this principle, it is said, puts us on the slippery slope to establishing a market for body parts. Auto parts, yes. Body parts, no. Start by paying people for their dead parents' kidneys, and soon we will be paying people for the spare kidneys of the living.

Well, what's wrong with that? the libertarians ask. Why should a destitute person not be allowed to give away a kidney that he may never need so he can live a better life? Why can't a struggling mother give her kidney so her kids can go to college?

The answer is that little thing called human dignity. We have a free society, but freedom stops at the point where you violate the very integrity of the self. We cannot allow live kidneys to be sold at market. It would produce a society in which the lower orders are literally cut up to serve as spare parts for the upper. No decent society can permit that.

But kidneys from the dead are another matter entirely. To be crude about it, whereas a person is not a commodity, a dead body can be. Yes, it is treated with respect. But it is not inviolable. It does not warrant the same reverence as that accorded a living soul.

The Pennsylvania program is not just justified, it is too timid. It seeks clean hands by paying third parties—the funeral homes—rather than giving cash directly to the relatives. Why not pay them directly? And why not $3,000 instead of $300? That might even address the rich/poor concern: after all, $3,000 is real money, even for bankers and lawyers.

The Pennsylvania program does cross a line. But not all slopes are slippery. There is a new line to be drawn, a very logical one: rewards for organs, yes—but not from the living.

The Talmud speaks of establishing a "fence" around the law, making restrictions that may not make sense in and of themselves but that serve to keep one away from more serious violations. The prohibition we have today—no selling of *any* organs, from the living or the dead—is a fence against the commoditization of human parts. Laudable, but a fence too far. We need to move the fence in and permit incentive payments for organs from the dead.

Why? Because there are 62,000 people desperately clinging to life, some of whom will die if we don't have the courage to move the moral line—and hold it.

From Charles Krauthammer, "Yes Let's Pay for Organs," *Time,* 5/17/99, p. 100. © TIME, Inc. Reprinted by permission.

1. What is the central issue that is being argued? _____

   _____

   _____

2. List the author's support for the argument.

   a. _____

   b. _____

   c. _____

3. What logical fallacies or propaganda devices can you identify?

   1. _____

   _____

   2. _____

   _____

   3. _____

4. How does the author respond to the opposing point of view?

   _____

   _____

5. What is your overall evaluation of this argument?

_____

_____

_____

_____

_____

SELECTION

"The line between news and entertainment has become blurred in most media."

GETTING THE PICTURE

Photographs have always been susceptible to manipulation, and today they can be altered in ways that are virtually undetectable. Examples, of course, abound. Models and movie stars who grace the covers of magazines and billboards really don't look exactly like their media images. Most of us are aware of these "too good to be true" images. But now the public has to be even more wary of manipulation by the media. Too often we read about reporters making up stories, altering information and quotes, and, in general, manipulating the truth. Recently, we learned that our government hired actors to pose as reporters in ads to push a particular agenda. Because not too many of us are going to abandon the quest to be informed, what do you think our rights and responsibilities as viewers are? The selection below discusses this issue and offers some suggestions for citizens to follow.

BIO-SKETCH

William P. Cunningham is professor emeritus at the University of Minnesota. In addition to writing environmental science textbooks, he has written many articles in the field of biology.

BRUSHING UP ON VOCABULARY

deregulation halting or reducing government regulation.

patsy a slang term for a scapegoat or fall guy.

stealth ad any ad that attempts to hide the marketer's identity and fool the consumer.

Excerpt from
ENVIRONMENTAL SCIENCE

by William P. Cunningham

Don't Believe Everything You See or Hear on the News

1   In our own everyday lives most of us are inundated by information and misinformation. Competing claims and contradictory ideas battle for our attention. The rapidly growing complexity of our world and our lives intensifies the difficulties in

knowing what to believe or how to act. Consider how the communications revolution has brought us computers, e-mail, cell phones, mobile faxes, pagers, the World Wide Web, hundreds of channels of satellite TV, and direct mail or electronic marketing that overwhelm us with conflicting information. We have more choices than we can possibly manage, and know more about the world around us than ever before, but, perhaps, understand less. How can we deal with the barrage of often contradictory news and advice that inundates us?

2   By now, most of us know not to believe everything we read or hear. "Tastes great . . . Low, low sale price . . . Lose 30 pounds in 3 weeks . . . You may already be a winner . . . Causes no environmental harm . . . I'll never lie to you . . . Two out of three doctors recommend . . ." More and more of the information we use to buy, elect, advise, judge, or heal has been created not to expand our knowledge but to sell a product or advance a cause.

3   For most of us, access to news is becoming ever more abundant and ubiquitous. Internet web logs comment on events even as they're happening. Cable television news is available around the clock. Live images are projected to our homes from all over the world. We watch video coverage of distant wars and disasters as if they are occurring in our living rooms, but how much do we really know about what's going on? At the same time that media is becoming more technically sophisticated, news providers are also becoming more adept at manipulating images and content to convey particular messages.

"The day you write to please everyone you no longer are in journalism. You are in show business."

—Frank Miller, Jr.

4   Many people watch TV news programs and read newspapers or web logs today not so much to be educated or to get new ideas as to reinforce their existing beliefs. A State of the Media study by the Center for Journalistic Excellence at Columbia University concluded that the news is becoming increasingly partisan and ideological. The line between news and entertainment has become blurred in most media. Disputes and disasters are overdramatized, while too little attention is paid to complex issues. News reports are increasingly shallow and one-sided, with little editing or fact checking. On live media, such as television and radio, attack journalism is becoming ever more common. Participants try to ridicule and demean their opponents rather than listening respectfully and comparing facts and sources. Many shows simply become people shouting at each other. Print media also is moving toward tabloid journalism, featuring many photographs and sensationalistic coverage of events.

5   According to the State of the Media Report, most television stations have all but abandoned the traditional written and edited news story. Instead, more than two-thirds of all news segments now consist of on-site "stand-up" reports or live interviews in which a single viewpoint is presented as news without any background or perspective. Visual images seem more immediate and are regarded as more believable by most people: after all, pictures don't lie, but they can give a misleading impression of what's really important. Many topics, such as policy issues, don't make good visuals, and therefore never make it into TV coverage. Crime, accidents, disasters, lifestyle stories, sports, and weather make up more than 90 percent of the coverage on a typical television news program. If you watched cable TV news for an entire day, for instance, you'd see on average, only 1 minute each about the environment and health care, 2 minutes each on science and education, and 4 minutes on art and culture. More than 70 percent of the segments are less than 1 minute long, meaning that they convey more emotion than

substance. People who get their news primarily from TV are significantly more fearful and pessimistic than those who get news from print media.

6   Partisan journalism has become much more prevalent since the deregulation of public media. From the birth of the broadcasting industry, the airwaves were regarded and regulated as a public trust. Broadcasters, as a condition of their licenses, were required to operate in the "public interest" by covering important policy issues and providing equal time to both sides of contested issues. In 1988, however, the Federal Communications Commission ruled that the proliferation of mass media gives the public adequate access to diverse sources of information. Media outlets no longer are obliged to provide fair and balanced coverage of issues. Presenting a single perspective or even a deceptive version of events is no longer regarded as a betrayal of public trust.

7   [1]A practice that further erodes the honesty and truthfulness of media coverage is the use of video news releases that masquerade as news stories. [2]In these videos, actors, hired by public relations firms, pose as reporters or experts to promote a special interest. [3]Businesses have long used this tactic to sell products, but a recent disturbing development is placement of news videos by governmental agencies. [4]For example, in 2004, the federal Department of Health and Human Services sent video stories to TV stations promoting the benefits of the recently passed but controversial Medicare drug law. The actors in these videos appeared to be simply reporting news, but, in fact, were presenting a highly partisan viewpoint. Critics complained that these "stealth ads" undermine the credibility of both journalists and public officials. Kevin W. Keane, a Health Department spokesman, dismissed the criticism, saying this is "a common, routine practice in government and the private sector." In 2004, the federal government paid $88 million to public relations firms and news commentators to represent administration positions on policy issues.

8   How can you detect bias in a news report? Ask yourself the following questions:

1. What political positions are represented in the story?
2. What special interests might be involved here? Who stands to gain presenting a particular viewpoint? Who is paying for the message?
3. What sources are used as evidence in this story? How credible are they?
4. Are statistics cited in the presentation? Are citations provided so you can check the source?
5. Is the story one-sided, or are alternate viewpoints presented? Are both sides represented by credible spokespersons, or is one simply a patsy set up to make the other side look good?
6. Are the arguments presented based on facts and logic, or are they purely emotional appeals?

9   We need to practice critical thinking to detect bias and make sense out of what we see and hear. Although the immediacy and visual impact of television or the Internet may seem convincing, we have to use caution and judgment to interpret the information they present. Don't depend on a single source for news. Compare what different media outlets say about an issue before making up your mind.

Source: "Don't Believe Everything You See" from William P. Cunningham, et al., *Environmental Science,* 9/e, pp. 8, 10. Copyright © 2007 McGraw-Hill Companies, Inc. Used with permission.

COMPREHENSION CHECKUP

True or False

Indicate whether the statement is true or false by writing T or F in the space provided.

_T_ 1. It is possible for a news provider to manipulate images and content.

_T_ 2. According to the author, news reports are increasingly one-sided.

_F_ 3. On live media, attack journalism is a thing of the past.

_F_ 4. More than three-quarters of all news segments consist of stand-up reports.

_F_ 5. Policy issues make up more than 90 percent of the coverage on a typical television news program.

_F_ 6. People who get news primarily from TV tend to be more optimistic than those who get their news from magazines or newspapers.

_T_ 7. In 2004, the federal government paid $88 million to public relations firms and news commentators to present administration positions on various issues.

_T_ 8. Kevin Keane apparently believes that stealth ads are common practices in government and the private sector.

Multiple Choice

Write the letter of the correct answer in the space provided.

_C_ 9. A key point the author makes is that
   a. complex issues get too much attention from the media
   b. news reports bend over backwards to present multiple points of view
   c. Americans are overwhelmed by conflicting information
   d. news and entertainment are presented as two separate and distinct entities

_____ 10. We can infer that the author of this selection is in favor of
   a. partisan journalism
   b. providing equal time on controversial issues
   c. allowing actors to pose as reporters or experts
   d. using so-called stealth ads

_____ 11. Which sentence among the following from paragraph 7 contains the most emotionally loaded language?
   a. sentence 1
   b. sentence 2
   c. sentence 3
   d. sentence 4

_____ 12. The author would probably agree with which of the following statements?
   a. Access to news is becoming ever more restricted.
   b. Print journalism and tabloid journalism are beginning to resemble each other in some respects.
   c. News reports are scrupulously checked to make sure the facts are accurate.
   d. Attack journalism is a thing of the past in live television.

_____ 13. All of the following are statements of opinion *except*
   a. "by now, most of us know not to believe everything we read or hear"
   b. "we have more choices than we can possibly manage, and know more about the world around us than ever before, but, perhaps, understand less"
   c. "a State of the Media study by the Center for Journalistic Excellence at Columbia University concluded that the news is becoming increasingly partisan and ideological"
   d. "the line between news and entertainment has become blurred in most media"

_____ 14. Which of the following best describes the author's attitude toward the current state of the news story?
   a. ambivalent
   b. concerned
   c. objective
   d. compassionate

_____ 15. A reasonable inference that can be drawn is that
   a. deregulation of the media has contributed to the rise in partisan journalism
   b. both sides of widely disputed issues continue to be presented
   c. actors posing as reporters are representing the government point of view in advertisements
   d. both a and c

_____ 16. Which of the following best describes the author's main purpose?
   a. to encourage the public to think critically about information presented by the media
   b. to inform the public about possible bias in news reports
   c. to persuade the reader to lobby the government to return regulation to the media industry
   d. both a and b

_____ 17. In paragraph 2 the author gives examples to demonstrate
   a. the stupidity of the public
   b. deceptive advertising techniques
   c. products to help people lose weight
   d. remedies for cancer

_____ 18. As used in paragraph 7, the words *erodes, masquerade, controversial,* and *disturbing* have a
   a. negative connotation
   b. positive connotation

_____ 19. The author expresses a negative bias toward all of the following *except*
   a. the Center for Journalistic Excellence at Columbia University
   b. e-mail, cell phones, mobile faxes, and pagers
   c. stealth ads
   d. cable television news

_____ 20. The author concludes the selection with a warning to
   a. practice critical thinking in order to detect bias in the media
   b. rely on only a single source you know and trust for daily news
   c. make up your mind about an issue after comparing different viewpoints
   d. both a and c

Vocabulary in Context

Each question below has a sentence from the selection and another sentence. A word is italicized in both sentences. Use the context clues in the two sentences to determine the meaning of the word.

1. "In our own everyday lives most of us are *inundated* by information and misinformation."

   He is such a dynamic speaker that he is *inundated* with requests to speak at various charitable events.

   Inundated means _____

2. "For most of us, access to news is becoming ever more abundant and *ubiquitous*."

   Commercials are *ubiquitous* on evening TV.

   Ubiquitous means _____

3. "Participants try to ridicule and *demean* their opponents rather than listening respectfully and comparing facts and sources."

   If you lie and cheat to get ahead in your career, you are likely to *demean* yourself.

   Demean means _____

4. "A State of the Media study by the Center for Journalistic Excellence at Columbia University concluded that the news is becoming increasingly *partisan* and ideological."

   His goal was to remain neutral and above *partisan* politics.

   Partisan means _____

5. "At the same time that media is becoming more technically sophisticated, news providers are also becoming more *adept* at manipulating images and content to convey particular messages."

   Karla is an *adept* tennis player; she has won many tournaments.

   Adept means _____

6. "People who get their news primarily from TV are significantly more fearful and *pessimistic* than those who get news from print media."

   With their continual fights, I am very *pessimistic* about their marriage surviving much longer.

   Pessimistic means _____

7. "News reports are increasingly *shallow* and one-sided, with little editing or fact checking."

   I think that she is a *shallow* person because her conversation is limited to discussions about hair and makeup.

   Shallow means _____

8. "A practice that further *erodes* the honesty and truthfulness of media coverage is the use of video news releases that masquerade as news stories."

   When government officials mislead the public, the public's trust in the government *erodes*.

   Erodes means _____

In Your Own Words

1. In a 2003 Gallup poll, 62 percent of the respondents stated that they believed news organizations are often inaccurate in their reporting. What factors do you think have led to the public's loss of confidence in the news media?

2. Do you primarily get your news from cable, local news channels, nightly network news, satirical comedy shows, the Internet, morning TV shows, or radio talk shows? Do you think the source of your news tends to be biased or slanted, or does it tend to be objective?

3. With the Internet, people can select only the news that interests them or that expresses views they already support. Do you think the ability to do this is going to encourage less tolerance and more polarization on the part of the public?

4. Do you think the nightly news has a liberal or a conservative bias? Give reasons for your view.

5. Do you think TV news programmers choose stories for their entertainment value or because they represent serious, important issues?

6. Do you think television has a vested interest in disasters? Does watching TV news make you feel like you are living in a world of perpetual crisis?

7. Media education is a mandatory part of the high school curriculum in Australia, Canada, and Great Britain. Do you think the United States should also make it a school requirement?

The Art of Writing

Keep track of the topics presented on a nightly newscast. Be sure to note how much time is devoted to discussions of crime, accidents, disasters, lifestyle stories, sports, weather, the environment, health care, science, education, art, and culture. How long does each segment last? What can you conclude about the information presented?

Internet Activity

Evaluate the following websites. What is the point of view of each? Do the websites reflect any biases?

Alliance for a Media Literate America:

www.nmec.org//medialit.html

Association for Media Literacy:

www.aml.ca

Media Alliance:

www.media-alliance.org

OUR HERITAGE: LEGAL AND POLITICAL

The next part of this chapter, on our legal and political heritage, includes excerpts from *John Adams* by David McCullough, *The Majesty of the Law* by Sandra Day O'Connor, and *American Art* by Wayne Craven. It also includes the Declaration of Independence and the Bill of Rights.

SELECTION

"There was no member of the Virginia delegation who did not own slaves, and of all members of Congress at least a third owned or had owned slaves."

GETTING THE PICTURE

Both John Adams, the second president, and Thomas Jefferson, the third president, died on the same day—the Fourth of July, 1826. Although both had wished to attend the fiftieth-anniversary celebration of the Declaration of Independence, neither was able to. Congress nevertheless paid tribute to both men, forever linking the two old "patriots"—Adams, the chief advocate of the Declaration, and Jefferson, its author. In his epitaph, Adams chose to say nothing of his political accomplishments, instead extolling the virtues of piety, humility, and industry. Jefferson wished to be remembered for his creative work. The inscription on his tombstone reads as follows:

Here Was Buried

THOMAS JEFFERSON

Author of the Declaration of American Independence,

Of the Statute of Virginia for Religious Freedom,

And Father of the University of Virginia

BIO-SKETCH

Historian David McCullough won the Pulitzer Prize for a biography of President Harry Truman in 1993 and again in 2001 for a biography of John Adams, our second president. He has said that the six years that it took him to write *John Adams* were the best years of his writing career.

BRUSHING UP ON VOCABULARY

redundant wordy or unnecessarily repetitious. Derived from the Latin *unda*, meaning "wave." When speakers or writers are wordy, they are said to have a *redundant* style because their "waves" of words go on and on, repeating themselves.

preamble an introductory statement; a preface. In Latin, *pre* means "before," and *ambular* means "to walk." The introductory portion of an essay or a speech is called a *preamble* because it comes first or "walks before."

mercenary a professional soldier hired to serve in a foreign army. The word can be traced back to the Latin *mercenarius*, meaning "one who works for wages." When Jefferson mentions "mercenaries" in the Declaration of Independence, he is referring to the Hessians who fought under the British flag in the Revolutionary War.

Excerpt from
John Adams
by David McCullough

JEFFERSON, ADAMS, AND THE DECLARATION OF INDEPENDENCE

1   Jefferson was to draft the declaration. But how this was agreed to was never made altogether clear. He and Adams would have differing explanations, each writing long after the fact.

2   According to Adams, Jefferson proposed that he, Adams, do the writing, but that he declined, telling Jefferson he must do it.

3   "Why?" Jefferson asked, as Adams would recount.

4   "Reasons enough," Adams said.

5   "What can be your reasons?"

6   "Reason first: you are a Virginian and a Virginian ought to appear at the head of this business. Reason two: I am obnoxious, suspected and unpopular. You are very much otherwise. Reason third: You can write ten times better than I can."

7   Jefferson would recall no such exchange. As Jefferson remembered, the committee simply met and unanimously chose him to undertake the draft. "I consented: I drew it [up]."

. . .

8   Congress had to review and approve the language of the drafted declaration before it could be made official. Deliberations commenced at once, continuing through the next morning, July 3, when mercifully the temperature had dropped ten degrees, broken by the storm of the previous day.

9   For Thomas Jefferson it became a painful ordeal, as change after change was called for and approximately a quarter of what he had written was cut entirely. Seated beside Benjamin Franklin, the young Virginian looked on in silence. He is not known to have uttered a word in protest, or in defense of what he had written. Later he would describe the opposition to his draft as being like "the ceaseless action of gravity weighing upon us night and day." At one point Franklin leaned over to tell him a story that, as a printer and publisher over so many years, he must have offered before as comfort to a wounded author. He had once known a hatter who wished to have a sign made saying, JOHN THOMPSON, HATTER, MAKES AND SELLS HATS FOR READY MONEY, this to be accompanied by a picture of a hat. But the man had chosen first to ask the opinion of friends, with the result that one word after another was removed as superfluous or redundant, until at last the sign was reduced to Thompson's name and the picture of the hat.

10   Beyond its stirring preamble, most of the document before Congress was taken up with a list of grievances, specific charges against the King—"He has

plundered our seas, ravaged our coasts, burnt our towns. He is at this time transporting large armies of foreign mercenaries to complete the works of death, desolation and Tyranny. . . ." And it was the King, "the Christian King of Great Britain," Jefferson had emphasized, who was responsible for the horrors of the slave trade. As emphatic a passage as any, this on the slave trade was to have been the ringing climax of all the charges. Now it was removed in its entirety because, said Jefferson later, South Carolina and Georgia objected. Some northern delegates, too, were a "little tender" on the subject, "for though their people have very few slaves themselves yet they had been pretty considerable carriers."

11   In truth black slavery had long since become an accepted part of life in all of the thirteen colonies. Of a total population in the colonies of nearly 2,500,000 people in 1776, approximately one in five were slaves, some 500,000 men, women, and children. In Virginia alone, which had the most slaves by far, they numbered more than 200,000. There was no member of the Virginia delegation who did not own slaves, and of all members of Congress at least a third owned or had owned slaves. The total of Thomas Jefferson's slaves in 1776, as near as can be determined from his personal records, was about 200, which was also the approximate number owned by George Washington.

. . .

12   In time Jefferson and Adams would each denounce slavery. Jefferson was to write of the degrading effects of the institution on both slave and master. Adams would call slavery a "foul contagion in the human character." But neither [they] nor any other delegate in Congress would have let the issue jeopardize a declaration of independence, however strong their feelings. If Adams was disappointed or downcast over the removal of Jefferson's indictment of the slave trade, he seems to have said nothing at the time. Nor is it possible to know the extent of Jefferson's disappointment or if the opposition of South Carolina and Georgia was truly as decisive as he later claimed. Very possibly there were many delegates, from North and South, happy to see the passage omitted for the reason that it was patently absurd to hold the King responsible for horrors that, everyone knew, Americans—and Christians no less than the King—had brought on themselves. Slavery and the slave trade were hardly the fault of George III, however ardently Jefferson wished to fix the blame on the distant monarch.

13   Of more than eighty changes made in Jefferson's draft during the time Congress deliberated, most were minor and served to improve it. But one final cut toward the conclusion was as substantial nearly as the excise of the passage on the slave trade, and it appears to have wounded Jefferson deeply.

14   To the long list of indictments against the King, he had added one assailing the English people, "our British brethren," as a further oppressor, for allowing their Parliament and their King "to send over not only soldiers of our common blood, but Scotch and foreign mercenaries to invade and destroy us." And therein, Jefferson charged, was the heart of the tragedy, the feeling of betrayal, the "common blood" cause of American outrage. "These facts have

given the last stab to agonizing affection, and manly spirit bids us renounce forever these unfeeling brethren," he had written. "We must endeavor to forget our former love for them."

15   This most emotional passage of all was too much for many in Congress, and to it Jefferson had added a final poignant note: "We might have been a free and great people together." Nearly all of this was removed. There was to be no mention of a "last stab," or "love," or of the "free and great people" that might have been.

16   Finally, to Jefferson's concluding line was added the phrase "with a firm reliance on the protection of divine Providence," an addition that John Adams assuredly welcomed. Thus it would read:

17   And for the support of this Declaration, with a firm reliance on the protection of divine Providence, we mutually pledge to each other our lives, our fortunes, and our sacred honor.

18   But it was to be the eloquent lines of the second paragraph of the Declaration that would stand down the years, affecting the human spirit as neither Jefferson nor anyone could have foreseen. And however much was owed to the writings of others, as Jefferson acknowledged, or to such editorial refinements as those contributed by Franklin or Adams, they were, when all was said and done, his lines. It was Jefferson who had written them for all time:

19   We hold these truths to be self-evident, that all men are created equal, that they are endowed by their Creator with certain unalienable rights, that among these are life, liberty, and the pursuit of happiness. That to secure these rights, governments are instituted among men, deriving their just powers from the consent of the governed.

· · ·

20   In old age, trying to reconstruct events of that crowded summer, both Thomas Jefferson and John Adams would incorrectly insist that the signing took place July 4.

21   Apparently there was no fuss or ceremony on August 2. The delegates simply came forward in turn and fixed their signatures. The fact that a signed document now existed, as well as the names of the signatories, was kept secret for the time being, as all were acutely aware that by taking up the pen and writing their names, they had committed treason. Whether Benjamin Franklin quipped "We must all hang together, or most assuredly we shall hang separately" is impossible to know, just as there is no way to confirm the much-repeated story that the diminutive John Hancock wrote his name large so the King might read it without his spectacles. But the stories endured because they were in character, like the remark attributed to Stephen Hopkins of Rhode Island. Hopkins, who suffered from palsy, is said to have observed, on completing his spidery signature, "My hand trembles, but my heart does not."

Source: "Jefferson, Adams, and the Declaration of Independence," reprinted with the permission of Simon & Schuster Adult Publishing Group from David McCullough, *John Adams,* pp. 119, 130–131, 134–136, 138. Copyright © 2001 by David McCullough.

COMPREHENSION CHECKUP

Multiple Choice

Write the letter of the correct answer in the blank provided; you may refer to the reading selection or to other sections of this book if necessary.

_____ 1. The mode of rhetoric in this selection is primarily
  a. narration
  b. description
  c. exposition
  d. persuasion

_____ 2. The overall pattern of organization is primarily
  a. cause and effect
  b. comparison-contrast
  c. example
  d. chronological order

_____ 3. In paragraph 1, Adams portrays himself as
  a. self-congratulatory
  b. defeated
  c. self-deprecatory
  d. gleeful

_C_ 4. In the debate over the wording of the Declaration, Jefferson
  a. became angry when changes were suggested
  b. was actively engaged in debating corrections
  c. remained silent
  d. fought vigorously for every word

_b_ 5. Jefferson was a proud representative of
  a. Delaware
  b. Virginia
  c. Massachusetts
  d. New York

_C_ 6. On his plantation, Jefferson   *200 slaves*
  a. hired only free men
  b. had only a few slaves
  c. had many slaves
  d. farmed with the aid of family members only

_C_ 7. The actual signing of the Declaration of Independence occurred on
  a. July 2
  b. July 4
  c. August 2
  d. December 26

_d_ 8. The state with the most recorded slaves was
  a. South Carolina
  b. Georgia
  c. Kentucky
  d. Virginia

_____ 9. Jefferson's Declaration
   a. listed grievances against the king
   b. defended the practice of slavery
   c. criticized the use of foreign mercenaries
   (d.) both a and c

_____ 10. In his original draft of the Declaration, in addition to his indictment of the king, Jefferson assailed
   (a.) the British people
   b. John Locke
   c. the Virginia delegation
   d. France

True or False

Indicate whether the statement is true or false by writing T or F in the blank provided.

__T__ 1. Washington and Jefferson owned a comparable number of slaves.

__T__ 2. By affixing their signatures to the Declaration, the delegates were committing an act of treason.

__F__ 3. John Hancock was large in stature.

__F__ 4. Approximately forty changes were made to Jefferson's Declaration.

__T__ 5. The most memorable lines in Jefferson's Declaration are contained in the second paragraph.

Vocabulary in Context

Cross out the incorrect word in each sentence, and write the correct word from the following list in the blank provided. (Use each word only once.)

ardent	desolate	eloquent	plundered
commence	diminutive	emphatic	poignant
denounced	downcast	excise	superfluous

__Commence__ 1. Once children turn 5 in the United States they usually ~~end~~ their formal schooling.

_____ 2. Santa's elves are known for their ~~large~~ size.

_____ 3. The audience applauded enthusiastically after the president delivered a stirring and ~~bland~~ speech.

_____ 4. He already had accumulated sufficient credits to graduate; any further credits were purely ~~essential~~.

_____ 5. After Carolyn ~~failed~~ her final exams, she was especially ecstatic.

_____ 6. In his closing argument, the prosecutor praised the defendant's heinous crime.

_____ 7. Mike professed his love to his sweetheart in a warm, loving, dispassionate manner.

_____ 8. When asked whether she wanted to be given a Lexus as her award, Carmen gave a very tentative nod "yes."

_____ 9. The grave-robbers protected the valuables in the tombs.

_____ 10. Conditions in the country were fertile after the drought destroyed the land.

_____ 11. The movie _Selena_, about the life of the late singer, was heartbreaking and unaffecting in places.

_____ 12. The surgeon's only recourse was to preserve the infected flesh after gangrene had set in.

In Your Own Words

1. The pursuit of happiness is one of the "unalienable rights" written into the Declaration. What do you think Jefferson meant by "the pursuit of happiness"? What do you think most Americans today require for a "happy life"?

2. Oscar Wilde once said, "In this world there are only two tragedies. One is not getting what one wants, and the other is getting it." What do you think he meant? Do you agree or disagree with him?

The Art of Writing

In a brief essay, respond to the item below.

Rabbi Harold Kushner says that an individual doesn't become happy by pursuing happiness. Instead, he says that "happiness is like a butterfly—the more you chase it, the more it flies away from you and hides. But stop chasing it, put away your net and busy yourself with other, more productive things than the pursuit of personal happiness, and it will sneak up on you from behind and perch on your shoulder." Explain Kushner's concept using examples from your own life.

Internet Activity

Visit the following website to learn more about John Adams.

http://www.whitehouse.gov/history/presidents

List several facts that were new to you and were not mentioned in the reading selection.

STUDY TECHNIQUE 9

Venn Diagrams

A Venn diagram is an illustration that shows similarities and differences between topics using a graphic of two overlapping circles. Notice the diagram below. In the circle on the left, characteristics specific only to Jefferson are listed; in the circle on the right, characteristics specific only to Adams are listed; in the overlapping area, characteristics shared by both Adams and Jefferson are listed.

Complete the Venn diagram comparing and contrasting Jefferson and Adams by listing more traits unique to each of these men and more traits they shared. Then write a paragraph comparing and contrasting the two men. You will find that it is much easier to write a comparison-contrast assignment after creating such a Venn diagram.

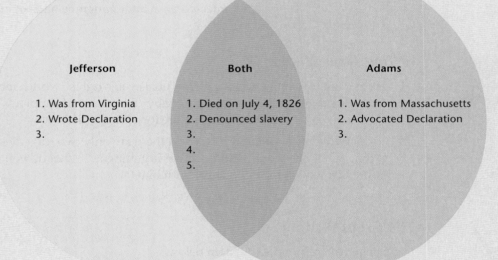

Jefferson

1. Was from Virginia
2. Wrote Declaration
3.

Both

1. Died on July 4, 1826
2. Denounced slavery
3.
4.
5.

Adams

1. Was from Massachusetts
2. Advocated Declaration
3.

INTRODUCTION TO DEDUCTIVE AND INDUCTIVE REASONING

Drawing Conclusions: Deductive and Inductive Reasoning

In the final step of analyzing a selection, the reader must evaluate the soundness of the author's reasoning. Often our evaluation is based on deductive or inductive reasoning.

Deductive Reasoning

The word *deduction* comes from the Latin *de*, meaning "from," and *duc*, meaning "to lead." In **deductive reasoning,** we move from a general principle and a specific example to reach a conclusion.

Here's an example of a deductive argument:

Major premise: All of Stephen King's books are enjoyable.

Minor premise: *From a Buick 8* is a book by Stephen King.

Conclusion: Therefore, *From a Buick 8* is enjoyable.

This deductive argument has two premises: First, the general principle (also called the *major premise*): "All of Stephen King's books are enjoyable." Second, the specific instance (or *minor premise*), "*From a Buick 8* is a book by Stephen King." Finally, it has a conclusion: "*From a Buick 8* is enjoyable." This type of deductive argument—with a major premise, a minor premise, and a conclusion—is called a **syllogism.** If both the major and minor premises are true, and the conclusion follows from the premises, then the conclusion must be true, and we have a *sound* argument. Since the conclusion follows from the premises, the argument is also *valid*.

Here's another example:

Major premise: If I have the flu, I won't feel good.

Minor premise: I feel good.

Conclusion: Therefore, I don't have the flu.

Again, we have both a major and a minor premise. If both of these premises are true, then the conclusion must be true because, again, the argument is valid.

Here's a third example:

Major premise: If I go to the store now, I'll miss the start of the basketball game on TV.

Minor premise: If I miss the start of the basketball game on TV, I'll be in a bad mood.

Conclusion: If I go to the store now, I'll be in a bad mood.

Again, if both premises are true, then the conclusion is also true, since it does follow from the two premises. (The argument is valid.)

But not all deductive arguments are valid. Look at this example:

Major premise: All of Stephen King's books are enjoyable.

Minor premise: The book I'm reading now is enjoyable.

Conclusion: Therefore, the book I'm reading now is a Stephen King book.

This argument is *invalid* because, while both premises may well be true, the conclusion does not follow from these premises. The book you're reading now might not be a Stephen King book. It might be an enjoyable book by another author.

Here's something else about deductive arguments: A deductive argument is sound only when both the premises are true. Let's go back to our second example:

Major premise: If I have the flu, I won't feel good.

Minor premise: I feel good.

Conclusion: Therefore, I don't have the flu.

What if this second premise is false. It says you feel good. But what if you really don't feel good. What if you really feel sick. If you don't really feel good, then you can't conclude that you don't have the flu. You very well might have the flu.

We can say this about deductive arguments: You can rely on the conclusion only if the argument is both sound and valid.

The next selection is the Declaration of Independence. The Declaration as a whole is considered a classic deductive argument. If pared down to its basic parts—major premise, minor premise, and conclusion—the syllogism would look like this:

Major premise: When a government becomes tyrannical in its treatment of its people, the people have a right to overthrow it and create a new government.

Minor premise: The government of Great Britain has become tyrannical in its treatment of Americans.

Conclusion: Therefore, Americans have a right to overthrow the British government and create a new government.

If these premises are true, then the conclusion must be true.

You can see that explaining deductive arguments can get complicated. What we have just said could only be called an introduction to deductive arguments. To learn more about them, you should take a course in logic.

Inductive Reasoning

Like *deduction,* the word *induction* comes from the Latin root *duc,* meaning "to lead," and *in,* meaning "into." In **inductive reasoning,** specific examples, evidence, or propositions lead to a more general conclusion.

Here's an example of inductive reasoning:

It's Wednesday, and you're trying to decide what restaurant to go to this weekend. You're thinking about three possibilities: Great Flavors, Hot and Spicy, and Healthy Stuff. So you start talking to your friends. Bill tells you that Great Flavors is all right, but nothing special. Tanya says that Hot and Spicy is too hot and spicy. Lisa says that she enjoyed Healthy Stuff. You talk to some other people too. They all tell you about the same thing. The food at Great Flavors is mediocre. Hot and Spicy goes overboard. And Healthy Stuff serves food that is nutritious *and* delicious. So you decide that you will probably have a good time at Healthy Stuff, and that's where you will go.

The argument here moves from specific information about three restaurants to a general conclusion about which restaurant would be most enjoyable.

As this example shows, a conclusion reached by inductive reasoning is only as sound as the quality of the information on which it is based. If the information on which you based your conclusion is bad, so will be your conclusion.

One problem with your conclusion might be that it was based on too little information. Perhaps you didn't ask enough people about your three restaurant options. Maybe if you had talked to more people, you would have started hearing negative opinions about Healthy Stuff. And maybe you would have started hearing positive opinions about Great Flavors or Hot and Spicy. From talking to more people, you might have reached a different conclusion. You might have concluded that you would likely have a good time at Hot and Spicy.

So inductive arguments lead to conclusions that are only *probably* true. You couldn't conclude from your survey that you would *certainly* have a good time at Healthy Stuff. You could only conclude that you would *probably* have a good time there. The better your information is, the more probable your conclusion will be true.

You can now see one important difference between deductive and inductive reasoning. Deductive reasoning produces conclusions that are either true or false. But inductive reasoning produces conclusions that are only probably true or false.

Exercise 2: Identifying Inductive and Deductive Arguments

Directions: After studying each example, indicate whether the argument is inductive or deductive by writing I or D in the blank provided. Be prepared to discuss whether the conclusion is valid or invalid.

_____ 1. The only passenger train running between Tucson and Los Angeles is operated by Amtrak. Wynona is taking a passenger train from Tucson to Los Angeles. So Wynona must be traveling on an Amtrak train.

_____ 2. I was at Mall of America this morning, and it was crowded with shoppers carrying shopping bags filled with recent purchases. So the economy must be doing well.

_____ 3. When I don't eat breakfast I start feeling weak around 10:30. I missed breakfast this morning, so I know I'm going to start feeling weak around 10:30.

_____ 4. Frida likes all kinds of jazz music. Marco gave Frida a jazz CD. Frida is going to like her new CD.

_____ 5. When the principal visited Lois Johnson's classroom, the children were running around the classroom talking and playing with each other, while Ms. Johnson yelled at them to take their seats and be quiet. The principal concluded that Ms. Johnson did not know how to maintain discipline.

_____ 6. Yomiko has noticed that many of the speakers at the seminars she attends are dull. Yomiko will be going to a seminar tomorrow. Yomiko expects that some of the speakers at the seminar will be dull.

DEDUCTIVE REASONING: AN EXAMPLE

SELECTION

GETTING THE PICTURE

The following is an annotated version of the Declaration of Independence. The annotations are based on information provided by Stephen E. Lucas, a professor of communication arts at the University of Wisconsin–Madison.

THE DECLARATION OF INDEPENDENCE
by THOMAS JEFFERSON

INTRODUCTION

A general statement

1   When in the course of human events, it becomes <u>necessary</u> for one people to dissolve the political bands which have connected them with another, and to assume among the Powers of the earth, the separate and equal station to which the Laws of Nature and Nature's God entitle them, a decent respect to the opinions of mankind requires that they should <u>declare the causes which impel them to the separation.</u>

Key word

Impersonal tone

Purpose stated

PREAMBLE

2   We hold these truths to be self-evident, that <u>all men are created equal</u>, that <u>they are endowed by their Creator with certain unalienable Rights</u>, that among <u>these are Life, Liberty and the pursuit of Happiness</u>.

Five propositions given

General philosophy of government

3   That <u>to secure these rights, Governments are instituted among Men</u>, deriving their just powers from the consent of the governed.

4   That <u>whenever any Form of Government becomes destructive of these ends, it is the Right of the People to alter or to abolish it</u>, and to institute a new Government laying its foundation on such principles and organizing its powers in such form, as to them shall seem most likely to effect their Safety and Happiness. Prudence, indeed, will dictate that Governments long established should not be changed for light and transient causes; and accordingly all experience hath shown that mankind are more disposed to suffer, while evils are sufferable, than to right themselves by abolishing the forms to which they are accustomed. But when a long train of abuses and usurpations pursuing invariably the same Object evinces a design to reduce them under absolute Despotism, it is their right, it is their duty, to throw off such government, and to provide new Guards for their future security.

Fifth is most crucial— asserts the right of revolution

5   Such has been the patient sufferance of these Colonies; and such is now the necessity which constrains them to alter their former Systems of Government. The history of the present King of Great Britain is a history of repeated injuries and usurpations, all having in direct object the establishment of an absolute Tyranny over these States. *To prove this, let Facts be submitted to a <u>candid</u> world.*

INDICTMENT OF GEORGE III

Four groups of facts listed

Proof : 28 grievances

Word <u>candid</u> implies an appeal to fair and unbiased

Group I charges 1–12: describe the abuse of king's executive power

6   He has <u>refused his Assent to Laws</u>, the most wholesome and necessary for the public good.

7   He has forbidden his Governors to pass Laws of immediate and pressing importance, unless <u>suspended in their operation</u> till his Assent should be obtained; and when so suspended, he has utterly neglected to attend to them. He has refused to pass other Laws for the accommodation of large districts of people, unless those people would relinquish the right of Representation in the Legislature, a right inestimable to them and formidable to tyrants only.

Charges are arranged by topics, not chronologically

8   He has called together legislative bodies at places unusual, uncomfortable, and distant from the depository of their public Records, for the sole purpose of fatiguing them into compliance with his measures.

Charges are purposely ambiguous: no names, dates, or places are identified

9   He has <u>dissolved Representative Houses repeatedly</u>, for opposing with manly firmness his invasions on the rights of the people.

10   He has refused for a long time, after such dissolutions, to cause others to be elected; whereby the Legislative powers, incapable of Annihilation, have returned to the People at large for their exercise, the State remaining in the mean time exposed to all the dangers of invasion from without, and convulsions within.

11   He has endeavoured to prevent the population of these States; for that purpose obstructing the Laws for Naturalization of Foreigners; refusing to pass others to encourage their migrations hither, and raising the conditions of new Appropriations of Lands.

12   He has <u>obstructed the Administration of Justice</u>, by refusing his Assent to Laws for establishing Judiciary powers.

13   He has made Judges dependent on his Will alone, for the tenure of their offices, and the amount and payment of their salaries.

14   He has erected a multitude of New Offices, and sent hither swarms of Officers to harass our People, and eat out their substance.

15   He has <u>kept among us, in times of peace, standing Armies</u> without the Consent of our legislatures.

16   He has affected to render the Military independent of and superior to the Civil power.

Group II charges 13–22: subjected America to unconstitutional measures

17   He has combined with others to subject us to a jurisdiction foreign to our constitution, and

unacknowledged by our laws; giving his Assent to their Acts of pretended Legislation:

18   For Quartering large bodies of armed troops among us:

19   For protecting them, by a mock Trial from punishment for any Murders which they should commit on the Inhabitants of these States:

20   <u>For cutting off our Trade with all parts of the world:</u>

21   <u>For imposing Taxes on us without our Consent:</u>

22   <u>For depriving us in many cases of the benefits of Trial by Jury</u>:

23   For transporting us beyond Seas to be tried for pretended offences:

24   For abolishing the free System of English Laws in a neighboring Province, establishing therein an Arbitrary government, and enlarging its Boundaries so as to render it at once an example and fit instrument for introducing the same absolute rule into these Colonies.

25   <u>For taking away our Charters</u>, abolishing our most valuable Laws, and altering fundamentally the Forms of our Governments:

26   For suspending our own Legislatures, and declaring themselves invested with power to legislate for us in all cases whatsoever.

Group III charges 23–27: the king is charged with violence and cruelty

27   He has abdicated Government here, by declaring us out of his Protection and waging War against us.

28   He has <u>plundered</u> our seas, <u>ravaged</u> our Coasts, <u>burnt</u> our towns, and <u>destroyed</u> the Lives of our people.

Emotionally charged verbs

29   He is at this time transporting large Armies of foreign Mercenaries to compleat the works of death, desolation and tyranny, already begun with circumstances of Cruelty & perfidy scarcely paralleled in the most barbarous ages, and totally unworthy of the Head of a civilized nation.

30   He has constrained our fellow Citizens taken Captive on the high Seas to bear Arms against their Country, to become the executioners of their friends and Brethren, or to fall themselves by their Hands.

31   He has excited domestic insurrections amongst us, and has endeavoured to bring on the inhabitants of our frontiers, merciless Indian savages, whose known rule of warfare, is an undistinguished destruction of all ages, sexes, and conditions.

Group IV final charge   32   In every stage of these Oppressions We have Petitioned for Redress in the most humble terms: <u>Our repeated Petitions have been answered only by repeated injury</u>. A Prince, whose character is thus marked by every act which may define a Tyrant, is unfit to be the ruler of a free people.

Colonies have appealed in vain

Denunciation of the British people   33   Nor have We been wanting in attentions to our British brethren. We have warned them from time to time of attempts by their legislature to extend an unwarrantable jurisdiction over us. We have re-minded them of the circumstances of our emigration and settlement here. We have appealed to their na-tive justice and magnanimity, and we have conjured them by the ties of our common kindred to disavow these usurpations, which would inevitably interrupt our connections and correspondence. <u>They too have been deaf to the voice</u> of Justice and of consanguin-ity. We must, therefore, acquiesce in the necessity, which denounces our Separation, and hold them, as we hold the rest of mankind, Enemies in War, in Peace Friends.

This section finishes the case for independence

Use of metaphor

Conclusion   34   We, therefore, the representatives of the united States of America, in General Congress, Assembled, appealing to the Supreme Judge of the world for the rectitude of our intentions, do, in the Name, and by Authority of the good People of these Colonies, sol-emnly publish and declare, That these United Colonies are, and of Right ought to be Free and Independent States; that they are absolved from all Allegiance to the British Crown, and that all political connection between them and the State of Great Britain, is and ought to be totally dissolved; and that as Free and Independent States, they have full Power to levy War, conclude Peace, contract Alliances, establish Com-merce, and to do all other Acts and Things which Independent States may of right do. And for the support of this Declaration, with a firm reliance on the protection of divine Providence, <u>we mutually pledge to each other our Lives, our</u> Fortunes and our sacred Honor.

Personal tone

A solemn vow from men of honor

Source: The Declaration of Independence. Annotation of the Declaration of Independence is based on information from Stephen E. Lucas, *The Stylistic Artistry of the Declaration of Independence,* 1989.

COMPREHENSION CHECKUP

Short Answer

In one or two sentences, answer the questions below.

1. In the very first sentence, Jefferson makes a claim that people are entitled by "the Laws of Nature and Nature's God" to separate and equal stations. What does this claim mean?

   _____

   _____

   _____

2. According to Jefferson's reasoning in paragraph 2, what truths does he claim are self-evident? What is meant by the term *self-evident?*

   _____

   _____

   _____

3. According to paragraph 3, what is the purpose of governments? From where do governments derive their power?

   _____

   _____

   _____

4. In paragraph 4, Jefferson responds to those who would throw off governments for "light and transient causes." What sort of cause does he say you need to "throw off governments"?

   _____

   _____

   _____

5. Jefferson hopes that a listing of specific acts of tyranny by George III will convince others that the American colonies are justified in separating themselves from England. List some factual evidence given by Jefferson to justify independence. What are the most serious complaints?

   _____

   _____

   _____

6. To whom is Jefferson addressing his Declaration?

   _____

   _____

   _____

7. What is Jefferson referring to in the next-to-the-last paragraph? Do you think the British Parliament accepted Jefferson's claim?

   _____

   _____

   _____

8. What does Jefferson announce in the last paragraph?

_____

_____

_____

9. Many reform movements have been inspired by Jefferson's Declaration. Do you think that Jefferson was aware that he was speaking to future generations?

_____

_____

_____

10. What is the overall tone of Jefferson's argument?

_____

_____

_____

Vocabulary Practice

From the following list, determine the antonym for each set of listed words.

abolish	despotism	endowed	prudence	solemnly
acquiesce	emigration	magnanimous	ravaged	transient

1. stingy; mean; petty; greedy   _____

2. preserved; guarded   _____

3. continuous; perpetual; everlasting   _____

4. foolishness; senselessness; rashness   _____

5. initiate; secure; support   _____

6. democracy; liberalism; liberty   _____

7. silly; jocularly   _____

8. immigration   _____

9. object; resist; dissent; refuse   _____

10. divested; deprived; forfeited   _____

In Your Own Words

The following painting is John Trumbull's *The Declaration of Independence*, which dates from 1818. It was commissioned by President James Madison to hang in the U.S. Capitol Rotunda in Washington, D.C. Trumbull, who fought in the Revolutionary War, also painted three other pictures illustrating the fight for American independence. In addition, he did a series of portraits of famous people from that period.

Study the composition of the painting. To portray the scene as realistically as possible, Trumbull consulted with Thomas Jefferson. All of the signers of the Declaration are present in the painting. The tallest figure, Jefferson, is handing a copy of the Declaration to John Hancock. To Jefferson's left is Benjamin Franklin, and to his right in the foreground is John Adams. What is the overall tone of the painting? What is the significance of the flags on the wall? Which figure is given the most importance?

The Declaration of Independence (1818) BY JOHN TRUMBULL

Architect of the Capitol

The Art of Writing

In a brief essay, respond to the items below.

1. The phrase "that all men are created equal" has caused considerable controversy. What do you think Jefferson meant by it? What is your interpretation of the phrase?

2. Do you think that the sort of rebellion advocated by Jefferson in the Declaration could ever be justified in today's world? In what circumstances?

Internet Activities

1. To learn more about Thomas Jefferson, go to

   www.monticello.org

   Click on "A Day in the Life of Jefferson" to follow Jefferson through a typical 24 hours during his retirement at Monticello. Then, to learn more about Jefferson's role in the Lewis and Clark Expedition, click on "Jefferson and the Expedition." Peruse this portion of the site to find a page of interest to you; print it and briefly summarize your findings.

2. To learn more about the Declaration of Independence and to view material from the collections of the Library of Congress, go to

   http://lcweb.loc.gov/exhibits/declara/declara1.html

   Click on either "Chronology of Events" or "Objects in the Exhibition." If you select the chronology, create a short time line of the events leading up to the signing of the Declaration. Or select an object in the current exhibition, and briefly describe it.

SELECTION

"The Bill of Rights was drafted intentionally in broad, sweeping terms, allowing meaning to be developed in response to changing times and current problems."

GETTING THE PICTURE

Opinion on the ratification of the U.S. Constitution was almost evenly divided between those who favored its passage and those who did not. Many were opposed because they feared that a strong federal government would usurp the power of the states and individual citizens. As a result, a compromise was reached: If the Constitution were approved, amendments would be added at a later date that would safeguard individual liberties. The ten amendments adopted later became the Bill of Rights.

BIO-SKETCH

Sandra Day O'Connor, the first woman justice on the U.S. Supreme Court, was appointed by President Ronald Reagan in 1981. Raised on a ranch in Arizona, she is the author, with her brother Alan, of the best-seller *Lazy B,* which describes her formative years. A graduate of Stanford University and Stanford University Law School, O'Connor, who graduated near the top of her class, initially could not find employment as a lawyer because of her sex. Instead, she was offered jobs as a legal secretary. In her book *The Majesty of the Law,* from which the following excerpt is taken, she discusses notable cases and reminisces about changes in the law since she first became an attorney and then a judge.

BRUSHING UP ON VOCABULARY

Federalists persons who favored a strong central government and the creation of a national bank. *The Federalist Papers* were a series of essays written primarily by Alexander Hamilton, James Madison, and John Jay to convince the voters of New York to adopt the Constitution.

Anti-Federalists persons who favored a weak central government and emphasized individual and states' rights. The Bill of Rights is considered a major accomplishment of the Anti-Federalists.

Excerpt from

The Majesty of the Law

by Sandra Day O'Connor

THE EVOLUTION OF THE BILL OF RIGHTS

1   The Bill of Rights is truly a remarkable document. Upon reading it, one cannot help but be struck by how concise it is. Countless thousands of pages have been written about it, but the Bill of Rights itself sums up our most precious

freedoms—more than two dozen fundamental rights—in fewer than five hundred words. And its brevity is not accidental. Before James Madison rose in Congress to read his first draft, he pored over hundreds of provisions suggested by various state ratifying conventions. He could have compiled them all into a lengthy document, but chose not to. He decided, quite deliberately, to single out only a handful of fundamental principles. His view was that enumerating additional rights of less significance would risk diminishing the document's importance. After all, a laundry list of lesser rights, such as the right to wear powdered wigs in public, would sit uneasily beside such fundamental liberties as freedom of speech and religion.

2   Madison was keenly conscious of the language he used in framing the Bill of Rights. The proposals offered by the various state conventions used tentative terms. An earlier state version of what became our Eighth Amendment provided that "excessive bail *ought not* to be required." Madison replaced the tentative terms with stronger ones, transforming suggestions into bold declarations. Thus, the Eighth Amendment declares in no uncertain terms that "excessive bail *shall not* be required." This kind of language does not *request* that the government afford the people certain freedoms; it *demands* it. It declares that they exist as a matter of natural law, and that the government has no authority to interfere with their exercise.

3   Likewise, the First Amendment does not *ask* the government to refrain from intervening in religious matters. It declares unflinchingly that "Congress *shall make no law* respecting an establishment of religion, or prohibiting the free exercise thereof." This strong language serves two purposes. It inspires and reassures those of us who hold the rights, and it warns any who would dare violate these rights that they may not do so.

4   The Bill of Rights is both simple and eloquent. The ten amendments are written in language that any literate American can understand and many can recite from memory. And at the same time that they are forcefully written, they are neither rigid nor inflexible. The Bill of Rights was drafted intentionally in broad, sweeping terms, allowing meaning to be developed in response to changing times and current problems. In many ways the Bill of Rights is like a novel by Faulkner or a painting by Monet: it does not change, but our understanding and perception of it may. Had the Bill of Rights been written in less broad terms, it might not have withstood the passage of time. The world today is a much different place than it was two centuries ago. We have different problems, different priorities, and different technologies than our ancestors had.

5   As a result, several of the amendments are as vital today—or more so—than when they were adopted. Consider the First Amendment's declaration that "Congress shall make no law . . . abridging the freedom of speech." In drafting this provision, the primary concern was to protect political speech: specifically, criticism of the government. In England, outspoken critics of the king had sometimes been labeled traitors and severely punished. It was thus of immense importance to the early Americans, in setting up their own government, to permit all kinds of political speech. More than two hundred years later, we

continue to value the importance of speech on political topics and afford it constitutional protection, no matter how controversial or despised its substance may be. Indeed, the First Amendment has been relied on to permit even neo-Nazis to march and speak in a city that included Holocaust survivors.

6   At the same time, the First Amendment has been invoked to protect speech on all sorts of topics far removed from politics—topics that its drafters could never have imagined. This has required the Supreme Court to grapple with a host of difficult issues. One case, for instance, questioned whether the First Amendment prohibits a high school principal from keeping stories about pregnancy and birth control out of the school paper. Another asked whether pharmacies must be permitted to advertise their prices for over-the-counter drugs. We have even had to decide whether New Hampshire residents who disagree with the state motto, "Live Free or Die," can use tape to cover that part of their license plates.

7   Nevertheless, the guarantee of "the freedom of speech" contained in the Bill of Rights is not absolute. The Court has held, for example, that obscene speech is not protected.

8   Further removed from the drafters' vision of the First Amendment are cases holding that the First Amendment protects conduct that conveys a particular message. Thus, the Court has ruled that a junior high school could not prohibit its students from wearing black armbands to protest the nation's involvement in the Vietnam War. And, more recently, the Court held that the First Amendment invalidates a statute criminalizing the burning of the American flag as a form of protest, although it does not invalidate a prohibition on nude dancing in public places.

9   Another constant and inexhaustible source of litigation has been the Fourth Amendment, which protects Americans against "unreasonable searches and seizures." This amendment was included in the Bill of Rights to outlaw in this country the much despised British practice of conducting unannounced house-to-house searches, pursuant to so-called writs of assistance.

10   But the Fourth Amendment has come to stand for much more. Technological advancements that Madison and his contemporaries could never have foreseen have made it possible for the government to conduct a search without ever entering a person's home. For example, wiretaps allow people's conversations to be monitored and recorded without their knowledge. The Court has held that to be a search. It has also determined that a search occurs when police officers use thermal imaging devices to "see" through walls. But this leads to further questions. Does it matter whether the technology is generally available to the public? How available is generally available? Do Fourth Amendment protections decrease as technology becomes even more advanced?

11   Questions like these are difficult, and no amount of study of James Madison's private notes will yield a conclusive answer.

12   Just as technology has made the Fourth Amendment a murkier area than our forebears could have suspected, biological science has complicated application of the Fifth Amendment. The Fifth Amendment guarantees that no one

"shall be compelled in any criminal case to be a witness against himself." We all know from watching TV police shows what the Fifth Amendment means: "You have the right to remain silent." The government cannot force you to testify against yourself if you are accused of a crime. The inspiration for this amendment can be traced all the way back to the Inquisition, where heretics were routinely tortured until they confessed their sins.

13   But today the government can often tell whether someone is guilty without an oral confession. It can test drivers' blood to see if they have been driving while intoxicated. Or it can analyze defendants' DNA structure to determine conclusively whether a single hair or body-fluid sample found at the scene of the crime belongs to them. The question for the Court has become whether the Fifth Amendment allows the government to compel the extraction and use of such evidence.

14   These amendments—the First, Fourth, and Fifth—were adopted in the infancy of our republic, but they remain a constant source of litigation, controversy—and inspiration—even in a new millennium. Time and technology have advanced, yet these provisions remain vital because our ancestors recognized the importance of framing our most basic rights in broad terms.

15   On the other hand, other of the amendments are little remembered today. Cited very rarely is the Third Amendment, which declares: "No soldier shall, in time of peace be quartered in any house, without the consent of the Owner, nor in time of war, but in a manner to be prescribed by law." This had been a very real problem in eighteenth-century England. Soldiers were put in people's homes, and the home-owner was made responsible for providing room and board. But this has never been a policy in our country. While the government may, in times of war, take young people out of their homes and draft them into the military, it rarely tries to put soldiers *into* people's houses.

16   There are two other amendments that do not enumerate any specific freedoms, but which were nonetheless of vital significance to those who drafted the Bill of Rights. They are the Ninth and Tenth Amendments.

17   The Ninth Amendment provides that the rights enumerated in the Bill of Rights are not the *only* rights possessed by the people. Probably the most famous example of an unenumerated right is the right to privacy. In *Griswold* v. *Connecticut,* the Court held that the Constitution protects a right of privacy, including the right of married couples to use contraceptives. The nature and description of unenumerated rights, and the extent to which they are subject to the highest level of judicial scrutiny, is hotly debated. But there is little doubt that some such rights do exist. And there is little doubt that we will see more litigation to test and define them.

18   The Tenth Amendment sets out in a single sentence the Anti-Federalists' main concern about the Constitution: that the new government not be permitted to usurp the sovereign authority of state governments: "The powers not delegated to the United States by the Constitution, nor prohibited by it to the States, are reserved to the States respectively, or to the people." The amendment makes clear that the power of the federal government is derived from the states, and that the Constitution is not construed to convey any more power to the

government than is absolutely necessary to carry out its enumerated functions. All other power belongs to the states.

19   This understanding is consistent with the sentiments of the Anti-Federalists, who recognized that state legislatures were closer to the people than the new national government and more accurately reflected the people's wishes. It is also consistent with the sentiments of the Federalists, who, while desiring a strong central government, wanted to preserve strong state governments to prevent the federal government from abusing its power.

20   Of course the Ninth and Tenth Amendments are not often relied upon by litigants. Like the Third Amendment, they have been largely ignored, at least for the time being. But this does not mean that they will not become more vital in the future. One would think that, after two centuries, we would have figured it all out. But we have not. More than two hundred years after the Bill of Rights was adopted, courts still grapple with many of the same questions. Thus, even though the First Amendment's freedom of speech clause and the Fourth Amendment's prohibition of unlawful searches have been subjects of litigation since the Framer's days, we their descendants are still working out the details.

21   And new questions are always being raised—questions that no one could have foreseen in our nation's earliest years. That is the beauty of the Bill of Rights. Along with the new questions come new understandings of what the amendments mean. For while the text of the Bill of Rights does not change, our perspective on it has evolved with the passage of time. The adoption of the Bill of Rights deserves our praise and thanksgiving. It is part of our American contribution to the notion of freedom and justice.

✔ COMPREHENSION CHECKUP

Multiple Choice

Write the letter of the correct answer in the blank provided.

_____ 1. The author's main idea is that
   a. some amendments in the Bill of Rights are no longer as relevant today as they were in earlier times
   b. the Bill of Rights is a remarkable document deserving of our praise and thanksgiving
   c. the Fourth Amendment has a broader meaning today than when it was originally adopted

_____ 2. The author's purpose and mode of writing is
   a. purpose in writing: to entertain; mode of writing: narrative
   b. purpose in writing: to inform; mode of writing: expository
   c. purpose in writing: to entertain; mode of writing: persuasive

_____ 3. The author's tone is
   a. angry
   b. indifferent
   c. instructive

_____ 4. The reader can logically infer that the author
   a. values the forcefulness of the Bill of Rights
   b. values the flexibility of the Bill of Rights
   c. both of the above

_____ 5. Who is the author's intended audience?
   a. high school and college students
   b. the general public
   c. teachers and other educators

_____ 6. The title of the selection implies that
   a. several amendments are just as vital today as they were in
      the past
   b. the Third Amendment will become more vital in the future
   c. while the wording of the Bill of Rights remains the same, its mean-
      ing has changed over time

_____ 7. The words *simple, eloquent,* and *remarkable* in reference to the Bill of
      Rights have a
   a. positive connotation
   b. negative connotation
   c. neutral meaning

_____ 8. As used in paragraph 2, *tentative* most nearly means
   a. experimental
   b. temporary
   c. weak

_____ 9. Complete the following analogy: ought not : shall not : : request :
      _____ (paragraph 2)
   a. demand
   b. gift
   c. ask

_____ 10. In paragraph 4, the author compares the Bill of Rights to a painting by
      Monet, implying that
   a. the Bill of Rights is a beautiful document
   b. the Bill of Rights is subject to varying interpretations
   c. the writing of the Bill of Rights was painstaking

_____ 11. In paragraph 15, the transition phrase *on the other hand* indicates
   a. cause and effect
   b. contrast
   c. comparison

_____ 12. Which of the following does the excerpt support as true?
   a. The Supreme Court grapples with difficult issues that could not
      have been foreseen by the framers.
   b. Advances in technology have had little effect on the justices' inter-
      pretation of the Bill of Rights.
   c. Unenumerated rights are those that the Supreme Court views as
      having little importance.

———— 13. Which of the following statements from the selection represents a fact rather than an opinion?
  a. "Questions like these are difficult, and no amount of study of James Madison's private notes will yield a conclusive answer."
  b. "The Bill of Rights is both simple and eloquent."
  c. "Indeed, the First Amendment has been relied on to permit even neo-Nazis to march and speak in a city that included Holocaust survivors."
  d. "One would think that, after two centuries, we would have figured it all out."

———— 14. Which of the following statements is correct?
  a. The Ninth Amendment provides that citizens have more rights than those specified in the first eight amendments.
  b. Unlike the first eight amendments, the Ninth and Tenth Amendments do not identify specific rights.
  c. The Tenth Amendment places limits on the powers of the federal government.
  d. All of the above.

In Your Own Words

1. In your opinion, which is the most important amendment to the Constitution? Give reasons for your choice.

2. How important is it for people to be aware of the Bill of Rights? Do you think those who apply to be U.S. citizens should have to demonstrate real understanding of the Constitution and the Bill of Rights?

3. What is it about the Bill of Rights that has made it such an enduring document? What is it about the document that makes it so difficult to emulate by other emerging democracies?

The Art of Writing

In a brief essay, respond to the item below.

Discuss some of the ways the Bill of Rights protects people who are wrongfully accused of a crime.

Internet Activity

The texts of opinions and transcripts of oral arguments appear on the Supreme Court's website at

www.supremecourtus.gov

Visit the site, choose an opinion of interest to you, and summarize it briefly.

THE BILL OF RIGHTS

Articles in Addition to, and Amendment of, the Constitution of the United States of America, Proposed by Congress, and Ratified by the Legislatures of the Several States, Pursuant to the Fifth Article of the Original Constitution.

AMENDMENT I

Congress shall make no law respecting an establishment of religion, or prohibiting the free exercise thereof; or abridging the freedom of speech, or of the press; or the right of the people peaceably to assemble, and to petition the Government for a redress of grievances.

AMENDMENT II

A well-regulated Militia, being necessary to the security of a free State, the right of the people to keep and bear Arms, shall not be infringed.

AMENDMENT III

No soldier shall, in time of peace be quartered in any house, without the consent of the Owner, nor in time of war, but in a manner to be prescribed by law.

AMENDMENT IV

The right of the people to be secure in their persons, houses, papers, and effects, against unreasonable searches and seizures, shall not be violated, and no Warrants shall issue, but upon probable cause, supported by Oath or affirmation, and particularly describing the place to be searched, and the persons or things to be seized.

AMENDMENT V

No person shall be held to answer for a capital, or otherwise infamous crime, unless on a presentment or indictment of a Grand Jury, except in cases arising in the land or naval forces, or in the Militia, when in actual service in time of War or public danger; nor shall any person be subject for the same offence to be twice put in jeopardy of life or limb; nor shall be compelled in any criminal case to be a witness against himself; nor be deprived of life, liberty, or property, without due process of law; nor shall private property be taken for public use, without just compensation.

AMENDMENT VI

In all criminal prosecutions, the accused shall enjoy the right to a speedy and public trial, by an impartial jury of the State and district wherein the crime shall have been committed, which district shall have been previously ascertained by law, and to be informed of the nature and cause of the accusation; to be confronted with the witnesses against him; to have compulsory process for obtaining witnesses in his favor, and to have the Assistance of Counsel for his defence.

AMENDMENT VII

In Suits at common law, where the value in controversy shall exceed twenty dollars, the right of trial by jury shall be preserved, and no fact tried by a jury, shall be otherwise reexamined in any Court of the United States, than according to the rules of the common law.

AMENDMENT VIII

Excessive bail shall not be required, nor excessive fines imposed, nor cruel and unusual punishments inflicted.

AMENDMENT IX

The enumeration in the Constitution, of certain rights, shall not be construed to deny or disparage others retained by the people.

AMENDMENT X

The powers not delegated to the United States by the Constitution, nor prohibited by it to the States, are reserved to the States respectively, or to the people.

 COMPREHENSION CHECKUP

Fill in the Blank

Identify the correct amendment and fill in the blank provided.

1. Lt. Col. Oliver North frequently cited the _____ Amendment privilege against self-incrimination when he refused to testify about the Iran-Contra scandal.

2. Rap artist Snoop Dogg (real name: Calvin Broadus) believes his lyrics are constitutionally protected by the _____ Amendment.

3. Today's debate over handgun control is based on the _____ Amendment.

4. The constant noise and glare of military planes at an airport interfered with the normal use of adjoining land as a chicken farm. The owner protested and was awarded just compensation because of the _____ Amendment.

5. A Jehovah's Witness feels his child is not required to salute the flag at school because of the _____ Amendment.

6. The _____ Amendment exists to answer the objections of those who thought that naming some rights but not all results in the government's claiming the power to prevent a person from "lying on his left side on a long winter's night."

7. Bail of $200,000 for a person who has robbed a store is prohibited under the _____ Amendment.

8. The Supreme Court let stand a Georgia decision that bans organized prayers before public school football games because of the _____ Amendment.

9. Under the _____ Amendment, a confession cannot be considered voluntary unless preceded by proper warnings (Miranda).

10. Because of Amendment _____, the national government can't place a soldier in a private citizen's home to live without the owner's permission (during peacetime).

11. Because of Amendment _____, a person cannot be made to wait years with a charge hanging over his or her head.

12. In 1971, the federal government sought to prohibit *The New York Times* from publishing the "Pentagon Papers." However, the Supreme Court ruled that such a prohibition was a violation under the _____ Amendment.

Vocabulary in Context

Complete each of the following by selecting the two words that make the best sense in the passage as a whole.

ascertained	compensation	disparage	grievances
impartial	infamous	infringed	redress

1. It was cruel of you to _____ me for attempting to get just _____ from my employer. After all, I deserve some money because it's against the law to fire people because of their age.

2. Sue _____ the facts about the _____ outlaw by searching through old newspapers and magazines.

3. You _____ on my right to breathe clean air when you smoked in our office. We have to share the same workspace, and we need to compromise. We need to find someone _____ to help us settle this dispute.

4. Annoyed by random locker searches, the students at Central High petitioned the school board for a _____ of their _____.

In Your Own Words

1. Why do you think these particular rights were considered important by the framers of the Constitution? If you were to write a contemporary Bill of Rights, what other rights would you include?

2. Phrases such as "due process of law" and "cruel and unusual punishment" are always open to interpretation. What are the advantages of such abstract language? Would more specific language have been better? Why or why not?

The Art of Writing

In a brief essay, respond to one of the items below.

1. Rewrite the Bill of Rights in modern, colloquial English, and illustrate each with a relevant example.

2. The Second Amendment is complicated and open to multiple interpretations. Do you think this amendment grants today's citizens the right to own guns? Or does it only grant them the right to carry guns in militias?

Internet Activity

Visit the Constitution Center website at

www.constitutioncenter.org

You can take a tour of the museum, review Supreme Court cases, or explore the Constitution and the Bill of Rights.

SELECTION

"Peale failed to create a truly grand state-type portrait . . ."

GETTING THE PICTURE

Most of us are accustomed to seeing George Washington on the dollar bill, but what did George Washington really look like? At Arizona State University, digital images were created using a plaster mask and bust of Washington made by French sculptor Jean Antoine Houdon when the president was 53. Computers then adjusted the digital images to represent key ages in his life. The new images, considered the most realistic to date, are available at Washington's Mount Vernon home. And the researchers concluded that he looks nothing like the Gilbert Stuart image on the dollar bill.

BIO-SKETCH

Wayne Craven, a leading historian of American sculpture, is professor emeritus of art history at the University of Delaware. He has written about American art from the Colonial period to the present time. His books include *Colonial American Portraiture*, *Sculpture in America,* and *American Art*, the textbook from which this excerpt is taken. He currently serves on the editorial board of the Smithsonian in American art.

BRUSHING UP ON VOCABULARY

Hessians German soldiers in the service of King George III of Great Britain during the Revolutionary War. The Hessians numbered about 30,000. On the night of December 25, 1776, General George Washington led his army across the Delaware River at Trenton, New Jersey, and surprised and defeated them.

Excerpt from
AMERICAN ART

by Wayne Craven

George Washington Paintings

1   As a young man, Charles Willson Peale (1741–1827) had been a clocksmith, silversmith, and saddler in Annapolis before deciding to become a portrait painter in the mid-1760s. In fact, he traded a newly made saddle for some lessons in painting.

2   Peale moved to Philadelphia just before the outbreak of the Revolutionary War, in which he served as an officer of the Continental Army, part of the time with General George Washington. The military and political struggles produced something the colonists had few of—American heroes. Late in 1778, Congress, meeting in Philadelphia, summoned its commander-in-chief for strategic planning sessions. During that period, Peale was commissioned by the Executive Council of Pennsylvania to paint a large portrait of the greatest American hero of all.

3   The full-length portrait was meant to glorify George Washington and incite patriotic pride and fervor in the breast of all who saw it. Peale made studies of the battlefields of Trenton and Princeton, where Washington had inflicted stinging defeats upon the British troops and captured over a thousand Hessians. The artist

made specific reference to the battle of Princeton in the background of his portrait by including Princeton College's Nassau Hall on the horizon. Hessian flags are conspicuous among the trophies of war that surround the general.

"A work of art cannot be satisfied with being a representation; it should be a presentation."

—Jacques Reverdy

4   Despite the opportunity his subject offered, Peale failed to create a truly grand state-type portrait—no American painter yet had experience in making such an heroic image. The military accouterments notwithstanding, Peale's *Washington* does not achieve the heroic grandeur and dignity usually associated with the great man. George Washington was a tall man, to be sure, but Peale's tendency to attenuate the human figure, and the small size of Washington's head, cause him to appear gangly and lacking in refined proportions. Moreover, the pose in which he placed Washington is so casual, even awkward, that it precludes any feeling of greatness or of a dramatic moment. Even the face of Washington is unheroic. Be they commander-in-chief or merchant, Peale was incapable of idealizing his subjects—this produced an accurate likeness, but not an heroic ideal. Peale's *Washington* gives us a truthful representation of our first national hero, but tells us of his greatness through the collection of objects that surround him, rather than through the man himself.

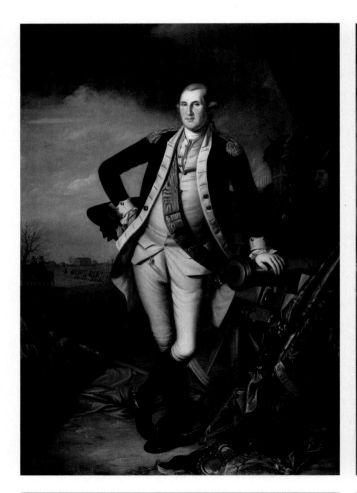

General George Washington before Princeton, (1779) CHARLES WILLSON PEALE

Photo: Gérard Blot. Réunion des Musées Nationaux/Art Resource, NY. Chateaux de Versailles et de Trianon, Versailles, France.

George Washington (The Lansdowne Portrait) (1796) GILBERT STUART

Acquired as a gift to the nation through the generosity of the Donald W. Reynolds Foundation. Photo Credit: National Portrait Gallery, Smithsonian Institution/Art Resource, NY.

5   Another extraordinary talent was Gilbert Stuart (1755–1828), who was born and grew up in Rhode Island. Realizing the need for training that was unavailable in America, Stuart embarked in 1777 for London, where he spent several destitute years before the well-known artist Benjamin West learned of his plight and took him into his own studio. Stuart quickly mastered the style of portrait painting and left West to set up his own studio, which became one of the most successful in London.

6   Stuart liked painting portraits because they could be completed quickly, and they were lucrative. By then he had developed a taste for elegant high living and was always in need of money. Despite numerous commissions, Stuart's extravagant lifestyle carried him ever deeper into debt, until his only recourse was flight to Ireland. There he worked from 1787 to 1792, achieving considerable success and acclaim, but again accruing such debts that it was once more necessary to flee or go to prison—and so he returned to America in 1793.

7   There, his portraits brought Stuart all the work he could handle, but ambitious to establish a practice among the new governmental leadership of the young republic, he moved to Philadelphia in 1794.

8   Stuart's first portrait of Washington was painted in Philadelphia in the Spring of 1795. It shows the subject, extremely sober and aloof, turned obliquely to the viewer's right. Dissatisfied, Stuart sought another sitting from the president in 1796. The result was the creation of two portraits that have ever since been the accepted image of the great man. The bust-length (Athenaeum) portrait shows the head turned to our left. The original unfinished portrait, now owned by the National Portrait Gallery, Stuart kept in his studio throughout his life, and from it produced well over one hundred replicas.

"A work of art is an exaggeration."

—André Gide

9   The third portrait (Lansdowne) is a full-length state portrait for which Stuart used the bust image (Athenaeum) for painting the head. Here, finally, was a portrait of Washington that equaled the adulation and hero-worship that had by then enveloped him. In fact, Stuart's image of Washington has often been criticized, beginning with Martha Washington, for not capturing an accurate likeness of the man. What it did capture, however, was an image that expressed what admirers over the centuries wished to think him—dignified, solemn, and stately, a statesman of international stature. Although Peale's may present a more accurate likeness, Stuart's portrait surpasses Peale's image in its idealization.

Source: "George Washington Paintings" from Wayne Craven, *American Art,* pp. 104, 107, 141, 143. Copyright © 2003 McGraw-Hill Companies, Inc. Used with permission.

✓ COMPREHENSION CHECKUP

Multiple Choice

Write the letter of the correct answer in the space provided.

    1. Charles Peale's painting of George Washington was criticized for all of the following reasons *except*
        a. Washington was portrayed too realistically
        b. Washington's head was too small for his body
        c. Washington was made to look too heroic
        d. Washington's pose was too casual

_____ 2. Gilbert Stuart moved from England to Ireland and then back to America because
     a. he did not earn much money from his portrait painting
     b. he had to flee from his debts
     c. he failed to complete paintings for which he had received money
     d. his wife was spending too much money

_____ 3. Stuart painted _____ portraits of Washington.
     a. one
     b. two
     c. three
     d. four

_____ 4. Martha Washington wanted Stuart to paint a
     a. more realistic portrait of Washington
     b. more heroic-looking painting
     c. more dignified and stately painting
     d. portrait that future admirers would accept

_____ 5. Peale practiced all of the following vocations *except*
     a. artist
     b. army officer
     c. musician
     d. silversmith

True or False

Indicate whether the statement is true or false by writing T or F in the space provided.

__F__ 6. Peale studied under the artist Benjamin West.

__T__ 7. Both Peale and Stuart painted full-length portraits of Washington.

__F__ 8. Stuart moved to Washington, D.C., to be closer to governmental leaders.

__F__ 9. Peale was well known for idealizing his subjects.

__T__ 10. Peale placed a building from Princeton College in the background of his painting of Washington.

Vocabulary in Context

In the paragraphs indicated, find a word that matches the definition given, and write the word in the space provided.

1. to extol; to honor with praise (paragraph 3) _glorify_
2. easily seen or noticed; readily observable (3) _conspicuous_
3. equipment of a soldier (4) _accouterments_
4. to make thin or slender (4) _attenuate_
5. makes impossible; prevents (4) _precludes_
6. lacking food, clothing, and shelter (5) _destitute_
7. distressing condition or situation (5) _plight_
8. profitable; money-making (6) _lucrative_
9. spending more than is necessary or wise (6) _extravagant_
10. serious; solemn (8) _sober_

11. reserved; reticent (8) _____Aloof_____

12. excessive admiration (9) _____Adulation_____

13. surrounded (9) _____Enveloped_____

Vocabulary Practice

Use each of the following words in a sentence. You may change or add endings. The paragraph number in parentheses tells you where the word is located in the story.

1. summoned (paragraph 2) _____

_____

2. incite (3) _____

_____

3. embarked (5) _____

_____

4. elegant (6) _____

_____

5. surpasses (9) _____

_____

In Your Own Words

Take this short true or false quiz (courtesy of the George Washington Mount Vernon Estate) to see how much you know. Circle T for true and F for false. Answers are at the end of the section.

George Washington

T F   1. Chopped down a cherry tree.

T F   2. Had wooden teeth.

T F   3. Once threw a silver dollar across the Potomac River.

T F   4. Was the first president to live in the White House.

T F   5. Wore a wig.

T F   6. Had two children with his wife, Martha.

T F   7. Was born on February 11, 1732.

T F   8. Attended college.

T F   9. Was the first man to sign the U.S. Constitution.

T F 10. Introduced the mule to America.

T F 11. Declined the opportunity to be king.

Paraphrasing

Paraphrase the following quotations. When you are finished, check to make sure the meaning of both statements is the same.

George Washington's "Rules of Civility and Decent Behavior in Company and Conversation"

1. Every action done in company ought to be done with some sign of respect to those that are present.

    _____

2. Show nothing to your friend that may affright him.

    _____

3. Show not yourself glad at the misfortune of another, even though he were your enemy.

    _____

4. Be not hasty to believe flying reports to the disparagement of anyone.

    _____

5. Play not the peacock, looking everywhere about you to see if you be well decked, if your shoes fit well, if your stockings set neatly and clothes handsomely.

    _____

6. Associate yourself with men of quality if you esteem your own reputation, for it is better to be alone than in bad company.

    _____

    _____

7. Be not apt to relate news if you know not the truth thereof.

    _____

8. Be not curious to know the affairs of others.

    _____

9. Undertake not what you cannot perform; but be careful to keep your promise.

    _____

10. Speak no evil of the absent, for it is unjust.

    _____

Internet Activity

Take a virtual tour of Mount Vernon at

www.mountvernon.org

Write a paragraph describing an object you found interesting or something new you learned about George Washington.

Answers to George Washington Quiz

1. False. The story about Washington chopping down a cherry tree seems to have been invented shortly after his death in 1799.

2. False. He had false teeth, but not wooden ones. They fit poorly, which may be one reason why Washington never smiled in portraits.

3. False. The Potomac River is more than a mile wide.

4. False. He is the only U.S. president who didn't live in the White House. It was completed after his presidency.

5. False. Washington kept his own hair, wearing it long and tied in a ponytail in the back. He powdered his hair, as was the custom of the day.

6. False. George Washington had no biological children. Martha was a widow with two young children when they married.

7. True. He was born February 11, but he celebrated his birthday on February 22.

8. False. The death of his father brought an end to his formal schooling.

9. True.

10. True. He introduced mules to America in the 1780s.

11. True.

TEST-TAKING TIP

Key Words That Often Appear in Essay Questions

Following is a list of key words that often appear in essay questions. If you are going to write a good answer to an essay question that uses one of these terms, you need to know what the term means.

analyze
to break down the subject into parts and discuss each part. You will discuss how the parts relate to each other.

comment on
to discuss or explain.

compare
to show differences and similarities, but with the emphasis on similarities.

contrast
to show differences and similarities, but with the emphasis on differences.

criticize
The narrow meaning of *criticize* is to examine something for its weaknesses, limitations, or failings. Does the theory, article, or opinion make sense? If not, why not? In a more general sense, criticize means to find both strengths and weaknesses. In this sense, the meaning of *criticize* is similar to the meaning of *evaluate*.

define
to state the meaning of a term, theory, or concept. You will want to place the subject in a category and explain what makes it different from other subjects in the category.

describe
to explain what something is or how it appears. You will need to draw a picture with words.

diagram
to make a chart, drawing, or graph. You will also want to label the categories or elements, and maybe provide a brief explanation.

discuss
to go over something fully. You will want to cover the main points, give different perspectives, and discuss strengths and weaknesses.

enumerate
to make a list of main ideas by numbering them.

evaluate
to examine for strengths and weaknesses. You will need to give specific evidence and may wish to cite authorities to support your position.

VOCABULARY   Unit 8

This unit begins with the word parts *-ology, geo-, helio-,* and *terr-;* moves on to *path-, ten-* or *tin-, fid-* and *cred-,* and *tact-* and *tang-;* and concludes with *-ject* and *locut-.*

logy—study or science of

astronomy	*astro-* means "pertaining to the stars," so *astronomy* is the science that studies such things as the origins, composition, and motions of the stars and planets.
astrology	the study that assumes and attempts to interpret the influence of the heavenly bodies on human affairs. Horoscopes are based on *astrology.*
seismology	the science and study of earthquakes.
sociology	the science or study of the origin, development, organization, and functioning of human society.
anthropology	*anthro-* means "man," so *anthropology* is the science that studies human beings, especially their origin, development, division, and customs.
paleontology	*paleo-* means "old," so *paleontology* is the science of the forms of life existing in past geological periods.

geo—earth; helio—sun; terr—earth, land

geology	the science that deals with the dynamics and physical history of the earth. A *geologist* studies the earth's crust and the way in which its layers were formed.
geography	the study of the surface of the earth, its division into continents and countries, and the climate, natural resources, and inhabitants of the regions.
geocentric	having or representing the earth as the center, as in the *geocentric* theory of the universe.
heliocentric	having or representing the sun as the center of the universe.
apogee	*apo-* means "off" or "away," so the *apogee* is the point in the orbit of the moon at which it is farthest from the earth; the highest point or most exalted point. Is Tiger Woods at the *apogee* of professional golf?
perigee	*Peri* means "near," so the *perigee* is the point in the orbit of the moon at which it is nearest to the earth; the lowest point.
territory	any large stretch of land or region.
terrain	a tract of land with reference to its natural features or military advantages. He purchased a home with five acres of hilly *terrain.*
terra firma	Latin for firm or solid earth. After the long ocean voyage, Shawn was grateful to be back on *terra firma.*
terrestrial	pertaining to, consisting of, or representing the earth. Coyotes are *terrestrial* animals.

path(o), pathy—feeling, suffering, emotion

antipathy	an aversion; a strong feeling against. Although Adella liked animals, she had a real *antipathy* toward cats.
apathy	lack of strong feeling, interest, or concern. Because of public *apathy*, no real reform was likely to occur.
pathos	the quality in life or art of evoking a feeling of pity or compassion. As the heroine lay dying, the musical score turned to *pathos*.
pathetic	causing or evoking pity either sympathetically or contemptibly. The fireman was haunted by the victim's *pathetic* cries for help.
pathological	characterized by an unhealthy compulsion; habitual; concerned with diseases. Unfortunately, you cannot trust her word because she is a *pathological* liar.

ten(t), tin—hold, cling, keep

tenacious	gripping firmly; holding fast. Despite their separation, he cannot rid himself of his wife; she has a *tenacious* hold on his feelings.
retentive	able to hold, keep, remember. Calla has an extremely *retentive* mind for facts and figures.
tenure	the length of time something is held; the status of holding a job permanently. Professors work hard to achieve *tenure*.
detention	being held back; forced delay or confinement. Because of Mike's behavior, he has a *detention* every day this week.
tenant	a person who pays rent to use land; to hold, occupy, or dwell in.
pertinent	relevant; holding to the point. Don't bother me with trivial details; I only want the *pertinent* information.

fid—faith(ful); cred—believe

fidelity	loyalty. The subjects pledged *fidelity* to their new king.
infidel	a person who does not believe in a particular religion; an unbeliever; a person who disbelieves a particular theory or belief.
confident	sure, certain, assured; a strong belief in oneself. Nina was utterly *confident* she would pass the bar exam and become a lawyer.
diffident	lacking faith in one's own ability, worth, or fitness; timid, shy.
credulous	willing to believe things even without proof; easily convinced. It is easy to play tricks on Charlotte; she is so *credulous* that she'll believe anything.
incredulous	not willing or able to believe; doubtful. Mona gave Sam an *incredulous* look when she found out he'd won the lottery.

tact, tang—touch

intangible	not able to be touched or grasped; vague, elusive. He has many fine *intangible* qualities like compassion and forthrightness.
tactile	perceptible to the touch.
intact	untouched; remaining sound or whole. When Juan found his wallet, it was still *intact* and held all of his credit cards and money.

ject—throw

dejected	to depress the spirits. The literal meaning of *deject* is "to throw down."
eject	to drive or force out; to throw out.
inject	The literal meaning of *inject* is "to throw in." She *injected* some humor into a dreary situation.
interject	*Inter* means "between," so an *interjection* is a remark "thrown into" a conversation, often abruptly. To interject means "to interrupt."
project	to throw forward; to predict; to cause to be heard clearly. The teacher easily *projected* her voice so that those sitting in the back of the class had no trouble hearing.

locut (loqu)—speak, talk

eloquent	graceful and forceful in speech. *e-* means "out," and *loqu-* means "speak," so the literal meaning is to "speak out." At the trial's end, the defense attorney gave an *eloquent* summation of the evidence favoring his client's innocence.
loquacious	talkative. Some people are more *loquacious* when they are nervous or uncomfortable.

Completing Verbal Analogies

One type of analogy can be expressed as "A is the study of B; C is the study of D." An example is given below.

                  A   B   C   D

__a__   astronomy : stars : : seismology : _____
        a. earthquakes
        b. dinosaurs
        c. rocks
        d. oceans

The answer is (a). *Astronomy* is the study of the stars, and *seismology* is the study of earthquakes.

Complete the following analogies.

_____ 1. sociology : human society : : geology : _____
        a. the lowest point
        b. the highest point
        c. the zodiac
        d. the earth

_____ 2. anthropology : human beings : : geography : _____
        a. the sun
        b. surface of earth
        c. the moon
        d. heavenly bodies

The following questions review previous analogy types. Some questions may contain vocabulary from previous units.

_____ 3. heliocentric : sun : : geocentric : _____
      a. stars
      b. atmosphere
      c. earth
      d. ocean

_____ 4. zenith : apogee : : nadir : _____
      a. distance
      b. moon
      c. perigee
      d. earth

_____ 5. interject : remark : : inject : _____
      a. intravenous
      b. vaccine
      c. person
      d. talking

_____ 6. anarchy : lawlessness : : apathy : _____
      a. military
      b. government
      c. people
      d. indifference

_____ 7. astrology : astronomy : _____ : : _____
      a. science : pseudoscience
      b. pseudoscience : science
      c. pseudoscience : horoscopes
      d. stars : planets

Now that you have studied the vocabulary in Unit 8, practice your new knowledge by completing the crossword puzzle on the next page.

Vocabulary 8

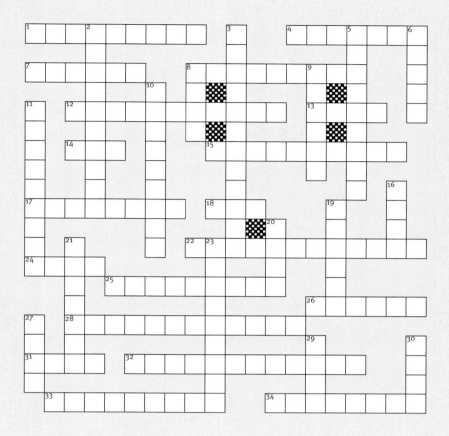

ACROSS CLUES

1. After the bitter custody battle, Sarah had _____ for her ex-husband.
4. She used her _____ sense to read the braille letters with her fingers.
7. Because of public _____, the voter turnout was low.
8. Because Jerry cut classes, he had to serve a _____ after school.
12. Samantha gave Matt an _____ look when she learned he had spent all his hard-earned money gambling in Las Vegas.
13. A word part meaning "throw."
14. A word part meaning "faith."
15. Susie is so _____ that her friends wonder when she pauses to breathe.
17. The Miami Hurricanes became _____ when they lost the college national championship game after the second overtime.
18. Abbreviation for what was once the eighth month.*
22. If you are interested in dinosaurs, you might want to take a course in _____.
24. A word part meaning "god."*

25. Oregon was a _____ before it became a state.
26. The landlord had to evict the _____ because he wasn't paying his rent.
28. Margaret Mead revolutionized the field of _____ with her research on the customs of the people of Samoa.
31. A word part meaning "hold."
32. The theory that regards the sun as the center of the universe.
33. If you are interested in social organization, you might study _____.
34. At the wedding ceremony, the couple pledged their undying _____ to each other.

DOWN CLUES

2. There are many _____ qualities like patience that go into making a successful leader.
3. A _____ liar might be able to pass a polygraph test.
5. Holding her son's head above the water, she maintained a _____ grip until they reached safety.

6. He did not want to _____ the annoying student from the class, but he finally had to tell him to leave.
8. A word part meaning "god."*
9. A baby rattlesnake can sometimes _____ more poison than a full-grown rattlesnake.
10. He wanted a summary report with only the _____ details on his desk by 5:00.
11. She felt _____ that she would do well on the test because she had studied hard.
16. A word part meaning "touch."
19. Was his election as president the _____ of his political career?
20. A word part meaning "science of."
21. The _____ was considered to be too rocky for any crops to grow.
23. The science of _____ is not to be confused with the pseudoscience of astrology.
27. A word part meaning "feeling."
29. A word part meaning "believe."
30. A word part meaning "many."*

*From a previous unit.

Evaluating the Evidence

The Thinker (1880) BY AUGUSTE RODIN

© The Cleveland Museum of Art, Gift of Ralph King, 1917.42

View and Reflect

Rodin originally sculpted *The Thinker* as part of his unfinished masterpiece *The Gates of Hell*. From his lofty perch at the top of the gate, *The Thinker* was meant to look down and ponder the sins of humanity. At the request of many patrons, Rodin increased the size of the original sculpture and made it freestanding. Today, it is one of the most widely recognized pieces of art in the world.

1. In this sculpture, Rodin tried to create a man "who did not just think with his head, but thought with his entire body." What do you think Rodin meant by this comment? Do you think he succeeded?

2. In 1970, a bomb was set at the base of an original Rodin *Thinker*, badly damaging the statue's feet. The museum decided against encasing the statue in protective glass or having it repaired. Do you think the museum made the right decision?

EVALUATING PERSUASIVE WRITING

Instead of sticking with neutral, objective language, authors sometimes use language with strong connotations, language designed to arouse the reader emotionally. This is often a sign of bias on the author's part and serves as a signal that the author is trying to influence you. Authors might exploit any or all of the following persuasive techniques:

1. Emotionally Loaded Language

This type of language is designed to appeal directly to your feelings rather than your reasoning abilities. In the example below, notice Dr. William Nolan's use of loaded words in his description of a severely disabled 90-year-old woman who has developed pneumonia. A decision must be made on whether to treat the pneumonia with penicillin or withhold the medication, which would likely cause death within three or four days.

> On the one hand, you cannot bear to see your **once vivacious** mother living the **painful, limited** life to which the stroke has **condemned** her. On the other hand, you hate to be the one to decide to let nature take its course. Until you are actually faced with such a decision, you probably won't be able to predict which course you would take.
>
> I'll tell you what choice I would make. I'd say, "Don't give her any penicillin. Keep her as comfortable as possible and let's see what happens. Maybe she'll have the resistance to fight off the pneumonia on her own and if she doesn't, she'll die a **peaceful** death. I don't want to be responsible for **condemning** my mother to a **living hell.**"
>
> *Source:* From William Nolen, "Deciding to Let Your Parents Die," permission from Blassingame, McCauley, and Wood. Reprinted from Deanne Milan, *Improving Reading Skills,* 2nd ed., New York: McGraw-Hill, 1992, p. 345.

2. Tear-Jerking Stories or References to People and Causes

In the following paragraph, the author describes the plight of the men and women, many of whom are immigrants making hourly wages one-third lower than other employees, who clean the nation's slaughterhouses and have "arguably the worst job in the United States."

> A brief description of some cleaning-crew accidents over the past decade says more about the work and the danger among slaughterhouse sanitation crews than any set of statistics. At the Monfort plant in Grand Island, Nebraska, Richard Skala was beheaded by a dehiding machine. Carlos Vincente, a twenty-eight-year-old Guatemalan who'd been in the United States for only a week, was pulled into the cogs of a conveyor belt at an Excel plant in Fort Morgan, Colorado, and torn apart. Salvador Hernandez-Gonzalez, an employee of DCS Sanitation, had his head crushed by a pork-loin processing machine at an IBP plant in Madison, Nebraska.

The same machine had fatally crushed the head of another worker, Ben Barone, a few years earlier. At a National Beef plant in Liberal, Kansas, Homer Stull climbed into a filthy blood-collection tank to clean it. Stull was overcome by hydrogen sulfide fumes. Two co-workers climbed into the tank and tried to rescue him; all three men died. Eight years earlier, Henry Wolf had been overcome by hydrogen sulfide fumes while cleaning the very same tank; Gary Sanders had tried to rescue him; both men died; and the Occupational Safety and Health Administration (OSHA) later fined National Beef for its negligence. The fine was $480 for each man's death.

Source: From Eric Schlosser, *Fast-Food Nation: The Dark Side of the All-American Meal,* pp. 83–85. Copyright © 2001 by Eric Schlosser. Reprinted by permission of the Houghton Mifflin Company. All rights reserved.

3. Figurative Language

In the example below, the author draws on figurative language to describe what's wrong with popular culture.

The popular culture, in its hierarchy of values, puts the joys of sex far above the happiness of motherhood. The women's magazines, the soaps, romance novels, and prime-time TV all celebrate career, sex, and the single woman. "Taking care of baby" is for Grandma. **Marriage and monogamy are about as exciting as a mashed potato sandwich.** That old triumvirate "the world, the flesh, and the devil" not only has all the best tunes, but all the best ad agencies.

Source: From Patrick J. Buchanan, *The Death of the West,* New York: St. Martin's Press, 2002, p. 43.

4. Manipulation of Tone

In the first paragraph, the author assumes an ironic tone when she says the United States has the safest food supply. In the second paragraph, she explains the problems inherent in the food production system by making an analogy.

One of the most insistent marketing messages we hear, trumpeted by both industry and regulators, is that the United States has the safest food supply in the world. Yet according to the Centers for Disease Control's best calculations, each year 76 million Americans—nearly one in four, and that's a lowball estimate—become infected by what they eat. Most find themselves for a few days dolefully memorizing a pattern of bathroom floor tiles. About 325,000 land in the hospital. Two million suffer drawn-out, sometimes lifelong, medical complications from unwittingly eating a contaminated morsel. More than 5,000—about 14 a day—die from indulging in what should be one of life's great pleasures. The "world's safest food supply" regularly doles out *E. coli* O157:H7 in hamburgers, *Salmonella* in alfalfa sprouts, *Listeria* in hot dogs, *Campylobacter* in Thanksgiving turkeys.

　　The site of modern meat production is akin to a walled medieval city, where waste is tossed out the window, sewage runs down the street, and feed and drinking water are routinely contaminated by fecal material. Each day, a feed-lot steer deposits 50 pounds of manure, as the animals crowd atop dark mountains composed of their own feces. "Animals are living in medieval conditions and we're living in the twenty-first century," says Robert Tauxe, chief of the CDC's foodborne and diarrheal diseases branch. "Consumers have to be aware that even though they bought their food from a lovely modern deli bar or salad bar, it started out in the sixteen hundreds."

Source: From Madeline Drexler, *Secret Agents: the Menace of Emerging Infections,* pp. 75, 86. Copyright © 2002 by the National Academy of Sciences.

5. Propaganda Techniques

These techniques include bandwagon, plain folks, name calling, and testimonials. In his final book before his death, noted historian Stephen Ambrose wrote about the Founding Fathers. He had less than positive feelings about Thomas Jefferson, our third president and author of the Declaration of Independence. He described Jefferson as having "a great mind and a limited character." In the following paragraph, Ambrose "name-calls" Jefferson "an intellectual coward.

> Thomas Jefferson, the genius of politics, could see no way for African Americans to live in society as free people. He embraced the worst forms of racism to justify slavery, to himself and those he instructed. The limitations he displayed in refusing both to acknowledge the truth of his own observations on the institution, and his unwillingness to do something, anything, to weaken and finally destroy it, brand him an intellectual coward. . . .

Source: From Stephen Ambrose, *To America: Personal Reflections of an Historian,* New York: Simon & Schuster, 2002, p. 4. (p. 414).

In the following example, David and Myra Sadker turn to a testimonial to demonstrate their point that there has always been criticism of the nation's public schools.

> "Everyone is aware today that our educational system has been allowed to deteriorate. It has been going downhill for some years without anything really constructive having been done to arrest the decline, still less to reverse its course. We thus have a chronic crisis: an unsolved problem as grave as any that faces our country today. Unless this problem is dealt with promptly and effectively, the machinery that sustains our level of material prosperity and political power will begin to slow down."
>
> Does this sound familiar, as though you just read it in today's newspaper? Actually, this was written in the 1950s by Admiral Hyman Rickover, a frequent critic of U.S. schools. And that's the point that a growing number of educators are making: School bashing is nothing new; it is as American as apple pie, an old tradition that has reached a new peak in recent years. In fact, these educators believe that not only is the current crescendo of criticism old hat, but it is terribly misguided, because today's schools are doing as well as they ever have—maybe, just maybe, they are doing better.

Source: From Myra Pollack Sadker and David Miller Sadker in *Teachers, Schools, and Society,* 5th ed., New York: McGraw-Hill, 2000, p. 251. Copyright © 2000 McGraw-Hill. Reprinted by permission The McGraw-Hill Companies, Inc.

When an author cites a testimonial, ask yourself the following questions:

- Is the writer an authority in that particular field?
- Is this the writer's specific area of competence?
- Is the writer biased?
- Is the writer likely to gain some advantage from the testimonial?

6. Psychological Appeals

The media frequently employs this technique to create ads that appeal directly to our desire for safety, power, prestige, sex, or popularity.

> For example, for Thanksgiving 2002, People for the Ethical Treatment of Animals (PETA) used a "turkey terror" campaign that appealed to Americans' fear of terrorism. The commercial depicts a terrorist takeover of a supermarket by a turkey. The store manager is shown "bound and gagged," with grocery shoppers cowering as the turkey warns that "innocent creatures will be beaten, scalded, and dismembered if anyone resists." The commercial ends with a plea to stop eating meat.
>
> *Source:* From Karen Huffman, et al., in *Psychology in Action,* 4th ed., pp. 59, 590. Copyright © 1994 John Wiley & Sons, Inc. This material is used by permission of John Wiley & Sons, Inc.

PETA Ad (Thanksgiving 2002)

Courtesy of People for the Ethical Treatment of Animals.

Fear induction is one of the most effective persuasive techniques. It is commonly used in advertisements and public service announcements, such as the one in the advertisement on the next page that was commissioned by the U.S. Department of Transportation. For fear tactics to work, (1) the appeal must engender a lot of fear, (2) the audience must believe the message, and (3) specific instructions for avoiding the danger must be presented.

These shoes were found 46 yards from
the crash caused by a drunk driver.
Carissa Deason was thrown 30 yards and
not even her father, a doctor, could save her.

Friends Don't Let Friends Drive Drunk

U.S. Department of Transportation/Ad Council.

7. Moral Appeals

Authors may seek to appeal to your sense of morality or fair play. In his book *Living a Life That Matters*, Rabbi Harold Kushner discusses the views of Kenneth Blanchard and the Reverend Norman Vincent Peale.

> Blanchard and Peale call for integrity in the business world both as a tactical advantage and as a matter of principle. If a company encourages employees to increase sales by dishonest means, that company might find its employees padding expense accounts or taking trade secrets to other companies when they move on. Both Blanchard and Peale urge their readers to ask themselves: "If we have to cheat to win, shouldn't we think twice about what business we're in?"
>
> *Source:* From Harold S. Kushner, *Living a Life That Matters*, New York: Anchor Books, 2001, p. 91.

8. Appeals to Authority

Authors may call attention to the integrity, intelligence, or knowledge of themselves or others to convince you to trust their judgment and believe them, as the following excerpt by James Steyer illustrates.

> If another adult spent five or six hours a day with your kids, regularly exposing them to sex, violence, and rampantly commercial values, you would probably forbid that person to have further contact with them. Yet most of us passively allow the media to expose our kids routinely to these same behaviors—sometimes worse—and do nothing about it.

If we don't start taking responsibility—as parents first, but also by demanding it from the huge media interests, as well as the government officials who are supposed to regulate them on behalf of the public interest—then we put our children at continued risk. We will raise generations of kids desensitized to violence, overexposed to reckless sex, and commercially exploited from their earliest years. And our culture will pay an ever-increasing price.

As a parent, as a national child advocate, as someone who teaches constitutional law and civil liberties courses at Stanford University, and as the head of one of the few independent children's media companies in the United States, I've had a unique vantage point. And from where I stand, the world of media and children is not a very pretty picture. In fact, I'm convinced that the huge influence of the "other parent" should be a matter of national concern for parents, policymakers, and responsible media executives alike.

Source: From James P. Steyer, *The Other Parent,* New York: Atria Books, 2002, pp. 5, 10, 16.

To evaluate persuasive writing, you want to become better at recognizing the techniques we have just discussed. You should also pay attention to the following:

- *Background:* Learn what you can about the author. What other books or articles has the author written? Is the author known for representing certain viewpoints? Is the author involved in advocacy organizations?

- *Assumptions:* Try to identify the values and principles that form the author's basic outlook. Do you agree with this outlook? Contrast the author's basic outlook to other possibilities. What are the values and principles behind opposing outlooks?

- *Organization:* Pay attention to how a piece of writing is organized. How is the author structuring the argument? Where are the reasons or explanations? Do the reasons support the conclusion?

In summary, authors who are trying to persuade do not usually write material that is entirely objective and meant solely to inform. Instead, they tend to make use of factual material to bolster their opinions and conclusions. By recognizing persuasive techniques and understanding the author's motives and underlying assumptions, you will be better able to avoid emotionalism and manipulation and to evaluate the persuasiveness or worth of the argument the author is making rationally and critically.

Are some people easier to persuade than others? In the next section, we will look at four major factors that make certain audiences susceptible to persuasion: personality traits, vulnerability, involvement, and reactance (resistance to persuasion). After reading the passage, complete the outline that follows.

CHARACTERISTICS OF THE AUDIENCE

1. *Personality traits:* The relationship between personality and persuasion is complex. Consider, as an example, self-esteem. Research shows that people with low self-esteem may be less confident of their opinions, but they also tend to be less attentive to persuasive arguments and are therefore harder to persuade. On the other hand, people with high self-esteem tend to be more confident of their opinions and are therefore harder to persuade. Interestingly, people with moderate self-esteem tend to be the easiest to influence. Because they pay attention to the message and they are somewhat unsure of their opinions, they tend to change their attitudes the most.

2. *Vulnerability:* Young children and adolescents are particularly vulnerable to certain appeals. Parents and health officials are thus understandably concerned about cigarette advertisements that apparently target these groups with "cool" cartoon-like characters. Adults are particularly susceptible to persuasive appeals if they are lonely, depressed, inexperienced, poorly educated, or physically isolated.

3. *Involvement:* The more actively an individual becomes involved in an idea or product, the more likely he or she is to be persuaded. If you can get someone to sign a petition or write a letter to a candidate, they are likely to become committed to your cause or product.

4. *Reactance:* Regardless of individual differences in personality, vulnerability, and involvement, most recipients of persuasive messages share a common need to believe they are free to choose and free to disagree. When people feel pressured, they often increase their resistance to persuasion—a phenomenon known as **reactance.** They may even rebel and do just the opposite. In one experiment, children were allowed to choose any brand of candy on display, except Brand X. Can you guess what the children did? Those who were told not to choose Brand X chose it significantly more often than those who were given a free choice.

Having concluded our brief look at persuasion, we encourage you to use what you have learned to critically evaluate the persuasive messages that bombard all of us every day. Many people needlessly worry about the dangers of subliminal advertising, hypnosis, and brainwashing, and then overlook the ordinary techniques that are used *effectively* to sell everything from toothpaste to presidential candidates. Developing your critical thinking skills and applying your new knowledge better equips you to deal with our complex, message-dense culture.

Source: "Characteristics of Audience" from Karen Huffman, et al., in *Psychology in Action,* 4th ed., pp. 59, 590. Copyright © 1994 John Wiley & Sons, Inc. This material is used by permission of John Wiley & Sons, Inc.

Exercise 1: Outlining

Directions: Below is an outline of the first two characteristics discussed above. Complete the outline for the remaining two characteristics.

I. Four major characteristics of an audience that affect ease of persuasion.
   A. Personality traits
      1. Because people with low self-esteem are less confident of their opinions and less attentive to persuasive arguments, they are harder to persuade.
      2. Because people with high self-esteem are more confident of their opinions, they are harder to persuade.
      3. Because people with moderate self-esteem pay attention to the message and are somewhat unsure of their opinions, they are the easiest to persuade.
   B. Vulnerability
      1. Young children and adolescents are vulnerable to persuasive appeals.
      2. Adults may also be susceptible to persuasive appeals.
         a. If they are lonely.
         b. If they are depressed.
         c. If they are inexperienced.
         d. If they are poorly educated.
         e. If they are physically isolated.

C. _____

  1. _____
     _____

  2. _____
     _____

D. _____

  1. _____
     _____

  2. _____
     _____

  3. _____

In the pages that follow, you will need to evaluate the author's reasoning to see how valid or persuasive it is.

DEATH AND DYING

Memory of the Garden at Etten, detail (1888)
BY VINCENT VAN GOGH

The State Hermitage Museum, St. Petersburg.

The Tragedy (1903) BY PABLO PICASSO

Chester Dale Collection, Image courtesy of the Board of Trustees, National Gallery of Art, Washington, D.C.

1. In what ways does Picasso convey sadness through his picture? In what ways does van Gogh?

2. In Picasso's painting, what does the young boy seem to be doing?

3. What do you think has happened to this family to make them so sad?

4. What is the setting in van Gogh's painting?

5. Which painting conveys a greater feeling of sadness?

The next four selections focus on death and dying. Carefully evaluate the evidence in each selection so that you can answer the questions that follow.

SELECTION

"Some will eventually be 'weaned' back to their own lung power. Others will never draw an independent breath again."

GETTING THE PICTURE

In the United States today, deciding how to treat the terminally ill or those in chronic pain is harder than ever because of the existence of life-prolonging medical technology. As a result, the whole concept of a "good death" has been called into question. One of the top fears of many Americans is dying in a hospital hooked up to machines. The author of this article, a physician, describes the dilemma of caring for a patient who has no realistic chance of recovery.

BIO-SKETCH

Elissa Ely graduated magna cum laude in 1978 from Wesleyan University and earned her M.D. from Harvard Medical School in 1988. Today she is a psychiatrist at the Massachusetts General Hospital. She is also a regular contributor to *The Boston Globe* and a featured commentator on *All Things Considered,* aired by National Public Radio. In addition, she has been a psychiatrist at Tewksbury Hospital and given lectures in psychiatry at Harvard Medical School.

BRUSHING UP ON VOCABULARY

cardiac pertaining to the heart.

respirator an apparatus to produce artificial breathing. Originally, this word came from the Latin *re,* meaning "again," and *spirare,* meaning "to breathe."

chintz cotton fabric with bright colors; borrowed from Hindi *chint* and Sanskrit *citra-s,* meaning "distinctive, bright, clear." The cheetah also gained its name from these words.

Dreaming of Disconnecting a Respirator

by ELISSA ELY

1 LATE ONE NIGHT—in the intensive care unit, one eye on the cardiac monitor and one on the Sunday paper, I read this story:

2 An infant lies in a hospital, hooked to life by a respirator. He exists in a "persistent vegetative state" after swallowing

a balloon that blocked the oxygen to his brain. This "vegetative state," I've always thought, is a metaphor inaccurately borrowed from nature, since it implies that with only the proper watering and fertilizer, a comatose patient will bloom again.

3   One day his father comes to visit. He disconnects the respirator and, with a gun in hand, cradles his son until the infant dies. The father is arrested and charged with murder.

4   In the ICU where I read this, many patients are bound to respirators. I look to my left and see them lined up, like potted plants. Some will eventually be "weaned" back to their own lung power. Others will never draw an independent breath again.

5   In Bed No. 2, there is a woman who has been on the respirator for almost two months. When she was admitted with a simple pneumonia, there were no clues she would come apart so terribly. On her third day, she had a sudden and enigmatic seizure. She rolled rapidly downhill. Her pneumonia is now gone, but her lungs refuse independence: She can't come off the machine.

6   I know little about this patient except that she is elderly and European. (It is the peculiar loss of hospital life that patients often exist here with a medical history, but not a personal one.) I sometimes try to picture her as she might have been: busy in a chintz kitchen smelling of pastries.

She might have hummed, rolling dough. Now there is a portable radio by the bed, playing Top Ten, while the respirator hisses and clicks 12 times a minute.

7   The family no longer visits. They have already signed the autopsy request, which is clipped to the front of her thick chart. Yet in their pain, they cannot take the final step and allow us to discontinue her respirator. Instead, they have retired her here, where they hope she is well cared for, and where she exists in a state of perpetual mechanical life.

8   I have dreamed of disconnecting my patient's respirator. Every day I make her death impossible and her life unbearable. Each decision—the blood draws, the rectal temperatures, the oxygen concentration—is one for or against life. No action in the ICU is neutral. Yet many of these decisions are made with an eye toward legal neutrality—and this has little to do with medical truth. The medical truth is that this patient exists without being alive. The legal neutrality is that existence is all that is required.

9   Late at night, reading in the ICU, the story of that father—so dangerous and impassioned—puts me to shame. I would never disconnect my patient from her respirator; it is unthinkable. But this is not because I am a doctor. It is because I feel differently toward her than the father toward his son.

10   I do not love her enough.

Source: Elissa Ely, "Dreaming of Disconnecting a Respirator," *Boston Globe,* July 1, 1989. Copyright © 1989 by Globe Newspaper Co. (MA). Reproduced with permission of Globe Newspaper Co. (MA).

 COMPREHENSION CHECKUP

Evaluating the Evidence

1. Is the author's primary purpose to inform or to persuade? What evidence do you have to support your conclusion?

    _____

    _____

    _____

2. What is the author's background? Does the author have the qualifications to write seriously about this topic?

_____

3. Does the article contain primarily facts or opinions?

_____

_____

   a. List some facts from the article:

_____

_____

_____

   b. List some opinions from the article:

_____

_____

_____

4. If the author has a strong bias, write it below. Can you give some examples of emotionally loaded language or material that has been included to create an emotional response on your part?

_____

_____

_____

_____

5. What is your opinion on the topic of euthanasia (mercy killing, assisted suicide)? Do you think that your opinion is biased? If so, does your bias interfere with your ability to evaluate what the author is saying fairly?

_____

_____

_____

6. Does the author use any specific propaganda devices? List them below. How did you react to these techniques?

_____

_____

_____

7. How would you describe the author's tone? What does the tone tell you about the author's bias?

_____

_____

Vocabulary in Context

Select the word that best completes the phrase.

enigmatic	impassioned	perpetually	vegetative	weaned

1. finally _____ from the bottle

2. *Mona Lisa's* _____ smile

3. delivered an _____ speech in favor of voting rights

4. _____ late to class

5. never went out; led a _____ life

The Art of Writing

The medical case of Terry Schiavo, the 26-year-old woman who lived for years in what doctors described as a "persistent vegetative state," sparked a fierce national debate about when life should end when no specific instructions are left by those who are incapacitated. Terry's husband was ultimately given the right by the courts to remove her feeding tube, thus effectively ending her life.

The following is an excerpt from an article on the autopsy results as reported in *The New York Times* on June 16, 2005:

> MIAMI, June 15—An exhaustive autopsy found that Terri Schiavo's brain had withered to half the normal size since her collapse in 1990 and that no treatment could have remotely improved her condition, medical examiners said on Wednesday. The autopsy results were released almost three months after Ms. Schiavo died after the court-ordered removal of her feeding tube. The report generally supported the contention of Ms. Schiavo's husband, Michael, accepted by judges in six courts over the years, that she was unaware and incapable of recovering. And it countered arguments by her family, who badly wanted to win custody of Ms. Schiavo, that she was responsive and could improve with therapy. At a news conference, Dr. Thogmartin said the condition of Ms. Schiavo's body was "consistent" with earlier medical findings that she was in a persistent vegetative state. Her parents, who believed she might some day eat and drink on her own or even speak, had rejected that diagnosis. But the courts accepted testimony from Ms. Schiavo's husband, Michael, that she would not want to stay alive in her condition. "This damage was irreversible," Dr. Thogmartin said of Ms. Schiavo's brain. "No amount of therapy or treatment would have regenerated the massive loss of neurons."

> Excerpt from "Autopsy Results of Terri Schiavo" as reported in *The New York Times*, 6/16/05.

Write a brief essay giving your opinion about how society should treat people who are in a "persistent vegetative state."

Internet Activity

Using a search engine like Google, find a website that deals with the issue of euthanasia, and analyze the website by answering the following questions.

1. *Author's purpose:* Is the author's primary purpose to inform or to persuade? Why do you think so?

2. *Emotional appeals:* Where does the author use language that is intended to arouse the reader emotionally? Give two examples of material that is included for its emotional appeal.

3. *Ethical appeals:* What information does the author include to persuade the reader to consider her or him an authority in this area or to trust his or her judgment on this subject?

4. *Logical appeals:* What logical or reasonable arguments does the author use? Is the author using inductive or deductive reasoning?

5. *Psychological appeals:* Is the author trying to manipulate the reader psychologically by appealing to the need for acceptance, power, prestige, and so on?

6. *Propaganda techniques:* What propaganda techniques does the author use? Are the techniques appropriate to his or her purpose? Cite specific examples.

7. *Tone:* What is the author's tone? Is the tone meant to influence or manipulate the reader? Give specific examples of how the author uses tone to affect the reader.

8. *Bias:* What is the author's specific bias? Where is the bias presented? At the beginning? The middle? The end?

Print one or two pages from the website.

SELECTION

"There is no blueprint, however, for a good death. Death can't be neatly packaged with a red bow. It is messy, irrational . . ."

GETTING THE PICTURE

The article below explores some fundamental questions about death and dying in the United States today.

BIO-SKETCH

Sheryl Gay Stolberg, a Washington correspondent for *The New York Times*, spent five years covering science and health policy but now covers Congress. Previously, she worked at the *Los Angeles Times* and *The Providence Journal* in Rhode Island. She graduated from the University of Virginia in 1983 and presently lives in Chevy Chase, Maryland, with her husband and two daughters.

BRUSHING UP ON VOCABULARY

melatonin a hormone important in regulating biorhythms.

hospice a health care facility or series of home visits for the terminally ill. Originally, a hospice was a rest house for travelers.

palliative a way of relieving a person from the symptoms of an illness without necessarily curing the disease.

The Good Death: Embracing a Right to Die Well

By SHERYL GAY STOLBERG

"The art of living well and the art of dying well are one."

—Epicurus

1   THE COLD BARE FACTS of Barbara Logan Brown's death are these: on July 17, 1996, Mrs. Logan Brown, a 38-year-old mother of two from Rochester, New York, died of AIDS, another statistic in an epidemic that has killed more than 362,000 Americans. Cancer had seeped into her brain; thrush had clogged her throat, making swallowing impossible. An intravenous diet of morphine had rendered her comatose.

2   Those are the cold bare facts. But there are other facts—achingly poignant, indeed, beautiful, some might argue—about Barbara Logan Brown's death. They are recounted here by Roberta Halter, herself a mother of four who cared for her dying friend and is today the guardian of Mrs. Logan Brown's son and daughter:

3   "The last time Barbara was able to go outside, she sat on the front porch. The girls and I went upstairs and took poster paint and painted a big huge smiley face above her bed. The next day, everyone put hand prints all over the wall. The children called it 'The Hands of Love,' and they started to paint messages on the wall. After the paint had dried, we let visitors come. By the end of the day, there were messages everywhere. It was kind of a tribute to her while she was still living. And it was wonderful."

4   It was in Mrs. Halter's view, a good death.

5   A good death. It is a provocative phrase.

A MYSTERY PROFANED

6   The Supreme Court has weighed in on one of the most divisive moral, legal, and medical questions of the day: whether the Constitution gives Americans a fundamental right to a physician's help in dying. The justices said it does not, leaving the battle over whether to permit or prohibit assisted suicide to rage on among lawyers and legislators, doctors and ethicists across the country.

7   While the court ruled on the constitutional issue, what remains unsettled—indeed, unsettling—is the idea at the heart of the assisted-suicide question: that for most Americans, modern medicine has made dying worse.

8   America is often called a "death-denying" society; each year the United States spends millions on efforts to conquer death, or at least to postpone it. The self-help shelves of bookstores overflow with such pearls as "Stop Aging Now!" and "Stay Young the Melatonin Way."

9   If Americans don't deny death, they often trivialize it, said Joan Halifax, a Zen Buddhist priest who founded the Project on Being with Dying in Santa Fe, New Mexico. "By the time a kid gets into high school, he has seen 20,000 homicides on television," she said. "Death as a mystery to be embraced, entered into and respected has been profaned in our culture."

10   Courtesy of the assisted-suicide debate, the concept of a good death has now emerged, though many experts reject the phrase as simplistic. Dr. Ira Byock, president of the Academy of Hospice and Palliative Medicine, prefers "dying well." Dr. Timothy Keay, an end-of-life care expert at the University of Maryland, says "the least worst death."

11   There is no blueprint, however, for a good death. Death can't be neatly packaged with a red bow. It is messy, irrational, most often filled with sorrow and

pain. More than two million Americans die each year; there are as many ways to die as to live. And so unanswerable questions arise: Not only what constitutes a good death and how can it be achieved, but who, ultimately, it is for—the person dying, or those going on living?

12   "I'm a little cynical about this whole notion of good death," said Dr. David Hilfiker, the founder of Joseph's House in Washington, which cares for homeless men dying of AIDS. "Death is really hard for most people. Why should people who are dying have to have a beautiful death? That's putting the burden on them to have some kind of experience that makes us feel good."

13   Indeed, said Dr. Sherwin B. Nuland, the author of "How We Die," the patient's needs often get lowest priority. "A good death," he said, "is in the eye of the beholder."

"Death, the last voyage, 14
the longest, the best."

—Thomas Wolfe

In centuries past, a good death was celebrated in art and literature as *ars moriendi,* the art of dying. Death marked salvation of the soul, neither an ending nor a beginning but, like birth, part of the cycle of life. "True philosophers," Plato wrote, "are always occupied in the practice of dying."

15   Buddhism is filled with stories of Zen masters who write poems in the moments before death, embracing it as the only time in life when absolute freedom may be realized. In the Middle Ages, Christian monks greeted one another with the salutation *Momento mori,* remember that you must die.

16   Today, it seems, most Americans would rather forget. Asked their idea of a good death, they say, "quick." Keeling over in the garden, trowel in hand, is one ideal, going to bed and not waking up another.

17   That is a reaction against medical technology; if Americans want anything from death, they want to remain in control, to avoid making their exits tethered to a machine. It is fear of a painful, lonely and protracted high-tech death that has fueled the movement to make assisted suicide legal.

18   "The classic idea of the good death is the sudden death," Dr. Nuland said, "but if you think seriously about it, that isn't what you want." "What you really want is a tranquil, suffering-free last few weeks where you have the opportunity for those near you to express what your life has meant to them."

19   A century ago such opportunities could be elusive. Infectious disease caused most deaths; cholera struck, and there was a burial two days later. Dr. Joanne Lynn, director of George Washington University's Center to Improve Care of the Dying, said: "When people went to bed and said 'If I should die before I wake,' they meant it."

20   Today the leading causes of death are heart disease, cancer, and stroke. For older people, disproportionately affected by these ailments, dying can drag on for months or years. Most women, Dr. Lynn said, have eight years of disability before they die; most men, five or six. It might seem, then, that people have time to plan for their deaths, but many don't take advantage. A study to be published in this week's *Annals of Internal Medicine* found that most seriously ill adults in the hospital do not talk to their doctors about being kept alive on life-support machines. They prefer not to discuss it.

21   Americans have been reticent to talk about death; only recently have doctors and families felt obliged to tell a terminally ill person that he was, in fact, dying. Often the truth simply went unremarked, like an elephant in the dining room.

22   In 1969, Elisabeth Kubler-Ross shattered the silence with "On Death and Dying." In it, she described the progression of a patient's coping mechanisms in five stages of dying: denial, anger, bargaining, depression and finally acceptance.

23   Dr. Byock, the author of "Dying Well," offers what he calls the "developmental model" of dying. When he began caring for the terminally ill 20 years ago, he noticed that when he asked patients how they were feeling, often the reply was something like this: "Despite it all, doctor, I am well."

24   The juxtaposition of wellness and dying seemed a paradox, but he has concluded that the two can exist side by side. "In dying," he said, "there are opportunities to grow even through times of severe difficulty, which we would label suffering."

25   In his view, dying well includes love and reconciliation, a settling of worldly affairs and a life's summing up, as stories are recounted and passed to new generations. By these standards, Barbara Logan Brown most certainly had a good death. "Barbara," Mrs. Halter said, "had an opportunity to put her life here on earth in order."

IN THE END, LIBERATION

26   Conventional wisdom holds that people die as they have lived; a crotchety old man in life will be a crotchety old man in death. Not so, say experts in end-of-life care: death can be both transforming and liberating.

27   Dr. Halifax, the Buddhist priest, tells of a woman whose daughter was a hospice nurse. Throughout her life, the mother had adhered to strict codes of politeness and propriety. A few days before her death, she began screaming in rage and pain.

28   As a nurse, her daughter knew that narcotics could subdue her mother's pain. But she chose to do nothing; the screaming, she believed, was her mother's way of finally expressing herself. "The screaming went on for four days and four nights," Dr. Halifax said. "And about an hour before she died, she lit up, and became extremely peaceful, and relaxed completely. And then she died."

29   Was it a good death? Dr. Halifax paused.

30   "A good death," she finally allowed, "sounds a little polite. It's like death with manners. I don't want to adorn death. Death is death."

Source: From Sheryl Gay Stolberg, "The Good Death: Embracing a Right to Die Well," from *The New York Times,* June 29, 1997, section 4, pp. 1, 4. Copyright © 1997 by The New York Times Co. Reprinted with permission.

 ## COMPREHENSION CHECKUP

Content and Structure

Choose the best answer for each of the following questions. You may refer back to the article.

1. The mode of rhetoric in this selection is primarily _____. (Explain the answer you give.) _____

_____

2. The pattern of organization in paragraph 3 is primarily
   a. comparison-contrast
   b. example
   c. chronological order
   d. cause and effect

3. In paragraphs 14–16, two types of death are contrasted. Describe the two types below.

   a. _____

   _____

   b. _____

   _____

4. Explain the cause and effect relationship in paragraph 17.

   Cause: _____

   Effect: _____

5. In paragraphs 18–20, Stolberg implies several contrasts. State three things being contrasted.

   a. _____

   _____

   b. _____

   _____

   c. _____

   _____

6. In paragraph 21, Stolberg uses a figure of speech to describe Americans' reluctance to speak of death. Identify and then explain the meaning of this figure of speech.

   _____

   _____

7. According to Dr. Byock, what does "dying well" include?

   a. _____

   b. _____

   c. _____

8. Explain the meaning of the phrase "death with manners" in the last paragraph.

   _____

9. Write the overall main idea of the selection below.

   _____

   _____

10. The author's purpose is to _____. (Explain the answer you give.)

    _____

11. To support her conclusion, the author primarily relies on
    a. statistics from research studies
    b. expert opinion from health-related fields
    c. her own observations and opinions

12. The author's tone throughout the article is
    a. loving
    b. angry
    c. serious
    d. humorous

Vocabulary in Context

For each italicized word from the article, use your dictionary to find the best definition according to the context.

1. other facts—achingly *poignant* (paragraph 2) _____

2. they often *trivialize* it (9) _____

3. has been *profaned* in our culture (9) _____

4. exits *tethered* to a machine (17) _____

5. lonely and *protracted* high-tech death (17) _____

6. a *tranquil,* suffering-free last few weeks (18) _____

7. such opportunities could be *elusive* (19) _____

8. *reticent* to talk about death (21) _____

9. *juxtaposition* of wellness and dying (24) _____

_____

10. *crotchety* old man (26) _____

11. *adhered* to strict codes (27) _____

12. politeness and *propriety* (27) _____

13. *subdue* her mother's pain (28) _____

14. to *adorn* death (30) _____

In Your Own Words

1. Do you think dying today is more dehumanizing than in the past? Why or why not?

2. Do you have a living will? Why are so many Americans reluctant to make provisions for death?

3. Dr. Jack Kevorkian, the so-called Dr. Death, insists that those in chronic pain with no chance of recovery have a right to a physician-assisted suicide with the administration of mercy-killing drugs. The Supreme Court has decided that no such general right can be found in the Constitution. Do you think that laws should be passed authorizing physician-assisted suicide? Or do you think that laws should be passed banning it?

4. The June 1997 issue of the *Journal of the American Medical Association* reported that "a new analysis of doctor-assisted suicide in the Netherlands suggests that caregivers there have increasingly taken the next, troubling step: ending patients' lives without their permission." The Netherlands has long been considered a model by advocates of assisted suicide in the United States. This new information seems to confirm the fears of U.S. opponents of assisted suicide, which remains illegal in most states. In the political cartoon on the next page, Steve Benson, an opponent of assisted suicide, addresses this troubling issue. Do you think that the acceptance of euthanasia would lead to a more relaxed attitude toward the taking of life in general, and toward taking the lives of those in need of constant attention in particular? What effect would this have on patients' ability to trust their doctors?

Cartoon Steve Benson by permission of Creators Syndicate.

The Art of Writing

In a brief essay, respond to one of the items below.

1. Compare and contrast the experience of dying described at the beginning of
    the selection to that described at the end. From the perspective of the patient,
    which one would you call a "good death"? From the perspective of the family?
    Be sure to provide arguments that support your position.

2. The Greek word parts *eu,* meaning "good," and *thanatos,* meaning "death,"
    appear in the word *euthanasia*, so the literal meaning of this term is "good
    death." Euthanasia is also thought of as "mercy killing." Euthanasia may be
    either active or passive: in the first case, death is deliberately inflicted,
    sometimes by a relative; in the second, life-support systems are withdrawn
    and the patient dies naturally. Controversy surrounding the morality of
    euthanasia has increased in recent years because of advances in medical
    technology that make it possible for human beings, both newborn and old,
    to be kept alive almost indefinitely, even when severely impaired. Where do
    you stand on euthanasia? Do you think life is sacred, so that euthanasia is
    always wrong? Do you think that the patient's ability to continue to enjoy
    life should influence the decision? Who should make the decision? The
    patient? The family? The doctor? The courts? Be sure to provide arguments
    that support your position.

Internet Activity

The websites on the next page (with very similar URLs) discuss euthanasia from
radically different perspectives. Visit the two sites and browse through their web

pages and links. After determining the point of view of each, list the various persuasive techniques they employ.

www.euthansia.com

www.euthanasia.org

"In the Mexican worldview, death is another phase of life, and those who have passed into it remain accessible."

GETTING THE PICTURE

In Mexican culture, the skeleton or skull is viewed as a symbol of resurrection, rather than as a symbol of death. Papier-mache figures like the one below commonly poke fun at particular people from many walks of life. In the United States, *el Dia de los Muertos* is often confused with Halloween, but unlike Halloween, the Mexican holiday is not considered scary or macabre. Actually, *el Dia de los Muertos* most closely resembles U.S. Memorial Day because both holidays show honor and respect for the dead.

© Spike Mafford/Getty Images.

SELECTION *continued*

BIO-SKETCH

Both writers of this textbook teach at the Stanford University Medical School.

BRUSHING UP ON VOCABULARY

indigenous originating from a particular country or region.

dogma a specific tenet or doctrine.

Excerpt from
CORE CONCEPTS IN HEALTH
by Paul M. Insel and Walton T. Roth

El Dia de los Muertos: The Day of the Dead

1   In contrast to the solemn attitude toward death so prevalent in the United States, a familiar and even ironic attitude is more common among Mexicans and Mexican Americans. In the Mexican worldview, death is another phase of life, and those who have passed into it remain accessible. Ancestors are not forever lost, nor is the past dead. This sense of continuity has its roots in the culture of the Aztecs, for whom regeneration was a central theme. When the Spanish came to Mexico in the sixteenth century, their beliefs about death, along with such symbols as skulls and skeletons, were absorbed into the native culture.

"A solemn funeral is   2   Mexican artists and writers confront death with humor and even sarcasm, depict-
inconceivable in the   ing it as the inevitable fate that all—even the wealthiest—must face. At no time is this
Chinese mind."   attitude toward death livelier than at the beginning of each November on the holiday
—Lin Yutang   known as *el Dia de los Muertos,* "the Day of the Dead." This holiday coincides with All
                        Souls' Day, the Catholic commemoration of the dead, and represents a unique blend-
                        ing of indigenous ritual and religious dogma.

"As men, we are all   3   Festive and merry, the celebration in honor of the dead typically spans two days—
equal in the presence   one day devoted to dead children, one to adults. It reflects the belief that the dead
of death."   return to Earth in spirit once a year to rejoin their families and partake of holiday
—Publius Syrus   foods prepared especially for them. The fiesta usually begins at midday on October 31,
                        with flowers and food—candies, cookies, honey, milk—set out on altars in each house
                        for the family's dead. The next day, family groups stream to the graveyards, where
                        they have cleaned and decorated the graves of their loved ones, to celebrate and com-
                        mune with the dead. They bring games, music, and special food—chicken with molé
                        sauce, enchiladas, tamales, and *pande muertos,* the "bread of the dead," sweet rolls in
                        the shape of bones. People sit on the graves, eat, sing, and talk with the departed
                        ones. Tears may be shed as the dead are remembered, but mourning is tempered by
                        the festive mood of the occasion.

4   During the season of the dead, graveyards and family altars are decorated with yellow candles and yellow marigolds—the "flower of death." In some Mexican villages,

yellow flower petals are strewn along the ground, connecting the graveyard with all the houses visited by death during the year.

5   As families cherish memories of their loved ones on this holiday, the larger society satirizes death itself—and political and public figures. The impulse to laugh at death finds expression in what are called *calaveras,* a word meaning "skeletons" or "skulls" but also referring to humorous newsletters that appear during this season. The *calaveras* contain biting, often bawdy, verses caricaturing well-known public figures, often with particular reference to their deaths. Comic skeletal figures march or dance across these pages, portraying the wealthy or influential as they will eventually become.

6   Whenever Mexican Americans have settled in the United States, *el Dia de los Muertos* celebrations keep the traditions alive, and the cultural practices associated with the Day of the Dead have found their way into the nation's culture. Books and museum exhibitions have brought to the public the "art of the dead," with its striking blend of skeletons and flowers, bones and candles. Even the schools in some areas celebrate the holiday. Students create paintings and sculptures depicting skeletons and skulls with the help of local artists.

7   Does this more familiar attitude toward death help people accept death and come to terms with it? Keeping death in the forefront of consciousness may provide solace to the living, reminding them of their loved ones and assuring them that they themselves will not be forgotten when they die. Yearly celebrations and remembrances may help people keep in touch with their past, their ancestry, and their roots. The festive atmosphere may help dispel the fear of death, allowing people to look at it more directly. Although it is possible to deny the reality of death even when surrounded by images of it, such practices as *el Dia de los Muertos* may help people face death with more equanimity.

Source: "El Dia de los Muertos: the Day of the Dead," from Paul M. Insel and Walton T. Roth, *Core Concepts in Health,* 9th ed., New York: McGraw-Hill, 2002, p. 579. Copyright © 2002 McGraw-Hill. Reprinted by permission The McGraw-Hill Companies, Inc.

 COMPREHENSION CHECKUP

Multiple Choice

Write the letter of the correct answer in the blank provided.

_____ 1. Which sentence best expresses the main idea of the selection?
   a. The festival of the Day of the Dead typically begins on October 31.
   b. The Mexicans view death as part of life and have a yearly celebration to remember and honor their loved ones who have died.
   c. Mexican artists treat death with humor and sarcasm.
   d. The souls of deceased children and deceased adults return on separate days.

_____ 2. The author's tone could best be described as
   a. arrogant
   b. pessimistic
   c. incredulous
   d. objective

_____ 3. The author's primary purpose is to
  a. persuade Americans to interact more with family members
  b. entertain the reader with personal stories celebrating a unique ritual
  c. inform the reader of the ways in which death is dealt with around the world
  d. explain the Day of the Dead celebration

_____ 4. In paragraph 2, the author says that Mexican artists and writers depict death as something "that all—even the wealthiest—must face." This means that
  a. "for certain is death for the born" (Gita)
  b. "as men we are all equal in the presence of death" (Syrus)
  c. "death is certain to all; all shall die" (Shakespeare)
  d. all of the above

_____ 5. The authors of this selection probably feel that
  a. a graveyard is no place for a celebration
  b. poking fun at death is in poor taste
  c. yearly celebrations such as the Day of the Dead may help people cope with their own inevitable death
  d. unlike the lighthearted attitude toward death reflected in U.S. culture, Mexicans exhibit an exceedingly solemn attitude

_____ 6. _Indigeneous_ ritual, as described in paragraph 2, is likely to be
  a. native
  b. inborn
  c. unnatural
  d. creative

_____ 7. From this selection you could conclude that
  a. the Day of the Dead celebrations continue to be popular with many Mexican immigrants to the United States
  b. the Day of the Dead celebration is popular only with non-Christians
  c. family and community members participate in the Day of the Dead celebration
  d. both a and c

_____ 8. A synonym for the word _equanimity_ as used in paragraph 7 is
  a. excitability
  b. indifference
  c. composure
  d. evasion

_____ 9. The word _tempered_ as used in paragraph 3 means
  a. property mixed
  b. tuned
  c. made less intense
  d. having a pleasant disposition

_____ 10. The Mexican celebration features all of the following _except_
  a. bread of the dead
  b. a mournful attitude throughout
  c. aromatic flowers
  d. vigils to honor loved ones

Topics and Supporting Details

Using the paragraph numbers in the text, match each paragraph with its topic.

1. Uses for the "flower of death" __4__

2. Satirical elements of the holiday __5__

3. Psychological and social benefits of the holiday __7__

4. Continuation of aspects of the holiday by Mexican immigrants to the United States __6__

5. Introduction and origin of the holiday __1__

6. Description of food and activities that make up the celebration __3__

7. Lively depiction of death by artists and writers __2__

Below are additional sentences about *el Dia de los Muertos*. Write the paragraph number in which the sentence is most likely to fit.

8. Mexican marigolds, called *zempascuchitl,* are particularly suited for the Days of the Dead festivities because of the strong, pungent aroma. __4__

9. Concepts of death and the afterlife existed in the ancient Maya and Aztec cultures. __1__

10. Mexican poets often write about death, comparing the fragility of life to a dream, a flower, a river, or a passing breeze. __2__

11. These *calaveras* often show individuals dancing with their own skeletons. __5__

12. A teacher at a Phoenix elementary school had her seventh-grade students create *ofrendas* during the Day of the Dead holiday. __6__

Synonyms

Match each word in column A with its synonym in column B.

Column A	**Column B**
_____ 1. accessible	a. native
_____ 2. bawdy	b. obtainable
_____ 3. depicting	c. common
_____ 4. equanimity	d. comfort
_____ 5. indigenous	e. spread
_____ 6. inevitable	f. unavoidable
_____ 7. partake	g. participate
_____ 8. prevalent	h. vulgar
_____ 9. solace	i. portraying
_____ 10. strewn	j. calmness

In Your Own Words

1. The goal of the ancient Greeks was to live a full life and then die with glory. What is your definition of a full life?

2. In the United States, many people reach adulthood without having seen a close family member or friend die. This stands in direct contrast to other parts of the world where death is visible daily. How do you think an early experience with death changes one's attitude toward the dying process?

3. Many psychologists and other medical professionals feel that the United States as a whole is a nation of "death deniers" and "death avoiders." They point out that we often avoid even saying the word "died," preferring euphemistic expressions such as "passed on." They also note that many people in our culture are in a constant search for the elusive "fountain of youth." These individuals are willing to use whatever cosmetic or surgical means are available to avoid looking their age. How do you feel about this issue?

4. Amish family members who lose a loved one are given community support for at least a year following their loss. That support, in addition to their strong religious convictions, appears to help the Amish heal. After several young Amish girls were killed in their classroom, many people were amazed to see the Amish extend that comfort to the family of the killer. How do you think these built-in traditions of offering help to others aid in the healing process?

The Art of Writing

Write a few paragraphs discussing one of the following questions.

1. Are some cultures better at providing support after the loss of a loved one than others?

2. What are the after-death practices of your specific culture? What are the funeral rites in your culture?

Internet Activity

To learn more about the Day of the Dead celebrations, consult the following websites:

www.public.iastate.edu/~rjsalvad/scmfaq/muertos.html

www.dayofthedead.com/html/traditions.htm#skullsandskeletons

REVIEW TEST: *Transition Words*

Write the correct word(s) in the blank provided.

1. The actual burial vault of King Tutankhamum was opened in 1923. The coffin was made of 242 pounds of pure gold and was sculpted into a jeweled effigy of the king himself. When the mummy inside was unwrapped, it _____ was covered with jewels.

    a. despite

    b. truly

    c. also

    d. besides

2. _____, the mummy was in a state of extreme decay, possibly from use of excessive amounts of embalming oil. The lengthy embalming process, which took over seventy days to complete, included thoroughly washing the body, removing the internal organs, covering the body with sodium, drying it, coating it with resin, and wrapping it in linen. Finally, the pharaoh was ready to be displayed to the public.
   a. In spite of
   b. However
   c. Again
   d. As well as

3. The media was ecstatic _____ this was the first time that a pharaoh's tomb had been discovered reasonably intact in the Valley of the Kings. They marveled at the precious objects the tomb contained, including gold sandals, rings, necklaces, bracelets, and amulets. And, in case the king wanted to travel, there were even two full-size gold chariots.
   a. because
   b. unlike
   c. to emphasize
   d. overall

4. _____ robbers had tunneled into King Tutankhamum's tomb shortly after he was interred, they had taken very little. About all they accomplished was to desecrate the holy site.
   a. Again
   b. Although
   c. Underneath
   d. Hence

5. _____, priests were called in to purify the site. They quickly resealed the tomb, and then they left behind curses to intimidate those who would attempt to enter the sacred shrine again.
   a. In spite of
   b. As noted
   c. So
   d. Yet

6. Inside the tomb over a hundred *ushabti*, three-foot-high statues of servants, were lined up _____ the king's body, ready to wait on him in death as they had waited on him in life.
   a. as indicated
   b. next to
   c. further
   d. right

7. King Tutankhamum ascended the throne at age 9, died at age 19, and never actually participated in a battle. _____, his tomb is crowded with images of him as a great warrior.
   a. Yet
   b. Finally
   c. Here again
   d. Thus

8. Tutankhamum became pharaoh after his childhood marriage to the daughter of the pharaoh Akhenaten. _____ his father-in-law Akhenaten, King Tutankhamum is not considered to be a great pharaoh.
   a. Overall
   b. Unlike
   c. Furthermore
   d. Without a doubt

9. _____, he was a totally innocuous one.
   a. As well as
   b. Once again
   c. Hence
   d. Instead

10. He has achieved fame solely _____ his tomb was discovered intact. Debris from other nearby tombs had covered the entrance hiding the tomb from view. _____ Carter removed the waste material on November 4, 1922, he discovered one stone step leading downwards. He uncovered fifteen more steps and then a blocked doorway. As Carter slowly worked his way into the tomb, he described it this way: "My eyes grew accustomed to the light, details of the room within emerged slowly, and gold—everywhere the glint of gold."
   a. again; Furthermore
   b. because; After
   c. nevertheless; Despite
   d. still; Once again

SELECTION

"No matter who opens a tomb and takes away its contents, that person is violating the intentions of those who sealed the tomb originally."

GETTING THE PICTURE

How often does a person's most cherished dream come true? After fifteen years of hard work, it happened to British archaeologist Howard Carter.

BIO-SKETCH

Mark Getlein is a painter and an author of textbooks on art-related subjects.

BRUSHING UP ON VOCABULARY

pillage to rob or plunder. *Pillage* is derived from the Old French word *piller*, meaning "spoils or booty."

propriety fitting or proper. *Propriety* is derived from the Latin *propietatem*, meaning "appropriateness."

perpetrator a person who carries out an evil, criminal, or offensive action. *Perpetrator* derives from the Latin word *perpetratus*, meaning "to bring into existence."

SELECTION *continued*

mummy the dead body of a human being preserved by the ancient Egyptian process of embalming. The first step in this process was to remove the deceased's brain through the nostrils by means of a long hook. Next, the liver, lungs, intestines, and stomach were removed. All of the organs were then preserved in separate receptacles. The body was soaked in salt water for a lengthy period and thoroughly dried. Later the body was stuffed and then swaddled in clean strips of linen.

Excerpt from
GILBERT'S LIVING WITH ART
by Mark Getlein

Whose Grave Is This Anyway?

1   When Howard Carter and his party opened the tomb of the Egyptian king Tutankhamum in 1922, there was rejoicing around the world. The tomb was largely intact, not seriously pillaged by ancient grave robbers, so it still contained the wonderful artifacts that had been buried with the young king more than three millennia earlier. Over the next several years Carter and his team systematically photographed and cataloged the objects from the tomb, then transported them to the Cairo Museum.

2   There is a certain irony in this story that raises complex ethical questions. Why are Carter and his party not called grave robbers? Why are their actions in stripping the tomb acceptable—even praiseworthy—when similar behavior by common thieves would be deplored? No matter who opens a tomb and takes away its contents, that person is violating the intentions of those who sealed the tomb originally. No matter what the motivation, a human body that was meant to rest in peace for all time has been disturbed. Should this not make us feel uncomfortable?

3   From the beginning some were uneasy about the propriety of unearthing Tutankhamum's remains. When Lord Carnarvon, Carter's sponsor, died suddenly from a mosquito bite, and several others connected with the project experienced tragedies, rumors arose about the "curse of King Tut." But Carter himself died peacefully many years later, and the talk subsided.

4   Perhaps it is the passage of time that transforms grave robbing into archaeology. Carter would no doubt have been outraged if, say, his grandmother's coffin had been dug up to strip the body of its jewelry. But after three thousand years Tutankhamum has no relatives still around to protest.

5   Perhaps it is a question of the words we use to describe such ancient finds. We speak of Tutankhamum's "mummy," and mummy is a clean, historical-sounding word. Parents bring their children to museums to see the mummies and mummy cases. We can almost forget that a mummy is the embalmed body of a dead human

Howard Carter Examining King Tut, 1922.

being, pulled out of its coffin so that we can marvel at the coffin and sometimes the body itself.

6   Or, perhaps the difference between grave robbing and archaeology lies in the motives of the perpetrators. Common thieves are motivated by greed, by their quest for money to be made by selling stolen objects. Carter and his team did not sell the treasures from Tutankhamum's tomb but stored them safely in the Cairo Museum, where art lovers from around the world can see them. They were, in effect, making a glorious gift to the people of our century and centuries to come (while at the same time, one must point out, acquiring significant glory for themselves).

7   The basic issue is a clash of cultural values. To the Egyptians, it was normal and correct to bury their finest artworks with the exalted dead. To us, the idea of all that beauty being locked away in the dark forever seems an appalling waste. We want to bring it into the light, to have it as part of our precious artistic heritage. Almost no one, having seen these magnificent treasures, would seriously propose they be put back in the tomb and sealed up.

8   In the end, inevitably, our cultural values will prevail, simply because we are still here and the ancient Egyptians are not. After three thousand years, Tutankhamum's grave really isn't his anymore. Whether rightly or wrongly, it belongs to us.

Source: From Rita Gilbert, "Whose Grave Is This Anyway?," in *Gilbert's Living With Art*, 6th ed. by Mark Getlein, New York: McGraw-Hill, 2002, p. 274. Copyright © 2002 McGraw-Hill. Reprinted by permission of The McGraw-Hill Companies, Inc.

✔ COMPREHENSION CHECKUP

(Answers can be found in the selection or the Review Test on pages 556–558.)

True or False

Indicate whether each statement is true or false by writing T or F in the blank provided.

_____T___ 1. Several people who were associated with unsealing King Tut's tomb died under mysterious circumstances.

_____T___ 2. King Tut's tomb was discovered close to its original condition.

_____F___ 3. Howard Carter was a British geologist.

_____T___ 4. Gold was featured predominantly inside King Tut's tomb.

_____F___ 5. The wondrous objects removed from King Tut's tomb were stored in the British Museum of Natural History.

Multiple Choice

Write the letter of the correct answer in the blank provided.

_____ 6. King Tut was a pharaoh who
   a. was relatively unimportant in Egyptian history
   b. died at an early age
   c. caused the death of Howard Carter
   d. both a and b

_____ 7. All of the following are true *except*
   a. the furnishings of King Tut's tomb were discovered largely intact
   b. in ancient Egypt, the burial of royalty was done in accord with elaborate rituals
   c. King Tut's coffin was made of pure gold
   d. Lord Carnarvon died before the discovery of King Tut's tomb

_____ 8. The contents of King Tut's tomb were
   a. resealed by Carter and Lord Carnarvon
   b. placed on display so that the public could view them
   c. sold to the highest bidder
   d. stolen by thieves and vandals

_____ 9. The ancient Egyptians
   a. buried their finest pieces of artwork with their dead
   b. took steps to embalm and preserve corpses
   c. tried to preserve royal tombs for eternity
   d. all of the above

_____ 10. The author of the article suggests all of the following *except*
   a. the passage of time transforms grave robbing into the study of archaeology
   b. archaeologists offer opportunities to experience other cultures
   c. archaeologists should stop invading and disturbing the burial sites of past civilizations
   d. King Tut's grave now belongs to humanity

Vocabulary in Context

Fill in the blanks using words from the following list. Use each word only once.

appalling	deplored	prevailed	sponsor
artifacts	heritage	propose	subsided
clash	marvel	quest	transformed
curse	precious	rejoicing	violating

1. After his anger _subsided_, he was quick to apologize to his wife for his outburst.

2. Michael's mother _deplored_ her son's slovenly ways because he failed to pick up anything in his room.

3. I would like to _propose_ a toast to the new bride and groom.

4. Having children _transformed_ her life.

5. There was much _rejoicing_ among the students when our team won the state football championship.

6. To someone who is dehydrated, a drop of water is very _precious_.

7. To determine whether _artifacts_ are genuine or fake without damaging them, scientists often use X-rays.

8. Be careful when you travel in foreign countries. You may be accused of _violating_ social customs you are unfamiliar with.

9. The amount of man-made debris that is found on beaches around the world is _appalling_.

10. He was on a _quest_ to identify his son's murderer. Nothing would stop him until he fulfilled his goal of seeing the murderer behind bars.

11. When I failed to pay the fortune-teller for her advice, she placed a _curse_ on my children and my children's children.

12. Genealogy is important to people who want to trace their family _heritage_.

13. When I look at the Eiffel Tower, I can only _marvel_ at the amount of work that went into its construction.

14. We are looking for a _sponsor_ for our softball team. Are there any volunteers?

15. Do you think that a red blouse and an orange skirt _clash_?

16. She successfully _prevailed_ on her teenagers to pass up a vacation with friends and join the family on a car trip.

In Your Own Words

1. Do you think it's appropriate to investigate ancient grave sites for archaeological purposes? Why or why not?

2. Do you think it's appropriate to display the bodies found in ancient graves in museums? Why or why not?

The Art of Writing

In a brief essay, respond to the item below.

In 2002, Zahi Hawass became the director of Egypt's Supreme Council of Antiquities. He has made it his mission to recover the ancient treasures of the Egyptian people. In 1983, Egypt passed a law declaring all new finds to be Egyptian property. Previously, many artifacts belonged to the person who found them. Hawass and his staff have contacted museums around the world informing them of Egypt's readiness "to make the most strenuous efforts to reclaim illegally exported antiquities." Hawass hopes artifacts will be returned from many of the most illustrious museums in Europe, including the Louvre. As he says, "there is no statute of limitations on stolen masterpieces." He uses many weapons in his fight to recover Egypt's treasures, such as posting names on the Internet, taking museum board members to court, and barring foreign archaeologists from working in Egypt. "Unfortunately, there is no 'curse of the mummies,'" he says. "I, however, am trying to fulfill that role."

Do you think museums should be compelled to return works of art that were taken many years ago from another country? What are some relevant considerations for whether antiquities should be returned to the country of origin? What if that country is politically unstable or near a place of tension and fighting? What about the many people who will no longer be able to visit the exhibits if they are moved a long distance away? How much opportunity will people have to learn about other cultures if countries begin taking back their antiquities?

Internet Activities

1. While the most famous mummies belong to the ancient Egyptians, other cultures and societies have also engaged in mummification. In 1995, the mummified body of a young Inca girl, probably a sacrificial victim, was discovered on the mountain of Nevado Impato. Evita Perón, the wife of Juan Perón, president of Argentina, died in 1952 and was embalmed. Her body disappeared in 1955 but was recovered and returned to Argentina in 1974, still perfectly preserved. Vladimir Lenin, the Russian revolutionary leader who died in 1924, is also preserved as a mummy. Today's more modern version of mummification uses cryogenics. Bodies are frozen in liquid nitrogen and then preserved in a steel container. Using an Internet search engine, such as Google or Yahoo! investigate the mummification or cryogenics process, and then write a short summary of your findings.

2. Do you believe in curses? When Howard Carter was warned that "death comes on wings to he who enters the tomb of a pharoah," he paid no attention. And yet his patron, Lord Carnarvon, died of a mosquito bite within days of unsealing King Tut's tomb. Other deaths quickly followed, including the death of a French scientist who visited the tomb shortly after its discovery, an X-ray specialist on his way to examine the mummy, and an American archaeologist who died of a mysterious virus soon after a visit. Mere coincidences? What do you think? Check out the following websites and write a paragraph arguing your position on whether there was a curse. Be sure to use transition words in your paragraph.

    http://www.civilization.ca/civil/egypt/egtut04e.html

    http://unmuseum.mus.pa.us/mummy.htm

    http://www.mummytombs.com/egypt/kingtut.htm

TEST-TAKING TIP

Key Words That Often Appear in Essay Questions (Continued)

explain to make clear; to give reasons. An explanation often involves showing cause-and-effect relationships or steps.

illustrate to use a diagram, chart, figure, or specific examples to explain something further.

interpret to say what something means. A question that asks for an interpretation usually wants you to state what something means to you. What are your beliefs or feelings about the meaning of the material? Be sure to back up your position with specific examples and details.

justify to give reasons in support of a conclusion, theory, or opinion.

list to put down your points one by one. You may want to number each of the points in your list.

outline to organize information into an outline, using headings and subheadings. Your outline should reflect the main ideas and supporting details.

prove to demonstrate that something is true by means of factual evidence or logical reasoning.

relate to discuss how two or more conclusions, theories, or opinions affect each other. You will want to explain how one causes, limits, or develops the other.

review to summarize or sometimes to summarize and then analyze critically.

summarize to put down the main points; to state briefly the key principles, facts, or ideas while avoiding details and personal comments.

trace to follow the course of development of something in a chronological or logical sequence. You will want to discuss each stage of development from beginning to end.

VOCABULARY Unit 9

Unit 9 covers vocabulary with the following word parts: *belli-*, *-cede*, and *-ces*; *-gnostos* and *cogni-*; *cur-*; *bene-* and *mal-*; *pos-* and *pon-*; *-trac(t)*; *viv-*; *voc-*.

belli—war

bellicose inclined or eager to fight; aggressively hostile. The situation worsened daily as each nation sounded more *bellicose* and less inclined to a peaceful resolution.

belligerent engaged in warfare; showing readiness to fight; hostile. Amanda thought that Todd's increasingly *belligerent* behavior must be due to using drugs.

Bellicose and *belligerent* are synonyms.

rebel a person who rises in arms against a ruler or government; a person who resists authority, control, or tradition. During the teenage years, many young people are *rebels:* They just can't tolerate their parents' authority.

cede, ces—go (back), yield, withdraw

cede	to yield or formally surrender to another. After the battle, the disputed land was *ceded* to the victorious party.
accede	to give one's consent or approval; to give up, agree. Mona refused to *accede* to her parents' wishes and give her child up for adoption. Instead, she vowed to raise him all by herself.
precede	to go or come before. In a traditional wedding ceremony in the United States, the bridesmaids *precede* the bride up the aisle.
recession	the act of receding or withdrawing; a period of economic decline.
secede	to stop being a member of a group. During the Civil War, Alabama was one of the states that *seceded* from the Union.

gnostos—know; cogni—know

agnostic	a person who believes that it is impossible to know whether or not there is a God.
cognitive	pertaining to the act or process of knowing; perception.
incognito	with one's identity hidden or unknown. Many movie stars, not wishing to be recognized by fans, travel *incognito*.
cognizant	being aware or informed of something. Were the parents *cognizant* that their child was suffering from depression?

cur(r)—run

concurrent	occurring or existing simultaneously or side by side. The literal meaning is "running together." What is the likelihood of an earthquake and a tornado happening *concurrently*?
cursive	handwriting in flowing strokes with the letters joined (running) together. Although I can read his printing, his *cursive* writing is often illegible.
cursory	going rapidly over something without noticing details; hasty; superficial. Eva gave the memo a *cursory* reading; she will review it again later when she has more time.
discursive	passing aimlessly from one subject to another; rambling. Because I hadn't seen Marilyn for a long time, our conversation was *discursive*, ranging from our health and our children to new books and movies.
incursion	an invasion of a place or territory; a raid. Has there been another *incursion* into enemy territory?
precursor	a person or thing that comes before and makes the way ready for what will follow; forerunner. Was the typewriter a *precursor* to the computer?
recur	to occur again. The literal meaning is "to run back." As soon as Sonia finishes her antibiotics, her ear infection *recurs*.

bene—well; mal—bad

benefactor	a person who has given money or other help as to a charity or school. An anonymous *benefactor* paid Truman's tuition to a private school.
beneficiary	a person or group that receives benefits. In his mother's will, Marco was named as her primary *beneficiary*.
benediction	a blessing; an utterance of good wishes.
benevolent	characterized by expressing goodwill or kindly feelings; kind; generous. Sascha's *benevolent* uncle paid for her trip to the United States.
malcontent	not satisfied with current conditions; ready to rebel.
malevolence	the quality or state of wishing evil or harm on others. In the fairy tale "Snow White and the Seven Dwarfs," the *malevolent* stepmother plots Snow White's death.
malfeasance	misconduct or wrongdoing committed by someone holding a public office. The congressman was accused of *malfeasance* for accepting expensive gifts from a lobbyist.
malign	to speak harmful untruths about someone; slander. Now that she is no longer around to defend herself, it seems unfair to *malign* her.

pos, pon—put, place

imposition	the laying on of something as a burden or obligation. Would it be too much of an *imposition* for you to watch Colby every day after school for the next two weeks?
depose	to remove from office or position, especially high office. The rebels did not succeed in *deposing* the tyrant.
deposition	the written statement of a witness, made under oath, but not in court, to be used later at a trial.

trac(t)—pull, draw

retract	to draw back; to withdraw. Threatened by the senator's attorneys, the paper was forced to *retract* a statement that it had made earlier in the week about the senator's extramarital affairs. A turtle can *retract* its head.
detract	to take something away, especially something worthwhile or attractive. Josie wanted to get contacts because she believed that her glasses *detracted* from her appearance.
traction	the power to grip or hold to a surface; moving without slipping; the act of drawing or pulling. When the tires lost *traction* on the wet road, the car began to skid.

viv—live

vivid	strikingly bright or intense; realistic; full of life; lively. The flower paintings of Georgia O'Keeffe are famous for their *vivid* colors.
revive	renew; restore to life or consciousness. After pulling the 2-year-old from the swimming pool, the paramedics worked frantically to *revive* her.

convivial	enjoying a good time with other people, such as at a party; sociable; friendly; jovial. Her new in-laws were so *convivial* that Kelly looked forward to spending the holidays with them.
vivisection	the action of cutting into or dissecting a living body. *Antivivisectionist* groups have caused many university researchers to abandon experiments on rhesus monkeys.

voc—call

vocal	having a voice; inclined to express oneself with words. The teacher told the class that she wanted them to be *vocal* and participate.
revoke	to call back or withdraw; to cancel. Because Tim failed to come home by midnight, his mother *revoked* his driving privileges for the next two weeks.
advocate	to support or urge by argument. *ad-* means "to," and *voc-* means "call," so the literal meaning is "to call to." The financial adviser was a strong *advocate* for staying out of debt.
vocation	a person's regular occupation or calling.
avocation	something a person does in addition to a principal occupation, especially for pleasure; hobby. His *vocation* is teaching, but his *avocation* is surfing.

Completing Verbal Analogies

Another common type of analogy can be expressed as "A is associated with B; C is associated with D." An example is shown below.

       A   B   C   D

___**b**___ lawyer : legal : : chef : _____
    a. fasting
    b. culinary
    c. comfort
    d. dieting

The answer is b. A *lawyer* is associated with the *legal* field, in the same way that a *chef* is associated with the *culinary* field.
    Complete the following analogies.

_____ 1. malefactor : bad : : benefactor : _____
    a. good
    b. money
    c. possessions
    d. poverty

_____ 2. belligerent : hostility : : convivial : _____
    a. aggressiveness
    b. eagerness
    c. rebelliousness
    d. friendliness

_____ 3. incognito : hidden : : cognizant : _____
    a. contented
    b. perceived

                      c. withdrawn
                      d. serious

_____ 4. accede : giving up : : recede : _____
                      a. accepting
                      b. moving back
                      c. pleading
                      d. believing

_____ 5. avocation : hobby : : vocation : _____
                      a. prayer
                      b. yelling
                      c. occupation
                      d. trip

    Now that you have studied the vocabulary in Unit 9, practice your new knowledge by completing the crossword puzzle on the next page.

Vocabulary 9

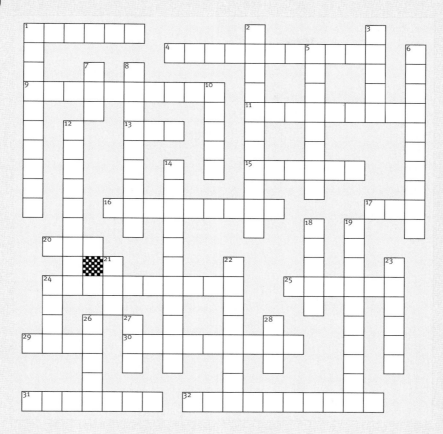

ACROSS CLUES

1. You _____ someone when you spread a false, mean-spirited story about that person.

4. The legislator committed _____ when he accepted a bribe.

9. The judge sentenced the defendant to _____ sentences of three and five years.

11. Prince William, dressed in casual clothes, traveled _____ throughout the United States.

13. A word part meaning "run."

15. Because Sascha had only been underwater for a minute, the paramedics were able to _____ her.

16. The supervisor was _____ of the fact that Carrie and Guillermo were leaving early every Friday.

17. A word part meaning "earth."*

20. A word part meaning "call."

24. An unknown _____ gave Maria enough money to complete her education.

25. Should we _____ a driver's license after only one DUI offense?

29. A word part meaning "yield."

30. His _____ of photography was more important to him than his vocation as a computer programmer.

31. The minute the legislator made the comment, he wished he could _____ it.

32. Kind people are considered to be _____.

DOWN CLUES

1. The employee complained all the time and was known as a _____.

2. The _____ countries were at war with each other.

3. A word part meaning "war."

5. Josh said he was an _____ because he did not know whether God exists.

6. The lawyer took the _____ of the witness to the car accident.

7. The abbreviation for what was once the eighth month.*

8. Was the icebox a _____ to the refrigerator?

10. A word part meaning "pull."

12. He sounded increasingly _____ and less likely to find a peaceful resolution.

14. After the funeral service, the priest delivered a short _____.

18. The army could sense that victory was near.

19. It was a real _____ to have her mother-in-law stay for two months in their tiny house.

21. The abbreviation for what was once the tenth month.*

22. Snow tires have better _____ on snow than regular tires.

23. South Carolina was the first state to _____ from the Union.

24. A word part meaning "good."

26. Darcy's allergies _____ every fall and spring.

27. A word part meaning "bad."

28. A word part meaning "put."

*From a previous unit.

Study Skills

Jean Puy. Study, or The Schoolgirl, c. 1933–34

Musée National d'Art Moderne, Centre Pompidou, Paris, France. Bridgeman Art Library. © 2009 Artists Rights Society (ARS), New York/ADAGP, Paris.

PART 5

Organizing Textbook Information

CHRISTO AND JEANNE-CLAUDE: *Wrapped Reichstag, Berlin,* 1971–95. © CHRISTO 1995.
PHOTO WOLFGANG VOLZ.

View and Reflect

The wrapping of the Reichstag required 1,076,000 square feet of fabric. It took
90 climbers and 120 installation workers to complete the project, which remained in
place for only two weeks. All of the projects done by Christo and Jeanne-Claude are
temporary, paid for by the artists, and all materials are recycled afterwards. The two
have been called "environmental artists" because they work in both rural and urban
environments. They force people to view familiar locations in new and different ways.

1. What do you imagine the building here would look like without the wrappings?
2. The Reichstag is Germany's parliament building. Do you think the wrapping of
   the Reichstag comments on politics? How?
3. Do you consider the wrapping of a large structure like the Reichstag art? Why or
   why not?

STUDYING TEXTBOOK CHAPTERS

In previous chapters of this book, you were introduced to various study techniques. You also practiced applying many of these techniques. In this chapter, we will review those techniques and introduce you to others that will help you study for your college classes. You will also have a chance to practice your newly acquired skills with a chapter on the arts from a cultural anthropology textbook.

SKIMMING

Skimming is a study technique very similar to SQ3R (see page 55). Skimming involves reading material quickly in order to gain a quick overview and identify the main points. As in SQ3R, you read the introduction to the chapter, the summary at the end of the chapter, the section titles and subtitles, and the first sentence of each section and many paragraphs. You also look at the illustrations and read the captions. Once you have skimmed the chapter, you should be able to state its main idea.

Skim through the section "Body Arts" (including the Introduction and Summary, see page 578), and then indicate whether each statement is true or false by writing T or F in the space provided.

_____ 1. People are only interested in things that are practical or useful.

_____ 2. It is only in the United States that people are concerned with altering their physical appearance.

_____ 3. In some places in Africa, hairstyle indicates that a woman is a widow.

_____ 4. Some societies alter body parts other than just hair and beards.

_____ 5. Native Americans sometimes put war paint on their faces.

_____ 6. In New Guinea, covering one's face with white clay signifies respect for the deceased.

_____ 7. The art of tattooing is practiced in very few places.

_____ 8. Tattooing is a modern art form.

_____ 9. Tattooing and scarification are more permanent than body paint.

_____ 10. Both Maori men and women had tattoos.

_____ 11. Among the Polynesians, the Marquesa were least likely to cover their bodies with tattoos.

_____ 12. Cutting or creating scars on the body is called scarification.

_____ 13. The aesthetic response is universal.

_____ 14. In a curing ceremony, Navajo singers are using both visual art and performance art.

SCANNING

Scanning is a technique for quickly finding answers to specific questions. People use scanning techniques daily in order to find information quickly. When you go to the phone book, you scan down through the list of names or businesses until you find the one you are looking for. You don't actually take the time to read every name. You may also scan through the TV guide, the dictionary, and newspaper ads.

Scan through the section "Performance Arts" (see page 582) to find the answers to the following specific questions. Scan titles and subtitles of sections to determine which sections are likely to have the answers. Once you have located the appropriate section, move your eyes rapidly across the information to locate the answers to the questions that follow.

1. In the _____ religious tradition, hymns are sung in unison to draw the congregation together to promote fellowship.

2. In the *voudon* religion, the spirits are called _____.

3. The era of the slave trade began around the _____.

4. _____ may cause illness or death when they possess someone.

5. According to the Tumbuka, a person is cured when he or she is returned to a correct balance between _____ and _____ forces.

6. A Navajo _____ is responsible for performing a curing ritual.

7. The singer creates images of the Holy People out of sand in what are called

_____.

8. The _____ ordered the Navajo not to make permanent images of them.

ANNOTATING

In Study Technique 1 (page 32), you learned how to underline or highlight information and then make notes to yourself in the margins. In the sample material that follows, we have demonstrated these skills for you in the Introduction and part of "Body Arts." Study this example and use it as a guide. Then practice your annotating skills on the sections "Beards," "Head Shaping," and "Altering Other Body Parts"(see page 579).

OUTLINING

In Study Technique 4 (page 128), we introduced you to outlining, an important study technique for organizing textbook information. Here we will illustrate the proper outlining format by giving you a sample outline for the section "Body Arts." You can then practice outlining the section "Performance Arts."

In a formal outline, main, first-level headings are enumerated with Roman numerals (I, II, III, etc.), second-level headings are enumerated with capital letters (A, B, C, etc.), third-level headings are enumerated with Arabic numbers (1, 2, 3, etc.), and fourth-level headings are enumerated with lowercase letters (a, b, c, etc.). Each level contains information that is more specific than the level above it.

Another rule for making a formal outline is that you cannot have a single subsection; you must have either no subsections or at least two. So, for example, section I cannot have only subsection A; it must have either no subsections or at least subsections A and B.

It takes time to outline textbook material, but the process of outlining helps you to organize and learn the material. If you have done a good job with your outline, you should be able to study from it without having to return to the original textbook material.

Study the outline below for the portion of the textbook chapter "Body Arts." Compare the outline with the text.

I. Body Arts
   A. Physical alterations
      1. Hairstyles
         a. Indicate woman's status (Africa, Hopi)
         b. Indicate clan membership (Omaha)
      2. Beards
         a. Demonstrate religious beliefs (for some)
         b. Denoted social status in ancient times
      3. Head shaping
         a. Universal until 18th century (France)
         b. Tight caps for babies (Netherlands)
         c. Elongation of skull (ancient Andeans and Egyptians)
         d. Headboards (Chinook)
      4. Other body parts
         a. Feet of wealthy girls bound (China)
         b. Holes cut in earlobes (Africa)
         c. Teeth filed to points (African pygmy)
         d. Rings placed on girls' necks (Africa)
         e. Plastic surgery used (Western nations)
   B. Painting of face and body
      1. Face
         a. Used for war (Native Americans)
         b. Used for religious rituals (Native Americans)
         c. Used to enhance social appearance (Native Americans)
      2. Body
         a. May have religious significance
         b. Could be a daily activity
   C. Tattooing and Scarification
      1. Tattooing
         a. Has long history as art form
         b. Practiced by ancient Egyptians, Bretons, Romans
         c. Outlawed by Christians
         d. Rediscovered by sailors in Pacific
         e. Could indicate social status
         f. Most elaborately practiced by Polynesians
         g. Conferred specific privileges
      2. Scarification
         a. Is more limited than tattooing
         b. Can be part of initiation rituals
II. Performance Arts

MAPPING

You were introduced to mapping in Study Technique 6 (page 177). Mapping is similar to outlining in that it includes main categories and subcategories. But in contrast to outlining, it is more visual and free-form. Look at the map based on the section "Body Arts." After studying the sample map, try to map the section "Performance Arts." Your goal in mapping is to create a good study guide.

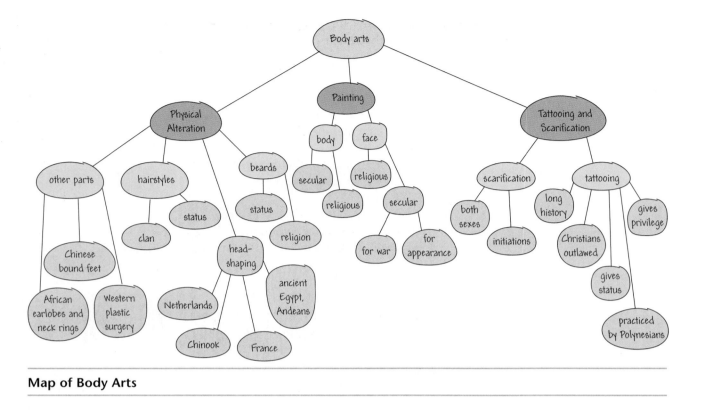

Map of Body Arts

COMPARISON-CONTRAST CHART

In Study Technique 5 (page 170), you were introduced to the comparison-contrast chart. Some material lends itself nicely to a comparison-contrast chart, and this is the case with the sections on the Tumbuka and the Navajo. Read these sections, and complete the chart below. In the first column, the categories to be compared and contrasted are listed; in the second and third columns, record the information for the Tumbuka and the Navajo that pertain to that category. We have provided the categories as a sample to help you get started. When you complete the chart, answer the questions that follow.

Comparison-Contrast Chart

Category	Tumbuka	Navajo
Practiced by		
Cause of illness		
Person who performs ceremony		

Comparison-Contrast Chart (*continued*)

Category	Tumbuka	Navajo
Role of sick person		
Time of ceremony		
Visual art involved		
Duration of ceremony		

What similarities did you discover about the Timbuka and the Navajo through the process of filling in the chart? What specific examples substantiate your conclusions?

VENN DIAGRAM

In Study Technique 9 (page 496), you learned to make a Venn diagram. Like the comparison-contrast chart, Venn diagrams are helpful for showing similarities and differences. As you will recall, the Venn diagram is made up of two interlocking circles. In the outside parts of the circles, you list the traits that are unique to each subject being discussed, while in the overlapping area you list the traits the two subjects share. The following textbook chapter discusses similarities and differences between tattooing and scarification. Complete the Venn diagram below with information from the textbook chapter. We have given you a few sample items to get you started.

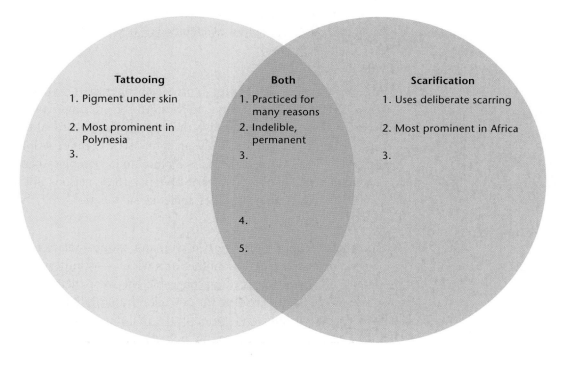

Tattooing
1. Pigment under skin
2. Most prominent in Polynesia
3.

Both
1. Practiced for many reasons
2. Indelible, permanent
3.
4.
5.

Scarification
1. Uses deliberate scarring
2. Most prominent in Africa
3.

SELECTION

Excerpt From
HUMANITY
by James Peoples

Art and the Aesthetic

Introduction

1   There is much more to human life than the acquisition of necessities like food, clothing, and shelter. There is also more to living than the production and use of things for
their utilitarian value. All peoples have both a sense of and a desire for the *aesthetic:*
those things that appeal to the eye, the ear, the taste, the touch, the emotions, and the
imagination. Such sensory experiences are important not only for their functional
value but because their color, form, design, sound, taste, or feel are pleasurable in
their own right. Commonly, these experiences are sought after to stimulate our im-
aginations and emotions through the creation of feelings of happiness, fear, or even
anger. These expressions of the aesthetic are what we generally call *art*.

2   Although art permeates most aspects of human activity, from clothing and furniture to music and theater, space constraints do not permit us to discuss all these
diverse forms of artistic expression. For this reason we limit our discussion to the
categories of body arts and performance arts.

Def.—aesthetic those things appealing to mind, senses, emotion

Def.—art is an expression of the aesthetic

Body Arts

MI   People around the world are highly creative in altering their physical appearance. Almost
3   anything that can be done to the body is probably being done or has been done in the
past. In Euro-American societies, for example, parts of the body are now being pierced
that few people even thought of as pierceable a decade or two ago. For convenience, we
focus on the body arts of physical alterations, body painting, and scarification.

3 types of body arts

Physical Alterations

MI   In most societies people attempt to physically alter their bodies. Head and body hair
4   is treated in many different ways. In Western societies hair is styled and often artifi-
cially colored. Some people shave their head, their beard, their legs and armpits.
Others let their beard and mustache grow and style them in various ways. Still others,
particularly middle-aged males, tempt vanity to have replacement hair grown on the
top of their head. In most Western societies these actions are mainly a matter of
fashion or personal taste; in other societies such actions may have deeper cultural
meanings.

5   ***Hairstyles***   In parts of Africa, a woman's status—for example, whether she is
unmarried or married, or is a mother or a widow—is indicated by hairstyle. Among
the Hopis, adolescent girls of marriageable age wear their hair in a large whorl on
each side of the head, creating the so-called butterfly hairstyle. After marriage they
will wear their hair long and parted in the middle. Children among the Omahas had
their hair cut in patterns indicating their clan membership.

6 **Beards** Wearing beards is not always a matter of personal taste and fashion. In many societies, such as Hasidic Jews, Mennonites, Amish, some Muslim sects, and Sikhs, wearing a beard is an act of religious belief. In the ancient world social status was frequently associated with beards. In Egypt only the nobility were allowed to wear beards. Not only did noblemen wear beards, but women of the nobility frequently wore artificial beards as well to indicate their social rank. In contrast, in ancient Greece only the nobility were allowed to be clean shaven; men of commoner status had to let their beards grow.

Henry Peabody/The National Archives.

7 **Head Shaping** Hair alterations are usually reversible, for hair will grow back. Other parts of the body are altered on a permanent basis. Cranial deformation or head shaping has been and is still widely practiced among the peoples of the world. The skull of a baby is soft and if the baby's head is bound the shape of the skull can be permanently changed, flattening the back or the forehead or lengthening the head. In parts of France cranial deformation was virtually universal until the eighteenth century. A baby's face was tightly wrapped in linen, resulting in a flattened skull and ears. In the Netherlands, babies once wore tight-fitting caps that depressed the front portion of the skull. The elite classes of the ancient Andean civilizations elongated the skull, as did the ancient Egyptians. For the first year of its life a Chinook baby was wrapped on a hard board, with another board bound against the top and front of the head. This technique resulted in a head with additional breadth. Some peoples of Central Africa bound the heads of female babies to create elongated skulls that came to a point on the back.

8 **Altering Other Body Parts** Some people permanently altered other parts of the body as well. In China the feet of female children of high-status families were bound at the age of 5 or 6 to deform the feet and keep them small. This was not only considered attractive, it was practiced as a visible indication of the fact that the family was sufficiently wealthy that its women did not have to do much physical labor. In parts of Africa and among some Native American peoples holes were cut in earlobes or the lower and upper lips were expanded so that earplugs and large lip plugs could be inserted. Some of these plugs were up to three inches in diameter. Some central

African Pygmy peoples file their front teeth into points, which in their culture enhances their attractiveness. In parts of Africa, a series of rings was placed around a girl's neck over a period of time, so that when she reached womanhood her shoulders were pressed down, her neck appeared longer, and she could wear multiple neck rings.

9   Such alterations continue in modern nations. Much of the lucrative work of plastic surgeons in contemporary Western nations is concerned with altering physical appearance by changing the shapes of the eyes, nose, mouth, and jowls, and increasing or decreasing the size of breasts, lips, thighs, hips, or waistlines.

10   ***Painting***   Painting is a less drastic and temporary manner of changing an individual's appearance. Some peoples paint only their faces, while others paint almost their entire bodies. Face painting is more common than body painting.

11   ***Face Painting***   Native American peoples commonly painted their faces for war. Among the Osage, before attacking their enemy, the men would blacken their faces with charcoal, symbolic of the merciless fire and their ferocity. In other Native American groups face painting was individualized, each man using different colors and designs to create a ferocious appearance. Sometimes the manner in which a man painted his face depended on a vision and his spiritual helpers. However, not all face painting was associated with war. Faces were commonly painted for religious rituals as well. In addition, many Native American peoples simply painted their faces to enhance their social appearance. Thus, Native Americans painted their faces for a variety of reasons—warfare, religious rituals, and social appearance—just like other peoples in the world.

12   ***Body Painting***   Body painting refers to painting the entire body, or most of it. Like face painting, body painting is found all over the world. In some cases, body painting has religious significance and meaning; in other cases, it is purely secular, designed to enhance the person's physical appearance. Many people in Papua, New Guinea, cover their faces and limbs with white clay when a relative or important person dies as a sign of mourning and respect for the deceased. Among the aboriginal peoples of Australia, bodies were painted with red and yellow ocher, white clay, charcoal, and other pigments. During rituals individuals were painted with elaborate designs covering most of the body. The colors and designs were standardized and had symbolic meaning. Ritual specialists who knew these designs did the painting for religious ceremonies. Outside of ritual contexts, for many Australian peoples, body painting was a secular and daily activity, performed by family members on one another. Individuals were free to use whatever colors and designs pleased them, so long as they were not ritual designs.

Tattooing and Scarification

13   Tattooing and the related practice of scarification are widespread practices. Tattoo designs, achieved by etching and placing a colored pigment under the skin, have been practiced by diverse peoples. When the skin is too dark for tattooing designs to be seen, people may use scarification, the deliberate scarring of the skin to produce designs on the body.

14   ***Tattooing***   Tattooing has a long history as an art form. Tattooing was practiced in ancient Egypt, as well as by the ancient Scythians, Thracians, and Romans in Europe. The ancient Bretons, at the time of the Roman conquest, were reported to have had

their bodies elaborately tattooed with the images of animals. In the fourth century A.D., when Christianity became the official religion of the Roman Empire, tattooing was forbidden on religious grounds. Tattooing virtually disappeared among European peoples until the eighteenth century, when it was discovered in the Pacific and Asia by sailors and reintroduced to Europe as purely secular art.

15   There is an important difference between body painting and tattooing and scarification: paint is removable; tattooing and scarification are indelible and permanent. As a result, tattooing and scarification are usually associated with societies in which there are permanent differences in social status. In these societies, the significance and meaning of tattoos varies. However, for the most part, the more fully tattooed an individual is, the greater the social status.

16   The adornment of the body by tattoos is most elaborate in the scattered islands of Polynesia. In fact, the word *tattoo* itself is Polynesian. The word, like the practice of tattooing sailors, came into use as the result of the voyages of Western explorers and whalers in the seventeenth and later centuries. Tongans, Samoans, Marquesans, Tahitians, the Maori of New Zealand, and most other Polynesian peoples practiced tattooing, which everywhere was connected to social distinctions such as class or rank, sex, religious roles, and specialization, Polynesian peoples are all historically related, so it is not surprising that marking the body with tattoos is found on almost all islands, albeit to different degrees and with somewhat different styles.

© Bob Krist/Corbis.

17   Many Maori had large areas of their bodies covered with tattoos, which could be placed on the torso, thighs, buttocks, calves, and, most notably, the face. Several instruments were used by skilled tattoo artists to incise the patterns characteristic of most Maori tattoos. One was a small chisel made of bone and etched into the skin with a hammer. Apparently, no anesthetic was used to relieve the pain and, in fact, tolerating the pain of the procedure may have been part of its cultural significance. To make pigment, several kinds of wood were burned for their ashes. After the artist made the cuts, pigment was rubbed into the wounds to leave permanent markings. The most skilled tattoo artists

18   Both Maori men and women wore tattoos, although men's bodies were more thoroughly covered. For both sexes, tattoos were seen not merely as body ornamentation or expression of one's personal identity. Having tattoos brought certain privileges. Men who did not undergo tattooing could not build canoe houses, carve wood, make weapons, or weave nets. Untattooed women could not help in the gardens with sweet potatoes, the Maori staple vegetable crop.

19   In all of Polynesia, it was the people of the Marquesas whose bodies were most covered by tattoos. The highest ranking chiefs even had tattoos on the soles of their feet. To the Marquesa, a thorough covering of the body was necessary to protect it from spiritual dangers.

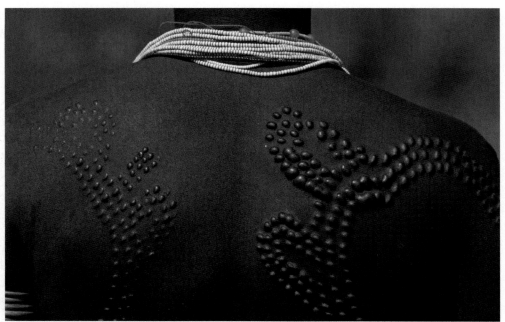

© Remi Benali/Corbis.

20   *Scarification*   Decorating the body by cutting and creating scars, or scarification, is more limited among the world's peoples than tattooing. As in tattooing, scarification is practiced for numerous reasons. Depending on the culture, both men and women may be scarred. Sometimes the scarred design is on the face; in other cases, the chest, breast, back, and even the legs and arms may be elaborately covered with such designs. Sometimes scarification forms part of the puberty rite. Among the Nuer of the southern Sudan, a series of horizontal cuts is made on the foreheads of men who have completed male initiation rituals. On young men, these cuts symbolically mark and communicate their maturity and courage. After they scarify, these cuts become permanent symbols of Nuer manhood.

Performance Arts

21   Performance arts encompass music, song, and dance, which use voice, instruments, and movement to delight the senses and communicate. Generally, music, song, and dance are closely interrelated, but may differ significantly, depending on whether they are religious or secular in nature. For convenience, we will focus on music in the Judeo-Christian religious tradition, the *voudon* religion of the Caribbean, and in the Navajo curing rituals.

The Judeo-Christian Religious Tradition

22 People raised in the Judeo-Christian religious tradition are quite familiar with the many functions of music in religious services. The lyrics of familiar hymns sung to praise God are an integral part of worship rituals. Music also helps to create the mood and sense of reverence for the service and is capable of altering the emotional state of the participants. The shared experience of singing in unison may help draw the congregation together, enhancing what many Christian denominations call their fellowship. In these and other ways, music is important in making the congregation receptive to the messages delivered by the sermon and prayers.

Music in the *Voudon* Religion

23 Music and other forms of performance art are essential to the religious experience for diverse peoples in all parts of the world. The *voudon* (voodoo) religion of the Caribbean heavily incorporates performance arts into religious ceremonies. Followers of *voudon* consider themselves to be people who "serve the spirits" (*loa*). Many *loa* originated and now live in West Africa, where the ancestors of modern Afro-Caribbean peoples were enslaved during the era of slave trade beginning about 1500. *Voudon* temples are elaborately decorated with sacred objects, paintings, and symbolic representations of various *loa*, which show the devotion of the worshippers and make the temple attractive to the spirits. Through drumming, music, and energetic dancing, *voudon* worshippers induce the *loa* to leave their spiritual homes and take over the bodies of those who worship them. When the *loa* possess their human servants, the latter speak with the voices of the *loa*, wear the *loa's* favorite clothing, eat their foods, drink their beverages, and generally assume their identities. Visiting petitioners with problems can ask questions of the worshipper *loa*, who may answer with directions about what course of action to take. *Voudon* drumming, music, and dancing are so totally integrated into temple rituals that the religion is unimaginable without it.

Tumbuka Diviner-Healers

24 Music is essential to the healing process among many African peoples. The Tumbuka of northern Malawi combine singing, drumming, and dancing in all-night curing sessions. Some kinds of illness are caused by a category of spirits called *vimbuza*. *Vimbuza* cause various kinds of illness and even death when they possess someone. The Tumbuka believe that health requires a balance between bodily cold and hot forces (similar to the bodily "humours" of old Europe). When *vimbuza* enter the body, they create an imbalance between hot and cold forces, leading to the buildup of heat that is culturally interpreted as sickness.

25 Tumbuka diviner-healers both diagnose illnesses and direct elaborate healing ceremonies that include drumming, music, and dance. The most essential part of the curing ritual is a shared musical experience in the context of a group gathering, with every individual present expected to contribute to the music making. Even patients themselves participate in the total experience by singing, clapping, and dancing. As the sick person dances to the accompanying rhythm of drums and music, the heat inside the person's body increases. This leads the possessing spirit to expend excess energy and cool off. By thus restoring the balance between hot and cold, the individual is cured, at least temporarily.

The Navajo Curing Rituals

26   For the Navajo of the American Southwest, art is part of curing rituals. In Navajo belief, the most common cause of illness is the loss of harmony with the environment, often caused by the person's violation of a taboo or other transgression. When illness strikes and a diagnosis is made, a Navajo "singer" (curer or medicine man) is called on to organize a complex curing ceremony.

27   In curing ceremonies, the singer addresses and calls on the Holy People, who are spiritual beings believed by Navajo to have the power to restore sick people to harmony and beauty. Ceremonies usually occur in a hogan (house) at night, and in theory the procedures must be executed perfectly for the cure to work.

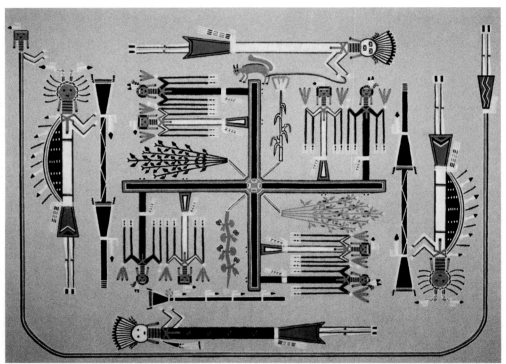

© Geoffrey Clements/Corbis.

28   For the ceremony the singer creates images of the Holy People out of sand, called sandpaintings. Navajo sandpaintings are visual and sacred representations that are created, used in a single ceremony, and then destroyed. Each sandpainting is part of a ceremony that also includes other sacred objects (such as rattles and prayer sticks) and lengthy songs or chants recited by the singer. The song/chants that are recited over the sandpainting and the patient may last for hours. Most song/chants tell of the myths depicted in the specific sandpainting.

29   There are literally hundreds of sandpaintings. Most ceremonies involve a combination of many sandpaintings used in association with particular chants. Because some are quite large and enormously detailed, they often take hours to create. But all must be exact representations of the ideal model of the mythical scene or event depicted. The images are stylized drawings of the Holy People, many of whom are depicted with weapons and armor. Most scenes represented in the sandpaintings are from particular myths familiar to the patient and audience.

30   Sandpaintings are made for the express purpose of inducing the Holy People to come to the hogan where the ceremony is held. During the ceremony, the patient is usually sitting on the sandpainting itself. The singer completes the transfer of power to the patient when he rubs the patient's body with the sand of the images of the Holy People. After each phase of the ceremony is finished, the sandpainting is destroyed, for the Holy People commanded the Navajo not to make permanent images of them.

31   Navajo sandpaintings certainly are works of art. Some Anglos who have seen them think it is a shame to destroy such beautiful images that singers and their helpers have worked so hard to create. But in the context of Navajo beliefs, sandpaintings are made for specific curing ceremonials held for particular patients. That purpose—not expressing the singer's creativity, making an artistic statement, celebrating Navajo culture, or publicly displaying the singer's talents—is their objective. For Navajo, fulfilling their purpose requires that the paintings not be permanent.

Summary

32
1. All cultures have artistic objects, designs, songs, dances, and other ways of expressing their appreciation of the aesthetic. The aesthetic impulse is universal, although cultures vary in their ways of expressing it and the social functions and cultural meanings they attach to it.

2. People raised in the Western tradition are inclined to think of art as something set apart from everyday life—as when we use the phrase "fine arts"—yet we all express ourselves aesthetically in many ways, including how we dress, decorate our houses, and eat our meals.

3. In addition to allowing people to express themselves aesthetically, art serves communicative functions by encoding meanings and messages in symbolic forms.

4. Art takes a multitude of forms, including body art. People around the world change their bodily appearance by such means as physical alterations, application of body paints, tattoos, and scarification. These decorations of the body are used for a variety of purposes, including beautification, expression of individual or group identity, display of privilege or social position, and symbolic indication of social maturity. The tattooing practices of the Maori of New Zealand and other Polynesians exemplify some of these functions.

5. Performance arts include the use of sound and movement for both aesthetic and communicative purposes. Often, performance art is tightly integrated into a people's spiritual and religious life, from Judeo-Christian worship services to possession trances in the *voudon* religion of the Caribbean.

6. Perhaps many forms of art began as "sacred" in that they were connected to the appeal to or worship of spiritual beings. Certainly, the religious elements of artistic expression are important not only in the history of Western art but also in the artistic traditions of people the world over. In their complex curing ceremonies, Navajo singers use both visual arts (sandpaintings) and performance arts (chants/songs) in appealing to the Holy People. Distinguishing "sacred" and "secular" art seems like a simple thing, but objects with religious significance are often used for practical purposes.

Source: "Art and the Aesthetic" from James Peoples, *Humanity,* 7/e, pp. 306–321. Copyright © 2006.

Preparing for and Taking Standardized Tests

At some point, many of you are likely to have to take standardized exams like the SAT, ACT, and GRE. Most standardized exams require you to read passages of varying lengths and then answer questions about the passages. Many of the passages come from literary works, textbooks, essays, news magazines, and documents similar to those you have been reading in *The Art of Critical Reading*. As with most exams, preparation for standardized exams is the key to doing well. Here are some tips:

1. Familiarize yourself with the types of directions and the types of questions that will be on the exam.

2. If possible, take a practice exam or answer sample questions allotting yourself the same amount of time you will have during the actual test.

3. Consider the scoring system. Should you guess? Most experts say that if you can eliminate at least two of the four choices, it's in your best interest to make an educated guess if you don't know the answer.

4. Experiment with the following methods for reading a passage. Determine which method works best for you before taking the big exam.

    • Read the passage carefully and then answer the questions.

    OR

    • Skim the passage, glance at the questions, reread the passage carefully, and then answer the questions.

    OR

    • Read the questions first, then read the passage carefully, and finally answer the questions.

5. Immediately determine the topic and the central theme or main idea of the passage you have read. Read to determine main ideas and to understand concepts. You can go back and look for details later.

6. Make sure you understand the first paragraph of a passage. This paragraph is extremely important. It often gives an overview of the passage, and the main idea is often located there.

7. Mark key parts of the passages or make short notes in the margins if permissible. For instance, you might write *MI* by the main idea and circle key transition words like *in contrast* or *in summary*. But be careful not to overmark.

8. Be sure to read all the possible answers carefully before choosing one. Remember that several answers may be partially correct; the correct answer is the one that most accurately and completely answers the question.

9. If the exam has more than one reading passage, perhaps start with a passage that is about something with which you are already familiar. It is also permissible to tackle the easier questions first.

10. If you must read a passage that you have little interest in, ask yourself what you might learn from the passage.

11. Be aware that your exam is likely to include all of the following:

    • Main idea questions that test your ability to identify the central point.

    • Detail questions that test your ability to locate specific pieces of information.

    • Inference questions that test your ability to understand the implications of the material.

    • Purpose questions that test your ability to understand why the author wrote the passage and who the intended audience is.

    • Vocabulary questions that test your ability to decipher the meaning of words from context clues.

    • Tone questions that test your ability to describe the author's attitude.

VOCABULARY   Unit 10

This is the last vocabulary unit. The first group of words in this unit concerns water, air, and life. The second group concerns sleep and light. The final group includes words using the prefix *in-,* but in several variant forms.

aqua, hydro—water; pneu—air, breathe, wind

aquarium	a tank or container filled with water in which collections of animals and plants live; also, the building where these collections are placed on exhibit.
aqueduct	*–duc* means "to lead," so this word means literally "to lead water." An *aqueduct* can be a pipe for bringing water from a distant place, or it can resemble a canal or tunnel. The Romans built *aqueducts* throughout their empire; many of these are still used today.
Aquarius	This is the constellation that looks like a man carrying water. If you were born between January 20 and February 18, your zodiac sign would be *Aquarius.*
hydrant	a large pipe with a valve for releasing water from a water main
hydroelectric	electricity generated by the energy of running water, usually water falling over a dam.
hydrologist	a person who studies water, including the cycle of evaporation and precipitation.
hydraulic	The literal meaning is "water tube." Today, *hydraulic* is a term used to describe a system operated by the movement of fluid, such as a *hydraulic* jack or *hydraulic* brakes.
pneumatic	containing wind, air, or gases; filled with or worked by compressed air. The tires on your car are *pneumatic* because they hold pressurized air.
pneumonia	An inflammation of the lungs that causes difficulty in breathing

nat—birth; bio—life

nature	the essential character of something; what has always been there from birth.
native	*Native* has two meanings: First, your *native* state or country is where you were born. Second, *native* plants, animals, and people are the ones that originally came from an area. Eucalyptus trees are not *native* to the United States; they were brought here from Australia.
nativity	A *nativity* scene is a birth scene, such as you might see at Christmas when the birth of Jesus is celebrated.
innate	*in-* here means "within," so your *innate* characteristics are those you were born with.
prenatal	before birth
postnatal	after birth
biography	an account of a person's life written by someone else
autobiography	Because *auto-* means "self," an *autobiography* is the story of one's own life written by oneself.

biochemistry	the study of the chemistry of life processes in both plants and animals.
biopsy	the removal of bits of living tissue for analysis
biodegradable	matter that is capable of breaking down or decomposing so that it can return to the life cycle.
symbiotic	the living together of two different organisms for mutual benefit

lum, luc—light; photo—light

luminary	a body or object that gives off light; a person who has attained eminence in a field or is an inspiration to others. Maya Angelou, Rita Dove, and other literary *luminaries* were invited to attend a conference on writing held at Vanderbilt University.
illuminate	to supply or brighten with light; to enlighten. Sylvia used a flashlight to *illuminate* the boxes in the cellar.
translucent	permitting light to pass through but not allowing things on the other side to be seen clearly; easily understood; clear. The glass on most shower doors is *translucent*.
lucid	easily understood; intelligible; sane; glowing with light. After the driver's *lucid* explanation of the events leading to the traffic accident, the police officer had no further questions.
photography	the art or method of making pictures by means of a camera
photogenic	forming an appealing subject for photography; producing or emitting light. A *photogenic* politician has an advantage.
photosynthesis	the process by which green plants form sugars and starches from water and carbon dioxide: This process occurs when sunlight acts upon the chlorophyll in the plant.

hypno(s), dorm, coma—sleep

hypnosis	an artificially induced trance resembling sleep that is characterized by a heightened susceptibility to suggestion.
dormitory	a building, as at a college, containing rooms for residents; a large room containing a number of beds and serving as communal sleeping quarters.
dormant	inactive, as in sleep; undeveloped. Although the volcano has been *dormant* for fifty years, scientists predict an eruption sometime this century.
coma	a state of prolonged unconsciousness including a lack of response to stimuli
comatose	lacking vitality or alertness; torpid

Additional meanings of *in*

As you learned in Unit 5, the Latin prefix *in-* has two distinct meanings: "not" as in the word *inactive*, and "within" or "into" as in the word *incarcerate* (meaning to put in jail or prison). In some English words, *in-* acts as an intensifier, with the meaning "very" or "completely."

infamous	This word does not mean "not famous." Rather, it means "famous but for the wrong reasons." *Infamous* refers to people who have a bad reputation or are notorious, such as Jesse James, Bonnie and Clyde, or Charles Manson.

invaluable	*Invaluable* does not mean "not valuable," but instead means something so valuable that it is priceless. Original copies of the Constitution, your mother's advice, and your grandmother's ring might all be considered *invaluable*.
inflammable	This word means "very flammable." If something is inflammable, it will burn easily. This word is related to the word *inflame*, which means "to catch fire." If something does *not* burn, it would be *non*flammable.
ingenious	*Ingenious* does not mean that a person is not smart. Instead, it means that a person is clever and creative. Inventors such as Thomas Edison and Alexander Graham Bell were *ingenious*.
ingenuous	being naïve about a subject; a childlike candidness. A spy cannot afford to be truly *ingenuous*, although at times she might want to pretend to be *ingenuous*.

Completing Verbal Analogies

Another common type of analogy can be expressed as "A is primarily concerned with B; C is primarily concerned with D." An example is shown below.

        A   B   C   D

___d___ dentist : teeth : : ophthalmologist : _____
        a. ears
        b. feet
        c. insects
        d. eyes

The answer is d. A *dentist* is primarily concerned with *teeth*, just as an *ophthalmologist* is primarily concerned with *eyes*.

Complete the following analogies.

_____ 1. terrarium : plants : : aquarium : _____
        a. dirt
        b. fish
        c. air
        d. water

_____ 2. pneumatic : air : : hydraulic : _____
        a. fluid
        b. tires
        c. nature
        d. wind

_____ 3. geologist : earth : : hydrologist : _____
        a. air
        b. nature
        c. dirt
        d. water

_____ 4. biography : someone else's life : : autobiography : _____
        a. one's horoscope
        b. one's own life
        c. one's birth date
        d. one's health

_____ 5. prenatal : events before birth : : postnatal : _____
    a. events leading up to birth
    b. innate characteristics
    c. events after birth
    d. state of alertness

_____ 6. sun : solar energy : : dams : _____
    a. hydroelectric power
    b. wind energy
    c. water resource
    d. thermonuclear energy

Now that you have studied the vocabulary in Unit 10, practice your new knowledge by completing the crossword puzzle on the next page.

Vocabulary 10

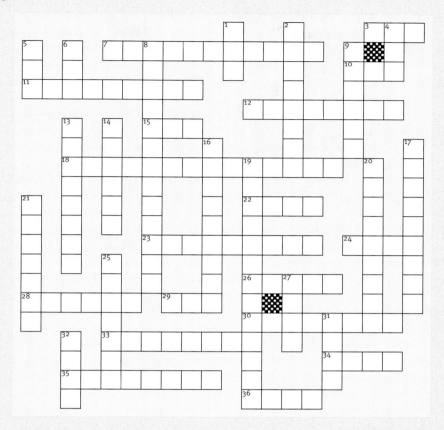

ACROSS CLUES

3. A word part meaning "call."*
7. Bathroom windows are often _____.
10. A word part meaning "born."
11. A relationship of mutual dependency.
12. Picasso, who attained great eminence in the field of art, is an artistic _____.
15. A word part meaning "life."*
18. _____ occurs when sunlight acts upon chlorophyll in a plant.
22. A word part meaning "sleep."
23. Hospital patients who lie in bed too long sometimes develop _____.
24. A word part meaning "air."
26. His writing was very _____ and clear.
28. It is in her _____ to be kind and caring.
29. A word part meaning "put or place."*

30. The driver hit his head on the windshield of the car and became _____.
33. The ancient Romans used an _____ system to move water from one city to another.
34. A word part meaning "water."
35. A birth scene.
36. A word part meaning "believe."*

DOWN CLUES

1. A word part meaning "run."*
2. Jeffrey Dahmer, a serial killer, became _____.
4. An abbreviation for what was once the eighth month.
5. A word part meaning "yield."*
6. A word part meaning "light."
8. The life story of your life written by you.
9. Researchers have concluded that shyness is an _____ characteristic that tends to stay with people throughout their lifetime.

13. A person under the influence of _____ is more susceptible to suggestion.
14. The _____ showed that the growth was benign.
16. Marilyn Monroe often played innocent, childlike, _____ roles.
17. The _____ brakes on your car contain a liquid.
19. The dams along the Colorado River produce _____ power.
20. The iMac computer has an _____ design.
21. In most states, if you park too close to a fire _____, you will get a ticket.
25. The volcano is currently _____, but is expected to erupt within the next decade.
27. A word part meaning "sleep."
31. A word part meaning "pull."*
32. A word part meaning "good."*

*From a previous unit.

Appendices

SECTIONS IN APPENDICES

Golconde (1953)
BY RENÉ MAGRITTE

© 2009 C. Herscovici, London/Artists Rights Society (ARS), New York. Banque d'Images, ADAGP / Art Resource, NY. Menil Collection, Houston, Texas, U.S.A.

Visual Aids

BAR GRAPHS

Bar graphs use vertical (top-to-bottom) or horizontal (left-to-right) bars to show comparisons. Usually, longer bars represent larger quantities. The title of the bar graph below is "Annual Earnings and Education." In this graph, the vertical bars represent the average earnings for the U.S. population in 2003 for increasing levels of education. The source of the data is the U.S. Census Bureau, U.S. Department of Commerce.

Annual Earnings and Education

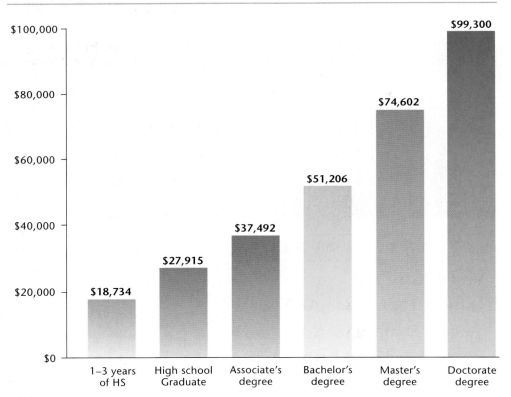

Source: Census 2004. U/S. Census Bureau, U.S. Department of Commerce.

After studying the graph, answer the questions below.

1. What is the average annual income for somebody with a bachelor's degree?

_____

2. What is the average annual income for somebody with an associate's degree?

   _____

3. What is the average annual income for somebody with a high school diploma?

   _____

4. What is the difference in average annual income between someone with an associate's degree and someone with a high school diploma? _____

5. What is the relationship between level of education and average annual income? _____

6. Would you expect the lifetime earnings of someone with a doctorate degree to be greater on average than for someone with a master's degree? _____

TABLES

Tables display information in rows (across) and columns (up and down). The table below demonstrates how two people (Joe and Roscoe) respond differently to the same stressors. Joe encounters a stressor, perceives it as stressful, and winds up with stress. Roscoe, on the other hand, encounters the same stressor, but perceives it in such a way as to avoid stress. Thus, we can see that an event has only potential for eliciting a stress reaction. Whether it actually does elicit a stress reaction depends on how it is perceived.

The Chronic Stress Pattern versus the Healthy Stress Pattern

STRESSOR	JOE (CHRONIC STRESS PATTERN)	ROSCOE (HEALTHY STRESS PATTERN)
Oversleeps—awakes at 7:30 instead of 6:30	Action: Gulps coffee, skips breakfast, cuts himself shaving, tears button off shirt getting dressed	Action: Phones office to let them know he will be late; eats a good breakfast
	Thoughts: I can't be late again! The boss will be furious! I just know this is going to ruin my whole day.	Thoughts: No problem. I must have needed the extra sleep.
	Result: Leaves home anxious, worried, and hungry	Result: Leaves home calm and relaxed
Stuck behind slow driver	Action: Flashes lights, honks, grits teeth, curses, bangs on dashboard with fist; finally passes on blind curve and nearly collides with oncoming car	Action: Uses time to do relaxation exercises and to listen to his favorite radio station
	Thoughts: What an idiot! Slow drivers should be put in jail! No consideration of others!	Thoughts: Here's a gift of time—how can I use it?

(Continued)

The Chronic Stress Pattern versus the Healthy Stress Pattern (*Cont.*)

STRESSOR	JOE (CHRONIC STRESS PATTERN)	ROSCOE (HEALTHY STRESS PATTERN)
Staff meeting	Action: Sits in back, ignores speakers, and surreptitiously tries to work on monthly report	Action: Listens carefully and participates actively
	Thoughts: What a waste of time. Who *cares* what's going on in all those other departments? I have more than I can handle keeping up with my own work.	Thoughts: It's really good to hear my coworkers' points of view. I can do my work a lot more effectively if I understand the big picture of what we're all trying to do.
	Results: Misses important input relating to his department; is later reprimanded by superior	Results: His supervisor compliments him on his suggestions.
Noon—behind on deskwork	Action: Skips lunch; has coffee at desk; spills coffee over important papers	Action: Eats light lunch and goes for short walk in park
	Thoughts: That's the last straw! Now I'll have to have this whole report typed over. I'll have to stay and work late.	Thoughts: I'll be in better shape for a good afternoon with a little exercise and some time out of the office.
Evening	Action: Arrives home 9 P.M., family resentful; ends up sleeping on couch; does not fall asleep until long into the morning	Action: Arrives home at usual time; quiet evening with family; to bed by 11 P.M., falls asleep easily
	Thoughts: What a life! If only I could run away and start over! It's just not worth it. I'll never amount to anything.	Thoughts: A good day! I felt really effective at work, and it was nice reading to the kids tonight.
	Results: Wakes up late again, feeling awful; decides to call in sick	Results: Wakes up early, feeling good

Table from Jerrold Greenberg, *Comprehensive Stress Management*, 10th ed. New York: McGraw-Hill, 2008, p. 11. Copyright © 2008 McGraw-Hill. Reprinted by permission of The McGraw-Hill Companies, Inc.

Directions: Indicate whether the statement is true or false by writing T or F in the blank provided. If you can't tell based on the information provided in the table, write CT. You may refer to the table.

_____ 1. Roscoe, stuck behind a slow driver, listens to the radio.

_____ 2. Joe, stuck behind a slow driver, causes an accident.

_____ 3. Roscoe is chastised by a superior.

_____ 4. Roscoe eats a salad before his walk in the park.

_____ 5. Joe openly tries to work on his monthly report at the staff meeting.

FLOWCHARTS

Flowcharts are often used in textbooks to show cause-and-effect relationships and the sequence of events. The action moves, or flows, in the direction of the arrows. The following flowchart, which appears in a psychology textbook, shows how stress triggers bodily effects, upsetting thoughts, and leading to ineffective behavior. Notice how each element worsens the others in a vicious cycle.

Stress: The Vicious Cycle

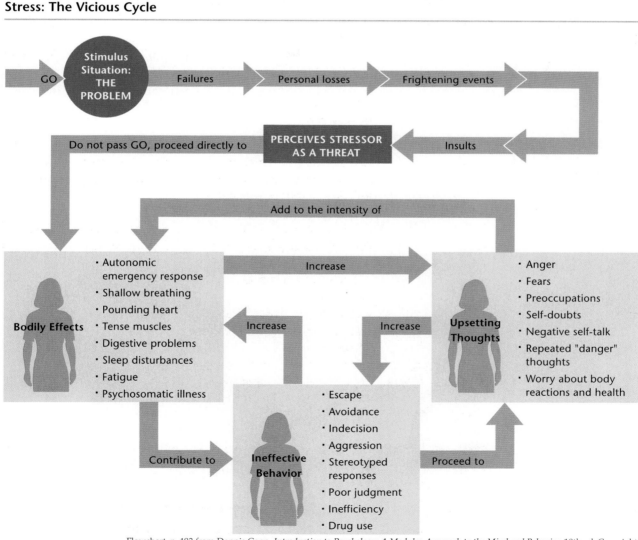

Flowchart, p. 483 from Dennis Coon, *Introduction to Psychology: A Modular Approach to the Mind and Behavior*, 10th ed. Copyright © 2006. Reprinted with permission of Wadsworth, a division of Thomson Learning: www.thomsonrights.com. Fax 800-730-2215.

Indicate whether the statement is true or false by writing T or F in the blank provided. If you can't tell based on the flowchart, write CT.

_____ 1. Avoidance decreases the bodily effects of stress.

_____ 2. Sleep disturbances contribute to ineffective behavior.

_____ 3. Shallow breathing increases upsetting thoughts like anger.

_____ 4. Poor judgment can lead to negative self-talk.

_____ 5. Anger can intensify digestive problems.

_____ 6. Exercise can reduce the bodily effects of stress.

MAPS

Maps are useful for presenting information visually. The legend, which indicates what color or shading represents, is the key to understanding the map. Maps may also have endnotes that explain the specific details. The following map, based on data from the *Statistical Abstract of the United States 2007*, shows the number of violent crimes that occurred in the United States as of 2004. Study the map, using the legend and the endnotes as a guide.

Some States Are Safer: Violent Crime in the United States

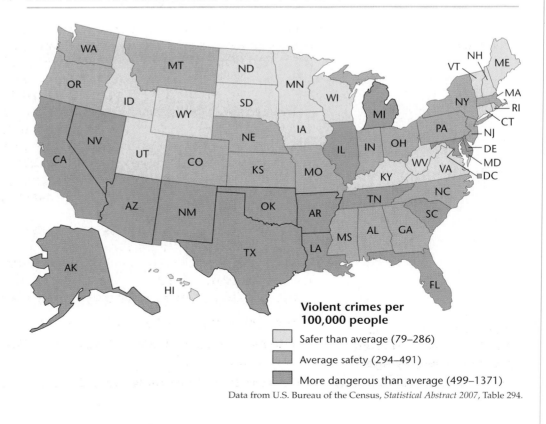

Violent crimes per 100,000 people

☐ Safer than average (79–286)

◼ Average safety (294–491)

◼ More dangerous than average (499–1371)

Data from U.S. Bureau of the Census, *Statistical Abstract 2007*, Table 294.

Violent crimes are murder, rape, robbery, and aggravated assult. The variation of violence among the states is incredible. Some states have a rate that is ten times higher than that of other states. With a rate of 79 per 100,000 people, North Dakota has the lowest rate of violence, while Florida, at 711, has the highest rate. The U.S. average rate is 466 (the total of the states' average rates of violence divided by 50). This total does not include Washington, D.C., whose rate is 1,371,17 times as high as North Dakota and almost 3 times the national average.

Using the information in the map and legend, answer the following questions.

1. According to the information given, violent crimes are _____, _____, _____, and _____.

2. _____ is the state with the lowest rate of violent crime.

3. The state with the highest rate of violent crime in the United States is _____.

4. How many states are considered to be safer than average? _____.

5. California, Arizona, and Nevada all have _____ rates of violent crime.

6. Hawaii has a safer-than-average rate, but Alaska has a _____ _____ safety rate.

PIE GRAPHS

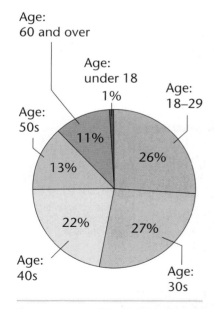

Percentage of Individuals Who Have Been Victimized by Identity Theft, by Age

Pie chart from Kapoor, *Personal Finance*, p. 193.

Age:
60 and over

Age:
under 18
1%

Age:
18–29

Age:
50s

11%

26%

13%

22%

27%

Age:
40s

Age:
30s

Pie graphs are illustrations that show percentages or proportions as pie-shaped sections of a circle. The whole interior of the circle represents 100 percent. The pie graph illustrates the percentage of people in each age bracket who have been victimized by identity theft, based on information provided by the Federal Trade Commission in April 2005.

According to the FTC, anyone can be a victim of identity theft. The biggest problem is that you may not know your identity has been stolen until something is already amiss. You may get bills for a credit card account you never opened; your credit report may include debts you never knew you had; a billing cycle may pass without your receiving a statement; or you may see charges on your statement that you didn't sign for, didn't authorize, and know nothing about.

Because identity theft is the fastest-growing financial crime, the FTC maintains the Identity Theft Data Clearinghouse and provides information to identify theft victims. You can call toll-free 1-877-ID-THEFT or visit www.consumer.gov/idtheft.

Using the information in the pie graph, answer the following questions.

1. What percentage of victims are in their 30s? _____

2. Which age group has the lowest percentage of identity theft? _____

3. What are the next two lowest groups? _____

4. What reasons do you suppose account for the two highest age groups of identity theft? _____

_____

5. What steps can you take to thwart identity thieves? _____

_____

6. What can you do to protect your social security number? _____

_____

CONSUMER LABELS

Consumer labels are designed to help consumers make wise choices about specific products. Since March 1999, the Food and Drug Administration has required the labels of dietary supplements to carry a "supplements facts" panel. In addition, because most supplements have not been evaluated by the FDA for safety or effectiveness, the label must carry a disclaimer.

What's in a Label?

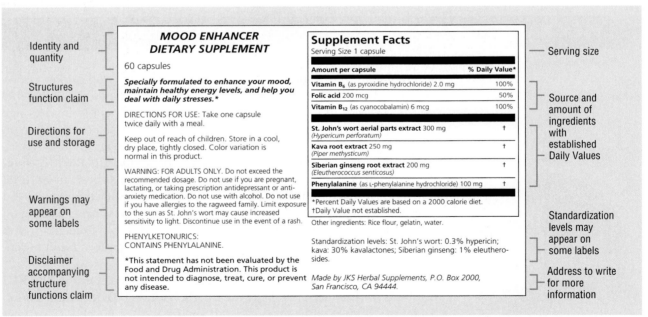

Figure from Paul M. Insel, *Core Concepts in Health*, 9th ed. New York: McGraw-Hill, 2002, p. 343.
Copyright © 2002 McGraw-Hill. Reprinted by permission of The McGraw-Hill Companies, Inc.

Using the information in the dietary supplement label, answer the following questions.

1. What is the meaning of *disclaimer?*_____
   a. a statement that reveals or lays open
   b. a statement that expresses disapproval
   c. a statement that repudiates or denies

2. One capsule of this product contains _____ mg of St. John's wort.

3. Is this product something that should be given to children? _____

4. What is the meaning of *warning*? _____
   a. notification of possible dangers
   b. directions about how much medicine to give
   c. praise of the product

5. What is the recommended dosage for this product? _____

6. Does this product claim to help you if you are suffering from stress? _____

7. Should you take this product if you are going to be in the sun for prolonged periods? _____
   a. Yes, there should be no adverse effect.
   b. No, the product increases the skin's sensitivity to sunlight.

8. Is it safe to take this product with alcohol? _____

LINE GRAPHS

A **line graph,** which takes the form of a line drawn in an L-shaped grid, shows the relationship between two variables. One of these variables is defined along the bottom, on the horizontal (across) axis of the grid. The other variable is defined along the side, on the vertical (up and down) axis of the grid. The line need not be straight; in fact, it is often jagged or curved. Often the bottom scale of the grid measures time (for example, minutes, years, or decades), and so the line graph shows changes over time.

The line graph below shows the decline in viewership of the nightly news telecasts of the three major networks—ABC, NBC, and CBS. According to NewsBusters, the viewership in 2006 dropped even further, to 21 million viewers.

Evening News Viewership, All Networks,
NOVEMBER 1980 TO NOVEMBER 2005

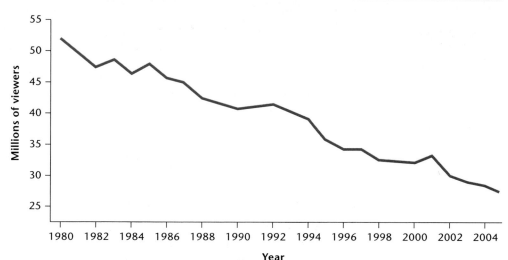

Graph from State of the News Media 2007, Project for Excellence
in Journalism. www.stateofthenewsmedia.org/2007

Using information from the line graph, answer the following questions.

1. The vertical axis is in _____ of viewers.

2. What was the approximate total decline in number of viewers from 1980 to 2005? _____

3. What probably was the reason for the increase in number of viewers in 2001?

    _____

4. What were the only other years that showed an increase in number of viewers?

    _____

5. What are possible reasons for the decrease in viewership of these newscasts?

    _____

6. What are your main sources of news information? _____

EXERCISE: VISUAL AIDS

On this page and the next are a bar graph, a line graph, and a map. The bar graph depicts life expectancy by year of birth. The line graph and the map depict the "graying of America," that is, the increasing proportion of elderly people in the U.S. population.

Life Expectancy by Year of Birth

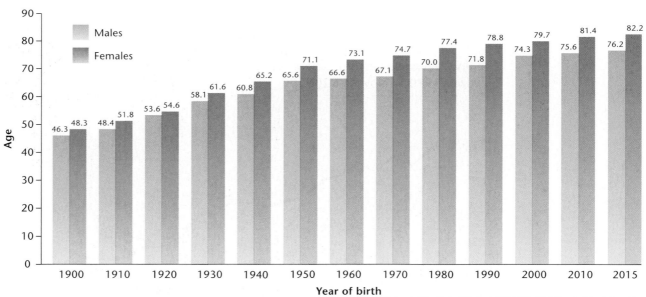

Source: *Statistical Abstract of the United States*, 2007; Table 98; *Historical Statistics of the United States, Colonial Times to 1970, Bicentennial Edition, Part 1, Series B, pp. 107–115.*

Median Age of U.S. Population

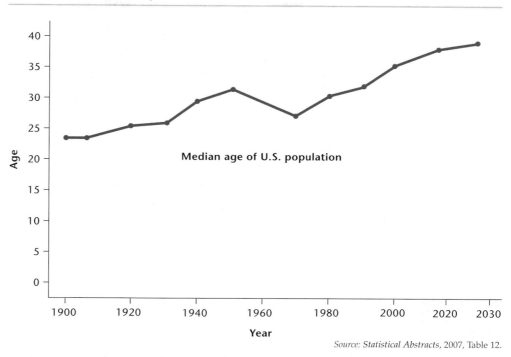

Source: Statistical Abstracts, 2007, Table 12.

As Florida Goes, So Goes the Nation: The Year 2025

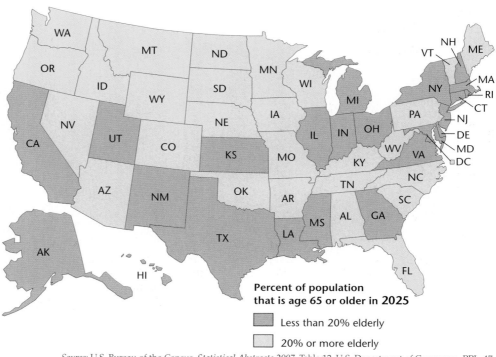

Percent of population that is age 65 or older in **2025**

Less than 20% elderly

20% or more elderly

Source: U.S. Bureau of the Census, *Statistical Abstracts 2007*, Table 12, U.S. Department of Commerce, PPL-47.

Note: The growing proportion of the elderly in the U.S. population is destined to have profound effects on U.S. society. By the year 2025, one-fifth of the population of 27 states is expected to be 65 or older. Today, at 16.8 percent, only Florida comes close to this.

Using the information in these three visual aids, answer the questions below:

1. The average life expectancy of a man born in 1980 is _____.

2. The average life expectancy of a woman born in 2000 is _____.

3. In one hundred years, 1900–2000, the life expectancy of males increased from _____ to _____ years.

4. In 1900, the median age of the U.S. population was approximately _____.

5. In 1940, the median age of the U.S. population was approximately _____.

6. In 2020, the median age of the U.S. population is projected to be approximately _____.

7. What do these visual aids tell us about the percentage of people age 65 or older in California? _____

8. What do these visual aids tell us about the percentage of people age 65 or older in Oregon? _____

Using a Thesaurus

The word *thesaurus* is derived from the Greek *thesauros,* meaning "treasure or treasury." A **thesaurus** is a "treasury" of related words. It is a dictionary of synonyms and antonyms presented alphabetically in categories. Unlike a dictionary, a thesaurus does not give the definition, pronunciation, or etymology of a word.

The purpose of a thesaurus is to enable you to be more precise in the words that you use so that you can express your thoughts exactly. It also enables you to choose alternate words so that you don't just repeat the same word over and over again. Many students find a thesaurus to be an invaluable resource in helping them select just the right word to use in an essay or homework assignment.

As an example, imagine that you have just written the following sentences:

Worn out by evading her pursuers, she now lay prostrate in the desert sand. Trying to conserve her insufficient supply of water, she drank sparingly from her canteen, fully aware that only a few insufficient drops remained.

Notice that the word *insufficient* has been used twice. Replacing the word with a synonym might improve the sentence and help to clarify your meaning. Turning to *Roget's College Thesaurus,* you find the following entry:

INSUFFICIENCY

Nouns—**1,** insufficiency; inadequacy, inadequateness; incompetence, IMPOTENCE; deficiency, INCOMPLETENESS, IMPERFECTION, shortcoming, emptiness, poorness, depletion, vacancy, flaccidity; ebb tide; low water; bankruptcy, insolvency (see DEBT, NONPAYMENT).

2, paucity; stint; scantiness, smallness, none to spare; bare necessities, scarcity, dearth; want, need, deprivation, lack, POVERTY; inanition, starvation, famine, drought; dole, pittance; short allowance *or* rations, half-rations.

Verbs—**1,** not suffice, fall short of (see FAILURE); run dry, run *or* give out, run short; want, lack, need, require; be caught short, be in want, live from hand to mouth; miss by a mile.

2, exhaust, deplete, drain of resources; impoverish (see WASTE); stint, begrudge (see PARSIMONY); cut back, retrench; bleed white.

Adjectives—**1,** insufficient, inadequate; too little, not enough; unequal to; incompetent, impotent; weighed in the balance and found wanting; perfunctory (see NEGLECT); deficient, wanting, lacking, imperfect; ill-furnished, -provided, *or* -stored; badly off.

2, slack, at a low ebb; empty, vacant, bare; out of stock; short (of), out of, destitute (of), devoid (of), denuded (of); dry, drained; in short supply, not to be had for love or money, not to be had at any price; empty-handed; short-handed.

3, meager, poor, thin, sparing, spare, skimpy, stinted; starved, half-starved, famine-stricken, famished; jejune; scant, small, scarce; scurvy, stingy; at the end of one's tether; without resources (see MEANS); in want, poor (see POVERTY); in DEBT. *Slang,* shy of, fresh out of.

Adverbs—insufficiently, *etc.*; in default, for want of; failing.

Antonyms, see SUFFICIENCY.

Notice that the synonyms are presented by parts of speech: nouns, verbs, adjectives, and adverbs. At the end of the entry, antonyms are listed.

Depending on the meaning you are trying to convey, you might choose to replace the word *insufficient* with *inadequate* or *meager*. For instance, your new sentence might now look like this:

> Worn out by evading her pursuers, she now lay prostrate in the desert sand. Trying to conserve her insufficient supply of water, she drank sparingly from her canteen, fully aware that only a few meager drops remained.

Exercise 1: Using a Thesaurus

Use a thesaurus to find two synonyms for each of the words below.

1. insufferable: _____ _____
2. frugal: _____ _____
3. enervate: _____ _____

Exercise 2: Recognizing Synonyms

Can you recognize the following well-known proverbs? They have been rewritten with synonyms for key words. Rewrite the proverbs to bring them back to their familiar form.

1. Birds of similar plumage assemble.

   _____

2. Sanitation is next to piousness.

   _____

3. An examined kettle does not bubble.

   _____

Now use your thesaurus to rewrite the following proverbs. Find synonyms for at least two words in each proverb.

4. You can't teach an old dog new tricks.

   _____

5. Where there's smoke, there's fire.

   _____

6. Look before you leap.

   _____

7. People who live in glass houses shouldn't throw stones.

   _____

Peter Mark Roget (1779–1869), an English physician, wrote the first thesaurus in 1852 at the age of 73. Since Roget's death, many editions of his thesaurus have been published, including editions that are now on the Internet, such as *Roget's International Thesaurus* www.bartleby.com/110/. Most computer word processing programs, such as MS Word, also feature a thesaurus.

MS WORD THESAURUS

The thesaurus that accompanies MS Word groups words into categories based on meaning. In MS Word, you highlight the word in your typed text that you want to replace, click on Tools, click on Language, and then click on Thesaurus. Below is a sample search for the word "art" as found in the title of this textbook, *The Art of Critical Reading.* The first MS Word Screen that appears is the one below.

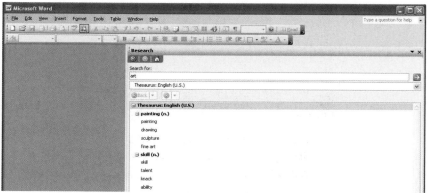

Screen capture MS Word thesaurus entry for the word "Art"

Two main meanings of "art" are given in bold. The meaning we are interested in is one related to "skill." Now click on the word "skill" (in regular type), and the following screen with more words will appear.

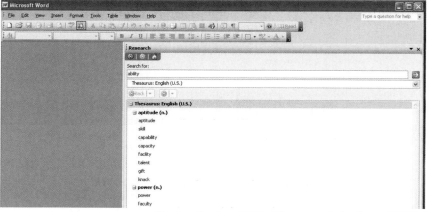

Screen capture from MS Word Thesaurus entry for the word "Ability"

You can continue to highlight words until you find the one that suits your needs. If you can't find something close enough, consult *Roget's International Thesaurus* or the following website: www.refdesk.com.

ROGET'S INTERNATIONAL THESAURUS

Roget's International Thesaurus is organized by categories. To search for a word, first consult the index found at the back of the book. The following is how the word "art" appears in the index of the *Roget's*.

ART

representation 349.1

knack 413.6

science 413.7

cunning 415.1

stratagem 415.3

visual arts 712.1

artistry 712.7

vocation 724.6

science 927.10

The numbers after each category indicate where that particular category is located in *Roget's*. Probably the best category for our purposes is 413.7, which appears as follows:

413 SKILL

7 art, science, craft; skill; technique, technic, **technics,** technology, technical knowledge or skill, technical know-how <nonformal>, field-work, **mechanics,** mechanism, method

Excerpts from *Roget's International Thesaurus,* 5th Edition by Peter Mark Roget and edited by Robert L. Chapman. Copyright © 1992 by HarperCollins Publishers, Inc. Reprinted by permission.

The words are listed in order of their relationship to the general classification—in this case, "skill." The words in bold are the most common words for each variation of use. If none of these words meet your needs, you can look in other sections of the general classification or return to the index to locate another general category.

Exercise 3: Using a Thesaurus

What synonyms can you find for the word "critical" as used in *The Art of Critical Reading?*

Look up "critical" in the thesaurus that is associated with your word processor. Follow the same procedure that we completed above with the word "art." Write the appropriate words that you locate on the line below.

Look up "critical" in the index of *Roget's International Thesaurus.* Find words that could be substituted for "critical" as it is used in *The Art of Critical Reading.* Write those words below.

Sample Summary

The following paragraph summarizes the plagiarism scandal described in Jody Wilgoren's article "School Cheating Scandal Tests a Town's Values" (pages 185–188).

A plagiarism scandal at Piper High School in Kansas caused deep divisions in a once close-knit community. Students in Christine Pelton's sophomore biology class were required to complete a leaf project worth 50 percent of their grade. Upon reviewing the projects, Ms. Pelton discovered with the aid of computer software that 28 of 115 students had plagiarized parts of their reports. Ms. Pelton gave those students zeros on the assignment. Both the principal and the superintendent initially backed Ms. Pelton, but after parental protests, the superintendent intervened and reduced the assignment from 50 percent of the final grade to only 30 percent. He also directed Ms. Pelton to deduct only 600 points instead of 1,500 points from those who were accused of plagiarizing. In protest, Ms. Pelton resigned her position. The resulting scandal pitted parent against parent. Some parents asserted that the leniency unfairly penalized those who did the assignment correctly and that students were being robbed of a valuable lesson in values. Others said that those who plagiarized did not fully understand the meaning of plagiarism. Teachers worried that their authority had been seriously undermined. And because of the media attention focused on Piper, residents feared that the incident made the entire community look bad.

Vocabulary Word Parts

Following is a list of the vocabulary word parts you studied in this text. The prefixes indicating numbers are listed first. The other word parts are listed in alphabetical order.

WORD PART	MEANING	EXAMPLE
uni	one	unify
mono	one	monogram
bi	two	bivalve
di	two	dichotomy
du(o)	two	duplex
tri	three	triplicate
qua(d)	four	quadrangle
tetra	four	tetrapod
quint	five	quintessence
pent	five	pentathlon
hex	six	hexagram
sex	six	sextet
sept	seven	September
hept	seven	heptagon
oct	eight	October
nov	nine	November
dec, dek	ten	December
a(n)	not, without	asymmetrical
ad	toward	admit
agogos	lead; bring together; excite	demagogue
ana	back; up; again	anachronism
aqua	water	aquarium
archy	rule	monarchy
auto	self, by oneself	autocracy
belli	war	belligerent
bene	well	benefactor
bio	life	biography
cap	head	caption
capt, cept	hold; seize; take	captivity
cede, ces	go (back); yield; withdraw	precede
chrono	time	chronology
cide	kill	genocide
circum	around	circumvent

WORD PART	MEANING	EXAMPLE
cogni	know	cognitive
coma	sleep	comatose
con	with	convert
corp	body	corporation
cracy	rule; strength; power	plutocracy
cred	believe	incredulous
cur(r)	run	recur
demos	people	democracy
deus	god	deity
dia	through; across; apart; thoroughly	diagonal
dis	apart; away	dismiss
dorm	sleep	dormant
duc	lead	induce
dys	bad; abnormal; difficult	dysentery
equi	equal	equitable
eu	good; well	eulogy
fid	faith(ful)	fidelity
frater, fratri	brother	fraternity
genus	birth; begin; race	genealogy
geo	earth	geocentric
gnostos	know	agnostic
graph	write	demography
helio	sun	heliocentric
homo	man	homicide
hydro	water	hydroelectric
hypno(s)	sleep	hypnosis
in	not; opposite; into; within	invert
inter	between; among	interpersonal
intra	within; inside	intrapersonal
ism	doctrine; theory	polytheism
ject	throw	inject
legis	law	legislature
locut (loqu)	speak, talk	loquacious
log(ue)	speech; word	dialogue
logy	science of; study of	seismology
lum, luc	light	translucent
macro	large, long	macrocosm
mal	bad	malign
mater, matri	mother	maternity
medius	middle	intermediate
meter	measure	pedometer
micro	small	microfilm
mis	hate; bad(ly)	misconstrue
mis, mit	send	mission
nat	birth	native
pater, patri	father	paternity
path(o), pathy	feeling; suffering; emotion	apathy
ped	child	pediatrician
phil(o)	love	philanthropist

WORD PART	MEANING	EXAMPLE
photo	light	photography
pneu	air; breathe; wind	pneumonia
polis	city	politician
poly	many	polytechnic
pos, pon	put; place	depose
potis	powerful	potent
pro	forward	progressive
re	back; again	remit
sacri	holy	sacred
sanct	holy	sanctuary
se	apart; away from	separate
sequ, secut	following	sequence
soror	sister	sorority
syn	same	synagogue
tact, tang	touch	tactile
temp	time; moderate	temperate
ten(t), tin	hold; cling; keep	detention
terr	earth, land	territory
theo	god	theocracy
trac(t)	pull; draw	traction
ven	come	prevent
vert	turn	divert
viv	live	revive
voc	call	vocal

Index

Index of Artists and Art Works

Stemware
OF THE 20TH CENTURY

THE TOP 200 PATTERNS

Park Lane by Mikasa.

Stemware

OF THE 20TH CENTURY

THE TOP 200 PATTERNS

Harry L. Rinker

HOUSE OF COLLECTIBLES

THE BALLANTINE PUBLISHING GROUP • NEW YORK

Important Notice. All of the information, including valuations,
in this book has been compiled from the most reliable sources,
and every effort has been made to eliminate errors
and questionable data. Nevertheless, the possibility of error, in a work of such
immense scope, always exists. The publisher will not
be held responsible for losses that may occur in the purchase,
sale, or other transaction of items
because of information contained herein. Readers
who feel they have discovered errors are invited
to write and inform us, so they may be corrected in
subsequent editions. Those seeking further information
on the topics covered in this book are advised
to refer to the complete line of *Official Price Guides*
published by the House of Collectibles.

Copyright © 1997 by Rinker Enterprises, Inc.

All rights reserved under International and Pan-American Copyright Conventions.

HC This is a registered trademark of Random House, Inc.

Published by: House of Collectibles
The Ballantine Publishing Group
201 East 50th Street
New York, NY 10022

Distributed by The Ballantine Publishing Group, a division of Random House, Inc., New York, and simultaneously in
Canada by Random House of Canada Limited, Toronto.

http://www.randomhouse.com

Manufactured in the United States of America

ISSN: 1094-3854

ISBN: 0-676-60084-0

Text design by Debbie Glasserman
Cover design by Kristine V. Mills-Noble
Cover photo © George Kerrigan

First Edition: November 1997

Contents

From Edinburgh Crystal's 1986/87 catalog.

Acknowledgments

This book was a team effort. Although my name appears on the cover as the author, dozens of individuals have contributed their expertise.

Gary S. Corns, Manager of the Imaging Services Design Team, spearheaded the efforts at Replacements, Ltd. His tolerance and patience concerning my requests for "just one more piece of information" and his willingness to answer those requests is much appreciated. Mark Klein, Director of Marketing, was instrumental in securing the cooperation of the Wedgwood Group and is responsible for Replacements' marketing of this and its companion volumes, *Dinnerware of the 20th Century* and *Silverware of the 20th Century*.

Chris Kirkman, Jamie L. Robinson, and other members of Replacements' curating staff were extremely helpful. They are research professionals and made me feel like a team member every time I visited in Greensboro.

Bob Page, Replacements' founder, is a source of inspiration each time I speak to him. I still have not decided which one of us loves what we do more. This book and its companion volumes would not have been possible without Bob's enthusiastic support and his willingness to provide access to Replacements' database.

My Replacements contacts continue to grow. I view Doug Anderson, Executive Vice President, as this project's cheerleader. I also thank Dale Frederiksen, Mark Donahue, Media and Marketing Coordinator, and Todd Hall for their efforts. Finally, a special thanks to Pat Thompson of Greensboro, North Carolina, who was my first contact at Replacements and is now an independent media consultant. She dreamed my dream for this project and opened the appropriate doors.

Dena George at Rinker Enterprises, Inc. was responsible for the price listings, for image management, and for working with manufacturers and their public relations firms in obtaining information and images. She was ably assisted by Nancy Butt. Additional support came from Dana Morykan, Kathy Williamson, Virginia Reinbold, and Richard Schmeltzle.

The cooperation received from manufacturers and their agents was most welcome. These include: Anchor Hocking Glass Corporation, Barbara Wolf, Manager of Merchandising Services; Baccarat, Shari James and Howard Hyde, Vice President of Sales and Marketing; Durand International, Peggy DeMarchi and Bernard Grigri, Director of Marketing; Edinburgh Crystal; Lenox Brands, Alice Kolator, Director of Public Relations, Ellen Denker, Archives, and Tracy Mitchell; Mikasa; Miller Rogaska Crystal, Marcy Karales; Noritake Co., Inc., Ellen Ladd; Orrefors, Inc., Robin Spink, Marketing; Princess House, Inc., Cathy Paulson and Kathy Butler; Sasaki, Yvette Rosado; *Tableware Today,* Amy Stavis, Editor and Publisher; Waterford Crystal, Scott J. Scordo, Creative Services Administrator; Waterford/Wedgwood, BC Design Inc., Bernadette Hoyt and Chie Riley, Librarian; Wedgwood USA, Stacey Lundy, Marketing Assistant; and Wedgwood, England, Clare Elsby, Communications Department.

The House of Collectibles staff, headed by Timothy J. Kochuba, is commended for its patience and fortitude in bringing this project to its conclusion. Randy Ladenheim-Gil served as project coordinator and editor, Simon Vukelj directed the marketing efforts, and Alex Klapwald supervised production.

Inevitably, with a project of this size and nature, many individuals whose names do not appear here also helped assemble data and performed other tasks that led to the publication and successful sale of this book. My thanks to all of these individuals. The talents they brought to the project are sincerely appreciated.

Finally, my thanks to you, the purchaser of this book. I hope you will find that it more than meets your expectations.

Introduction

My earliest stemware memories involve eating, not drinking. When we ate at the dining room table rather than the kitchen nook, my mother often used her sherbet glasses to serve dessert. The sherbet stems rarely held sherbet—we were not a sherbet family. Instead, the glasses were filled with pudding or rich, creamy Abbots ice cream, topped with crushed walnuts or cherries and chocolate syrup, the latter ingredients coming from my uncle's drugstore.

My parents owned a set of crystal. Although I remember seeing several sets of eight glasses in the china closet, I have no memories of the exact shapes or patterns. But I do remember the color—the stems were light pink.

When I was cleaning out my parents' home, I found a set of eight cocktail glasses stored in a box. They had black glass stems and a frosted, conical-shaped bowl. They looked neat, so I kept them. They were still housed in the box in which I had found them when I began the research on this book. Now they reside in my corner cupboard. Mother always said, "Practice what you preach." Since I advocate using family heirlooms, I would be remiss in not doing so myself.

Having only vague memories of my parents' stemware, I called several of my aunts and uncles to ask about their stemware and to see what memories they had of the stemware at my parents' and grandparents' houses. I was surprised to discover that their memories were as vague as mine.

My parents, my brother, and I lived with my Prosser grandparents at their home on High Street in Bethlehem, Pennsylvania, between 1946 and 1948. When one of my aunts recalled a set of light green stems stored on a top shelf in Grandma Prosser's kitchen, I had a brief flashback of them. I cannot remember them with any degree of certainty, but if they existed, they probably were an inexpensive, mass-produced depression glass set. Grandpa Prosser was not a big spender—he had ten children to raise!

While each of my aunts and uncles owned some stemware, none owned a set containing six or more shapes. In fact, none of them knew the make and pattern of their stemware. Aunt Jeannette's memories centered around the use of her sherbet glasses. Dessert served in sherbet glasses appears to have been the height of elegance achieved in my mother's family.

Surprised that my aunts and uncles did not know more about their stemware, I began asking employees, friends, and others I met about their tableware. Even though most could name the manufacturer and pattern of their dinnerware and flatware, almost no one knew the same about their stemware, which I found fascinating. If I were searching for a reason to write this book, I would have to look no further.

As a young adult in the 1960s, I bought a home in suburbia and was heavily into the casual lifestyle of the patio and backyard grill. Serving wine at informal parties was just coming into vogue. Needing wine glasses for an upcoming event, I remember hopping into my car and driving to Almart, one of the first discount chain stores in Pennsylvania's Lehigh Valley, at the Lehigh Shopping Center, and buying an inexpensive boxed set of eight glasses. They were Japanese. I was more interested in what went into the glasses than in the glasses themselves.

Today, the lifestyle I embraced in the 1960s is considered casual by the tabletop industry. It is an eclectic, mix-and-match lifestyle—not everything has to be coordinated. It is nice to know where I fit in.

My corner cupboard contains several dozen stems, representing a half dozen patterns. One pattern has two stems, another has eleven. Too lazy to wash my stemware by hand, I put it into the dishwasher. Many pieces do not enjoy a relatively long life. When stems are broken and replacements are needed, I never take a surviving stem to the store and attempt to match it. Instead, I go shopping, find a pattern I like, and buy a boxed set of six or twelve. Having grown up in an "it's too good to throw out" environment, I cannot bring myself to discard the broken sets. Further, as a user of whatever happens to be in the front of the cupboard, my table stemware usually has an identity crisis.

Since working on this book, I have resolved to do better. I am reviewing my stemware to determine which patterns I like and which I do not. Once I have made that determination, I plan to research the patterns I like and learn their history, as well as that of their manufacturers and designers. There is truth in the concept that the love of objects is in direct proportion to what one knows about them. Patterns I love will be expanded.

Further, matched stemware will be the order of the day on my table in the future. Because of my work on this book, I now realize the attention and care stemware manufacturers give to designing patterns that complement all styles of dinnerware. There is no universal pattern. I have accepted the fact that since I own multiple sets of dinnerware, I should own multiple sets of stemware. (I confess to being somewhat concerned about my lifestyle becoming more formal and less casual!)

As I learn more about my stemware, exploring my likes and dislikes, and as I use it more frequently, I challenge you to do the same. There is something about using stemware that appears to slow life down, to create a brief, reflective pause. Given today's fast-paced lifestyle, this may be just what the doctor ordered.

As an antiques and collectibles writer and appraiser, I frequently am asked by individuals to value their tableware services and recommend someone, sometimes anyone, who will buy them. I always ask my clients if they have talked with their children to ask if they would like them. The stock answer is "They do not want them."

My response is twofold. First, be patient. The nostalgia gene is a late bloomer. Many young adults who said no to their parents' queries in their thirties have deep-seated regrets by their forties. Second, use your tableware, especially when your children and their families visit. It only takes a few meals to change how your children view your family tableware heirlooms.

The true value of objects is not monetary, but the memories associated with them. Use creates those memories. Stemware, dinnerware, and flatware were not created to be merely displayed in a china cabinet or stored in a buffet. They were made and sold to be used. It is a point we should never forget.

How does one determine what constitutes the top 200 patterns of 20th-century stemware? The most obvious approach is to research production and sales records and make a list. However, this information is not readily available. Manufacturers jealously guard such statistics, and making them public provides the competition with valuable information that could be used against them.

If sales and production statistics were the only criteria used to develop the Top 200 Patterns list, the result would be far different from the list that appears in this book. There would be more patterns from the first decades of the twentieth century and far fewer contemporary patterns. Such a list would reflect past, not present, tastes.

The Top 200 Pattern list that appears in this book is based on today's market demand. The patterns listed are those that are most often requested by individuals who are seeking replacement pieces—they are the top 200 patterns currently in use.

An analysis of the Top 200 Pattern list reveals several key marketing and use trends. Many of the patterns are still in production. Because manufacturers and distributors often limit the number of retailers allowed to sell their product, many individuals have turned to mail-order catalogs and replacement services to replace or add pieces to their contemporary stemware. The Replacements, Inc., letterhead now indicates the ability to supply "Discontinued & Active" china, crystal, and flatware.

The Top 200 Pattern list contains no pressed glass stemware patterns from the pre-1920 period. In fact, there are only a limited number of patterns whose origins date between 1920 and 1940. The vast majority of the patterns on the list were first designed and marketed following World War II, with many of them dating from the post-1970s period.

Stemware of the 20th Century: The Top 200 Patterns is designed to serve a number of purposes. There is more to this book than a list of forms and their values.

First, the book provides the basic guidelines needed to select, use, and care for stemware. As the old adage goes, the more one knows about something, the more one appreciates it. This book offers the reader an opportunity to learn about stemware—how stemware and its use in the art of fine dining evolved, the history of its manufacturers, and the unique story of some patterns.

Second, this book shows the tremendous variety of patterns readily available to decorators or those who wish to acquire new stemware. There are dozens of choices for most decorating styles; every pattern is illustrated. Take a few minutes, flip through the pages, and marvel at the ingenuity of those who designed and manufactured the patterns.

This book contains information on over 200 stemware patterns. The 25 extra patterns are a bonus—better to share this information, since it was available, than to discard it!

Two points must be clarified at this point, relating to the use of the term *pattern*. Pattern and shape are not synonymous. Pattern describes a specific design motif. Shape describes the body form of the suite and its matching pieces. A pattern may appear on more than one shape. Heisey's Orchid and Rose Points are patterns, not shapes. Occasionally, the body form is the pattern. Lenox Crystal's Antique and Fostoria's Jamestown patterns are two examples. In this instance, variation is achieved by color.

Third, the checklist approach identifies which forms are available within each pattern. When a pattern includes accessory pieces that match the stems, they are also listed. Although this book's principal focus is stemware, its overall subject is the tabletop. If one wishes only to acquire a stemware suite (fluted champagne glass, goblet, iced beverage glass, wine glass), then every pattern listed is a possibility. If one's goal is to set a table with matched stems and accessories, then the choice of patterns narrows.

The checklist also serves as a hunting list. Many individuals will be surprised at the number of forms in some patterns.

Fourth, this book answers the question: About how much will I have to pay to replace a piece or expand my stemware? The pricing is retail and realistic. However, prices are not absolute. Price guides are exactly what their name implies—guides. Most individuals buy with a budget in mind. Realistic prices allow the user to determine which patterns are affordable and which are not.

Stemware of the 20th Century is one title from a series of three books focusing on tableware. If you find it helpful and informative, you may also be interested in its two companion titles—*Dinnerware of the 20th Century* and *Silverware of the 20th Century*.

I

GUIDELINES FOR SELECTING, USING, AND CARING FOR STEMWARE

Photo courtesy of Lenox, Inc.

CHAPTER 1

A Brief History of Stemware

Glass was as prized as gold and silver in ancient Rome. Its difficulty of manufacture and its fragile nature made it a luxury available only to the wealthy. Glass remained a luxury item until a series of technological, chemical, and marketing advances that occurred during the nineteenth century made glassware available to everyone.

There are basically two types of glass—soda-based glass and lead- or flint-based glass. Early glass was made from a soda-based formula. In 1675, George Ravenscroft of England developed a glass formula that today serves as the foundation for lead crystal glass. His flint-glass formula created a heavier, clearer, and more brilliant glass. In the mid-1860s, American glass manufacturers perfected the formula for a soda-lime glass, a lighter, less-expensive glass, but one that lacked the clarity and brilliance of crystal glass. Unlike earlier soda-based formulas, the soda-lime formula was ideal for mass-produced, pressed glass. It quickly became the glass of choice for machine-made glassware.

Before proceeding, it is necessary to discuss the meaning of the word *crystal*. To the purist, crystal defines glassware made from mineral quartz. It is the formula, not color, that defines the piece. The purist also thinks of crystal as handmade rather than machine-produced. In fact, it can be either. To the public, crystal is a generic term for any fine glassware. Many collectors use the term as a color, equating crystal with clear. "A clear colorless glass of superior quality," a dictionary definition, combines these points.

For the purposes of this book, crystal means a lead- or flint-based glass that is clear in color. It can be plain or decorated, handblown or machine-made. Its association with fine quality is assumed.

UNDERSTANDING THE CRYSTAL GLASSMAKING PROCESS

Silica (sand), litharge (a fused lead monoxide), and potash or potassium carbonate are the principal ingredients in crystal glass. Smaller quantities of additional chemicals are added to give glass qualities such as durability, clarity, sparkle, and reflectivity. The exact formula differs from manufacturer to manufacturer and is a closely guarded secret. Orrefors crystal consists of sand (55 percent), red lead oxide (30 percent), potash (13 percent) and other ingredients (2 percent). The quality of the three initial ingredients and of what constitutes the 2 percent are the keys.

The ingredients are placed into a batch-mixing machine. A small quantity of broken crystal is added to this mixture or *batch*, as the mix is known. The final composition is placed into a crucible, or melting pot, and heated to 1400°C in a natural gas-fired or electric furnace. Thirty-six hours later, the mix is a molten crystal ready for use.

Making Handblown Crystal Stemware

Glassblowing today uses almost the same techniques and methods used during the eighteenth and nineteenth centuries. Although technological advances have taken place in furnace construction, glass formulas, and molds, skilled craftsmen still play a pivotal role in glassmaking.

Making a piece of handblown crystal stemware requires teamwork. Commercial glassware, such as stemware, often consists of a team of seven individuals—the gaffer, who controls the flow of work; the stem maker; the blower; the gatherer; two foot and stem gatherers; and one or two assistants. Timing is critical; the process must be carefully orchestrated. Footed items are made by two teams, one making the bowl, the other the foot. A master craftsperson assembles the two while the crystal is still soft and pliable.

A craftsperson, called a *blower*, gathers a quantity of crystal from the furnace on the end of a hollow blowing rod. He or she uses a twisting motion to keep the glass from falling to the floor. The *gather* is smoothed with a wooden block that has been soaked in water. The wooden block is shaped to correspond to the basic outline of the piece being made.

The blower blows through the rod to create the cavity inside the crystal gather. Using an iron mold to control the outer shape, he or she blows the piece to its full shape. Pincers, puncellas, punty irons, tongs, and shearing scissors are other tools used to achieve a piece's final shape.

A skilled blower must exhibit tremendous dexterity and coordination of hands, breath,

In this illustration from a period Tiffin catalog, a glassworker is seen scoring lines.

and strength. Traditionally, blowers learn their trade by making medium-sized tumblers. As their skill level increases, they graduate to centerpieces, bowls, vases, and complicated pieces of all shapes and sizes. Some blowers specialize in the intricate assembly of liquor and wine glasses.

Once a piece is shaped and becomes solid, it is *annealed*, a process that allows the crystal to slowly reach room temperature. Annealing eliminates the stress that can be caused by too-rapid cooling and contraction. Annealing takes place in a *lehr*, or cooling oven, the piece often traveling through it on a conveyor belt.

Any blown object begins life as an enclosed shape. Before decoration can begin, the surplus glass, or *moil*, is removed by shearing or *cracking off* the unwanted cap. Shearing is a hand process; cracking off is done by machine. A score line is cut around the top of the piece with a diamond. A gas flame is then applied, creating a thermal stress that snaps off the top. The remaining rough edge is either reheated and smoothed out or ground smooth.

Decorating Crystal Stemware

Crystal stemware is decorated in a variety of methods, for example, by cutting and engraving. The method of decoration is instrumental in determining the wall thickness of a piece of stemware—the deeper the decorative motif, the thicker the glass.

The cutting process, because of its tedious nature, can take several days on larger pieces. Even smaller pieces can take several hours. Patterns are geometric in form. Cutting requires infinite patience, precision, and physical strength. There is no margin for error. Once a piece is cut, it goes to the polisher, whose efforts add sparkle to the finished product.

Engraved decoration begins with an ink outline of the desired motif or script placed on the glass blank. This design is drawn freehand, using chalk and engraver's ink. Designs are executed using small copper wheels fitted to a lathe and coated with an abrasive paste mixed with oil. The paste is applied constantly throughout the cutting process. By cutting the design to various depths, the engraver achieves a finely detailed finished product. Variation in design is achieved through a wide selection of copper wheel diameters and varying degrees of roughness of the grinding paste.

As seen, a single piece of stemware is not the product of a single individual but of dozens of skilled individuals, from designer to polisher. Understanding the intricate manufacturing processes involved allows a fuller appreciation for the beauty and quality of crystal stemware.

GLASSMAKING IN THE UNITED STATES

Within a year of arriving in America, the Jamestown, Virginia, settlers established a glass factory. The first American glassmakers were German and Polish in origin. Although Virginia had an abundant supply of raw ingredients and timber, this first effort failed due to quarreling among the glassmakers, as well as among those governing the colony. No examples of Jamestown glass have survived. Attempts to establish glasshouses in Massachusetts, New York, and Pennsylvania in the seventeenth century also failed.

Casper Wistar, a German immigrant, established the first successful American glass factory in Salem, New Jersey, in 1739. With the assistance of other immigrant German-trained glassmakers, Wistar's factory produced a variety of bottles and tableware, including bowls, dishes, and pitchers. The factory remained in operation until 1780. Several employees moved to Glassboro, New Jersey, and established a factory at that location.

William Henry Stiegel, an immigrant from Cologne, Germany, established his first glasshouse near his iron foundry in Lancaster County, Pennsylvania. A few years later, he built a second furnace near Manheim, Pennsylvania. Stiegel produced a high-quality glass that competed openly with glass imported from England and the Continent. His product line included enamel-decorated and engraved pieces. Shapes included pocket flasks, small jugs, footed salt dips, and tumblers. By 1774, Stiegel was in debtor's prison and his factory was closed.

Glassmaking in America was established on a permanent basis in the period immediately following the American Revolution. Glass factories were opened in Boston, Cape Cod, New York, Philadelphia, and Pittsburgh. By the second quarter of the nineteenth century, Pittsburgh had become the center of the American glass industry.

There are three basic methods used to make glass—free blown, mold blown, or pressed. Prior to the seventeenth century, glass was free blown. By the mid-eighteenth century two-, three-, and four-part molds were used. Stiegel used a dip or part-sized mold to add ribs and diamonds to his pieces.

The first American patent for pressed glass was awarded to J. P. Bakewell of Bakewell and Company in Pittsburgh for an "improvement in making glass furniture knobs." Other patents followed in the 1820s. In 1828, Deming Jarvis of the Boston and Sandwich Glass Company, Sandwich, Cape Cod, patented an "improved" method to mechanically press molten glass.

The ability to press glass greatly increased production capabilities. Early soda-based glass, used primarily for free blown and mold blown, did not prove viable for mold pressing. Manufacturers turned to flint- or lead-based glass. Many of the earlier molds included ornate designs as a way of disguising production problems. The resulting products named this period of American glass production the "Lacy Period."

When collectors talk about the era of American pressed glass, they refer to the period between 1825 and 1915. It is a mistake to assume that glass production was completely mechanized. Many tasks were still done by hand, such as taking the molten glass to the pressing machine.

Lead oxide is a key ingredient in lead or flint glass. When the American Civil War created a lead shortage, American glassmakers began searching for an alternative glass formula. William Leighton Sr., a Scottish immigrant and an employee of Hobbs, Brockunier and Company of Wheeling, West Virginia, developed in 1864 a soda-lime glass formula that eliminated the need for lead oxide. In addition to saving lead, the new formula could be pressed easily, it produced finer detail, and, because it was lighter in weight, it cost less to ship. Production costs dropped by two-thirds. The only difficulty was the new soda-lime glass was not as light-reflective as lead or flint glass.

The expanding of the shape vocabulary was another major result of the development of soda-lime glass. Previously, most glass objects were decorative—serving accessories such as butter dishes, candlesticks, centerpieces, compotes, creamers, jugs, pitchers, salt cellars, sugar bowls, and so on. Suddenly, stemware—from goblets to wine glasses—was available in hundreds of different patterns at a relatively modest cost.

As production costs declined, glass manufacturers were encouraged to experiment. Color formulas were perfected. Amethyst, blue, green, and yellow supplemented clear glass formulas. Opalescent qualities were introduced, and opaque white milk glass became an industry standard. At the end of the nineteenth century, art glass and Bohemian glass were in vogue. America had fallen in love with glass.

Late nineteenth-century American technological advances in glass cutting, coupled with a new wave of Eastern European-trained glassworkers, created the "Brilliant Period," 1880–1920, of American cut class. The *Russian* pattern was patented by T. G. Hawkes & Company in 1882. Cut glass stemware played a major role in popularizing cut glass.

Glass design closely mirrors furniture design. After all, glass serves as an important complement, reflecting the richness of the wood and the elegance of porcelain and silver flatware and tableware. In the 1850s and 1860s, glass patterns favored Grecian and classical motifs. By the 1870s, naturalism, with its realistic portrayals of flowers, animals, and the human form, was dominant. Geometric patterns, for example, Daisy and Button, were the order of the day between 1880 and 1900. Colonial Revival patterns, with their fluted, block, and thumbprint designs, were popular during the first two decades of the twentieth century.

As one reads the brief histories of the American glass companies in the main section of this book, several points will become evident. The American glass industry is very much a family business. It often is multigenerational. Many new firms began as family members decided to go in separate directions. As the nineteenth century progressed, the center of the American glass industry moved west, into Ohio and Indiana. The search for an abundant, inexpensive fuel— natural gas—was the key factor.

Mergers and consolidations were continual. In 1891, The United States Glass Company, a glass combine, was created. Its formation was instrumental in maintaining the strength of America's glass industry during the first three decades of the twentieth century.

The depression had a heavy impact on the American glass industry. The companies that were able to survive enjoyed a period of prosperity during World War II and the ten years that followed. By the 1950s, increased production costs, union difficulties, and a flood of cheap foreign imports resulted in the closing of many American glass factories. Again, the companies that were able to weather the tough times of the 1960s emerged in the 1980s and 1990s as viable concerns, in part due to their purchase and inclusion as divisions of national and international firms specializing in tabletop wares.

The glass dinnerware service arrived in the 1920s and 1930s. A variety of plate sizes and a cup and saucer were added to many older and new patterns. Glass became very inexpensive. It was the age of the five-cent tumbler. Elaborate, neoclassical etched designs dominated. Entire pattern lines were expanded by producing pieces in amber, blue, pale green, and pink, in addition to crystal or clear. Clearly, the decades between World War I and World War II were a golden age for American manufacturers of glass stemware and dinnerware.

World War II had a positive effect on the American glass industry. With extra money in her pocket, Rosie the Riveter was in a buying mood. Since stemware and other glassware were abundant, she bought plenty of it.

Following the war, the bridal market blossomed. The good times extended through the end of the 1950s. Capitalizing on this trend, American glass manufacturers heavily targeted the bridal market. Sales in this market were the survival key for many companies.

The American lifestyle did an about-face in the 1950s, as it moved from a formal to a casual focus. As America turned modern, glass stemware and dinnerware no longer meshed with contemporary tastes. Melamine dinnerware and brightly colored aluminum tumblers were popular. The only stemware in many homes was inexpensive, foreign-made drinking glasses for daily use and an all-purpose wine glass for guests. Stemware simply did not fit into the lifestyle of the beatnik and hippie.

The Yuppies and Dinks of the mid-1970s and the conspicuous consumption of the current Me and X generations are responsible for the stemware renaissance. Today's lifestyle is casually formal. Once again, homes are being built with separate dining rooms. Home entertaining involves an elegantly appointed table with dinnerware, stemware, flatware, and other decorative accessories.

The tabletop industry also deserves part of the credit for this revival. During the 1960s and 1970s, major dinnerware manufacturers recognized the importance of expanding their lines, thus they offered a full range of tabletop products. Renewed emphasis was placed on designing a wide range of shape lines and patterns to complement dozens of different lifestyles. The quality of products improved across the board; the only negative was a reduction in the number of forms in many suites.

The 1970s saw Asian and European manufacturers take a renewed interest in the American market. Several manufacturers established American divisions, while others opened elaborate marquis stores in key cities. Aggressive marketing was focused toward middle- and upper-income buyers.

New marketing techniques, such as targeted mail-order catalog sales, has further enhanced stemware sales. Many mass merchandisers now carry brand-name, rather than generic, stemware. Manufacturer name recognition is once again a major selling point in the 1990s.

Finally, stemware is enjoying a big boost from the rediscovery and reuse of family heirloom stemware by today's young adults. Manufacturers have responded by performing annual production runs of discontinued patterns. Some manufacturers, such as Princess House, have created their own matching service. A few buy and resell discontinued patterns, but most rely on replacement services to meet this need.

The 1980s and 1990s stemware renaissance means that stemware will continue to play a vital role in the twenty-first century. Optimism within the tabletop community abounds.

THE EVOLUTION OF LENOX CRYSTAL

In 1827, James Bryce was a newly arrived immigrant from Scotland. He traveled to Pittsburgh, Pennsylvania, where he apprenticed with the glassmaking firm of Bakewell, Page, and Bakewell. He continued with that company and its successors for six years, at which time he joined Mulvaney and Ledlie, a Pittsburgh manufacturer of lamps and flint glass tableware.

In 1847, James Bryce, Robert Bryce, Fred McKee, and others founded Bryce McKee and Company and built their own glass factory. Numerous partnership changes took place between 1854 and 1882. In 1858, the company presented its products at the 26th Exhibition of the Franklin Institute in Philadelphia. One of today's most popular designs, *Antique*, was developed during this period. Several patents were obtained relating to the glass-forming process, one as early as 1869. The company eventually evolved into Bryce Brothers and established a reputation for the innovative production and design of tableware, giftware, and other glass products.

In 1893, James Bryce sold his original factory in Pittsburgh and purchased the idle Smith-Brudewold Glass Company factory in Hammondville, near Mount Pleasant, Pennsylvania. Within a few years, the factory proved to be inadequate to meet the demand for the company's lead crystal stemware, bowls, vases, and so on.

After raising $20,000 from local bond sales and receiving a donation of land from Mount Pleasant, Bryce Brothers built a new factory in the borough of Mount Pleasant. The new $35,000 plant opened on October 12, 1896. Restaurants, hotels, private clubs, and others nationwide purchased Bryce Brothers handblown lead crystal in a wide range of decorating techniques. As the years progressed, Bryce Brothers' high-quality crystal was found at U.S. embassies, consulates, and legations throughout the world.

When Lenox Incorporated, a company that had become preeminent in the field of fine china, wished to offer crystal of comparable quality to its accounts, it began discussions with Bryce Brothers. In 1965, Lenox acquired Bryce Brothers and changed its name to Lenox Crystal, Incorporated. Within two years, 96 percent of the stores that retailed Lenox china also carried Lenox crystal, and 85 percent of the brides registering for china also chose crystal.

Operations continued for several years at the old Bryce Brothers factory. However, the seventy-five-year-old multistory construction did not lend itself to efficient fuel usage, good process layout, or significant expansion. Construction began on the present one-story, 145,000-square foot plant in 1969. Lenox chose to build the facility in Mount Pleasant, near the old factory, to keep its valuable skilled workforce. The company also conducted extensive research in the United States and Europe to design the plant and equipment in the most cost-effective manner, while retaining the quality of the product. When the new factory opened in October 1979, it was the first facility built in the United States since 1905 that was devoted exclusively to the production of handblown lead crystal.

In 1976, Lenox Crystal introduced its first line of handblown, undecorated, lead crystal gift items. A major breakthrough in the glass-melting technique occurred in 1979, with the introduction of the first fully continuous, electrically heated glass-melting furnace. Production began in 1981 of heavily blown, deeply cut stemware with a considerably higher lead content. One year later, Lenox Crystal developed the capability for producing high-quality, sand-etched inscriptions and photographic images, thus enabling the company to make presentation pieces for use by the White House and high government officials.

In August 1988, Lenox Crystal opened a new outlet warehouse at its facility in Mount Pleasant. Seconds are offered at reduced rates. Lenox Crystal currently has nine such outlets nationwide.

Today, Lenox Crystal, Inc. enjoys a reputation in the Mount Pleasant community as a "well-established business run by men of the best business reputation." Visitors traveling in western Pennsylvania are invited to visit Lenox Crystal's showroom in Mount Pleasant, a short distance from the New Stanton or Donegal exits of the Pennsylvania Turnpike.

The Lenox Crystal Plant in Mt. Pleasant, Pennsylvania. *Photo courtesy of Lenox, Inc.*

CHAPTER 2

Stemware Finesse—Selecting and Using the Stemware That Is Right for You

Your daily drinking glasses are a form of stemware. Yet, most individuals do not think of them as such, for two main reasons. First, they usually are flat-bottomed tumblers. Stemware does not have to have a stem. A well-designed crystal tumbler is every bit as elegant as a crystal stem. Second, because they are designed for daily use and washing in a dishwasher, the glass body tends to be thick and the pattern simple. To keep costs modest, most are made utilizing a soda-lime formula. Users view them as being disposable, not precious.

Consider adding a touch of class to your daily life. Seek out stemware patterns that feature the iced beverage glass in the form of a tumbler. Many modern crystal tumblers are as durable as their less expensive soda-lime counterparts.

Casual lifestyles, from beatnik to suburban patio, reigned supreme from the beginning of the 1960s through the end of the 1970s. Stemware played a minor role in most households during this period. It was quite common to own only one stemware form from a suite, most likely the wine. Society had an "all-purpose" mind-set. The ideal was achieved when a single stemware form served multiple purposes. Far more champagne was drunk from wine glasses than from fluted champagne during these two decades.

Life was so casual that no social stigma was attached to using stemware that did not match. In fact, some decorators encouraged this eclectic approach.

The challenge to design stemware that complemented and accented the casual lifestyle was welcomed by stemware manufacturers. They responded positively, and many new shapes and patterns evolved.

By the late 1980s, two major lifestyle changes occurred. The highly informal casual lifestyle of the 1960s and 1970s was transformed into one that stressed casual elegance, that is, casual with a touch of class. There also was a return to traditional values, particularly in the family. Once again, the dining room rather than the patio or den assumed a primary role for meals and entertaining. Stemware benefited significantly from both changes.

Young adults purchasing stemware for the first time began buying full stemware suites. Older adults followed suit. Tables were set with glassware that complemented stemware. Everything matched.

Other individuals asked their parents or grandparents for stemware they had lost interest in or had placed in storage. While treasured, these heirloom pieces are being used today. Since most of this stemware was acquired without cost, owners are eager to purchase additional forms to their sets or to increase the number of pieces in forms they already own.

SELECTING YOUR STEMWARE

You are the most important person your stemware needs to please. Properly chosen, it provides a sense of excitement and pride each time you use it.

Select your stemware to complement your dinnerware. Most of the time, both will appear on your table. If your dinnerware pattern is formal, choose a classic stemware shape and pattern. If your dinnerware has a country flare, select a stemware shape and pattern that has a rugged, rustic look to it. Use the same procedure to select a flatware pattern.

The goal is a totally coordinated tabletop design. Lenox Brands and Waterford/Wedgwood are among the manufacturers who have expanded their lines to include a full range of tabletop products. This allows them to design stemware, dinnerware, and flatware patterns that can be fully coordinated. Before searching elsewhere, check with your dinnerware manufacturer. Assuming that the company is still in business, determine whether they have coordinating stemware and flatware that complements your dinnerware pattern. If they do, give it careful consideration.

What are you looking for in your stemware? Gorham Crystal recommends considering the following wants:

- You want your crystal to be beautiful.
- You want your crystal to be fashionable.
- You want a timeless design.
- You want your crystal to be functional.
- You want your crystal to reflect you.

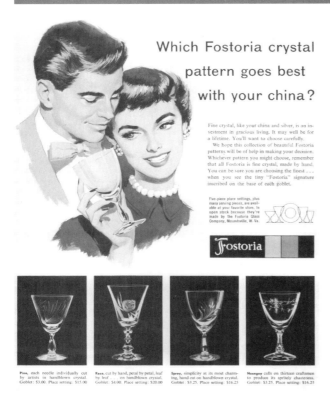

Period magazine advertisment for Fostoria crystal.

Select carefully. Do not rush. Chances are, you will live with your choices for several decades, if not your lifetime. Check the full range of buying sources, from the local department store to replacement services. Do not settle for second best. Keep looking until you find the pattern that is right for you.

How will you know when you find the right pattern? The answer is simple. You will fall in love with it. Do not be surprised if it is love at first sight. Trust your heart.

When selecting stemware, adopt four criteria—use, cost, quality, and quantity. Select a stemware pattern that is versatile, one that finds a ready home in a variety of color settings and decorative motifs. Take along a piece of your dinnerware, wallpaper, and/or drapery fabric when shopping. It is far better to discover that a pattern will not work before purchasing it rather than afterward.

A stemware pattern should blend with the decorating decor of the setting and the room in which it is used. If the room has a Colonial or Early American theme, a shape with strong fluting or a traditional pressed pattern is appropriate. If the room setting is contemporary, the shape should be futuristic, the pattern simple.

Buy the best that you can afford. Most manufacturers offer stemware in three or four price categories. There is a pattern just right for everyone's budget.

It is a mistake to settle for your second or third pattern choice because you cannot afford your first choice. Many stemware services for eight began as a service for two. Add to your stemware as you can afford it. So what if the process takes years? It is the end result that is important.

There are many measures of quality—from the design of the shape line and pattern to the reputation of the manufacturer and the retailer from whom the stemware was purchased. The first decision you should make is whether or not you want lead crystal stemware. If you select lead crystal, the option preferred by most individuals, you are limiting your choices. The Top 200 Pattern list contains patterns that have a crystal content of less than 24 percent lead or that are manufactured using the soda-lime formula.

Focus on shape line and pattern. Conduct a broad search. Popular shapes and designs are found in a variety of interpretations. Make sure you have seen all of these variations before making your final selection.

Do not select a pattern until you have seen the entire shape line. While the pattern design may be extremely appealing on the goblet, it may lose its appeal on the iced tea glass. Actually create a place setting of the suite. Seeing the pieces in combination will make your final decision much easier.

The number of patterns greatly exceeds the number of shape lines. A typical manufacturer will offer a dozen or more patterns utilizing the same shape line. Also keep in mind that manufacturers discontinue patterns. There may be patterns of which you are completely unaware if you are using a modern catalog from a manufacturer. Many retailers do not carry a manufacturer's full line. Make it a point to ask if other patterns are available.

Quantity involves the number of individual forms available within the shape line. Most patterns offer the typical four-piece suite—fluted champagne, goblet, iced tea glass, and wine; however, some patterns also contain both a claret, a liquor/cocktail glass, a juice, a champagne/sherbet, a low sherbet, a low- and high-stemmed water goblet, a parfait, and an oyster cocktail. Do not forget about accessory pieces such as bowls, single and double candlesticks, centerpiece bowls, creamers, several styles of plates, relishes, salt and pepper sets, and sugar bowls.

As the twentieth century progressed, the number of forms available within a shape line decreased, one reason older patterns are so popular with today's younger users. They offer a wider variety of stems and serving accessories than many contemporary patterns.

USING YOUR STEMWARE

Use your stemware—use it, but do not abuse it. Stemware will break when dropped or when carelessly handled. Always pick up a stemmed piece by its stem, never by its rim or foot. Rims and feet are fragile and can be easily damaged.

There are only a few basic rules for setting a table with stemware. The menu and style of the meal determines which stemware is required. When the meal is formal, the water goblet is placed above the knifepoint and the wine glass or glasses are arranged to the right of it. A fluted champagne can be placed to the right of the wine glass, or it can be placed behind or in between the goblet and wine glass, thus creating a triangular presentation.

When the meal is informal, a goblet or iced tea glass and/or a wine glass is placed to the right of the dinner plate above the knife. A separate side table with cups and saucers and stemware is appropriate for buffets.

When planning a dinner party using your stemware, the following hints will help make the event festive and memorable:

- When dinner is ready, fill the glasses three-fourths full and refill them throughout the meal.
- Water, wine, and other beverages should be poured from the right.
- Pour water without lifting the glass from the table.
- Serve chilled water.
- Never leave the area in front of your guest bare. Exchange one stem for another until dessert time.

If you store your stemware in cabinets with blind cupboard doors, you do not have to be concerned with its appearance. However, if you are storing stemware in a china cabinet with a glass door or sides, display the pieces horizontally, by shape. If you own multiple patterns of stemware, display light body, blown patterns on top with heavier cut stems toward the bottom. Antique stemware also should be displayed near the bottom. Coordinate the display with other glassware accessories.

Do not hesitate to change your stemware service. As your personal tastes change or you redecorate, your stemware pattern may no longer be appropriate. When this occurs, consider purchasing new stemware.

What about the cost? Put the issue into perspective. How much do you spend every three to five years for a new car or every ten years for a new television set? These costs can easily exceed the cost of a new stemware service. Further, consider the percentage of the original purchase price you receive when you trade in or sell your five-year-old car. The depreciation in value of your stemware service, assuming you purchased it new, is likely to be less.

Your old set of stemware has value. But how much? Write to a replacement service and ask for a quote.

Not all value is monetary. Since stemware is designed to serve several generations, consider passing your old stemware along to your children or your friends' children as a starter set. If no one wants it, consider selling it.

In summary, stemware should not reside in storage, as nothing is gained by its sitting on a shelf. Its true value rests in its use—stemware adds a touch of elegance to your life.

STEMWARE PATTERNS AND THE DESIGN STYLES THEY COMPLEMENT

Selecting the right stemware pattern is critical to creating the ambiance you desire. Choices abound. Throughout this book, you will find pattern groupings designed to assist you in the selection process.

These pattern suggestions are only the beginning of the selection process. Review all of the patterns in this book and add or subtract additional patterns to create your working list. Once you have assembled your working list, it is easy to choose the pattern that works best for you.

You probably noted during your review that some patterns appear quite similar. Popular patterns were offered with slight variations by a number of manufacturers. You also observed that there is a wide variety of pattern interpretations within a single shape or pattern theme. This is why stemware is so exciting and offers so much. There is a pattern just right for everyone's taste.

Many of these group listings could easily be expanded to include a dozen or more patterns. Since the desire to limit is implicit in these suggestions, five was selected as an ideal working number.

There is no right or wrong choice. The choice that counts is the one that pleases you. Further, who said you had to limit your choice to one? There is nothing wrong with owning two or three sets of stemware.

A TOWLE® SILVER COMPANY

CHAPTER 3

Caring for Your Stemware

The best way to care for your stemware service, whether it is a family heirloom, a bridal gift nurtured into a complete stemware suite, or a newly acquired pattern to complement your latest dinnerware, is to use it. Each use renews the joy and excitement associated with owning fine stemware. And each use enhances the love you feel for the pattern and the pieces comprising it. After all, do we not take the best care of the things we most cherish?

Although it may appear delicate, twentieth-century stemware is designed to be used. Is it breakable? Absolutely. Does this mean it has to be handled with kid gloves? Absolutely not.

The survival key is reasonable care. Initially, you must systematically practice care techniques. Within a short time, they become automatic, second nature. In the future, when you are retrieving or storing your stemware, remember the points discussed in this chapter. There is little doubt that you will ask, "Isn't it amazing how easy and enjoyable it is to use fine stemware on a regular basis?"

PROPERLY STORING STEMWARE

There are two steps to properly storing stemware. The first involves a thorough analysis of the space in which you intend to store or display your stemware. The second involves examining exactly how you store your stemware within that space.

Analyzing Your Storage Space

Take a moment and consider a few worst-case scenarios. Design your storage space to eliminate the potential dangers you identified.

If your storage unit is a hanging cupboard, make sure it is securely bolted to the wall. The same applies to shelves. All too often, hanging cupboards and shelves are secured at only two locations, which is not enough. If one bolt or screw fails, the cabinet or shelf will tilt or fall. Most hanging cabinets and shelves are not designed to hold their positions with only one bolt or screw in place.

Always secure a hanging cupboard with a minimum of three screws at its top and one or more "L" braces at its bottom. Instead of securing a shelf with only two braces, each just slightly in from the left and right ends, add one or two braces in the middle. If you are going to err, err on the side of too much, rather than too little support.

Carefully check the weight-bearing potential of shelving in kitchen cabinets and china closets. Far too many units have shelves whose only supports are small quarter-inch triangular metal clips at each of the corners. If any one of these fails, the shelf will collapse. Damage is often several shelves deep.

Do the shelves in your kitchen cabinet sag in the middle? You would be surprised at how many do. Consider strengthening the load-bearing capacities of your shelves with one or two supporting rods or block columns. Usually a column located in the center, an equal distance from the sides, front, and back, is sufficient. However, if the shelf is long, use two columns at the one-third and two-third points of the shelf's length.

Be extra careful when determining each column's length. Each should fit snugly between shelves, but should not raise the top shelf or depress the bottom shelf, even slightly. The columns are to assist in load bearing, not take over the responsibility of the end brackets.

Most storage cabinets consist of multiple shelves. When inserting additional support columns, line them up directly on top of each other. When offset, they do not have the same load-sharing capabilities as when aligned.

Purchase a line level, the kind contractors use to make sure a chalk line is level, at the hardware store. Use it twice a year to check the level of your shelves. When you find that a glass or wood shelf is no longer level across its entire surface, replace it. Once wood or glass develops a bend, it is cheaper to replace it than to straighten it.

How deep are your shelves? Far too many pieces of stemware are broken each year by individuals reaching for a piece located on the back of a shelf and, in doing so, knocking or striking a piece in front. While common sense dictates that stemware in the front should be removed before back pieces, few individuals actually practice this safety measure.

What is the ideal shelf size? This is not an easy question to answer. One solution is to base the depth on the maximum width of four stems, plus one inch. This provides a one-quarter-inch separation between each stem and the back wall of the storage unit. If you are fortunate enough to work with a kitchen cabinet designer and have available space, explore a stepped shelf approach.

Many older homes have a Butler's or storage pantry. Often these pantries contain cabinets with deep shelves on one side for dinnerware and cabinets with narrow shelves slightly deeper than a single piece of stemware on the other side. Impractical in today's home? Perhaps. However, if you are constructing a new home and have the funds and space, consider asking the architect or builder to include a modern storage pantry off of the kitchen.

Stemware and barware are not synonymous. Some contemporary kitchens contain mounted ceiling track units for storing stemware. These work fine for glasses designed for bar use. Crystal stemware should always be stored in an upright position; its stems are not designed to withstand the abuse that track storage produces.

A viable working shelf height is far more important than shelf depth. Most kitchen cabinets are too high; users must stand on their tiptoes or on a kitchen stool to reach the upper shelves. This method of storage considerably increases the damage risk to stemware. You need to be able to see what you are doing and have solid footing when handling your stemware, which is why many people prefer to store their stemware in china closets. However, just as storage shelves can be too high, they also can be too low. Many individuals have trouble bending. Stemware should be handled in a natural position; the ideal stemware storage level is waist to shoulder height.

Check the heating and lighting conditions in your storage area. Rapid changes in temperature can damage stemware. Do not store your stemware in cabinets that are attached to or rest against an outside wall of your home. Some comfortable winter evening, place your hand on one of your home's outside walls. You will be surprised to discover how cold it is.

Keep stemware storage units away from heating sources, including direct sunlight. A buffet or china cabinet that is directly above or beside a heating source is an invitation to disaster. Wood and glass have few problems adjusting to gradual changes in temperature. When the change is rapid, something has to give. Remember getting into your car on a sunny winter day and being surprised at how warm it was? The sun heats up the inside of a closed storage unit in exactly the same way. Prolonged exposure to heat also causes some glass to develop a milky, cloudy appearance.

Do not expose your stemware to direct sunlight. Some glass changes color, often assuming a light-purple hue, when exposed to excessive sunlight.

Storage and Display Methods

An ideal storage space is one that is roomy enough so no stemware surfaces touch one other. Contact can cause chipping, hairline cracks, or damage to the surface—avoid it!

Mail-order catalogs, department stores, jewelry shops, and other places that sell fine stemware offer protector cases. A typical storage unit holds twelve stems. Most cases have foam dividers and a zipper for easy access.

Do not stack glass accessory pieces, such as bowls and punch cups, inside of each other. Stacking guarantees damaged rims and scratches. If stacked glassware becomes stuck, fill the top unit with cold tap water and submerge the bottom one in warm tap water. Separation should be possible within a few minutes. Wrapping the stuck pieces in a warm towel is another solution, which works especially well when attempting to free a stuck bottle stopper.

A china cabinet is essentially open storage. Arrange your stemware so it is attractively displayed—tall pieces in the back, the most appealing part of the pattern to the front, and rows offset from each other.

Dust is an enemy of glass. A fine layer of dust can make a glass shelf slippery. The simple act of walking by a china cabinet or a large truck rumbling past the house can provide enough vibration to cause a stem to move.

Dust is an abrasive—it can scratch the bottom of a glass. If you question this, pick up an older piece of stemware, turn it upside down, and rake lightly across its bottom. Chances are the bottom will contain irregular scratch marks, which result from drawing the stem across dust and dirt and textured surfaces, such as table linens.

Once a month, gently wipe your stemware with a soft cloth. The key is to prevent any accumulation of dust on surfaces. Be extra careful when handling stemware that has not been used or cleaned for several months. The surface dust can act like a lubricant, causing the stem to slip from your grasp.

Conservation Materials (100 Standing Rock Circle, Reno, NV 89511) produces Dust Bunny, a 17″ × 17″ white cloth that attracts and holds dust particles but is not chemically treated. The synthetic fiber acquires a high static charge during wiping that attracts the dust particles. The cloth can be washed and reused. The Toy Tender, available from Jim Tolliver (900 County Road, AO99, Edgewood, MN 87015), consists of a set of three 100 percent Australian lamb wool dusters. They are great for toys and also work well for stemware. Fluffing out the wool loads it with static electricity. When soiled, one need only to swirl the duster in sudsy water, rinse thoroughly, and dry.

PROPERLY WASHING STEMWARE

Stemware can be washed by hand or by using a dishwasher. Every manufacturer of crystal stemware recommends hand washing. It is advice worth following. Using a dishwasher puts your stemware at risk. Having stated this, some modern patterns have been designed to be dishwasher-safe. Check carefully to determine whether your pattern is one of them.

Washing by Hand

Remove any diamond jewelry before washing and drying stemware. In fact, remove any jewelry that has the potential to scratch or cut.

Before beginning the washing process, take a moment to remind yourself that stemware is slippery when wet. A water coating eliminates surface tension. Properly support each piece at all times.

Gently rinse stemware prior to washing. Make washing the final, not the only, cleaning process. When washing by hand, place a rubber mat or towel in the bottom of the sink as a cushioning device to help prevent damage if a piece slips from your hand during the washing process. Also consider providing similar cushioning underneath the area where you will be drying the stemware.

A double sink is ideal. Use one side for washing and the other for rinsing. Both the wash water and rinse water should be warm to the touch. When the water cools, consider emptying the sinks and refilling them. If a double sink is not available, fill a large bowl or plastic tub with warm water for rinsing.

Place stems into the water sideways. If the water is too hot and the stem bottom is inserted first, the glass may crack. Grooves in cut glass stemware can be cleaned using a small soft brush, but be gentle.

The wash water should remain soapy. A mild household detergent works best, especially if the rinsing process is done effectively. Do not use abrasives of any kind.

Gorham recommends adding some vinegar to the water to give crystal a "brand-new" sparkle. Mikasa suggests that a few drops of bluing or ammonia will achieve the same effect. *Do not do this* if your pattern contains gold or platinum decoration.

Dry stemware while it is still warm with a soft, lint-free cloth. Again, the exception is stemware with gold or platinum decoration. These pieces should be allowed to cool before drying. Air drying works fine if you have sufficient space to arrange the stemware so pieces do not touch one other.

To Use or Not to Use the Dishwasher—That Is The Question

As you have already seen, the basic answer is no. However, the ideal may not be practical. At least consider the following points if you adopt this risky approach.

Dishwasher controls have reached the point where they can be programmed to perform a myriad of differing tasks. Wash and rinse temperatures should never exceed those recommended by the manufacturer. Carefully read and *reread* the machine's instruction manual.

It is critical to select the correct washing agent and water temperature. While some washing agents and rinse aids are practically harmless when used at reasonable temperatures, they can do a lot of damage when used at high temperatures. Cascade, Dishwasher ALL, and Calgonite are among the safer choices for U.S. and Canadian users.

Evaporation in a hot atmosphere is the process used for drying in dishwashers. Occasionally, this process leaves a deposit on stemware, the result of the washing agent drying on the stemware before the rinse cycle begins. The fault rests with the dishwasher, not your stemware. If this scum is allowed to build up, it is difficult to remove. As soon as you notice a problem, call the dishwasher's local service agent and request that your dishwasher be serviced.

Dishwasher vibration can cause pieces to strike against each other. Most modern dishwashers have plastic covered racks that prevent movement of dishes.

The key to safe dishwasher use is to resist the temptation to overload the dishwasher so the dishes are washed in one, not two loads. Overloading is an invitation to trouble. In this case, it is the user, not the dishwasher, that is responsible for any damage.

Never open the dishwasher until its cycle is completed and the interior of the machine has returned to room temperature. Make it a firm rule to wait at least one hour. Glass cannot tolerate abrupt changes in temperature. Exposing dishwasher-heated glass to room temperature is an invitation to breakage.

HANDLING STEMWARE

Use care when handling stemware. "Two hands" is a good rule. Do not put weight on the edge or rim of stemware—these parts are fragile and vulnerable to chipping.

Always support hollowware pieces with one hand on the bottom. This is critical when picking up any hollowware piece that is filled with liquid. Handles are great, but extra support helps to lessen the load.

PROPERLY TRANSPORTING STEMWARE

If you are moving, it is best to leave the packing of your fine stemware to specialists, who possess the skill to do the job right. They will wrap each piece separately and surround each within a box or barrel with excelsior or plastic peanuts to prevent the packages from coming into contact with each other. Check the moving company's insurance policy, and make sure it provides *replacement* cost coverage for any damaged pieces.

If you insist on packing and moving your own stemware, follow these simple rules:

- Pack in uniform-sized boxes. This makes stacking the boxes easier during the moving process.
- Use medium-sized boxes. The final packing weight per box should not exceed twenty to twenty-five pounds.

- Reinforce the bottoms of all boxes with an extra piece of cardboard or foam before packing anything in the box.
- Wrap each piece separately, first with soft white tissue paper and then with bubble wrap with $1/2''$ to $1''$ sized bubbles.
- When placing pieces in a box, make sure there is cushioning around all sides of the wrapped unit. Do not make the mistake of assuming that a box with dividers provides adequate protection for individual pieces. If the piece is free to move, it is not properly packed.
- Do not forget to add padding on the top before closing and sealing the box.
- Mark the box with a detailed list of its contents.
- Call your insurance agent and make sure your homeowner's insurance covers your stemware while in transit.
- Say a prayer that everything arrives undamaged, which is why professional movers are recommended.

In summary, your stemware was designed and manufactured to be used, not to reside in a museum. Treat it with the respect it deserves and it will last for generations.

Fine stemware, especially when it is a family heirloom, adds an aura of elegance to even the simplest of meals. There isn't a meal from morning until night when it is not appropriate and welcome.

A Fostoria Crystal advertisement.

DISASTER-PROOFING YOUR STEMWARE

If you live in an area subject to earthquakes, tornadoes, or flooding, consider the tips that follow from Scott M. Haskins' *How To Save Your Stuff from a Disaster*, published by Preservation Help Publications (P.O. Box 1206, Santa Barbara, CA 93102).

Scientists working with representatives of the Getty Museum have developed a product called Quake Wax *(Editor's note: Quake Wax is now being sold under the brand name Be Still My Art—Museum Mounting Wax*)*. "Quake Wax is a sticky synthetic wax that can be used between the base of a small to medium object and a table top or shelf to anchor it down. The object can be picked up at any time and Quake Wax will not stain the furniture surface. Other materials, like Plastellina or other 'fixing' materials which contain oil, should be avoided as they can stain furniture and objects alike. Use it [Quake Wax] . . . to make sure objects don't rattle around and break against each other during the shake.

- Install clasps or hooks on cabinet doors. They usually pop open, even during a moderate shake, and let everything inside fall to the floor.
- A lip on the front of a shelf will help keep objects in their place. They will have a harder time 'walking' off as everything vibrates.
- Replace glass shelves in curio cabinets (which break and crash down on other items . . . they are heavy too) with Lucite or Plexiglas shelves. They can be made to order at your local glass shop. Help to hold them in place with Quake Wax."

*Be Still My Art—Museum Mounting Wax is manufactured by Conservation Materials, 100 Standing Rock Circle, Reno, NV 89511.

CHAPTER 4

Expanding or Replacing Pieces from Your Stemware Service

Thinking of increasing your favorite stem from four to six or eight pieces? After using your stemware, have you decided to expand your suite to include additional stem shapes or to seek additional glass forms that complement your stems? Perhaps you or a guest accidentally broke a stem—what should you do?

The answer is simple. Take advantage of the wide range of opportunities from antiques and collectibles periodicals to replacement services that are available for expanding or replacing your stemware.

There is a direct correlation between the amount you will pay per piece and the time you are willing to spend in the hunt. However, the hunt has costs. If you spend two or three hours of your time and several dollars in postage and telephone calls and only save five dollars on a piece, you need to rethink your approach. Even though the cost may be slightly higher, finding a source that can immediately supply the pieces you need often is the most economical solution.

DOCUMENTING YOUR PATTERN

You already know the manufacturer, the name of your pattern, and exactly what it looks like. Many of the people you contact will also recognize the manufacturer and pattern name but may have trouble visualizing it. You need to help them.

Begin by making a tracing of the pattern. Place a thin piece of tissue paper around the bowl of the stem. Rub lightly with a soft lead pencil to capture the design. If unsuccessful, do a freehand drawing of the pattern. Make your drawing as exact and detailed as possible so it can be used as an overlay for matching purposes.

Put three measurements on the rubbing or drawing: (1) the height of the stem, (2) the diameter of the bowl, and (3) the diameter of the base. If you wish, trace the edge of the base and then turn the stem over and do the same for the top. Finally, do a freehand drawing of the bowl shape and the stem portion.

After having gone to all of this trouble, make several photocopies of the final result. This will prevent you from having to repeat the process later. Keep two or more copies on file.

If you retained a copy of the manufacturer's catalog or brochure that came with your stemware, photocopy it. A magazine advertisement featuring the pattern also provides valuable reference information.

If you have access to a good 35mm camera, consider taking a series of photographs of each stem shape and any matching accessories. Because of its reflective quality and the fact that most pieces are clear, photographing glass requires patience and trial and error.

Take your picture from an angle slightly above the height of the stem. In other words, shoot down on it a little, which will provide a sense of depth for the stem in the finished photograph. If you have the capabilities, take two close-up photographs, one of the pattern on the bowl and the second of the stem portion.

It is critical that the picture be in focus. Photograph details with a close-up or telephoto lens. Make sure you have enough depth of field when photographing stemware pieces.

Beware of reflected light from nearby objects, the backdrop, and lighting. Do not use a flash, even at an angle, as the light will bounce back from the stem right into the camera lens. Consider photographing the stem inside of a box with a solid background. A shoe box is one possibility. Another approach is to take the photograph in a shaded area. While this eliminates shadows, it is not always a solution to the reflection problem. Bracket your exposure a half stop in either direction.

Use a solid color backdrop. Test several different photographic angles to ensure that the color is not reflected in the bowl of the stem. Place a ruler beside the piece to provide size information.

Include a card with your name, address, and telephone number in the photograph. This enables individuals who are searching on your behalf to know who to contact upon finding a match.

Given the difficulties involved in photographing stemware, consider calling several local photographers to determine the cost to have your pieces done professionally. If the cost is within your budget, this is a quick and painless solution.

KNOW EXACTLY WHAT YOU ARE SEEKING

Lack of adequate information is one of the primary reasons why individuals do not respond to want requests. You need to be specific—the more information you provide, the better.

If your goal is to expand your stemware suite or purchase accessories, send the seller a list of the pieces you already own, as well as a list of those pieces you are seeking. The seller may have pieces that are not on your list, and you will certainly want to know about these.

Clearly indicate the condition level at which you wish to purchase a piece. If you want a piece in excellent condition, that is, virtually free of any defects, state this specifically. Indicate whether you are willing to accept a stem whose lip or base has been ground to remove chips or flakes. However, the more emphasis you place on "like new" condition, the more difficult it will be to locate the pieces you desire.

The standard approach is to ask for quotes. Some individuals prefer to indicate on their list what they are willing to pay, usually noting that this is a maximum price and that they hope to receive lower quotes. The reality is that virtually every quote will be at the willing-to-pay price.

Indicate your full name, address, and day and evening telephone numbers on any request you distribute. Today, sellers are far more likely to telephone than to write.

BUYING OPTIONS

You have more buying options than you realize. Utilizing a replacement service is the most obvious choice. However, before exploring that sales venue, consider the following additional possibilities. Using your imagination, you probably can add to the list.

Garage sale circuit. This is not as dumb as it sounds, especially if you have one of the more popular patterns and attend garage sales frequently. This is the cheapest buying source you will find.

In most cases, the seller wants to sell the pieces as a lot rather than individually. Buy them all. The spare pieces provide an inexpensive backup if you break a piece. If you try to buy only a few pieces, do not be surprised if the seller's asking price is almost equal to the entire lot. Sellers know that what remains will be worth considerably less because the set has been split.

Do not be afraid to hand out your want list to individuals who appear to be garage sale regulars. You cannot be everywhere at once. Dozens of eyes searching on your behalf are better than two eyes.

Friends and neighbors. If you have a friend or neighbor who has a stemware set that matches your pattern, do not hesitate to say, "If you ever tire of that set and want to get rid of it, call me." Never underestimate the power of positive suggestion.

When using your stemware for a party or family gathering, mention your desire to expand your service or find replacement pieces. You will be amazed at what people remember. Again, your chances for success increase proportionally to the number of people who are looking on your behalf.

Post your want list on church, grocery store, or service club bulletin boards. Make sure you attach a photograph or drawing to this list, which will help catch an individual's attention.

Antiques malls. Antiques malls are becoming increasingly aware of the importance of securing want lists and passing them on to their dealers. Many have bulletin boards and are more than willing to post buyers' want lists.

Many antiques malls allow their dealers to place business cards in their booths. When walking through the mall, collect the cards from those dealers who feature stemware services and send them a copy of your want list. If the booth is devoted to replacement dinnerware, stemware, and/or flatware, consider calling the dealer and talking with him or her directly.

Antiques shows. Many antiques shows include dealers who specialize in the replacement of stemware and flatware. Take the time to talk with them to discuss your specific needs.

Talk with generalist dealers who offer only one or two services. Antiques show dealers only bring a small portion of their merchandise to shows. They may have exactly what you are seeking at home. Practice the old adage, "It never hurts to ask."

Antiques and collectibles trade periodicals. Most antiques and collectibles trade periodicals have a classified advertisement section. Many also offer business card classifieds, an advertisement measuring $3^1/_2" \times 2"$, the standard business card size. Follow a traditional business card approach when designing your advertisement. Place a "want" or "seeker" advertisement, keeping it short and simple, for example, "WANTED. Quotes on Gorham's King Edward pattern stemware. Name, telephone number with area code." You should have no difficulty limiting your request to twenty words or less.

There are over fifty antiques and collectibles trade periodicals. In addition to using a strong regional paper, consider placing your advertisement in one or more of the following national publications:

The Daze, P.O. Box 57, Otisville, MI 48463
Antique Week, P.O. Box 90, Knightstown, IN 46148
Warman's Today's Collector, 700 East State Street, Iola, WI 54990
Antique Trader Weekly, P.O. Box 1050, Dubuque, IA 52004
Maine Antique Digest, P.O. Box 1429, Waldoboro, ME 04572
Collectors News, 506 Second Street, Grundy Center, IA 50638

Manufacturer. Some patterns remain in production for decades. Before assuming that the pattern you inherited or purchased has been discontinued, check with the manufacturer. While some shapes may no longer be available, others may.

Some manufacturers maintain a small inventory of out-of-production pieces so they can fulfill replacement demands. A few maintain a file of individuals who are looking for specific pieces should they be contacted by those wishing to sell discontinued items back to the manufacturer.

A few manufacturers and distributors, for example, Princess House, have their own matching services. Occasionally, some manufacturers will reproduce a pattern and fill any outstanding orders. These pieces are sold at premium prices.

Mail-order catalogs. If your pattern is still in production, the manufacturer does not sell direct, and you cannot find a source within a reasonable driving distance, consider contacting a mail-order catalog firm specializing in the sale of stemware, other tabletop wares, and giftware. Barrons (P.O. Box 994, Novi, MI 48376), Michael C. Fina (508 Fifth Avenue, New York, NY 10036), and Ross-Simons (9 Ross-Simons Drive, Cranston, RI 02920) are three examples.

Mail-order catalogs generally sell at full retail. In addition, customers pay a shipping and handling charge. Surprisingly, many replacement services sell current production material at a slight discount. It would be wise to do some comparison shopping before ordering.

REPLACEMENT SERVICES

Ordering from a replacement service is the quickest and easiest way to expand or replace an item from your stemware service. Today's replacement services are very customer-oriented.

Most replacement services have a staff of skilled researchers who are more than willing to assist you in identifying any stemware pattern. Send them a set of your photocopies, drawings, or photographs. Within a few weeks, you will receive a letter providing you with the name of the pattern and a list of pieces available. If the research efforts prove negative, you will be informed of this as well.

Most replacement services automatically add your name to their records. If they do not have the pieces you need, they will contact you when they locate them. A few services offer a "call collect" program. You provide a number that can be called collect within a few hours of the service's entering a piece in their sales inventory.

Replacement services acquire material in a variety of conditions. When reviewing a quote, pay close attention to the condition of the piece being offered. If you are uncertain about a piece's condition, call for clarification. You may find the same piece in identical condition listed at two separate prices. When you find a bargain price, take advantage of it.

Many replacement services also offer repair services. If a piece of your stemware has a small chip or flake, consider having it repaired. Repairs are done under the assumption that the piece will be put back into use. The restoration cost may be less than buying a replacement. Also, if the piece is scarce, you can use it until an unbroken one is available.

Finally, order only from a replacement service that offers a money-back guarantee, no questions asked. This is the most important aspect of doing business by mail. If you have a problem, call immediately. As indicated previously, complete customer satisfaction is the goal.

Replacements, Ltd. (P.O. Box 26029, Greensboro, NC 27420/1-800-737-5223), worked closely with the House of Collectibles and me in the preparation of this book. I have visited its warehouse and have used its curating library. I strongly recommend contacting Replacements, Ltd., whenever you are exploring replacement service options.

FINDING A REPLACEMENT SERVICE

You will find advertisements for replacement services in a wide range of periodicals—from magazines such as *Family Circle* to Sunday newspaper supplements to antiques and collectibles trade newspapers such as *Antique Week* (P.O. Box 90, Knightstown, IN 46148). Check several publications, begin your search with a list of a half dozen or more possibilities.

Read replacement service advertisements carefully. Some specialize only in patterns from one or two companies. Others offer an extremely wide range of replacement services that also may include stemware, dinnerware, flatware, tabletop accessories, and contemporary collectibles.

David J. Maloney Jr.'s *Maloney's Antiques & Collectibles Resource Directory, 3rd Edition* (Dubuque, IA: Antique Trader Books: 1995) contains the most comprehensive list of replacement (matching) services available. Look under his Dinnerware, Glass, and Flatware general headings. Maloney provides a full mailing address, telephone number, and brief description of each firm's specialities. He also provides a list of firms that repair dinnerware.

Do not hesitate to ask family or friends who have used a replacement service about their experiences. Personal recommendations often are the best.

CHAPTER 5

Keys to Using This Book

This book has three specific goals: (1) to assist you in the selection and care of the stemware patterns you decide are right for you; (2) to provide a checklist of forms that were manufactured as part of or in conjunction with those stemware patterns; and (3) to enhance your appreciation of your stemware selections by providing historical information about their manufacturers and occasionally about the patterns themselves.

Do not ignore the previous chapters as they contain a wealth of information. Chapter 3 is a must-read. Even the most experienced glassware user will learn something new.

ORGANIZATION

The heart of this book is an alphabetical listing—first by manufacturer and then by pattern—of over 200 of the most requested patterns from replacement services. A brief history introduces each manufacturer.

Pattern names correspond to those used by the manufacturer. For consistency, the water goblet has been selected as the form of choice for illustration. Illustrations contain the details necessary for pattern identification.

An alphabetical approach is also used within the listings. Listings are by form, shape is a qualifying adjective of a form.

A pattern name index is provided. The same pattern name was used by different manufacturers. In every case, the pattern designs differ slightly. If you own a pattern, know its name, and want to locate it quickly, use the pattern name index.

UNDERSTANDING THE CHECKLIST FORMAT

Pattern listings are based on a checklist approach. The goal is to provide a complete list of forms and shapes made in the pattern. All basic forms and shapes are included. A few forms and shapes, those that had limited production and do not appear regularly for sale in the marketplace, are missing. Encyclopedic checklists are built over time. The checklists in this edition represent a strong start.

Not all manufacturers use the same terminology for the same form. This book does; the same form terms are used consistently from pattern to pattern.

Understanding the method used for listing forms is essential when locating the correct price. Some forms were manufactured with variations. Often a manufacturer produced two water goblets in the same pattern, one with a tall stem and one with a short stem. The overall height of the two goblets can be the same. When this occurs, the short stem is described as "Water Goblet, low." Also, some candy dishes were designed with and without a lid. The following listing methodology was used. A candy dish with a lid is listed as "Candy Dish, covered." A candy dish originally with a lid that is now missing is listed as "Candy Dish, covered, no lid." Finally, a candy dish that was designed to be "open" (it never had a lid) is described simply as "Candy Dish." An orphan lid will be listed as "Lid, candy dish."

Forms may be found individually priced, like "Cup" or "Saucer," or as a unit, like "Cup and Saucer." Discrepancies sometimes exist between the price of the set and the sum of its pieces. As a rule, it is less expensive to buy a set than individual pieces.

The glassware industry has generous manufacturing tolerances. A 4" oyster cocktail can range in size from $3^3/_4$" to $4^1/_4$". Because many individuals wish to purchase exact replacement matches for their stemware, known size variations are listed separately. In most instances, there is no difference in price, nor should there be. The issue is not value, but knowing the degree of variation within the form.

The size of each piece has been included when available. Sizes included in this book are measured in either diameter/length or height. The following chart will help determine the dimension that applies:

SIZE IN DIAMETER/LENGTH		SIZE IN HEIGHT	
Ashtray	Nappy	Candlestick	Jug
Bonbon	Plate	Compote	Pitcher
Bowl	Platter	Creamer	Shaker

SIZE IN DIAMETER/LENGTH		SIZE IN HEIGHT	
Celery	Relish	Cruet	Stemware
Coaster	Salver	Cup	Sugar
Dish	Tray	Decanter	Tumbler
Mayonnaise	Vegetable	Jar	Vase

Two exceptions would be the sizes included with lids and saucers. A size listed with a lid is the size of the piece to which the lid belongs. A size listed with a saucer is the size of the cup that goes with the saucer.

SEEKING A PRECISE PATTERN MATCH

Close does not count when seeking replacement or additional pieces for a stemware pattern. The match must be exact.

Five items must be examined to ensure that a replacement piece matches the stemware pattern—bowl, stem, base, pattern, and color.

When a manufacturer creates a stemware pattern that proves to be extremely popular, other manufacturers will produce their own version of the pattern. Though the two pieces may appear identical at first glance, a close inspection will reveal subtle variations—there has to be, as designs are patented. An exact copy represents a patent infringement. The stem may differ slightly or the shape of the bowl may vary a little. Eventually, design patents do expire. Pride of manufacture still prevents a direct copy.

Matching a competitor's popular color is an entirely different matter. The same color can be achieved through a variety of formulas. Hence, many manufacturers produce pieces in color hues that match those of their competitors.

A precise match occurs only when the bowl, stem, base, pattern, and color are identical. Begin by holding the two pieces at arm's length, then bring them forward for a closer inspection. A noticeable difference means the pieces are not an exact match.

PRICING NOTES

The prices that appear in this book are based upon what one would pay to purchase a specific piece of stemware from a seller specializing in stemware replacement. They are price guidelines, not price absolutes. Price is of the moment, contingent on supply and demand and a host of other variables.

Prices are based on the assumption that a piece is in fine condition, that is, it shows no visible damage at arm's length and shows only minor defects upon close inspection. Visible defects such as chips and rough edges lower a piece's value significantly, often by 50 percent or more.

The glassware patterns that appear in this book are mass-produced. As a result, it pays to comparison shop. Replacement services are price-competitive. Further, each brings its own interpretation of value to the patterns it sells. The interpretation can differ significantly from seller to seller.

A number of patterns included in this book are currently in production and available for sale at authorized sales centers and through mail-order catalogs, usually at the manufacturer's suggested retail price. Before buying from these sources, check the prices for these patterns from replacement services. The replacement service price may occasionally be lower than the manufacturer's suggested retail price. Replacement services buy a large portion of their inventory on the secondary market. When they buy at favorable prices, they can pass along these savings to their customers. However, replacement services charge premium prices for pieces from discontinued patterns or discontinued forms from a current production pattern.

Individuals who remember or who still retain the sales receipts or price lists showing what they paid initially for their pieces sometimes have difficulty accepting the price quotes they receive from replacement services. While they may need only a piece or two, the replacement service probably bought an entire service so it could make these pieces available. When considered in this light, replacement service prices are not out of line.

A REQUEST FOR YOUR HELP

As much as I would like it to be, this book is not comprehensive. Glassware manufacturers do not maintain reference archives. Last year's advertisements, catalogs, and price lists are discarded when the current year's sales materials arrive. Design and production records are kept for a few years and then trashed. Historical records are lost when one company acquires another. Contemporary manufacturers focus on the future, not the past.

Over a decade ago, Replacements, Ltd., in Greensboro, North Carolina, began assembling a dinnerware, stemware, flatware, and collectibles reference library. Today, its holdings are the best research source on the subject in the United States. Replacements, Ltd., generously made its library available to me. However, even in this great collection, there are gaps.

You can help fill them. If you have information about a pattern to add to this book, please share it. A few possibilities include: (1) promotional literature about your pattern, for example, a pamphlet describing how it was made, its designer, and/or special features; (2) a brochure and/or price list of available forms and shapes; (3) pieces in your service that do not appear on the checklist; and (4) manufacturers' promotional literature about how to care for your stemware.

While I would love to have your original copy, a photocopy will do. First, appropriate information will be incorporated into the next edition of this book. Second, I will make a duplicate copy and send it to the Replacements, Ltd., library.

Finally, although I tried to make this book error-free, I am certain that some errors slipped through the cracks. I cannot correct them if you do not point them out to me.

Please send any information you have that expands my research database and your comments, positive or negative, to: Stemware Pattern Research, Rinker Enterprises, Inc., 5093 Vera Cruz Road, Emmaus, PA 18049. Your assistance will be most appreciated.

GENERAL CRYSTAL PIECE TYPE GUIDE
CRYSTAL AND CUPS ARE MEASURED TOP TO BOTTOM

CODE	DESCRIPTION	CODE	DESCRIPTION
G	Water Goblet	CR	Creamer (Standard Size)
GL	Low Goblet	SU	Sugar Bowl (Standard Size)
T	Iced Tea (can also be flat)	CNS	Single Candlestick (under 6" tall)
ST	Sherbert/Champagne	PIT	Pitcher (48 oz. or larger)
SL	Low Sherbert	PLA	Plate (7–8")
W	Wine	REL	Relish or Celery
CLA	Claret (Large Wine)	CS	Cup and Saucer Set (Standard Size)
LC	Liquor Cocktail	SFL	Fluted Champagne
CO	Cordial	FR	Fruit Bowl (Individual Size)
J	Juice (can also be flat)	CA	Cake Plate (all styles)
PAR	Parfait	*TUM	Flat or Footed Tumbler (Not T or J size)
OC	Oyster Cocktail	S/P	Salt and Pepper Set (with lids)

*Price stated for TUM also applies to barware such as hi-ball, old fashioned, and double old fashioned.

SAMPLE OF TYPICAL PIECE TYPES
(Sizes and shapes vary between patterns and manufacturers.)

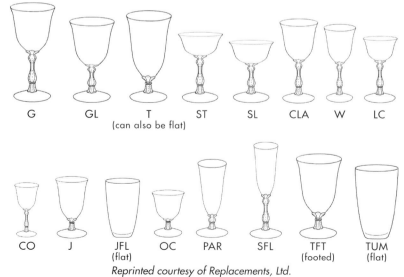

Reprinted courtesy of Replacements, Ltd.

CHAPTER 6

Stemware Glossary

This glossary is designed to help the reader understand the terminology used to describe the shapes, methods of decoration, types of stemware bodies, and manufacturing and aging terms encountered when discussing stemware.

Terminology and the meaning of terms changes over time. Today, a *nappy* is an open, shallow, flat-bottomed serving dish. In the 1940s, it most often meant a round or heart-shaped candy dish with an applied oval handle. Some terms have become obsolete, for example, sherbet. Others have acquired a generic meaning, even though their initial meaning has been retained, for example, stem.

Acid Polishing: A process by which the gray cutting is smoothed and polished through immersion in acid.

Annealing: The process of reheating a piece of finished glass which is then gradually cooled. Annealing increases the strength of glass.

Blank: An undecorated piece of glassware that usually is destined for further processing or decoration.

Blown Glass: Glass forced into shape by air pressure. The pressure can be either human or machine-produced (compressed air). The glass is either free blown or mold blown.

Cased Glass: Glassware in which a layer of colored glass is applied over a layer of clear glass. The colored glass often is cut away to create all or a portion of the decorative motif.

Cooper Wheel Engraving: A decorating process involving the use of various sizes of cooper wheels to cut the design into the piece, a method that requires great skill and experience on the part of the cutter.

Compote: A footed bowl, open or lidded, designed to hold candy, fruit, or jelly, depending on its size, also known as a comport.

Crimped: A decorative shape motif by which the outer rim of a piece of glassware is tooled to produce large scallops or undulations.

Cruet: Any stoppered bottle. Commonly used to describe bottles designed to hold oil, vinegar, or other liquid dressings.

Crystal: (1) glass made with a lead oxide, (2) a term synonymous with fine glassware, and (3) used to describe glass that is clear.

Etching: A decoration process whereby the design is eaten into the ware by acid.

Finial: A decorative handle or knob, usually on the lid of a piece.

Flared Bowl: A bowl with its rim tooled outward to form a wider outer edge.

Flatware: (1) tableware that is more or less flat and is usually formed as a single piece, for example, a plate, and (2) a generic term describing eating and serving utensils.

Form: Describes the purpose for which an object was created and/or the use that it serves, for example, a goblet or plate.

Frosted Glass: A semi-opaque glass with a gray, textured surface produced by sandblasting, acid baths, or powdered glass fired to its surface.

Giftware Industry: A general term describing a group of manufacturers who produce objects traditionally given as gifts. In some cases, these objects have shapes, forms, and patterns that match or complement dinnerware, stemware, and flatware.

Gray Cutting: A form of opaque and gray glass decoration that results from cutting with an abrasive wheel.

Hollowware: An object with depth and volume, for example, a glass or pitcher.

Ice Jug: A glass pitcher that has extra glass around its pouring lip to prevent ice cubes from falling into a glass.

Intaglio: Decoration that is beneath the surface, the opposite of embossing.

Iridescent Glass: Glassware to which a special coating has been applied to create a rainbow effect when light strikes the piece.

Jug: Another name for a pitcher.

Lead Crystal: Glass in which lead is one of the main ingredients. Lead oxide lends a brilliance and durability to glass. It is responsible for the bell-like tone that emanates when the glass is struck. Full lead crystal must contain over 24 percent lead oxide.

Lehr: A type of annealing oven in which a conveyor belt carries the ware slowly through descending temperatures.

Line: Glass items made for sale by a company on a regular basis.

Mold Marks: Ridges indicating the points at which the mold that formed a piece was separated to facilitate the removal of the ware.

Nappy: Any round or square dish used for various serving purposes.

Optics: Crystal glassware that has an attractive, rippled decoration in its body.

Pattern: Decorative motif on the surface of an object.

Polished Cutting: A design cut into glassware by an abrasive wheel, then polished either by acid or by a buffing wheel to remove the gray effect caused by the abrasive compound.

Pressed Glass: Glassware that is formed in a mold. The actual pressing can be done by machine or hand. Both shape and design may be molded at the same time.

Rolled Edge: A rim treatment in which the edge is slightly turned up or under.

Sham Bottom: The heavy, solid base on tumblers that adds weight and demonstrates the clarity or color of the glass.

Shape: Physical characteristics (appearance) of a piece of glassware.

Sherbet: Stemware form used to serve a variety of desserts, ranging from cut fruit to ice cream.

Stem: (1) The portion of a piece of glassware separating the bowl from the foot, also known as the standard in large serving pieces, or (2) synonymous with stemware.

Stemware: A generic term referring to fine glassware.

Suite: Refers to a place setting of a goblet, wine, fluted champagne, and iced beverage glass in a matching pattern. Occasionally used to describe all of the pieces in a pattern.

Tabletop Industry: General term describing a group of manufacturers who produce dinnerware, stemware, flatware, and complementary decorative accessories.

COMMON STEMWARE NAMES AND THEIR USES

Brandy	Used for brandy and other after-dinner liqueurs. Also used to serve ice and other desserts.
Champagne, fluted	Used for sparkling wines, parfaits, and specialty drinks.
Champagne, saucer	Used for sparkling wines, sorbet, and iced seafood.
Cordial	Used for dinner liqueurs.
Double Old Fashioned	Used for drinks on the rocks (with ice).
Goblet	Usually used for serving water, also can be used for red wine, which usually is served in a larger and more rounded glass than white wine, occasionally used for parfaits and other desserts.
Highball	Used for mixed drinks, soft drinks, milk, and so on.
Iced Tea	Used for water with ice, iced tea, and other iced drinks.
Martini	Used for martinis and occasionally desserts such as ice cream.
Pilsner (Beer Glasses)	Used for beer, iced beverages, and soft drinks.
Wine	Used for serving wine, usually white, also can be used for red wine.

II

STEMWARE PATTERNS

CHAPTER 7

The Patterns

ANCHOR HOCKING GLASS CORPORATION
Lancaster, Ohio

On December 31, 1937, the Anchor Cap Corporation acquired all of the properties, assets, and business of The Hocking Glass Company. The new company was named The Anchor Hocking Glass Company. Both companies were well-established within the glass industry, and each was the result of several previous mergers.

The Hocking Glass Company incorporated on November 2, 1905, to manufacture plain and decorated, pressed, blown, machine, hotel bar and kitchen tableware, tumblers, stemware, illuminating glassware, packers' ware, glass novelties, and specialties. Its plant was in Lancaster, Ohio.

The Hocking Glass Company played a pioneering role in the development of glassmaking machinery. In 1928, the company made the first automatic pressed tableware. Several lines of mold-etched dinnerware soon followed. The Hocking Glass Company also was an industry leader in the development of color dinnerware. Amber, blue, canary, and green appeared occasionally in the early and mid-1920s. Rose, also known as pink, flamingo, and cerise, was made between 1926 and 1942. Topaz first appeared in 1928. Mayfair's blue, a medium tone, began around 1930. Royal ruby was introduced in 1939; its popularity extended into the 1960s. In the 1950s, many Royal ruby molds were used to produce pieces in forest green.

In 1924, The Hocking Glass Company acquired 87 percent of the capital stock of the Lancaster Glass Company, founded on May 31, 1908. The company manufactured glassware similar to that produced by Plant No. 1 of The Hocking Glass Company. After acquiring the remaining 13 percent of the stock in 1933, The Hocking Glass Company dissolved the Lancaster Glass Company prior to its merger with the Anchor Cap Corporation in 1937.

Between 1924 and 1928, The Hocking Glass Company acquired a 60 percent interest in The Standard Glass Manufacturing Company that operated plants in Canal Winchester and Bremen, Ohio. The company specialized in the cutting and polishing of glass tumblers, stemware, and tableware. In May 1940, The Standard Glass Manufacturing Company became a wholly owned subsidiary of The Anchor Hocking Glass Company.

In April 1931, The Hocking Glass Company acquired 50 percent of the capital stock of the General Glass Corporation for the purpose of acquiring the properties of the Turner Glass Company, in receivership since 1930, and having previously manufactured glass tumblers, jars, and bottles. Turner had plants in Winchester, Ohio, and Terre Haute, Indiana. After acquiring the remaining stock, The Hocking Glass Company dissolved The General Glass Corporation prior to its merger with the Anchor Cap Corporation.

In August 1941, the Anchor Hocking Glass Corporation opened a new glass factory in Connellsville, Pennsylvania. Company expansion continued. In 1942, the Anchor Hocking Glass Corporation acquired a 97 percent interest in the Maywood Glass Company, a manufacturer of glass jars and bottles, based in Los Angeles, California. In 1944, The Carr-Lowrey Glass Company, a Baltimore manufacturer of machine-made perfume, cosmetic, and toilet water bottles in flint and opal glass, became a wholly owned subsidiary. Tropical Glass & Box Company of Jacksonville, Florida, joined the Anchor Hocking family in 1954.

In 1962, a new glass factory opened in Houston, Texas. Warehousing facilities were expanded in Los Angeles in 1962 and Chicago in 1963. On July 1, 1963, the International Division of Anchor Hocking was established. In 1969, the company changed its name to the Anchor Hocking Corporation to more accurately reflect its diversified status. By the early 1970s, the company operated eighteen plants, enjoyed a huge export trade, and billed itself as "the world's largest manufacturer of glass tableware."

Anchor Hocking Glass Corporation, Mayfair, pink, transparent (also called Open Rose)

Mayfair, also known as Open Rose, was produced from 1931 to 1937. It is one of the most collected patterns of depression glass, and was made in pink, blue, green, and yellow. The pink color was created in both a transparent and a frosted pink. Pink and blue are the most common colors, while green and yellow pieces are much harder to find. A few pieces were also produced in crystal.

There have been many reproductions of this pattern, though the colors and some dimensions differ from the original forms. Shot glasses, cookie jars, salt and pepper shakers, and juice pitchers are all known to have been reproduced.

Bowl, 8¼″	$40.00
Bowl, cereal, 5½″	30.00
Bowl, covered, 10″	100.00
Bowl, handled, 11¾″	50.00
Butter Dish, covered	100.00
Cake Plate, footed, 10″	35.00
Candy Dish, covered, 8¾″	70.00
Celery Dish, 10″	35.00
Cocktail, 4″	75.00
Cookie Jar, covered, no lid	40.00
Cream Soup Bowl, 5″	35.00
Creamer, 3⅞″	30.00
Cup, 2⅛″	25.00
Decanter, with stopper, 10⅝″	200.00
Iced Tea, flat, 5¼″	55.00
Iced Tea, footed, 6½″	40.00
Juice, flat, 3½″	50.00
Juice, footed, 3¼″	90.00
Pitcher, 6″	60.00
Pitcher, 8½″	125.00
Plate, dinner, 9½″	40.00
Plate, grill, 9½″	35.00
Plate, luncheon, 8½″	25.00
Platter, oval, handled, 12″	35.00
Relish, four-part, 8⅜″	30.00
Salt and Pepper Shakers, pair, flat	70.00
Sandwich Server, center handle, 11½″	50.00
Saucer	12.00
Sherbet, footed, 3¼″	22.00
Sugar, open, 2⅞″	40.00
Tumbler, 4¼″	30.00
Tumbler, footed, 5¼″	45.00
Water Goblet, 5¾″	70.00
Whiskey, 2¼″	85.00
Wine, 4½″	75.00

THE TOP FIVE PATTERNS COLONIAL REVIVAL

ANCHOR HOCKING, MISS AMERICA

DUNCAN & MILLER, SANDWICH

FOSTORIA, AMERICAN

IMPERIAL, CAPE COD

WATERFORD, COMERAGH

Anchor Hocking Glass Corporation, Miss America, pink (also called Diamond)

Anchor Hocking's Miss America, also known as Diamond, was produced from 1935 to 1937. Pink and green were the most common colors, although some pieces can be found in crystal and ruby red.

As with many depression-glass patterns, Miss America had been re-created, though the colors are noticeably different from the originals. Butter dishes, salt and pepper shakers, pitchers, and tumblers have all been reproduced.

Bowl, cereal, 6¼″	$25.00
Bowl, fruit, 9″	90.00

Bowl, oval, 10″	30.00	Plate, bread and butter, $5^3/_4$″	17.00
Cake Plate, footed, 12″	45.00	Plate, dinner, $10^1/_4$″	25.00
Candy Dish, covered, $7^1/_8$″, no lid	100.00	Plate, salad, $8^1/_2$″	35.00
Candy Dish, covered, $11^3/_4$″	175.00	Platter, oval, $12^1/_4$″	35.00
Celery, $10^1/_2$″	32.00	Relish, four-part, $8^3/_4$″	35.00
Coaster	25.00	Salt and Pepper Shakers, pair	80.00
Compote	30.00	Saucer	10.00
Creamer, footed	20.00	Tumbler, $4^1/_2$″	45.00
Cup	20.00	Water Goblet, $5^1/_2$″	70.00
Iced Tea, $5^3/_4$″	120.00	Wine, $3^3/_4$″	75.00
Pitcher, 8″	150.00		

David Hall McConnell (1858–1937) founded the California Perfume Company (CPC) in the mid-1880s. After an initial career selling books house to house, McConnell became convinced that perfume also could be sold in this manner. McConnell and his wife, Lucy Emma, produced the first CPC products in their home, and McConnell sold them along with his books. McConnell's philosophy was simple: "I learned . . . that the proper and most advantageous way of selling goods was to be able to submit the goods themselves to the people."

Heliotrope, Hyacinth, Lily-of-the-Valley, Violet, and White Rose were the first five perfumes manufactured. Within a short time, the line was expanded to include other perfumes and toilet articles. By 1894, McConnell's operation occupied four floors of a Manhattan building. In 1897, he built a three-story laboratory in Suffern, New York.

Mrs. P. F. E. Albee was the company's first "General Traveling Agent," acknowledged as the first "Avon Lady." By the mid-1930s, the sales force had grown to over 30,000 agents, and the sales volume was measured in millions.

McConnell incorporated the California Perfume Company in January 1916. After doing business as Allied Products, Inc., the parent company became Avon Allied Products, Inc. The trade name Avon was adopted in 1929 because of the similarity of the landscape surrounding the laboratories in Suffern, New York, to that of Avon, England. Avon Products, Inc., the distributor of Avon cosmetics, toiletries, and giftware, is a division of Avon Allied Products, Inc.

In 1936, Avon experimented in Kansas City, Missouri, Oklahoma City, and Wichita with the concept of dividing a geographic region into territories in an effort to reach customers in urban and suburban areas. Each territory was served by a representative and manager. After World War II ended, this became the universal Avon sales structure. By 1949, Avon had 2,500 employees, 65,000 representatives, $25 million in sales, and facilities in New York City, Suffern, Kansas City, Middletown, Ohio, Chicago, and Pasadena, California.

In 1954, the first "Ding-Dong, Avon Calling" television commercial aired. In 1964, the New York Stock Exchange began trading Avon stock. The same year saw the introduction of the "advance callback" brochure selling plan, where the representative left a mini-brochure at customers' homes and returned for orders. In 1972, Avon moved into its new world headquarters at 9 West 57th Street in New York City. Sales topped the billion-dollar mark.

Avon Products, Inc., introduced its ruby red Cape Cod 1876 Collection in 1975 with the Cape Cod cruet. A water goblet and wine goblet followed in 1976. Over forty shapes have been produced for the Cape Cod 1876 Collection. Since many pieces were sold for only a few years and then discontinued, some are available only on the secondary/replacement market.

Avon, Cape Cod, ruby, cut

Avon's Cape Cod was fashioned after an Early American pressed glass called "Sandwich" glass. It was inspired by the classic Roman Rosette pattern designed over a century ago in Cape Cod, Massachusetts.

Bell, 6½″	$15.00
Bowl, 8¾″	20.00
Bowl, cereal, 7½″	15.00
Bowl, fruit, 5″	12.00
Bowl, fruit, 8¾″	20.00
Box, heart-shaped	15.00
Butter Dish, covered, ¼ lb.	30.00
Cake Plate, pedestal, 3½″ × 10¾″	50.00
Candlestick, 2⅜″	10.00

Candlestick, 8¾″	37.00
Candy Dish, 6″	12.00
Champagne, 5¼″	10.00
Condiment Dish	12.00
Creamer, 3¾″	10.00
Cruet, with stopper, 5½″	12.00
Cup and Saucer, 3¼″	15.00
Decanter, 9½″	35.00
Hurricane Lamp	20.00
Iced Tea, 5½″	10.00
Mug, 5″	15.00
Napkin Rings, set of four	20.00
Ornament	15.00
Pie Plate, 10⅞″	30.00
Pitcher, 8¼″	55.00
Plate, bread and butter, 5¾″	10.00
Plate, dessert, 7½″	10.00
Plate, dinner, 11″	15.00
Platter	25.00
Salt and Pepper Shakers, pair, 4½″	20.00
Salt Shaker, 4½″	10.00
Sauce Boat, 8″	25.00
Sugar, open, 3¼″	10.00
Sugar, open, 3½″	10.00
Tray, two-tiered, brass handle	30.00
Tumbler, footed, 3¾″	10.00
Vase, 8″	20.00
Water Goblet, 6″	10.00
Wine, 4⅝″	7.00

Baccarat is a small town on the banks of the Meurthe River on the slopes of the Vosges Mountains in the French region of Lorraine. Baccarat crystal's origins date to 1764, when the Bishop of Metz, who owned large tracts of woodlands in the Lorraine region, including the town of Baccarat, wrote to King Louis XV protesting the flood of Bohemian glass products into France. King Louis XV granted a charter to the Bishop of Metz to establish a glass factory in Baccarat. The first products were mirrors and windowpanes.

After the French Revolution and the Napoleonic Wars, the company was revitalized by Gabriel-Aime d'Artigures, a crystal manufacturer determined to shift production from industrial glass to superior full lead crystal. In 1823, Baccarat received a gold medal at a national exhibition in Paris. As a result, King Louis XVIII placed a royal commission for a set of glasses. Orders soon poured in from France and abroad. Baccarat parlayed this into an aggressive international marketing effort. Eventually, the company established branches in Bombay, Saint Petersburg, Moscow, Sydney, Persia, Egypt, and North America.

In 1841, Baccarat introduced its famed Harcourt pattern with its flat cut rib. The pattern is still popular over 150 years later. In 1849, Baccarat presented balloon glasses, the harbinger of all gourmet wine glasses.

Baccarat crystal has won numerous prestigious awards in the last 200 years, including the Medaille d'Or at the 1867 and 1878 World's Fairs. In 1907, Baccarat became the first factory to manufacture crystal perfume bottles. In 1916, George Chevalier, a promising young artist, joined Baccarat. For the next fifty years, Chevalier designed crystal stemware, lamps, flagons, and animal sculptures.

In 1948, Baccarat opened a store in New York City on 57th Street. In 1964, the company celebrated its bicentenary with a retrospective at the *Musée des Arts Decoratifs* in Paris. In 1970, Baccarat invested in state-of-the-art furnaces that facilitated the continuous pouring of optically pure molten crystal.

In 1992, the French luxury conglomerate Goupe du Louvre became the main shareholder in Baccarat. In 1995, the company opened its American flagship store at 625 Madison Avenue at 59th Street in New York City, showcasing the entire Baccarat product range of traditional and contemporary giftware. Stores also opened in Nancy and Lyon, France, and Maranuchi, Tokyo, Japan.

Baccarat, Capri, crystal, optic

Baccarat, Harmonie, crystal, cut

Originally designed in the latter part of the nineteenth century for the Maharani of Baroda in India, this service was revived in 1969 and has proved to be a best-seller ever since.

Champagne, 5¼″	$55.00
Champagne, fluted, 7³/₈″	60.00
Claret, 6″	60.00
Cocktail, 4″	55.00
Cordial, 3⁵/₈″	50.00
Iced Tea	55.00
Water Goblet, 7¼″	60.00
Water Goblet, low, 6³/₄″	60.00
Wine, 5¼″	60.00

Decanter, 13³/₄″	$350.00
Highball, 5½″	70.00
Iced Tea	75.00
Vase, 9⁷/₈″	400.00
Vase, straight, 12″	500.00
Water Goblet	70.00

Baccarat, Massena, crystal, cut

Baccarat, Montaigne, crystal, optic

Massena is named after an illustrious field marshal of France during the reign of Napoleon I. Napoleon had nicknamed him "The cherished child of victory." Massena was introduced in 1979.

This pattern was created in 1890. It has an optic effect, which is a fluting on the interior of an outwardly smooth bowl that casts intriguing shadows on a table or tablecloth.

Bowl, 6$^{7}/_{8}$″	$350.00
Champagne, 5$^{3}/_{4}$″	120.00
Champagne, fluted, 8$^{1}/_{2}$″	120.00
Claret, 6$^{3}/_{8}$″	110.00
Cordial, 5$^{3}/_{8}$″	110.00
Decanter, 13$^{1}/_{4}$″	550.00
Finger Bowl, 4$^{1}/_{2}$″	110.00
Highball, 5$^{1}/_{2}$″	110.00
Old Fashioned, 3$^{5}/_{8}$″	100.00
Water Goblet, 7$^{1}/_{2}$″	130.00
Water Goblet, low, 7″	120.00
Wine, 5$^{7}/_{8}$″	110.00

Champagne, 4$^{7}/_{8}$″	$50.00
Champagne, fluted, 6$^{7}/_{8}$″	55.00
Claret, 5$^{3}/_{4}$″	55.00
Cordial, 3$^{1}/_{8}$″	50.00
Iced Tea	55.00
Tumbler, flat, 3$^{1}/_{8}$″	50.00
Water Goblet, 7″	55.00
Water Goblet, low, 6$^{3}/_{8}$″	55.00
Wine, 4$^{7}/_{8}$″	55.00

In 1901, Myron L. Case, Andrew W. Herron, Casey Morris, Fred L. Rosemond, and Addison Thompson, owners of the National Glass Company of Pennsylvania, incorporated the Cambridge Glass Company in Ohio. A plant was erected in Cambridge to take advantage of the good supply of natural gas and silica sand in the region.

Arthur J. Bennett, an East Coast importer of china and glassware, with strong roots in the English glass and ceramic industry, was hired to manage the new firm. A crystal water pitcher designed by Bennett was the first piece of glass produced by the Cambridge Glass Company in May 1902.

After a period of financial difficulties between 1907 and 1910, Bennett purchased the entire factory, including the machinery and property, for $500,000. An able manager, Bennett stabilized the company and opened a second plant in Byesville, Ohio. The Byesville plant ceased operations in 1917.

By the 1920s, the Cambridge Glass Company employed over 700 skilled workers. All products were handmade; no automatic machines were used. Over 5,000 molds were required to produce the company's extensive line of giftware, novelties, stemware, tableware, and tumblers. Bennett personally designed many of these pieces. The Cambridge Glass Company received international recognition for its pressed and blown pieces in crystal and color.

Cambridge maintained showrooms in Chicago, Dallas, Denver, Los Angeles, New York, and Philadelphia. The Cambridge Glass Company products were shipped to every state, as well as to Australia, Europe, and other parts of the world.

In 1939, Bennett sold his controlling interest in the company to W. L. Orme, his son-in-law. Many new designs and colors were created. Orme introduced the famous Square pattern around 1950. On June 17, 1954, Orme notified his employees that operations would cease. Orie J. Mosser, a plant manager who had been with the company for fifty years, turned the final key.

The company was sold to new owners. In March 1955, still using the name of the Cambridge Glass Company, the factory reopened. Sales were modest. The company changed hands again in 1956. Finally, in 1958, the plant closed for the last time.

In November 1960, the Imperial Glass Company of Bellaire, Ohio, acquired the Cambridge name and the company's remaining assets, including molds, patents, samples, and stock. Imperial placed a number of the Cambridge molds back into production. Since the molds were not changed in any way, it is difficult to distinguish some Cambridge/Imperial pieces. Only when a different color or decoration was used can the origin be clearly assigned.

Cambridge Glass Company, Chantilly, crystal, etched (No. 3625)

The second stemware line in the 3600 series, No. 3625 with the Chantilly Etching on Blank 3625 in crystal, was produced from 1939 to the plant's closing in 1958.

Basket, handled, footed, 6″	$50.00
Bonbon, handled, 5¼″	35.00
Bonbon, handled, footed, 6″	40.00
Bonbon, handled, footed, 7½″	40.00
Bowl, flared, three-toed, 10″	70.00
Bowl, four-toed, 11″	90.00
Bowl, four-toed, oval, 12″	90.00
Bud Vase, 10″	37.00
Butter Dish, covered, ¼ lb.	60.00
Cake Plate, handled, 13½″	70.00
Candlestick, 5″	32.00
Candlestick, double light, 6″	55.00
Candlestick, triple light, 6″	65.00
Candy Dish, covered, 8″, no lid	50.00
Champagne, 6″	32.00
Cheese and Cracker, 13½″	100.00
Claret	35.00
Coaster, 3¾″	20.00
Cocktail, 5⅝″	32.00
Compote, 5″	35.00
Compote, 5½″	40.00
Cordial, 4⅝″	70.00
Creamer, 3⅜″	35.00
Creamer, flat, 2½″	35.00
Creamer, footed, 3¾″	35.00
Creamer, mini, 2⅛″	32.00
Creamer, mini, 3⅛″	32.00
Cruet, with stopper	45.00
Cup and Saucer	50.00
Decanter, footed	100.00
Ice Bucket	65.00
Ice Bucket, chrome handle	70.00
Iced Tea, footed, 7¾″	37.00
Jug, 20 oz.	55.00
Jug, 32 oz.	65.00
Jug, 76 oz.	100.00
Juice, footed, 5⅜″	35.00
Mayonnaise, two-piece	50.00
Mayonnaise, three-piece	65.00
Mayonnaise, four-piece	85.00
Oyster Cocktail	35.00
Pickle, 7⅜″	45.00
Plate, bread and butter, 6½″	25.00
Plate, dinner, 10½″	60.00
Plate, handled, 6″	35.00
Plate, handled, footed, 8″	40.00
Plate, salad, 7½″	30.00
Plate, salad, 8″	30.00
Plate, salad, 8⅝″	30.00
Plate, three-toed, 12″	70.00
Plate, torte, 14″	90.00
Plate, torte, three-toed, 13″	85.00
Relish, two-part, 6″	35.00
Relish, two-part, 7″	35.00
Relish, three-part, 6½″	35.00
Relish, three-part, 8″	40.00
Relish, three-part, 9½″	50.00
Relish, three-part, 12″	75.00
Relish, five-part, 12″	75.00
Salt and Pepper Shakers, pair, chrome lids	60.00
Salt and Pepper Shakers, pair, plastic lids	60.00
Salt and Pepper Shakers, pair, no lids	37.00
Seafood Icer, with liner	65.00
Sherbet, 4⅞″	35.00
Sugar, mini, 2½″	32.00
Sugar, mini, 2⅜″	32.00
Sugar, open, footed, 2½″	35.00
Sugar, open, footed, 3″	35.00
Tray, for sugar and creamer	35.00
Tumbler	35.00

Vase, footed, 6″	35.00	Creamer, footed, mini, 2³/₄″	40.00
Vase, footed, 8″	40.00	Cup, footed, 2¹/₂″	45.00
Vase, footed, 9″	60.00	Cup and Saucer, footed, 2¹/₂″	50.00
Vase, footed, 11″	90.00	Ice Bucket, with tongs	180.00
Vase, footed, 12″	90.00	Iced Tea	50.00
Water Goblet, 7³/₄″	35.00	Mayonnaise, with ladle	80.00
Wine	35.00	Nut Cup, 3″	90.00
		Parfait, 6¹/₄″	90.00
		Plate, 8¹/₂″	50.00
		Plate, footed, 8″	45.00
		Plate, salad, 7¹/₂″	30.00
		Relish, two-part, 8″	60.00
		Relish, three-part, 6³/₄″	65.00
		Relish, three-part, 8″	65.00
		Relish, three-part, 9⁵/₈″	65.00
		Relish, three-part, 11″	65.00
		Relish, three-part, 12″	65.00
		Salt and Pepper Shakers, pair, no lids	45.00
		Salt Shaker, chrome lid	35.00
		Seafood Icer, with liner, 4³/₄″	140.00
		Sherbet, 4³/₄″	30.00
		Sugar, open, footed, 3″	40.00
		Sugar, open, footed, mini, 2¹/₄″	40.00
		Tumbler, footed, 7″	35.00
		Vase, 9³/₄″	100.00
		Water Goblet, 8³/₈″	50.00

Cambridge Glass Company, Rose Point, crystal, etched (No. 3121)

Design No. 3121 with the Rose Point etching on crystal blanks was produced from late 1936 to the factory's closing in 1958. The Imperial Glass Co. also produced this line after acquiring the rights to the Cambridge molds and etchings.

Ashtray, 4³/₈″	$70.00
Bonbon, 5″	50.00
Bonbon, 6″	50.00
Bonbon, 7¹/₈″	50.00
Bonbon, 8¹/₄″	50.00
Bonbon, footed, 9³/₄″	50.00
Bowl, four-toed, 12¹/₂″	95.00
Butter, covered, round	230.00
Candlestick, triple light, 5¹/₈″	75.00
Candy Dish, no lid, 7″	165.00
Champagne, 6³/₈″	32.00
Cocktail, 6″	40.00
Compote, 5¹/₄″	70.00
Compote, 6¹/₄″	70.00
Creamer, footed, 4″	40.00

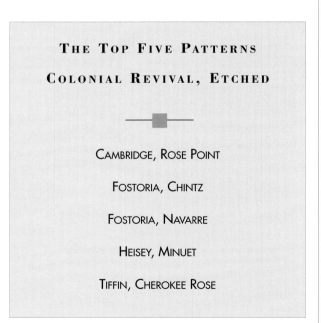

THE TOP FIVE PATTERNS

COLONIAL REVIVAL, ETCHED

CAMBRIDGE, ROSE POINT

FOSTORIA, CHINTZ

FOSTORIA, NAVARRE

HEISEY, MINUET

TIFFIN, CHEROKEE ROSE

Cambridge Glass Company, Rose Point, crystal, etched, gadroon stemware, optic (No. 3500)

The No. 3500 stemware line, commonly known as gadroon, was Cambridge's first stemware line produced with Rose Point etching. The Rose Point etching on crystal blanks was offered from 1935 to 1958.

Champagne, 6½″	$40.00
Claret	110.00
Cocktail	45.00
Cordial	110.00
Iced Tea, footed	55.00
Juice, footed	35.00
Oyster Cocktail	40.00
Parfait	100.00
Sherbet	35.00
Tumbler	40.00
Water Goblet	55.00
Wine	85.00

Cambridge Glass Company, Wildflower, crystal, etched (No. 3121)

A wide assortment of crystal pieces was produced in the Wildflower pattern during the 1940s and 1950s, as well as a few colored pieces.

Bonbon, handled, 5½″	$50.00
Bonbon, handled, 5¾″	50.00
Bonbon, handled, 7″	60.00

Bowl, flared, four-toed, 10″	75.00
Bowl, flared, four-toed, 12″	75.00
Bowl, footed, handled, 11″	90.00
Bowl, oval, four-toed, handled, 12″	90.00
Bud Vase, 10″	60.00
Butter Dish, ¼ lb.	175.00
Cake Plate, handled, 13½″	80.00
Candlestick, 4⅝″	37.00
Candlestick, 5¼″	37.00
Candy Dish, covered, 8″	70.00
Celery, 11½″	60.00
Celery, three-part, 9″	60.00
Celery, three-part, 12″	75.00
Celery, five-part, 12″	75.00
Champagne, 6⅜″	37.00
Claret	75.00
Cocktail, 6″	37.00
Compote, 5½″	55.00
Compote, 6½″	55.00
Cordial	75.00
Creamer, footed, 3¾″	40.00
Cruet, no stopper	40.00
Ice Bucket, 5⅝″	160.00
Iced Tea	40.00
Juice, 5⅝″	35.00
Mayonnaise	50.00
Mayonnaise Underplate, 8″	20.00
Oyster Cocktail, 4½″	37.00
Parfait	50.00
Pickle, footed, 9½″	75.00
Pitcher	175.00
Plate, 7½″	35.00

Plate, 8½″	45.00	Salt and Pepper Shakers, pair	75.00
Plate, bread and butter, 6½″	25.00	Sherbet, 4¾″	37.00
Plate, dinner, 10½″	75.00	Sugar, mini, footed, 2⅜″	37.00
Plate, footed, handled, 8″	50.00	Sugar, open, footed, 3″	35.00
Plate, salad, 8″	35.00	Tumbler, flat, 5⅜″	50.00
Plate, service, four-toed, 12″	65.00	Tumbler, footed, 7″	40.00
Plate, torte, 14″	75.00	Vase, footed, 6″	75.00
Relish, 7″	50.00	Vase, footed, 8″	90.00
Relish, two-part, 6″	50.00	Vase, footed, 11″	100.00
Relish, two-part, 7″	50.00	Vase, footed, 13″	150.00
Relish, three-part, 6½″	50.00	Water Goblet	45.00
Relish, three-part, handled, 8″	75.00	Wine, 5¾″	60.00

DUNCAN & MILLER GLASS COMPANY
Washington, Pennsylvania

In 1874, George Duncan Sr. became the sole owner of the Ripley Glass Company, a Pittsburgh, Pennsylvania, glass company that manufactured bar glasses and flint glassware. Within a short period, James E. Duncan Sr., George's son, and Augustus H. Heisey, George's son-in-law, joined the business, which was renamed George Duncan & Sons.

Many early Duncan patterns are attributed to Heisey, who eventually left the firm in 1895 to found his own firm in Newark, Ohio. John Ernest Miller, a Duncan designer, achieved worldwide acclaim. He is best known for the Three Face pattern.

In 1891, George Duncan & Sons joined the United States Glass Company's glass trust. When a fire destroyed the company's plant in 1892, Duncan severed its ties with the trust. After exploring a number of alternative sites to rebuild, Duncan selected Washington, Pennsylvania, and built his factory on Jefferson Avenue. The first glassware from the Washington plant was produced on February 9, 1893.

In 1900, the company was incorporated as Duncan & Miller, specializing in the manufacture of fine glassware and shipping its products throughout the world. The company used the slogan, "The Loveliest Glassware in America."

Duncan & Miller's Canterbury was introduced during World War II in response to the shortage of imported fine crystal. Teardrop, Pattern No. 301, is perhaps the best known of all Duncan & Miller tableware patterns. Sandwich was designed to have the feel and characteristics of Sandwich Glass, one of America's early glass manufacturers in Sandwich, Massachusetts, whose operations ceased in 1888.

In 1955, Duncan & Miller was sold. Many of the molds and equipment went to the United States Glass Company of Tiffin, Ohio, which was to continue producing a line of wares under a Duncan & Miller division. Several Duncan & Miller employees went to Tiffin to assist with the transition. Others found employment in nearby glass factories and cutting plants, for example, Glassport, Pennsylvania, and New Martinsville, West Virginia. Although the official closing date of the factory was June 24, 1955, the fourteen-pot furnace was not turned off until August 30. With all outstanding orders filled, the remaining stock was sold at bargain prices.

Buyers were sought for the Duncan & Miller plant. Andy Brothers, a Washington, Pennsylvania, company that recapped tires, was in the process of renovating the factory when it burned to the ground on June 29, 1956.

Duncan & Miller Glass Company, Canterbury, crystal (Pattern 115, Stem 5115$^1/_2$)

Duncan & Miller produced Canterbury glassware until 1955, when the plant closed, and Tiffin Glass Co. acquired the molds.

Ashtray, 3″	$15.00
Ashtray, 4$^1/_2$″	17.00
Ashtray, 5$^1/_2$″	17.00
Ashtray, rectangular, 3$^1/_2$″ × 2$^1/_4$″	10.00
Ashtray, rectangular, 4$^1/_2$″ × 3$^1/_2$″	12.00
Ashtray, rectangular, 6$^1/_2$″ × 4$^3/_4$″	20.00
Basket, oval, handled, 9$^1/_2$″ × 10″	75.00
Bowl, flared, 12″	60.00
Bowl, flared, oval, 13″	65.00
Bowl, fruit, 7$^1/_2$″	17.00
Bowl, oval, 10″	40.00
Bowl, salad, crimped, 9″	35.00
Bowl, salad, crimped, 10″	40.00
Bowl, salad, shallow, 12″	40.00
Candlestick, 3″	45.00
Candlestick, double light, 6$^1/_2$″	60.00
Candy Dish, covered, divided, handled, 8″	50.00
Candy Dish, covered, footed, 9″	50.00
Celery, 11″	25.00
Champagne, 4$^1/_4$″	17.00
Cheese and Cracker Set, two-piece	50.00
Cigarette Box, covered, 4$^1/_2$″ × 3$^1/_2$″	40.00
Claret, 5″	32.00
Cocktail, 4$^1/_4$″	17.00
Compote, 5$^1/_2$″	25.00
Condiment, two-part, 8″	30.00

Cordial	20.00
Creamer and Sugar Set, with tray	50.00
Creamer and Sugar Set, with tray, mini	40.00
Cruet, with stopper, 5$^5/_8$″	40.00
Cup and Saucer, 2$^3/_4$″	22.00
Finger Bowl, 4$^1/_4$″ × 2″	15.00
Iced Tea, footed, 6$^1/_4$″	17.00
Juice, footed, 4$^1/_4$″	17.00
Marmalade and Underplate, with ladle	25.00
Mayonnaise and Underplate, with ladle	30.00
Mayonnaise and Underplate, divided, with two ladles	40.00
Mint Tray, 4″	20.00
Nappy, 5″	15.00
Nappy, handled, 5$^1/_4$″	22.00
Nappy, handled, 9″	27.00
Old Fashioned, 3$^1/_4$″	15.00
Oyster Cocktail, 4″	17.00
Pickle, 8″	25.00
Pitcher, 4$^3/_4$″	25.00
Pitcher, 9$^1/_4$″	40.00
Plate, bread and butter, 6″	15.00
Plate, dinner, 11″	50.00
Plate, handled, 7$^1/_2$″	20.00
Plate, luncheon, 8$^1/_2$″	20.00
Plate, salad, 7$^1/_2$″	17.00
Plate, sandwich, handled, 11$^1/_2$″	60.00
Plate, torte, 14″	75.00
Relish, two-part, 6″	22.00
Relish, two-part, 8$^1/_8$″	27.00
Relish, two-part, 8$^5/_8$″	27.00
Relish, two-part, handled, 10$^1/_2$″	35.00
Relish, three-part, 8″	30.00
Relish, three-part, 11$^1/_4$″	30.00
Relish, four-part, 11$^1/_4$″	35.00
Relish, five-part, 12″	40.00
Rose Bowl, 5″	20.00
Salt and Pepper Set, with tray	50.00
Salt and Pepper Shakers, pair, 3$^3/_4$″	40.00
Sherbet, 3$^5/_8$″	17.00
Tumbler, 3$^3/_4$″	12.00
Tumbler, 4$^1/_2$″	15.00
Tumbler, 6$^1/_4$″	17.00
Tumbler, footed, 6$^1/_4$″	15.00

Vase, 5½″	25.00
Vase, 8″	30.00
Vase, 12″	50.00
Water Goblet, 6″	17.00
Water Goblet, low, 5³/₈″	17.00
Wine	25.00

Water Goblet, 7¼″	35.00
Wine	35.00

Duncan & Miller Glass Company, Chantilly, crystal, cut (Cutting 773, Stem 5115½)

Bowl, crimped, 10½″	$60.00
Candlestick, double light	60.00
Candy Dish, covered, 8″	75.00
Champagne, 5½″	32.00
Cocktail, 5⅛″	32.00
Compote, 7½″	60.00
Cordial, 4³/₈″	75.00
Creamer	35.00
Iced Tea, footed	40.00
Juice, footed, 4⅛″	25.00
Mayonnaise and Underplate, with ladle	75.00
Nappy, 6″	40.00
Oyster Cocktail	30.00
Plate, 7½″	25.00
Plate, 8½″	35.00
Plate, handled, 7½″	40.00
Plate, sandwich, handled, 11½″	60.00
Plate, torte, 14″	75.00
Relish, two-part, 6″	40.00
Relish, three-part, 9″	50.00
Relish, five-part, 12″	60.00
Sugar	35.00

Duncan & Miller Glass Company, First Love, crystal, etched (Pattern 111, Stem 5111½)

Ashtray, 3″	$30.00
Ashtray, 6½″	40.00
Bowl, flared, 11¼″	100.00
Bowl, oval, 11½″	80.00
Candlestick, 4½″	40.00
Candlestick, double light, 5³/₄″	75.00
Candy Dish, covered, 8½″, no lid	60.00
Celery, 9″	60.00
Champagne, 5″	40.00
Cigarette Box, 4½″	80.00
Cocktail, 4½″	40.00
Compote, 5½″	60.00
Cordial, 3½″	80.00
Creamer, 3⅝″	45.00
Cup and Saucer, flat, 2⅝″	50.00
Cup and Saucer, footed, 2³/₈″	50.00
Ice Bucket	175.00
Iced Tea, 6½″	40.00
Juice, 5¼″	40.00
Mayonnaise, with ladle	45.00
Nappy, 7¼″	50.00
Nappy, handled, 7⅛″	50.00
Oyster Cocktail, 3⅞″	40.00
Plate, Canterbury Shape, 6³/₈″	40.00
Plate, Canterbury Shape, 7⅞″	40.00
Plate, Canterbury Shape, 8⅞″	40.00
Plate, sandwich, 13½″	80.00

Plate, square, 6″	40.00	Basket, handled, 7″	115.00
Plate, Terrace Blank, 6⅛″	40.00	Bowl, cereal, 7″	10.00
Plate, Terrace Blank, 7½″	40.00	Bowl, crimped, 11¼″	55.00
Plate, Terrace Blank, 8½″	40.00	Bowl, dessert, 6″	10.00
Relish, two-part, 8″	60.00	Bowl, flared, 11¾″	55.00
Relish, two-part, 8½″	60.00	Bowl, fruit, 3½″	10.00
Relish, three-part, 8¼″	70.00	Bowl, fruit, 5″	15.00
Relish, three-part, 8⅜″	70.00	Bowl, gardenia, 11½″	50.00
Relish, four-part, 9″	70.00	Bowl, heart-shaped, handled, 6″	25.00
Relish, five-part, 12″	70.00	Bowl, salad, 10″	70.00
Salt and Pepper Shakers, pair	80.00	Bowl, salad, shallow, 12″	75.00
Salt and Pepper Shakers, pair, no lids	55.00	Butter Dish, covered, ¼ lb.	75.00
Salt Shaker, no lid	40.00	Butter Dish, covered, round	100.00
Sherbet, 4″	40.00	Cake Salver, footed, 11½″	25.00
Sugar, open, flat, 3¼″	45.00	Cake Salver, footed, 13″	30.00
Vase, 6¾″	60.00	Candlestick, 4″	30.00
Vase, 10″	100.00	Candy Dish, covered, footed, 8½″	60.00
Water Goblet, 6¾″	40.00	Celery, 10¼″	25.00
Wine, 5⅜″	65.00	Champagne, 5″	20.00
		Cheese and Cracker Set, two-piece	40.00
		Cheese Dish, covered	100.00
		Cigarette Box, covered, 3½″	35.00
		Coaster, 4½″	12.00
		Cocktail, 4¼″	15.00
		Compote, crimped, 5½″	20.00
		Creamer, footed, 4¼″	15.00
		Creamer, footed, mini 3¼″	15.00
		Creamer and Sugar Set, with tray, mini, three pieces	45.00
		Cruet, with stopper, 5¾″	35.00
		Cup, 2⅛″	15.00
		Cup and Saucer, 2⅛″	17.00
		Cup and Saucer, 2¼″	17.00
		Deviled Egg Server, 12¼″	65.00
		Ice Cream Dish, 4¼″	15.00
		Iced Tea, flat, 5¼″	25.00
		Iced Tea, footed, 5⅜″	22.00
		Jar, covered, 8¼″	55.00
		Jar, covered, 8⅝″	55.00
		Juice, flat, 3¾″	15.00
		Juice, footed, 3¼″	15.00
		Mayonnaise and Underplate, with ladle	35.00
		Nappy, handled, 5″	15.00
		Nappy, handled, 5½″	15.00
		Oil Cruet, with stopper, 5¾″	55.00

Duncan & Miller Glass Company, Sandwich, crystal (Pattern 41)

Duncan & Miller's Sandwich pattern was named after the town of Sandwich, Massachusetts, on Cape Cod. The Sandwich design was produced from 1924 to 1955, when some of the molds were sold to other companies. It was available in amber, cobalt blue, crystal, green, pink, and red.

Ashtray, 3⅞″	$15.00
Ashtray, square, 2⅞″	12.00
Basket, 11¾″	225.00

Old Fashioned, 3¼"	22.00	Salt and Pepper Shakers, pair, 2½", no lids	15.00
Oyster Cocktail, 2¼"	17.00	Sherbet, 4¼"	12.00
Oyster Cocktail, 2¾"	17.00	Sugar, open, footed, 3¼"	15.00
Parfait, 5¼"	25.00	Sugar, open, footed, mini, 2¾"	15.00
Pickle, 7"	20.00	Sugar Shaker	35.00
Pitcher, 8"	125.00	Sundae, 3⅜"	15.00
Plate, 8¼"	15.00	Syrup Pitcher	40.00
Plate, bread and butter, 6"	12.00	Tray, for condiment set, 8"	25.00
Plate, dessert, 7⅛"	12.00	Tray, for salt and pepper set, 6⅛"	15.00
Plate, dinner, 9½"	30.00	Tray, mint, 7¾"	27.00
Plate, handled, 11½"	40.00	Tray, oval, for creamer and sugar set, 8"	20.00
Plate, salad, 8"	15.00	Tumbler, flat, 4⅜"	17.00
Plate, service, 13¼"	55.00	Tumbler, footed, 3¾"	12.00
Plate, torte, 12"	40.00	Tumbler, footed, 4⅞"	15.00
Plate, torte, 13"	50.00	Vase, flared, 3"	17.00
Plate, torte, large, 16¼"	100.00	Vase, flared, 4¾"	27.00
Relish, two-part, 5½"	22.00	Vase, footed, 10"	65.00
Relish, two-part, 6"	22.00	Water Goblet, 5⅞"	20.00
Relish, two-part, 7"	27.00	Wine, 4⅜"	22.00
Relish, three-part, 12"	35.00		
Relish, three-part, rectangular, 10½" × 6¾"	35.00		
Relish, four-part, handled, 10"	40.00		

DUNCAN AND MILLER DIVISION
UNITED STATES GLASS COMPANY

Duncan's Early American

Sandwich Glass

Pattern Number 41

Catalog 93
Page 1

Duncan & Miller Glass Company, Teardrop, crystal (Pattern 301, Stem 5301½)

Duncan & Miller's Teardrop pattern was produced from 1934 to 1955 in crystal only. The design was available in full dinnerware sets as well as in stemware.

Ashtray, 3¼"	$15.00
Ashtray, 5"	17.00

Basket, oval, 10″	125.00	Relish, two-part, 8³/₈″	27.00
Bonbon, 6″	25.00	Relish, three-part, 11³/₄″	30.00
Bowl, crimped, 11¹/₂″	90.00	Relish, four-part, 12″	35.00
Bowl, flared, 11¹/₂″	90.00	Relish, five-part, 12″	40.00
Bowl, handled, 12″	90.00	Salt Shaker	17.00
Butter Dish, covered, 6″	65.00	Salt Shaker, chrome lid	17.00
Candy Dish, covered, 8″	75.00	Salt Shaker, no lid	12.00
Candy Dish, heart-shaped, 7¹/₂″	50.00	Sherbet, 2³/₈″	17.00
Champagne, 4³/₈″	17.00	Sugar, open, footed, 3¹/₄″	20.00
Champagne, 5¹/₈″	17.00	Sundae, 3³/₈″	17.00
Champagne, 5³/₈″	17.00	Sundae, 3⁵/₈″	17.00
Cheese Stand, 3¹/₄″	27.00	Sundae, 3⁷/₈″	17.00
Claret, 5¹/₈″	32.00	Tray, 8″	17.00
Claret, 5³/₈″	32.00	Tumbler, flat, 6″	15.00
Coaster, 3″	15.00	Tumbler, footed, 4³/₈″	17.00
Cocktail, 4⁵/₈″	17.00	Tumbler, footed, 5″	17.00
Cordial, 3⁷/₈″	35.00	Tumbler, footed, 5¹/₄″	17.00
Creamer, footed, 4″	20.00	Water Goblet, 6⁷/₈″	17.00
Creamer, mini, 2³/₄″	17.00	Water Goblet, 7¹/₄″	17.00
Creamer and Sugar Set, with tray,		Water Goblet, low, 5¹/₂″	17.00
mini, three pieces	60.00	Wine, 4³/₄″	30.00
Cruet, with stopper	45.00	Wine, 5″	30.00
Cup, 2¹/₂″	20.00		
Cup, footed, 2³/₄″	20.00		
Cup and Saucer, footed, 2³/₄″	25.00		
Iced Tea, flat, 5³/₄″	15.00		
Iced Tea, footed, 6″	17.00		
Juice, flat, 3¹/₂″	12.00		
Juice, footed, 4″	17.00		
Mayonnaise	25.00		
Mayonnaise Underplate	25.00		
Nappy, 5″	25.00		
Nut Dish, two-part, 6″	25.00		
Oyster Cocktail, 2⁵/₈″	17.00		
Pickle, 7¹/₄″	25.00		
Pitcher, 8¹/₂″	100.00		
Plate, 6³/₈″	17.00		
Plate, 7¹/₂″	17.00		
Plate, 10¹/₂″	50.00		
Plate, lemon, 7¹/₄″	22.00		
Plate, torte, 14″	75.00		
Relish, 8¹/₂″	25.00		
Relish, two-part, 5¹/₂″	27.00		
Relish, two-part, 6″	27.00		
Relish, two-part, 6¹/₄″	27.00		
Relish, two-part, 7³/₄″	27.00		

Duncan & Miller Glass Company, Willow, crystal, cut (Stem D3)

Bowl, flared, 12¹/₂″	$95.00
Bowl, footed, 10¹/₂″	85.00
Bowl, salad, 10¹/₂″	95.00
Candlestick	45.00
Candlestick, double light	65.00
Candy Dish, covered, 6″	95.00
Celery, 11″	65.00

Celery, 11³/₈″	50.00	Oyster Cocktail, 4″	27.00
Champagne, 4³/₄″	27.00	Plate, 7¹/₂″	35.00
Cheese and Cracker Set, handled, 11″	90.00	Plate, 8³/₄″	35.00
Cocktail, 4¹/₂″	27.00	Plate, torte, 14″	95.00
Compote, 7¹/₂″	70.00	Relish, three-part, handled, 12″	70.00
Cordial, 4¹/₂″	45.00	Relish, five-part, 10″	80.00
Creamer	35.00	Relish, five-part, 12″	90.00
Highball, 5⁵/₈″	35.00	Sherbet	27.00
Iced Tea, footed, 6¹/₂″	35.00	Sugar, open, 2⁵/₈″	40.00
Juice, footed, 5¹/₈″	27.00	Tray, center handle, 11″	85.00
Mayonnaise, three-piece	90.00	Water Goblet, 6¹/₄″	32.00
Old Fashioned, 3¹/₄″	35.00	Wine, 5¹/₄″	45.00

J. G. Durand, a member of the Durand family of the northern province of France, founded a crystal glass company in 1815. Today, that company has grown into the largest producer of glassware consumer products. Its products are exported to 135 countries. Approximately 25 percent of its production is shipped to the United States.

J. G. Durand markets its crystal products in the United States under a variety of labels—Cristal J. G. Durand, Cristal D'Arques, Luminare, Arocroc, Arcopal, Arcuisine, Arcolflam, and Arcoflam Clearline. Cristal J. G. Durand is the premier collection of J. G. Durand CIE. Its development was made possible by Durand's invention of tooling that enabled it to produce the first entirely machine-made, 24 percent and over, lead crystal. Developing machinery that imitates the art of handblown crystal has been a major goal of the company.

J. G. Durand's wide variety of products makes it one of the most diversified companies in the tabletop houseware and decorative accessories markets. Its mixture of traditional, transitional, and contemporary trendsetting designs allows the company to reach a wide audience whose tastes range from classic opulence to modern simplicity.

Durand International, Longchamp, crystal, cut

This popular pattern, produced by Durand International's Cristal D'Arques division, is still produced in the fluted champagne, iced tea, water goblet, and wine glass forms.

Ashtray, 6¼″	$12.00
Bonbon, footed, 6″	15.00
Bowl, 4¾″	12.00
Bowl, footed, 6⅛″	22.00
Bowl, footed, 8¾″	30.00
Bowl, fruit, 8¾″	25.00
Bowl, fruit, footed, 4¼″	10.00
Brandy, 5¼″	15.00
Bud Vase, 3¼″	12.00
Butter Dish, covered, ¼ lb.	30.00
Cake Plate, footed, 12½″	25.00
Candle, votive, 3¼″ × 2½″	15.00
Candlestick, 6¾″	15.00
Candy Dish, covered, 4¾″	30.00
Candy Dish, covered, footed, 4¼″	30.00
Candy Dish, covered, footed, 6″	35.00
Champagne, 5⅝″	7.00
Champagne, fluted, 8⅛″	7.00
Champagne Bucket, 7¾″	75.00

Cordial, 4⅝″	7.00
Creamer, 3½″	12.00
Decanter	40.00
Decanter, ship	40.00
Highball, 5⅜″	7.00
Ice Bucket, 5½″	40.00
Iced Tea, 7″	12.00
Juice, flat, 4″	15.00
Old Fashioned, 3¾″	7.00
Picture Frame, 3½″ × 5″	12.00
Picture Frame, 5″ × 7″	15.00
Pitcher, 9½″	40.00
Plate, dessert, 7¾″	15.00
Relish, two-part, 12½″	20.00
Salt and Pepper Shakers, pair, 3″	25.00
Sherbet	7.00
Sherry	7.00
Shot Glass, 2¼″	7.00
Sugar, covered, 4½″	20.00
Sugar, covered, 2½″, no lid	12.00
Sugar, open, 4½″	12.00
Tray, rectangular, 15¾″ × 8¾″	20.00
Tumbler, flat, 5″	7.00
Vase, 5¼″	25.00

Vase, 9¾″	40.00
Vase, footed, 4¾″	25.00
Vase, footed, 7″	30.00
Vase, footed, 9″	40.00
Water Goblet, 7¼″	7.00
Wine, 5¾″	7.00
Wine, 6½″	7.00

**Durand International, Tuilleries/Villandry,
crystal, cut**

The Tuilleries stemware line, produced by Durand International's Cristal D'Arques division, was discontinued in 1987. This stemware design is very similar to the Villandry barware line, which is still in production.

Bowl, fruit, 4⅜″	$17.00
Bowl, salad, 8¾″	30.00
Candy Dish, covered, 4¼″	35.00
Champagne, fluted, 6½″	17.00
Cordial, 3¾″	15.00
Decanter	35.00
Highball	17.00
Ice Bucket, 5¼″ × 5″	35.00
Iced Tea	17.00
Old Fashioned, 3½″	15.00
Tumbler	15.00
Vase, 9¾″	30.00
Water Goblet, 6⅛″	20.00
Wine, 5¼″	20.00

Villandry tumblers by Cristal D'Arques.
Photo couresy of J. G. Durand International.

THE TOP FIVE PATTERNS
TRADITIONAL

DURAND, VERSAILLES

GORHAM, KING EDWARD

LENOX, NAVARRE

WATERFORD, ARAGLIN

WATERFORD, LISMORE

Durand International, Versailles, crystal, cut

Produced by Durand International's Cristal D'Arques division, the Versailles pattern is still produced in the cordial, fluted champagne, water goblet, and wine glass forms.

Champagne, 5″	$15.00
Champagne, fluted	17.00
Cocktail	15.00
Cordial, 3⁷/₈″	12.00
Highball	15.00
Iced Tea	15.00
Sherry	12.00
Water Goblet, 6⁵/₈″	15.00
Wine, 4⁷/₈″	15.00

EDINBURGH CRYSTAL
Edinburgh, Scotland

Edinburgh glass is part of Scotland's proud heritage. Glass has been made for over three centuries within the city's boundaries, initially in the Citadel in the port of Leith, and finally in the Norton Park area of the city. In the early 1660s, Leith glasshouses produced bottles and commercial-quality drinking glasses. By the end of the eighteenth century, fine crystal and window glass was being made. The nineteenth century witnessed the decline of the crystal glass industry in Leith and in Portobello, its neighbor. By the middle of the century, Leith's glasshouses were once again producing bottles for brewers, distillers, and wine importers.

Although in decline in Leith, manufacturing of fine crystal glassware continued in the heart of Edinburgh. John Ford's, later the Royal Holyrood Glass Works, became flint glass manufacturers to Queen Victoria. The company was noted for its cut and engraved crystal glass, as well as for colored glass and novelty paperweights. When Ford's closed in 1904, the Edinburgh and Leith Flint Glass Works were the sole producers of crystal glass in the city.

The Edinburgh and Leith Flint Glass Company was established in 1867, an outgrowth of the estate of John Thomas, who operated a glass factory at No. 33 Leith Walk, the main thoroughfare from Edinburgh to Leith. By 1873, Alexander Jenkinson, who also ran a pottery and glass retail shop at 10 Princes Street, was associated with the firm. Shortly thereafter, the company moved to Norton Park in the newly developed district, just off Easter and London Roads. Three generations of Jenkinsons managed the company.

In 1921, Stanley Noel Jenkinson was instrumental in combining the company with Thomas Webb and Sons, Stourbridge, to form Webb's Crystal Glass Company. In 1955, the Edinburgh company was renamed Edinburgh Crystal Glass Company. In 1964, the company became part of Dema Glass, the glass division of Crown House.

After almost a decade at the Norton Park site, the company moved to a completely new facility at Penicuik, ten miles south of Edinburgh. By 1974, glassmaking and decorating were being done at the Penicuik location.

Edinburgh Crystal, Thistle, crystal, cut

Champagne	$60.00
Champagne, fluted	65.00
Claret	65.00
Cordial	60.00
Highball	60.00
Hock	70.00
Iced Tea	65.00
Old Fashioned	55.00
Old Fashioned, double	60.00
Sherry, 6″	65.00
Shot Glass, 2½″	65.00
Water Goblet	65.00
Whiskey, 3¼″	65.00
Wine	65.00

The thistle flower of Scotland was the inspiration for this Edinburgh pattern.

Edinburgh Crystal's Thistle, from the company's 1986–87 catalog.

FACTORY TOUR INFORMATION

Edinburgh Crystal welcomes thousands of visitors each year to its factory tours at Penicuik. Tours begin at the Visitor Centre, where the story of Edinburgh crystal is told via an exhibition and a video presentation. The Visitor Centre is open Monday through Saturday from 9:00 A.M. until 5:00 P.M. and on Sunday from 11:00 A.M. until 5:00 P.M. Tours leave Monday through Friday at 9:15 A.M. and 3:30 P.M. A Factory Shop offers a wide variety of Edinburgh and regional products. For information, contact Edinburgh Crystal Visitor Centre, Eastfield, Penicuik, Midlothian, EH26 8HB, or telephone 011-44-1-968-675128.

The Federal Glass Company was established around 1900. The company's initial products were handmade and included pressed crystal wares that were sold plain or decorated. Federal needle-etched blown goblets are commonly found. Mass production was emphasized as Federal directed its efforts toward manufacturing large quantities to meet the public's demands.

A leader in introducing automation to the glass industry, the Federal Glass Company was one of the largest manufacturers of machine-made jugs and tumblers by the 1920s. During this decade, Federal introduced stemware and refreshment sets that featured an iridescent and a luster treatment. The company's 1926 catalog included its first machine-made, color glass—*Optic* tumblers in Springtime green.

Federal's green was phased out around 1936. Amber and Golden Glow were introduced in 1931 and made until 1942. Rose Glow (pink) was made between 1933 and 1941. During the 1930s, Federal introduced a wide range of machine-pressed, modeled, color dinnerware with etched designs. Dinnerware in Madonna blue (a medium shade) was made between 1933 and 1934, and an iridescent amber color was used from 1934 to 1935. Federal also was a pioneer in the area of hand-painted and stenciled decoration on tumblers.

In the 1940s, the Federal Glass Company became a major supplier of institutional wares, creating products to serve motels, restaurants, universities, and other institutions around the world. In 1958, the Federal Paper Board Company acquired the Federal Glass Company. New ownership was unable to reinvigorate the company. On January 31, 1979, Federal ceased its manufacturing operations.

Federal Glass Company, Sharon, pink (also called Cabbage Rose)

Sharon was produced in pink, green, and amber, with a few pieces produced in crystal, from 1935 to 1939.

Bowl, cereal, 6″	$25.00
Bowl, fruit, 5″	17.00
Bowl, fruit, 8½″	40.00
Bowl, fruit, 10½″	45.00
Bowl, soup, 7¾″	60.00

Butter Dish, covered, round, no lid	32.00	Pitcher, without ice lip	175.00
Cake Plate, footed, $11\frac{1}{2}''$	50.00	Plate, bread and butter, $6''$	25.00
Candy Dish, covered	75.00	Plate, dinner, $9\frac{1}{2}''$	50.00
Champagne, $2\frac{3}{8}''$	17.00	Plate, salad, $7\frac{1}{2}''$	30.00
Cream Soup Bowl, $5''$	55.00	Platter, oval, $12\frac{1}{2}''$	55.00
Creamer, $3\frac{1}{2}''$	22.00	Salt and Pepper Shakers, pair, no lids	40.00
Cup	17.00	Saucer	17.00
Iced Tea	60.00	Sugar, covered	30.00
Lid, candy dish	30.00	Tumbler, flat, $4\frac{1}{8}''$	50.00
Pitcher, with ice lip	200.00	Vegetable, oval, $9\frac{1}{2}''$	40.00

The Fostoria Glass Company broke ground for a glass factory in Fostoria, Ohio, on January 1, 1888. As an incentive to the owners, the town of Fostoria gave the company free land and promised free gas for the furnaces. Within six months of opening, the factory was producing a line of glass bottles, shakers, and utilitarian ware.

Tragedy struck. The natural gas that seemed so plentiful unexpectedly ran out. The Fostoria Glass Company immediately announced that it was constructing a new glass factory in Moundsville, West Virginia. When the new factory opened in 1891, the company expanded its product line to include candelabra, cologne bottles, jars, oil lamps (some hand-painted), perfume items and vanity boxes. Needle-etched and blown stemware followed.

The history of the Fostoria Glass Company is linked with the Dalzell family. W. A. B. Dalzell, William F. Dalzell, David B. Dalzell, David Dalzell Jr., and Kenneth Dalzell all played major roles in managing and directing the company.

Fostoria's stemware and tableware included a wide variety of products in crystal and color. Color tableware was introduced in 1924. Fostoria competed actively with Cambridge, Heisey, and Westmoreland. It is hard not to miss the color similarities between Fostoria's Azure blue and Cambridge's blue, and the pattern similarities between Fostoria's June and Navarre etchings and Cambridge's Rose Point and Heisey's Orchid etchings.

The Fostoria Glass Company changed with the times. When pressed and needle-etched glass stemware fell from favor, the company turned to plate and master etchings. Color was used more frequently. When teas and luncheons were replaced by brunches and cocktail parties, Fostoria added new patterns, shapes, and forms to its line.

The Fostoria Glass Company marketed aggressively. The sales force concentrated on better-quality retailers, from jewelry to department stores. Model boutiques were established in larger department stores. The company supported its Fostoria sales force with an extensive national advertising campaign. Strong personal contact between buyer and retailer was the goal. A major effort was directed toward targeting the bridal market. The company even published its own magazine, *Creating with Crystal*. Fostoria's efforts were highly successful.

In 1965, the Fostoria Glass Company acquired the Morgantown Glass Company of Morgantown, West Virginia, for its molds, colors, and production of lead crystal. Fostoria kept the Morgantown molds in production at the Morgantown site until 1971. Although a few Morgantown pieces were kept in the Fostoria line, most were closed out at Fostoria outlet stores. Fostoria simply could not create strong buyer interest in lead crystal.

Foreign competition intensified in the 1970s. In 1983, the Lancaster Colony Corporation purchased the Fostoria Glass Company. In 1986, the Moundsville factory closed, and the remaining stock in the warehouse was sold. Collectors thrilled at the opportunity to acquire many one-of-a-kind items, for example, experimental, morgue, and trial pieces.

Fostoria Glass Company, American, crystal, pressed (Blank 2056)

American Blank 2056, a pressed glass line, was produced in crystal and green. Crystal was produced from 1915 to 1982. Fostoria's American pattern is the longest running line in glassmaking history.

Almond, oval, 2³/₄″	$15.00
Almond, oval, 3³/₄″	17.00
Almond, oval, 4¹/₂″	17.00
Appetizer Tray, square	27.00
Ashtray, oval, 3⁷/₈″	10.00
Ashtray, oval, 5¹/₂″	17.00
Ashtray, square, 3″	10.00
Ashtray, square, 5″	50.00
Banana Split, 9″ × 3¹/₂″	350.00
Basket, reed handle, 7″ × 9″	90.00
Bell	350.00
Bonbon, three-toed, 6″	20.00
Bonbon, three-toed, 7″	20.00
Bonbon, three-toed, 8″	20.00
Bowl, baby, 4¹/₂″	50.00
Bowl, cupped, 7″	60.00
Bowl, floating garden, 10″	50.00
Bowl, floating garden, 11″	50.00

Bowl, floating garden, oval, 10″	35.00
Bowl, floating garden, oval, 11″	40.00
Bowl, fruit, 13″	75.00
Bowl, fruit, flared, 4¹/₂″	15.00
Bowl, fruit, footed, 12″	250.00
Bowl, fruit, footed, 16″	200.00
Bowl, fruit, shallow, 13″	65.00
Bowl, handled, 4¹/₂″	15.00
Bowl, handled, 8¹/₂″	50.00
Bowl, handled, 10³/₈″	40.00
Bowl, lily pond, footed, 12″	60.00
Bowl, oval, 4¹/₂″	15.00
Bowl, oval, deep, 11³/₄″	45.00
Bowl, rolled edge, 11¹/₂″	50.00
Bowl, round, 7¹/₄″	195.00
Bowl, round, 10″	25.00
Bowl, round, footed, 5¹/₈″	200.00
Bowl, square, handled, 4¹/₂″	17.00
Bowl, three-toed, 10¹/₄″	50.00
Bowl, wedding, covered, square, footed, 6¹/₂″	100.00
Bowl, wedding, square, footed, 6¹/₂″	55.00
Box, candy, covered, three-part	80.00
Bud Vase, cupped, 6″	25.00
Bud Vase, cupped, 8¹/₄″	25.00
Bud Vase, flared, 6¹/₄″	25.00
Bud Vase, flared, 8¹/₄″	25.00
Butter Dish, covered, ¹/₄ lb.	35.00
Butter Dish, covered, round, 7¹/₄″	130.00
Cake Plate, handled, 10″	35.00
Cake Plate, three-toed, 12″	25.00
Cake Salver, round, 10″	75.00
Cake Salver, square, 10″	100.00
Candlestick, 3″	17.00
Candlestick, 7″	60.00
Candlestick, double light, 4³/₈″	35.00
Candlestick, octagonal base, 6¹/₄″	32.00
Candy Dish, hexagon footed, 5″	50.00
Celery, 10″	30.00

Celery Vase, straight, 6″	50.00	Mayonnaise, divided, 6¼″	30.00
Champagne, 4¾″	15.00	Muffin Tray, handled, 10″	35.00
Champagne, flared, 4⅜″	17.00	Mug, beer, handled, 4½″	65.00
Champagne, hexagon footed, 4¾″	17.00	Mug, youth, handled, 3¼″	45.00
Cigarette Box, covered, 4¾″	40.00	Mustard, covered, with spoon	50.00
Claret, 4¾″	40.00	Nappy, 4¼″	15.00
Coaster, 3¾″	10.00	Nappy, 5¼″	15.00
Cocktail, 2⅞″	15.00	Nappy, 6½″	15.00
Compote, covered, 6⅛″	45.00	Nappy, 7″	27.00
Compote, covered, 9″	55.00	Nappy, 8″	30.00
Condiment Tray, cloverleaf	165.00	Nappy, 8¼″	40.00
Cookie Jar, covered, 8⅞″	250.00	Nappy, covered, 5″	35.00
Cordial, 3⅛″	30.00	Nappy, flared, 6¼″	27.00
Cream Soup and Saucer, 5″	60.00	Nappy, flared, 7″	40.00
Creamer, footed, 3¾″	15.00	Nappy, flared, 8¼″	45.00
Creamer, footed, mini, 2⅝″	12.00	Nappy, fruit, 3¾″	17.00
Creamer and Sugar Set, with tray,		Nappy, handled, 5″	15.00
three pieces	35.00	Old Fashioned, double, 3⅜″	25.00
Creamer and Sugar Set, with tray,		Olive Dish, rectangular, 6″	17.00
mini, three pieces	35.00	Oyster Cocktail, 3⅝″	15.00
Cruet, with stopper, 6½″	35.00	Party Server, 5¼″	45.00
Cup, footed, 2⅝″	12.00	Party Server, with two metal	
Cup and Saucer, footed, 2⅝″	17.00	spoons, 5¼″	50.00
Decanter, with stopper, 9¼″	100.00	Pickle, rectangular, 8″	17.00
Finger Bowl, with underplate, 4½″	75.00	Pickle Jar, with glass lid, 6⅛″	495.00
Hat, 2½″	25.00	Picture Frame	15.00
Hat, 3″	35.00	Pitcher, pint, 5⅜″	25.00
Hat, 4″	45.00	Plate, bread and butter, 6″	10.00
Hurricane Lamp, base only, 3″	360.00	Plate, dinner, 9½″	20.00
Ice Bucket, metal handle, 6½″	80.00	Plate, ice cream, brick, 5¾″	60.00
Iced Tea, flat, 5″	30.00	Plate, lemon, covered, 5½″	50.00
Iced Tea, flat, flared, 5¼″	35.00	Plate, salad, 7¾″	15.00
Iced Tea, footed, flared, 5¾″	25.00	Plate, salad, crescent, 7½″ × 4⅜″	50.00
Iced Tea, handled, 5¾″	200.00	Plate, sandwich, 9″	15.00
Jam, covered, 4¼″	50.00	Plate, sandwich, 10½″	27.00
Jam, covered, 6¾″	50.00	Plate, sandwich, 11½″	40.00
Jug, 7¼″	50.00	Plate, torte, 14″	50.00
Jug, 8″	75.00	Plate, torte, 18″	100.00
Jug, ice lip, 6½″	65.00	Plate, torte, 20″	125.00
Juice, flat, 4¾″	15.00	Plate, torte, 24″	300.00
Juice, footed, 3¼″	15.00	Plate, watercress, 8″	35.00
Marmalade, covered, with spoon and		Plate, youth, 6″	65.00
underplate, 3⅝″	75.00	Platter, oval, 10½″	45.00
Mayonnaise, 2¾″	15.00	Platter, oval, 12″	55.00
Mayonnaise, 4¾″	25.00	Preserve Bowl, covered, two handles,	
Mayonnaise, 5¾″	25.00	7¾″, no lid	50.00

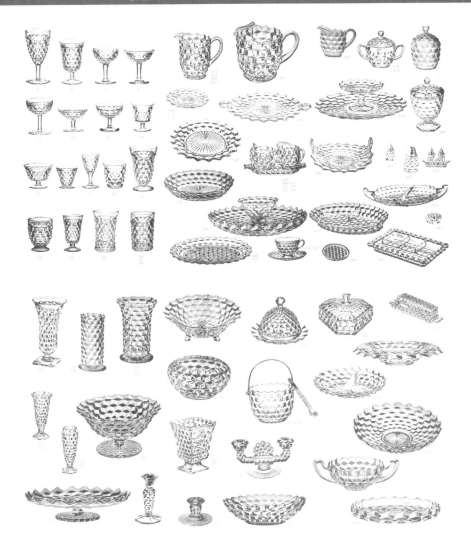

American by Fostoria, from a period company catalog.

Punch Bowl, footed, high, 14″	250.00
Punch Bowl, footed, low, 14″	225.00
Punch Bowl, footed, low, 18″	350.00
Punch Cup, flared	10.00
Punch Cup, straight	10.00
Relish, oval, two-part, 12″	20.00
Relish, three-part, 9½″	37.00
Relish, three-part, 10½″	37.00
Relish, oval, four-part, 6½ × 9″	65.00
Relish, square, four-part, 10⅞″	150.00
Rose Bowl, 3½″	25.00
Rose Bowl, 5″	35.00
Salt and Pepper Set, with tray, mini, plastic lids, 2″	32.00
Salt and Pepper Shakers, pair, chrome lids, 3½″	30.00
Salt Dip, individual, 2″	15.00
Sauce Boat and Underplate	75.00
Saucer	5.00
Sherbet, 3½″	15.00
Sherbet, flared, 3¼″	15.00
Sugar, covered, 6¼″	45.00
Sugar, covered, handled, 5¼″	27.00
Sugar, mini, 2½″	15.00
Sugar, open, 2⅜″	15.00
Sugar Shaker, 4⅝″	75.00
Sundae, 3⅛″	15.00
Tidbit, three-toed, round, 7¼″	25.00
Toothpick	25.00
Tray, center handle, 12″	45.00
Tray, oval, handled, 6″	50.00
Tray, oval, handled, 10½″ × 5″	65.00
Tray, rectangular, 5″ × 2½″	100.00
Tray, rectangular, 10½″ × 7½″	80.00
Tray, round, 12″	150.00
Tricorne, handled, 5″	15.00
Tricorne, three-toed, 11″	50.00
Trophy Bowl, footed, handled, 8″	125.00
Trophy Bowl, handled, 12½″	50.00
Tumbler, flat, 3⅝″	15.00
Tumbler, flat, 4″	17.00
Tumbler, flat, flared, 4⅛″	30.00
Tumbler, footed, 4⅜″	17.00
Vase, 7″	100.00
Vase, flared, 5⅜″	35.00
Vase, flared, 7⅜″	80.00

Vase, flared, 9¼″	100.00
Vase, flared, swung, 9½″	295.00
Vase, footed, 6½″	100.00
Vase, square, footed, 9¾″	50.00
Vase, straight, 8″	90.00
Vase, straight, 10″	50.00
Vase, swung, 10½″	230.00
Vase, urn, 6½″	35.00
Vase, urn, 7½″	45.00
Vegetable, oval, 9″	30.00
Vegetable, oval, divided, 10″	40.00
Water Goblet, hexagon footed, 6⅞″	25.00
Water Goblet, low, 5¼″	15.00
Wedding Bowl, covered, 8¼″, no lid	55.00
Whiskey, 2½″	25.00
Wine, hexagon footed, 4½″	20.00

Fostoria Glass Company, Argus, olive green, pressed (Blank 2770)

The Argus Blank 2770, a pressed glass line made by special arrangement with the Henry Ford Museum, was produced in crystal, olive green, cobalt, ruby, and gray. Olive green was produced from 1963 to 1982.

Bowl, fruit, 5″	$20.00
Champagne, 5⅛″	15.00
Compote, covered	50.00
Creamer, 5⅞″	25.00
Highball, flat, 5¼″	25.00
Iced Tea, footed, 6⅝″	25.00
Juice, flat, 2⅞″	20.00

Old Fashioned, 3⁷/₈″	25.00
Plate, 8¹/₈″	20.00
Sugar, covered, footed, 6¹/₄″	35.00
Water Goblet, 6¹/₂″	20.00
Wine, 5″	22.00

Fostoria Glass Company, Bridal Belle, crystal, cut, platinum band (Blank 6072, Decoration 639)

The Bridal Belle Decoration 639 on Celeste Blank 6072 in crystal with a platinum band and polished cutting was originally produced from 1957 to 1973. The champagne, iced tea, water goblet, and wine were reissued in 1980 as part of the Nostalgia line, a special promotion to reissue many popular discontinued patterns.

Fostoria Glass Company, Argus, ruby, pressed (Blank 2770)

The Argus Blank 2770, a pressed glass line made by special arrangement with the Henry Ford Museum, was produced in crystal, olive green, cobalt, ruby, and gray. Ruby was produced from 1964 to 1982.

Bowl, fruit, 5″	$25.00
Champagne, 5¹/₈″	27.00
Compote, covered	75.00
Creamer, 6″	35.00
Highball, 5¹/₄″	30.00
Iced Tea, footed, 6³/₄″	37.00
Juice, flat, 2⁷/₈″	32.00
Old Fashioned, 3⁷/₈″	30.00
Plate, 8″	25.00
Sugar, covered, 6¹/₈″	45.00
Water Goblet, 6¹/₂″	32.00
Wine, 4⁷/₈″	35.00

Champagne, 4⁷/₈″	$32.00
Cordial, 3¹/₈″	60.00
Iced Tea, footed, 6³/₈″	40.00
Juice, footed, 4⁷/₈″	32.00
Plate, 7¹/₂″	35.00
Water Goblet, 6³/₈″	35.00
Wine, 4⁷/₈″	50.00

Fostoria Glass Company, Buttercup, crystal, etched (Blank 6030, Etching 340)

The Buttercup Etching 340 on Astrid Blank 6030 in crystal was produced from 1942 to 1959. The champagne, iced tea, sherbet, both water goblets, and wine were reintroduced in 1980 as part of the Nostalgia line, a promotion to reissue popular discontinued patterns.

Ashtray, $2^5/_8''$	$25.00
Bowl, 6″	20.00
Bowl, flared, 12″	75.00
Bowl, fruit, 13″	75.00
Bowl, handled, 10″	60.00
Bowl, lily pond, 12″	65.00
Bowl, salad, 9″	60.00
Bowl, salad, $10^1/_2''$	65.00
Bowl, salad, 11″	65.00
Candlestick, 4″	20.00
Candlestick, $5^1/_2''$	30.00
Candlestick, 6″	30.00
Candlestick, double light, $5^1/_2''$	40.00
Candlestick, triple light, 8″	50.00
Candy Dish, covered, $3^3/_4''$	100.00
Celery, 11″	50.00
Champagne, $5^5/_8''$	30.00
Cocktail, $5^1/_4''$	25.00
Compote, 5″	40.00
Cordial, $3^7/_8''$	50.00
Creamer, footed, $3^3/_4''$	30.00
Cup and Saucer, footed, $2^1/_2''$	35.00
Iced Tea, footed, 6″	35.00

Juice, footed, $4^5/_8''$	25.00
Mayonnaise and Underplate, with ladle	75.00
Oyster Cocktail, $3^3/_4''$	25.00
Pickle, 8″	35.00
Plate, bread and butter, 6″	20.00
Plate, dinner, $9^1/_2''$	60.00
Plate, luncheon, $8^1/_2''$	30.00
Plate, salad, $7^5/_8''$	25.00
Plate, salad, crescent, $7^1/_2''$	45.00
Plate, sandwich, 11″	40.00
Plate, torte, 14″	75.00
Plate, torte, 16″	100.00
Relish, two-part, $6^1/_2'' \times 5''$	30.00
Relish, three-part, $10'' \times 7^1/_4''$	40.00
Saucer	12.00
Sherbet, $4^3/_8''$	25.00
Sugar, open, footed, $3^1/_8''$	30.00
Tray, center handle, $11^1/_4''$	50.00
Water Goblet, $7^7/_8''$	35.00
Water Goblet, low, $6^1/_4''$	30.00
Wine, 6″	35.00

Fostoria Glass Company, Carousel, crystal, cut (Blank 6080, Cutting 863)

The Carousel Cutting 863 on Fascination Blank 6080 in crystal was produced from 1958 to 1975.

Champagne, $4^3/_4''$	$30.00
Claret, 6 oz., $5^3/_4''$	40.00
Claret, 8 oz., $5^3/_4''$	40.00

Cocktail, $4^3/_8''$	30.00
Cordial, $3^1/_2''$	55.00
Iced Tea, footed, $5^1/_2''$	30.00
Juice, footed, $4^3/_8''$	30.00
Plate, $7^1/_2''$	30.00
Water Goblet, $6^3/_4''$	35.00
Wine, $5^1/_8''$	40.00

Fostoria Glass Company, Century, crystal, pressed (Blank 2630)

The Century Blank 2630 in crystal is a pressed glass line that was produced from 1950 to 1982.

Ashtray, $2^3/_4''$	$15.00
Bonbon, three-toed, $7^3/_8''$	32.00
Bowl, cereal, $6''$	20.00
Bowl, flared, $8''$	60.00
Bowl, flared, $12''$	50.00
Bowl, flared, footed, $10^3/_4''$	60.00
Bowl, fruit, $5''$	15.00
Bowl, handled, $4^1/_2''$	15.00
Bowl, lily pond, $8^3/_8''$	55.00
Bowl, lily pond, $11^1/_4''$	70.00
Bowl, oval, handled, $10''$	50.00
Bowl, salad, $8^1/_2''$	65.00
Bowl, salad, $10^1/_2''$	75.00
Bud Vase, footed, $6^1/_4''$	40.00
Butter Dish, covered, $^1/_4$ lb.	70.00
Cake Plate, handled, $9^1/_2''$	60.00
Candlestick, $4^1/_2''$	20.00
Candlestick, double light, $7''$	35.00

Candlestick, triple light, $7^3/_4''$	40.00
Candy Dish, covered, $7''$	50.00
Champagne, $4^3/_8''$	25.00
Cheese and Cracker Set	85.00
Cheese Stand, $2^3/_4''$	35.00
Cocktail, $4^1/_8''$	25.00
Compote, $4^3/_8''$	35.00
Creamer, footed, $4^1/_4''$	22.00
Creamer, footed, mini, $3^3/_8''$	22.00
Creamer and Sugar Set, with tray	50.00
Creamer and Sugar Set, with tray, mini	60.00
Cruet, $4^3/_4''$, no stopper	25.00
Cup, footed, $2^5/_8''$	20.00
Cup and Saucer, footed, $2^5/_8''$	25.00
Ice Bucket, metal handle, $4^7/_8''$	80.00
Iced Tea, footed, $5^7/_8''$	35.00
Jam, covered, footed, $6''$	60.00
Jam, footed, $3^7/_8''$	35.00
Juice, footed, $4^3/_4''$	25.00
Mayonnaise, $3''$	32.00
Muffin Tray, handled, $9^1/_2''$	60.00
Mustard, covered, with spoon, $4''$	50.00
Nappy, handled, $4^1/_2''$	15.00
Oyster Cocktail, $3^3/_4''$	25.00
Pickle, $8^1/_2''$	27.00
Pitcher, pint, $5^7/_8''$	65.00
Plate, bread and butter, $6^1/_8''$	15.00
Plate, dinner, $9''$	45.00
Plate, dinner, $10^1/_2''$	30.00
Plate, luncheon, $8^1/_2''$	25.00
Plate, salad, $7''$	20.00
Plate, torte, $14''$	50.00
Plate, torte, $16''$	60.00
Platter, oval, $12''$	65.00
Relish, two-part, $7^1/_2''$	35.00
Relish, three-part, $9^3/_8''$	40.00
Relish, three-part, $11^1/_8''$	40.00
Salt and Pepper Shakers, pair, chrome lids	40.00
Salt and Pepper Shakers, pair, no lids	35.00
Salt Shaker	20.00
Sandwich Tray, handled, $11^1/_4''$	50.00
Saucer	7.00
Snack Tray, $10^1/_2''$	40.00
Sugar, open, footed, $4''$	22.00

Sugar, open, footed, mini, 3¼″   25.00
Tidbit, two-tiered, metal handle, 10¼″   60.00
Tidbit, three-toed, 8¼″   45.00
Tray, center handle, 11½″   60.00
Tray, for creamer and sugar set,
   mini, 7¼″   20.00
Tray, handled, 9⅛″   55.00
Tricorne, three-toed, 7½″   32.00
Vegetable, oval, 9½″   55.00
Water Goblet, 6″   32.00
Wine, 4⅝″   35.00

Fostoria Glass Company, Chintz, crystal, etched, optic (Blank 6026, Etching 338)

Chintz Etching 338 on Greenbriar Blank 6026 in crystal with an optic bowl was produced from 1940 to 1973. The champagne, iced tea, sherbet, both water goblets, and wine were reintroduced in 1980 as part of the Nostalgia line, a promotion to reissue popular discontinued patterns.

Bonbon, 7″ $45.00
Bowl, flared, handled, 12″   125.00
Bowl, footed, handled, 5″   35.00
Bowl, fruit, 5″   35.00
Bowl, handled, 8½″   70.00
Bowl, handled, 10″   100.00

Bowl, handled, 10½″   100.00
Cake Plate, handled, 10″   75.00
Candlestick, 4″   30.00
Candlestick, 5½″   40.00
Candlestick, double light, 3½″   40.00
Candlestick, triple light, 6″   60.00
Candy Dish, covered, three-part   150.00
Celery, 11″   45.00
Champagne, 5½″   30.00
Claret, 5½″   50.00
Cocktail, 5″   25.00
Compote, 4⅝″   50.00
Compote, 5½″   50.00
Cordial, 3⅞″   45.00
Creamer, footed, 3⅞″   30.00
Cup and Saucer, 2½″   45.00
Finger Bowl, 4½″   60.00
Iced Tea, footed, 6″   35.00
Juice, footed, 4¾″   25.00
Mayonnaise and Underplate,
   with ladle   75.00
Mayonnaise Underplate   20.00
Nappy, 6″   35.00
Oyster Cocktail, 3⅝″   20.00
Pickle, 8″   40.00
Plate, bread and butter, 6″   20.00
Plate, dinner, 9½″   60.00
Plate, luncheon, 8½″   35.00
Plate, salad, 7½″   30.00
Plate, torte, 16″   125.00
Platter, 12″   100.00
Relish, two-part, square   40.00
Relish, three-part, 10″ × 7½″   50.00
Relish, five-part   50.00
Sauce Boat, 4⅜″   55.00
Sherbet, 5″   25.00
Sugar, mini, footed, 2⅞″   25.00
Sugar, open, footed, 3½″   30.00
Tidbit, three-toed, 8¼″   30.00
Tray, center handle, 11½″   60.00
Tricorne, 4⅝″   25.00
Tumbler, footed   30.00
Vegetable, 9½″   100.00
Water Goblet, 7⅝″   35.00
Water Goblet, low, 6⅛″   25.00
Wine, 5⅜″   50.00

Fostoria Glass Company, Christiana, crystal, cut (Blank 6030, Cutting 814)

Christiana Cutting 814 on Astrid Blank 6030 in crystal was produced from 1942 to 1969. The champagne, iced tea, sherbet, both water goblets, and the wine were reintroduced in 1980 as part of the Nostalgia line, a promotion to reissue popular discontinued patterns.

Champagne, 5⅝″	$35.00
Cocktail, 5¼″	30.00
Cordial, 3¾″	55.00
Finger Bowl, 4¼″	45.00
Iced Tea, footed, 6″	40.00
Juice, footed, 4½″	35.00
Oyster Cocktail, 3¾″	35.00
Plate, 7⅝″	30.00
Plate, luncheon, 8½″	30.00
Sherbet, 4⅜″	32.00
Water Goblet, 7⅞″	40.00
Water Goblet, low, 6⅜″	30.00
Wine, 5⅞″	50.00

Fostoria Glass Company, Classic Gold, crystal, gold band (Blank 6080, Decoration 641)

Classic Gold Decoration 641 on Fascination Blank 6080 in crystal with a gold band was produced from 1958 to 1982.

Champagne, 4¾″	$25.00
Claret, 6 oz., 5¾″	30.00
Claret, 8 oz., 5¾″	35.00
Cocktail, 4⅜″	25.00
Cordial, 3⅝″	40.00
Iced Tea, footed, 5⅝″	25.00
Juice, footed, 4⅜″	25.00
Plate, 7½″	25.00
Water Goblet, 6¾″	25.00
Wine, 5⅛″	40.00

THE TOP FIVE PATTERNS

COUNTRY

FOSTORIA, COLONY

FOSTORIA, WHEAT

GORHAM, GENTRY

WATERFORD, COLLEEN

WESTMORELAND, PANELED GRAPE

Fostoria Glass Company, Colony, crystal, pressed (Blank 2412)

The Colony Blank 2412 in crystal, a pressed glass line, was produced from the late 1920s to 1973.

Ashtray, 3″	$12.00
Ashtray, 3¹/₂″	15.00
Ashtray, 4¹/₂″	15.00
Ashtray, round, 3″	12.00
Ashtray, round, 4¹/₂″	15.00
Ashtray, round, 6″	20.00
Bonbon, 5″	15.00
Bonbon, 6¹/₄″	17.00
Bonbon, three-toed, 6³/₄″	17.00
Bowl, 4¹/₂″	12.00
Bowl, 5¹/₂″	15.00
Bowl, 9″	45.00
Bowl, flared, 8¹/₄″	50.00
Bowl, flared, 11″	50.00
Bowl, footed, 5³/₄″	20.00
Bowl, fruit, 10″	40.00
Bowl, fruit, low, 14″	65.00
Bowl, handled, 4³/₄″	15.00
Bowl, handled, 8¹/₂″	35.00
Bowl, handled, 10¹/₂″	35.00
Bowl, lily pond, 9″	30.00
Bowl, lily pond, 10″	40.00
Bowl, lily pond, 13″	45.00
Bowl, low, footed, 10¹/₂″	75.00
Bowl, oval, footed, 11″	50.00
Bowl, rolled edge, 9″	40.00
Bowl, salad, 9″	40.00

Bud Vase, 6¹/₄″	17.00
Butter Dish, covered, ¹/₄ lb.	60.00
Cake Plate, handled, 10″	25.00
Candlestick, 3³/₈″	15.00
Candlestick, 7″	25.00
Candlestick, 9″	30.00
Candlestick, double light 6¹/₄″	30.00
Candy Dish, covered, 6¹/₂″	50.00
Candy Dish, covered, footed	75.00
Celery, 9⁵/₈″	20.00
Celery, 11¹/₂″	30.00
Champagne, 3⁵/₈″	15.00
Cheese and Cracker Set	45.00
Cocktail, 3⁷/₈″	12.00
Compote, 4″	20.00
Compote, covered, 6¹/₄″	50.00
Cream Soup Bowl, 5″	40.00
Creamer, footed, 3⁷/₈″	12.00
Creamer, footed, mini, 3″	12.00
Creamer and Sugar Set, with tray, mini, three-piece	35.00
Cruet, with stopper, 5⁷/₈″	45.00
Cup, footed, 2¹/₂″	12.00
Cup and Saucer, footed, 2¹/₂″	17.00
Finger bowl, 4³/₄″	15.00
Iced Tea, footed, 5¹/₂″	22.00
Jam, covered, 6″	40.00
Juice, footed, 4⁵/₈″	15.00
Lid, butter dish, ¹/₄ lb.	22.00
Mayonnaise Bowl and Underplate	40.00
Mayonnaise Bowl and Underplate, with ladle	45.00
Muffin Tray, handled, 8³/₈″	40.00
Nappy, 4¹/₂″	12.00
Nappy, 5″	12.00
Nut Dish, 5³/₄″	25.00
Oyster Cocktail, 3³/₈″	12.00
Pickle, 8″	15.00
Pickle, 9¹/₂″	20.00
Pickle, rectangular, 8″	15.00
Pitcher, 5⁷/₈″	70.00
Pitcher, 7³/₄″	90.00
Pitcher, 8¹/₂″	150.00
Plate, bread and butter, 6¹/₈″	12.00
Plate, dinner, 9″	45.00
Plate, lemon, handled, 6¹/₂″	15.00

Plate, luncheon, 8¼″	15.00	Bonbon, 7½″	$32.00
Plate, salad, 7⅜″	15.00	Bowl, salad, 11″	45.00
Plate, torte, 13″	50.00	Butter Dish, covered, ¼ lb.	60.00
Plate, torte, 15″	75.00	Candlestick, 6″	25.00
Plate, torte, 18″	100.00	Champagne, 4½″	25.00
Platter, 12½″	50.00	Cocktail, 4½″	30.00
Relish, two-part, 9″	25.00	Cordial, 2⅞″	45.00
Relish, three-part, 13⅛″	30.00	Creamer, flat, 3½″	25.00
Rose Bowl, 6″	50.00	Creamer, flat, mini, 3¼″	20.00
Salt and Pepper Shakers, pair,		Cup and Saucer, flat, 2⅜″	30.00
gold lids	50.00	Iced Tea, footed, 6¼″	35.00
Sandwich Tray, handled, 11½″	35.00	Juice, footed, 4½″	25.00
Saucer	7.00	Mayonnaise and Underplate	40.00
Snack Tray, 10½″	20.00	Pitcher, 5½″	40.00
Sugar, footed, mini, 2¾″	12.00	Pitcher, 7⅛″	60.00
Sugar, open, footed, 3½″	12.00	Pitcher, 8¼″	80.00
Tidbit, footed, 7⅝″	35.00	Plate, 7¼″	22.00
Tidbit, three-toed	20.00	Plate, dinner, 10″	40.00
Tumbler, flat, 3⅝″	20.00	Plate, serving, 13⅝″	30.00
Tumbler, flat, 3⅞″	20.00	Plate, square, 8⅜″	22.00
Tumbler, flat, 4⅞″	25.00	Plate, torte, 13¾″	70.00
Vase, flared, 7½″	40.00	Saucer	10.00
Vase, flared, 7¾″	45.00	Sugar, open, flat, 2¾″	25.00
Vegetable, oval, 10½″	35.00	Tray, 7⅜″	20.00
Vegetable, oval, divided, 10½″	40.00	Water Goblet, 5⅞″	35.00
Water Goblet, 5¼″	22.00		
Wine, 4¼″	35.00		

Fostoria Glass Company, Contour, crystal, S-shaped stem (Blank 6060)

The Contour Blank 6060 in crystal was produced from 1955 to 1971.

Fostoria Glass Company, Corsage, crystal, etched, optic (Blank 6014, Etching 325)

Corsage Etching 325 on Blank 6014 in crystal with an optic bowl was produced from 1935 to 1959. The champagne, iced tea, water goblet, and wine were reintroduced in 1980 as part of the Nostalgia line, a promotion to reissue popular discontinued patterns.

Bonbon, three-toed, 7³/₈″	$25.00
Bowl, flared, 12″	75.00
Bowl, footed, 4″	35.00
Bowl, handled, 9″	75.00
Bowl, handled, 10″	75.00
Bud Vase, 8″	60.00
Cake Plate, handled, 10″	60.00
Cake Plate, handled, 10¹/₂″	60.00
Candlestick, 5¹/₂″	40.00
Candlestick, double light	45.00
Candlestick, triple light	50.00
Candy Dish, covered, three-part	100.00
Celery	40.00
Champagne, 5³/₈″	30.00
Claret, 5⁷/₈″	35.00
Cocktail, 5″	30.00
Compote, 4¹/₂″	45.00
Cordial, 3³/₄″	50.00
Creamer, footed, 4¹/₈″	30.00
Cup, flat, 2¹/₂″	30.00
Cup and Saucer, flat, 2¹/₂″	35.00
Finger Bowl, 4⁵/₈″	40.00
Iced Tea, footed, 6″	32.00
Juice, footed, 4³/₄″	25.00
Oyster Cocktail, 3³/₄″	25.00
Pickle	35.00
Plate, bread and butter, 6¹/₈″	25.00
Plate, dinner, 9¹/₂″	50.00
Plate, luncheon, 8″	35.00
Plate, salad, 7″	30.00
Plate, torte, 13″	75.00
Relish, two-part	50.00
Relish, three-part, 12¹/₄″	55.00
Relish, four-part	75.00
Relish, five-part	75.00
Sherbet, 4¹/₂″	22.00
Sugar, footed, mini, 2⁷/₈″	27.00
Sugar, open, footed, 3¹/₂″	30.00
Tidbit, three-toed	30.00
Tricorne, 4⁵/₈″	30.00
Tumbler, footed, 5¹/₂″	30.00
Water Goblet, 7³/₈″	32.00
Wine, 5¹/₄″	35.00

Fostoria Glass Company, Debutante, gray mist bowl (Blank 6100)

The Debutante Blank 6100 with a gray mist bowl was produced from 1962 to 1982.

Brandy, 2⁷/₈″	$25.00
Champagne, 4³/₈″	20.00
Claret, 5³/₈″	35.00
Finger Bowl	25.00
Iced Tea, footed, 6³/₄″	22.00
Plate, 7¹/₂″	22.00
Water Goblet, 6⁵/₈″	22.00
Wine, 5⁵/₈″	25.00

Fostoria Glass Company, Dolly Madison, crystal, cut (Blank 6023, Cutting 786)

Dolly Madison Cutting 786 on Colfax Blank 6023 in crystal with cut flutes on the bottom of the bowl was produced from 1939 to 1973. The champagne, iced tea, sherbet, water goblet, and wine were reintroduced in 1980 as part of the Nostalgia line, a promotion to reissue popular discontinued patterns.

Bonbon, 5$\frac{1}{2}$″	$50.00
Bonbon, 7″	50.00
Bowl, flared, 11$\frac{1}{2}$″	100.00
Bowl, flared, 12″	100.00
Bowl, footed, 9$\frac{1}{8}$″	120.00
Bowl, handled, 10$\frac{1}{2}$″	40.00
Cake Plate, handled, 12″	50.00
Candlestick, 4$\frac{1}{2}$″	40.00
Candlestick, double light	50.00
Celery, 10″	50.00
Champagne, 4$\frac{7}{8}$″	30.00
Cocktail, 4$\frac{3}{8}$″	30.00
Compote, 4$\frac{3}{4}$″	50.00
Cordial, 3$\frac{1}{2}$″	50.00
Creamer, footed, 4$\frac{1}{8}$″	32.00
Creamer, footed, mini, 3$\frac{1}{2}$″	30.00
Cruet	55.00
Cup, footed, 2$\frac{1}{2}$″	30.00
Cup and Saucer, footed, 2$\frac{1}{2}$″	35.00
Ice Bucket, 6$\frac{1}{4}$″	150.00
Iced Tea, footed, 5$\frac{3}{4}$″	40.00
Juice, footed, 4$\frac{1}{2}$″	30.00
Mayonnaise, with ladle	45.00
Mayonnaise and Underplate	45.00
Mayonnaise and Underplate, with ladle	60.00
Mayonnaise Ladle, 5″	20.00
Muffin Tray, 10″	40.00
Nappy, 6$\frac{1}{2}$″	50.00
Olive Dish, 6″	40.00
Oyster Cocktail, 3$\frac{5}{8}$″	32.00
Pickle, 3$\frac{5}{8}$″	32.00
Plate, 7$\frac{1}{2}$″	25.00
Plate, bread and butter, 6$\frac{1}{8}$″	22.00
Plate, dinner, 9$\frac{3}{8}$″	40.00
Plate, luncheon, 8$\frac{1}{2}$″	30.00
Plate, torte, 13$\frac{3}{4}$″	75.00
Plate, torte, 14″	75.00
Plate, two-handled, 8″	40.00
Relish, three-part, 11$\frac{3}{4}$″	50.00
Salt and Pepper Shakers, pair, 2$\frac{1}{2}$″	50.00

Salt Shaker, chrome	25.00
Salt Shaker, no lid	15.00
Sherbet, 4$\frac{3}{8}$″	32.00
Sugar, footed, mini, 3″	30.00
Sugar, open, footed, 3$\frac{7}{8}$″	32.00
Tumbler, footed	30.00
Water Goblet, 6$\frac{3}{8}$″	40.00
Wine, 4$\frac{3}{4}$″	45.00

Fostoria Glass Company, Engagement, crystal, platinum band (Blank 6092, Decoration 648)

Engagement Decoration 648 on Priscilla Blank 6092 in crystal with a platinum band was produced from 1960 to 1982.

Champagne, 5$\frac{1}{2}$″	$30.00
Cordial, 3$\frac{1}{2}$″	50.00
Finger Bowl	25.00
Iced Tea, footed, 6$\frac{3}{8}$″	35.00
Juice, footed, 4$\frac{3}{4}$″	25.00
Plate, 8″	25.00
Water Goblet, 7$\frac{1}{8}$″	35.00
Wine, 5$\frac{1}{4}$″	40.00

VERSAILLES BY CRISTAL D'ARQUES *(Durand International).*

TUILLERIES/VILLANDRY BY CRISTAL D'ARQUES *(Durand International).*

ANTIQUE BLUE BY LENOX CRYSTAL.
Photo courtesy of Lenox, Inc.

DESIRE BY LENOX CRYSTAL.
Photo courtesy of Lenox, Inc.

NAVARRE BLUE *(left)* AND CLEAR BY LENOX CRYSTAL.
Photo courtesy of Lenox, Inc.

WEATHERLY BY LENOX CRYSTAL.
Photo courtesy of Lenox, Inc.

ARCTIC LIGHTS
FLUTED CHAMPAGNE
STEMWARE XY701
PARK LANE
CHAMPAGNE COOLER
SN101

ARCTIC LIGHTS BY MIKASA.

PARK LANE
STEMWARE
SN101

PARK LANE BY MIKASA.

RICHMOND GOLD BY MILLER ROGASKA CRYSTAL.
Photo courtesy of Reed & Barton.

RHYTHM BY NORITAKE.
Photo courtesy of Noritake Company Limited.

Troy *(gold trim, left)* and Paris *(platinum trim)* by Noritake.
Photo courtesy of Noritake Company Limited.

Illusion, designed by Nils Landberg for Orrefors.
Photo courtesy of Orrefors.

PRELUDE, DESIGNED BY NILS LANDBERG FOR ORREFORS.
Photo courtesy of Orrefors.

WINGS BY SASAKI CRYSTAL.
Photo courtesy of Sasaki.

LISMORE BY WATERFORD CRYSTAL.
Photo courtesy of Waterford Crystal.

FROM LEFT TO RIGHT, WEDGWOOD CRYSTAL'S MONARCH, MAJESTY, SOVEREIGN, AND ROYAL GOLD *(not in listings)*.
Photo courtesy of BC Design Incorporated.

Fostoria Glass Company, Firelight, crystal, mother of pearl bowl, optic (Blank 6080¹/₂, Decoration 657)

Fostoria Glass Company, Georgian, crystal, cut (Blank 6097, Cutting 885)

Firelight Decoration 657 on Fascination Blank 6080¹/₂ in crystal with a loop optic mother of pearl iridescent bowl was produced from 1962 to 1981.

Georgian Cutting 885 on Sheraton Blank 6097 in crystal with hand-cut flutes on the bottom of the bowl was produced from 1961 to 1982.

Champagne, 4³/₄″	$40.00
Claret, 5³/₄″	45.00
Cocktail, 4³/₈″	40.00
Cordial, 3⁵/₈″	70.00
Iced Tea, footed, 5¹/₂″	40.00
Juice, footed, 4¹/₄″	30.00
Plate, 7″	30.00
Water Goblet, 6³/₄″	50.00
Wine, 5¹/₈″	55.00

Champagne, 5¹/₄″	$32.00
Claret, 6″	40.00
Cordial, 3¹/₂″	55.00
Iced Tea, footed, 6¹/₂″	40.00
Juice, footed, 4⁵/₈″	30.00
Old Fashioned, 3″	35.00
Old Fashioned, double, 3³/₄″	35.00
Water Goblet, 5⁷/₈″	40.00
Wine, 4¹/₂″	50.00

From a 1960s Fostoria pamphlet entitled "How to Select Your Table Crystal."

Fostoria Glass Company, Golden Lace, crystal, gold band (Blank 6085, Decoration 645)

Golden Lace Decoration 645 on Petite Blank 6085 in crystal with a gold band and crystal print was produced from 1959 to 1975.

Champagne, 5¼″	$40.00
Cordial, 3½″	65.00
Iced Tea, footed, 6⅛″	45.00
Juice, footed, 4½″	40.00
Water Goblet, 6⅝″	45.00
Wine, 5″	65.00

Fostoria Glass Company, Heather, crystal, etched, optic (Blank 6037, Etching 343)

Heather Etching 343 on Silver Flutes Blank 6037 in crystal with an optic bowl was produced from 1949 to 1971. The champagne, iced tea, sherbet, both wa-

ter goblets, and the wine were reintroduced in 1980 as part of the Nostalgia line, a promotion to reissue popular discontinued patterns.

Bonbon, footed, 7⅛″	$40.00
Bonbon, footed, 7⅜″	35.00
Bowl, flared, 10¾″	50.00
Bowl, fruit, 5⅛″	32.00
Candlestick, 4½″	40.00
Candy Dish, covered, 6¾″	80.00
Champagne, 6″	32.00
Cocktail, 5″	35.00
Compote, 4⅜″	50.00
Cordial, 4″	60.00
Creamer, footed, 4¼″	30.00
Cruet, 6⅛″	80.00
Iced Tea, footed, 6¼″	32.00
Jam, covered, 4″, no lid	50.00
Juice, footed, 4⅞″	30.00
Mayonnaise and Underplate	45.00
Oyster Cocktail, 4″	25.00
Parfait, 6⅛″	45.00
Pickle, 8⅝″	40.00
Plate, 8⅝″	40.00
Plate, bread and butter, 6⅛″	22.00
Plate, dinner, 9½″	55.00
Relish, two-part, 7⅜″	35.00
Relish, three-part, 11⅛″	45.00
Salt and Pepper Shakers, pair	65.00
Sherbet, 4⅞″	30.00
Snack Plate, 8½″	45.00
Sugar, open, footed, 4⅛″	30.00
Tidbit, three-toed, 8¼″	40.00
Water Goblet, 7⅞″	35.00
Water Goblet, low, 6½″	32.00
Wine, 6″	50.00

Fostoria Glass Company, Heritage, crystal, pressed (Blank 2887)

The Heritage Blank 2887 in crystal, a pressed glass line, was produced from 1979 to 1982.

Bowl, fruit, 5″	$15.00
Candy Dish, covered	30.00
Champagne, 5¹/₈″	15.00
Coaster	7.00
Compote, footed	25.00
Highball, 5¹/₄″	15.00
Iced Tea, footed, 7¹/₈″	17.00
Mayonnaise, with ladle	15.00
Old Fashioned, double, 4″	12.00
Plate, 8″	15.00
Tidbit, chrome handle, 8″	25.00
Tidbit, two-tiered	25.00
Water Goblet, 7¹/₄″	15.00
Wine, 6¹/₈″	17.00

Fostoria Glass Company, Holly, crystal, cut (Blank 6030, Cutting 815)

Holly cutting 815 on Astrid Blank 6030 in crystal was produced from 1942 to 1980. The champagne, iced tea, sherbet, both water goblets, and the wine were reintroduced in 1980 as part of the Nostalgia line, a promotion to reissue popular discontinued patterns.

Champagne, 5⁵/₈″	$35.00
Cocktail, 5¹/₄″	25.00
Cordial, 3⁷/₈″	45.00
Creamer, footed, 3³/₄″	30.00
Cup, footed, 2³/₈″	32.00
Cup and Saucer, footed, 2³/₈″	40.00
Iced Tea, footed, 6″	35.00
Juice, footed, 4⁵/₈″	25.00
Oyster Cocktail, 3³/₄″	32.00
Pickle, 8″	40.00
Plate, 6″	32.00
Plate, 8¹/₂″	32.00
Relish, two-part, 8¹/₂″	45.00
Relish, three-part, 12″	50.00
Salt and Pepper Shakers, pair, mini, no lids	25.00
Salt Shaker, 2⁵/₈″	30.00
Salt Shaker, mini	30.00
Salt Shaker, no lid	20.00
Sherbet, 4³/₈″	30.00
Sugar, mini, 2¹/₄″	30.00
Sugar, open, footed, 3¹/₄″	30.00
Tray, center handle, 11¹/₂″	60.00

Water Goblet, 7⅞″	35.00
Water Goblet, low, 6¼″	35.00
Wine, 6″	50.00

Fostoria Glass Company, Invitation, crystal, platinum band (Blank 6102, Decoration 660)

Invitation Decoration 660 on Silhouette Blank 6102 in crystal with a platinum band was produced from 1963 to 1982.

Bowl, footed, 10″	$30.00
Brandy	35.00
Champagne, 5⅛″	30.00
Champagne, fluted, 7⅝″	35.00
Claret	35.00
Cocktail, 5½″	25.00
Creamer, footed	20.00
Finger Bowl	25.00
Iced Tea, footed, 6⅝″	35.00
Plate, 7″	25.00
Plate, 8″	25.00
Relish, two-part	25.00
Relish, four-part	30.00
Relish, five-part	35.00
Sugar, footed	20.00
Water Goblet	35.00
Wine, 5⅞″	35.00

Fostoria Glass Company, Jamestown, pressed (Blank 2719)

Jamestown Blank 2719, a pressed glass line produced in amber, amethyst, blue, brown, crystal, green, pink, and ruby, was produced from 1958 to 1982. Amber and blue were produced during the entire production lifetime.

Amber

Bowl, fruit, 4½″	$22.00
Bowl, salad, 10″	40.00
Bowl, serving, handled, 10″	45.00
Butter Dish, covered, 8″	75.00
Cake Plate, handled, 9½″	35.00
Celery, 9″	30.00
Champagne, 4⅛″	15.00
Creamer, footed, 3⅞″	25.00
Iced Tea, footed, 6″	22.00
Jam, covered, 6⅛″	65.00
Juice, footed, 4¾″	17.00
Muffin Tray, handled, 9⅜″	50.00
Pickle, 7⅝″	30.00
Pitcher, 7″	85.00
Plate, 8¼″	20.00
Plate, torte, 14″	50.00
Relish, two-part, 9⅛″	35.00
Salt and Pepper Shakers, pair, chrome lids, 3½″	40.00
Salver, 7″ × 10″	85.00
Sauce Dish, covered, 4½″	35.00
Sherbet, 4¼″	15.00

Sugar, open, footed, 3½″	25.00	Water Goblet, 5⅞″	22.00
Tumbler, flat, 4¼″	22.00	Wine, 4⅜″	25.00
Tumbler, flat, 5⅛″	25.00		
Water Goblet, 5⅞″	20.00		
Wine, 4⅜″	22.00		

Blue

Crystal

Crystal was produced only until 1970.

Bowl, fruit, 4½″	$22.00	Bowl, fruit, 4½″	$22.00
Bowl, salad, 10″	60.00	Bowl, salad, 10″	50.00
Bowl, serving, handled, 10″	70.00	Bowl, serving, handled, 10″	60.00
Butter Dish, covered, 8″	100.00	Butter Dish, covered, 8″	75.00
Cake Plate, handled, 9½″	45.00	Cake Plate, handled, 9½″	35.00
Celery, 9″	35.00	Celery, 9″	30.00
Champagne, 4⅛″	22.00	Champagne, 4¼″	20.00
Creamer, footed, 4″	30.00	Creamer, footed, 4″	30.00
Iced Tea, 6⅛″	25.00	Iced Tea, 6″	25.00
Jam, covered, 6⅛″	65.00	Jam, covered, 6⅛″	65.00
Juice, 4¾″	22.00	Juice, 4¾″	20.00
Muffin Tray, handled, 9⅜″	75.00	Muffin Tray, handled, 9⅜″	50.00
Pickle, 7⅝″	30.00	Pickle, 7⅝″	30.00
Pitcher, 7″	125.00	Pitcher, 7″	100.00
Plate, 8″	25.00	Plate, 8¼″	22.00
Plate, torte, 14″	65.00	Plate, torte, 14″	55.00
Relish, two-part, 9⅛″	35.00	Relish, two-part, 9⅛″	35.00
Salt and Pepper Shakers, pair, chrome lids, 3½″	50.00	Salt and Pepper Shakers, pair, chrome lids, 3½″	45.00
Salver, 7″ × 10″	125.00	Salver, 7″ × 10″	100.00
Sauce Dish, covered, 4½″	50.00	Sherbet, 4¼″	20.00
Sherbet, 4¼″	22.00	Sugar, open, footed, 3½″	27.00
Sugar, open, footed, 3½″	30.00	Tumbler, flat, 4¼″	25.00
Tumbler, flat, 4¼″	22.00	Tumbler, flat, 5¼″	25.00
Tumbler, flat, 5⅛″	25.00	Water Goblet, 5⅞″	22.00
		Wine, 4¼″	22.00

Green		Pink	
Green was produced only until 1974.		*Pink was introduced in 1959.*	
Bowl, fruit, $4^{1}/_{2}''$	$22.00	Bowl, dessert, $4^{1}/_{2}''$	$40.00
Bowl, salad, 10″	50.00	Bowl, salad, 10″	60.00
Bowl, serving, handled, 10″	60.00	Bowl, serving, handled, 10″	70.00
Butter Dish, covered, 8″	75.00	Butter Dish, covered, 8″	100.00
Cake Plate, handled, $9^{1}/_{2}''$	35.00	Cake Plate, handled, $9^{1}/_{2}''$	50.00
Celery, 9″	30.00	Celery, 9″	45.00
Champagne, $4^{1}/_{4}''$	20.00	Champagne, $4^{1}/_{4}''$	25.00
Creamer, footed, 4″	30.00	Creamer, footed, 4″	30.00
Iced Tea, $6^{1}/_{8}''$	25.00	Iced Tea, footed, 6″	32.00
Jam, covered, $6^{1}/_{8}''$	65.00	Jam, covered, $6^{1}/_{8}''$	75.00
Juice, $4^{3}/_{4}''$	20.00	Juice, footed, $4^{3}/_{4}''$	25.00
Muffin Tray, handled, $9^{3}/_{8}''$	50.00	Muffin Tray, handled, $9^{3}/_{8}''$	75.00
Pickle, $7^{5}/_{8}''$	30.00	Pickle, $7^{5}/_{8}''$	40.00
Pitcher, 7″	100.00	Pitcher, 7″	150.00
Plate, $8^{1}/_{4}''$	20.00	Plate, 8″	25.00
Plate, torte, 14″	55.00	Plate, torte, 14″	65.00
Relish, two-part, $9^{1}/_{8}''$	35.00	Relish, two-part, $9^{1}/_{8}''$	50.00
Salt and Pepper Shakers, pair, chrome lids, $3^{1}/_{2}''$	45.00	Salt and Pepper Shakers, pair, chrome lids, $3^{1}/_{2}''$	50.00
Salver, 7″ × 10″	100.00	Salver, 7″ × 10″	125.00
Sherbet, $4^{1}/_{4}''$	20.00	Sauce Dish, covered, $4^{1}/_{2}''$	50.00
Sugar, open, footed, $3^{1}/_{2}''$	30.00	Sherbet, $4^{1}/_{4}''$	22.00
Tumbler, flat, $4^{1}/_{4}''$	22.00	Sugar, open, footed, $3^{1}/_{2}''$	25.00
Tumbler, flat, $5^{1}/_{8}''$	25.00	Tumbler, flat, $4^{1}/_{4}''$	25.00
Water Goblet, $5^{7}/_{8}''$	20.00	Tumbler, flat, $5^{1}/_{4}''$	25.00
Wine, $4^{3}/_{8}''$	25.00	Water Goblet, $5^{7}/_{8}''$	30.00
		Wine, $4^{3}/_{8}''$	30.00

Ruby

Ruby was introduced in 1964.

Bowl, dessert, 4½"	$40.00
Bowl, salad, 10"	60.00
Bowl, serving, handled, 10"	70.00
Butter Dish, covered, 8"	100.00
Cake Plate, handled, 9½"	50.00
Celery, 9"	45.00
Champagne, 4¼"	25.00
Creamer, footed, 4"	30.00
Iced Tea, footed, 6⅛"	32.00
Jam, covered, 6⅛"	75.00
Juice, footed, 4¾"	25.00
Muffin Tray, handled, 9⅜"	75.00
Pickle, 7⅝"	40.00
Pitcher, 7"	125.00
Plate, 8"	25.00
Plate, torte, 14"	65.00
Relish, two-part, 9⅛"	50.00
Salt and Pepper Shakers, pair, chrome lids, 3½"	50.00
Salver, 7" × 10"	125.00
Sauce Dish, covered, 4½"	50.00
Sherbet, 4¼"	22.00
Sugar, open, footed, 3½"	30.00
Tumbler, flat, 4¼"	27.00
Tumbler, flat, 5¼"	27.00
Water Goblet, 5⅞"	32.00
Wine, 4½"	32.00

Fostoria Glass Company, June, crystal, etched, optic (Blank 5098, Etching 279)

June Etching 279 on Blank 5098 in crystal with an optic bowl was produced from 1928 to 1951. The champagne, claret, iced tea, and water goblet were reintroduced in 1980 as part of the Nostalgia line, a promotion to reissue popular discontinued patterns.

Ashtray	$25.00
Bonbon	20.00
Bowl, cereal, 6½"	25.00
Bowl, salad, 10"	35.00
Cake Plate, handled, 10"	30.00
Candlestick, 2"	20.00
Candlestick, 3"	20.00
Celery, 11¾"	45.00
Champagne, 6"	30.00
Cheese and Cracker Set	50.00
Chop Plate, 13"	30.00
Claret, 6"	40.00
Cocktail, 5⅛"	30.00
Compote, 5"	30.00
Compote, 6"	30.00
Cordial, 3⅞"	35.00
Cream Soup Bowl, footed	25.00
Cream Soup Saucer	15.00
Creamer, footed	20.00
Cup, footed, 2½"	30.00
Cup and Saucer, footed, 2½"	35.00
Finger Bowl Underplate, 6¼"	15.00
Ice Bucket	75.00
Iced Tea, 6"	32.00

Juice, 4³/₈″	25.00
Mayonnaise and Underplate	35.00
Nappy, three-toed, 6″	15.00
Oyster Cocktail, 3³/₄″	25.00
Parfait, 5¹/₄″	35.00
Plate, bread and butter, 6″	15.00
Plate, dinner, 9¹/₂″	25.00
Plate, dinner, 10¹/₄″	35.00
Plate, grill, 10″	50.00
Plate, luncheon, 8³/₄″	22.00
Plate, salad, 7¹/₂″	20.00
Platter, 12″	40.00
Platter, 15″	50.00
Relish, three-part, 8¹/₂″	25.00
Saucer	10.00
Seafood Icer, with liner, 2⁵/₈″	50.00
Seafood Icer, 2³/₄″, no liner	45.00
Sherbet, 4¹/₄″	25.00
Sugar, covered, footed	50.00
Sugar, open, footed	20.00
Tumbler, footed, 5¹/₄″	25.00
Vegetable, oval, 9″	40.00
Vegetable, oval, 10″	45.00
Water Goblet, 8¹/₄″	32.00
Whiskey,	35.00
Wine, 5³/₈″	35.00

claret, iced tea, sherbet, water goblet, and wine were reintroduced in 1980 as part of the Nostalgia line, a promotion to reissue popular discontinued patterns.

Champagne, 5¹/₂″	$32.00
Claret, 6″	40.00
Cocktail, 5″	30.00
Cordial, 4″	45.00
Creamer, footed, 4¹/₄″	32.00
Iced Tea, footed, 6″	35.00
Juice, footed, 4³/₄″	30.00
Oyster Cocktail, 3⁵/₈″	30.00
Plate, 8¹/₂″	32.00
Sherbet, 4⁵/₈″	30.00
Sugar, open, footed, 3⁷/₈″	32.00
Tumbler, footed, 5⁵/₈″	32.00
Tumbler, footed, 6⁵/₈″	32.00
Water Goblet, 7¹/₂″	35.00
Wine, 5¹/₂″	40.00

Fostoria Glass Company, Mademoiselle, crystal (Blank 6033)

Mademoiselle Blank 6033 in crystal was produced from 1949 to 1971.

Fostoria Glass Company, Laurel, crystal, cut (Blank 6017, Cutting 776)

Laurel Cutting 776 on Sceptre Blank 6017 in crystal was produced from 1938 to 1959. The champagne,

Champagne, 4³/₄″	$22.00
Coaster, with spoon rest, 4³/₄″	15.00
Cocktail, 4¹/₄″	17.00
Cordial, 3³/₄″	32.00
Finger Bowl	17.00

Highball, 4⅞″	17.00	Bowl, handled, 8½″		60.00
Iced Tea, footed, 5⅞″	25.00	Bowl, handled, 10½″		75.00
Juice, footed, 4⅝″	17.00	Bowl, oval, 10″		75.00
Old Fashioned, 3⅛″	17.00	Bowl, square, 6″		30.00
Oyster Cocktail, 3⅞″	17.00	Bowl, square, handled, 4″		20.00
Parfait, 5⅝″	22.00	Cake Plate, handled, 10″		65.00
Plate, 8½″	22.00	Candlestick, 4″		30.00
Plate, dinner, 9½″	30.00	Candlestick, 5½″		35.00
Plate, salad, crescent, 7⅜″	27.00	Candlestick, double light, 4½″		40.00
Relish, 8½″	30.00	Candlestick, triple light, 6″		60.00
Scotch, 4⅝″	17.00	Candy Dish, covered, three-part		150.00
Seafood Icer, with liner, 2¾″	30.00	Celery, 11″		50.00
Seafood Icer, with liner, 4½″	30.00	Champagne, 5⅝″		30.00
Sherbet, 4″	17.00	Claret, 6¼″		35.00
Water Goblet, 6¼″	25.00	Cocktail, 5¼″		27.00
Whiskey, 3¼″	17.00	Compote, 4¾″		45.00
Whiskey Sour, 3⅝″	17.00	Cordial, 3⅞″		65.00
Wine, 4¾″	27.00	Creamer, footed, 4″		32.00
		Cup, footed, 2½″		30.00
		Cup and Saucer, footed, 2½″		45.00
		Finger Bowl, 4½″		50.00
		Ice Bucket, 4⅜″		150.00
		Iced Tea, footed, 5⅞″		35.00
		Jam, covered, 7½″		90.00
		Juice, footed, 4¾″		27.00
		Mayonnaise, three-piece		90.00
		Oyster Cocktail, 3⅝″		32.00
		Pickle, 8″		40.00
		Plate, bread and butter, 6″		20.00
		Plate, dinner, 9½″		60.00
		Plate, luncheon, 8½″		30.00
		Plate, salad, 7½″		25.00

Fostoria Glass Company, Meadow Rose, crystal, etched, optic (Blank 6016, Etching 328)

Meadow Rose Etching 328 on Wilma Blank 6016 in crystal with an optic bowl was produced from 1936 to 1975. The champagne, claret, iced tea, sherbet, and water goblet were reintroduced in 1980 as part of the Nostalgia line, a promotion to reissue popular discontinued patterns.

Bonbon, 7″	$50.00	Plate, torte, 14″		75.00
Bowl, flared, 12″	80.00	Plate, torte, 16″		100.00
Bowl, flared, handled, 5″	30.00	Relish, two-part, 7¾″		50.00
Bowl, footed, handled, 12″	80.00	Sherbet, 4⅜″		27.00
		Sugar, footed, mini, 2⅞″		30.00
		Sugar, open, footed, 3⅝″		32.00
		Tidbit, three-toed, 8¼″		40.00
		Tray, center handle, 11″		50.00
		Tricorne, 4⅝″		25.00
		Tumbler, footed, 5⅜″		32.00
		Vase, 5″		100.00
		Vase, footed, 10″		150.00
		Water Goblet, 7⅝″		35.00
		Wine, 5½″		40.00

Fostoria Glass Company, Navarre, etched, optic (Blank 6016, Etching 327)

Navarre Etching 327 on Wilma Blank 6016 with an optic bowl was produced in blue, crystal, and pink. It was Fostoria's most popular pattern in 1982.

Blue

Fostoria's blue Navarre was produced from 1937 to 1982.

Bell	$120.00
Champagne, 5½″	50.00
Champagne, continental, 8⅛″	75.00
Claret, 4½ oz., 6″	75.00
Claret, 6½ oz., 6¼″	75.00
Iced Tea, footed, 5⅞″	55.00
Water Goblet, 7⅝″	55.00
Wine Magnum, 7¼″	150.00

Crystal

Fostoria's crystal Navarre was produced from 1936 to 1982.

Bell	$50.00
Bonbon, footed, 7⅜″	35.00
Bowl, flared, 12″	70.00
Bowl, footed, 10½″	65.00
Bowl, footed, handled, 5″	25.00
Bowl, footed, handled, 10½″	75.00
Bowl, handled, 4⅜″	20.00
Bowl, oval, 10″	70.00
Bowl, square, 6″	25.00
Bowl, square, handled, 4″	20.00
Brandy, 5½″	50.00
Cake Plate, handled, 10″	75.00
Cake Plate, oval, 10½″	75.00
Candlestick, 4″	35.00
Candlestick, 5½″	35.00
Candlestick, double light, 4½″	45.00
Candlestick, double light, 5″	45.00
Candlestick, triple light, 6″	60.00
Candlestick, triple light, 6¾″	60.00
Candy Dish, covered, three-part	125.00
Celery, 9″	40.00
Celery, 11″	50.00
Champagne, 5⅝″	30.00
Champagne, continental, 8⅛″	60.00
Claret, 4½ oz., 6″	45.00
Claret, 6½ oz., 6¼″	50.00
Cocktail, 5⅛″	30.00
Compote, 3¼″	32.00

Compote, 4½″	40.00	Relish, five-part, 13¼″	100.00
Compote, 4¾″	40.00	Salt and Pepper Shakers, pair,	
Cordial, 3⅞″	75.00	flat, 3¼″	75.00
Cracker Plate, 11″	50.00	Salt and Pepper Shakers, pair,	
Creamer, footed, 3¾″	30.00	footed, 3½″	125.00
Creamer, mini	22.00	Saucer	10.00
Cup, flat, 2½″	30.00	Sherbet, 4⅜″	30.00
Cup and Saucer, flat, 2½″	40.00	Sherry, 6⅛″	60.00
Finger Bowl, 4½″	50.00	Sugar, mini	25.00
Highball, 4⅞″	45.00	Sugar, open, footed, 3½″	30.00
Ice Bucket, 4⅜″	125.00	Tidbit, three-toed, 8¼″	35.00
Ice Bucket, 6″	150.00	Tricorne, three-toed, 4⅝″	32.00
Iced Tea, footed, 5⅞″	50.00	Tumbler, footed, 5⅜″	32.00
Juice, footed, 4⅝″	32.00	Vase, 5″	100.00
Mayonnaise, three-piece	75.00	Water Goblet, 7⅝″	50.00
Nappy, handled, 5″	32.00	Wine, 5½″	55.00
Nut Dish, three-toed, 6¼″	30.00	Wine Magnum, 7¼″	75.00
Old Fashioned, double, 3⅝″	45.00		
Oyster Cocktail, 3¾″	32.00		
Pickle, 8″	35.00		
Pickle, 8½″	35.00		

Pink

Fostoria's pink Navarre was produced from 1937 to 1978.

Plate, bread and butter, 6¼″	25.00		
Plate, dinner, 9½″	50.00		
Plate, luncheon, 8⅝″	32.00		
Plate, salad, 7½″	27.00	Bell	$100.00
Plate, torte, 14″	75.00	Champagne, 5⅝″	35.00
Plate, torte, 16″	100.00	Champagne, continental, 8⅛″	55.00
Relish, two-part, square, 6″	45.00	Claret, 4½ oz., 6″	55.00
Relish, two-part, square, 7½″	55.00	Claret, 6½ oz., 6⅛″	55.00
Relish, three-part, 10″ × 7½″	60.00	Iced Tea, footed, 5⅞″	35.00
Relish, three-part, 12″	60.00	Water Goblet, 7⅝″	40.00
Relish, four-part, 10″	65.00	Wine Magnum, 7¼″	75.00

Fostoria Glass Company, Nosegay, crystal, cut (Blank 6051¹/₂, Cutting 834)

Fostoria Glass Company, Pine, crystal, cut (Blank 6052¹/₂, Cutting 835)

Nosegay Cutting 834 on Courtship Blank 6051¹/₂ in crystal was produced from 1953 to 1972. The champagne, iced tea, water goblet, and wine were reintroduced in 1980 as part of the Nostalgia line, a promotion to reissue popular discontinued patterns.

Champagne, 4¹/₂″	$32.00
Cocktail, 3⁷/₈″	32.00
Cordial, 3¹/₈″	50.00
Creamer, flat, 3¹/₂″	40.00
Iced Tea, footed, 6¹/₈″	35.00
Juice, footed, 4⁵/₈″	32.00
Oyster Cocktail, 3³/₄″	35.00
Plate, 8¹/₂″	35.00
Snack Plate, Contour blank, 10″	60.00
Sugar, open, flat, 3″	40.00
Water Goblet, 6¹/₄″	40.00
Wine, 4¹/₂″	40.00

Pine Cutting 835 on Continental Blank 6052¹/₂ in crystal was produced from 1953 to 1972.

Butter Dish, covered, ¹/₄ lb.	$80.00
Candlestick, 2¹/₄″	27.00
Champagne, 4³/₈″	25.00
Cocktail, 4″	25.00
Cordial, 3¹/₄″	40.00
Creamer, flat, 3¹/₂″	30.00
Creamer, flat, mini, 3″	25.00
Cup, flat, 2³/₈″	27.00
Cup and Saucer, flat, 2³/₈″	32.00
Iced Tea, footed, 6¹/₈″	27.00
Juice, footed, 4⁷/₈″	25.00
Mayonnaise and Underplate	50.00
Oyster Cocktail, 3⁷/₈″	22.00
Plate, 7¹/₄″	25.00
Plate, 7¹/₂″	25.00
Plate, 7⁵/₈″	25.00
Plate, 8¹/₂″	25.00
Plate, dinner, 10″	50.00
Relish, two-part, 7⁵/₈″	40.00
Relish, three-part, 10³/₄″	40.00
Salt and Pepper Shakers, pair, chrome lids	50.00
Salt Shaker, no lid	15.00
Sugar, footed, mini, 2¹/₂″	25.00
Sugar, open, 2⁷/₈″	30.00
Water Goblet, 5⁷/₈″	25.00
Wine, 4¹/₂″	40.00

Fostoria Glass Company, Renaissance Gold, crystal, gold bands (Blank 6111, Decoration 678)

Renaissance Gold Decoration 678 on Illusion Blank 6111 in crystal with gold bands and crystal print was produced from 1968 to 1982.

Champagne, 5¹/₈″	$50.00
Claret, 6″	55.00
Cordial, 3⁷/₈″	90.00
Iced Tea, footed, 6⁵/₈″	60.00
Water Goblet, 7¹/₈″	60.00
Wine, 6¹/₈″	55.00

Fostoria Glass Company, Richmond, crystal, gold band (Blank 6097, Decoration 654)

Richmond Decoration 654 on Sheraton Blank 6097 in crystal with a gold band was produced from 1961 to 1982.

Bell, 5¹/₂″	$40.00
Bowl, footed, 10″	30.00
Champagne, 5¹/₈″	27.00
Claret, 6″	30.00
Cordial, 3¹/₂″	50.00
Creamer, footed	30.00
Cup and Saucer, footed, 2³/₈″	37.00
Iced Tea, footed, 6³/₈″	32.00
Juice, footed, 4³/₄″	25.00
Plate, 7¹/₂″	27.00
Water Goblet, 6³/₄″	32.00
Wine, 5″	40.00
Wine Magnum, 6³/₄″	50.00

Fostoria Glass Company, Romance, crystal, etched (Blank 6017, Etching 341)

Romance Etching 341 on Sceptre Blank 6017 in crystal was produced from 1942 to 1971. The champagne, claret, iced tea, sherbet, water goblet, and wine were reintroduced in 1980 as part of the Nostalgia line, a promotion to reissue popular discontinued patterns.

Ashtray, 2⁵/₈″	$20.00
Bowl, 6″	25.00
Bowl, footed, 12″	80.00
Bowl, fruit, 13″	90.00
Bowl, handled, 10″	75.00
Bowl, lily pond, 11″	70.00
Bowl, oval, handled, 13¹/₂″	100.00
Bowl, salad, 9″	60.00

Bowl, salad, 10½"	75.00	Vase, footed, 10"	125.00
Bowl, soup, 8"	50.00	Water Goblet, 7³/₈"	32.00
Bud Vase, footed, 6"	60.00	Wine, 5½"	40.00
Candlestick, 4"	30.00		
Candlestick, 5"	40.00		
Candlestick, 5½"	40.00		
Candlestick, double light, 5½"	50.00		
Candlestick, triple light, 8"	60.00		
Candy Dish, covered, round	125.00		
Celery, 11"	50.00		
Champagne, 5½"	25.00		
Claret, 5⁷/₈"	40.00		
Cocktail, 5"	30.00		
Compote, 3¼"	40.00		
Compote, 5"	40.00		
Compote, 7½"	70.00		
Cordial, 3⁷/₈"	50.00		

Fostoria Glass Company, Rose, crystal, cut (Blank 6036, Cutting 827)

Rose Cutting 827 on Rutledge Blank 6036 in crystal was produced from 1951 to 1973. The champagne, iced tea, sherbet, water goblet, and wine were reintroduced in 1980 as part of the Nostalgia line, a promotion to reissue popular discontinued patterns.

Cracker Plate, 11¼"	50.00		
Creamer, footed, 3³/₄"	30.00		
Cup, footed, 2½"	32.00		
Cup and Saucer, footed, 2½"	40.00		
Iced Tea, footed, 6"	32.00		
Juice, footed, 4³/₄"	30.00		
Mayonnaise, with ladle, 5"	50.00	Champagne, 4⁷/₈"	$37.00
Oyster Cocktail, 3½"	30.00	Cocktail, 4¹/₈"	30.00
Pickle, 8"	35.00	Cordial, 3³/₈"	50.00
Plate, bread and butter, 6¹/₈"	20.00	Creamer, 3½"	40.00
Plate, dinner, 9"	75.00	Creamer, flat, mini, 3¼"	35.00
Plate, luncheon, 8"	35.00	Cup and Saucer, 2½"	50.00
Plate, salad, 7"	25.00	Iced Tea, footed, 6¹/₈"	40.00
Plate, salad, crescent	50.00	Juice, footed, 4⁵/₈"	35.00
Plate, sandwich, 11"	60.00	Oyster Cocktail, 3⁵/₈"	37.00
Plate, torte, 13⁷/₈"	70.00	Parfait, 5⁷/₈"	45.00
Plate, torte, 16"	100.00	Plate, 7½"	35.00
Relish, three-part, 10"	40.00	Plate, 8½"	35.00
Relish, three-part, 12¼"	50.00	Relish, two-part, 7⁵/₈"	60.00
Salt and Pepper Shakers, pair, 2⁵/₈"	75.00	Relish, three-part, 10³/₄"	70.00
Salt Shaker, no lid	20.00	Salt and Pepper Shakers, no lids	50.00
Sherbet, 4⁵/₈"	32.00	Sherbet, 4¹/₈"	35.00
Sugar, open, footed, 3¼"	30.00	Sugar, flat, mini, 2½"	35.00
Tray, center handle, 11½"	60.00	Sugar, open, 2³/₄"	40.00
Tumbler, footed, 5½"	27.00	Water Goblet, 6³/₄"	37.00
Vase, 5"	60.00	Wine, 4⁷/₈"	55.00
Vase, 10"	100.00		
Vase, footed, 6"	75.00		
Vase, footed, 7½"	75.00		

Fostoria Glass Company, Sheffield, crystal, platinum band (Blank 6097, Decoration 653)

Fostoria Glass Company, Shell Pearl, crystal, mother of pearl bowl, loop optic (Blank 6055, Decoration 633)

Sheffield Decoration 653 on Sheraton Blank 6097 in crystal with a platinum band was produced from 1961 to 1982.

Champagne, 5¼″	$35.00
Claret, 6″	45.00
Cordial, 3⅝″	55.00
Creamer, flat, 3⅝″	40.00
Creamer, flat, mini, 3″	35.00
Cup, flat, 2½″	35.00
Cup and Saucer, flat, 2½″	45.00
Iced Tea, footed, 6½″	40.00
Juice, footed, 4¾″	35.00
Plate, 7½″	35.00
Plate, 8½″	35.00
Sugar, flat, mini, 2½″	35.00
Sugar, open, flat, 2⅞″	40.00
Water Goblet, 6¾″	37.00
Wine, 5″	40.00
Wine Magnum, 6¾″	55.00

Shell Pearl Decoration 633 on Marilyn Blank 6055 in crystal with a loop optic mother of pearl iridescent bowl was produced from 1954 to 1974.

Bowl, oval	$25.00
Champagne, 4½″	32.00
Cocktail, 4″	30.00
Cordial, 3⅜″	55.00
Creamer	20.00
Creamer, mini	15.00
Iced Tea, footed, 6¼″	40.00
Juice, footed, 4⅞″	35.00
Mayonnaise and Underplate, with ladle	50.00
Oyster Cocktail, 4⅛″	32.00
Plate, optic, 7″	15.00
Plate, serving, 14″	35.00
Relish, two-part	25.00
Relish, three-part	30.00
Salt and Pepper Shakers, pair, chrome lids	40.00
Snack Plate, 10″	30.00
Sugar	20.00
Sugar, mini	15.00
Water Goblet, 6⅛″	40.00
Wine, 4⅝″	50.00

Fostoria Glass Company, Shirley, crystal, etched (Blank 6017, Etching 331)

Fostoria Glass Company, Silver Flutes, crystal, optic (Blank 6037)

Shirley Etching 331 on Sceptre Blank 6017 in crystal was produced from 1938 to 1956.

Silver Flutes Blank 6037 in crystal with an optic bowl was produced from 1949 to 1971.

Bonbon, three-toed, 7″	$45.00
Bowl, flared, 12″	80.00
Candlestick, double light	45.00
Champagne, 5½″	30.00
Claret, 5⅞″	45.00
Cocktail, 5″	30.00
Cordial, 3⅞″	45.00
Creamer, footed, 3¾″	32.00
Creamer, footed, mini, 3⅛″	32.00
Cup and Saucer, footed, 2½″	30.00
Iced Tea, 6″	32.00
Juice, 4¾″	30.00
Nut Dish, three-toed, 6″	45.00
Oyster Cocktail, 3⅝″	30.00
Pickle, 8″	30.00
Plate, 6⅛″	20.00
Plate, 7½″	30.00
Salt Shaker, no lid	20.00
Saucer	10.00
Sherbet, 4½″	30.00
Sugar, open, footed, 3½″	32.00
Tumbler, footed, 5½″	30.00
Water Goblet, 7½″	32.00
Wine, 5½″	50.00

Champagne, 6″	$25.00
Cocktail, 5⅛″	25.00
Cordial, 4″	35.00
Iced tea, footed, 6⅛″	25.00
Juice, footed, 4⅞″	22.00
Oyster Cocktail, 4″	25.00
Parfait, 6⅛″	27.00
Sherbet, 4⅞″	25.00
Water Goblet, 7⅞″	25.00
Water Goblet, low, 6½″	25.00
Wine, 6″	35.00

Fostoria Glass Company, Sweetheart Rose, crystal, cut (Blank 6092, Cutting 877)

Sweetheart Rose Cutting 877 on Priscilla Blank 6092 in crystal was produced from 1960 to 1974.

Champagne, 5$^1/_2$"	$32.00
Cordial, 3$^5/_8$"	55.00
Iced Tea, footed, 6$^3/_8$"	40.00
Juice, footed, 4$^7/_8$"	35.00
Plate, 7$^1/_2$"	32.00
Water Goblet, 7"	40.00
Wine, 5$^1/_4$"	45.00

Fostoria Glass Company, Trousseau, crystal, platinum band (Blank 6080, Decoration 642)

Trousseau Decoration 642 on Fascination Blank 6080 in crystal with a platinum band was produced from 1958 to 1982.

Bowl, footed, 10"	$40.00
Champagne, 4$^3/_4$"	25.00
Claret, 6 oz., 5$^3/_4$"	30.00
Claret, 8 oz., 5$^3/_4$"	35.00
Cocktail, 4$^3/_8$"	25.00
Cordial, 3$^5/_8$"	40.00
Creamer, footed	20.00
Finger Bowl	15.00
Iced Tea, footed, 5$^1/_2$"	32.00
Juice, footed, 4$^3/_8$"	25.00
Plate, 7"	20.00
Plate, 8"	25.00
Relish, two-part	25.00
Relish, four-part	35.00
Relish, five-part	45.00
Sugar, footed	20.00
Water, Goblet, 6$^3/_4$"	27.00
Wine, 5$^1/_8$"	30.00

Fostoria Glass Company, Wedding Ring, crystal, platinum band (Blank 6051$^1/_2$, Decoration 626)

Wedding Ring Decoration 626 on Courtship Blank 6051$^1/_2$ in crystal with a platinum band was produced from 1953 to 1975. The champagne, iced tea, water goblet, and wine were reintroduced in 1980 as part of the Nostalgia line, a promotion to reissue popular discontinued patterns.

Bowl, footed, 10"	$40.00
Bowl, salad, 9"	40.00
Candlestick, 4"	25.00

Champagne, 4³/₈″	25.00	Candlestick, 2³/₈″	$40.00
Cocktail, 3⁷/₈″	25.00	Champagne, 4¹/₂″	37.00
Cordial, 3¹/₈″	40.00	Cocktail, 3⁷/₈″	32.00
Creamer, footed, 3¹/₂″	25.00	Cordial, 3¹/₈″	55.00
Creamer, mini	20.00	Creamer, 3¹/₂″	40.00
Cup	15.00	Creamer, flat, 3⁵/₈″	40.00
Iced Tea, footed, 6¹/₈″	27.00	Cup, 2¹/₂″	40.00
Juice, footed, 4⁵/₈″	25.00	Cup and Saucer, 2¹/₂″	45.00
Mayonnaise and Underplate,		Iced Tea, footed, 6¹/₈″	37.00
with ladle	60.00	Juice, footed, 4⁵/₈″	30.00
Oyster Cocktail, 3³/₄″	25.00	Mayonnaise and Underplate,	
Relish, two-part	25.00	with ladle	80.00
Relish, four-part	30.00	Oyster Cocktail, 3³/₄″	40.00
Relish, five-part	35.00	Plate, 7¹/₂″	32.00
Saucer	10.00	Plate, 8¹/₂″	32.00
Sugar, 2⁵/₈″	25.00	Salt and Pepper Shakers, pair,	
Sugar, mini	20.00	chrome lids	70.00
Tray, for creamer and sugar, mini	25.00	Snack Plate, Contour blank, 9⁵/₈″	30.00
Water Goblet, 6¹/₄″	30.00	Sugar, open, 2³/₈″	40.00
Wine, 4¹/₂″	40.00	Sugar, open, flat, 2³/₄″	40.00
		Water Goblet, 6¹/₄″	40.00
		Wine, 4¹/₂″	45.00

**Fostoria Glass Company, Wheat, crystal, cut
(Blank 6051¹/₂, Cutting 837)**

Wheat Cutting 837 on Courtship Blank 6051¹/₂ in crystal was produced from 1953 to 1973. The champagne, iced tea, water goblet, and wine were reintroduced in 1980 as part of the Nostalgia line, a promotion to reissue popular discontinued patterns.

**Fostoria Glass Company, Willowmere, crystal,
etched, optic (Blank 6024, Etching 333)**

Willowmere Etching 333 on Cellini Blank 6024 in crystal with an optic bowl was produced from 1938 to 1970. The champagne, claret, iced tea, sherbet, water goblet, and wine were reintroduced in 1980 as part of the Nostalgia line, a promotion to reissue popular discontinued patterns.

Champagne, 5⅝″	$30.00
Claret, 5¾″	45.00
Cocktail, 4¾″	30.00
Compote, 4¾″	55.00
Cordial, 3¾″	70.00
Creamer, 3¾″	30.00
Creamer, footed, 4″	30.00
Creamer, footed, mini, 3¼″	25.00
Creamer and Sugar Set, with tray, mini, three pieces	80.00
Cup and Saucer, 2½″	40.00
Iced Tea, footed, 5¾″	37.00
Juice, footed, 4⅝″	30.00
Oyster Cocktail, 3½″	30.00
Plate, 7½″	30.00
Plate, bread and butter, 6⅛″	25.00
Plate, torte, 14″	75.00
Saucer	12.00
Sherbet, 4⅜″	30.00
Sugar, open, footed, 3½″	30.00
Tray, center handle, 11¼″	80.00
Tumbler, footed, 5¼″	32.00
Vegetable, round, 11″	70.00
Water Goblet, 7⅛″	35.00
Whipped Cream, 7⅛″	50.00
Wine, 5⅜″	45.00

Jabez Gorham established the Gorham Company in Providence, Rhode Island, in 1831 for the purpose of manufacturing sterling flatware and hollowware. John Gorham, Jabez's son, developed many of the techniques and processes that enabled Gorham to become one of the world's leading silversmiths. Between 1865 and 1915, Gorham Crystal was the recipient of the Grand Prize Medal, the Gold Medal, and many other international awards at World's Fairs and other exhibitions for its hand-hammered silver tables and highly ornate and imaginative hollowware pieces in sterling and gold.

Gorham has enjoyed a high visibility in Washington, D.C.—Gorham pieces were purchased by the Lincoln, Grant, and Bush administrations. Sports fans immediately recognize its custom-designed sports trophies, including the Borg-Warner Trophy for the Indianapolis 500, the Davis Cup for tennis, and the America's Cup for yachting.

In 1967, Gorham became a division of Textron, Inc., of Providence, Rhode Island. The company expanded its line to include a full range of tabletop products.

In 1970, Gorham acquired the Flintridge China Company of Pasadena, a china manufacturer. Gorham doubled its china manufacturing capabilities over the next eight years, however china production ceased on December 31, 1984.

Gorham made the same commitment to its crystal stemware as it did to its silver pieces, allowing no substitute for fine design and quality craftsmanship. Today, Gorham is a division of Lenox Brands.

Gorham Crystal, Althea, crystal, cut

Ashtray, 4½"	$20.00
Biscuit Barrel, 7¾"	80.00
Bonbon, 4⅜"	50.00
Bonbon, 5¾"	50.00
Bowl, 4⅜"	60.00
Bowl, 6¾"	60.00
Bowl, 7½"	60.00
Bowl, footed, 6⅜"	100.00
Bud Vase, 4⅞"	40.00
Bud Vase, 5⅝"	40.00

Sugar, covered, 4¼"	50.00
Sugar, open, 3¾"	40.00
Vase, 5⅜"	40.00
Vase, 7¾"	40.00
Water Goblet, 7"	40.00

Gorham Crystal, Bamberg, crystal, cut

Candlestick	$60.00
Champagne	60.00
Champagne, fluted	80.00
Claret	80.00
Cocktail	60.00
Cordial, 4⅛"	70.00
Creamer	70.00
Decanter, 10½"	350.00
Iced Tea	85.00
Juice	60.00
Parfait	60.00
Pitcher	300.00
Sugar	70.00
Water Goblet	85.00
Wine	80.00

Butter Dish, covered, ¼ lb.	80.00
Candy Dish, covered, 4⅛"	50.00
Candy Dish, covered, 6⅛"	50.00
Centerpiece, 12⅛"	50.00
Champagne, 4⅝"	35.00
Creamer, 2⅜"	30.00
Creamer, 2¾"	30.00
Highball, 5¼"	30.00
Iced Tea	40.00
Marmalade, 5¾"	30.00
Old Fashioned, 3½"	30.00
Relish, three-part, 12½"	50.00
Salt and Pepper Shakers, pair, 2¾"	50.00
Salt and Pepper Shakers, pair, 5¼"	50.00

Decanter, 12½″	145.00
Hock	30.00
Iced Tea, footed, 6⅞″	30.00
Punch Bowl, 7⅝″	260.00
Water Goblet, 7½″	27.00
Water Goblet, low, 6⅞″	27.00
Wine, 4⅞″	25.00
Wine, 5⅝″	27.00
Wine, 5¾″	25.00

Gorham Crystal, Chantilly, crystal, cut

Champagne	$55.00
Champagne, fluted	65.00
Cordial	60.00
Iced Tea	65.00
Juice	60.00
Pitcher	275.00
Water Goblet	65.00
Wine	65.00

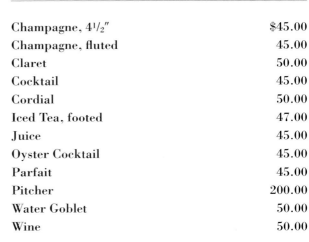

Gorham Crystal, Crown Point, crystal, cut

Champagne, 4½″	$45.00
Champagne, fluted	45.00
Claret	50.00
Cocktail	45.00
Cordial	50.00
Iced Tea, footed	47.00
Juice	45.00
Oyster Cocktail	45.00
Parfait	45.00
Pitcher	200.00
Water Goblet	50.00
Wine	50.00

Gorham Crystal, Cherrywood, crystal, cut

Brandy, large	$40.00
Brandy, small	35.00
Champagne, 4⅝″	32.00
Champagne, fluted, 7⅝″	27.00
Claret, 6¼″	32.00
Cocktail, 3¾″	30.00
Cordial, 3⅞″	30.00
Cordial, tall	40.00

Gorham Crystal, de'Medici, crystal, cut

Champagne, $5^1/_8''$	$50.00
Cordial	50.00
Iced Tea, footed	55.00
Water Goblet, 7''	60.00
Wine, 6''	60.00

Gorham Crystal, Florentine, crystal, cut

Champagne, $5^3/_8''$	$45.00
Champagne, fluted, $8^1/_2''$	55.00
Iced Tea, footed	55.00
Water Goblet	55.00
Wine	55.00

Gorham Crystal, First Lady, crystal, platinum trim

Champagne, $4^5/_8''$	$27.00
Cocktail, $4^1/_8''$	27.00
Cordial, $3^3/_4''$	30.00
Iced Tea	32.00
Juice, $6^1/_2''$	27.00
Water Goblet, $6^5/_8''$	30.00
Wine, $5^1/_2''$	30.00

Gorham Crystal, French Cathedral, crystal, cut

Champagne	$40.00
Champagne, fluted	45.00
Iced Tea, footed	45.00
Water Goblet	45.00
Wine	45.00

Gorham Crystal, Gentry, crystal

Champagne, fluted	$25.00
Claret	25.00
Cocktail	25.00
Cordial	25.00
Iced Tea	25.00
Juice	25.00
Oyster Cocktail	25.00
Parfait	25.00
Pitcher	125.00
Sherbet	25.00
Water Goblet, $6^5/_8''$	25.00
Water Goblet, low	25.00

Gorham Crystal, Jolie, crystal, cut

Champagne	$15.00
Champagne, fluted, $8^5/_8''$	15.00
Cocktail	20.00

Cordial	25.00
Iced Tea, $8^1/_8''$	17.00
Juice	20.00
Oyster Cocktail	20.00
Parfait	20.00
Pitcher	100.00
Sherbet	15.00
Water Goblet, $8^1/_4''$	15.00
Wine	15.00

Gorham Crystal, King Edward, crystal, cut

Biscuit Barrel, $7^1/_4''$	$70.00
Bowl, $6^3/_4''$	50.00
Bowl, $7^1/_4''$	50.00
Bowl, $7^1/_2''$	50.00
Bowl, 9"	50.00
Brandy, large	35.00
Brandy, small	30.00
Centerpiece, $10^1/_2''$	70.00
Champagne	20.00
Champagne, fluted, $7^3/_8''$	25.00
Creamer, $3^1/_8''$	22.00
Iced Tea, footed, $7^1/_8''$	27.00
Lid, butter dish, $1/_4$ lb., $5^7/_8''$	35.00
Pitcher, $8^3/_8''$	100.00
Punch Bowl, 8"	240.00
Salt and Pepper Shakers, pair, $4^1/_2''$	37.00
Sugar, covered, 4"	30.00
Sugar, open, 4"	25.00
Water Goblet, $7^1/_8''$	25.00
Wine, 6"	25.00

Gorham Crystal, Lady Anne, crystal, cut

Champagne, $5^5/_8''$	$20.00
Champagne, fluted, $8^5/_8''$	25.00
Highball, $6''$	15.00
Iced Tea, footed, $7^5/_8''$	27.00
Old Fashioned, double, $4''$	15.00
Water Goblet, $7^5/_8''$	25.00
Wine, $6^7/_8''$	25.00

Gorham Crystal, Lady Anne Gold, crystal, cut, gold trim

Champagne	$30.00
Champagne, fluted, $8^3/_4''$	30.00
Claret	30.00
Cocktail	30.00
Cordial	40.00
Iced Tea, $7^5/_8''$	32.00
Juice	30.00
Oyster Cocktail	30.00

Parfait	35.00
Sherbet	30.00
Water Goblet, $7^5/_8''$	30.00
Water Goblet, low	30.00
Wine, $7''$	30.00

Gorham Crystal, La Scala, crystal, cut

Champagne, $5''$	$55.00
Champagne, fluted	55.00
Cocktail	55.00
Cordial, $4''$	55.00
Iced Tea, footed	70.00
Juice	60.00
Parfait	55.00
Water Goblet	60.00
Wine, $5^1/_4''$	65.00

Gorham Crystal, Laurin Gold, crystal, optic, gold trim

Champagne	$15.00

Champagne, fluted, 9″	15.00
Claret	15.00
Cocktail	15.00
Cordial	20.00
Iced Tea, 7$\frac{1}{8}$″	17.00
Juice	15.00
Oyster Cocktail	15.00
Parfait	15.00
Sherbet	15.00
Water Goblet, 7$\frac{3}{4}$″	15.00
Water Goblet, low	15.00
Wine, 7$\frac{1}{4}$″	15.00

Gorham Crystal, Rosewood, crystal, cut

Champagne, 4$\frac{7}{8}$″	$70.00
Claret	70.00
Cocktail, 3$\frac{3}{4}$″	70.00
Cordial	80.00
Iced Tea, footed	75.00
Water Goblet, 6$\frac{7}{8}$″	80.00
Wine, 4$\frac{5}{8}$″	80.00

Gorham Crystal, Nocturne, crystal, cut

Champagne, 5″	$30.00
Champagne, fluted	40.00
Decanter, 9$\frac{1}{2}$″	185.00
Iced Tea, footed	55.00
Old Fashioned, 3$\frac{1}{2}$″	50.00
Water Goblet	55.00
Wine	55.00

Gorham Crystal, Tivoli, crystal, cut

Champagne, 5$\frac{1}{4}$″	$60.00
Champagne, fluted	60.00
Cocktail	60.00
Cordial, 4$\frac{1}{2}$″	60.00
Iced Tea	70.00
Juice	65.00
Parfait	60.00
Water Goblet	65.00
Wine	60.00

A. H. HEISEY AND COMPANY
Newark, Ohio

Augustus H. Heisey, who was born in Hanover, Germany, and emigrated to the United States in 1843, began his glass industry career as a clerk with the King Glass Company of Pittsburgh. In 1870, Heisey married Susan Duncan, daughter of George Duncan, owner of the Ripley Glass Company. In 1874, George Duncan deeded a one-quarter interest in his business, renamed George Duncan & Sons, to each of his two children, James and Susan. In 1879, two years after George Duncan's death, James Duncan and Heisey purchased the remaining one-half interest from the Duncan estate. In the 1880s, Heisey applied for and obtained several design patents. In 1891, the United States Glass combine acquired George Duncan & Sons.

By 1893, Heisey had begun to formulate plans to strike out on his own. He selected Newark, Ohio, as the site for his new venture because of an abundant supply of natural gas, inexpensive labor, and active recruitment by the New Board of Trade. In April 1896, Heisey opened a sixteen-pot furnace in Newark. Eventually, the plant would expand to three furnaces and employ over 700 people.

Early production was confined to pressware, barware, and hotelware. In the late 1890s, Heisey introduced colonial patterns with flutes, scallops, and panels. They were so well received that Heisey (the company, not the man) retained at least one colonial pattern in its line until the factory closed.

George Duncan Heisey, a son of Augustus Heisey, designed the famous "Diamond H" trademark in 1900; the company registered it in 1901. By 1910, Heisey was aggressively marketing its glass through national magazines. In 1914, blown ware was first manufactured. Not content with traditional pulled stemware, the company introduced fancy-pressed stemware patterns in the late 1910s.

Edgar Wilson, another son of Augustus Heisey, became president in 1922 following Augustus's death. He was responsible for most of the colored Heisey glass. While some colored glass was made earlier, the first pastel colors and later the deeper colors, like cobalt and tangerine, were manufactured in quantity in the 1920s and 1930s. By Edgar Wilson's death in 1942, colored glassware had virtually disappeared from the market.

T. Clarence Heisey, another son of Augustus Heisey, assumed the presidency of the company. A shortage of manpower and supplies during World War II curtailed production. Many animal figures were introduced in the 1940s. An attempt was made to resurrect colored glass in the 1950s. Increasing production costs and foreign competition eventually resulted in the closing of the Heisey factory in December 1957.

The Imperial Glass Corporation of Bellaire, Ohio, bought the Heisey molds in 1958, but only a small number were kept in production, primarily those patterns Heisey had produced when it ceased operations. Some pieces still carried the Heisey mark; however, in January 1968, Imperial announced it would no longer use it.

A. H. Heisey & Company, Crystolite, crystal, blown (Pattern 1503)

Crystolite, introduced in 1938, was produced in amber, crystal, Sahara and Zircon/limelight.

Ashtray, 3$^1/_4$″	$30.00
Ashtray, 3$^1/_2$″	30.00
Bonbon, 6$^1/_4$″	55.00
Bonbon, 7″	55.00
Bonbon, 7$^1/_4$″	55.00
Bowl, dressing, 5″	60.00
Bowl, oval, 7″	80.00
Candlestick, 2$^1/_8$″	40.00
Candlestick, 4″	40.00
Candlestick, double light	50.00
Candy Dish, covered, 5$^1/_2$″	70.00
Candy Dish, covered, 7″	75.00
Celery, 12$^1/_2$″	60.00
Centerpiece, 13$^1/_8$″	120.00
Champagne, 3$^7/_8$″	40.00
Cheese Stand, 2$^7/_8$″	60.00
Cheese Stand, 5$^1/_2$″	60.00
Cigarette Box, 4″	80.00
Cigarette Holder, 4″	45.00
Claret	50.00

Coaster, 4″	20.00
Cocktail, 3$^5/_8$″	40.00
Compote, 4$^3/_4$″	60.00
Creamer, 2$^3/_4$″	45.00
Creamer, 3$^3/_4$″	45.00
Creamer and Sugar Set, with tray	95.00
Creamer and Sugar Set, with tray, mini	65.00
Cruet, 3$^5/_8$″, no stopper	40.00
Cruet, with stopper, 4$^3/_4$″	85.00
Cup and Saucer, 2$^3/_8$″	50.00
Ice Bucket, 4$^1/_2$″	160.00
Iced Tea, flat, 5$^7/_8$″	40.00
Iced Tea, footed, 6$^3/_8$″	40.00
Jug, 8″	120.00
Juice, footed, 4$^7/_8$″	40.00
Mayonnaise and Underplate	70.00
Mayonnaise and Underplate, with ladle	80.00
Mayonnaise Underplate, 8″	27.00
Nappy, 5$^3/_8$″	50.00
Oyster Cocktail, 3$^1/_2$″	40.00
Pickle, 9″	55.00
Plate, dinner, 10$^1/_2$″	80.00
Plate, salad, 7$^1/_4$″	40.00
Plate, salad, 8$^1/_4$″	40.00
Plate, sandwich, 12″	90.00
Plate, sandwich, 14″	100.00
Plate, torte, 11″	75.00
Plate, torte, 14″	90.00
Punch Bowl, 6$^1/_4$″	400.00
Relish, two-part, 6$^3/_4$″	60.00
Relish, three-part, 9$^1/_2$″	70.00
Relish, three-part, 12$^1/_2$″	70.00
Relish, four-part, 9″	80.00
Salt and Pepper Shakers, pair	75.00
Saucer	15.00
Sugar, mini, 1$^7/_8$″	40.00
Sugar, open, 2$^1/_4$″	45.00

Sugar, open, $3^5/_8''$	45.00
Tumbler, flat, $4^1/_4''$	40.00
Vase, 3"	60.00
Vase, footed, 6"	70.00
Water Goblet, $5^7/_8''$	40.00

A. H. Heisey & Company, Heisey Rose, crystal, etched (Etching 515)

Heisey Rose was produced from 1949 to 1957.

Ashtray, 3"	$40.00
Bowl, dressing, 8"	70.00
Bowl, fruit, crimped, 10"	70.00
Bowl, fruit, crimped, 12"	90.00
Bowl, fruit, three-toed, 11"	80.00
Bowl, gardenia, 10"	75.00
Bowl, gardenia, 13"	100.00
Bowl, oval, footed, 11"	165.00
Bowl, salad, 7"	65.00
Bowl, salad, 9"	75.00
Bud Vase, footed, 8"	50.00
Bud Vase, footed, 10"	60.00
Butter Dish, covered, square, 6"	170.00
Cake Salver, $13^1/_2''$	150.00
Candlestick, $3^5/_8''$	50.00
Candy Dish, covered, seahorse handles, $8^1/_2''$	210.00
Celery, 12"	75.00
Champagne, $4^5/_8''$	45.00
Cheese and Cracker Set, 12"	150.00
Claret	140.00
Cocktail	60.00

Compote, $3^5/_8''$	75.00
Cordial, $4^1/_4''$	180.00
Creamer, footed, 4"	50.00
Creamer, footed, mini, 3"	50.00
Cup and Saucer	50.00
Finger Bowl	50.00
Iced Tea, footed, $6^3/_4''$	50.00
Jam, open, 7"	65.00
Juice, footed, $5^1/_2''$	40.00
Mayonnaise	60.00
Oyster Cocktail, footed	70.00
Plate, dinner, $10^1/_2''$	175.00
Plate, salad, $8^1/_2''$	40.00
Plate, sandwich, 11"	100.00
Plate, sandwich, 14"	150.00
Plate, service, $10^1/_2''$	90.00
Plate, torte, $13^3/_4''$	95.00
Relish, three-part, round, 7"	70.00
Relish, three-part, 11"	80.00
Relish, four-part, round, 9"	85.00
Salt and Pepper Shakers, pair, footed	90.00
Seafood Icer, with liner	90.00

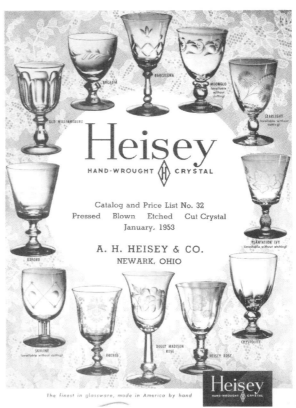

The cover of Heisey's 1953 catalog #32.

Sherbet, 3³/₄″	45.00	Pickle, 13″	45.00
Sugar, footed, 4″	50.00	Plate, luncheon, 8¹/₄″	32.00
Sugar, footed, mini, 3″	50.00	Plate, salad, 7″	20.00
Tray, center handle, 14″	150.00	Relish, three-part, 7″	40.00
Tray, for cream and sugar set,		Salt and Pepper Shakers, pair	75.00
individual, 8″	50.00	Sherbet, 3¹/₂″	40.00
Vase, footed, 7″	70.00	Sugar, footed	50.00
Vase, footed, fan, 7″	75.00	Tumbler, footed, 5³/₈″	40.00
Vase, footed, violet, 3¹/₂″	50.00	Water Goblet, 8″	40.00
Water Goblet, 6³/₈″	50.00	Wine	75.00
Wine	125.00		

A. H. Heisey & Company, Minuet, crystal, etched (Etching 503)

Minuet was produced from 1939 to the 1950s.

Bowl, footed, 6″	$25.00
Bowl, footed, handled, 6″	30.00
Bowl, oval, 12″	75.00
Candlestick	40.00
Celery, 12″	50.00
Champagne, 6¹/₄″	40.00
Claret	50.00
Cocktail, 6″	35.00
Compote, 5¹/₂″	50.00
Cordial, 5³/₈″	150.00
Creamer, footed	50.00
Cup and Saucer	70.00
Finger Bowl	60.00
Iced Tea, footed, 6⁷/₈″	50.00
Juice, footed, 5¹/₈″	40.00
Oyster Cocktail, 3¹/₂″	45.00

A. H. Heisey & Company, Orchid, crystal, etched (Etching 507)

Orchid was produced from 1940 to 1957.

Ashtray, 3″	$40.00
Bowl, crimped, 10″	75.00
Bowl, dressing, 8″	70.00
Bowl, gardenia, 13″	80.00
Bowl, salad, 7″	50.00
Butter Dish, covered, square,	
6¹/₄″, no lid	135.00
Candlestick, 3¹/₂″	50.00
Candlestick, double light	80.00
Celery, 12″	60.00
Celery, 13″	60.00
Champagne, 6¹/₈″	40.00
Cheese Stand, 5¹/₂″	65.00
Cheese Stand, 6¹/₄″	65.00
Cheese Stand, 6⁵/₈″	65.00
Cocktail, 5¹/₂″	45.00
Compote, 3³/₄″	70.00

Cordial, 4³/₄″	170.00
Creamer, footed, 4″	50.00
Cup and Saucer, footed, 2³/₄″	70.00
Finger Bowl	90.00
Iced Tea, footed, 6⁵/₈″	50.00
Jam, open, 6¹/₂″	60.00
Juice, footed, 5³/₈″	45.00
Mayonnaise, 5¹/₂″	60.00
Mayonnaise and Underplate	70.00
Mayonnaise Underplate, 7³/₈″	30.00
Mint Dish, 5¹/₂″	65.00
Oyster Cocktail	65.00
Plate, dinner, 10¹/₂″	150.00
Plate, salad, 7¹/₄″	35.00
Plate, torte, 13⁵/₈″	95.00
Relish, three-part, round, 7¹/₄″	80.00
Relish, four-part, round, 9″	90.00
Salt and Pepper Shakers, pair	90.00
Sherbet, 4″	40.00
Sugar, mini, 2³/₄″	50.00
Sugar, open, footed, 3⁷/₈″	50.00
Water Goblet, 8³/₈″	50.00
Water Goblet, low, 6″	45.00
Wine, 5¹/₄″	85.00

A. H. Heisey & Company, Plantation, crystal, pressed (Pattern 1567)

The first Plantation pieces were produced in 1946.

Ashtray, 3¹/₂″	$35.00
Bowl, fruit, crimped, 9¹/₂″	75.00
Bowl, fruit, crimped, 12″	90.00
Bowl, gardenia, 9¹/₂″	90.00
Bowl, gardenia, 13″	100.00
Bowl, gardenia, footed, 11¹/₂″	125.00
Bowl, salad, 9″	90.00
Butter Dish, covered, ¹/₄ lb., 7″	100.00
Cake Salver, 13″	100.00
Candlestick, double light	75.00

Candy Dish, covered, 5″	100.00
Celery, 13″	50.00
Champagne, 4¹/₄″	32.00
Claret	70.00
Coaster, 4″	50.00
Cocktail	40.00
Compote, 5″	50.00
Cordial	125.00
Creamer, footed	40.00
Cruet, with stopper	50.00
Cup and Saucer	40.00
Iced Tea, footed	65.00
Juice, footed	50.00
Mayonnaise and Underplate, 5¹/₄″	60.00
Nappy, 5″	25.00
Nappy, 5¹/₂″	25.00
Oil Cruet, with stopper, 6³/₈″	135.00
Oyster Cocktail, 3³/₄″	35.00
Plate, salad, 8¹/₂″	35.00
Plate, sandwich, 14″	80.00
Plate, torte, 14″	80.00
Relish, three-part, 11″	65.00
Relish, four-part, round, 8″	75.00
Relish, five-part, oval, 13″	100.00
Salt and Pepper Shakers, pair	57.00
Sugar, footed, open, 4³/₈″	37.00
Vase, footed, flared, 5″	40.00
Vase, footed, flared, 9″	80.00
Water Goblet	50.00
Wine	75.00

In 1901, a group of investors from Wheeling, West Virginia, and Bellaire, Ohio, founded the Imperial Glass Company. Bellaire had a long-established glassmaking tradition. The Imperial factory was the newest of fourteen glasshouses built in the city. Ed Muhleman, previously with the Crystal Glass Works of Bridgeport, Ohio, supervised the construction and served as the company's manager. The first Imperial glass was manufactured on January 13, 1904. The company's products were mass-market directed—jelly glasses, tumblers, and assorted tableware.

Victor G. Wicke, owner of a selling agency in New York, was hired as Imperial's secretary and sales manager. Imperial's success was guaranteed by one of its first orders, approximately twenty different items to be supplied to almost 500 F. W. Woolworth stores. McCrory and Kresge also became major Imperial customers.

Between 1910 and 1920, machine-made glassware flooded the market. Imperial responded by introducing a number of new glassware lines. "Nuart" iridescent ware was introduced. Next came "Nucut" crystal, a pressed reproduction of English cut glass pieces. "Nucut" sold well as a premium. The Grand Union Tea Company distributed a large amount. In the 1950s, "Nucut" was reintroduced as "Collectors Crystal" and once again became very popular.

The depression and the continuing loss of market share to mass-production glass factories forced Imperial to declare bankruptcy in 1931. The plant continued to operate through court-appointed receivers. The Imperial Glass Corporation, a new entity, was formed during July and August of 1931. An order from the Quaker Oats Company for a premium similar to Cape Cod helped revive the company. In 1937, Imperial launched Candlewick, its best-selling line.

In 1940, Imperial acquired the Central Glass Works of Wheeling, established in 1860. It proved to be the first of a number of acquisitions, including A. H. Heisey and Company in 1958 and the Cambridge Glass Company in 1960.

In 1973, Imperial became a subsidiary of the Lenox Glass Corporation. In 1981, Lenox sold the company to Arthur Lorch, a private investor living in New York, who in turn sold it to Robert Stahl, a Minneapolis, Minnesota, liquidator, in 1982. In October 1982, Imperial declared bankruptcy. Consolidated-Colony, a partnership of Lancaster Colony Corporation and Consolidated International, purchased Imperial in December 1984. Most of the company's molds were sold. Maroon Enterprises of Bridgeport, Ohio, purchased the buildings and property in March 1985.

Imperial Glass Corporation, Candlewick, crystal (Line 3400)

Ashtray, 3¹/₄″	$12.00
Ashtray, 4″	12.00
Ashtray, 5″	12.00
Ashtray, 6″	12.00
Ashtray, blue, 4″	12.00
Ashtray, pink, 6″	12.00
Ashtray Set, colored, three pieces	40.00
Ashtray Set, three pieces	35.00
Bonbon, 6¹/₂″	25.00
Bowl, divided, 10″	95.00
Bowl, float, 11″	65.00
Bowl, handled, 7″	25.00
Bowl, heart-shaped, 5¹/₂″	25.00
Bowl, heart-shaped, handled, 5″	27.00
Bowl, round, 8¹/₄″	65.00
Bowl, round, 10″	65.00
Bowl, three-toed, 4¹/₂″	90.00
Bud Vase, 6″	85.00
Butter Dish, covered, ¹/₄ lb.	135.00
Butter Dish, round, 5¹/₂″, no lid	45.00
Butter Pat, 4⁵/₈″	15.00
Candleholder	45.00
Candlestick, 3¹/₂″	17.00
Candlestick, double light	30.00
Candlestick, flower, 5¹/₄″	55.00
Candy Box, covered, 6¹/₂″	55.00
Candy Dish, covered, 7″	135.00
Candy Dish, covered, three-part, 6¹/₂″	95.00
Candy Dish, 7″, no lid	65.00
Celery, 13¹/₄″	50.00

Champagne, 5¹/₄″	20.00
Cigarette Box, 4³/₈″	60.00
Coaster, 4″	10.00
Cocktail, 4⁵/₈″	17.00
Compote, 5¹/₂″ × 3″	30.00
Cordial, 4¹/₂″	45.00
Creamer, footed, 3¹/₂″	17.00
Creamer, footed, 4⁷/₈″	17.00
Creamer, footed, mini, 3″	15.00
Creamer, mini, 2¹/₂″	15.00
Creamer and Sugar Set, with tray, mini, three pieces	55.00
Creamer and Sugar Set, with tray, three pieces	60.00
Cruet, 6⁵/₈″, no stopper	45.00
Cruet, 7⁷/₈″, no stopper	50.00
Cruet, with stopper, 5⁵/₈″	75.00
Cruet, with stopper, 6⁵/₈″	75.00
Cup and Saucer, flat, 2¹/₈″	15.00
Cup and Saucer, footed, 2⁷/₈″	15.00
Deviled Egg Server, 11¹/₂″	155.00
Iced Tea, 6³/₈″	25.00
Juice, 4³/₄″	20.00
Lid, marmalade	22.00
Marmalade, covered, 4³/₄″, no spoon	50.00
Marmalade, covered, with spoon	55.00
Mayonnaise, 5¹/₂″	15.00
Mayonnaise, divided, 5¹/₂″	32.00
Mayonnaise and Underplate, divided, 5¹/₂″	45.00
Mayonnaise Ladle, 6″	15.00
Mayonnaise Underplate, 7″	20.00
Mayonnaise Underplate, 8″	20.00
Mint Dish, heart-shaped, 4¹/₄″	15.00
Mint Tray, 8¹/₂″	30.00
Nappy, handled, 6″	25.00
Nut Dish, heart-shaped, 5¹/₂″	15.00
Pastry Tray, 11³/₄″	50.00
Pepper Shaker, plastic lid	12.00
Pickle, 8¹/₂″	32.00
Plate, 7¹/₄″	12.00
Plate, 8″	12.00
Plate, canapé, 6″	25.00
Plate, salad, crescent, 8¹/₄″	60.00
Plate, torte, 13″	50.00
Plate, two-handled, 5″	45.00

Plate, two-handled, 7″	12.00
Plate, two-handled, 10″	35.00
Relish, two-part, 7¼″	25.00
Relish, two-part, 8¼″	25.00
Relish, two-part, oval, 11″	35.00
Relish, two-part, square, 7½″	115.00
Relish, three-part, 10½″	65.00
Relish, four-part, 9½″	32.00
Relish, five-part, 11″	70.00
Relish, five-part, 13″	95.00
Relish, six-part, 10½″	70.00
Salad Fork, 9½″	25.00
Salad Spoon, 9½″	25.00
Salt and Pepper Shakers, pair, footed, 5″, no lids	35.00
Salt and Pepper Shakers, pair, no lids	15.00
Salt and Pepper Shakers, pair, plastic lids	25.00
Salt and Pepper Shakers, pair, silverplate lids	25.00
Salt Dip, 2¼″	15.00
Salt Shaker, chrome lid	12.00
Salt Shaker, footed, 5″	25.00
Salt Shaker, footed, 5″, no lid	17.00
Salt Shaker, no lid	7.00
Salt Shaker, plastic lid	12.00
Seafood Icer, with liner, 4¼″	110.00
Sugar, footed, mini, 2½″	15.00
Sugar, open, footed, 3¼″	17.00
Sugar, open, footed, 4¼″	17.00
Tidbit Set, heart-shaped, three pieces	55.00
Tray, 5″	22.00
Tray, for creamer and sugar set, individual, 6¾″	22.00
Tray, for vinegar set, 8″	45.00
Tray, handled, 8″	45.00
Tray, oval, 9″	40.00
Tumbler, flat, 5¾″	25.00
Vase, crimped, plain top, 8″	45.00
Wafer Tray, center handle, 6″	27.00
Water Goblet	25.00

Imperial Glass Corporation, Candlewick, crystal (Other Stemware Lines)

Cocktail, 2³⁄₈″	$22.00
Iced Tea, 5⁷⁄₈″	30.00
Juice, 4″	15.00
Old Fashioned, 3³⁄₈″	32.00
Sherbet, 2⅛″	15.00
Tumbler, flat, 5³⁄₈″	20.00
Water Goblet, 4¾″	17.00

Imperial Glass Corporation, Cape Cod, crystal (Line 1600)

Champagne	$15.00
Iced Tea	17.00
Juice	15.00
Water Goblet	20.00

**Imperial Glass Corporation, Cape Cod, crystal
(Line 1602)**

Ashtray, 4¼″	$15.00
Ashtray, double, 5½″	20.00
Baked Apple, 5¾″	15.00
Bowl, footed, 9¼″	75.00
Bowl, fruit, 4⅛″	15.00
Bowl, fruit, 12½″	80.00
Bowl, oval, 11¼″	85.00
Cake Plate, footed, 10½″	55.00
Cake Stand, round, patterned, 11″	85.00
Champagne, 5″	12.00
Claret, 5½″	15.00
Cocktail, 3½″	12.00
Cocktail, 4⅝″	12.00
Compote, 4½″	40.00
Cordial, 3¾″	15.00
Creamer, 4⅝″	17.00
Creamer, footed, 4″	17.00
Cruet, 5¼″, no stopper	20.00
Cruet, patterned, round handle, with stopper	30.00
Cruet, round, patterned handle, with stopper	30.00
Cruet, with stopper, 5¼″	30.00
Cup and Saucer, footed, 2¾″	17.00
Decanter, 8½″	80.00
Decanter, 9½″	80.00
Finger Bowl, 5″	15.00
High Ball, 4⅛″	15.00
Iced Tea, flat, 5¼″	15.00
Iced Tea, footed, 6″	15.00

Juice, flat, 4½″	15.00
Juice, footed, 5¼″	15.00
Lid, marmalade	10.00
Marmalade, covered, 3¼″, no lid	22.00
Marmalade, covered, no spoon	32.00
Mayonnaise, 5½″	17.00
Mayonnaise and Underplate	35.00
Mayonnaise Underplate, 7″	10.00
Nut Dish, 3″	30.00
Nut Dish, 4⅛″	30.00
Old Fashioned, 3⅜″	15.00
Oyster Cocktail, 3¾″	15.00
Parfait, 5⅞″	15.00
Pitcher, pint, 6″	50.00
Plate, 7″	12.00
Plate, 8¼″	12.00
Plate, bread and butter, 6¾″	12.00
Plate, footed, 7″	12.00
Plate, torte, 13⅝″	40.00
Plate, torte, 14″	40.00
Plate, torte, 14½″	40.00
Plate, torte, 16½″	40.00
Plate, torte, 17″	40.00
Plate, torte, large, 16¼″	65.00
Plate, torte, large, 16½″	65.00
Relish, 9½″	35.00
Relish, five-part, 11¼″	65.00
Salt and Pepper Shakers, pair, chrome lids, 4″	25.00
Salt and Pepper Shakers, pair, plastic lids	25.00
Salt and Pepper Shakers, pair, 3¼″, no lids	17.00
Salt and Pepper Shakers, pair, no lids	17.00
Salt and Pepper Shakers, pair, mini, no lids	12.00
Salt and Pepper Set, with tray, no lids	32.00
Salt Shaker, chrome lid	20.00
Salt Shaker, plastic lid	12.00
Salt Shaker, 3″, no lid	10.00
Salt Shaker, 3¼″, no lid	10.00
Salt Shaker, mini, no lid	7.00
Sherbet, 3¼″	10.00
Spider, divided, 9½″	45.00
Spider, handled, 4¾″	35.00

Spider, handled, 8¹/₈″	35.00
Sugar, open, 4¹/₄″	17.00
Sugar, open, footed, 3¹/₂″	17.00
Sundae, 3³/₄″	10.00
Tumbler, footed, 5¹/₂″	15.00
Vase, 8¹/₂″	60.00
Water Goblet, 6¹/₄″	15.00
Water Goblet, low, 5¹/₄″	15.00
Water Goblet, low, 5¹/₂″	15.00
Whiskey, 2⁵/₈″	15.00
Wine, 3⁷/₈″	15.00
Wine, 4¹/₂″	15.00

Imperial Glass Corporation, Old Williamsburg, crystal (Line 341)

Bowl, gardenia, footed, 10″	$75.00
Bowl, salad, 9″	65.00
Cake Stand, 11″	80.00
Candlestick, 7¹/₂″	45.00
Candy Dish, covered, footed, 7″	100.00
Candy Dish, covered, footed, 10″	125.00
Celery, 13″	50.00
Champagne, 4³/₄″	15.00
Claret	17.00
Cocktail	17.00
Compote, 4¹/₂″	30.00
Compote, 6″	40.00
Creamer and Sugar, covered, handled	50.00
Creamer and Sugar, mini	30.00
Creamer and Sugar, open	35.00
Cruet, with stopper	30.00
Finger Bowl, 4¹/₂″	15.00

THE TOP FIVE PATTERNS EARLY AMERICAN

FOSTORIA, ARGUS

FOSTORIA, JAMESTOWN

IMPERIAL, OLD WILLIAMSBURG

LENOX, ANTIQUE

TIFFIN, KING'S CROWN

Iced Tea, flat	20.00
Iced Tea, footed	22.00
Juice, flat	17.00
Juice, footed	20.00
Mayonnaise, three pieces	40.00
Nappy, 4″	20.00
Nappy, 5¹/₂″	20.00
Nappy, 6″	25.00
Nappy, 7″	25.00
Nappy, 8″	25.00
Old Fashioned, double	22.00
Pickle, 9″	40.00
Pitcher, pint	50.00
Pitcher, quart	75.00
Plate, 6″	12.00
Plate, 7″	12.00
Plate, 8″	12.00
Plate, torte, 13″	35.00
Relish, three-part, 10″	50.00
Relish, five-part, 13″	60.00
Salt and Pepper Shakers, pair	25.00
Sherbet	15.00
Tray, round, 10″	25.00
Tumbler	17.00
Water Goblet, 6³/₄″	17.00

Water Goblet, low, 6½″   17.00
Wine, 5³/₈″   22.00

Imperial Glass Corporation, Twist, crystal (Line 110)

Champagne, 4³/₈″	$20.00		
Claret, 4⁷/₈″	27.00		
Cocktail, 3³/₄″	15.00		
Cordial, 3⁵/₈″	20.00		
Cup, 2″	22.00		
Iced Tea, flat	20.00		
Iced Tea, footed	22.00	Sherbet	20.00
Juice, flat	15.00	Tumbler	17.00
Parfait, 6¼″	22.00	Water Goblet, 6³/₈″	22.00
Plate, 8³/₈″	20.00	Wine, 4½″	22.00

OLD WILLIAMSBURG

341 9 oz. Tall Goblet	341 9 oz. Low Goblet	341 6 oz. Tall Sherbet	341 4-1/2 oz. Low Sherbet	341 3 oz. Cocktail	341 4-1/2 oz. Claret	341 5 oz. Ftd. Juice	341 12 oz. Ftd. Ice Tea

341 12 oz. Ice Tea (no foot)	341 13 oz. Double Old Fashion	341 8 oz. Tumbler	341 5 oz. Juice	341/16—1 Pint Pitcher	341/24—1 Quart Pitcher

341/902 Sugar and Cream Set. Handled	341/30 Sugar and Cream Set	341/122 Individual Sugar and Cream Set	341/96 Salt and Pepper Set	341/119 4 oz. Cruet and Stopper

341/355 Ftd. Jar and Cover (Height 10″)	341/354 Ftd. Jar and Cover (Height 7″)	341/66B 4-1/2″ Compote	341/45C—6″ Ftd. Compote	341/1D 6″ Plate	341/3D 7″ Plate	341/5D 8″ Plate

JEANNETTE GLASS COMPANY
Jeannette, Pennsylvania

The Jeannette Glass Company was established in 1898. It originally produced handblown, narrow-mouthed bottles. When manufacturing this style no longer proved profitable, the factory converted to semiautomatic methods and turned out wide-mouthed glass containers for foodstuffs. By 1910, Jeannette Glass was producing automobile headlight lenses and glass brick, known as sidewalk tile.

The Jeannette Glass Company introduced a line of pressed table and kitchenware in the 1920s. Jeannette's popular Depression Era patterns include Adam (1932–1934), Cherry Blossom (1930–1939), Cube or Cubist (1929–1933), Doric (1935–1938), Doric and Pansy (1937–1938), Floral or Poinsettia (1931–1935), Hex Optic or Honeycomb (1928–1932), Homespun or Fine Rib (1939–1949), Iris and Iris Herringbone (1928–1932, 1950s, and 1970s), Sunburst or Herringbone (late 1930s), Sunflower (1930s), Swirl or Petal Swirl (1937–1938), and Windsor or Windsor Diamond (1936–1946). The company also made glass candy containers for other firms and individuals during the 1920s.

In 1952, Jeannette Glass purchased the McKee Glass Corporation from the Thatcher Glass Company, which enabled them to expand into the production of heat-resistant and industrial glass.

The Jeannette Glass Company experienced several periods in the post–World War II era when its stemware enjoyed a strong popularity with the American buying public. Anniversary (1947–1949, late 1960s to mid-1970s), Floragold or Louisa (1950s), Harp (1954–1957), Holiday or Buttons and Bows (1947 through the mid-1950s), and Shell Pink Milk Glass (1957–1959) were among the most popular patterns. The Iris pattern was so popular that it easily made the transition from a pre-war to post-war pattern.

The Jeannette Glass Company ceased its operations in the mid-1980s.

Jeannette Glass Company, Cherry Blossom, pink

Cherry Blossom was manufactured in pink, green, Delphite (opaque blue), crystal, Jadite (opaque green), and red. It was produced from 1930 to 1939. In the listing that follows, AOP means "all over pattern," and PAT means "pattern at top."

Bowl, cereal, 5³/₄″	$40.00
Bowl, fruit, 4³/₄″	25.00
Bowl, fruit, 8¹/₂″	75.00
Bowl, fruit, three-toed, 10¹/₂″	85.00
Bowl, handled, 9″	75.00
Bowl, handled, 11″	60.00
Bowl, oval, 9″	70.00
Bowl, soup, flat, 7³/₄″	75.00
Butter Dish, covered	125.00
Cake Plate, three-toed, 10¹/₄″	50.00
Coaster	12.00
Creamer, 3¹/₂″	30.00
Cup, 2¹/₄″	25.00
Cup and Saucer, 2¹/₄″	40.00
Iced Tea	17.00
Pitcher, AOP, 6³/₄″	125.00
Pitcher, PAT, flat, 8″	90.00
Pitcher, PAT, footed, 8″	100.00
Plate, bread and butter, 6″	20.00
Plate, dinner, 9″	40.00
Plate, grill, 9¹/₄″	45.00
Plate, salad, 7″	25.00
Platter, oval, 11″	50.00
Platter, round, 13″	60.00
Platter, round, divided, 13″	75.00

Saucer	15.00
Sherbet	20.00
Sugar, covered, 4⁵/₈″	60.00
Tray, sandwich, 10¹/₂″	50.00
Tumbler, flat, PAT, 3¹/₂″	25.00
Tumbler, flat, PAT, 4¹/₄″	40.00
Tumbler, flat, PAT, 5″	60.00
Tumbler, footed, AOP, 3³/₄″	25.00
Tumbler, footed, AOP, round foot, 4¹/₂″	50.00
Tumbler, footed, AOP, scalloped foot, 4¹/₂″	55.00

Jeannette Glass Company, Iris, crystal

Iris was manufactured mainly in crystal and iridescent, with some pieces produced in pink and green. Most crystal pieces were produced between 1928 and 1932, though additional pieces were created in the 1940s and 1950s, and some candy dishes and vases were made as late as the 1970s.

Bowl, cereal, 5″	$100.00
Bowl, fruit, beaded edge, 4¹/₂″	50.00
Bowl, fruit, beaded edge, 8″	90.00
Bowl, fruit, ruffled edge, 11¹/₂″	25.00
Bowl, fruit, straight edge, 11″	75.00
Bowl, salad, ruffled edge, 9¹/₂″	25.00
Bowl, sauce, ruffled edge, 5″	15.00
Bowl, soup, 7¹/₂″	150.00
Bud Vase, 9″	35.00
Butter Dish, covered, round	55.00
Candlestick, double light	25.00

Candy Dish, covered	125.00	Plate, dinner, 9″	50.00
Champagne, 4″	22.00	Plate, luncheon, 8″	100.00
Coaster	75.00	Plate, sandwich, 11³/₄″	40.00
Cocktail, 4¹/₄″	25.00	Saucer	15.00
Creamer, footed, 3¹/₂″	15.00	Saucer, demitasse	20.00
Cup	20.00	Sherbet, 2¹/₄″	25.00
Cup, demitasse	25.00	Sugar, covered, 5¹/₂″	32.00
Iced Tea, footed, 6⁵/₈″	40.00	Sugar, open, 3¹/₄″	17.00
Juice, flat, 4″	125.00	Tumbler, footed, 6¹/₈″	25.00
Nappy, 5″	12.00	Vase, 9″	50.00
Pitcher, footed, 9¹/₂″	50.00	Water Goblet	37.00
Plate, 5¹/₂″	15.00	Wine, 4¹/₄″	22.00

Walter Scott Lenox and Jonathan Coxon Sr. founded the Ceramic Art Company in Trenton, New Jersey, in 1889. Lenox acquired sole ownership in 1894. In 1906, he formed Lenox, Inc.

Lenox's goal was to create an American-made ware that resembled Belleek, a thin porcelain of high quality manufactured in Ireland. Lenox's breakthrough came when Tiffany and Company in New York displayed its first complete dinner service and when President Woodrow Wilson ordered a set of Lenox dinnerware for the White House.

In the 1960s, Lenox decided to expand its tabletop product lines. Following its practice of keeping its production American-based, Lenox acquired Bryce Brothers, a glassmaking firm established in 1896 to manufacture handblown stemware for hotel and household use. The company's factory was in Mt. Pleasant, Pennsylvania. Bryce Brothers' stemware was etched, engraved, and hand-decorated.

Like many other glass manufacturers, Bryce Brothers had introduced colored glassware to their line in the 1920s. The company was known for stemware that featured a crystal top and a colored stem. Lenox Corporation acquired Bryce Brothers in 1965 and renamed it Lenox Crystal.

Lenox Crystal patterns were designed to coordinate with the complete selection of Lenox China. An aggressive marketing program geared toward brides was launched, making Lenox Crystal a leading choice of American brides. The vice president of the United States and the U.S. State Department's embassies around the world use Lenox Crystal.

Other post-1960 acquisitions included Art Carved, Inc., Dansk International, Hartmann Luggage, the Imperial Glass Corporation, Kirk Stieff and its wholly owned subsidiary Gorham Silver, and H. Rosenthal Jewelry Corporation. Today, the company's various divisions are grouped under the Lenox Brands umbrella.

In 1985, Lenox dedicated a new plant in Oxford, North Carolina, to manufacture Lenox fine china gifts. The Kinston, North Carolina, plant, opened in 1991, enables Lenox to keep pace with the rapid growth in the china industry.

Lenox Crystal, Allegro, Allegro Shape, crystal

Champagne, 5⅝"	$37.00
Champagne, fluted, 8⅜"	40.00
Iced Tea, 8⅜"	40.00
Water Goblet, 8¼"	40.00
Wine, 7⅝"	40.00

Lenox Crystal, Antique, Antique Shape, blue

Champagne, 5"	$22.00
Iced Tea, 6⅝"	25.00
Water Goblet, 6¾"	25.00
Wine, 5"	25.00

Lenox Crystal, Allure, Bel Canto Shape, crystal

Champagne, 5⅝"	$40.00
Champagne, fluted	45.00
Iced Tea, 6⅝"	40.00
Water Goblet, 7⅝"	40.00
Wine, 6¾"	45.00

Allure by Lenox. *Photo courtesy of Lenox, Inc.*

Lenox Crystal, Antique, Antique Shape, crystal

Champagne, 5″	$30.00
Highball, 5″	32.00
Iced Tea, 6³/₄″	32.00
Juice, 6″	30.00
Old Fashioned, 3³/₈″	32.00
Water Goblet, 6³/₄″	32.00
Wine, 5″	32.00

Lenox Crystal, Ariel, Allegro Shape, crystal, platinum trim

Champagne, 5⁵/₈″	$45.00
Champagne, fluted, 8³/₈″	45.00
Iced Tea, 8¹/₄″	45.00
Water Goblet, 8¹/₄″	45.00
Wine, 7³/₄″	45.00

Lenox Crystal, Aria, Aria Shape, crystal

Champagne, 6¹/₄″	$40.00
Champagne, fluted, 9¹/₄″	27.00
Iced Tea, 8″	30.00
Water Goblet, 8¹/₂″	27.00
Wine, 7⁵/₈″	27.00

Lenox Crystal, Atrium, Allegro Shape, crystal, gold trim

Champagne, 5⁵/₈″	$35.00
Champagne, fluted, 8³/₈″	40.00
Iced Tea, 8³/₈″	40.00
Water Goblet, 8³/₈″	40.00
Wine, 7⁵/₈″	45.00

Lenox Crystal, Autumn, Barclay Shape, crystal, gold trim

Champagne, 5$^{1}/_{8}$″	$80.00
Iced Tea	80.00
Water Goblet	90.00
Wine	90.00

Lenox Crystal, Brookdale, Romance Shape, crystal, cut

Champagne, 5$^{1}/_{4}$″	$40.00
Iced Tea, 6$^{1}/_{2}$″	40.00
Juice, 5$^{1}/_{4}$″	40.00
Water Goblet	40.00
Wine	40.00

Lenox Crystal, Blue Mist, Expression Shape, blue

Champagne, 5″	$17.00
Champagne, fluted	20.00
Iced Tea, 6$^{3}/_{8}$″	25.00
Water Goblet, 7$^{1}/_{8}$″	25.00
Wine, 6$^{1}/_{4}$″	25.00

Lenox Crystal, Castle Garden, Bel Canto Shape, crystal, etched

Champagne	$40.00
Champagne, fluted	40.00
Iced Tea, 6$^{5}/_{8}$″	40.00
Water Goblet, 7$^{5}/_{8}$″	40.00
Wine, 6$^{3}/_{4}$″	40.00

Lenox Crystal, Charleston, Liberty Shape, crystal, cut

Bell, $6^{1}/_{4}''$	$45.00
Brandy, 5''	45.00
Champagne	32.00
Champagne, fluted, 8''	32.00
Highball, $5^{7}/_{8}''$	15.00
Iced Tea, $6^{3}/_{4}''$	37.00
Old Fashioned, double, 4''	15.00
Pitcher, pint, $5^{1}/_{8}''$	70.00
Water Goblet, $7^{1}/_{2}''$	32.00
Wine, $6^{3}/_{4}''$	32.00

Lenox Crystal, Clarity, Romance Shape, crystal, cut

Champagne	$27.00
Champagne, fluted, $8^{3}/_{8}''$	27.00
Iced Tea, $7^{3}/_{8}''$	30.00

Water Goblet, $7^{3}/_{4}''$	27.00
Wine, 7''	27.00

Lenox Crystal, Classic Laurel, Classic Shape, crystal, cut, gold trim

Champagne	$45.00
Champagne, fluted, $8^{3}/_{4}''$	45.00
Iced Tea	45.00
Water Goblet	45.00
Wine	45.00

Lenox Crystal, Classic Shell, Classic Shape, crystal, gold or platinum trim

Champagne	$40.00
Champagne, fluted	40.00
Iced Tea	40.00
Water Goblet, 8''	40.00
Wine, $7^{1}/_{4}''$	40.00

Lenox Crystal, Desire, Dimension Shape, crystal, platinum trim

Champagne, 5″	$27.00
Champagne, fluted, 7⁵/₈″	27.00
Iced Tea, 6¹/₄″	27.00
Water Goblet, 7″	30.00
Wine, 6³/₈″	32.00

Lenox Crystal, Eternal, Barclay Shape, crystal, gold trim

Champagne, 5¹/₈″	$37.00
Iced Tea, 6⁵/₈″	45.00
Water Goblet	45.00
Wine	45.00

Lenox Crystal, Eclipse, Allegro Shape, crystal, gold trim

Champagne, 5⁵/₈″	$35.00
Champagne, fluted	35.00
Iced Tea, 8¹/₄″	35.00
Water Goblet, 8¹/₄″	35.00
Wine	35.00

Lenox Crystal, Fair Lady, Bel Canto Shape, crystal, etched, platinum trim

Champagne, 5¹/₂″	$50.00
Champagne, fluted	50.00
Iced Tea, 6³/₄″	50.00
Water Goblet, 7¹/₂″	55.00
Wine, 6⁵/₈″	55.00

Lenox Crystal, Firelight, Statuesque Shape, crystal

Champagne	$27.00
Champagne, fluted, 9½″	27.00
Iced Tea, 8¼″	30.00
Water Goblet, 8½″	27.00
Wine, 7¾″	27.00

Lenox Crystal, Fontaine, Bel Canto Shape, crystal, etched, gold trim

Champagne, 5½″	$50.00
Champagne, fluted	55.00
Iced Tea	50.00
Water Goblet	50.00
Wine, 6¾″	55.00

Lenox Crystal, Green Mist, Expression Shape, green

Champagne, 5″	$25.00
Champagne, fluted	27.00
Iced Tea	30.00
Water Goblet, 7⅛″	30.00
Wine, 6¼″	32.00

Lenox Crystal, Firelight Gold, Statuesque Shape, crystal, gold trim

Champagne	$30.00
Champagne, fluted	$30.00
Iced Tea, 8¼″	32.00
Water Goblet, 8½″	30.00
Wine	30.00

Lenox Crystal, Hayworth, Bel Canto Shape, crystal, gold trim

Champagne, 5⅝″	$45.00
Champagne, fluted	50.00
Iced Tea, 6⅝″	50.00
Water Goblet, 7½″	50.00
Wine, 6⅝″	50.00

Lenox Crystal, Intrigue, Dimension Shape, crystal, gold trim

Champagne, 5⅛″	$30.00
Champagne, fluted, 7⅝″	30.00
Iced Tea, 6¼″	30.00
Water Goblet, 7⅛″	32.00
Wine	32.00

Intrigue by Lenox. *Photo courtesy of Lenox, Inc.*

Lenox Crystal, Lace Point, Dimension Shape, crystal, etched, platinum trim

Champagne	$45.00
Champagne, fluted	50.00
Iced Tea	45.00
Water Goblet, $7^{1}/_{8}''$	45.00
Wine, $6^{1}/_{4}''$	50.00

Lenox Crystal, Liberty, Column Shape, crystal, cut, gold trim

Champagne	$55.00
Champagne, fluted, $8^{7}/_{8}''$	55.00
Iced Tea	55.00
Water Goblet	55.00
Wine	55.00

Lenox Crystal, Laurent, Belmont Shape, crystal, gold trim

Champagne, $5''$	$30.00
Iced Tea, $6^{1}/_{2}''$	32.00
Juice, $5^{1}/_{8}''$	30.00
Water Goblet	32.00
Wine	32.00

Lenox Crystal, Madison, Aria Shape, crystal, platinum trim

Champagne	$30.00
Champagne, fluted, $9^{1}/_{4}''$	30.00
Iced Tea	32.00
Water Goblet, $8^{1}/_{2}''$	30.00
Wine, $7^{5}/_{8}''$	30.00

Lenox Crystal, Mansfield, Romance Shape, crystal, gold trim

Champagne, 5¹/₄″	$32.00
Iced Tea, 6⁵/₈″	35.00
Water Goblet, 7″	35.00
Wine	35.00

Lenox Crystal, McKinley, Column Shape, crystal, gold trim

Champagne, 5³/₄″	$40.00
Champagne, fluted, 9″	25.00
Iced Tea, 7⁵/₈″	30.00
Water Goblet, 8³/₈″	25.00
Wine, 7³/₈″	25.00

Lenox Crystal, Maywood, Bel Canto Shape, crystal, platinum trim

Champagne, 5⁵/₈″	$45.00
Champagne, fluted, 8″	45.00
Iced Tea, 6⁵/₈″	45.00
Water Goblet, 7¹/₂″	45.00
Wine, 6⁵/₈″	45.00

Lenox Crystal, Monroe, Aria Shape, crystal, gold trim

Champagne	$30.00
Champagne, fluted, 9¹/₄″	30.00
Iced Tea, 7⁷/₈″	32.00
Water Goblet, 8¹/₂″	30.00
Wine, 7⁵/₈″	30.00

Lenox Crystal, Montclair, Romance Shape, crystal, platinum trim

Champagne, $5^3/_8''$	$32.00
Iced Tea	35.00
Water Goblet, 7"	37.00
Wine	37.00

Lenox Crystal, Navarre, Navarre Shape, blue, etched

Champagne	$45.00
Champagne, fluted	50.00
Iced Tea, $5^7/_8''$	45.00
Water Goblet	50.00
Wine	50.00

Lenox Crystal, Moonspun, Dimension Shape, crystal, etched, platinum trim

Champagne	$40.00
Champagne, fluted, $7^5/_8''$	40.00
Iced Tea, $6^1/_4''$	40.00
Water Goblet, $7^1/_8''$	40.00
Wine, $6^3/_8''$	40.00

Lenox Crystal, Navarre, Navarre Shape, crystal, etched

Champagne	$50.00
Champagne, fluted, 8"	50.00
Iced Tea	50.00
Water Goblet, $7^5/_8''$	50.00
Wine, $6^1/_2''$	50.00

Lenox Crystal, Radiance, Belmont Shape, crystal, cut

Champagne, 5″	$35.00
Iced Tea	35.00
Water Goblet, 7″	45.00
Wine, 6¹/₈″	50.00

Lenox Crystal, Solitaire, Barclay Shape, crystal, platinum trim

Champagne, 5¹/₈″	$32.00
Iced Tea, 6⁵/₈″	37.00
Water Goblet	37.00
Wine	37.00

Lenox Crystal, Sea Swirl, Statuesque Shape, crystal, cut

Champagne	$40.00
Champagne, fluted, 9¹/₂″	40.00
Iced Tea, 8³/₈″	40.00
Water Goblet, 8³/₈″	45.00
Water Goblet, 8⁵/₈″	45.00
Wine, 7³/₄″	45.00

THE TOP FIVE PATTERNS CONTEMPORARY

LENOX, ALLEGRO

LENOX, SEA SWIRL

LENOX, WINDSWEPT

MIKASA, OLYMPUS

SASAKI, WINGS

Lenox Crystal, Starfire, Allegro Shape, crystal, cut

Champagne, 5⅝″	$35.00
Champagne, fluted, 8⅜″	40.00
Iced Tea, 8⅜″	35.00
Water Goblet, 8¼″	37.00
Wine	37.00

Lenox Crystal, Weatherly, Belmont Shape, crystal, platinum trim

Champagne, 5″	$35.00
Iced Tea, 6½″	40.00
Water Goblet, 7″	40.00
Wine	40.00

Lenox Crystal, Tuxedo, Romance Shape, crystal, gold etched

Champagne, 5¼″	$45.00
Iced Tea, 6½″	55.00
Water Goblet, 7″	55.00
Wine	55.00

Lenox Crystal, Wheat, Dimension Shape, crystal, etched, platinum trim

Champagne, 5⅛″	$35.00
Champagne, fluted	35.00
Iced Tea	35.00
Juice	35.00
Water Goblet	35.00
Wine	35.00

Lenox Crystal, Windswept, Statuesque Shape, crystal

Candlestick, $7^{1}/_{8}''$	$35.00
Champagne	25.00
Champagne, fluted, $9^{1}/_{2}''$	25.00
Highball, $6''$	15.00
Iced Tea, $8^{1}/_{4}''$	30.00
Water Goblet, $8^{5}/_{8}''$	25.00
Wine, $7^{7}/_{8}''$	25.00

Mikasa, meaning "The Company," was established in 1948. It is a designer, developer, and marketer of a wide range of tabletop products, including casual and formal dinnerware, crystal stemware and serving pieces, stainless steel flatware, and gifts and decorative accessories.

Mikasa owns no manufacturing facilities. Instead, it relies on its thirty-plus-year relationship with more than 150 manufacturers in twenty-two countries to produce its products. Mikasa takes pride in the fact that its manufacturers blend the master craftsmanship of old-world artisans with the most advanced technology of the twentieth century.

The Mikasa Crystal collection features the highest-quality crystal, enhanced by the cutting and application of rich metallic bands. Patterns range from formal to casual.

Mikasa, Arctic Lights, crystal, cut, Prestige Collection (Pattern XY701)

Brandy, 5³/₄″	$25.00
Candleholder, 8″	30.00
Champagne, 6¹/₂″	25.00
Champagne, fluted, 10³/₄″	25.00
Cordial, 7″	25.00
Decanter	85.00
Highball, 5¹/₄″	25.00
Hock, 8¹/₄″	30.00
Ice Bucket, 5″	55.00
Iced Tea, 8¹/₂″	25.00
Old Fashioned, double	25.00
Pitcher	75.00
Water Goblet, 9″	25.00
Wine, 8¹/₈″	25.00

Mikasa, Briarcliffe, crystal, platinum trim, Transitional Stemware (Pattern TS102)

Champagne, fluted, 9³/₄″	$27.00
Cordial	30.00
Iced Tea	25.00
Old Fashioned, double, 3⁵/₈″	22.00
Water Goblet, 8³/₈″	27.00
Wine, 8¹/₈″	27.00

Mikasa, Cameo, crystal, cut, Prestige Stemware (Pattern 57640)

Champagne, 6³/₈″	$35.00
Champagne, fluted	35.00
Cordial, 5¹/₂″	35.00
Iced Tea	45.00
Water Goblet	45.00
Wine, 7¹/₄″	45.00

Mikasa, Gold Crown, crystal, cut, gold trim, Transitional Stemware (Pattern 40061)

Champagne, 6″	$35.00
Champagne, fluted, 8½″	37.00
Cordial, 5⅛″	35.00
Iced Tea, 7″	37.00
Water Goblet	37.00
Wine	37.00

Mikasa, Olympus, crystal, cut, gold trim, Prestige Collection (Pattern XY703)

Bud Vase, 9¼″	$25.00
Champagne, fluted, 10⅞″	20.00
Cordial, 7″	20.00
Highball, 5⅜″	15.00
Iced Tea, 8⅜″	20.00
Water Goblet, 9″	20.00
Wine, 8¼″	20.00

Mikasa, Jamestown, crystal, gold trim, Transitional Stemware (Pattern T2703)

Candlestick, 7⅞″	$15.00
Champagne, fluted, 9¼″	15.00
Cordial	17.00
Iced Tea, 8⅛″	15.00
Old Fashioned, 3⅜″	12.00
Water Goblet, 9⅛″	15.00
Wine, 8¾″	15.00

Mikasa, Park Avenue, crystal, cut, Transitional Stemware (Pattern TS115)

Brandy	$25.00
Candlestick, 6¼″	20.00
Champagne, fluted	25.00
Cordial, 6⅜″	25.00
Highball, 5⅜″	20.00
Iced Tea	25.00

Water Goblet	25.00
Wine	25.00

Mikasa, Park Lane, crystal, Park Lane Collection (Pattern SN101)

Candlestick, 8″	$17.00
Candy Dish, covered, footed	35.00
Champagne, 5¹/₈″	12.00
Champagne, fluted, 8³/₄″	12.00
Condiment Jar, covered	25.00
Cordial, 5″	10.00
Decanter	55.00
Highball, 5³/₄″	10.00
Iced Tea, 7³/₈″	12.00
Mug, 4³/₈″	12.00
Old Fashioned, 3³/₄″	10.00
Old Fashioned, double, 3⁷/₈″	10.00
Pitcher	60.00
Rose Bowl, 5″	45.00
Water Goblet, 6⁷/₈″	10.00
Wine, 6³/₈″	10.00

Mikasa, Seamist, crystal, frosted stem, Fashion Stemware (Pattern 24211)

Champagne, fluted, 9¹/₂″	$40.00
Cordial, 6¹/₄″	40.00
Iced Tea, 6⁵/₈″	37.00
Water Goblet, 9¹/₄″	40.00
Wine, 8³/₈″	40.00

Mikasa, Seamist, coral, frosted stem, Fashion Stemware (Pattern 24253)

Champagne, fluted, 9¹/₂″	$40.00
Cordial, 6¹/₄″	40.00
Iced Tea, 6⁵/₈″	37.00
Water Goblet, 9¹/₄″	40.00
Wine, 8³/₈″	40.00

Mikasa, Seville, crystal, rib optic, Prestige Stemware (Pattern 59000)

Champagne	$35.00
Champagne, fluted	37.00
Cordial	35.00
Iced Tea	37.00
Water Goblet	37.00
Wine	37.00

Mikasa, Wheaton, crystal, gold trim, Transitional Stemware (Pattern TS101)

Brandy	$25.00
Champagne, fluted	25.00
Iced Tea, $6^3/_4''$	25.00
Water Goblet, $8^1/_4''$	25.00
Wine, 8″	25.00

Mikasa, Versailles, crystal, cut, Transitional Stemware (Pattern 40062)

Champagne, 6″	$35.00
Champagne, fluted	35.00
Cordial, $5^1/_4''$	32.00
Iced Tea, 7″	40.00
Old Fashioned, $3^1/_2''$	35.00
Water Goblet, 8″	35.00
Wine, $7^1/_8''$	40.00

Rogaska is located in the foothills of the Alps in the small, recently independent country of Slovenia. Italy's Murano, where the art of glassblowing originated, lies to the west. To the north is the Czech Republic and Slovakia, where glass cutting was perfected. Rogaska itself has a glassmaking tradition that is almost 200 years old. The Rogaska Crystal Factory employs about 1,200 workers, many of whom are from the region surrounding the city.

John Miller, founder of Waterford USA and its president for over twenty-five years, saw the same potential in the Rogaska Factory in the 1980s that he saw in Waterford in the 1950s. He challenged Rogaska to think of itself as a world-class crystal manufacturer on the same level as companies like Baccarat, Orrefors, and Waterford. Miller designed and introduced a line of crystal that fit the "bridge" classification—excellent design and quality but moderately priced. Mikasa's Signature and Waterford's Marquis lines were viewed as direct competitors.

Prior to working with John Miller, Rogaska only manufactured crystal under the private label of a retailer, for example, Macy's Gallia. Because the Miller name added credibility, Rogaska agreed to market crystal under its own name, provided that the name Miller was attached to it. The Rogaska Factory allows only Miller Rogaska to distribute its crystal under the "Rogaska" name. Today, Miller Rogaska is part of Reed & Barton.

Miller Rogaska Crystal, Richmond, crystal (Pattern 2903)

Bowl, 5¼" $50.00

Bowl, 8⅛"	50.00
Brandy, 4¾"	25.00
Candlestick, 7⅞"	25.00
Champagne, 6⅛"	25.00
Champagne, fluted, 8⅜"	25.00
Cordial, 5½"	25.00
Decanter, 10¾"	100.00
Highball, 5"	15.00
Highball, 5¼"	15.00
Hock	35.00
Iced Tea, 7¼"	30.00
Old Fashioned, double, 4"	15.00
Pitcher, 7"	130.00
Salt and Pepper Shakers, pair	50.00
Water Goblet, 7⅞"	25.00
Wine, 7⅛"	25.00
Wine, balloon	35.00

Miller Rogaska Crystal, Richmond Gold, crystal, gold trim (Pattern 5703)

Champagne, fluted, 8¼″	$32.00
Highball, 5¼″	30.00
Hock	37.00
Iced Tea, 7⅛″	35.00
Old Fashioned, double, 4″	30.00
Water Goblet, 7⅞″	32.00
Wine, 7⅛″	32.00
Wine, balloon, 8¾″	37.00

NORITAKE
Japan

Ichizaemon Morimura, one of the founders of Noritake, established Morimura-kumi, a Japanese exporting company, in Tokyo in 1867, as well as an import shop in New York to sell traditional Japanese goods.

Attending a Paris World's Fair inspired Morimura to establish a porcelain factory—Nippon Toki Kaisha Ltd., the forerunner of Noritake, in Nagoya, Japan, in 1904. This factory produced the first Japanese white porcelain dinnerware plate. Dinnerware sets for export soon became the company's principal product. In 1932, bone china dinnerware was added to the product line.

The ceramic factory was heavily damaged during World War II. Between 1946 and 1948, the company sold its dinnerware under the "Rose China" label because it did not match the quality of the earlier Noritake. By 1948, quality levels once again met earlier standards. Noritake Company, Inc., established to sell tableware in the United States, was organized that same year. By 1961, Noritake had firmly ensconced itself as a leading producer of every type of dinnerware—bone china, earthenware, ironstone, porcelain, and stoneware.

If the company was to grow, it had to seek new, but related directions. As a result, it expanded its product line to include crystal glassware, a complement to its dinnerware lines.

During the 1960s, Noritake established two factories for the manufacturer of glassware, one making handmade, mouth-blown, full-lead crystal stemware and the other producing sturdy, colorful, casual glassware. Noritake's Paris and Troy crystal patterns and Sweet Swirl casual glassware have proven extremely popular. Noritake also has been successful in marketing a variety of quality crystal giftware.

Today, Noritake has companies, branches, and/or plants in Australia, Canada, Eastern Europe, Germany, Guam, Ireland, the Philippines, Sri Lanka, the United Kingdom, and the United States to manufacture and distribute its products. Crystal is made in Eastern Europe, Germany, and Japan. In 1981, the company changed its name to Noritake Company Limited.

Noritake, Paris, crystal, platinum trim

Brandy, $5^1/_2''$	$17.00
Champagne, $5^3/_8''$	17.00
Champagne, fluted, $8^1/_2''$	17.00
Iced Tea, $7^5/_8''$	17.00
Water Goblet, $7^1/_2''$	17.00
Wine, $7''$	17.00

Noritake, Troy, crystal, gold trim

Champagne, $5^3/_8''$	$17.00
Iced Tea, $7^5/_8''$	17.00
Water Goblet, $7^5/_8''$	17.00
Wine, $7''$	17.00

Noritake, Rhythm, crystal, platinum trim

Champagne, $4^3/_8''$	$27.00
Iced Tea, $7''$	35.00
Water Goblet, $7''$	32.00
Wine, $5^1/_2''$	32.00

Noritake, Virtue, crystal, etched

Champagne, $5^3/_8''$	$45.00
Champagne, fluted, $8^1/_2''$	45.00
Iced Tea, $7^5/_8''$	45.00
Water Goblet, $7^1/_2''$	50.00
Wine, $7''$	50.00

ORREFORS
Orrefors, Sweden

The first glassworks was built in Orrefors in 1898. In the early years, output consisted primarily of jars, lamp shades, perfume vials, table glass, and large pieces. Advances were achieved through the recruitment of workers from other glassworks, such as Kosta, and from the Continent, and by copying glass from more advanced producers.

Production at Orrefors did not become significant until the 1910s, when the glassworks was acquired by Johan Ekman of Gothenburg. In his desire to stress artistic design, Ekman engaged the services of Simon Gate, a portrait and landscape painter, in 1916. Artist Edward Hald arrived the following year. Thus began a tradition of close cooperation between a skilled glassblower and a gifted designer at Orrefors. Products included functional, mass-produced household glass with wide public appeal and art glass in the form of engraved and polished pieces.

Orrefors' international breakthrough came at the 1925 Paris Exhibition. From the Hotel de Ville, the Town Hall of Paris, the Swedish pavilion borrowed a magnificent glass goblet, designed by Simon Gate, which had been presented as a gift to the City of Paris from the City of Stockholm in 1922. Orrefors and the designer received the prestigious Grand Prix award. The publicity surrounding this award attracted gifted glassblowers to Orrefors. The union of glassblowers and artists led to the joint development of techniques such as "Graal" and "Ariel" and to the further development of the traditional Bohemian copper-wheel engraving.

Success led to the arrival of new designers. Graphic artist Vicke Lindstrand arrived in 1928 and created new painted and engraved motifs. Nils Landberg and Sven Palmqvist came at the end of the 1920s as engravers, apprentices, and, after serving as assistants to Simon Gate and Edward Hald, became full-fledged glass artists during the 1930s.

Intensive experimentation and a continuous search for a new means of expression generated results. Orrefors helped launch the concept of Swedish Modern at the 1939–1940 New York World's Fair. Nils Landberg's "Tulip Glass" and Ingeborg Lundin's "Apple" illustrate the graceful, daring glass of the 1950s. Palmqvist's centrifuged bowls created a worldwide stir.

Today, Orrefors continues to create a fresh new approach to color while maintaining its traditional emphasis on elegant, rounded shapes. While its art glass pieces continue to explore the limitless possibilities of glass design, the company's household glass generates its income. It is for this reason that art glass designers also lend their creative talents to developing new household glass products.

Nils Landberg. *Photo courtesy of Orrefors.*

NILS LANDBERG (1907–1991)

After completing his studies at the Swedish Crafts Association School in Gothenburg (1923–1925), Nils Landberg attended the engraving school at Orrefors (1925–1927) and stayed on as a trainer designer under Simon Gate and Edward Hald. Orrefors catalogs of the 1930s and 1940s include a number of restrained, almost nondescript, commercial designs in clear crystal with engravings of animals, equestrian groups, neoclassical figures, and Viking ships.

The slender glass for which Landberg is internationally recognized first appeared in the late 1940s. In 1953, the Tulip series was introduced, with its elongated forms stretching the glass's elasticity and the skills of the glassblowers to the limit. Landberg wanted his pieces gathered and handblown, "manufactured in a natural way," as he described the process.

Landberg expanded the Tulip series in the 1950s by adding new shapes and colors. Thin, globular, and teardrop models evolved. The Illusion and Susan series joined the stemware line; these were complemented with a selection of glassware that was lightly engraved with floral and linear patterns.

Landberg remained at Orrefors until 1972. His fluid shapes are a hallmark of Orrefors and continue to inspire more recent designers such as Lagerbielke. The pieces Landberg designed are included in the collections of the National Museum in Stockholm, the Röhsska Museum in Gothenburg, the Museum of Modern Art in New York, and the Akademie der Bildende Künste in Stuttgart, Germany. Landberg spent his retirement years in the Orrefors community.

Sven Palmqvist. *Photo courtesy of Orrefors.*

SVEN PALMQVIST (1906–1984)

Palmqvist's love of glass began as a young boy when he assisted glassblowers in local glasshouses in his native province of Småland. His education included the engraving school at Orrefors (1928–1930), the College of Technology in Stockholm (1931–1933), and the Royal Academy of Arts, Stockholm (1934–1936). After two years spent studying and traveling in Europe, Palmqvist joined Orrefors in time to assist in the firm's entry for the 1937 International Exposition in Paris.

Palmqvist made major contributions in glass technology and design. Kraka, Ravenna, and Fuga, three major processes, are credited to him. The dazzling church mosaic patterns in the Italian city of Ravenna inspired the Ravenna technique. The Fuga bowl was made possible by Palmqvist perfecting the centrifuge process at Orrefors.

Palmqvist's approach to glass was simple: "Machine made glass should be as simple and functional as possible, although that doesn't preclude its being beautiful. Handmade art glass should be very elegant. I don't believe in any in-between."

In addition to his technological contributions, Palmqvist designed a wide range of Orrefors' standard glassware in shapes and patterns ranging from lightly engraved handblown pieces to undecorated molded examples. Rhapsody is a Palmqvist design.

Palmqvist also designed outdoor sculpture and architectural columns. His two walls of glass blocks interspersed with Ravenna sections for the Swedish Broadcast and TV network in Stockholm earned him worldwide acclaim. He won the Grand Prix in 1957, along with many other international design awards.

Palmqvist retired from Orrefors in 1972. He was a freelance designer for the firm until his death in 1984.

Orrefors, Coronation, crystal, cut

Champagne, 4¹/₂″	$40.00
Champagne, fluted	40.00
Claret	40.00
Cocktail, 3³/₈″	45.00
Cocktail, V-shape, 4¹/₂″	45.00
Cordial, 2⁵/₈″	40.00
Cordial, 3³/₈″	40.00
Finger Bowl, 4¹/₄″	50.00
Iced Tea	45.00
Juice	40.00
Oyster Cocktail	45.00
Parfait	45.00
Sherbet	40.00
Tumbler, flat, 4¹/₈″	40.00
Water Goblet, 5³/₄″	45.00
Water Goblet, 6″	45.00
Wine, 4¹/₂″	45.00

Orrefors, Illusion, crystal (Pattern 1799)

Illusion was designed by Nils Landberg.

Champagne, 5¹/₈″	$30.00
Champagne, 5¹/₄″	30.00
Champagne, fluted, 8³/₈″	35.00
Claret, 7¹/₄″	35.00
Cordial, 5″	32.00
Decanter, 13″	235.00
Iced Tea, footed, 9³/₈″	35.00
Martini, 5¹/₂″	35.00
Old Fashioned, 3″	30.00
Old Fashioned, double, 3⁷/₈″	32.00
Pitcher, 6³/₄″	100.00
Pitcher, 7¹/₄″	100.00
Schnapps, 6⁷/₈″	32.00
Sherry, 6″	32.00
Tumbler, 3³/₈″	30.00
Tumbler, flat, 5³/₄″	32.00
Water Goblet, 8¹/₄″	35.00
Wine, 6″	35.00
Wine, 6¹/₂″	35.00

Orrefors, Rhapsody (Pattern 1850)

Rhapsody was designed by Sven Palmqvist.

Orrefors, Prelude, crystal, cut (Pattern 1800)

Prelude was designed by Nils Landberg.

Champagne, $5^{1}/_{4}''$	$35.00
Champagne, fluted, $8^{1}/_{2}''$	45.00
Claret, $7^{3}/_{8}''$	45.00
Cocktail, $5^{1}/_{2}''$	37.00
Cordial, $5^{1}/_{4}''$	40.00
Decanter, $11^{1}/_{2}''$	240.00
Iced Tea, footed, $9^{3}/_{8}''$	45.00
Martini, $5^{5}/_{8}''$	40.00
Old Fashioned, $3''$	35.00
Old Fashioned, double, $3^{7}/_{8}''$	40.00
Pitcher, $7^{1}/_{8}''$	140.00
Schnapps, $6^{7}/_{8}''$	37.00
Sherry, $5^{3}/_{4}''$	37.00
Tumbler, $3^{3}/_{8}''$	40.00
Tumbler, $5^{1}/_{2}''$	45.00
Water Goblet, $8^{1}/_{4}''$	45.00
Wine, $6''$	45.00
Wine, $6^{5}/_{8}''$	45.00

Crystal

Champagne, $5^{3}/_{8}''$	$30.00
Claret, $6''$	40.00
Cordial, $4^{1}/_{8}''$	32.00
Cordial, $4^{3}/_{8}''$	32.00
Iced Tea	40.00
Schnapps, $4^{3}/_{4}''$	35.00
Sherry, $5''$	32.00
Tumbler, flat, $2^{3}/_{4}''$	32.00
Water Goblet, $7^{1}/_{4}''$	40.00
Wine, $5^{1}/_{4}''$	35.00

Smoke

Champagne, 5³/₈″	$25.00
Claret, 6″	32.00
Cocktail, 4¹/₈″	25.00
Cordial, 4¹/₄″	25.00
Decanter, 9¹/₄″	100.00
Decanter, 9³/₄″	100.00
Decanter, cordial, 9¹/₄″	75.00
Iced Tea	35.00
Old Fashioned, 3¹/₄″	25.00
Old Fashioned, double, 3¹/₂″	25.00
Pitcher, 7″	140.00
Schnapps, 4³/₄″	22.00
Sherry, 5″	25.00
Sherry, 5³/₄″	25.00
Water Goblet, 7³/₈″	32.00

PRINCESS HOUSE, INC.
North Dighton, Massachusetts

Princess House, Inc., is a direct seller of household and tabletop wares headquartered in North Dighton, Massachusetts. It sells its wares primarily through mail-order catalogs and a network of 15,000 independent consultants who demonstrate Princess House products in approximately 500,000 homes each year.

In 1993, Princess House, Inc., was a division of the Colgate-Palmolive Company, with affiliates in Australia, Canada, England, and Mexico. Today, the company is privately owned.

Princess House, Inc., Heritage, crystal

Beer Glass, 5½″	$7.00
Bell	17.00
Bowl, centerpiece, 11⅞″	55.00
Bowl, cereal, 5½″	10.00
Bowl, fruit, 9¾″	22.00
Bowl, revere, 5″	12.00
Bowl, revere, 10″	35.00
Bowl, salad, 9⅞″	40.00
Brandy, 4½″	5.00
Bud Vase, 3¾″	17.00
Bud Vase, 4″	17.00
Bud Vase, 4¼″	17.00
Bud Vase, 5″	17.00

Bud Vase, 5½″	17.00
Bud Vase, 7″	17.00
Bud Vase, 10″	17.00
Bud Vase, 10¼″	17.00
Butter Dish, covered, round	15.00
Cake Plate, dome cover, footed, 12¼″	50.00
Candle Lamp, 9″	30.00
Candy Dish, covered, 7¼″	15.00
Candy Dish, covered, 7¾″	15.00
Candy Dish, covered, 8½″	15.00
Candy Dish, covered, 9″	15.00
Candy Dish, covered, apple, 5½″	15.00
Champagne, 4⅞″	5.00
Champagne, fluted, 10″	15.00
Champagne, tulip	12.00
Chip and Dip Set, 11¼″	30.00
Cocktail, 5″	5.00
Cooler, 7⅛″	5.00
Creamer, 2¾″	10.00
Decanter, 15″	27.00
Fruit, apple, 3¼″	17.00
Fruit, pear, 3¼″	17.00
Gravy Boat	25.00
Hurricane Lamp, 11¾″	27.00
Ice Bucket, 5½″	35.00
Ice Bucket, 5⅝″	35.00
Iced Tea	7.00
Iced Tea, flat, 6¾″	5.00
Jar, utility, 6¼″	20.00

Jar, utility, 9″	22.00	Plate, luncheon, 8″	7.00
Juice, 4¹/₂″	5.00	Platter, oval, 18″	40.00
Juice, flat, 3¹/₂″	5.00	Punch Bowl, with twelve punch cups	
Margarita, 7″	10.00	and ladle	75.00
Mug, 5¹/₈″	12.00	Salt and Pepper Shakers, pair, 4¹/₄″	12.00
Mug, 5¹/₂″	12.00	Sherbet, 4³/₈″	7.00
Parfait, 6¹/₈″	5.00	Sugar, covered	10.00
Pilsner, 7¹/₂″	7.00	Sugar, open, 2⁵/₈″	7.00
Pitcher, 5¹/₂″	27.00	Tumbler, flat, 5″	5.00
Pitcher, 6¹/₄″	27.00	Vase, 8⁵/₈″	25.00
Pitcher, 9¹/₂″	27.00	Vase, 11″	40.00
Pitcher, 10¹/₂″	27.00	Water Goblet	7.00
Pitcher, pint, 6¹/₂″	25.00	Wine, 6″	7.00

Japan's Sasaki Crystal was established in 1902. Today, this family-owned business is one of the largest privately held and operated manufacturers and distributors of fine crystal products. It is committed to providing customers with affordable, innovative designs of lasting quality.

In 1977, Sasaki Inc., a subsidiary of the parent company, opened offices in New York. Within a short period, it became one of the leaders in the tabletop industry. Today, the company offers a full assortment of fine crystal stemware, porcelain and stoneware dinnerware, stainless steel flatware, fine crystal, and art glass giftware.

Sasaki also is known for its double-rolled edge commercial dinnerware, used by such restaurants as Vong, the Zen Palate, the Rattle Snake Grill, and Jo Jo's. In addition, restaurants such as Le Cirque in New York City have commissioned Sasaki to manufacture dinnerware bearing their logo.

Sasaki draws on a large pool of talent, including furniture, industrial, jewelry, and textile designers, architects, interior decorators, and sculptors to develop new product lines. Sasaki's Double Helix flatware, designed by Ward Bennet, is on permanent exhibit at the Museum of Modern Art in New York.

ETUSO YAMAGISHI

Etuso Yamagishi, designer of the Wings pattern, was born in Nagano, Japan, in 1953. After graduating from the Tokyo University of Arts, he joined Sasaki Glass Co., Ltd.

Yamagishi designed the Wings suite between 1980 and 1982, which consists of sixteen items—stemware, candleholder, compote, dinner bell, jewelry tray, plate, and perfume bottle. Between 1982 and 1986, Yamagishi developed a series of crystal music instruments, including an Alpen horn, bell, harp, and xylophone.

In 1986, Yamagishi moved to New York and was employed by Vignell Associates. From 1987 to 1988, he worked for Sasaki Crystal in New Jersey, where he designed the Charade, Engagement, and Omnia suites.

Yamagishi moved back to Tokyo and the Sasaki Glass Co., Ltd., in 1998. In 1996, Yamagishi became their marketing and chief planning manager.

**Sasaki, Wings, crystal, frosted stem
(Pattern A2923)**

Wings was designed by Etsuo Yamagishi.

Champagne, $4\frac{1}{2}''$	$40.00
Champagne, fluted	50.00
Cigarette Holder	70.00
Cocktail, $4\frac{1}{8}''$	50.00
Cordial, $3\frac{7}{8}''$	45.00
Decanter, 12″	160.00
Hock, 7″	80.00
Iced Tea, $6\frac{3}{8}''$	50.00
Juice, $3\frac{7}{8}''$	45.00
Pitcher, $8\frac{3}{8}''$	200.00
Pitcher, bar, no handle, 6″	130.00
Port, $4\frac{7}{8}''$	50.00
Sherbet, 4″	50.00
Sherry, $4\frac{7}{8}''$	55.00
Water Goblet	45.00
Wine	50.00

STUART CRYSTAL
Wordsley, Stourbridge, England

Glassmaking arrived in England's Stourbridge district when a group of Huguenot craftsmen fled religious persecution in Europe at the end of the sixteenth century. They were attracted to the Stourbridge region because of its fine clay for use in making crucibles and coal, a new fuel used for firing the furnaces.

Two hundred years later, glass manufacture had progressed from window and bottle making to fine tablewares. Four new cone glasshouses were built close to the new Stourbridge Canal in Wordsley. Two of these cones, the Redhouse (now preserved as a working museum) and the Whitehouse, were to become part of the home of Stuart Crystal.

At age eleven, in 1827, Frederick Stuart was apprenticed to Richard Bradley Ensell at the Redhouse. Ensell died a few months later, and his son sold the business to the Rufford family, owners of the Heath Glassworks in Stourbridge. Stuart continued his training with the Ruffords. In 1834, Messrs. Hodgetts and Davies, glassmakers from Dudley, leased the Redhouse. Stuart left to work for Messrs. John Parrish & Company, a glass-cutting business.

The fine glass pieces exhibited by Stourbridge glassmakers at the 1851 Crystal Palace Exhibition in London called attention to the high-quality products originating in this region. Richard Mills and Thomas Webb asked Frederick Stuart to form a partnership and to establish a new glasshouse with their sons. The Albert Glasshouse, the last of the Stourbridge cones, was built a few hundred yards away from the Redhouse on Bridge Street in Wordsley. Following a larger order for the steamship *Great Eastern* in 1876, the firm became major contractors to the shipping trade until the last voyage of the R. M. S. *Queen Elizabeth* in 1970.

By 1880, George Mills had expressed a preference for making chandeliers and lighting wares, while Frederick Stuart and three of his sons were more enamored with the glassmaking next door at the Redhouse. When Philip Pargeter, who was responsible for the rediscovery of cameo glass, decided not to renew his lease on the Redhouse, the Stuarts assumed the lease and formed Stuart & Sons. Between 1880 and 1900, William and Robert Stuart became major innovators of intricate Victorian colored glass, producing between 600 and 1,000 new designs each year. Frederick Jr., Frederick's second son, specialized in the development of color mixes.

Expansion of form and design continued throughout the twentieth century. John Hambrey's cutting shop gave Stuart an individual style of cut crystal. Bohemian artist Ludwig Kny added a lively style of polished engraving. A Stuart acid polishing technique allowed the company to market rich Rock Crystal Wine Services in America, some fifteen years after the original work had been written off as being too expensive commercially.

In 1921, Stuart built a new ten-pot furnace between the old Whitehouse cone and canal. The name "Stuart Crystal" and the practice of etching the name *Stuart* on every piece produced were introduced for the first time in 1927.

In 1934, Harrod's mounted an exhibition of pieces from Stuart, Foley China, and Royal Staffordshire pottery, designed by new artists such as Eric Ravilious, Dame Laura Knight, and Graham Sutherland. Geoffrey Stuart, a member of the fourth generation of the Stuart family, contributed a number of Art Deco designs using a combination of straight cuts and carved intaglio lines.

Inexpensive utility ware, colored glass, and transferred enamels supported the business through the early 1950s, when the world market for crystal glass was reestablished. Stuart trained a new generation of glass cutters to meet the demand. Many of the new designs from this period were the creation of G. John Luxton, A.R.C.A., a designer who joined the firm in 1948.

In 1966, Stuart Crystal established a factory in South Wales. In 1980, the firm assumed the management of Strathearn Glass at Crieff in the heart of Scotland. A gilding and decorating studio at the Board School Works, Chepstow, was opened in 1983.

Throughout its long history, Stuart Crystal has been managed by members of the Stuart family. Most of its fourth-generation members retired in the 1970s, replaced by fifth-generation family members.

Stuart Crystal, Hampshire, crystal, cut

Champagne, $4^1/_2''$	$60.00
Cigarette Holder	70.00

Claret	60.00
Cocktail, $4^1/_8''$	60.00
Cordial, $3^7/_8''$	60.00
Finger Bowl	50.00
Hock, $7''$	80.00
Iced Tea, footed, $6^3/_8''$	85.00
Juice, footed, $3^7/_8''$	60.00
Old Fashioned	80.00
Oyster Cocktail	80.00
Pitcher, $8^3/_8''$	200.00
Pitcher, bar, no handle, $6''$	130.00
Plate, $7''$	100.00
Plate, $8''$	125.00
Port, $4^7/_8''$	70.00
Sherbet, $4''$	50.00
Sherry, $4^7/_8''$	60.00
Tumbler	70.00
Water Goblet	80.00

J. Beatty and Sons built a large glasshouse in Tiffin, Ohio, in 1888 to sell blown and pressed glassware in the United States and abroad. In 1892, Tiffin Glass Company became part of the U. S. Glass Company, a combine based in Pittsburgh, Pennsylvania. The Tiffin plant was designated as factory "R."

Initially, factory "R" made only pressed tumblers and barware. However, by the early 1900s, production had expanded to include lighter-weight stemware and brilliant cut glass. From 1910 to 1920, the product line was expanded further, with the addition of blown, cut, and etched dinnerware and stemware patterns in crystal and color. Shapes included cake plates, candleholders, candy dishes, centerpieces, decanters, jugs, and vases. The Flanders line, made between 1914 and 1935, included over seventy shapes.

Tiffin billed itself as "America's Prestige Crystal . . . within reach of the limited budget." During the depression, Tiffin made hundreds of patterns, its output doubling that of Cambridge and A. H. Heisey. Tiffin purchased Heisey blanks to meet its production requirements. The company's famed "Lady Stems" were made between 1939 and 1956.

Tiffin's profits carried many other plants in the U. S. Glass Company. Several operations making inexpensive glassware were closed or sold during the depression. In 1937, the main office of the U. S. Glass Company moved from Pittsburgh to the Tiffin factory in Steubenville.

In 1938, C. W. Carlson Sr. became president of the U. S. Glass Company. Under his leadership and that of his son, C. W. Carlson Jr. Tiffin was rejuvenated. New shapes and colors were added to the Tiffin line. Swedish-trained craftsmen were responsible for the handblown, handcrafted Swedish line, introduced in 1940.

By 1951, Tiffin was the only U. S. Glass Company plant in operation. U. S. Glass Company purchased Duncan & Miller in 1955 and moved some of the company's molds and glassmakers to Steubenville. The new Duncan patterns by Tiffin included Countess and Wistaria.

In the 1950s, Tiffin Modern was introduced. The line featured free-flowing accent pieces such as ashtrays, flower baskets, and vases in a variety of colors, including twilight and smoke, twilight and green, ruby and crystal, and crystal and smoke. C. W. Carlson Sr. retired in 1959.

The early 1960s proved to be very difficult for the U. S. Glass Company. It declared bankruptcy in 1962 and closed the Tiffin factory. Production resumed under the "Tiffin Art Glass Corporation," a firm created by C. W. Carlson Jr. and several former Tiffin employees. Tiffin Art Glass produced high-quality, etched stemware and other glass accent pieces. The company also offered a "Pattern Matching Program," annually manufacturing retired patterns. The phrase "Tiffin is Forever" was used to publicize the program.

Tiffin purchased the molds and equipment of the T. G. Hawkes Cut Glass Company, in Corning, New York, in 1964. Hawkes' Delft Diamond and Laurel were continued in production.

Continental Can purchased the Tiffin factory in 1966, selling it in 1968 to the Interpace Corporation, a holding company of Franciscan china. Interpace kept many Tiffin patterns in production, including Palais Versailles. In addition, Madeira, made in colors identified as Blue, Citron, Cornsilk, Ice, Plum, Olive, and Smoke, was created to coordinate with Franciscan dinnerware patterns.

Tiffin was sold once again in 1980, this time to Towle Silversmiths. Towle began importing blanks from Eastern Europe. In 1984, Towle closed the Tiffin factory and donated the land and buildings to the city of Tiffin.

Jim Maxwell, a former Tiffin Glass cutter, bought the Tiffin molds and equipment. The Tiffin trademark is now a registered trademark of Maxwell Crystal, Inc. In 1992, Maxwell placed four Hawkes and Tiffin patterns back into production.

Tiffin, Cherokee Rose, crystal, etched (No. 17399—teardrop stem)

Cherokee Rose, produced in crystal only, was one of Tiffin's most popular patterns made during the 1940s and 1950s.

Bowl, crimped, 12″	$75.00
Bowl, fruit, 6″	30.00
Bowl, salad, 7″	45.00
Bowl, salad, 10″	75.00
Bud Vase, 6⁵/₈″	37.00

Bud Vase, 8¹/₈″	50.00
Bud Vase, 10⁵/₈″	55.00
Celery, 10¹/₂″	75.00
Champagne, 5³/₄″	27.00
Claret	60.00
Cocktail, 5¹/₂″	32.00
Compote, 6″	50.00
Cordial	60.00
Creamer	30.00
Finger Bowl, 5″	35.00
Iced Tea	37.00
Juice, 5″	27.00
Oyster Cocktail	30.00
Parfait	60.00
Plate, 6″	20.00
Plate, beaded, 8¹/₈″	30.00
Plate, luncheon, 8″	25.00
Relish, three-part, 6⁵/₈″	60.00
Relish, three-part, 12¹/₂″	60.00
Sherbet, 4¹/₄″	32.00
Sherry	45.00
Sugar, open, flat, 3¹/₄″	37.00
Tray, center handle, 12″	100.00
Water Goblet	35.00
Wine, 5⁷/₈″	45.00

Tray, center handle, 12″	100.00
Water Goblet, 8¹/₈″	35.00
Wine, 5⁷/₈″	45.00

Tiffin, Cherokee Rose, crystal, etched (No. 17403)

Cherokee Rose, produced in crystal only, was one of Tiffin's most popular patterns made during the 1940s and 1950s.

Bowl, crimped, 12″	$75.00
Bowl, fruit, 6″	30.00
Bowl, salad, 7″	45.00
Bowl, salad, 10″	75.00
Bud Vase, 6⁵/₈″	37.00
Bud Vase, 8¹/₈″	50.00
Bud Vase, 10⁵/₈″	55.00
Celery, 10¹/₂″	75.00
Champagne, 5⁷/₈″	27.00
Claret	60.00
Cocktail, 5¹/₂″	32.00
Compote, 6″	50.00
Cordial	60.00
Creamer	30.00
Finger Bowl, 5″	35.00
Iced Tea, 6¹/₂″	37.00
Juice, 5″	27.00
Oyster Cocktail	30.00
Parfait	60.00
Plate, 6″	20.00
Plate, beaded, 8¹/₈″	30.00
Plate, luncheon, 8″	25.00
Relish, three-part, 6⁵/₈″	60.00
Relish, three-part, 12¹/₂″	60.00
Sherbet, 4¹/₄″	32.00
Sherry	45.00
Sugar, open, flat, 3¹/₄″	37.00

Tiffin, Elyse, crystal, cut (No. 17863)

Champagne, 5³/₄″	$40.00
Claret	45.00
Cocktail	40.00
Cordial, 5″	45.00
Finger Bowl	45.00
Iced Tea	50.00
Juice	40.00
Nappy	45.00
Plate, salad, 8″	50.00
Water Goblet, 7³/₈″	60.00

Tiffin, June Night, crystal, etched (No. 17392)

June Night, available in crystal only, was produced during the 1940s and 1950s. It was produced on four Tiffin stemware lines, including No. 17378, No. 17392, No. 17441, and No. 17471.

Bowl, crimped, 12″	$140.00
Bowl, fruit, 6″	40.00
Bowl, salad, 7″	60.00
Bowl, salad, 10″	125.00
Bud Vase, 6″	35.00
Bud Vase, 8″	50.00
Bud Vase, 10½″	55.00
Champagne, 6⅛″	32.00
Claret	50.00
Cocktail, 5¼″	32.00
Cordial, 5⅛″	50.00
Creamer, flat, 3⅛″	40.00
Finger Bowl, 4¾″	40.00
Iced Tea, footed	35.00
Juice, footed	25.00
Oyster Cocktail	30.00
Parfait	40.00
Plate, 6½″	30.00
Plate, luncheon, 8″	40.00
Relish, three-part, 6½″	75.00
Relish, three-part, 12½″	125.00
Sherry	50.00
Sugar, open, 3⅛″	40.00
Water Goblet, 7⅞″	35.00
Wine, 5½″	45.00

Tiffin, King's Crown (No. 4016)

King's Crown, also known as Thumbprint, was introduced by the U. S. Glass Co. in the late 1800s. The U. S. Glass Co.'s Tiffin Division continued to produce this pattern into the 1960s. Tiffin's King's Crown plates can be distinguished from similar patterns produced by other manufacturers by the star design that appears in the center.

King's Crown was produced by various manufacturers in crystal, with cranberry, ruby, gold, or platinum flashing.

Cranberry flashed

Ashtray, 4″	$12.00
Ashtray, 5¼″	20.00
Bonbon, crimped, handled, 8¾″	55.00
Bowl, 5¾″	27.00
Bowl, crimped, footed	37.00
Bowl, flared, footed	60.00
Bowl, fruit, footed, 6½″	50.00
Bowl, salad, 9¼″	70.00
Bud Vase, 9″	42.00
Bud Vase, 12¼″	90.00
Cake Plate, center handle, 12″	75.00
Cake Salver, 12″	37.00
Candleholder, double light, 5½″	45.00
Candy Dish, covered	45.00
Candy Dish, covered, footed	40.00
Champagne, 3″	15.00
Champagne, 3¼″	15.00
Cheese and Cracker Set	80.00

Cheese Stand	27.00
Chip and Dip Set	100.00
Cigarette Box, covered	60.00
Claret, 4³/₈″	25.00
Cocktail, 4″	17.00
Compote, 7″	75.00
Creamer	32.00
Cup	10.00
Finger Bowl, 4″	17.00
Highball, 5¹/₂″	17.00
Iced Tea	17.00
Juice, 4″	15.00
Mayonnaise, divided	32.00
Mayonnaise and Underplate, with ladle	65.00
Nappy, 5³/₄″	20.00
Nappy, flared, handled, 8¹/₂″	37.00
Oyster Cocktail	20.00
Pitcher	100.00
Plate, bread and butter, 5″	10.00
Plate, dinner, 10″	50.00
Plate, handled, 9¹/₄″	40.00
Plate, salad, 7¹/₂″	20.00
Plate, torte, 14¹/₂″	75.00
Relish, five-part, 14″	85.00
Saucer	10.00
Snack Plate, 9³/₄″	20.00
Sugar	32.00
Sundae	20.00
Tray, 9¹/₂″	40.00
Tumbler	20.00
Water Goblet, 5⁵/₈″	20.00
Wine, 3¹/₂″	22.00
Wine, 4″	22.00

Ruby flashed

Ashtray, 4″	$12.00
Ashtray, 5¹/₄″	15.00
Bonbon, crimped, handled, 8³/₄″	45.00
Bowl, 5³/₄″	20.00
Bowl, crimped, footed	30.00
Bowl, flared, footed	50.00
Bowl, fruit, footed, 6¹/₂″	40.00
Bowl, salad, 9¹/₄″	55.00
Bud Vase, 9″	35.00
Bud Vase, 12¹/₄″	70.00
Cake Plate, center handle, 12″	50.00
Cake Salver, 12″	30.00
Candleholder, double light, 5¹/₂″	35.00
Candy Dish, covered	35.00
Candy Dish, covered, footed	40.00
Champagne, 3″	10.00
Champagne, 3¹/₄″	10.00
Cheese and Cracker Set	65.00
Cheese Stand	20.00
Chip and Dip Set	75.00
Cigarette Box, covered	45.00
Claret, 4¹/₂″	15.00
Cocktail	15.00
Compote, 7″	65.00
Creamer	25.00
Cup	7.00
Finger Bowl, 4″	17.00
Iced Tea	15.00
Juice, 4″	12.00
Mayonnaise, divided	25.00

Mayonnaise and Underplate, with ladle	50.00
Nappy, 5³/₄″	15.00
Nappy, flared, handled, 8¹/₂″	30.00
Oyster Cocktail	15.00
Pitcher	75.00
Plate, bread and butter, 5″	7.00
Plate, dinner, 10″	35.00
Plate, handled, 9¹/₄″	30.00
Plate, salad, 7³/₈″	12.00
Plate, torte, 14¹/₂″	50.00
Relish, five-part, 14″	70.00
Saucer	7.00
Snack Plate, 9³/₄″	15.00
Sugar	25.00
Sundae	15.00
Tray, 9¹/₂″	30.00
Tumbler	15.00
Water Goblet, 5⁵/₈″	15.00
Wine, 3¹/₂″	15.00
Wine, 3³/₄″	15.00

Parfait	125.00
Pitcher, 9¹/₄″	450.00
Plate, 8″	100.00
Shot Glass, 2¹/₈″	95.00
Tumbler, flat, 5¹/₈″	110.00
Tumbler, footed, 2³/₄″	110.00
Water Goblet	125.00
Wine	125.00

Tiffin, Montclair, crystal, platinum trim (No. 17651)

Champagne, 5³/₈″	$25.00
Claret	30.00
Cocktail, 5¹/₂″	25.00
Cordial, 4³/₄″	40.00
Finger Bowl	30.00
Iced Tea, 5⁷/₈″	30.00
Juice, 4¹/₂″	27.00
Nappy	25.00
Oyster Cocktail	25.00
Parfait	30.00
Plate, salad, 8¹/₈″	25.00
Water Goblet, 7″	25.00
Wine	25.00

Tiffin, Melrose Gold, crystal, etched, gold trim (No. 17356)

Champagne	$110.00
Champagne, fluted	110.00
Claret	125.00
Cocktail	110.00
Cordial	150.00
Iced Tea, footed	110.00
Juice	100.00
Oyster Cocktail	110.00

Tiffin, Ondine, crystal, cut (No. 17708)

Champagne, $6^{1}/_{4}''$	$100.00
Champagne, fluted	100.00
Claret	110.00
Cocktail	100.00
Cordial	120.00
Iced Tea	110.00
Juice	100.00
Oyster Cocktail	100.00
Parfait	100.00
Water Goblet	120.00
Wine	

Tiffin, Palais Versailles, crystal, cut, gold trim (No. 17594)

Champagne, $5^{1}/_{8}''$	$85.00
Claret	100.00
Cocktail	85.00

Cordial	100.00
Finger Bowl, $4^{1}/_{2}''$	100.00
Iced Tea	100.00
Juice	90.00
Nappy	120.00
Plate, salad, 8″	90.00
Seafood Icer, with liner, $4^{3}/_{4}''$	130.00
Water Goblet	100.00
Wine, $6^{3}/_{8}''$	110.00

Tiffin, Westchester, crystal, gold trim (No. 17679)

Champagne	$60.00
Claret	70.00
Cocktail	60.00
Cordial, 4″	70.00
Finger Bowl	75.00
Iced Tea	65.00
Juice	60.00
Nappy	75.00
Plate, salad, 8″	75.00
Water Goblet	70.00
Wine	65.00

Tiffin, Wistaria, pink bowl (No. 17477)

Champagne, $4\frac{1}{2}''$	$35.00
Champagne, fluted	40.00
Claret	35.00
Cocktail, $4\frac{1}{2}''$	35.00
Cordial	45.00
Iced Tea	40.00
Juice, $5\frac{1}{2}''$	37.00
Oyster Cocktail	35.00
Parfait	40.00
Plate, $8\frac{1}{8}''$	35.00
Water Goblet, $6''$	40.00
Wine	35.00

Waterford Crystal traces its lineage to a crystal manufacturing business established by George and William Penrose in 1783. Although this initial effort to manufacture crystal and other glassware in Waterford lasted only sixty-eight years, the products that were produced enjoyed an unequaled reputation that survives today.

The end of flint glass production in Dublin around 1893 marked the demise of almost three centuries of glassmaking in Ireland. In 1902, sand from Muckish in Donegal was brought to the Cork Exhibition, where London glassblowers used a small furnace and made drinking glasses cut in an "early Waterford style." This attempt to revive an interest in glassmaking in Ireland failed.

In 1947, almost fifty years later, a small glass factory was established in Ballytuckle, a suburb of Waterford, approximately one and one-half miles from the Penrose glasshouse on the western edge of the city. Apprentices were trained by immigrant European craftsmen who were displaced as a result of World War II.

The management of Waterford Crystal dedicated its efforts to matching the purity of color, inspired design, and the highest-quality levels of eighteenth- and nineteenth-century Waterford glass. Capturing the brilliance of the traditional, deeply incised cutting patterns of earlier Waterford pieces provided an additional challenge.

Waterford Crystal continued to grow and prosper, eventually moving to a forty-acre site in Johnstown, near the center of Waterford. In the 1980s, computer technology improved the accuracy of the raw materials mix, known in the crystal industry as the "batch." Improvements in furnace design and diamond-cutting wheels enabled Waterford craftspeople to create exciting new intricate glass patterns. Two additional plants in County Waterford helped the company meet its manufacturing commitments.

Waterford Crystal stemware consists of essentially twelve stem shapes with a variety of cutting patterns, extending the range to over thirty suites. The Hibernia suite, with its heavily decorated convex pillar flutes with alternating panels of fine diamond cutting, preserves the early eighteenth-century design influence. The most popular shape is the more modern lines of the Lismore pattern, followed by the rich diamond cutting of Alana. Some of the most popular stemware patterns have been adapted to suit items of giftware, providing an opportunity to acquire matching bowls, vases, and other accessories to enhance a table setting.

In addition to producing stemware, giftware, and lighting, Waterford Crystal also executes hundreds of commissioned pieces. Waterford Crystal trophies, used for some of the world's most prestigious sporting events, are the best known examples. All Waterford Crystal can be identified by the distinctive "Waterford" signature on the base of the item.

WATERFORD CRYSTAL GALLERY AND FACTORY TOURS

The Waterford Crystal Gallery contains one of the world's finest displays of crystal. This 9,000-square-foot facility was opened to the public in May 1986. The Gallery houses many exhibition pieces, including the replicas of many sporting trophies and examples of the ever-changing Masterpiece Collection.

The Waterford Crystal Gallery is open Monday through Friday, 9 A.M. until 6 P.M. and Saturday, throughout the summer months, 10 A.M. until 1 P.M., subject to alterations as circumstances demand.

Tours of the Waterford Crystal factory can be arranged at the Gallery Reception. Tours depart between 10:15 A.M. and 2:30 P.M. Reservations are recommended. (Telephone for more information at +353 51 73311.)

THE HISTORY OF WATERFORD CRYSTAL, 1783–1851

George and William Penrose established a crystal manufacturing business in the busy Irish port of Waterford in 1783. Their initial investment of £10,000 was substantial. The glasshouse, situated on a piece of land they owned adjacent to Merchants' Quay on Anne Street in the heart of Waterford city, produced "plain and cut flint glass, useful and ornamental." John Hill, a glassmaker from Stourbridge in England, was instrumental in establishing the operation. Within a short period, the glasshouse employed between fifty and seventy workers.

In 1799, Jonathan Gatchell and members of the Ramsey and Barcroft families purchased the glasshouse from the Penroses. They then established the Waterford Flint Glass manufactory. Gatchell became the sole proprietor around 1810, following the death of his second partner, Ramsey. Unfortunately for Gatchell, parliament enacted a duty on the export of flint glass from Ireland during the same year.

Gatchell died in 1823, leaving a wife and three young children. At the time, the business was once again a partnership, consisting of Gatchell, his brothers James and Samuel, and his son-in-law Joseph Walpole. Gatchell's will provided that his son George would enter the business in 1835, when he turned twenty-one. George formed another partnership with George Saunders, an employee. In 1850, Saunders left. George had to either find another partner who had adequate capital or sell the business.

In 1851, George sent a magnificent Waterford entry to the 1851 London Crystal Palace Exhibition. In spite of the attention this piece received, he, a victim of excessive taxation and a lack of operating capital, was forced to close the glasshouse.

Waterford Crystal, Alana, crystal, cut (No. 600/132)

Brandy, $5^1/8''$	$65.00
Champagne, $4^1/8''$	50.00
Champagne, fluted, $7^3/8''$	50.00
Claret, $5^7/8''$	50.00
Cocktail, $4''$	45.00
Compote, $4^1/2''$	140.00
Cordial, $3^1/2''$	40.00
Decanter, $10^3/4''$	255.00
Decanter, $13^1/4''$	255.00
Decanter, ship, $9^1/2''$	300.00
Decanter, ship, $10''$	300.00
Decanter, wine, with stopper, $12^3/4''$	260.00
Dessert, footed, $3^1/8''$	75.00
Highball, $5''$	50.00
Highball, $5^5/8''$	50.00
Hock, $7^3/8''$	65.00
Iced Tea, footed	60.00
Jug, $6''$	180.00
Jug, $6^3/4''$	180.00
Jug, pint, $5^1/4''$	130.00
Juice, $3^7/8''$	50.00
Old Fashioned	45.00
Old Fashioned, double	45.00
Plate, $6''$	30.00
Plate, $8''$	35.00
Port	45.00
Roly Poly	45.00
Sherry, $5^1/8''$	40.00
Shot Glass	40.00
Tumbler, flat, $3^1/2''$	50.00

Tumbler, flat, $5^1/8''$	50.00
Water Goblet, $7''$	50.00
Wine	50.00

Waterford Crystal, Araglin, crystal, cut (No. 612/394)

Champagne, fluted	$45.00
Claret, $7^1/8''$	45.00
Cordial	45.00
Iced Tea, footed	60.00
Old Fashioned	40.00
Old Fashioned, double	40.00
Sherry	40.00
Water Goblet	45.00

Waterford Crystal, Ashling, crystal, cut (No. 600/786)

Champagne, $4^1/8''$	$60.00
Champagne, fluted	60.00

Claret, 5⅞"	70.00
Cocktail, 4⅛"	60.00
Cordial, 3½"	50.00
Decanter, 13¼"	300.00
Hock	65.00
Iced Tea	85.00
Jug	175.00
Juice	65.00
Old Fashioned	60.00
Plate, 6"	35.00
Plate, 8"	40.00
Port, 4⅜"	65.00
Sherry	60.00
Tumbler, flat, 5⅛"	65.00
Water Goblet, 6⅞"	70.00
Wine	65.00

Waterford Crystal, Avoca, crystal, cut (No. 605/583)

Champagne, 5¼"	$60.00
Champagne, fluted, 7⅜"	60.00
Claret, 6½"	60.00
Cocktail	60.00
Cordial	60.00
Dessert	60.00
Hock	60.00
Iced Tea	75.00
Juice	65.00
Old Fashioned	55.00
Port	60.00
Sherry, 5¼"	50.00
Tumbler	65.00
Water Goblet, 7"	60.00

Waterford Crystal, Avalon, crystal, Marquis Collection

Champagne, fluted, 8⅞"	$40.00
Iced Tea	50.00
Water Goblet, 8½"	40.00
Wine	40.00

**Waterford Crystal, Ballymore, crystal, cut
(No. 618/270)**

Champagne, fluted, 8¼″	$45.00
Claret	45.00
Cordial	40.00
Iced Tea	55.00
Old Fashioned	45.00
Sherry	45.00
Water Goblet	45.00

**Waterford Crystal, Ballyshannon, crystal, cut
(No. 608/309)**

Champagne, fluted	$45.00
Claret	45.00
Cordial	40.00
Iced Tea, footed	60.00
Old Fashioned	45.00

Old Fashioned, double	45.00
Sherry	45.00
Water Goblet	45.00

**Waterford Crystal, Carina, crystal, cut
(No. 612/190)**

Brandy	$45.00
Champagne, fluted, 8½″	45.00
Claret, 7⅛″	45.00
Cordial, 4⅝″	35.00
Cordial, 5¼″	35.00
Iced Tea, footed	60.00
Old Fashioned, 3⅝″	45.00
Old Fashioned, double	45.00
Sherry, 5¼″	45.00
Water Goblet, 8″	45.00

Waterford Crystal, Castlemaine, crystal, cut (No. 612/494)

Champagne, fluted, $8^{3}/_{8}''$	$45.00
Claret, $7^{1}/_{8}''$	45.00
Cordial, $4^{5}/_{8}''$	40.00
Iced Tea	70.00
Old Fashioned, $3^{1}/_{2}''$	45.00
Sherry	45.00
Water Goblet, $7^{7}/_{8}''$	45.00

Waterford Crystal, Clare, crystal, cut (No. 600/131)

Champagne, $4^{1}/_{8}''$	$80.00
Champagne, fluted, $7^{1}/_{4}''$	90.00
Claret, $5^{7}/_{8}''$	90.00
Cocktail, $3^{3}/_{4}''$	70.00
Cocktail, $4''$	70.00
Cordial, $3^{1}/_{2}''$	60.00
Decanter, spirit	300.00
Decanter, wine	300.00
Dessert, footed, $3^{1}/_{8}''$	110.00
Finger Bowl	110.00
Hock	110.00
Iced Tea	100.00
Jug	200.00
Juice, flat, $3^{1}/_{2}''$	80.00
Old Fashioned, $3^{3}/_{8}''$	85.00
Plate, $6''$	50.00
Plate, $8''$	60.00
Port	80.00
Sherry, $5^{1}/_{8}''$	70.00
Tumbler	70.00
Water Goblet	85.00
Wine	80.00

THE TOP FIVE PATTERNS MID-CENTURY MODERN

■

FOSTORIA, WEDDING RING

IMPERIAL, CANDLEWICK

LENOX, TUXEDO

ORREFORS, ILLUSION

WATERFORD, CLARIA

Claria by Waterford. *Photo courtesy of BC Design Incorporated.*

Waterford Crystal, Claria, crystal, Marquis Collection

Champagne, fluted, 9″	$25.00
Iced Tea, 8″	27.00
Water Goblet, 8½″	25.00
Wine, 8″	25.00

Waterford Crystal, Colleen, crystal, cut, short stem (No. 602/137)

Ashtray, 3½″	$40.00
Brandy, 5″	70.00
Champagne, 3⅜″	60.00
Champagne, 4⅜″	60.00

Champagne, fluted, 6″	70.00		Cocktail	50.00
Claret, 4³/₄″	60.00		Cordial, 3⁷/₈″	45.00
Cocktail, 3⁵/₈″	60.00		Highball	50.00
Compote, 4¹/₂″	150.00		Hock, 7³/₈″	80.00
Cordial, 3¹/₄″	45.00		Iced Tea, footed, 6³/₈″	75.00
Decanter, 10³/₄″	300.00		Old Fashioned	55.00
Decanter, 13¹/₄″	300.00		Old Fashioned, double	55.00
Finger Bowl, 4″	90.00		Sherry	50.00
Highball	55.00		Tumbler	50.00
Hock, 7¹/₂″	70.00		Water Goblet, 7″	70.00
Iced Tea, footed	75.00		Wine	70.00
Jug, 5¹/₂″	200.00			
Juice, flat, 3¹/₂″	45.00			
Old Fashioned, 3¹/₂″	60.00			
Old Fashioned, double	60.00			
Plate, 6″	40.00			
Plate, 8″	45.00			
Port, 3⁷/₈″	60.00			
Sherbet, 3¹/₈″	90.00			
Sherry, 4¹/₄″	50.00			
Tumbler, flat, 3¹/₂″	55.00			
Tumbler, flat, 4¹/₂″	55.00			
Water Goblet, 5¹/₄″	60.00			
Wine, 4¹/₂″	70.00			

Waterford Crystal, Comeragh, crystal, cut (No. 605/271)

Champagne, 5¹/₄″	$80.00
Champagne, fluted	80.00
Claret	80.00
Cocktail	80.00
Cordial, 3⁷/₈″	60.00
Decanter, 13″	300.00
Dessert	80.00
Finger Bowl, 3⁷/₈″	100.00
Hock, 7¹/₄″	100.00
Iced Tea	100.00
Juice	70.00
Old Fashioned, 3³/₈″	80.00
Port, 4¹/₂″	70.00
Sherry, 5¹/₄″	70.00
Shot Glass, 2³/₈″	60.00
Tumbler	70.00
Water Goblet	90.00

Waterford Crystal, Colleen, crystal, cut, tall stem (No. 605/137)

Brandy, 5³/₈″	$65.00
Champagne	70.00
Champagne, fluted, 7³/₈″	70.00
Claret, 6¹/₂″	70.00

Waterford Crystal, Curraghmore, crystal, cut (No. 690/127)

Champagne, $5^{1}/_{2}''$	$80.00
Champagne, fluted, $8^{1}/_{8}''$	85.00
Claret, $7^{1}/_{8}''$	85.00
Cocktail	75.00
Cordial, $4^{3}/_{4}''$	65.00
Decanter, spirit	300.00
Decanter, wine	300.00
Dessert	80.00
Finger Bowl	90.00
Hock	95.00
Iced Tea	95.00
Jug	200.00
Juice, footed	75.00
Old Fashioned	75.00
Plate, 6″	50.00
Plate, 8″	60.00
Port	80.00
Sherry, $6^{1}/_{4}''$	70.00
Tumbler, flat, $3^{1}/_{2}''$	70.00
Tumbler, flat, $4^{3}/_{8}''$	70.00
Tumbler, flat, $4^{5}/_{8}''$	70.00
Water Goblet	85.00
Wine, $6^{1}/_{4}''$	80.00

Waterford Crystal, Glenmore, crystal, cut (No. 604/899)

Champagne, $4^{3}/_{4}''$	$65.00
Champagne, fluted	65.00
Claret	65.00
Cocktail, $4^{1}/_{4}''$	65.00
Cordial, $3^{3}/_{4}''$	50.00
Decanter, spirit	250.00
Decanter, wine	250.00
Finger Bowl	80.00
Hock	65.00
Iced Tea	90.00
Jug	160.00
Juice	60.00
Old Fashioned, $3^{1}/_{2}''$	65.00
Plate, 6″	40.00
Plate, 8″	45.00
Port, $4^{1}/_{2}''$	60.00
Sherry, $5^{1}/_{2}''$	60.00
Tumbler	65.00
Water Goblet, 7″	85.00
Wine	65.00

Waterford Crystal, Hanover, crystal, gold trim, Marquis Collection

Brandy, 5¼″	$35.00
Bud Vase, 4″	40.00
Champagne, fluted, 8¾″	30.00
Decanter, 12¼″	140.00
Highball, 5⅞″	27.00
Iced Tea	37.00
Old Fashioned, double, 4″	27.00
Water Goblet, 8½″	32.00
Wine, 7⅝″	32.00
Wine, balloon, 8⅝″	40.00

Waterford Crystal, Kenmare, crystal, cut (No. 607/854)

Champagne, 4¾″	$65.00
Champagne, fluted	65.00
Claret	65.00
Cocktail, 4⅝″	60.00
Cordial, 3⅞″	50.00
Decanter, 13″	300.00
Dessert	65.00
Hock	75.00
Iced Tea	90.00
Jug	200.00

Hanover, Waterford Marquis Collection. *Photo courtesy of BC Design Incorporated.*

Juice	80.00
Old Fashioned, 3½"	65.00
Plate, 6"	40.00
Plate, 8"	50.00
Port, 5"	65.00
Sherry, 5⅜"	65.00
Tumbler	50.00
Water Goblet	80.00
Wine	60.00

Waterford Crystal, Kinsale, crystal, cut (No. 607/926)

Champagne, 4¾"	$70.00
Champagne, fluted	70.00
Claret, 6"	90.00
Cocktail, 4¾"	65.00
Cordial, 3⅞"	60.00
Decanter, spirit	275.00
Decanter, wine	275.00
Finger Bowl	80.00
Hock	75.00
Iced Tea	95.00
Jug	180.00
Juice	65.00
Old Fashioned, 3⅝"	75.00
Plate, 6"	45.00
Plate, 8"	55.00
Port, 5"	65.00
Sherry, 5⅜"	60.00
Tumbler, flat, 5"	75.00
Water Goblet, 6¾"	90.00
Wine	80.00

Waterford Crystal, Kildare, crystal, cut (No. 605/270)

Champagne	$45.00
Champagne, fluted	45.00
Claret, 6½"	45.00
Cocktail	45.00
Cordial, 4"	40.00
Creamer, 3⅞"	65.00
Decanter	225.00
Dessert	45.00
Hock	50.00
Iced Tea, footed	60.00
Juice	50.00
Old Fashioned	45.00
Port	45.00
Sherry, 5¼"	45.00
Sugar, open, 2¼"	65.00
Tumbler	50.00
Water Goblet	45.00
Wine	45.00

Waterford Crystal, Kylemore, crystal, cut
(No. 607/853)

Brandy, $5^1/_4''$	$80.00
Champagne, $4^3/_4''$	70.00
Champagne, fluted, $7^7/_8''$	80.00
Claret, $6''$	80.00
Cocktail, $4^3/_4''$	65.00
Cordial, $4''$	55.00
Decanter, spirit	300.00
Decanter, wine	300.00
Dessert	75.00
Finger Bowl, $2^3/_8''$	90.00
Highball	60.00
Hock, $7^1/_2''$	100.00
Iced Tea	95.00
Jug	200.00
Juice, flat, $3^5/_8''$	70.00
Old Fashioned, $3^5/_8''$	65.00
Old Fashioned, double	65.00
Port, $5''$	65.00
Plate, $6''$	50.00
Plate, $8''$	60.00
Sherry, $5^3/_8''$	60.00
Tumbler, flat, $5''$	60.00
Water Goblet, $6^3/_4''$	80.00
Wine	80.00

Waterford Crystal, Laurent, crystal, cut,
Marquis Collection

Champagne, fluted, $8^1/_2''$	$30.00
Iced Tea, $7^5/_8''$	35.00
Water Goblet, $7^5/_8''$	30.00
Wine, $7^1/_8''$	30.00

Waterford Crystal, Lismore, crystal, cut
(No. 600/318)

Biscuit Barrel, $6^3/_4''$	$150.00
Bowl, round, $5''$	100.00
Bowl, round, $7''$	100.00
Brandy	50.00
Champagne, $4^1/_8''$	45.00
Champagne, fluted, $7^1/_4''$	45.00

Claret, 5$^7/_8$″	45.00
Cocktail	45.00
Compote, 4$^1/_2$″	130.00
Cordial, 3$^1/_2$″	40.00
Decanter, 9$^1/_2$″	245.00
Decanter, 10$^1/_4$″, no stopper	230.00
Decanter, 12$^7/_8$″	245.00
Decanter, 13$^1/_2$″	245.00
Decanter, ship, 10″	240.00
Decanter, spirit, 10$^5/_8$″	240.00
Decanter, spirit, 12$^1/_2$″	240.00
Decanter, wine, 13$^1/_4$″	240.00
Finger Bowl	80.00
Highball, 5$^3/_4$″	50.00
Hock, 7$^1/_2$″	65.00
Iced Tea, footed, 6$^3/_8$″	60.00
Irish Coffee	80.00
Jug, 6$^1/_4$″	160.00
Juice, footed, 4″	50.00
Old Fashioned, 3$^3/_8$″	45.00
Old Fashioned, double	45.00
Plate, 8″	40.00
Plate, ice, 6″	35.00
Port	65.00
Salt Shaker, 3$^7/_8$″	50.00
Sherbet, footed, 3″	60.00
Sherry, 5$^1/_8$″	40.00
Shot Glass	40.00
Tumbler, flat, 5$^1/_8$″	45.00
Water Goblet, 6$^7/_8$″	45.00
Wine	45.00

Waterford Crystal, Lucerne, crystal (No. 695/992)

Champagne, fluted	$45.00
Iced Tea	55.00
Water Goblet	45.00
Wine	45.00

Waterford Crystal, Maeve, crystal, cut (No. 604/678)

Brandy	$50.00
Champagne	45.00
Champagne, fluted	45.00
Claret	45.00
Cocktail	45.00
Cordial	40.00
Dessert	40.00
Highball	50.00
Hock	45.00

Maeve by Waterford. *Photo courtesy of Waterford Crystal.*

Powerscourt by Waterford. *Photo courtesy of BC Design Incorporated.*

Iced Tea, footed	60.00	Claret, 7¹/₈″	85.00
Juice	45.00	Cocktail, 5¹/₄″	80.00
Old Fashioned	45.00	Cordial, 4⁵/₈″	60.00
Port	45.00	Decanter, spirit	300.00
Sherry, 5³/₈″	40.00	Decanter, wine	300.00
Tumbler, flat, 5″	45.00	Dessert	85.00
Water Goblet	45.00	Finger Bowl, 3⁷/₈″	100.00
Wine	45.00	Hock, 7¹/₂″	105.00
		Iced Tea	85.00
		Jug	200.00
		Juice, footed	65.00
		Old Fashioned, 3¹/₂″	70.00
		Plate, 6″	50.00
		Plate, 8″	60.00
		Port	70.00
		Sherry, 6³/₈″	70.00
		Tumbler, flat, 4³/₈″	70.00
		Tumbler, flat, 4⁵/₈″	70.00
		Water Goblet, 7⁵/₈″	85.00
		Wine, 6³/₈″	80.00

Waterford Crystal, Powerscourt, crystal, cut (No. 690/124)

Champagne, 5³/₈″	$80.00
Champagne, fluted, 8¹/₈″	85.00

Waterford Crystal, Rosslare, crystal, cut
(No. 607/927)

Champagne, $4^3/_4''$	$70.00
Champagne, fluted	70.00
Claret, 6"	85.00
Cocktail, $4^3/_4''$	70.00
Cordial, 4"	60.00
Decanter, spirit	275.00
Decanter, wine	275.00
Dessert	70.00
Hock	80.00
Iced Tea	100.00
Jug	180.00
Juice	70.00
Old Fashioned	65.00
Plate, 6"	55.00
Plate, 8"	65.00
Port, 5"	70.00
Sherry, $5^3/_8''$	65.00
Tumbler, flat, 5"	70.00
Water Goblet, $6^3/_4''$	85.00
Wine	75.00

Waterford Crystal, Sheila, crystal, cut
(No. 604/175)

Champagne, $4^3/_4''$	$55.00
Champagne, fluted, $7^1/_8''$	65.00
Claret	60.00
Cocktail, $4^1/_8''$	60.00
Cordial, $3^7/_8''$	45.00
Decanter, $12^3/_4''$	300.00
Dessert	60.00
Finger Bowl	70.00
Hock	65.00
Iced Tea	80.00
Jug, $6^3/_4''$	160.00
Juice, flat, $3^5/_8''$	60.00
Old Fashioned, $3^1/_2''$	60.00
Plate, 6"	40.00
Plate, 8"	45.00
Port, $4^1/_2''$	65.00
Sherry, $5^1/_2''$	50.00
Tumbler, flat, 5"	60.00
Water Goblet, 7"	65.00
Wine	65.00

Waterford Crystal, Tramore, crystal, cut
(No. 601/678)

Champagne, 4⁵/₈″	$55.00
Champagne, fluted	55.00
Claret, 5¹/₄″	60.00
Cocktail, 3″	60.00
Cocktail, 4¹/₄″	60.00
Cordial, 2⁷/₈″	50.00
Decanter, 12¹/₂″	270.00
Decanter, 13″	270.00
Hock, 7¹/₂″	90.00
Iced Tea	85.00
Jug, 6¹/₄″	200.00
Juice, 3⁷/₈″	60.00
Old Fashioned, 3³/₈″	60.00
Plate, 6″	30.00
Plate, 8″	35.00
Port, 4″	60.00
Sherry, 4¹/₂″	60.00
Tumbler, flat, 5″	60.00
Water Goblet, 5⁵/₈″	65.00
Wine, 5¹/₈″	60.00

Waterford Crystal, Wynnewood, crystal, cut
(No. 695/993)

Champagne, fluted	$45.00
Iced Tea	55.00
Water Goblet	45.00
Wine	45.00

From a family firm with approximately 2,000 employees in 1966, Wedgwood became a public company comprising eight factories employing around 5,500 people in the United Kingdom and overseas. Today the company accounts for 25 percent of the British ceramic tableware industry's output and 25 percent of its exports.

In 1969, Wedgwood acquired King's Lynn Glass Ltd., renaming it Wedgwood Glass. The acquisition of Galway Crystal Company of Galway, Erie, followed in 1974. Ronald Stenett-Wilson was the first chief designer for Wedgwood Glass. Lead crystal candlesticks, drinking glasses, decanters, ornamental objects, including paperweights, and stemware were among the products manufactured.

In 1986, Waterford and Wedgwood merged. The Wedgwood Group, now a division of Waterford Wedgwood, consists of six major divisions: Wedgwood, Coalport, Johnson Brothers, Mason's Ironstone, Wedgwood Hotelware, and Wedgwood Jewellery.

Wedgwood's stemware sales in America were modest. Given Waterford's strong position in the stemware market, Wedgwood crystal stemware is no longer available in the United States, except on the secondary/replacement market.

Wedgwood Crystal, Dynasty, crystal

Brandy	$30.00
Champagne	60.00
Champagne, fluted	60.00
Cordial	55.00
Highball	65.00
Hock	60.00
Iced Tea	70.00
Old Fashioned, double	60.00
Water Goblet	70.00
Wine	60.00

Wedgwood Crystal, Majesty, crystal

Brandy, $5^1/_8''$	$35.00
Bud Vase, $6^1/_8''$	45.00
Bud Vase, $7^1/_2''$	45.00
Champagne	50.00
Champagne, fluted	50.00
Cordial	45.00
Highball	55.00
Hock	50.00
Iced Tea, $8^3/_4''$	55.00
Old Fashioned, double	50.00
Water Goblet, $8^7/_8''$	55.00
Wine	50.00

Wedgwood Crystal, Monarch, crystal, cut

Brandy	$30.00
Champagne	50.00
Champagne, fluted	50.00

Cordial	45.00
Highball	55.00
Hock	50.00
Iced Tea	60.00
Old Fashioned, double	50.00
Water Goblet	60.00
Wine	50.00

Wedgwood Crystal, Sovereign, crystal

Brandy	$35.00
Champagne	55.00
Champagne, fluted	55.00
Cordial	50.00
Highball	60.00
Hock	60.00
Iced Tea	65.00
Old Fashioned, double	55.00
Water Goblet	65.00
Wine	55.00

Westmoreland traces its history to the East Liverpool Specialty Glass Company and the influence of Major George Irwin. Irwin was instrumental in moving the company from East Liverpool, Ohio, to Jeannette, Pennsylvania, to take advantage of the large natural gas reserves in the area. Specialty Glass, a new Pennsylvania company, was established in 1888. When the company ran out of money in 1889, Charles H. and George R. West put up $40,000 for 53 percent of the company's stock. The name was changed to Westmoreland Specialty Company.

Initially, Westmoreland made candy containers and a number of other glass containers. In 1910, the company introduced its Keystone line of tableware. Charles West had opposed the move into tableware production, and the brothers split in 1920. George West continued with the Westmoreland Specialty Company. In 1924, the company changed its name to the Westmoreland Glass Company.

Westmoreland made decorated wares and colonial era reproductions, for example, dolphin pedestal forms, in the 1920s. Color, introduced to the tableware lines in the early 1930s, was virtually gone by the mid-1930s. Amber, black, and ruby colors were created in an attempt to bolster the line in the 1950s.

In 1937, Charles West retired and J. H. Brainard assumed the company's helm. Phillip and Walter Brainard, J. H.'s two sons, joined the firm in 1940. In an effort to cut costs, all cutting and engraving work was eliminated in the 1940s. The grinding and polishing of glass ceased in 1957. New molds were not made until the milk glass surge in the early and mid-1950s.

The milk glass boom was over by 1958. While continuing to produce large quantities of milk glass in the 1960s, Westmoreland expanded its product line to include crystal tableware and colored items. The effort was unsuccessful. Attempts to introduce color into the milk glass line also proved disappointing. Further, by producing two grape milk glass patterns, Beaded Grape and Paneled Grape, Westmoreland found that its products were competing against each other. The company kept its doors open, albeit barely, by appealing to the bridal trade through advertisements in magazines such as *Better Homes and Gardens*.

In a search for any possible capital, an on-site gift shop was opened on April 12, 1962. The shop produced a steady cash flow. Shortly after the shop opened, Westmoreland began selling seconds, imperfect but totally usable pieces. Previously, pieces that did not meet the company's high standards were destroyed. Thus, another valuable source of cash was found.

By 1980, J. H. Brainard was searching for a buyer for the company. After turning down a proposal from a group of company workers, Brainard sold Westmoreland Glass Company to

David Grossman, a St. Louis–based distributor and importer, best known for his Norman Rockwell Collectibles series. Westmoreland's demise came on January 8, 1984, when factory operations ceased. Most of the molds, glass, historic information, catalogs, and furniture were sold at auction.

Westmoreland Glass Company, Paneled Grape, milk glass (Pattern 1881)

Paneled Grape is the most popular pattern in the Westmoreland Glass Company's history. It was produced from the 1940s to the factory's closing in the early 1980s. Paneled Grape was manufactured in many different forms, including complete dinner and luncheon sets.

Appetizer Set	$60.00
Ashtray, 4″	15.00
Ashtray, 5″	15.00
Ashtray, 6½″	20.00
Basket, oval, 6½″	30.00
Bowl, crimped, 6¼″	40.00
Bowl, cupped, 9″	50.00
Bowl, flared, footed, 5″	50.00
Bowl, footed, 6½″	60.00
Bowl, footed, 8¼″	60.00
Bowl, footed, 9½″	60.00
Bowl, fruit, footed, 2⅝″	20.00
Bowl, ivy, 7″	50.00
Bowl, oval, 6½″	40.00
Bowl, oval, 10″	45.00
Bowl, oval, footed, 11″	50.00
Bowl, oval, scalloped rim, 11½″	50.00
Bud Vase, 4¼″	30.00
Bud Vase, 5¾″	30.00
Bud Vase, 6″	30.00
Bud Vase, 8⅜″	30.00
Bud Vase, 9″	30.00
Bud Vase, 11½″	30.00
Bud Vase, 18″	35.00
Butter Dish, ¼ lb.	35.00
Cake Salver, footed	35.00
Cake Salver, footed, skirted	40.00
Candlestick, 4″	20.00
Candlestick, three-light	300.00
Candy Dish, covered, 5¼″	35.00
Candy Dish, covered, 6¼″	35.00
Candy Dish, covered, footed, 7¾″	50.00
Champagne	20.00
Compote, 5″	30.00
Compote, 6½″	30.00
Compote, 9″	35.00
Cordial	20.00
Creamer, 4¾″	22.00
Creamer, 5″	22.00
Creamer, 5¼″	22.00
Creamer, mini, 3¾″	20.00
Cruet, 4¾″	30.00
Cup, footed, 2½″	20.00
Cup and Saucer, footed, 2½″	25.00
Gravy Boat and Underplate	35.00
Honey Dish, 5⅛″	40.00
Iced Tea, flat, 5¾″	20.00
Juice	15.00
Lid, cheese	30.00
Mayonnaise, footed, 4″	25.00
Mayonnaise and Underplate	35.00
Nappy, 4½″	25.00
Old Fashioned	15.00

Parfait	25.00	Salt and Pepper Shakers, pair, 4″,	
Pitcher, 8$\frac{1}{8}$″	100.00	no lids	27.00
Pitcher, 9″	100.00	Salt Shaker, 4$\frac{3}{4}$″	20.00
Pitcher, pint, 5$\frac{1}{4}$″	50.00	Salt Shaker, 4″, no lid	12.00
Planter, 4$\frac{3}{4}$″	35.00	Salt Shaker, 4$\frac{3}{4}$″, no lid	12.00
Planter, 8$\frac{1}{2}$″	35.00	Salt Shaker, flat, 4″	20.00
Planter, 8$\frac{3}{4}$″	35.00	Sauce Boat Underplate, 9$\frac{1}{4}$″	20.00
Plate, bread and butter, 6″	15.00	Saucer	7.00
Plate, dinner, 10$\frac{1}{2}$″	35.00	Sherbet, 3$\frac{5}{8}$″	20.00
Plate, luncheon, 8$\frac{1}{2}$″	25.00	Sugar, covered, 5$\frac{1}{4}$″	30.00
Plate, serving, 14$\frac{1}{2}$″	40.00	Sugar, open, 3$\frac{3}{8}$″	22.00
Puff Box, covered, square, 5$\frac{1}{4}$″	32.00	Sugar, open, 4$\frac{1}{4}$″	22.00
Puff Box, covered, square,		Tumbler	20.00
no lid	22.00	Vase, 6″	40.00
Punch Bowl Stand, 5$\frac{1}{4}$″	100.00	Vase, 6$\frac{3}{4}$″	40.00
Relish, four-part, 8$\frac{3}{4}$″	40.00	Vase, 15″	45.00
Rose Bowl, 4″	30.00	Vase, celery, 6″	30.00
Rose Bowl, 5″	30.00	Vase, flared, 5$\frac{5}{8}$″	35.00
Salt and Pepper Shakers, pair	40.00	Vase, footed, 9$\frac{1}{8}$″	40.00
Salt and Pepper Shakers, pair, footed	40.00	Vase, footed, 11$\frac{1}{2}$″	45.00
Salt and Pepper Shakers, pair, 3$\frac{1}{2}$″,		Water Goblet, 6″	20.00
no lids	27.00	Wine, 4″	20.00

Appendix: The Top Patterns

Top 25 Crystal Patterns (Alphabetically)

Alana by Waterford (Cut)
Allure by Lenox
American—Clear by Fostoria (Stem #2056, Pressed)
Araglin by Waterford (Cut)
Candlewick—Clear by Imperial (Stem #3400)
Cape Cod—Clear by Imperial (#1600 & #1602)
Castle Garden by Lenox (Etched)
Century by Fostoria (Pressed)
Cherrywood—Clear by Gorham (Cut)
Chintz by Fostoria (Etched)
Colleen—Short Stem by Waterford (Cut)
Colony by Fostoria (Pressed)
Desire by Lenox (Platinum Trim)

Engagement by Fostoria (Platinum Trim)
Hanover by Waterford (Cut, Gold Trim)
Holly by Fostoria (Cut)
Kildare by Waterford (Cut)
King Edward by Gorham (Cut)
Lady Anne by Gorham (Cut)
Lismore by Waterford (Cut)
Moonspun by Lenox (Etched, Platinum Trim)
Navarre—Clear by Fostoria (Etched)
Rose Point—Clear by Cambridge (Stem #3121, Etched)
Sheffield by Fostoria (Platinum Band)
Wedding Ring by Fostoria (Platinum Band)

Top 26–50 Crystal Patterns (Alphabetically)

Ashling by Waterford (Cut)
Ballyshannon by Waterford (Cut)
Carina by Waterford (Cut)
Chantilly by Gorham (Cut)
Colleen—Tall Stem by Waterford (Cut)
Elyse by Tiffin/Franciscan #17683 (Cut)
Heisey Rose by Heisey (Etched)
Intrigue by Lenox (Gold Trim)
Kenmare by Waterford (Cut)
Kylemore by Waterford (Cut)
Maeve by Waterford (Cut)
Majesty by Wedgwood
Massena by Baccarat (Cut)

Meadow Rose—Clear by Fostoria (Etched)
Monroe by Lenox (Gold Trim)
Montclair by Lenox (Platinum Trim)
Navarre—Blue by Fostoria (Etched)
Navarre—Clear by Lenox (Etched)
Orchid by Heisey (Stem #5025, Etched)
Powerscourt by Waterford (Cut)
Prelude—Clear by Orrefors (Cut)
Romance by Fostoria (Etched)
Rose by Fostoria (Cut)
Solitaire by Lenox (Platinum Trim)
Weatherly by Lenox (Platinum Trim)

Top 51–100 Crystal Patterns (Alphabetically)

Althea by Gorham (Cut)
Antique—Blue by Lenox
Antique—Clear by Lenox
Arctic Lights by Mikasa #XY701 (Cut)
Argus—Ruby by Fostoria (Stem #2770, Pressed)
Ariel by Lenox (Platinum Trim)
Bamberg by Gorham (Cut)
Brookdale by Lenox (Cut)
Cape Cod—Clear by Imperial (Stem #1600)
Castlemaine by Waterford (Cut)
Charleston by Lenox (Cut)
Crown Point by Gorham (Cut)
Curraghmore by Waterford (Cut)

Dolly Madison by Fostoria (Cut)
Dynasty by Wedgwood
Eternal by Lenox (Gold Trim)
Firelight—Clear by Lenox
French Cathedral by Gorham (Cut)
Georgian by Fostoria (Cut)
Hayworth by Lenox (Gold Trim)
Heather by Fostoria (Etched)
Heritage—Clear by Fostoria (Pressed)
Invitation by Fostoria (Platinum Trim)
Iris—Clear by Jeannette Glass
Jamestown—Blue by Fostoria (Pressed)
Jamestown—Clear by Mikasa #T2703 (Gold Trim)

Jamestown—Pink by Fostoria (Pressed)
Jamestown—Ruby by Fostoria (Pressed)
June—Clear by Fostoria (Stem #5098, Etched)
June Night by Tiffin # 17392 (Etched)
La Scala by Gorham (Cut)
Laurel by Fostoria (Cut)
Mansfield by Lenox (Gold Trim)
Maywood by Lenox (Platinum Trim)
Monarch by Wedgwood (Cut)
Nocturne by Gorham (Cut)
Palais Versailles by Tiffin/Franciscan #17594
  (Cut, Gold Trim)
Paneled Grape—Milk Glass by Westmoreland

Park Lane by Mikasa #SN101
Rhythm—Clear by Noritake (Platinum Trim)
Richmond by Miller Rogaska
Rosslare by Waterford (Cut)
Sheila by Waterford (Cut)
Shell Pearl by Fostoria
Tivoli by Gorham (Cut)
Trousseau by Fostoria (Platinum Trim)
Tuilleries/Villandry by Durand (Cut)
Virtue—Clear by Noritake (Etched)
Willowmere by Fostoria (Etched)
Wynnewood by Waterford (Cut)

Bibliography

General References

Chefetz, Sheila. *Antiques For The Table: A Complete Guide to Dining Room Accessories for Collecting and Entertaining.* New York; Viking Studio Books, 1993.

Husfloen, Kyle. *Collector's Guide to American Pressed Glass: 1825–1915.* Radnor, Pa.: Wallace-Homestead, 1992.

Klein, Dan, and Ward Lloyd, eds. *The History of Glass.* London: Orbis Publishing, 1984.

Newman, Harold. *An Illustrated Dictionary of Glass.* New York: Thames and Hudson, 1977.

General Identification and Price References

Florence, Gene. *Collectible Glassware from the 40's, 50's, 60's. . . .* 3rd ed. Paducah, Ky.: Collector Books, 1996.

Florence, Gene. *Collector's Encyclopedia of Depression Glass.* 12th ed. Paducah, Ky.: Collector Books, 1996.

Florence, Gene. *Elegant Glassware of the Depression Era: An Identification and Value Guide.* 7th ed. Paducah, Ky.: Collector Books, 1997.

Florence, Gene. *Stemware Identification: Featuring Cordials with Values 1920s–1960s.* Paducah, Ky.: Collector Books, 1997.

Florence, Gene. *Very Rare Glassware of the Depression Years: Identification and Values.* 5th series. Paducah, Ky.: Collector Books, 1997.

Kovel, Ralph and Terry. *Kovels' Depression Glass & American Dinnerware Price List.* 5th ed. New York: Crown Trade Paperbacks, 1995.

Luckey, Carl F. *An Identification & Value Guide to Depression Era Glassware.* 3rd ed. Florence, Ala.: Books Americana, 1994.

Pickvet, Mark. *The Official Price Guide to Glassware.* New York: House of Collectibles, 1995.

Replacements, Ltd. *Replacements, LTD.'s Crystal ID Guide.* Greensboro, N. C.: Replacements, Ltd., n.d.

Marks Reference

Pullin, Anne Geffken. *Glass Signatures Trademarks and Trade Names: from the Seventeenth to the Twentieth Century.* Lombard, Ill.: Wallace-Homestead, 1986.

Company Histories and Price References

Anchor Hocking. *Corporate History of Anchor Hocking Glass Corporation.* Lancaster, Ohio: Anchor Hocking, n.d.

Archer, Margaret and Douglas. *Imperial Glass.* Paducah, Ky.: Collector Books, 1978.

Bennett, Harold and Judy. *The Cambridge Glass Book.* Des Moines, Iowa: Wallace-Homestead, 1970.

Bickenheuser, Fred. *Tiffin Glassmasters.* Book III. Grove City, Ohio: Glassmasters Publications, 1985.

Bredehoft, Neila. *Heisey Rose.* Newark, Ohio: Heisey Collectors of America, 1983.

Bredehoft, Neila. *Heisey's Orchid Etching.* Newark, Ohio: Heisey Collectors of America, 1983.

Bredehoft, Neila, *The Collector's Encyclopedia of Heisey Glass: 1925–1938.* Paducah, Ky.: Collector Books, 1986.

Duncan, Alastair. *Orrefors Glass.* Woodbridge, Suffolk: Antique Collectors' Club, 1995.

Felt, Thomas G. *A. H. Heisey & Company: A Brief History.* Newark, Ohio: Heisey Collectors of America, 1996.

Garrison, Myrna and Bob. *Imperial Cape Cod: Tradition to Treasure.* Arlington, Tex.: Myrna and Bob Garrison, 1982.

Kerr, Ann. *Fostoria: An Identification and Value Guide of Pressed, Blown & Hand Molded Shapes.* Paducah, Ky.: Collector Books, 1994.

Kovar, Lorraine. *Westmoreland Glass: 1950–1984.* Marietta, Ohio: Antique Publications, 1991.

Krause, Gail. *The Encyclopedia of Duncan Glass.* Washington, Pa.: The Krauses, 1976.

Long, Milbra, and Emily Seate: *Fostoria Stemware: The Crystal for America.* Paducah, Ky.: Collector Books, 1995.

National Cambridge Collectors, Inc. *Colors in Cambridge Glass.* Paducah, Ky.: Collector Books, 1984.

National Imperial Glass Collectors' Society. *Imperial Glass Encyclopedia.* Vol. I, A–Cane. Marietta, Ohio: The Glass Press, 1995.

Nye, Mark A. *Cambridge Stemware.* Miami, Fla.: Mark A. Nye, 1985.

Page, Bob and Dale Frederiksen. *Tiffin is Forever: A Stemware Identification Guide.* Greensboro, N. C.: Page-Frederiksen Publishing, 1994.

Piña, Leslie. *Fostoria: Serving the American Table 1887–1986.* Atglen, Pa.: Schiffer Publishing, 1995.

Wetzel, Mary M. *Candlewick: The Jewel of Imperial.* Rev., 1990 Price Guide. Hillside, Mich.: Ferguson Communications, 1981.

Wetzel-Tomalka, Mary M. *Candlewick: The Jewel of Imperial.* Book II. 2nd Printing 1996. Notre Dame, Ind.: Mary M. Wetzel-Tomalka, 1995.

Wilson, Chas West. *Westmoreland Glass.* Paducah, Ky.: Collector Books, 1996.

Index

REPLACEMENTS, LTD.
The World's Largest Retailer of Discontinued and Active China, Crystal, Flatware and Collectibles

In 1981, Bob Page, an accountant-turned-flea-marketer, founded Replacements, Ltd. Since then, the company's growth and success can only be described as phenomenal.

Today, Replacements, Ltd. locates hard-to-find pieces in over 80,000 patterns - some of which have not been produced for more than 100 years. Now serving over 2 million customers, with an inventory of 4 million pieces, they mail up to 250,000 inventory listings weekly to customers seeking additional pieces in their patterns.

The concept for Replacements, Ltd. originated in the late 1970's when Page, then an auditor for the state of North Carolina, started spending his weekends combing flea markets buying china and crystal. Before long, he was filling requests from customers to find pieces they could not locate.

"I was buying and selling pieces primarily as a diversion," Page explains. "Back when I was an auditor, no one was ever happy to see me. And, quite frankly, I wasn't thrilled about being there either."

Page began placing small ads in shelter publications and started building a file of potential customers. Soon, his inventory outgrew his attic, where he had been storing the pieces, and it was time to make a change. "I reached the point where I was spending more time with dishes than auditing," Page says. "I'd be up until one or two o'clock in the morning. Finally, I took the big step: I quit my auditing job and hired one part-time assistant. Today I'm having so much fun, I often have to remind myself what day of the week it is!"

Replacements, Ltd. continued to grow quickly. In fact, in 1986, Inc. Magazine ranked Replacements, Ltd. 81st on its list of fastest-growing independently-owned companies in the U.S. "Our growth has been incredible," says Page, who was named 1991 North Carolina Entrepreneur of the Year. "I had no idea of the potential when I started out."

Clear standards of high quality merchandise and the highest possible levels of customer service are the cornerstones of the business, resulting in a shopping experience unparalleled in today's marketplace. Page also attributes much of the success of Replacements, Ltd. to a network of nearly 1,500 dedicated suppliers from all around the U.S. The company currently employs about 500 people in an expanded 225,000 square foot facility (the size of four football fields).

Another major contributor to the company's fast growth and top-level customer service is the extensive computer system used to keep track of the inventory. This state-of-the-art system also maintains customer files, including requests for specific pieces in their patterns. It is maintained by a full-time staff of over 20 people and is constantly upgraded to ensure customers receive the information they desire quickly and accurately.

For those who are unsure of the name and/or manufacturer

Greensboro, North Carolina Facility